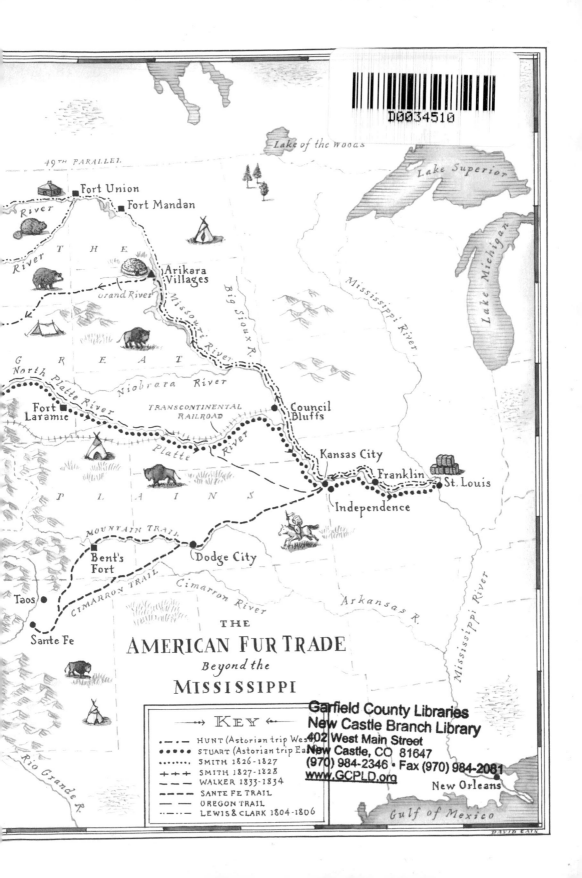

THE
AMERICAN FUR TRADE
Beyond the
MISSISSIPPI

Garfield County Libraries
New Castle Branch Library
402 West Main Street
New Castle, CO 81647
(970) 984-2346 • Fax (970) 984-2081
www.GCPLD.org

KEY

. _ . _ .   HUNT (Astorian trip West)
• • • • •   STUART (Astorian trip East)
. . . . . .   SMITH 1826-1827
+ + +   SMITH 1827-1828
_ _ _   WALKER 1833-1834
_ . _ _   SANTE FE TRAIL
_ _ _   OREGON TRAIL
. _ . . _   LEWIS & CLARK 1804-1806

Garfield County Libraries
New Castle Branch Library
402 West Main Street
New Castle, CO 81647
(970) 984-2346 • Fax (970) 984-2081
www.GCPLD.org

Fur,
Fortune,
and
Empire

OTHER BOOKS BY ERIC JAY DOLIN

Leviathan: The History of Whaling in America

Political Waters

Snakehead: A Fish Out of Water

Smithsonian Book of National Wildlife Refuges

Eric Jay Dolin

FUR, FORTUNE, —and— EMPIRE

The Epic History of the
Fur Trade in America

W. W. NORTON & COMPANY · New York London

Frontispiece: *Fur Traders Descending the Missouri*, by George Caleb Bingham, 1845

Copyright © 2010 by Eric Jay Dolin

All rights reserved
Printed in the United States of America
First Edition

Endpaper: Map © 2010 by David Cain

For information about permission to reproduce selections from this book,
write to Permissions, W. W. Norton & Company, Inc.,
500 Fifth Avenue, New York, NY 10110

For information about special discounts for bulk purchases, please contact
W. W. Norton Special Sales at specialsales@wwnorton.com or 800-233-4830

Manufacturing by RR Donnelley, Harrisonburg
Book design by Judith Stagnitto Abbate /Abbate Design
Production managers: Andrew Marasia and Julia Druskin

Library of Congress Cataloging-in-Publication Data

Dolin, Eric Jay.
Fur, fortune, and empire : the epic history of the fur trade in America / Eric Jay Dolin.
p. cm.
Includes bibliographical references and index.
ISBN 978-0-393-06710-1
1. Fur trade—North America—History. 2. Fur trade—West (U.S.)—History.
3. Frontier and pioneer life—North America. 4. Europeans—North America—History.
5. Imperialism—History. 6. Europe—Colonies—America. 7. North America—History.
8. North America—Ethnic relations. 9. North America—Discovery and exploration—European.
10. North America—Economic conditions. I. Title.
E46.D65 2010
381'.456850973—dc22

2010016212

W. W. Norton & Company, Inc.
500 Fifth Avenue, New York, N.Y. 10110
www.wwnorton.com

W. W. Norton & Company Ltd.
Castle House, 75/76 Wells Street, London W1T 3QT

1 2 3 4 5 6 7 8 9 0

To Jennifer

CONTENTS

THE HISTORY OF NORTH AMERICAN EXPANSION MIGHT almost be written in terms of the fur trade. Europeans were early attracted to the North American coast by the hope of reaping profits from this trade, and after the beginning of settlement revenue from it was the principal means of sustenance to the early English, French, and Dutch colonies. . . . Many a nameless trader, intent only upon his trade and caring nothing for the name of discoverer, has been the first white man to set foot upon lands credit for the discovery of which has gone to others. . . .Before him was the wilderness; behind him, over paths he himself had made, poured in an ever advancing tide of settlement. . . . Thus the fur trader has blazed the way across the continent.

◆•◀▶•◆

—ARTHUR H. BUFFINTON,
*paper presented to the Colonial Society of Massachusetts
by Samuel Eliot Morison, January 1916*

INTRODUCTION

British fur trading scene, eastern North America, from 1777.

"THE BIBLE AND THE BEAVER WERE THE TWO MAINSTAYS OF" the Plymouth Colony in its early years. So wrote historian James Truslow Adams in 1921.[1] Given that the Pilgrims were Puritan separatists who went to America to escape religious persecution, I understood Adams's reference to the Bible. It was central to the Pilgrims' way of life, and its teachings helped them maintain purpose and hope in the face of extremely trying circumstances. But I had no idea why he had thrown beavers into the mix. Intrigued, I read more, and soon the reference to beavers made sense. For more than a decade after their arrival in America, the Pilgrims' main source of income for purchasing supplies and paying off their debts had come from the sale of beaver pelts shipped to London—pelts they obtained by trading with the Indians.[2] Thus the beaver was critical to the colony's survival. This discovery was a surprise to me. What else didn't I know about the American fur trade? The answer was quite a lot.

The fur trade was a powerful force in shaping the course of American history from the early 1600s through the late 1800s, playing a major role in the settlement and evolution of the colonies, and in the growth of the United States. Millions of animals were killed for their pelts, which were used according to the dictates of fashion—and human vanity. This relentless pursuit of furs left in its wake a dramatic, often tragic tale of clashing cultures, fluctuating fortunes, and bloody wars.

In time the fur trade determined the course of empire. It spurred the colonization of eastern North America, and the fierce competition to control the region's fur trade pitted European nations against one another, transforming the New World into a battleground and ultimately leading to the expulsion of the Swedes, Dutch, and French from the continent. Disputes over the fur trade were also a factor in causing the American Revolution and the War of 1812, and as the trade spread to the shores of the Pacific, it became a critical force in expanding the United States and establishing its boundaries, especially in the Northwest.

Fur traders and trappers were typically the first white men the Indians had ever seen, and the dynamics of the fur trade dramatically influenced their culture, often for the worse. No less affected was a whole host of North American species, as the trade swept like a lethal wave over the land. Although the traffic in furs never caused the extinction of a species, in a few cases it came mighty close.

Much more than a recounting of economic, military, cultural, and ecological influences, however, the story of the American fur trade boasts a cast beyond the scope of a Hollywood epic (in a sense *The Good, the Bad, and the Ugly* might be an appropriate title)—at once the honest and the twisted, hedonists and visionaries, Founding Fathers and prodigal sons. And perhaps the most memorable characters of all are the animals that made the fur trade possible, especially the beaver, the sea otter, and the buffalo.

Thousands of books and articles have been written on the American fur trade. In 1902, in his classic 1,029-page *The American Fur Trade of the Far West*, Hiram Martin Chittenden warned his readers, "In fixing upon a logical order of presenting the subject much embarrassment has been experienced on account of the heterogeneous character of the material to be dealt with. The events have been so diverse, and have borne so little relation to each other, that the task of making a connected narrative has been well-nigh impossible."[3] Whereas Chittenden focused almost exclusively on the Western fur trade in the nineteenth century, the scope of this book is much broader. Nevertheless I found there to be a clear and compelling narrative. I also discovered that the narrative had a logical ending, for the conservation movement that emerged in the late 1800s and early 1900s coincided with the widespread implementation of laws regulating the killing of fur-bearing animals. This book, therefore, does not address the American fur trade as it evolved during the twentieth and twenty-first centuries, nor does it cover the current highly charged political and ethical debate over animal rights and the propriety or—many would say—the impropriety of wearing fur. What it does offer is the extraordinary story of the fur trade of old, when the rallying cry was, "Get the furs while they last."

PART I

Furs Settle
the New World

PREVIOUS PAGE | Discovery of the Hudson
River, *by Alfred Bierstadt, 1874.*

"As Fine a River as Can Be Found"

Henry Hudson.

*T*HE ENGLISH EXPLORER HENRY HUDSON AND HIS CREW OF sixteen sailed the eighty-five-foot *Halve Maen* (*Half Moon*) out of Amsterdam on April 4, 1609, to find a northeasterly route to the riches of the Orient. There is no record of what Hudson thought as he watched the city's skyline recede into the distance, but he was convinced he was on a fool's errand, so a sense of foreboding, perhaps resignation, must have prevailed. In 1608, in the employ of the English trading giant the Muscovy Company, Hudson had sailed in the same direction with the same charge, only to have his progress blocked by impenetrable pack ice. His own experience and those of other explorers, including the famed Dutchman Willem Barents, had shown, Hudson believed, that the northeasterly route was a dangerous illusion. Moreover Hudson was growing increasingly persuaded by intelligence brought back by the English explorers John Smith and George Weymouth, on their voyages west across the Atlantic, that the fabled passage to the Orient likely lay in that direction somewhere along the coast of the New World. Despite these misgivings Hudson apparently didn't share his concerns with the directors of the Dutch East India Company, who were bankrolling the voyage. After all, they still viewed the northeast route as the only viable course, evidence to the contrary notwithstanding. Some of Hudson's doubts about the voyage, however, must have filtered back to the company, because just before he departed the company amended his instructions, explicitly ordering him to sail the *Half Moon* to the northeast and "to think of discovering no other route or passage."[1]

One month later the *Half Moon* ran headlong into a "sea . . . full of ice" off the northern coast of Russia. Not surprised, Hudson took advantage of this opportunity and gave his increasingly disputatious crew a choice: They could return to Amsterdam, having failed to discover anything of significance, or they could take a gamble and strike out across the Atlantic, using either Smith's or Weymouth's journals as their guide. Following Smith would take them far down the American coast, where Smith believed there was a sea that led to the Orient, while Weymouth's course would have them seek the passage in the northern reaches of present-day Canada. The crew chose to gamble, and Hudson placed his faith in Smith. Hudson now had what he most desperately wanted—a chance for vindication.[2]

After a stormy voyage that battered the ship and split one of the masts in two, Hudson and his men reached Nova Scotia in mid-July. They sailed in a southwesterly direction for more than a month, coming close to the English settlement at Jamestown, Virginia, and then traveling a bit farther south before doubling back up the coast. Toward the end of August, Hudson and his men became the first Westerners known to enter Delaware Bay, but the phalanx of sandbars and shoals they soon discovered dispelled any thoughts that this was the passage to the Orient.[3] So they left the bay, proceeded farther up the coast, and in mid-September, as the sun beat back the last wisps of morning fog, the *Half Moon* sailed "between two headlands, and entered . . . into as fine a river as can be found, wide and deep, with good anchoring ground on both sides."[4] The *Half Moon* was riding on the river that would one day bear Hudson's name.

Fervently hoping that he had finally found the passage he was looking for, Hudson slowly made his way upriver. Things looked promising at first. The river was "a mile broad," bounded by stark palisades, and as deep as fourteen fathoms in places.[5] Over the course of a little more than a week and roughly

150 miles, however, the river's banks closed in and the bottom rose up to the point where the *Half Moon* could go no farther. Hudson had reached a dead end in the vicinity of what is now Albany, New York. After retracing his steps Hudson sailed out of the river's mouth in early October, then back across the Atlantic to inform his employers of the disappointing news.

Hudson didn't deliver the news himself. For reasons that remain unclear, instead of sailing straight for Amsterdam he put in at Dartmouth, England, only to be detained by English authorities who wanted him to "serve" his "own country" rather than work on behalf of England's bitter rival, the Dutch.[6] Although Hudson never made it back to Holland, news of his voyage did, in the form of his log and an accompanying report written by Emanuel van Meteren, a Dutchman living in London who had been instrumental in getting Hudson to sail under the Dutch flag in the first place. When Dutch merchants heard of Hudson's discoveries, they were intrigued because he had brought back information that suggested great profits, courtesy of the Indians he had encountered on his trip.[7]

What the merchants learned was that when Hudson had anchored the *Half Moon* below the river's mouth, the ship had been visited by Indians clad in "deer skins," "mantles of feathers," and "good furs."* In fact they were eager to trade, "very civil," and "very glad" to see the Europeans. Many times over the course of the next month, as Hudson made his way up and down the river, the Indians offered the Europeans corn, oysters, beans, grapes, tobacco, pompions (pumpkins), and beaver and otter skins in exchange for "trifles . . . beads, knives, and hatchets." Unfortunately such amicable relations were not the rule. One of Hudson's men was killed by an arrow through the neck while returning from a reconnaissance mission to check the depth of the river, and then, just a few days before the *Half Moon* returned to Europe, two vicious skirmishes left as many as ten Indians dead.[8] These skirmishes were overlooked, for van Meteren's report spoke of "friendly and polite" Indians along the "upper part" of the river, having "an abundance of provisions, skins, and furs, of martens and foxes, and many other commodities."[9] Reading about those skins and furs was understandably exciting because the fur trade was a lucrative business in Europe, in which the Dutch sought to play a larger role.

---

*Many of the older quotes used in this book employ archaic and at times confusing spellings of words, for example, "furres" instead of "furs." I have changed those spellings to conform to modern usage, unless making such a change would alter the meaning or detract from the power of the quote, in which case the old spelling is retained.

HE ROOTS OF THE FUR TRADE GO BACK TO PREHISTORIC TIMES, when humans relied on furs to protect them from the elements, an eminently sensible and necessary survival strategy, given that humans are one of the least hirsute or, if you prefer, the most naked of all mammals.[10] Indeed, the Bible informs us that, prior to banishing Adam and Eve from Eden, God "clothed them" in "garments of skins [furs]." As humans multiplied, so too did the use of furs, worn not only functionally for warmth but later for beauty and to signify rank and luxury. Ancient Egyptians traded with the Arabians and the Phoenicians for furs, coloring them with vegetable dyes. The Greeks imported furs from the Libyans as well as the Scythians, who lived north of the Caspian Sea and trimmed their clothes with beaver and otter skins. The Romans imported animal pelts from Germany, and when their senators replaced their traditional wool togas with "Gothic furs," people called the senators *Pellete*.[11]

During medieval times an astonishingly wide array of skins entered the stream of commerce and were traded north and south, east and west. Furs flowed from Germany, Ireland, and Scotland to London; from Spain, North Africa, and Sicily to Paris; from Sweden, Portugal, and Bulgaria to Bruges, and in other directions as well. Russia, to the east, also emerged as a major entrepôt, sending skins to the West. All these furs were cleaned, cut, stitched, and dyed by an ever-growing cadre of professionals, and made into a wide array of products, including robes, hats, gloves, and bedding. As a result the expanding fur trade helped to bring formerly insular countries and cultures into the nexus of an increasingly interdependent and connected world.[12]

Furs became an incredibly important sign of class distinction and wealth, creating a symbolic divide between nobility and commoner. A torrent of sumptuary laws put furs and people in their proper place. In 1337 King Edward III of England limited the wearing of fur to the royal family, to "Prelates, Earls, Barons, Knights and Ladies," and to church officials who had a yearly benefice of at least one hundred pounds.[13] In 1429 King James I of Scotland declared that silk clothes adorned with the best furs and ornamented with pearls or gold were to be worn only by men who had attained at least the rank of knight, or who had earned more than two hundred marks annually. Town councilors and aldermen were allowed to wear fur-lined gowns, while others of lesser rank were "enjoined to equip themselves in such grave and honest apparel as befits their station."[14] Wealthy merchants "of humble origin," spent extravagantly on furs to show the world that they were worthy of ascending a rung or two higher on the rigid ladder of social success.[15] As for commoners, they weren't literally left out in the cold. They too wore furs, but usually had to content themselves with the least desirable ones, such as those taken from more common animals, like goats, sheep, cats, dogs, and rabbits.[16]

The widespread use of furs notwithstanding, it was the nobility and the royal families who had the biggest impact on the fur trade. To help anchor their station within the rarefied air of the aristocracy, nobles purchased immense quantities of furs, but they were mere amateurs when compared with the royals, who, having almost unlimited resources, bought furs without restraint. King Henry IV of England, for example, had a single nine-part robe composed owf no fewer than twelve thousand squirrel and eighty ermine skins. And for her wedding to the French king Charles VIII, Anne of Brittany was clothed in a flowing robe adorned with gold thread, jewels, and 160 sable skins. The enormity of such extravagance becomes clearer when one considers that in the early 1200s it could take an English carpenter forty days to earn enough to purchase a single rabbit lining, and that one of King Henry VIII's gowns, which included 100 sable and 560 squirrel skins, cost roughly two hundred pounds, or about six thousand times the daily wage of one of the plasterers working at the time for the king at Eltham Palace.[17]

Not all monarchs viewed the wearing of furs in an uncritically positive light. Although Charlemagne, king of the Franks during the late eighth and early ninth centuries, willingly wore fine furs on state occasions, he held a dim view of those who believed that clothes made the man. So, when he became concerned that his courtiers had grown too fond of their luxurious wardrobes, he commanded them to put on their best clothes and go hunting with him on a particularly cold, rainy, and windswept day. The elements didn't bother Charlemagne in the least, since he was wrapped in a thick, water-repellent sheepskin cloak. His entourage, however, was soon drenched to the skin, their fancy silk and fur robes caked in mud. The stage was now set for Charlemagne to teach his noblemen a lesson. He led the shivering party back to the castle, and had them stand by the fire. As the robes dried, they shrank and shriveled, becoming very expensive rags. According to the Scottish historical novelist Sir Walter Scott, Charlemagne "gloried in his own plain sheepskin cloak, which had neither suffered by the storm nor by the heat, and exhorted the tattered crew by whom he was surrounded, to reserve silk and furs for days of ceremony, and to use in war and in the chase the plain but serviceable dress of their ancestors.[18]

While Charlemagne enjoyed poking fun at his noblemen's slavish attachment to their furs, the medieval chronicler Adam of Bremen perceived something far more sinister in the fur fad sweeping Europe in the eleventh century. The pious cleric took a particularly dim view of the flood of furs emanating from Russia, where, he said, "they are [as] plentiful as dung," and he worried that, "for our damnation . . . we strive as hard to come into the possession of a marten skin as if it were everlasting salvation." As a final salvo he claimed that it was because of this sacrilegious longing for furs, and the pernicious role of Russia in providing them, "that the deadly sin of luxurious pride" had enveloped the West.[19]

Sinful or not, demand for furs remained strong while dynasties waxed and waned. By the early 1600s, however, a problem arose because the European supply of furs was diminishing. For centuries trappers had combed the forests, meadows, streams, and rivers of Europe and lands farther east, killing an untold number of animals for their pelts.[20] The populations of fur-bearing animals were everywhere in steep decline. That is why Hudson's report of furs elicited such excitement in Holland. Just as the traditional sources of furs were petering out, another source was ready to be exploited, in America.

*H*UDSON WAS HARDLY THE FIRST WESTERNER TO discover the bounty in furs that lay across the Atlantic. That distinction belongs to the Norsemen, who sailed to North America early in the eleventh century and established a fleeting settlement in a place they called Vinland, whose location is still debated among historians but was most likely somewhere along the coast of Canada.[21] When the Icelander Thorfinn Karlsefni and his crew met the local Indians, they soon began trading, according to the saga of Eric the Red. The Indians were particularly interested in "red cloth, for which they offered in exchange peltries. . . . [F]or perfect unsullied skins the Skrellings [Indians] would take red stuff a span in length, which they would bind around their heads."[22]

Five centuries later Europeans began arriving off the coast of North America in greater numbers, witnessing firsthand the almost unbelievable abundance of furs in the New World. Though many of these Europeans were explorers searching for a route to the East, or gold or silver mines, and were not particularly interested in obtaining furs, they gladly did so when the opportunity arose. In 1524, for example, the Italian explorer Giovanni da Verrazano sailed *La Dauphine* into Casco Bay, in present-day Maine, and came across Indians "clothed in the skins of bear, lynx, sea-wolf, and other animals." Possibly suspicious or fearful of Europeans as a result of earlier contacts, the Indians refused to let Verrazano land. "If we wanted to trade with them for some of their things," Verrazano wrote, "they would come to the seashore on some rocks where the breakers were most violent, while we remained on the little boat, and they sent us what they wanted to give on a rope, continually shouting to us not to approach the land." In this manner, the Indians lowered down their furs, while the Europeans sent back "knives, hooks for fishing, and sharp metal," the only items the Indians desired.[23] And ten years later, in July 1534, near Chaleur Bay in northern New Brunswick, the French explorer Jacques Cartier encountered Indians who seemed almost *too* eager to trade. While a few of Cartier's men were exploring the coast in one of their boats, a large group of Micmac Indians on the shore raised furs aloft on sticks and waved them back and forth, while making gestures imploring the Europeans to land. Having just one boat and but a few men, the wary Europeans declined to be drawn in and continued on their way, whereupon seven boats full of Indians pursued them, "making many signs of love and mirth, as it were desiring our friendship." The Europeans urged the Indians to turn back, but still they came until two warning shots fired over their heads sent them paddling away in fright. Soon, however, the Indians returned, and when they got too close, the Europeans jabbed at them with lances until they departed. The next day nine boats full of Indians approached Cartier's two ships, "making signs that they came to traffic with us." This time Cartier sent two of his men ashore, with knives and "other iron wares, and a red hat to give unto their captain." These goods were warmly received, and the Indians traded all their furs, including the ones they were wearing. Before leaving, the now-naked Indians indicated that they would return the next day with more skins, and they did.[24]

*W*HILE EXPLORERS DABBLED IN THE FUR TRADE, IT WAS fishermen who took it to the next level. Intent on satisfying growing local demand for fish, Europeans sailed across the Atlantic during the early sixteenth century to find new fishing grounds, and off the coast of Newfoundland they found what appeared to be a mother lode—enormous shoals of gigantic cod.[25] At first fishermen had little contact with Indians or their furs, because fishing operations were conducted offshore.[26] The fisher-men would bait their hooks, throw the line overboard, haul the hooked fish aboard, and send it through an assembly line, with a series of stations located on tables running along the side of the ship. The first man in the chain would lop off the fish's head, the second would slice open the belly and rip out the guts, while the third would cut out the bones and pitch the fish into the salt-ing barrel full of brine, where it would cure for twenty-four hours, then be pressed and stored in the hold for the return voyage.

Over time this form of "green," or "wet," fishing was increasingly sup-planted by "dry" fishing, which shifted much of the operation to land. For months at a stretch, fishermen would live onshore with their ship anchored nearby. Each morning they would row their boats to sea and return with their catch. The fish were processed in the same manner as was done offshore, with one important difference: After pitching the fish into a salting barrel to cure, they would splay them out on rocks or wooden platforms called flakes to dry in the sun. Dry fishing was more efficient and cost effective than wet fishing since it required less salt, saved on cargo space, allowed the fishermen to fish longer, and produced a rock-hard product with an almost infinite shelf life.[27]

With fishermen on land for long periods of time, Indians began bringing furs to the fishermen's camps to trade. Since many of the fishermen returned yearly to the same location, the trade became cyclical, the Indians saving up their furs in preparation for the trading season, and the Europeans stocking up on trade items before leaving home. And the furs weren't always of local origin. As word spread that the Europeans were here to trade, inland Indians started packing up their furs and making annual excursions to the coast, while coastal Indians, acting as middlemen, also obtained pelts from the interior tribes to trade to the fishermen.

Originally a sideline to fishing, fur trading took center stage toward the end of the sixteenth century. Furs were almost the perfect commodities. The Indians did all the work collecting them, they could be bought with relatively inexpensive European wares, they were easy to transport, and commanded high prices back home. Of all the European fishermen who pursued this trade, it was the French who did so with the most drive, determination, and success, leading them to increasingly leave "their old vocation [of fishing] for the more lucrative trade in bear-skins and beaver-skins."[28] In this way "the great fish-ing industry . . . became the mother of the fur-trade."[29]

King Henry IV of France enthusiastically supported expanding the French fur trade in North America. He believed that it would bolster the failing treasury, provide an outlet for French trading goods, and strengthen and expand his empire. To help achieve these goals, Henry granted a group of Frenchmen monopoly rights to the fur trade in the region of the St. Lawrence River in 1599 on the condition that they annually transport fifty colonists to the area. Although Henry's hopes for rapid colonization were dashed—primarily because the monopolists were more interested in furs than settlements—the fur trade prospered. While these monopolists, and others who followed, established the first permanent fur-trading outpost in North America, at Tadoussac, and then another at Quebec, French entrepreneurs operating beyond the monopolists' control were also busy gathering pelts.[30]

*T*HUS WHEN HUDSON ARRIVED OFF THE COAST OF NOVA SCOTIA in the summer of 1609, the French trade in the region was already well established. In the vicinity of LaHave, six Indians—one of whom even spoke a few words of French—told Hudson "that the Frenchmen do trade with them." Three days later Indians visited the *Half Moon* rowing "French shallops [small open boats]" and looking to trade "beaver skins and other fine furs" for "red gowns," as well as other items that the "French trade with them."[31] It is doubtful that these encounters surprised Hudson or his men. Europeans were well aware of the inroads the French had made into the North American fur trade, and no European merchants were more envious of their success than the Dutch.

By the early 1600s the Dutch already had a thriving trade with Russia, bartering European goods for Muscovy furs. This trade, which kept scores of ships traveling back and forth from Amsterdam to Archangel, was highly favorable to the Dutch, since the Russians kept tariffs on imports and exports very low. Still, no tariffs were better than low ones, so when the Dutch merchants learned that a bounty in furs lay across the Atlantic, a place where duties wouldn't apply and furs could be had for various "trinkets," they set their sights on expanding their trade to the West. Moreover, this new source of furs would help make up for the diminished supply coming from Europe and Russia. Initially the Dutch tried to horn in on the French trade along the St. Lawrence.[32] But the role of interlopers in territory claimed and defended by the French was not one that the Dutch relished. Fortunately for them there was an alternative location: Courtesy of Hudson they now knew of a "fine" river, hundreds of miles from the French, with many "friendly" Indians who were eager to trade furs. And if the Dutch were lucky, most of those furs would come from beavers, whose pelts were particularly valued back home.

2

The Precious Beaver

*A vicious-looking beaver, with humanlike
eyes, from a book published in 1703.*

THE DAWN OF THE SEVENTEENTH CENTURY WAS A HORRIBLE
time for beavers. Killed by trappers for hundreds of years, the beaver had been just one of many furs in the universe of fashion, and a lesser one at that. Precious sables, martens, and ermines were among the fur elite; beavers were not. Then, toward the end of the 1500s, the evolution of style transformed the beaver hat into a necessary accoutrement for the well bred and well heeled. Suddenly the beaver—one of the world's most intriguing creatures—became the most sought-after commodity of the fur trade. Its popularity would not be surpassed for more than two hundred years.[1]

Since the beaver plays such a central role in this book, a brief digression on the animal's natural history is in order. There are two species of beaver—the European or Eurasian (*Castor fiber*) and the North American (*Castor canadensis*)—both of which belong to the largest group of mammals, the order Rodentia, or "gnawers," which includes other toothy members such as squirrels, porcupines, and rats. The European and the North American beaver differ in their number of chromosomes and a few behavioral characteristics but otherwise are largely indistinguishable; hence the generic term "beaver" will be used from now on. Beavers grow up to four feet long, and weigh as much as 110 pounds, although they average 40 to 50. The only larger rodent is the capybara, or "water hog," of South America, which also reaches four feet, but can pack as many as 150 pounds onto to its beefy frame. Both the modern beaver and the capybara, however, are lilliputian compared with the extinct giant beaver, which roamed ancient forests alongside woolly mammoths, and may have been up to seven feet long and have weighed nearly 500 pounds.[2]

A head-to-tail tour of the beaver reveals a range of fascinating features. Up front the four curved orange incisors, two each jutting from the upper and lower jaws, are the perfect combination of form and function, allowing the beaver to gnaw and chip its way through tree trunks up to three feet in diameter.[3] Such abrasive work would quickly wear down average mammalian teeth to the gums, but the beaver's incisors are designed to withstand this punishment and remain sharp. Their first line of defense is that they never stop growing, so what is worn away is quickly replaced. And second, the power of abrasion is an ally. The outer edge of each incisor is extremely dense and hard enamel, while the inner edge is much softer dentine. Thus the inner sides of the teeth wear down more quickly than the outer, keeping them beveled like a chisel, a profile that is further honed by the way in which upper and lower teeth slide past one another each time the mouth opens and closes. However, if one of the incisors breaks off or goes out of alignment, disaster can ensue. No longer impeded by its opposite, an incisor will continue growing, curving back on itself, making it impossible for the beaver to eat, resulting in a slow painful death by starvation. And if the errant tooth is angled in a certain way, it can impale and kill the beaver by puncturing its skull. The mighty incisors are backed up by sixteen deeply ridged molars, and this formidable toothy assemblage is embedded in the beaver's impressively large and sturdy skull, whose jaw is powered by massive muscles that create the brute chomping force needed to fell a tree, as well as the strength to grind the beaver's fibrous vegetarian fare, consisting of the bark and small twigs of deciduous trees, the leaves and roots of various aquatic plants, and terrestrial grasses, flowering plants, and berries.[4]

At the beaver's hind end is its most arresting and recognizable feature, the flat, lozenge-shaped tail, which accounts for a quarter or more of the animal's length. While the muscular base of the tail is furry, the rest of it appears to be covered with overlapping scales, such as one might see on a fish or a snake; but appearances deceive, and the scales are merely skin-deep indentations. A highly versatile appendage, the beaver's tail serves as a support to help the beaver sit upright while scanning its surroundings or gnawing through trees; as a fat reserve; a rudder in the water; and as a body-temperature regulator. It is also an alarm system. When the tail is slapped violently against the surface of the water, it generates a resounding crack that can be heard hundreds of yards away, warning other beavers of danger.[5]

The beaver's tail has even played a minor role in the history of religious dietary restrictions. As the author Mark Kurlansky points out, among the Catholic Church's edicts during the medieval era was one forbidding its followers from eating " 'red-blooded' meat on holy days . . . arguing that it was 'hot,' associated with sex, which was also forbidden on holy days." The church, however, had no problem with its followers eating meat that came from animals that lived underwater, for such meat was viewed as "cold" and apparently unlikely to excite libidinous passions. This dispensation was mistakenly extended to beaver tails because, the reasoning went, they were often immersed in water and therefore must be "cold." Thus, for the 166 holy days during the year, including all Fridays, Catholics could dine on beaver tails without guilt.[6] How many actually did so is unknown, but it may have been quite a few, because many who have tasted the beaver's fatty tail claim it to be quite a delicacy. Indians, too, viewed it as a delicacy, but they also saw the tail in a wholly different light than did the church. Instead of a suppressor of sexual desire, the beaver's tail was actually regarded by the Indians as an aphrodisiac that could help maintain an erection. Not surprisingly the tail was usually reserved for the sachem or chief, and was, as a seventeenth-century English observer of Indians in lower New England noted, "of such masculine virtue, that if some of our Ladies knew the benefit thereof, they would desire to have ships sent of purpose, to trade for the tail alone."[7]

The beaver is enveloped in a lustrous fur coat, usually chestnut brown or reddish in color, but at times black, and on very rare occasions white. The fur comprises two types of hair: the longer, coarser guard hairs, and the softer, woollier undercoat, which together achieve astounding densities ranging from 12,000 to 23,000 hairs per square centimeter. This thick coat provides added buoyancy in water, shields the flesh from the sharp teeth and claws of predators, and keeps the beaver dry and warm. The coat is thickest in the winter, and beavers that live in more northern and colder climates tend to have the thickest pelts of all, which were most prized in the fur trade. In contrast pelts obtained during the summer molting season or in warmer, southern climates were not as plush and therefore were less commercially desirable.[8]

Although beavers can be found living along the banks of rivers and streams, they prefer ponds. If beavers happen upon a natural pond, they may easily build a lodge or dig a burrow at the edge of the water and move in.[9] But if there are no ponds in the area they will often create one; it's for a good reason, after all, that beavers are called nature's engineers. Using a structurally impressive combination of logs, branches, mud, and stones, laboriously placed along the axes of streams, beavers construct mighty dams that halt the gurgling rush of water down hillsides and through valleys, thereby inundating the land and forming a pond. To build these natural masterpieces, beavers rely on raw materials that are close at hand, the most important of which is wood, provided by willows, aspens, birches, and other deciduous trees.[10] Alone or sometimes in pairs, the beaver sets to work with its powerful incisors, gnawing, cutting, and chipping away the wood near the base of the tree in a V-shaped pattern, often laboring for hours at a time, until the tree is left balancing precariously on a narrow point or wedge of wood, often no thicker than a pencil. With one more cut or a providential gust of wind, the connecting wood fibers rupture as the tree begins to fall. Sensing the vibrations through its teeth or hearing the wood crack, the beaver scampers out of harm's way. Then the tree topples to the ground—except when it doesn't. If the tree gets caught in nearby branches, it will remain standing, or listing as the case may be.[11] Some people claim that beavers can predict which way a tree will fall, or that they cut the tree so that it falls in the direction of their choosing. This is not true, and a small number of beavers are so clueless on this account that, failing to get out of the way of the crashing lumber, they end up serving as their own executioners, crushed to death by the tree they have just felled.[12]

Beaver dams in fact reflect the constraints of the environment and the proclivities of the builder. The severed branches and logs, held fast in the vice-like grip of the beaver's jaws, are dragged into the water to commence construction. Where the current is strong, the dam is usually slightly bowed upstream to best deflect the pressure of the water, and the dam's foundation is made up of stout limbs driven a short way into the mud, like pilings, and sometimes secured by stones. In more sluggish streams the dam may be perpendicular or concave to flow, and the foundation comprised of sticks, stones, and mud laid on the bottom. From these crude beginnings the beavers build up the width and height of the dam, carefully placing interlocking logs and branches across the expanding structure, and adding stones, mud, grass, and other debris to hold the dam together, give it bulk, and decrease its porosity. A single stream might have one dam or many, creating successive ponds dotting the terrain like a strand of liquid pearls.[13]

A family of beavers can construct a small dam in a few days, a thirty- to forty-foot dam in a week or so, and a thousand-foot dam in a couple of years, but no matter the length, dams are never truly completed. There are always walls to be shored up and holes to be patched, and the beavers' seemingly instinctive aversion to the sound of running water makes them very attentive repairmen indeed. Usually many generations of beavers will work on the same dam, which can range in length from a few feet to more than a thousand yards, and in height from barely eight inches to eighteen feet. Regardless of their size and age, dams don't last forever. Eventually the beavers will exhaust the easily accessible local supply of wood, and when they do, it is time to move on.[14]

HUMANS VIEW BEAVERS AS NATURE'S WORKAHOLICS, industrious to a fault, and that is why phrases such as "busy as a beaver," and "eager beaver" are part of the vernacular. "Most people have the idea," claimed Enos Mills, an American naturalist who spent twenty-seven years observing beavers in the wild, "that the beaver is always at work; not that he necessarily accomplished much at this work, but that he is always doing something." This is, however, a mistaken assumption. "The fact remains," Mills continued, "that under normal conditions he [the beaver] works less than half the time, and it is not uncommon for him to spend a large share of each year in what might be called play. He is physically capable of intense and prolonged application, and, being an intelligent worker, even though he works less than half the time he accomplishes large results."[15]

It is hard to overestimate beavers' extraordinary impact on the world around them. When Westerners launched their first explorations of the New World, the North American beaver was likely the most widespread and successful mammal on the continent, found "living almost everywhere there was water, from the Arctic tundra to the deserts of Northern Mexico."[16] About the only places beavers weren't found were in present-day Florida, the western edge of the arid Southwest, and farthest reaches of the frigid North. Population estimates for beavers at this time range from sixty to two hundred million.[17] The effect of the beaver on the environment, even now but more then, remains profound. Beaver ponds reduce turbidity and encourage the settling of sediment, resulting in clearer water, deeper penetration of the sun, and the blossoming of vegetable life. They create valuable wetland habitat for a great variety of animals and plants. When abandoned dams are finally breached, pond bottoms are exposed and are soon colonized by grasses, flowers, shrubs, and trees. Beaver dams are also critical to water conservation and flood control. Wetlands soak up rain, slowly releasing during dry spells, and the dams themselves offer essential service during severe storms, providing a bulwark against the rampaging waters and limiting the damaging impacts of downstream erosion.[18]

IVEN THE MYRIAD OF REMARKABLE CHARACTERISTICS AND skills that the beaver displays, it is not surprising that it has fascinated humans for thousands of years. Many Indian tribes have legends prominently featuring the beaver. Northeastern Algonquian peoples spoke of the world originally being enveloped by water, and of enormous beavers, otters, and muskrats diving into the depths retrieving heaps of mud, which the Great Spirit Manitou molded into the landforms that became the earth. One Algonquian tribe, the Amikona, or "People of the Beaver," believed they were descended from the carcass of the original beaver. The Cheyenne saw the world precariously supported by a great wooden beam, which had been partly gnawed through by the snow-white beaver of the Far North, the father of mankind. If the beaver got angry it would gnaw all the way through the beam, and the earth would fall into a dark abyss. To avoid this fate the Cheyenne refused to eat beaver or touch its skin. And the Paiute of California said that the beaver used its tail to bring fire from the East, and that is why the tail was naked—all the hair was burned off.[19]

While Indians have created legends about beavers, Westerners have created their own mythology, rife with hyperbole and fantastic claims. Beginning with the beaver's mouth, the Roman natural philosopher Pliny the Elder claimed, "The bite of this animal is terrible. . . . If they seize a man by any part of his body, they will never loose their hold until his bones are broken and crackle under their teeth."[20] Although a beaver's bite would no doubt be quite serious, Henry David Thoreau correctly noted in the nineteenth century that observers such as Pliny have "a livelier conception of an animal which has no existence, or of an action which was never performed, than most naturalists have of what passes before their eyes."[21]

Many medieval writers, including Dante Alighieri, believed that beavers were fish eaters. The beaver supposedly dangled its tail in the water, causing a fatty substance to be released that attracted the fish, whereupon the beaver, sensing the arrival of its meal, spun around and seized the fish in its mouth.[22] The eighteenth-century French natural historian Georges-Louis LeClerc, comte de Buffon, even went so far as to state baldly, "a beaver has a scaly tail because he eats fish." This last outrageous claim was too much for George Cartwright, an English entrepreneur who spent sixteen years on the Labrador coast in the late eighteenth century trading in furs and fishing. "I wonder much that Monsieur Buffon had not . . . [a scaly tail] himself for the same reason; for I am sure that he has eaten a great deal more fish, than all the beavers in the world put together."[23]

One of the oldest and most unusual myths surrounding the beaver involves the animals' testicles, hunters, and castoreum, a yellowish, pungent excretion that beavers use to mark their territory, and that was long thought by humans to have curative powers. The basis of this myth is the belief that castoreum is contained in the testicles, and since hunters often pursued beavers to obtain this valuable medicinal substance, the beavers would cut off their testicles as a means of escape.[24] The best explication of the castration myth comes from one of Aesop's Fables—"The Beaver and His Testicles"—written in the sixth century B.C.: "It is said that when the beaver is being chased by dogs and realizes that he cannot outrun them, he bites off his testicles, since he knows that this is what he is hunted for. I suppose there is some kind of superhuman understanding that prompts the beaver to act this way, for as soon as the hunter lays his hands on that magical medicine, he abandons the chase and calls off his dogs." Aesop drew from this story the following moral—"If only people would take the same approach and agree to be deprived of their possessions in order to live lives free from danger; no one, after all, would set a trap for someone already stripped to the skin."[25] The moral notwithstanding, the myth has many holes. First, castoreum is found not in the testicles but in the beaver's castor sacs. Second, the tale of the testicles fails to explain how female beavers, which were also chased for their castoreum, escaped the hunters' clutches. Finally, even if castoreum were found in a beaver's testicles, and male beavers were willing to castrate themselves to live another day, they simply wouldn't be able to do it because not only are the beaver's testicles very small, but they are also located inside the beaver's body, making them inaccessible to the animal's sharp incisors.

Some myths revolve around the beavers' mode of transporting wood back to their dams and lodges. A seventeenth-century observer claimed that to perform this operation, one beaver would lay a log on his shoulder, keeping it in place with his forepaw, then all the beavers would form a chain, holding "each other's tails like a team of horses," and pull the log to their "habitation."[26] Conrad Gesner, a sixteenth-century Swiss naturalist, had an even more unusual view of how this happened. The first step after felling a tree was for the beaver "company" to select one of the "oldest" beavers among them, "whose teeth could not be used for cutting," get him on his back, and "upon his belly lade all their timber, which they so ingeniously work and fasten into the compass of his legs that it may not fall." Alternatively the "company" could "constrain some strange beaver whom they meet withal, to fall flat on his back," and make him the transport vehicle for the wood. Whatever platform was selected, the "company" then dragged the beaver by the tail to the pond. Gesner didn't doubt the accuracy of this account because he knew of beavers that had been "taken that had no hair on their backs." And that was good news for the beaver, because Gesner claimed that hunters, upon seeing such bald beavers, and "in pity of their slavery or bondage," would "let them go away free."[27]

Few qualities of the beaver have attained more mythic status than its supposed intelligence. As John James Audubon and John Bachman observed, "the sagacity and instinct of the beaver have from time immemorial been the subject of admiration and wonder. The early writers on both continents have represented it as a rational, intelligent, and moral being, requiring but the faculty of speech to raise it almost to an equality, in some respects, with our own species."[28] Indeed, the number of authors who have seen fit to comment on the amazing "sagacity" of the beaver, and to compare this animal's mental capabilities favorably with our own, is impressive.[29]

In the end, however, all this intellectual adoration cannot hide the truth. As Lewis S. Morgan asserted in his 1868 classic *The American Beaver*, "In intelligence and sagacity . . . [the beaver] is undoubtedly below many of the carnivora."[30] Scientific statistical analysis supports Morgan's contention. One way that biologists measure intelligence is by calculating the encephalization quotient (EQ), which compares the size or weight of an animal's brain to "the expected brain size." The latter, in turn, is the average ratio of brain weight to body weight across all the species within a certain taxonomic grouping— for example, a class, order, or family. On this scale the beaver is about average, having an EQ of 0.9, which "is intermediate between that of terrestrial rodents of similar size and . . . squirrels."[31]

*I*T WASN'T, HOWEVER, THE BEAVER'S UNUSUAL PHYSICAL MAKE-UP, its engineering prowess, its work ethic, or its purported intelligence that most excited humans; rather it was the products provided by this rodent. Long before the arrival of Europeans, the beaver was a "commissary" to the North American Indians.[32] They roasted the entire beaver and ate its succulent meat. They cut the beaver's flesh into thin strips, cooked them over a low fire or on a rock under the hot sun, until they were dry and brittle. Then they pounded them, often along with berries, into a paste that was mixed with animal fat and molded into pemmican cakes that lasted for months, if not years, and provided sustenance for sojourns in the wilderness. Less an item of status than a life necessity, beaver pelts were stitched together into warm winter coats, mittens, and moccasins. Tanned beaver skins produced a thin, sturdy leather perfect for belts and summer dresses and shirts, as well as quivers and bags. The beaver's scapula was used in religious ceremonies, and even its teeth, decorated with carved lines and circles, or colors, were used by tribes, especially in the Pacific Northwest, to make dice for a game of chance.[33]

Westerners, on the other hand, saw beavers primarily as profit centers. The two most valuable commodities the animals afforded were castoreum and fur. For thousands of years humans killed beavers to get their castor sacs. Once dried, the syrupy and yellowish castoreum turns into a hard, reddish brown, waxy mass, with a musky, slightly sweet odor. Mixed with alcohol, injected into the body, or ingested as shavings or in pill form, castoreum has been touted as a remedy for a dizzying array of maladies, including headaches, epilepsy, rheumatism, insomnia, insanity, poor vision, and fleas. And at least since the ninth century, castoreum has also been used as a fixative in perfume, to make the scent last longer.[34]

By the late 1500s beaver fur had become as sought after as castoreum, for that is when hats made from beaver felt came into vogue. At its most elemental the felt-making process involves taking an animal's shorn fur, agitating, rolling, and compressing the fibers in the presence of heat, moisture, and sometimes grease, to the point where the fibers intertwine so tightly that they form a strong fabric. Although virtually any fur can be used in this process, beaver is "the raw material *par excellence* for felt" because the hairs of the beaver's woolly undercoat are barbed, which makes them ideal for interlocking with one another, creating an exceptionally dense, pliable, and waterproof felt that maintains its shape even in the toughest conditions.[35]

Given that the early history of hats is murky at best, it is not known when or where the first beaver felt hat was made.[36] The oldest reference to a beaver hat comes from Geoffrey Chaucer's late-fourteenth-century *Canterbury Tales*, which mentions a "merchant" sporting a "Flandrish beaver hat."[37] Over the next two centuries an expanding cadre of professional hatters met the growing demand for "beavers" or "castors," as beaver felt hats were called. And toward the end of the reign of Queen Elizabeth I, high-quality beaver hats were the most expensive and desired hats not only in England but throughout Europe, where the size and shape of one's beaver hat had already become a symbol of one's stature in society.[38] The exponential growth in the trade in beaver hats was a mortal blow to the European beaver. As demand for pelts grew, an extinction problem first coursed through Europe, with the circle of death eventually reaching Russia.

*D*ESPITE THE PAUCITY OF BEAVER AND OTHER FURS IN Europe and Russia, and the promise of the fur trade along the Hudson, the Dutch merchants did not rush across the Atlantic to reap the rewards. A trip to the New World was a major investment, which entailed considerable risk. It took time to plan the trip, gather a crew, and outfit the ship. As a result the first Dutch fur-trading voyage to follow in Hudson's wake didn't leave Amsterdam until 1611, roughly a year after van Meteren's intriguing report on Hudson's voyage arrived in Holland.

While the Dutch were planning to capitalize on Hudson's discovery, Hudson himself was heading toward his doom. In the spring of 1610, with the backing of a small group of English merchant adventurers, Hudson finally got his chance to captain a voyage that had as its goal the search for the Northwest Passage to the Orient. Since his last trip had disabused him of the notion that the passage could be found along the coast of America, where John Smith thought it might be, this time Hudson planned to follow George Weymouth's lead and find the passage farther north, in Canada.[39] In late April, Hudson and his crew of twenty-two, including his young son, John, sailed out from London on board the *Discovery*.

Although Hudson reached what would later be known as Hudson Bay, he did not find the passage he was seeking. What he did find, however, was that his crew could be pushed only so far. During a miserable winter on the edge of James Bay (south of Hudson Bay), while the *Discovery* was immobilized in pack ice and the crew was slowly wasting away, some of the men began complaining bitterly about Hudson's leadership. They were especially upset with the way the captain dispensed the dwindling provisions, and with his intention to continue searching for the passage come spring, thereby placing them all in further jeopardy, instead of admitting defeat and returning to England. By the time the ice broke up in early June 1611, freeing the *Discovery* to sail again, the growing discontent of the men erupted into mutiny.

One morning, as Hudson emerged from his cabin in his nightclothes, the mutineers grabbed him and "bound his arms behind him." They forced him, along with his son, and seven other men—"the poor, sick and lame" among them—into the *Discovery*'s shallop, "without meat, drink, clothes, or other provision." For a short while the shallop was towed behind the ship; then the line was severed, and the nine men were set adrift amidst the ice floes. As the shallop disappeared from view, the mutineers searched the ship for food, finding some that Hudson had apparently hidden in the hold. But then, like an apparition, the shallop reappeared in the distance, and the mutineers immediately "set the mainsail and topsails, and flew away as though from an enemy."[40] The haunting image of Hudson, his son, and the other men, huddled together in the shallop as the *Discovery* raced away, condemned to what must have been a slow and agonizing death, ranks as one of the most tragic and despairing scenes in the annals of maritime history.

The *Discovery* finally reached London in the late summer of 1611, with eight crewmen on board. Six years passed before four of them were charged with the murder of Hudson and the other men who had been forced onto the shallop. The mutineers pleaded not guilty, and all were acquitted. No trace of Hudson and his fellow castaways, has ever been found.[41]

3

New Amsterdam Rising

Dutch fur traders at Manhattan.

NOT MUCH IS KNOWN ABOUT THE FIRST DUTCH FUR-TRADING voyage to the Hudson, other than that it was sponsored by the Van Tweenhuysen Company in 1611, on a ship called the *St. Pieter* (*St. Peter*), and that it was successful enough to encourage the company to send forth the *Fortuyn* (*Fortune*) the following year, captained by Adriaen Block.[1] On that equally successful trip Block had the field to himself, and when he returned to America in the winter of 1612–13, it appeared that his luck would hold. Seven weeks after arriving on the Hudson River, however, Block saw a ship in the distance.[2] It was a Dutch ship, captained by Thijs Volckertz Mossel, and funded by a rival group of Amsterdam merchants. It too had come to trade.

Block bristled at the sight of this interloper, and the situation worsened when Mossel attempted to "spoil the trade" for Block, offering the Indians twice the amount of goods that Block had been paying for each beaver pelt. To avoid further competition, in which the price for pelts would only rise as the Indians played the rivals off against each other, the two captains set a fixed amount that they would pay per pelt. They also agreed to split the trade, with

Mossel receiving one-third of the pelts while the rest went to Block. But Mossel inflamed matters when, just prior to sailing home, he left behind one of his crew, a West Indian named Juan Rodrigues, along with eighty hatchets, a few knives, a sword, and a musket. Mossel swore to Block that Rodrigues had run away, and that the goods were his wages for the voyage, but Block suspected that Rodrigues had been left intentionally, with orders by Mossel to trade with the Indians on his behalf until the ship returned next season. It even appears that Block tried unsuccessfully to kidnap Rodrigues in an effort to thwart the competition.[3]

The controversy between Block and Mossel followed them back to Amsterdam, where their respective employers took up the cause, each arguing that they had the sole right to the fur trade along the river. Prince Maurice, Holland's leading nobleman, listened intently to both sides before telling them to resolve their differences. The merchants, however, couldn't agree to anything. The options of dividing the trade, combining forces, or having one competitor buy out the other were all equally repugnant. Determined and undaunted, each of the merchant companies sent a threatening letter warning the other to back off; and both proceeded to send another ship to America.[4]

Late in 1613 the two ships entered the Hudson, and the arguments commenced soon after. Mossel and Hendrick Christiaensen, representing the feuding merchants, were furious at the others for trespassing on what they felt was "their" river. While Christiaensen "tried to quarrel and make trouble" between the crews, using "many proud, heated and abusive words," Mossel took a more direct approach, ramming a canoe full of Indians on their way to Christiaensen's ship to trade for furs, and then hacking the canoe to pieces, while the Indians fled in terror. One eyewitness suggested that Mossel had resorted to such violent action because he possessed inferior goods, and did not think he could successfully compete for the Indians' furs. Mossel's solution was to threaten to drive away the Indians unless he was given part of the "skin-trade."[5]

Before things spiraled further out of control, Block himself arrived on the *Tijger*, in January 1614, and took control of the situation. Block, Christiaensen's superior in the same company, offered Mossel a deal. Block would take three out of every five furs traded with the Indians, leaving the other two for Mossel. Not long after the agreement was reached, a series of disasters upended their compromise. First the *Tijger* burned to the waterline, allegedly by accident. Second, members of Block's crew took Mossel's ship by force,

and after a series of failed negotiations and a subsequent firefight, the mutineers sailed to the West Indies to become pirates. Then, in May, two other
Dutch ships, each sponsored by a different set of merchants, arrived, forcing
Block and Mossel to rip up their earlier agreement, replacing it with one in
which each of the four parties would receive one-quarter of the furs traded
on the river.[6]

Despite these skirmishes the ships returned to Amsterdam in the summer
of 1614, bringing back a formidable cache of skins, with Block and Christiaensen alone accounting for 2,500, most of which were beaver.[7] Still, given the
rancor, the delays, the lawsuits that resulted, to say nothing of the lost ships,
the merchants were not happy with the returns on their investments. Yet their
anger proved short lived. On March 27, 1614, Holland's parliament, the States
General, issued a *General Octroy*, or general charter, which invited anyone
who had discovered "new Passages, Havens, Countries or Places" to obtain
a monopoly on trading in those areas, lasting for four voyages. Rather than
fight one another, the once-antagonistic merchants who had sent ships to the
Hudson in 1613–14 decided to bury their differences and band together, forming the New Netherland Company. In doing so they applied for a monopoly,
not only to trade in and around the river but also up and down the coast. The
fact that they didn't actually discover the Hudson or its surrounds did not
bother them in the least; nor did it trouble the States General, which granted
the merchants' application on October 14, 1614, giving them exclusive rights
to trade anywhere on the coast, from the fortieth to the forty-fifth lines of
latitude—roughly from present-day Philadelphia, Pennsylvania, to Bangor,
Maine—an area that was christened "New Netherland."[8]

To anchor its operations in the area, the New Netherland Company
quickly built a trading post on the Hudson, allowing its employees, or factors,
to trade year round. The post, called Fort Nassau, was built in 1614, on Castle
Island, near present-day Albany. It was a formidable redoubt, surrounded by
a breastwork, or palisade, fifty-eight feet on a side and an eighteen-foot-wide
moat, armed with two heavy and eleven light cannon, and occupied by a gar-
rison of ten to twelve men.[9] While the fort seemed impregnable, the island
was not. Repeated flooding forced the company to abandon Fort Nassau and
three years later to build a new fort nearby, also on the banks of the Hudson.

Being on the Hudson and near the confluence of another major river, the
Mohawk, Fort Nassau was an excellent trading hub, strategically located to
benefit from the flow of furs coming downriver from the beaver-rich hinter-

lands. It also provided the Dutch fur traders a place to retreat and fight. In reality, however, fighting was not a viable option. The Dutch were well aware that their pitiful defenses were no match for the Indians, who greatly outnumbered them. This was especially true of the Mohawk, who were part of the Iroquois League of Five Nations, the most powerful Indian alliance in eastern America, which also included the Oneida, the Onondaga, the Cayuga, and the Seneca. So the Dutch tried their best to maintain good relations with the Mohawk, as well as the Mahican (or Mohican) Indians, who inhabited much of the land to the east of the fort.

The New Netherland Company's monopoly expired in 1618 and was not renewed, most likely because the States General was contemplating establishing a private company—in which the government would have a financial interest—that would be responsible for trading activities in America. The end of the monopoly resulted in a virtual free-for-all that lasted five years. Any group that wanted to mount a trading expedition to the Hudson could, and ships representing rival Amsterdam merchants joined those of the still-dominant New Netherland Company.[10] As word spread that the Dutch were ready to trade, an increasing number of Indians brought furs to the posts on the Hudson, as well as to Dutch ships cruising the river. The Dutch in turn journeyed to the South River (the Delaware) and the Fresh River (the Connecticut), and as far east as Narragansett Bay, seeking additional trading opportunities.

*W*ITH MORE THAN A DECADE'S WORTH OF EXPERIENCE, THE Dutch were slowly building up a viable fur trade in America. As Adriaen van der Donck observed in his 1655 *A Description of New Netherland*, there were persuasive reasons for this success. "The country is truly suited and well situated for commerce: One, because it has fine and fertile land on which everything grows aplenty; two, because its fine rivers and navigable waterways reach many places and enable produce to be collected for purposes of trading; three, because the Indians, without labor and exertion on our part, provide us with a handsome and considerable peltry trade that can be assessed at several tons of gold annually."[11]

The trading bonds between the Dutch and the Indians grew stronger over time because both provided what the other wanted. The Dutch side of the equation was simple: The more furs the better, and the best fur of all was beaver. In exchange the Dutch gave the Indians a variety of European goods, including knives, metal pots, glassware, and duffels—coarse, durable, and usually colored pieces of woolen cloth. Guns and liquor, which would soon profoundly alter Indian life in America, were rarely used during this early stage of the Dutch fur trade.[12]

Particularly key to the trading activities were shell beads, which the Dutch called *sewan, sewant*, or *ȝeewand*, and the Indians and the English called *wampumpeag, peag*, or *wampum*. There were two types of wampum: White beads, cut from the inner whorls of whelk shells, and so-called black beads, which were really dark purple and worth twice as much as the white, from the edges of quahogs. Indians along much of the eastern seaboard used wampum for ceremonial purposes, as jewelry, as indicators of status, to pay tribute or to compensate for a wrong, as peace offerings, and as a medium of trade between tribes.[13] A seventeenth-century European observer noted that wampum "answers all occasions with them, as gold and silver doth with us."[14] Quickly realizing the importance of wampum as a form of currency they could use to buy furs, the Dutch provided the Indians with metal drills and polishing tools, and soon beads were being manufactured at a rapid rate.[15]

Thus began the close relationship between the Dutch and the Indians of Long Island, who produced so much wampum that the Dutch referred to Long Island as *sewan-hacky*, or "land of the shells."[16] The Dutch would trade European goods to the Indians of Long Island in exchange for wampum, and then use it to trade for furs with other Indians. From this point forward, and for much of the seventeenth and early eighteenth centuries, wampum would have an enormous impact on the colonial fur trade. As a nineteenth-century historian succinctly stated, "Wampum was the magnet which drew the beaver out of the interior forests."[17]

*S*OME HAVE ARGUED THAT EARLY EUROPEAN FUR TRADERS, including the Dutch, took advantage of the Indians, but in fact the Indians rarely saw it that way.[18] As the French Jesuit priest Paul Le Jeune observed in 1634 during his stay with the Montagnais, an Algonquian tribe in eastern Canada, the Indians were somewhat amused by the Europeans' great desire for furs and their willingness to part with valuable trade goods to get them. Le Jeune heard his "host say one day, jokingly, *Missi picoutau amis- cou*, 'The Beaver does everything perfectly well, it makes kettles, hatchets, swords, knives, bread; and, in short, it makes everything' . . . showing me a very beautiful knife [he said], 'The English have no sense; they give us twenty knives like this for one Beaver skin.' "[19] Joking aside, the point remains that usually both sides in the trade gave things they didn't value highly in exchange for things they did, and therefore both sides thought they were getting the better deal.[20]

Although Indians held beavers in high regard, they had no problem killing them. They had done so for thousands of years to provide food and clothing, and to serve other utilitarian purposes. But such killing was not indiscriminate, and "they killed animals only in proportion as they had need of them," noted the seventeenth-century French historian and statesman Nicolas Denys. "They never made an accumulation of skins of moose, beaver, otter, or others, but only so far as they needed them for personal use."[21] With the arrival of the Europeans, however, the nature of the Indians' relationship with beavers and other fur-bearing animals changed radically. As the historian William Cronon observed, "Formerly, there had been little incentive for Indians to kill more than a fixed number of animals. . . . Precolonial trade enforced an unintentional conservation of animal populations, a conservation which was less the result of enlightened ecological sensibility than of the Indians' limited social definition of 'need.' "[22] The opportunity to obtain European goods, however, altered this equation and the Indians' "definition of 'need.' " When they discovered that all that the Europeans wanted in exchange for their goods were relatively common furs, the Indians launched themselves wholeheartedly into this trade, much to the detriment of local animal populations.[23]

In effect the fur trade enabled the Indians to improve their standard of living and their status within their tribe and within the broader Indian community at little cost. The Indians' interest in European goods, however, must not be confused with the desire to accumulate wealth or become rich. Unlike the Europeans, for whom becoming richer through trade was the chief goal, the Indians had no interest in that pursuit. Their goals were more practical and sacred in nature.[24] Metal hatchets, knives, and kettles, as well as metal-tipped arrows fashioned from those kettles, performed better and lasted longer than the stone counterparts the Indians traditionally used, and gave the owners of such items added "prestige" among their peers.[25] Indians coveted imported glass beads and the shiny copper and brass objects for ornamental and ceremonial purposes; the latter because such objects were thought to be imbued with "spiritual power."[26] European fabric, especially when colored

red or blue, was in high demand not only because it was easily made into durable, flexible, lightweight, and relatively weatherproof clothing, but also because it was cheaper than beaver: As the historian Laurel Thatcher Ulrich so cogently put it, Indians in northeastern America "gave up . . . [fur] clothing not because it was inferior to English cloth but because it had become too valuable to wear."[27] Trading beaver pelts for wampum was also seen as particularly advantageous transaction.[28]

A similar logic held for the Europeans. The iron wares, the cloth, and the various trinkets they traded were fairly common items, in many instances produced specifically for the Indian trade, and therefore of little intrinsic value. Thus trading them for beaver pelts and other valuable furs was an extremely sound business decision.

This is hardly to suggest, however, that the Europeans were always fair traders, or that they always treated the Indians with respect. They most certainly did not. For example, in 1622 a Dutch merchant ascending the Connecticut River to trade with the Sequin Indians decided that the best way to obtain wampum was to kidnap the local chief and hold him hostage until the ransom of 140 fathoms of wampum belt was paid.[29] Still, taking the broad view, the notion that Indians were routinely duped or mistreated in their trades with the Europeans, at least at this early period of colonization, is simply not true. After all, the Indians were in a very real sense the customers of the European traders, and one of the key ways of maintaining a profitable relationship with one's customers is to treat them at least civilly. The traders knew that if they abused that relationship, their Indian partners would be partners no more.[30] Nor were the Indians novices when it came to trade. They had been trading among themselves, and across the length and breadth of North America, for thousands of years, and in the century before the Dutch arrived on the Hudson, Indians had honed their skills trading with a range of European explorers, fishermen, and fur traders. If anything, in the early years of the fur trade it was often the Europeans who were taken advantage of by the Indians, who quickly learned the value of furs and became adept at playing traders off against one another to drive up prices.[31] As Roger Williams, the highly principled founder of the colony of Rhode Island, who viewed Indians with much more respect and sympathy than did most of his fellow European colonists, observed in 1643, "whoever deals or trades with them [the Indians], had need of wisdom, patience, and faithfulness in dealing; for they frequently say, 'you lie: you deceive me.' They are marvelous subtle in their bargains to save a penny, and very suspicious that Englishmen labor to deceive them: therefore they will beat all markets, and try all places, and run twenty, thirty, yea forty miles and more, and lodge in the woods, to save six pence."[32]

It would be a mistake, however, to view the fur trade in purely economic, utilitarian, or spiritual terms. To the Indians especially the trade was an important means of forging bonds between individuals and groups. When an Indian exchanged furs with a trader for a metal hatchet, for example, "it wasn't," as Cronon notes, "simply two goods that were moving back and forth. There were *symbols* passing between them as well. The trader might not have been aware of all those symbols, but for the Indian the exchange represented a statement about friendship. The Indian might expect to rely on the trader for military support, and to support him in return."[33] Thus the trade in furs functioned diplomatically, cementing alliances between the Indians and the Europeans that helped to determine the balance of power not only among Indian tribes, but also among the Europeans who would soon be vying for control of the continent.

*T*HE ENGLISH POSED THE BIGGEST THREAT TO THE NEW hegemony established by the Dutch. In 1606 King James I had claimed for England the vast expanse of the North American continent that fell between the thirty-fourth and the forty-fifth parallels of latitude, roughly from present-day Cape Fear, North Carolina, to Bangor, Maine. One year later, and two years before Hudson had even arrived on the scene, the English established their first permanent settlement in America at Jamestown, Virginia. This didn't bode well for the Dutch, given that it wasn't until 1614 that they laid claim to New Netherland, which fell entirely within the realm that the English had already declared was theirs. And although Jamestown, located just above the thirty-seventh parallel, lay to the south of New Netherland, it was clear by the late teens that the English were forging ahead in their efforts to colonize farther to the north.[34]

The New Netherland Company, well aware of English designs, decided that the best way to parry the English and to keep New Netherland was to emulate the English and encourage colonization. In 1620 the directors of the company became aware of an opportunity to lure potential colonists away from the English. This chance was provided by a group of religious separatists, the Pilgrims, who were then living in Holland, and who showed interest in relocating to America. The Pilgrims had already obtained a patent from an English company to settle in America, but they were still trying to figure out a way to fund their trip when the Dutch stepped in.

The directors submitted a petition to the States General in February 1620, noting with great urgency that the king of England was eager to "people" New Netherland "with the English Nation," and thus "by force . . . render fruit-less" the Dutch "possession and discovery" of that land. There was, however, a way in which the States General might be able to avoid this outcome. The directors said there was, at this moment, "a certain English Preacher [John Robinson]," residing in Leiden, "versed in the Dutch language," who "has the means of inducing over four hundred families to accompany him hither [to New Netherland], both out of this country and England." If the States General were to transport these Pilgrims to America, protect them, and give them freedom to pursue their religion, then they would relocate and thereby preserve Holland's "rights" to those lands.[35]

The States General took a dim view of this petition. First, the parliament was already well along in the planning stages for a private company, which would oversee activities in America, and it was felt that this new entity should make any decisions about colonization. Second, Holland was intent on going to war with Spain, and now was no time to antagonize England, a potential ally in that war, by colonizing land the English thought was theirs. So on April 11, 1620, the States General rejected the petition. But by then it was academic, since in the interim the Pilgrims had accepted a land patent from a group of London investors called the Merchant Adventurers, which ultimately led the Pilgrims to establish the English colony of Plymouth on the shores of Massachusetts Bay.[36]

FINALLY, IN JULY 1621, AFTER YEARS OF PLANNING, THE States General chartered the Dutch West India Company, a privately owned monopoly that was charged with making war on Spain and funding the war by developing trade throughout a huge portion of the globe, including North America.[37] Before the company could do anything, however, it needed to be solvent, and that meant attracting investors, a task that was hindered by the company's emphasis on fighting. Therefore, over time, the company's statements and literature began touting the benefits of trade more than the need for war, and ultimately profits became the company's prime goal.[38] One of the company's original supporters, William Usselincx, offered a cogent argument for the strategic value of money as a motivator. "If one wants to get money," said Usselincx, "something has to be proposed to the people which will move them to invest. To this end, the glory of God will help with some, harm to Spain with others, with some the welfare of the Fatherland. But the principal and most powerful inducement will be the profit each man can make for himself."[39] That is why the West India Company focused much of its efforts on establishing a province in the vicinity of the Hudson, where the fur trade, if managed properly, could generate a steady stream of income.

It took the directors of the West India Company a little more than two years to get the company's financing in order. Almost as difficult as raising capital was rounding up settlers. These were prosperous times in Holland, and it was well nigh impossible to find Dutchmen willing to relocate to the wilds of America. But one small group was eager to emigrate: the Walloons, as the Dutch called them—French-speaking Protestant refugees, driven from Belgium by Spanish persecution.[40] Before approaching the Dutch, however, the Walloons—fifty-six families in all—turned toward England. Knowing that their neighbors in Leiden, the Pilgrims, had established an English colony in America, the Walloons wanted to do the same. So in July 1621 they petitioned King James I of England for permission to settle in Virginia, and the petition was forwarded for consideration to the Virginia Company, in charge of granting land patents for that part of America. Although the Virginia Company wanted to encourage colonization, and appeared willing to let the Walloons settle in Virginia, it had no interest in paying for transportation. Since the Walloons couldn't fund the trip themselves, negotiations went no further.

Rather than give up, the Walloons redirected their search for a sponsor and appealed to Holland. Their timing was propitious. The States General had recently created the West India Company, and both the company's directors and the politicians knew that settlers would be needed to anchor the company's new province in America. Therefore when the Walloons presented themselves as prospective settlers, the Dutch welcomed them. And, with the pledge of land in exchange for six years' working for the company, thirty Walloons left Holland on the *New Amsterdam*, in late January 1624, bound for the Hudson.[41]

The settlers arrived in early May, setting foot first on Manhattan Island. From there most made their way upriver to where Albany now stands, to inhabit the soon-to-be-constructed Fort Orange. Others settled on a small island near the mouth of the river (Governor's Island today), while still others fanned out to establish posts along the Delaware River and the Connecticut River.[42] The settlers were pleasantly surprised by their new surroundings, which were nothing like the savage wilderness many of them had imagined. "Here," one of them wrote in a letter home, "we found beautiful rivers, bubbling fountains flowing down into the valleys . . . agreeable fruits in the woods . . . considerable fish . . . good tillage land . . . [and] especially, free coming and going, without fear of the naked natives of the country. Had we cows, hogs, and other cattle fit for food . . . we would not wish to return to Holland, for whatever we desire in the paradise of Holland, is here to be found."[43]

The Walloons' arrival signaled the end of an era. No longer would Dutch fur traders have free rein along the coast. From then on all fur trading in the region was the company's business. And if anyone had any doubts as to what fur the company wanted most, all they needed to do was look at the seal of the new province, with a beaver squarely in its center, surrounded by a string of wampum.[44]

The province fared well the first year and half of its existence. On September 23, 1626, the *Arms of Amsterdam* sailed from New Netherland, arriving in Amsterdam on November 4, bringing with it both news from America and a hold full of cargo. The next day Pieter Schaghen, one of the directors of the West India Company, wrote a letter to the States General, telling the "High and Mighty Lords" that "our people are in good heart and live in peace there," that they had a successful harvest, and that they had "purchased the Island Manhattes from the Indians for the value of 60 guilders."[45] Soon after this purchase, Peter Minuit, New Netherland's first governor, gave Manhattan a new name—New Amsterdam—and then, in an effort to improve security and administration, he had the province's farflung colonists relocate to New Amsterdam, where he built Fort Amsterdam at the southwestern tip of the island to watch the harbor's mouth and guard against enemy attacks.

Although the purchase of Manhattan was hardly negligible, it seemed at the time less significant than the cargo aboard the *Arms of Amsterdam*: 7,246 beaver skins, 853 ½ otter skins, 48 mink skins, 36 wildcat skins, 33 mink, and 34 rat skins. When this is added to the 4,000 beaver skins New Netherland had sent home in 1624, and the 5,295 it had sent the following year, it becomes clear that the provincial fur trade was progressing rather nicely.[46] But, as the Dutch well knew, they were not the only ones looking for furs in America.

*T*HROUGH THE MID-1620S THE FRENCH FUR TRADE IN AMERICA was marked by instability and strife. Monopolies were granted and rescinded on a regular basis, and new companies came and went, with free-lance traders consistently cutting into company profits. Periods of open trade resulted in a free-for-all, in which scores of traders competed with one another for furs. Trading posts fell apart due to neglect and decay. And the much-hoped-for colonization of the region commonly referred to as "New France" never materialized; in 1625 there were only twenty permanent settlers in Quebec, who were greatly outnumbered by the transient fur traders. Despite these problems, however, the fur-trading business remained strong. In an average year as many as fifteen to twenty thousand furs, virtually all beaver, were shipped to France.[47] During this period French and Dutch interactions were very limited, with only a few instances when fur traders from one group tried to gather furs in what amounted to the other's backyard.

While the French were busy far to the north, the English were active in the south. In late April 1607, after a four-month voyage across the Atlantic in exceedingly cramped conditions, the hundred or so English settlers onboard the *Susan Constant*, the *Godspeed*, and the *Discovery* arrived on the coast of America at the mouth of Chesapeake Bay. A few weeks later, about forty miles from the ocean, on a densely wooded and swampy peninsula jutting out into the present-day James River, the ships' passengers stepped ashore, inaugurating the Jamestown Colony.[48] The most colorful of the settlers was twenty-seven-year-old John Smith, who by his own reckoning had already lived a life worthy of the history books, having survived a shipwreck, pirated in the Mediterranean, fought as a mercenary for the Dutch and the Hungarians, been enslaved by a Turkish pasha, and beheaded three men in duels.[49] When Smith—one of the colony's leaders, and for a time its president—had chance to survey his new surroundings, it seemed to him as if he had stepped ashore in paradise. As he would later recall, "Heaven and earth never agreed better to frame a place for man's habitation."[50] He marveled at the profusion of fish and vegetation, along with a great variety of animals, including beaver, otters, mink, and wildcats, all of which had fur coats suitable for trade.[51] This latter discovery was no surprise. Smith was very familiar with the voyages of fellow Englishmen—Sir Walter Raleigh, Martin Pring, George Weymouth, and Jamestown colonist Bartholomew Gosnold—who had preceded him to America. Each of these explorers had seen evidence of America's fur wealth, and some of them even obtained pelts from the Indians.[52] Therefore when Smith arrived in Jamestown he knew that furs could be one of the colony's greatest assets.

Despite the Indians' eagerness to trade furs, Smith and the other leaders of the colony had little time for or interest in such transactions. Theirs was a more basic struggle—to keep the colonists alive and fed. Nevertheless an illicit fur trade soon developed between the Indians and the crews who manned the supply ships sent from England. The sailors raided the ship's holds, taking goods to trade with the Indians for furs, baskets, and other commodities. To amend their profits the sailors enlisted the support of colonists, who surreptitiously acted as factors, stealing supplies from the fort and using them to trade with the Indians, and then passing the items received to the sailors in return for a cut of the profits. Over the span of six or seven weeks this secret trade resulted in the disappearance of two or three hundred axes, chisels, hoes, and pickaxes, as well as vast quantities of shot and powder. One ship's master later admitted that the furs and other goods he had obtained by this means generated a profit of thirty pounds back in England.

Rail as he did against this "damnable and private trade," there was little Smith could do about it before he departed the colony in the fall of 1609. Over the next ten to fifteen years the Jamestown colony did profit from the fur trade, as scores of traders traversed the region, but by the early 1620s, Virginia had already shifted much of its commercial energy toward tobacco.[53]

Thus, just when New Amsterdam was emerging on the world's stage, this small Dutch fur-trading province had little to fear from French competition in New France or from the Englishmen in Jamestown. However, there was a growing English threat to the north, and it came from the Leiden Pilgrims whom the Dutch had rejected as potential colonists in 1620.

— 4 —

"The Bible and the Beaver"

The Landing of the Pilgrims in Plymouth,
Sarony and Major, 1846.

VIRTUALLY EVERYBODY KNOWS THAT THE PILGRIMS WHO sailed on the *Mayflower* were religious dissenters from the Church of England who hoped to establish a colony in America where they would be free to practice their Puritan religion as they saw fit.[1] But that is only half the story. Although religious goals were foremost in the Pilgrims' minds, the Merchant Adventurers, the company sponsoring the voyage, had distinctly less spiritual ambitions. Everyone on that ship was expected to earn their keep and generate dividends for the company in one way or another. If the Pilgrims failed to achieve this goal, the colony would likely fail as well. Nobody was more aware of the economic imperative hanging over the voyage than William Bradford, one of the Pilgrims' leaders. And during the sixty-five days that the *Mayflower* spent at sea before sighting land at the tip of Cape Cod, Bradford must often have wondered which of the New World's many commodities—fish, furs, or timber—would enable this venture to earn a profit. As it turned out, the beaver, an animal that had been extinct in England for at least one hundred years, provided the answer.[2] And more to the point, beaver pelts, something that none of the *Mayflower*'s passengers had ever seen before, would prove to be their economic lifeline for the future.[3] As James Truslow Adams noted, "The Bible and the beaver were the two mainstays of the young colony. The former saved its morale, and the latter paid its bills, and the rodent's share was a large one."[4]

On the eve of the Pilgrims' departure all signs pointed to failure: The entire run up to that moment had been a series of disasters, disappointments, and frustrations, producing an atmosphere of growing anxiety and foreboding. In June the Pilgrims discovered, much to their astonishment, that the Merchant Adventurers had yet to secure transportation for the voyage, forcing the Pilgrims to purchase a ship, the *Speedwell*, to get them from Holland to Southampton. By the time the Pilgrims finally arrived in England in late July 1620, the company had acquired another ship, the *Mayflower*, but everything else surrounding the voyage remained in disarray.

The original agreement drawn up by the company seemed fair to the Pilgrims. It would bind them for seven years, during which they would work four days of every week generating returns for the company and two days for themselves, with the last day set aside for worship. Each colonist older than sixteen would get one free share in the venture, and during the seven-year period all living costs and supplies would be provided out of the company's joint stock. When the seven years concluded the shareholders would split the profits, and the colonists would own the land their houses stood on and the houses themselves.[5] But then—unilaterally and the last minute—the Merchant Adventurers, fearing that earnings would not be sufficient, altered the terms of the agreement. Now the Pilgrims would be required to devote all their time to company business, and the land and the houses would be common property, subject to division among the shareholders on a pro-rata basis—conditions the Pilgrims viewed as being "fitter for thieves & bond-slaves then honest men."[6]

Although the Pilgrims' representative signed the hastily revised agreement, the larger group refused to compromise, greatly offending the company's representative, Thomas Weston, who stormed off, leaving the Pilgrims "to stand on their own legs." On his way out Weston refused even to pay the one hundred pounds needed for the *Mayflower* and the *Speedwell* to satisfy all their debts and clear port, thereby forcing the Pilgrims to sell some of their precious supplies. It was a bitter sale, which Bradford said, left the Pilgrims with "scarce . . . any butter, no oil, not a sole to mend a shoe," and not enough swords, muskets, or armor to protect themselves adequately.[7] Also problematic was the issue of who would be making the voyage. Because of mounting fears about the terms of their employ, the voyage itself, and what perils might await them in America, many Pilgrims backed out, leading the company to add fifty-two nonseparatists to the passenger manifest, a move that alarmed the Pilgrims, who viewed these "Strangers" with considerable suspicion.

Problems continued when the first attempt to leave England was aborted. The *Speedwell* didn't live up to its name, leaking so badly that it couldn't be repaired, becoming a total loss. By early September the situation was dire. Although the *Mayflower* was packed to more than capacity, the would-be colonists had already eaten nearly half their provisions, and by leaving so late in the season, the ship was bound to encounter inclement weather on the notoriously tempestuous Atlantic. When the *Mayflower* finally did set sail, on September 6, 1620, Bradford noted, perhaps with more than a tinge of optimism, that they were accompanied by a "prosperous wind."[8] Unfortunately it didn't last long.

The *Mayflower* soon encountered "many fierce storms, with which the ship was shroudly shaken, and her upper works made very leaky."[9] The flooding and cracking of timbers were so bad that many onboard wanted to turn back, but with makeshift repairs and prayers to God, they continued, finally sighting the tip of Cape Cod two months later on the morning of November 9. The Pilgrims deemed what they saw in the distance to be a "goodly" land that was "wooded to the brink of the sea."[10] As much as the forests beckoned, they quickly realized that they were in the wrong place. Their land patent gave them permission to settle in the vicinity of the Hudson, not some two hundred miles to the north, so they began sailing south only to have their progress arrested by "dangerous shoals and roaring breakers" near the Cape's elbow.[11] Deciding that safety was more important than fidelity to the terms of an English patent, the Pilgrims turned around and on November 11 came to anchor in the relatively calm waters of modern Provincetown Harbor. A little over a month later, after a difficult and often frustrating expedition to find a suitable spot for a settlement along the coast, the *Mayflower*'s tired and sickly passengers stepped ashore in Plymouth.

*I*T WAS A STRANGELY DESOLATE PLACE. ALTHOUGH THERE were "cornfields" and other signs that Indians had cleared the land, there were no Indians, and no physical record of native settlement.[12] Yet just fifteen years earlier Samuel de Champlain, on one of his explorations of the American coast, had drawn a beautiful map of this area, showing it to be a thriving Indian community with numerous wigwams, planted fields, and Indians walking along the shore. The dramatic shift was attributable to the "great sickness" or plague. Sometime around 1616–19 an epidemic had struck the region, most likely sparked by a contagion introduced by European fishermen or fur traders, to which the Indians had never been exposed and to which they had no immunity. Although the exact cause and nature of the epidemic is still debated among historians, its impact is not.[13] The few thousand Indians living in the vicinity of Plymouth were virtually exterminated, while tribes farther away suffered devastating losses, with up to 90 percent mortality. The Pilgrims viewed this outcome as God's work, with a seventeenth-century historian noting that "divine providence [had thereby] made way for the quiet peaceable settlement of the English in the depopulated territory of those [Indian] nations."[14] Another historian of that era claimed that with the epidemic, "Christ (whose great and glorious works the Earth throughout are altogether for the benefit of his Churches and chosen) not only made room for his people to plant; but also tamed the hard and cruel hearts of these barbarous Indians."[15] But if this was God's work, it was truly horrific. One of the Pilgrims, exploring the coast, commented that so many thousands of Indians had been struck down that they had been unable to "bury one another; their skulls and bones were found in many places lying still above ground, where their houses & dwellings had been; a very sad spectacle to behold."[16]

With the Plymouth colonists having come ashore at the onset of winter, there was no talk of trade or profit making. Survival was the paramount goal; the rest could wait. By March 1621, as the land began its verdant turn toward spring, Plymouth was a community on the edge. Nearly half of the 102 people who had boarded the *Mayflower* lay dead, and of those that remained, only six or seven were "sound" enough to minister to the sick. On March 16, however, the colonists' fortunes took a turn for the better. That morning a tall, confident Indian walked "boldly" into the midst of Plymouth, at first alarming the colonists. But alarm turned to amazement when the Indian "saluted" and shouted out, "Welcome Englishmen!"[17]

Samoset was an Abenaki sachem from Pemaquid Point in Maine, who had learned "broken English" from fishermen who frequented the coast. He asked for beer, and the colonists fed him "strong water probably [probably aqua vitae], and biscuit, and butter, and cheese, & pudding, and a piece of a mallard, all of which he liked well." Samoset told them about Patuxet, the area in which they had settled, and of the local Indians, especially Massasoit, the great sachem of the nearby Pokanoket.[18] Samoset spent the night, and the next morning the colonists gave him "a knife, a bracelet, and a ring." They asked him to bring these to Massasoit and have him and his men visit Plymouth, bringing with them "such beaver skins as they had to truck [trade]."[19]

Massasoit, along with Samoset and a large group of warriors, arrived at Plymouth five days later. This meeting was especially auspicious. First, it resulted in a treaty of peace between the Plymouth Colony and the Pokanoket. Second, it introduced the colonists to Squanto or Tisquantum, a Patuxet Indian who had been kidnapped from the area in 1614 by the Englishman Thomas Hunt, and sold as a slave in Spain, only to end up living in England. In 1619 Squanto accompanied the English explorer Thomas Dermer on a voyage to New England, and in the summer of 1620, when Indians on Martha's Vineyard attacked Dermer's expedition, Squanto was taken prisoner and eventually placed under Massasoit's care. During the negotiations over the peace treaty with the Pilgrims, Squanto used his facility in English to serve as Massasoit's interpreter. Once the treaty was concluded Squanto stayed with the colonists, becoming not only their interpreter but also, according to Bradford, "a special instrument sent of God for their good beyond their expectation." Squanto taught the colonists how to plant corn, where to catch fish and obtain "other commodities," and also served as their guide to the surrounding countryside.[20]

*T*HE INITIAL MEETING BETWEEN MASSASOIT AND THE COLOnists was also significant because it inaugurated Plymouth's fur trade. The Plymouth men had asked Massasoit to bring beaver pelts to trade, and he did.[21] Six months later the Plymouth men set out on their first fur-trading expedition. On September 18, 1621, around midnight, Miles Standish, Plymouth's military leader, along with nine colonists, Squanto, and two other Indians, began sailing their shallop north along the coast to visit the

Massachusetts Indians. In addition to procuring furs the men hoped to "see the Country" and "make Peace" with the Indians.[22]

Over the next four days the expedition explored what is now Boston Harbor and the lands surrounding it. Seeing such a beautiful, broad, deep, and protected harbor, fed by mighty rivers, the Plymouth men realized they had made a mistake. This would have been a much better location to settle than Plymouth, which had a relatively shallow harbor and no great rivers connecting it to the fur-rich hinterlands. But although the men wished "they had been there seated," it was too late to make a change.[23]

Finding Indians to trade with proved difficult. On his visit to the area in 1614 John Smith had declared it to be "the Paradise of all those parts." The harbor's islands, which he estimated might have had nearly three thousand inhabitants, were planted with corn, fruit trees, and beautiful, well-tended gardens. The coast was cultivated as well, and had "great troupes of well proportioned people."[24] The scene that greeted Standish and his men, in contrast, was of a ravaged landscape, with overgrown fields and all the people "dead or removed."[25] The same disease that had hit Plymouth had killed most of the native population, and many others had succumbed to intertribal warfare. When Standish finally found a small group of extremely fearful Indians a few miles inland, and made clear to them that he and his men had come in peace and wanted "to truck," the Indians relaxed. The women accompanied the men back to their boat; along the way they "sold their [fur] coats from their backs, and tied boughs about them, but with great shamefacedness (for indeed they are more modest than some of our English women are)." Before departing with "a good quantity of beaver," Standish promised to return.[26]

The success of this expedition did not come soon enough to satisfy Weston. He had expected the colonists to start generating profits almost instantaneously upon arriving in America, and when the *Mayflower* returned to England in April 1621, its cargo being ballast and a few Indian artifacts, Weston exploded. He dashed off a sharply worded letter to John Carver, the first governor of Plymouth, complaining about the empty ship and warning the colonists to do better next time. "That you sent no lading . . . is wonderful," wrote Weston sarcastically, "and worthily distasted. I know your weakness was the cause of it, and I believe more weakness of judgment, then weakness of hands. . . . . Consider that the life of the business depends on the lading of this ship." This letter arrived in Plymouth, onboard the *Fortune*, in November 1621. In the interim Carver had died and Bradford had been elected governor, so it was up to him to take up the reply, which was essentially: You insult us with your unfounded accusations, we were barely able to stay alive and bury our dead much less engage in trade, and we hope you will forget our "offenses" and move on.[27]

In addition to Weston's excoriating missive the *Fortune* brought thirty-seven colonists, a new land patent to the area where the Pilgrims had settled, and a renewed plea from the Merchant Adventurers for the colonists to consent to the harsh terms that had been proposed just prior to their departure from England—namely that all their days for seven years be devoted to earning returns for the company. The contract still rankled, but the colonists felt they had no choice, so they signed. Wanting to prove their worth to the company, the colonists quickly loaded the *Fortune* with "two hogsheads of beaver and otter skins," worth five hundred pounds—roughly 60 percent of the value of the ship's cargo—and sent it back to England.[28] Ironically, given its name, the ship had the misfortune of being captured by a French man-of-war on its return and stripped of its cargo before being allowed to sail to its destination. The Merchant Adventurers were understandably dismayed by the loss, but they were also encouraged by the fact that the colonists had sent any furs at all. The colonists had clearly gotten the message, and from then on the company expected furs to be part of every shipment.

*T*HE COMPANY HAD FROM THE START WANTED THE COLONISTS to succeed at fur trading, but it did little to help them achieve this goal. Despite the fact that it was common knowledge that to obtain furs from the Indians one needed items to trade, the company failed to supply the *Mayflower* with the traditional goods that would appeal to the Indians. Thus, when the colonists began bartering for furs, they had, as Bradford observed, to rely on the "few trifling commodities [they had] brought with them at first."[29] The colonists pleaded with the Merchant Adventurers to stock them adequately, but the response was anemic at best. Largely left to shift for themselves, the colonists improvised.

The leaders of Plymouth soon realized that the Indians wanted corn, and once the colonists' harvests improved, they were quick to convert their surplus corn into beaver pelts.[30] The colonists also took advantage of opportunities to obtain European trading goods whenever possible, as when the English ship *Discovery* sailed into Plymouth harbor in August of 1622. Fitted out for the Indian trade, the ship had plenty of beads and knives. The *Discovery*'s captain, Thomas Jones, was happy to sell these goods to the colonists, but since he knew he had the upper hand, he imposed a high price. In no position to haggle, the colonists offered "coat-beaver at three shillings per pound, which in a few years after yielded twenty shillings [and] by this means they were fitted again to trade for beaver."[31] On another occasion, in 1626, hearing that an English plantation or settlement, on Monhegan Island, off the coast of Maine, was ready to "break up," Bradford and fellow Pilgrim Edward Winslow, along with a few other colonists, took a boat and "went thither," purchasing five hundred pounds' worth of trading goods, one hundred pounds of which came from a French ship that had been cast ashore a few months earlier.[32]

AVING THE GOODS TO TRADE FOR BEAVERS IS ONLY half of the equation; you also need beavers. And here, several factors—biology, geography, and the impacts of the plague—posed serious obstacles. Because beavers do not migrate over great distances and have a relatively low reproductive rate, intense hunting can easily wipe out local populations. Thus the pressures of the fur trade quickly stripped all the beavers from the woods and meadows in the vicinity of Plymouth. And because Plymouth lacks large navigable rivers, there was no easy route for furs from the interior to be transported to the Pilgrims. Finally the plague wiped out many of the local Indians who would have been the Pilgrims' most logical trading partners, and who could have served as a bridge to tribes farther away, where furs were more plentiful.

The colonists overcame these obstacles by traveling up and down the coast, seeking out Indians who had furs to trade. Standish's trip to Boston Harbor in 1621 was the first such expedition, and it was followed by others, including one in 1625, when Edward Winslow and fellow colonists loaded a shallop with corn and sailed "40 or 50 leagues to the eastward," to Maine, where they ascended the Kennebec River and traded their corn with the local Indians for "700 pounds of beaver, besides some other furs."[33] These ventures, although they might appear insignificant, loomed very large in the life of the colony. As Bradford wrote, during these early years of Plymouth's existence, "there was no other means [beside the trade in furs] to procure . . . food which they so much wanted, and clothes also."[34]

Reliance on the Indians as suppliers of pelts would become a leitmotif for the American fur trade for more than two hundred years, during which time the Indians became, according to the historian Harold Hickerson, "a kind of vast forest proletariat whose production was raw fur and whose wages were drawn in goods."[35] As William Wood, an Englishman who lived in Massachusetts for four years, wrote in 1634, the colonists were not well suited to take up the hunt. The "wisdom" of the beaver "secures them from the English who seldom or never kills any of them, being not patient to lay a long siege or to be so often deceived by their cunning evasions, so that all the beaver which the English have comes first from the Indians whose time and experience fits them for that employment."[36]

The Indians employed many hunting methods in their pursuit of beaver. They used traps on land and nets in the water, baited with the wood the beavers ate. Sometimes the Indians' dogs would catch the beavers.[37] Indians would also damage parts of the dam, and shoot the beavers with arrows and spears when they came to mend the breach, or, if the pond was frozen over, the hunters might kill the beaver by taking advantage of its need for air. In the latter case the Indians first destroyed the beaver lodge, forcing the beavers to escape through plunge holes into the water. Knowing that the beavers would seek out "the hollow and thin places between the water and ice, where they can breathe," the Indians would find these spots using their clubs, one side of which was tipped with a "whale's bone," while the other had a sharpened "iron blade." The Indians tapped the ice with the tip of the bone, and when a hollow space was found, flipped the club over and used the blade to make a hole, "looking to see if the water is stirred up by the movement or breathing of the beaver." If it was, they used a "curved stick" and their club to grab the beaver and smash its skull.[38]

The dead beavers were then given to the Indian women to be skinned, a relatively tedious job that began with cutting off the beaver's legs at their base, then slitting the animal from the underside of the chin to the tail. Starting at the edges, the pelt was slowly sheared and pulled away from the body, making every effort to cut off as much of the meat and fat as possible. After further cleaning and preparation, the oval pelts would travel one of two paths. Many were cut into rectangular pieces and stitched together by the Indians, then worn as robes for a year or more before being traded to the Europeans. This coat beaver, or *castor gras* as the French called it, was the most valuable because nearly all of the pelt's coarse guard hairs—which stick out beyond the soft woolly undercoat, and would otherwise have to be time-consumingly plucked out and discarded during the felting process— were already removed as a result of the constant friction between the pelt and the Indians' bodies. As an added bonus the Indians' perspiration thickened the remaining hairs, making them easier to felt and giving them a lustrous sheen.

Pelts not incorporated into robes were stretched on branch hoops, using animal sinews threaded through the edges, and dried in the shade for a day or two. The pelt was then scraped to remove the last vestiges of meat or fat, and dried some more. When the pelt was finally removed from the stretcher, it was as stiff as a board and ready for trade and transport. Such pelts, called parchment beaver, or *castor sec*, by the French still had guard hairs in place, and therefore were of lesser value than *castor gras*. No matter how the pelts were prepared, it was extremely important that it be done properly, because shoddy work could lead to maggot and moth infestation, rendering the pelts worthless.[39]

*T*HE PLYMOUTH COLONY HAD PLENTY OF COMPETITION FOR THE fur trade. Along the coast small plantations were cropping up, virtually all of which planned to earn their keep by trading for furs.[40] The most surprising and least successful of these plantations was the one established by none other than Thomas Weston. Early in 1621 Weston decided to "divorce" himself from the company of Merchant Adventurers and strike out on his own, thinking that he knew much better than the Pilgrims how to make a business of trading furs in America. The company warned the Plymouth Colony of his plans to establish a settlement nearby and absorb as much of the trade as possible for himself, and perhaps to take what supplies he wanted from the colonists either by force or guile.[41]

A year later, when Weston sent more than "60 lusty men" to start his operations, he showed that he had learned almost nothing about achieving success in America. The men, who soon proved to be "rude fellows," whom the historian Samuel Eliot Morison claimed "were the riffraff of the London slums," came with virtually no food or supplies, and only through the kindness of the colonists, who allowed them to stay in Plymouth, did they make it through the next few months.[42] In the fall Weston's men moved to Wessagussett, near modern-day Weymouth on the edge of Boston Harbor. Totally out of their element, the men not only fell apart physically, unable even to feed themselves adequately, but also antagonized the nearby Massachusetts Indians, who in turn became aggressive toward them. When the Plymouth colonists learned from their ally Massasoit that the Massachusetts Indians were planning to destroy the small settlement at Wessagussett as well as Plymouth, they went on the offensive. Along with a small force Standish visited Wessagussett, the plan being to foil the Indians' plans by killing as many of them as possible. After inviting some Indians into a house under the pretense of sharing a meal, Standish and his men sprang their trap, stabbing the Indians to death. The brief battle spread beyond the house, with more Indians being killed and Standish's men emerging victorious.[43]

Saved from certain death, most of Weston's men decided that they had had enough and got in their ship and sailed to Maine. Not long after they departed, Weston arrived in America in a most curious fashion. The Council of New England—the organization that controlled the issuance of land patents for northern New England and the governance of the region—had ordered Weston to stay away from the area, so he disguised himself as a blacksmith, assumed an alias, and crossed the Atlantic on a fishing vessel, landing on the coast north of the Merrimack River.[44] Hearing of the "ruin and dissolution" of his colony, Weston sailed south to see what could be done, but his shallop was caught in a storm and wrecked on the shore of Ipswich Bay, where he was captured by Indians and stripped of all of his possessions. Barefoot and with only the shirt on his back, he made his way to a nearby trading post, borrowed clothes and finaly traveled to Plymouth, where he had the temerity to ask its leaders to stake him some beaver so that he could get back on his feet while he waited for one of his ships to resupply him. Although they remained angered with their erstwhile supporter for castigating them and failing to send them promised supplies, Plymouth's leaders took pity on this forlorn character, and decided that brotherly forgiveness was the order of the day. They gave Weston one hundred beaver skins and sent him on his way. Weston ultimately established a base of operations in Virginia and made a few trading trips to Maine, but, true to form, he "never repaid" the colonists for their kindness, as Bradford bitterly recalled, and instead offered only "reproaches and evil words." After a few years Weston returned to England, where he died in debt.[45]

*A*NOTHER SOURCE OF COMPETITION FOR THE PLYMOUTH Colony was the scores of ships frequenting New England, whose crews had come to fish and trade for furs. By 1624 there were already nearly forty English ships alone cruising Maine's coast.[46] Although the Plymouth colonists didn't like sharing potential profits with these itinerant traders, it was what the fishermen traded that bothered Plymouth the most. To gain an edge in the fur trade, these "interlopers" trafficked in guns. This was not a new development (for many years fishermen-traders from various countries had traded firearms with the Indians), but by the mid- to late 1620s its scope had expanded. And as the Indians became more familiar with guns and their great value in hunting and warfare, their desire for guns only grew stronger, making them even more eager to trade furs to arm themselves. Thus each year more guns made their way into Indian hands.

The arming of the Indians greatly alarmed the Plymouth Colony. Their main defense against Indian aggression had been their superiority in fire-power, but now that superiority was challenged. Writing about these times, Bradford gave full vent to his emotions. "Oh! that princes and parliaments would take some timely order to prevent this mischief [supplying Indians with guns and powder], and at length suppress it, by some exemplary punishment upon some of these gain thirsty murderers (for they deserve no better title) before their colonies in these parts be over thrown by these barbarous savages, thus armed with their own weapons, by these evil instruments, and traitors to their neighbors and country."[47] Making matters worse, the English fishermen were openly flouting King James I's 1622 proclamation prohibiting trading firearms to the Indians, a law put in place specifically to protect his majesty's subjects overseas.[48]

Virtually powerless to stop the fishermen from engaging in this trade, the Plymouth colonists were not the only ones who were impotent. In June 1623 Capt. Francis West sailed to America on the *Plantation*, at the behest of the Council of New England, which had given him the grandiose title of "Admiral of New-England." Outraged that these upstart fishermen were ignoring the requirement that they obtain a license from and pay a fee to the council before fishing or trading along the coast, it instructed West to compel the fishermen to comply. Outmanned and outgunned, West failed miserably, finding that his foes were "stubborn fellows," much too "strong" to be put in their place by the likes of him and his meager force.[49]

*W*HILE PLYMOUTH HAD NO RECOURSE AGAINST THE TRAN-
sient fishermen-traders, it was an entirely different situation when
men settled nearby and began trading guns for furs, as was the case with
Thomas Morton and his associates, who set up operations on the shores of
Boston Harbor. Born in Devon around 1576 to an Anglican family of some
aristocratic bearing, and trained in law, Morton referred to himself as "Thomas
Morton of Clifford's Inn, Gent." Others were less kind. Bradford designated
him a "kind of pettifogger" who had "more craft than honesty," Winslow
labeled him "an arrant knave," and the nineteenth-century historian Charles
Francis Adams said that Morton was "a born Bohemian and reckless libertine,
without either morals or religion."[50] Whatever else he was, however, his ideas
about life and, in particular, commerce in guns were too disturbing for Plymouth to accept without a fight.

Morton first visited America in 1622, then returned in 1625 with a captain
Wollaston, a few other men of means, and "a great many" indentured servants
who were obliged to work for Wollaston and the other overseers for a period
of years, the goal being to set up fishing and fur-trading operations along the
shores of Massachusetts Bay. This motley band settled Mt. Wollaston (now
Quincy), but in less than a year Wollaston, whom Bradford called a "man of
pretty parts," had grown pessimistic about the future of such an outpost, and
he particularly wanted to avoid having to suffer through another long, cold
New England winter. So he took most of his servants to Virginia, leaving the
rest of them, one of his associates, and Morton behind. Virginia was much
more to Wollaston's liking, and he soon sold his servants for a considerable
profit, requesting that another contingent of them be delivered from Mt. Wollaston forthwith.[51]

This turn of events alarmed Morton, because he knew that soon Wollaston would be asking him to head south as well. Between his three-month
visit in 1622, and his more prolonged stay in Mt. Wollaston, Morton had fallen
unabashedly in love with New England and its commercial potential, and he
wanted to settle there for good. In *New English Canaan*, published in 1637,
Morton mused rhapsodically about this new land, which had captured his
imagination in the same way it had John Smith's years earlier. "And when
I had more seriously considered, of the beauty of the place, with all her fair
endowments," wrote Morton, "I did not think that in all the known world it
could be paralleled. . . . For in mine eye, 'twas Nature's Masterpiece, her chief-

est magazine of all where lives her store: If this land be not rich, then is the whole world poor."[52]

Instead of succumbing to Captain Wollaston's entreaties to send more servants south, Morton began to sow dissension among those who had stayed behind, telling them that if they went south they too would be sold. At the same time he held out another option for their consideration. If they agreed to join with him and settle in this area, Morton promised to break their bonds of servitude, treat them as equals, and share with them the fruits of their labor. Such emoluments were sufficient to incite a mini-insurrection, during which Wollaston's other associate was cast out, and Morton, or "Mine Host" as he later liked to be called, and his minion established a trading post that he christened "Mare-mount," or literally "hill by the sea." But the Pilgrims, who greatly distrusted Morton and his heathenish ways, referred to this settlement as "Merie-Mount," which has come down to us as "Merrymount," a most appropriate designation given what transpired there.[53]

Merrymount quickly became an unusually free and conspicuously rowdy community bent on having fun while making money. Morton established warm relations with the local Indians, viewing them more as friends and coconspirators than ignorant natives and potential enemies. Morton respected how the Indians honored their aged, and he admired their compassion, humor, joie de vivre, and willingness to share pretty much everything but their wives. He was further impressed that they had no jails or gallows "furnished with poor wretches."[54] Indeed, if Morton had had to choose between being among the Pilgrims at Plymouth or the Indians, he would have chosen the latter without question.

Using guns for barter, "Mine Host" and his followers soon were overseeing a thriving beaver-pelt trade with the Indians.[55] In May 1627, to celebrate the success of his venture, Morton held a celebration for his men, the local Indians, and all other comers, replete with beer, poetry, dancing, and an eighty-foot maypole topped with the antlers of a large buck, which served, Morton said, "as a fair sea mark for directions; how to find out the way to mine Host of Ma-re Mount." A sexually provocative song composed for the wild event implored, "Lasses in beaver coats come away, Yee shall be welcome to us night and day." The song's refrain was even bawdier:

Drink and be merry, merry, merry boys,
Let all your delight be in Hymen's joys,
Lo to Hymen now the day is come,
About the merry Maypole take a Room.[56]

The priggish and straitlaced Puritans of the Plymouth Colony viewed these proceedings with growing horror. Commenting on the situation at Merrymount, Bradford claimed that Morton and his men

Fell to great licentiousness and led a dissolute life, powering out themselves into all profaneness. And Morton became lord of misrule, and maintained (as it were) a school of Atheism. And after they had got some good into their hands, and got much by trading with ye Indians, they spent it as vainly, in quaffing & drinking both wine & strong waters in great excess, and, as some reported, ten pounds worth in a morning. They also set up a Maypole, drinking and dancing about it many days together, inviting the Indian women, for their consorts, dancing and frisking together, (like so many fairies, or furies rather) and worse practices. As if they had anew revived & celebrated the feasts of the Roman Goddess Flora, or the beastly practices of the mad Bacchanalians.[57]

The colonists were also bothered by Merrymount's commercial success. Each beaver that went to Morton and his men was one less that could potentially have gone to Plymouth, and Plymouth's leaders hated being undercut in the trade that was literally keeping them afloat. But much more worrisome to the Plymouth Colony than either Merrymount's "great licentiousness" or its profit was Morton's supplying the Indians with guns and teaching them how to shoot. Had his only offense been outcompeting Plymouth in trade or sinking to the depths of moral depravity, at least in the eyes of the Puritans, Morton likely would have been left to his own devices, while still being roundly cursed by his neighbors.[58] But with the trade in guns Morton had crossed the line and set the stage for his ultimate downfall.[59]

It didn't matter that the Indians had shown no inclination to turn their guns on the English but had used them primarily for hunting—the Pilgrims' fear of what might happen was enough cause for alarm. Bradford wrote of the "terror" felt by the settlers living "straglingly" along the coast, with "no strength in any place," who met gun-toting Indians in the woods. If Morton was not stopped, the argument ran, the arming of the Indians would only escalate. And by early 1628 all signs indicated that such an escalation was already taking place. Morton had requested that more "pieces" be sent over from England, and the Indians had, according to Bradford, become "mad" to get guns, and would give anything they owned to attain them, "accounting their bows & arrows but baubles in comparison."[60]

In the spring of 1628 representatives of all the plantations in the vicinity of Boston Harbor that felt most threatened by Morton met to consider their options. Realizing that none of them had the power to confront Morton on their own, or even as a combined force, they turned to Plymouth for support. As the most populous and powerful settlement in the area, and the one that potentially had the most to lose from the actions of Morton and his rowdies, Plymouth rose to the challenge. Persuasion was chosen as the first line of attack, and the aggrieved plantations wrote to Morton "in a friendly & neighborly way," imploring him to stop trading guns to the Indians. Morton responded with a scathing letter, inquiring by what right the plantations questioned his activities, and claiming that he would continue to "trade pieces with the Indians" despite the displeasure it had aroused. Holding out hope that Morton was amenable to reason, the plantations sent a second joint letter, in which they advised Morton to be "more temperate in his terms," and pointed out that he was violating King James's 1622 ban on trading guns with Indians. They also added a subtle warning, telling Morton that "the country could not bear the injury he did."

Morton's response was anything but subtle, declaring "the king was dead and his displeasure with him." Then he threw in a warning of his own. If anyone tried to "molest" him, it was they who should be worried: He would be ready for them.[61] This insolence was too much for the plantations to tolerate, and they decided to take Morton by force. With each of the plantations contributing money to a battle fund, Plymouth outfitted Miles Standish and eight men, and sent them to apprehend "the lord of misrule."

What transpired next depends on who is doing the telling. According to Morton, whose account is filled with characteristic braggadocio, "the Separatists envying the prosperity and hope of the plantation at Mare Mount," particularly its success with the beaver trade, "made up a party" to capture him, claiming that he was "a great monster." Morton made light of the force sent against him, calling them the "nine Worthies of New Canaan," and derisively labeling Standish, who was small in stature, as "Captain Shrimp." Morton claimed that Standish and his men caught him "by accident" at Wessagussettt, a mile or so from Merrymount, and that they were so joyous to have "obtained" their "great prize" that they "fell to tippling" and gorging themselves on food. Morton did not partake in the festivities, so he could remain alert, and escape if the opportunity presented itself.

That night, when the six men guarding him, including one who was lying beside him in bed, drifted into a deep sleep, Morton arose and made his way silently through two locked doors. But just as he thought he had escaped unnoticed, the second door slipped from his grip and slammed shut. This woke the guards and Standish, who Morton claimed, "took on most furiously, and tore at his clothes for anger, to see the empty nest, and their bird gone."

Standish caught up with Morton at Merrymount and pleaded with him to surrender and lay down his arms, so that he could be sent back to England. Morton, who claimed to be "the son of a soldier," at first declined, but after thinking of all the "worthy blood"—not his, theirs—that would be spilled in a fight, he relented when Standish promised not to harm him or any of his men. Despite this agreement Morton claimed that when he opened the door, "Captain Shrimp" and his men "fell upon him, as if they would have eaten him," and that the only reason they didn't "slice" him with a sword was because one of Standish's men, an old soldier, admonished the "worthies for their unworthy practices."[62]

Bradford's account lacks both the drama and the indignation of Morton's version. There is no mention of the encounter and stealthy escape at Wessagussett. Instead, when Standish arrived at Merrymount, "mine host" was already holed up in one of his houses, the doors and windows barred, with his men about him and "diverse dishes of powder & bullets ready on the table." Morton at first ignored Standish's summons to yield, preferring to cast "scoffs and scorns" at his attackers. Then, fearing that Standish would break down the walls of the house, Morton and some of his men exited through the front door, guns by their side. But they were all "so steeled with drink" that they couldn't even raise their "pieces" to aim, much less shoot any of the force arrayed against them. Morton wanted to shoot Standish, but before he could make an attempt, Standish stepped forward, grabbed the gun, and took hold of Morton. So ended the Battle of Merrymount, the only casualty one of Morton's men, who was so drunk that "he ran his own nose upon the point of a sword" one of Standish's men was holding up as he entered the house.[63]

Whichever of these stories is more accurate, the end result was the same. Morton received a mock trial and was held prisoner on the rocky Isle of Shoals, ten miles off the coast of New Hampshire and Maine, until a ship was found to take him back to England. Stripped of its leader, Merrymount dissolved and was renamed Mount Dagon in 1629, only to burn to the ground the next year.[64]

W HILE THE PLYMOUTH COLONISTS DEALT WITH MORTON, they simultaneously developed an interesting relationship with the Dutch. It began in March 1627, when Isaack de Rasière, the secretary of New Amsterdam, wrote governor Bradford a letter. Although the Dutch had known about the Plymouth Colony since its inception, this letter was the first formal contact between the two. De Rasière noted that the Dutch had often traveled by shallop up the coast and traded with Indians within a half day's journey of Plymouth, and being in such close proximity, the Dutch thought it was time to introduce themselves formally. De Rasière congratulated the English on the success of their colony and held out the hand of friendship. In particular he wanted to establish a mutually beneficial trading arrangement with Plymouth, and therefore offered to sell them Dutch wares in exchange for beaver or otter skins, and he added that if the English didn't desire these things, he hoped they would nonetheless be willing to sell the Dutch furs and other useful items "for ready money."[65]

Bradford responded with similar politesse, affirming Plymouth's desire to trade, but he also warned the Dutch to stop trading with the Indians to the southwest of Cape Cod, in and around Buzzard's and Narragansett bays. That land, he maintained, was claimed by England, a fact that gave Plymouth the right to expel intruders—a right Bradford implied they would exercise if the Dutch didn't back off. De Rasière responded that the Dutch had a claim to that land as well, and would continue to trade with the Indians as they pleased, but for the time being neither side took this dispute any farther. Instead they began trading.

With trumpets blaring to announce his arrival, de Rasière visited Plymouth in October 1627. He laid out for the colonists' perusal a great range of items, including tobacco, three types of colorful cloth, and sugar. The most important thing de Rasière brought with him, however, was wampum. Largely ignorant of wampum's great value in the Indian trade, the Plymouth colonists listened intently as he told them "how vendible it was" at Fort Orange, and how it had enabled the Dutch to obtain a great many furs. Then, in a not-so-subtle effort to direct Plymouth's trading attention to the northeast and away from southwestern areas where the Dutch were most active, de Rasière said that there was no doubt that if the English acquired wampum it would be a great boon to their fur trade in Maine, along the Kennebec River. Convinced by this pitch, Plymouth's leaders purchased fifty pounds' worth of the shell beads.[66]

The purchase of wampum and the focus on Maine meshed perfectly with Plymouth's evolving plans for the fur trade. After Winslow's successful trip to Maine in 1625, which yielded seven hundred pounds of beaver, there had been others to the same general vicinity. To get this trade on a firmer footing, Plymouth obtained a patent to the land along the Kennebec in 1628, and that same year they established a trading house on the river, at the site of present-day Augusta, and stocked it with clothing, blankets, corn and other food-stuffs, as well as other commodities that the Indians had shown a willingness to trade for furs. The colonists also stocked the post with the wampum they had recently purchased, but to their dismay found that it wasn't as "vendible" in Maine as de Rasière had predicted, at least in the short term. The inland Indians who came to the new trading post were unfamiliar with wampum and were at first reluctant to accept it in trade. Within two years time, however, that reluctance had been replaced by desire, with Bradford noting that from then on the Indians "could scarce ever get enough" wampum.[67]

*T*HE ACQUISITION OF WAMPUM AND THE EXPANSION OF TRAD-ing activities in Maine coincided with a radical restructuring of the economic underpinnings of the Plymouth Colony. In 1628 eight of the leading men in the community, including Bradford, Winslow, and Standish, assumed the burden of paying off the colony's £1,800 debt to the Merchant Adventur-ers in return for a six year monopoly to the region's fur trade. With Isaac Allerton, the former assistant governor of the Plymouth Colony, as their lead sales agent in London, the eight so-called undertakers expected to export a steady stream of furs and quickly draw down the debt, and they got off to a good start, sending nearly £700 worth of beaver to England their first year.[68]

The undertakers' stake in Maine's fur trade increased in 1629 when Aller-ton and a few other investors came to them with a proposition. Allerton's group had decided to launch a fur-trading post on the Penobscot River, and they wanted the undertakers to join as partners in this venture and/or supply the post with trading goods and food. This offer placed the undertakers in an uncomfortable position. If they refused to join the venture *or* supply the post, they risked offending and possibly losing the support of Allerton's group, which included the undertakers' main financial backers. On the other hand, if the undertakers didn't become partners in the Penobscot post but provided it with supplies, they would be aiding the competition, and likely reducing the profitability of the fur-trading post they had set up on the Kennebec River just a year earlier.

Making the decision more problematic was the undertakers' distrust and dislike of the man chosen to run the Penobscot post—Edward Ashley—"a very profane young man," according to Bradford, who had earlier offended the Pilgrims' sensitivities by living with the Indians, going "naked among them," and adopting "their manners." In the end the undertakers overlooked their concerns about Ashley, and signed on as partners and suppliers. It wasn't long, however, before Ashley lived up to their worst fears. Although he quickly gathered a "good parcel of beaver," Ashley refused to pay back the undertakers for any of the supplies they had given him, and then he had the gall to ask for more. And Ashley's familiarity with the Indians had, Bradford claimed, led him to commit "uncleanness with Indian women," an unpardonable sin in the Pilgrims' eyes. But what got Ashley into the most trouble was his trading "powder and shot" with the Indians, an offense that led to his arrest and imprisonment in England. With Ashley out of the way, the undertakers took over operations at the Penobscot trading post in 1630.[69]

*J*UST FOUR YEARS AFTER THE PILGRIM'S COLONIAL EXPERIment had begun, Edward Winslow wrote glowingly about the promise of the fur trade in New England. "Much might be spoken of the benefit that may come to such as shall plant here, by trade with the Indians for furs, . . . [for] the English, Dutch and French return yearly many thousand pounds profit by trade only."[70] During the balance of the 1620s Winslow and his fellow colonists made good on that promise. The Plymouth Colony had solidified its presence in the fur-rich region of Maine, and despite Dutch designs, was also branching out toward the southwest, establishing another trading post on the underside of Cape Cod, at the head of Buzzard's Bay, on the site of modern Sandwich. The combination of surplus corn harvests, wampum, and other commodities now coming more regularly from England gave Plymouth the means to expand the fur trade, while the colony's new financial arrangement and the undertakers' monopoly allowed for visions of a debt-free future. Indeed, by the dawn of the 1630s all the signs seemed to be pointing to the colony's continued success in the fur trade. Yet within ten years that trade simply disappeared.

PART II

*Clash of
Empires*

PREVIOUS PAGE | George Washington in the
Uniform of a British Colonel, *by Charles
Willson Peale, 1772.*

5

Competition, Conflict, and Chicanery

John Winthrop, by Samuel Harris, 1806.

AD THE PLYMOUTH UNDERTAKERS ADVERTISED FOR the candidate to be their representative in London, they could hardly have found a more promising applicant than Isaac Allerton. A respected member of the community—one of the original passengers on the *Mayflower* and the fifth signatory of the Mayflower Compact—he seemed to be the perfect choice. Surely such a man would act in the undertakers' best interests, especially since he was one of them. By 1630, however, he had resigned, leaving them facing an unholy financial mess.

Rather than sell furs and apply the profits to paying off the debt and supporting the colony, Allerton had taken a more self-serving path. Charging exorbitant amounts for supplies and engaging in duplicitous bookkeeping practices as well as questionable private expenditures, he not only squandered most of the profits but also allowed the undertakers' debt to more than double. Reflecting on this sorry state of affairs, Bradford ruefully observed that the entire colony had been "hoodwinked."[1]

With Allerton gone, however, and a new accountant tracking business expenditures, the undertakers fervently hoped that their fortunes would improve. But with continuing access to a good supply of furs being cut off as a result of French incursions in the north and competition from the Dutch—and other Englishmen—in the southwest, the unfortunate undertakers' bridge to economic viability was slowly crumbling: The imperial battle for America's fur trade had begun.

Soon after Allerton resigned, the French struck a blow at Plymouth's fur trade in an attack that was quick, bloodless, and almost comical in its execution. When a French ship arrived at Plymouth's Penobscot trading post in 1631, the men onboard, including a Scotsman acting as interpreter, claimed that they had long been at sea and had no idea where they were, and since the ship was leaking they asked for permission to land to make repairs. Permission granted, they came ashore, whereupon the Scotsman, conversing with a few of the "servants," discovered that their "master and the rest of the company" were at Plymouth fetching supplies. This information caused the Frenchmen suddenly to become quite interested in the guns on the wall racks of the trading post's main house, and they took them down for a closer look. Seemingly unaware of the trap being set, the servants responded affirmatively when asked whether the guns were loaded. With that the Frenchmen stopped admiring the guns and pointed them at the servants, bidding "them not to stir, but quietly" gather all that was of value. Soon the Frenchmen were on their way, enriched by £500 of goods and three hundred pounds of beaver pelts.[2]

Four years later the French attacked the post again, when Charles de Menou, sieur d'Aulnay, sailed into Penobscot Bay with orders from the Acadian governor "to clear the coast unto Pemaquid and Kennebec of all persons whatsoever." D'Aulnay commandeered the post's shallop which was offshore, and forced its men to pilot in his ship. On shore he took possession of the post and "purchased" all of its supplies at prices he set, claiming that he would pay the dispossessed Englishmen later, *if* they ever came to get what he owed them. Having finished the fire sale, d'Aulnay, "with a great deal of compliment and many fine words," gave the Plymouth men a small amount of food, crammed them into their shallop, and sent them home. When the ousted traders shared their story, it roused the colony's ire and spurred Plymouth's leaders to seek revenge and attempt to recapture the post.[3]

The Plymouth men consulted with their Puritan neighbors at the Massachusetts Bay Colony, which had been founded in 1629, to see if they would lend their support. Although the Massachusetts men approved of the retaliatory strike, they would not provide any funding, so Plymouth had to go it alone. They hired a three-hundred-ton ship, captained by a Mr. Girling and "well fitted with ordnance." If Girling succeeded in driving off the French his reward would be seven hundred pounds of beaver; but if he failed he would get nothing. To assist Girling, Plymouth sent a bark with a crew of twenty, led by the fearless and resolute Miles Standish. In the bark's hold, stored for safekeeping until the French were defeated, lay the sizable heap of beaver pelts that would be Girling's payment.

The expedition was a complete disaster. Pigheaded and rash, Girling disregarded the agreed-upon strategy, which was to give the French a chance to parley and voluntarily lay down their arms in the face of a well-armed foe. Instead Girling "began to shoot at distance like a mad man," and because the French were well protected by earthen breastworks, he "did them no hurt at all." Standish, alarmed and angered, convinced Girling that he would have better luck if he got closer to the targets, but it was too late. When Girling advanced he was able to get off only a few shots before exhausting his powder. At Girling's urging Standish reluctantly went to the nearest English plantation and obtained additional powder to continue the assault. By this time, however, Standish had grown suspicious of Girling's intent, having heard "by intelligence" that the incompetent captain intended to seize the bark and take all the furs. Rather than risk this Standish delivered the powder to Girling, then headed home with the pelts still onboard. His plan dashed, Girling bothered the French no more and sailed away.[4]

After Standish's return the Plymouth Colony attempted yet again to get the Massachusetts Bay Colony to support an expedition against the French. And for the second time the Massachusetts men, while continuing to be sympathetic, declined, citing financial limitations. But the real reason the Massachusetts men demurred was that they had no interest in helping Plymouth's fur trade at the expense of their own. From its founding, the Massachusetts Bay Colony viewed the fur trade as a means to maintain itself and pay off its investors.[5] In 1630, just a year after the colony received its royal charter, "the most highly developed enterprise in New England was the exportation of furs by the Pilgrims," and the Massachusetts men wanted to share in that success.[6] The possibilities of the fur trade astounded the Reverend Francis Higginson, one of the earliest Massachusetts Bay settlers. "It is almost incredible," he wrote in 1629, "what great gain some of our English planters have had by our

Indian corn." For proof he pointed to a man who sowed thirteen gallons of corn, which cost 6s. 8d. and was able to trade the resulting crop to local Indians for £327 of beaver, generating profits of nearly 1,000 percent.[7]

Before the Massachusetts Bay Colony could emulate Plymouth's success, it had to gain access to furs. This posed a problem. Most of the fur-bearing animals in the vicinity of Boston Harbor had been killed to feed the trade, forcing the Massachusetts Bay men to look farther afield. But when they did they found that the Plymouth Colony had gotten there first. This caused John Winthrop, the governor of the Massachusetts Bay Colony, to complain bitterly in 1634, with more than a twinge of commercial jealousy, that Plymouth had "engrossed all the Chief places of trade in N:E: viz.: Kennebec, Penobscot, Narragansett, and Connecticut."[8] Therefore, whenever the Massachusetts Bay Colony had an opportunity to beat Plymouth in the race for furs, it took it. Indeed, after the Plymouth men had been run out of the Penobscot post, merchants from the Massachusetts Bay Colony launched their own trade with the post's new French tenants, exchanging provisions, powder, and shot for furs and other goods, a move greatly decried by Plymouth's leaders, who had expected less predatory and more brotherly behavior on the part of their God-fearing neighbors.[9]

*T*HE PENOBSCOT AFFAIR WAS NOT THE FIRST TIME THAT THE Maine fur trade caused friction between the Plymouth and the Massachusetts Bay Colonies. In April 1634 there took place an event that Bradford said was "one of the saddest things that befell them since they came." John Hocking, a fur trader from the English plantation at Piscataway (now Portsmouth, New Hampshire), sailed up the Kennebec with a small crew, intending to go above the Plymouth Colony's trading post and intercept all the furs the Indians brought downriver. When Hocking reached the post, John Howland, the post's headman, told him that all the furs in the area belonged to Plymouth, demanding that Hocking and his men leave at once. Hocking responded that he would continue, Plymouth be damned, and trade there "as long as he pleased." Howland shouted back that he would be compelled to remove Hocking by force. Unimpressed by this show of bravado, Hocking "bid [Howland] . . . to do his worst" and then sailed upriver, anchoring out of sight of the post.[10]

Howland and four of his men pursued Hocking a short time later, and when they reached him, Howland again implored Hocking to leave peacefully. Spewing "foul" words, Hocking refused and then demanded to know whether Howland intended to shoot him. No, Howland replied, but he promised to send him away, and with that, ordered his men to cut Hocking's cables so that his boat would drift downriver. With one cable cut, Hocking warned Howland's men not to cut the other, and when they attempted to do so, Hocking grabbed his pistol and placed it against the temple of one of Howland's men, Moses Talbott. "Don't shoot him, shoot me instead!" Howland screamed, adding that Talbott was just following orders, and that "if any wrong was done it was himself that did it."[11] Ignoring Howland's plea, Hocking pulled the trigger, killing Talbott instantly. Before he could shoot again one of Talbott's "fellows (who loved him well)," shot Hocking, "who fell down and never spoke a word."[12] Leaderless, the rest of Hocking's men beat a hasty retreat.

Hocking's men told their fellow colonists at Piscataway that Hocking was the victim rather than the instigator, and that he was killed "without provocation." When this story filtered back to the Massachusetts Bay Colony, a great furor arose. Not only did the thought "of cutting one another's throats for beaver" alarm the populace, but the murders themselves had violated the sixth commandment, "Thou shalt not kill." When one of Hocking's relatives lodged a complaint with Governor Winthrop, "desiring that justice might be done upon the offender," the Massachusetts Bay Colony sprang into action.[13] Winthrop imprisoned John Alden, one of Plymouth's magistrates, who just happened to be in Boston at the time, on the grounds that he was at the Kennebec trading post when the murders occurred and should be called to account, even though he was not directly implicated in the shootings.[14]

Plymouth's leaders, outraged that their "neighbors," who had "no jurisdiction over them," had imprisoned a member of their colony and forced him to stand in court, sent Standish to tell their side of the story and gain Alden's release. Winthrop set Alden free, but only after Standish promised to appear in court and answer the charges. In the meantime Lords Say and Brooke, the owners of the Piscataway plantation, sent some pointed advice to Plymouth's governor, Thomas Prince: "We could, for the death of Hocking, have dispatched a man-of-war and beat down your houses at Kennebec about your ears; but we have thought another course preferable"—namely gathering together representatives from the Plymouth, Massachusetts Bay, and the Piscataway plantations to review the case and render a decision. But when the day came, nobody from Piscataway appeared, so the officials from Plymouth and Massachusetts Bay "fell into a fair debating of things," and devised their own ruling. They concluded that Hocking had infringed on Plymouth's rights, that he was to blame for the deadly altercation, and that his death was an excusable although deeply regretted homicide.[15]

The Hocking incident and the French takeover of the Penobscot post further stoked the Massachusetts Bay Colony's interest in the Maine fur trade, underscoring the Plymouth Colony's relative weakness and inability to protect its interests in that area. As a result Massachusetts Bay traders, as well as other English traders along the coast, gradually pushed the Plymouth fur traders aside, virtually eliminating them from Maine by the end of the 1630s. At the same time that Plymouth was being shut out of the northern fur trade, a similar dynamic was taking place to the south and west, where the Dutch—and to a much greater extent other English colonists—were putting the squeeze on Plymouth.

*I*N THE LATE 1620S, WHEN NEW AMSTERDAM AND PLYMOUTH were still enjoying a reasonably friendly if guarded relationship, the Dutch told the English about a wonderful place—the fertile and fur-rich lands along the Connecticut River. The Dutch invited the English to settle there and leave behind their present relatively "barren quarter." Bradford viewed this invitation as a magnanimous gesture, but the Dutch had an ulterior motive—they assumed that if the English settled along the river they would come under Dutch control, thereby giving the Dutch the opportunity to consolidate their claim on the region while adding to the population of their still-small colony. Plymouth's leaders initially rejected the invitation, but they had a change of heart after a visit from a Mahican sachem named Wahginnacut.[16]

In 1631 Wahginnacut, whose people lived in the Connecticut River valley, journeyed to both Plymouth and Massachusetts Bay with an offer. If the English settled along the Connecticut River, Wahginnacut would supply them with corn and eighty beaver skins each year, and the English would also be able to pursue the fur trade on their own. Wahginnacut hoped that the English would become allies against the Pequot, who had been attacking Wahginnacut's people and evicting them from their lands. The Massachusetts Bay leaders politely declined, but their Plymouth counterparts were intrigued, especially since they had only recently learned of Allerton's betrayal and were desperate to expand their trading activities. To find out if Wahginnacut's offer was worth accepting, Plymouth sent Winslow on a reconnaissance mission to the Connecticut River the next year, and he reported that it was "a fine place." This was followed by trading forays that were "not without profit."[17]

Plymouth's leaders finally decided in 1633 to stake a claim to the Connecticut River valley. In July, Bradford and Winslow met with Governor Winthrop and urged the Massachusetts Bay Colony to join with Plymouth to build a trading post on the Connecticut River in order to keep the Dutch out. When Winthrop refused, Bradford and Winslow sweetened the deal, offering to launch the venture if Massachusetts Bay would partner with them and promise to provide financial support in later years. But Winthrop could not be swayed, later writing that the Bay Colony's leaders "thought [it] not fit to meddle with" the project. Finally Bradford and Winslow asked Winthrop if he was opposed to Plymouth going it alone, and when Winthrop said no, Plymouth began preparing to head to the valley. But, as Plymouth would soon find out, the Dutch were already there.[18]

*W*HATEVER DESIRE THE DUTCH INITIALLY HAD FOR THE people of Plymouth to settle in the Connecticut River valley had evaporated by early 1633. The Dutch viewed the valley as their backyard and the English as potential invaders, who would not only displace the Dutch fur trade but the Dutch themselves if they had the chance. The Dutch were well aware of an English land patent that had been awarded to Lords Say and Brooke, among others, in 1631, which gave them title to a huge swath of land from Rhode Island to New York, including the Connecticut River valley. And the Dutch very likely had heard about Wahginnacut's overtures to the Plymouth and Massachusetts Bay colonies. Then, in 1633, came an event that only heightened the growing animosity and distrust the Dutch had for the English in America.[19]

The English ship *William* arrived at Fort Amsterdam on April 18, and its supercargo, the Dutchman Jacob Eelkes, declared his intention to trade for furs farther up the Hudson. Eelkes was the very same man who, in 1622, as an employee of the Dutch West India Company, had seized a Sequin Indian chief and held him for the ransom of 140 fathoms of wampum. Summarily dismissed by the Dutch for this heinous action, he had thrown his allegiance to the English, and was now back in America to use his knowledge of the fur trade to benefit his new bosses.

What happened next was a sort of "comic opera."[20] After getting drunk with Eelkes, Wouter van Twiller, the recently installed director general of New Amsterdam, remained mute while Eelkes and the Dutch adventurer David de Vries engaged in a heated argument that had both men claiming rights to the river and its furs by virtue of discovery. Eelkes claimed that Henry Hudson was English and therefore the river was an English possession, to which de Vries responded that Hudson was a Dutch employee at the time, and therefore the river was most certainly Dutch. A few days later Eelkes weighed anchor and began sailing upriver, while all van Twiller could rouse himself to do was break out the wine, drink up, and exhort his fellow Dutchmen to halt the Englishmen's advance—a call that elicited mocking laughter but no action.[21]

The daring de Vries could hold back his condemnation no longer. He scolded van Twiller for being weak, and said that if he had been in charge he would have bombarded Eelkes's ship with cannon fire from the fort, "and have prevented him from going up the river," adding, "The English are of so haughty a nature, they think everything belongs to them. I should send the ship *Soutberg* after him, and drive him out of the river."[22] A few days later van Twiller, urged to action by de Vries, sent three armed ships upriver to expel the intruder. By the time the ships arrived in the vicinity of Fort Orange, Eelkes had already begun trading, but it took the overwhelming Dutch force only a short while to round up Eelkes and his crew and transport them back to Fort Amsterdam, from which they and their ship were sent back to England. Spurred on by this incident, as well as knowledge of the impending English settlement of the Connecticut River valley, van Twiller proceeded with the construction of a small fort on the Connecticut River in the vicinity of what is now Hartford. Completed in June 1633, it was named "Fort Good Hope."[23]

Soon thereafter Plymouth forged ahead with its plan for a trading post on the Connecticut, purchasing from the Indians land six miles above the Dutch fort, and outfitting a "great new bark," captained by William Holmes, with all the supplies necessary to construct the post. When Holmes reached Fort Good Hope in early October, the fort's commander demanded to know where he was headed. Upon hearing that the Plymouth men planned to "seat" themselves above the fort and trade with the Indians, the commander ordered the Englishmen to "strike and stay" or be fired upon. Holmes defiantly responded that since he had a commission from the governor of Plymouth, it was his sworn duty to continue. The commander unleashed a few more choice threats, but his resolve didn't match his words, and he let the English pass. After reaching their destination, on the site of modern-day Windsor, the Plymouth men quickly "clapped up" their prefabricated frame house and built palisades around it for protection.[24]

When van Twiller learned of the Plymouth Colony's impudence, he sent its leaders a letter pointing out that the Dutch had already laid claim to the Connecticut River, and requesting that the Plymouth men leave at once. Totally ineffectual, this letter was followed by van Twiller's sending forth seventy armed men from Manhattan, with instructions to intimidate the English into leaving but not to use force. Upon seeing that the English were well defended, and that "it would cost blood" to dislodge them, the Dutch commander opted "to parley" instead, ultimately withdrawing his troops and returning to Manhattan "in peace."[25] With this the Plymouth men commenced trading with the Indians, happy that the Dutch had not proved to be quite the obstacle to settlement that Plymouth's leaders had feared. There was, however, another, much bigger obstacle to Plymouth's ambitions in the Connecticut River valley—their fellow Englishmen.

*I*N 1630 PLYMOUTH WAS THE MOST POPULOUS OF ALL NEW England colonies, with roughly three hundred people, but within five years the "great migration" of Puritans from England catapulted the Massachusetts Bay Colony into the lead with four to five thousand inhabitants.[26] Many of these people were crowded along the coast and wanted for a variety of reasons to move on. Some felt physically hemmed in, others sought to find a place where they could pursue their own brand of religion beyond the reproachful eyes of the Puritan leaders of Massachusetts Bay, and still others were seeking new economic opportunities. For this last group the fur trade was the most compelling draw. Even before the vast tide of humanity descended on the Massachusetts Bay Colony, many of its earliest residents pursued this trade. For example, in 1629 Mathew Craddock, the first governor of the colony, established a fur-trading and shipbuilding post on the Mystic River, just three miles from Charlestown, in the area of modern-day Medford.[27] Six years later Simon Willard led a dozen families on a seventeen-mile march inland to found the town of Concord, choosing this location in large part because it was well situated for the fur trade, with plenty of streams and ponds, and a river running through it.[28]

At first it appeared that the Massachusetts men weren't interested in exploiting the Connecticut River valley. After all, in July 1633 Winthrop had declined Bradford and Winslow's invitation to establish a joint trading post on the river. In doing so, however, Winthrop was, as one historian has politely observed, exhibiting "some disingenuousness."[29] The leaders of the Massachusetts Bay Colony wanted to settle the Connecticut River valley not only to take advantage of its furs but also its rich agricultural lands—they just didn't want Plymouth as a partner. Within weeks of refusing Plymouth's invitation Winthrop sent the *Blessing of the Bay* on a trip to the Connecticut River, Long Island, and New Amsterdam, where the Puritans presented van Twiller with a commission from Winthrop stating that "the King of England had granted the river and country of Connecticut to his own subjects; and therefore desired them [the Dutch] to forbear to build there." Despite this thinly veiled threat, van Twiller "kindly entertained" his guests and sent them on their way.[30] A few days after the *Blessing of the Bay* returned to Boston, Winthrop received a letter from van Twiller recommending that the two colonies leave it up to the English king and the Dutch States General to "agree concerning the limits and parting of their quarters, that as good neighbors we might live in these heathenish countries."[31] But King Charles I was too busy dealing with a variety of domestic and international problems to concern himself with such distant colonial disputes, leaving the Massachusetts Bay Colony to deal with the issue as it saw fit. And the Massachusetts men soon made their choice— they were heading to Connecticut.

JOHN OLDHAM'S FUR-TRADING VENTURE TO THE CONNECTI-cut River in 1633 proved decisive in making this choice. During the summer Oldham and three companions traveled what would later be called the "Old Connecticut Path," an Indian trail that started in Cambridge, Massachusetts, and wound its way over hills and through valleys, ending at the river near present-day Hartford.[32] When the expedition returned in September with many furs, and spoke so glowingly about the prospects for trading, and the fertility of the dark, rich soil in the region, the Connecticut River valley became an exceedingly attractive destination for those seeking to get away from the confines of the Massachusetts Bay Colony and start a new life.[33]

The floodgates for emigration opened in 1635, when a large group of colonists from Massachusetts Bay made their way to the Connecticut River, settling in Hartford, Wethersfield, as well as right on top of Plymouth's trading post at Windsor. The post's agent was alarmed by this great influx, writing to Bradford that "the Massachusetts men are coming almost daily, some by water, some by land. . . . I will do what I can to withstand them. I hope they will hear reason; as that we were here first, and entered with much difficulty and danger, both in regard of the Dutch and Indians, and bought the land."[34] The Massachusetts men, however, were not interested in reasoning with Plymouth about ownership, for they believed that "God . . . in a fair way of providence tendered" the land to them. Shocked at this cavalier and pernicious claim of divine right, Bradford admonished the intruders not to "cast . . . a covetous eye upon that which is your neighbor's and not yours," but this and other remonstrations had no effect whatsoever. The Massachusetts men greatly outnumbered Plymouth's meager force, they had all the power, and they weren't going anywhere. The Plymouth Colony didn't even consider retaliating but instead sought to make "peace . . . upon as good terms as they could get." Those terms turned out to be not very good at all, leaving the Plymouth men with only one-sixteenth of the land they had originally occupied, with the rest going to the newcomers. "Thus was the controversy ended," wrote Bradford, "but the unkindness not so soon forgotten."[35]

The Bay colonists were not the only ones seizing furs in Connecticut. Independent traders and fisherman were competitors, along with other English settlements, such as the one at the mouth of the Connecticut River, established in October 1635, when John Winthrop, Jr., sent a bark with twenty men to lay claim to the area. The fact that the Dutch had purchased this land from the local Indians three years earlier didn't bother Winthrop in the least; since it was part of an English land patent, he viewed the Dutch as trespassers. When Winthrop's men arrived they ripped down the arms of the Dutch government, which had been hanging from a tree, and "engraved a ridiculous face in their place."[36] By the time van Twiller sent a sloop to chase off the English it was too late. With two cannons at the ready, Winthrop's men repelled the puny Dutch force without firing a shot. The English fort and fur-trading post soon became known as Saybrook, in honor of Lords Say and Brooke, two of the patentees.[37]

By 1636 there were nearly eight hundred Massachusetts émigrés in Connecticut, further marginalizing the few Plymouth settlers who remained and making it more difficult for them to benefit from the region's fur trade.[38] That same year Plymouth's situation worsened when William Pynchon, one of the leaders of the Bay Colony, established a fur-trading post on the Connecticut River at a place called Agawam—now Springfield, Massachusetts— upriver from Plymouth's trading operations at Windsor. Pynchon's post soon absorbed most of the fur traffic on the river.[39]

With Plymouth bullied by the French to the north and pushed aside by the English to the southwest, the colony's fur trade suffered, and just when it seemed that things could get no worse, they did. Since jettisoning Allerton, Plymouth's leaders had blithely assumed that their financial difficulties were over. But they were shocked by the results of an audit of their fur-trade accounts in 1636. According to their agents in England, Plymouth still had considerable debts, despite having shipped roughly £12,000 worth of beaver and other furs to England between 1631 and 1636, an amount that, according to Bradford, should have cleared their entire account and then some.[40] It appeared that Plymouth's leaders had been hoodwinked again, but much of the blame must be laid at their own feet. Given their past experience, the leaders should have been much more engaged in overseeing their economic destiny. Hemmed in on all sides and unable to defend its interests, the colony found its fur trade slowly atrophying. For the remainder of the decade the colony sent fewer furs back to England each successive year, and by 1640 the trade had for all practical purposes ceased.[41]

*A*S PLYMOUTH'S FUR FORTUNES SANK, THE TRADE THRIVED throughout the rest of New England, spurred by growing demand. The rising colonial population led to an increase in the local consumption of beaver hats. Even in the Bay Colony, where the general court passed a law in 1634 that forbade the purchasing or wearing of beaver hats (except those already owned), because they were seen as promoting the twin sins of vanity and pride, such hats remained sought-after.[42] And in Europe the wearing of furs remained an important sign of class distinction. As one contemporary Frenchman observed, "Bachelors, Doctors of Law, Emperors, and Doctors of Medicine are vested in furs which represent the mysteries of Theology, the maxims of politics, and the secrets of medical science. . . . Of all the ornaments which luxury has invented there are none so glorious, so august, and so precious as furs. . . . The privileges and honors of Furriers and Skinners surpass quite rightly those of all other crafts."[43] English furriers who made beaver hats were given an added economic boost in 1638 when King Charles I declared that thenceforth England would no longer import foreign-made beaver hats, and that all beaver hats made in England for English consumption had to be made of 100 percent beaver, not mixed with other inferior furs, such as rabbit.[44]

When New England's fur traders pondered the future there was one particularly troubling sign. Fur-bearing animals were being hunted to commercial extinction over broader areas, requiring Indians to travel longer, over more tenuous supply routes, to bring furs to the scattered English trading posts. But New England's traders believed that there was one way to improve their prospects: If they could take over the lucrative Dutch fur trade, profitability might be ensured.

— 6 —

"Many Hounds Are the Hare's Death"

Peter Stuyvesant,
by Thomas Gimbrede, 1826.

NEW ENGLANDERS HAD LONG BEEN JEALOUS OF THE DUTCH
fur trade. For years they had heard stories about the many thousands
of beaver pelts and other furs the Dutch annually exported to Holland, and
they dreamed of diverting those furs into English hands. In 1635 an anonymous writer complained that the Dutch were "a great hindrance to the English
colonies in their trade of beaver."[1] Two years later Plymouth's old foe Thomas
Morton claimed that the Dutch were earning twenty thousand pounds per
year from the sale of beavers, and he urged his countrymen to take steps to
keep the Dutch from strengthening their hold on the region's fur trade, arguing that "it would be adjudged an irreparable oversight to protract time, and
suffer the Dutch" to expand their reach into the fur-rich hinterlands to the
west and north of the English colonies.[2]

While these sentiments were being voiced, efforts to displace the Dutch
were already under way, as English settlers began sweeping into the Con-

necticut River valley. Such efforts were, as the historian Arthur Buffinton pointed out, part of a larger historical tide: "This movement [into the valley] . . . preceded by fur-trading operations, and in the case of Springfield caused by them, must be regarded as the first of a series of clashes with the Dutch which were to end in their expulsion from the North American seaboard. Rivalry over the fur trade must be reckoned as the earliest in time, and one of the most important, of the causes contributing to that end."[3] Indeed, from the late 1630s until the mid-1660s, when the English drove the Dutch from the continent, the fur trade was a frequent and serious source of friction between the two.

While the English were settling in Connecticut, New Netherland was still experiencing serious growing pains. The Dutch West India Company had established New Netherland as a fur-trading operation first and a colony second. On the trading side, although the company's men were sending large amounts of furs back to Holland, the company's directors were not impressed. As early as October 1629 they wrote to the States General that the fur trade of New Netherland "is right advantageous; but one year with another, we can, at most, bring home only fifty thousand guilders."[4] This income paled in comparison to the profits the company was generating from its other ventures, including the systematic plundering of Spanish shipping, which in one particularly noteworthy engagement had resulted in the capture of seventeen galleons loaded with silver and goods valued at twelve million guilders.[5] Simply put the company viewed New Netherland as an economic backwater, and treated it as such.

New Netherland was faring no better with regard to colonization. In 1630 it had only about three hundred residents, and nobody back home was rushing to immigrate to America. By 1640 New Netherland's population had grown hardly at all.[6] The same year, in a bid to reverse the colony's fortunes, the company opened trade to anyone who wanted to pursue it, and immigrants from Holland as well as New England began swelling New Netherland's ranks. But then the emerging colony was knocked on its heels as a result of an extremely bloody war with the local Indians, precipitated by Director General Willem Kieft's ill-advised demand that they pay taxes in the form of furs, corn, and wampum in return for the military protection the Dutch provided.[7] Only after the war had ended and the much-despised Kieft was replaced by Peter Stuyvesant in 1647 did New Netherland begin to fulfill the promise of becoming a thriving colony.

HROUGHOUT THE 1630S AND UP THROUGH STUYVESANT'S arrival, New Netherland pursued the fur trade with considerable success, sending tens of thousands of beaver pelts and other furs back to Amsterdam.[8] One setback, however, came in the winter of 1634, when New Netherland's traditional trading partners, the Mohawk, ceased coming to Fort Orange. Since the fur trade was the colony's sole source of income, this was an economic disaster. The Dutch suspected that the French had lured the Mohawk away by offering them better or more goods in exchange for their furs. To woo them back the Dutch sent twenty-two-year-old Harmen Meyndertsz van den Bogaert, along with two companions and five Mohawk guides, to visit the Mohawk on their own turf.[9]

After traveling almost to the shores of Lake Oneida, the expedition reached the main Mohawk village. When van den Bogaert told one of the tribal chiefs that he had brought no presents—a traditional prerequisite to trading—and was only there for a "visit," the chief became enraged. He shouted at van den Bogaert, accused the Dutch of being "scoundrels," and told them that when the French came to trade they not only offered "gifts," but they also gave the Mohawk more wampum and better goods for their furs than the Dutch. When van den Bogaert had had enough, he let fly a few insults of his own, which softened the Indians' demeanor. One of them laughed and said, "You must not be angry. We are happy that you have come here."

The elders of the tribe "said that they wanted to be . . . friends, and that [the Dutchmen] must not be afraid," to which van den Bogaert replied that they were not. After the Indians had "conferred for a long time," an "old man" placed his hand on van den Bogaert's chest, and upon discovering that his heartbeat was steady and slow declared that the Dutchmen "were not afraid." With that the Indians presented van den Bogaert with a beaver coat, saying, "It is for your journey, because you are so tired." Then the real bargaining began.

The Indians said they would rather trade with the Dutch, but before they would do so, they wanted assurances that the exchange rate for one large beaver pelt would be set at four hands of wampum and four hands of cloth.[10] Van den Bogaert did not have the "authority" to make such a deal, and he said that he would have to first check with his "chief," the director of New Netherland. "You must not lie," one of the Indians replied, "and come in the spring to us and bring us all an answer. If we receive four hands, then we shall trade our pelts with no one else." When the Dutch agreed to these terms early the following year, trade between the Dutch and the Mohawk resumed.

N ONETHELESS EXTERNAL THREATS TO THE DUTCH TRADE mounted. Not long after the English swooped into the Connecticut Valley, Sweden attempted to usurp the Dutch fur trade on the Delaware River. This venture commenced after Peter Minuit, who had been unceremoniously sacked as the governor of New Netherland, went to Sweden with a commercial proposition. If the crown would back him and his associates, they would establish a fur-trading company on the banks of the Delaware, locating it strategically between the English to the south in Virginia, and the Dutch to the north in New Netherland. The deal struck, Minuit loaded two ships with cloth, liquor, and other trading goods and sailed to the Delaware, arriving there in the spring of 1638. He landed a short way up one of the Delaware's tributaries, called the Minquas Kill, on the west side of the river, south of modern Philadelphia. Even though both the English and the Dutch claimed this area by right of discovery, neither had actually purchased the land from the Indians, so Minuit now did. New Sweden was officially open for business, and Minuit and his men began building Fort Christina to serve as the main trading post and to protect them from attack.[11]

When Kieft learned of New Sweden he sent Minuit a letter claiming that the entire Delaware River was Dutch territory and warning him to desist: "In case you proceed with the erection of fortifications and cultivation of soil and trade in peltries or in any wise attempt to do us injury," Kieft concluded, "we do hereby protest against all damages, expenses and losses, together with all mishaps, bloodsheds and disturbances, which may arise in future time therefrom and . . . we shall maintain our jurisdiction in such manner, as we shall deem most expedient."[12] Minuit was not impressed by such verbiage, and he knew that the struggling Dutch colony was in no position to back up its threats at the moment, so he ignored Kieft and completed the construction of Fort Christina. Throwing himself into the fur trade, Minuit subsequently left for Europe in June 1638, with 2,212 furs, including nearly 1,800 beaver pelts as well as an assortment of otter and bearskins.[13] All Kieft could do was watch and complain that Minuit had "attracted all the peltries to himself by means of liberal gifts."[14] A fragile truce between New Sweden and New Netherland continued until an English ship arrived on the Delaware River in April 1641.

The ship was from the colony of New Haven, which had been established in 1638 on the banks of the Quinnipiac River in Connecticut, by men from Massachusetts. The ship was there because its captain, George Lamberton, had visited the Delaware in the winter of 1638–39 on a trading expedition. Lamberton knew that the Dutch and the Swedes had footholds on the river, but there was still, he thought, plenty of room for people from New Haven. When he returned home and told his associates about the river, its furs, and the lush countryside, they were intrigued. The New Haven colonists were already feeling a bit cramped for space, and the fur trade with the local Indians had not lived up to expectations, making the wide-open and productive Delaware region all the more inviting. So Lamberton and his associates created the Delaware Company, with the express purpose of establishing a settlement on the Delaware. Lamberton's visit in the spring of 1641 was intended to get that settlement started by purchasing land from the Indians, his instructions being to pick a location "not yet occupied by any Christian Nation."[15]

Lamberton bought large swaths of land on both sides of the river and built a trading post below the Swedes' Fort Christina, at a place called Varkens Kill, on the east side of the Delaware in the vicinity of modern Salem, New Jersey. Soon thereafter about sixty people from New Haven arrived, mostly fur traders, and began settling in. At the end of the summer Lamberton returned to New Haven, where his glowing reports about the area's potential for a vibrant fur trade encouraged the town to officially extend the reach of the New Haven colony to the banks of the Delaware. No longer just a commercial enterprise, the Delaware Company was now an arm of the colonial government.

When Lamberton returned to Varkens Kill in the spring of 1642, however, he discovered that this location was not well suited for carrying on the fur trade. It was not only below the Swedes at Fort Christina, but also the Dutch, who even farther up the Delaware had built Fort Nassau, opposite the confluence of the Schuylkill River. This meant that the Swedes and the Dutch had first crack at the furs brought downriver by the Indians. To remedy this situation Lamberton built a second trading post on land he had purchased the year before, at the mouth of the Schuylkill, on the west side of the Delaware, directly across from the Dutch at Fort Nassau.

ITH THE ARRIVAL OF THE ENGLISH, THE SWEDES AND THE
Dutch, who had been warily eyeing one another, set their sights on
ousting the new competitor in their midst. The Swedes struck first. Soon after
Lamberton arrived in 1641, the commander at Fort Christina sailed down to
Varkens Kill, fired warning shots, planted stakes emblazoned with the Swedish coat of arms around the new post, and sent one of his men to tell Lamberton that he was on Swedish land and must leave immediately. Lamberton
ignored this ultimatum and sent a threatening letter to the Swedes, claiming
that he had proper title to all the land he had purchased along the river, and
cautioning them to stay away.[16]

Next it was New Netherland's turn to tangle with the English, but in a
much more convincing fashion. Another contingent of New Haven settlers,
led by Robert Cogswell, sailed to the Delaware in the spring of 1642, and on
the way stopped briefly at New Amsterdam.[17] When Kieft learned of their
mission, he warned Cogswell "not to build or plant on the South River, lying
within the limits of New Netherland . . . as [those lands] . . . lawfully belong
to us."[18] Not wanting to miss a potential opportunity to gain new colonists,
Kieft added that if the New Haven men swore "allegiance" to Holland and the
Dutch West India Company, they could settle where they pleased. Cogswell
assured Kieft that his group intended to settle beyond the Dutch sphere, but if
they couldn't find such a place, they would settle on Dutch lands and become
loyal subjects. Satisfied, Kieft let Cogswell continue his journey, which ended
with his arrival at Lamberton's trading post at the mouth of the Schuylkill.

Cogswell undoubtedly thought that the post was on English land, since
it was part of Lamberton's purchase, but the Dutch vehemently disagreed,
and on May 15, 1642, Kieft and his council, "having received unquestion-
able information that some English had the audacity to land" opposite Fort
Nassau, resolved to drive them out.[19] Kieft ordered his men at Fort Nassau,
supplemented by two armed sloops sent from New Amsterdam, to "compel
[the English] . . . to depart directly in peace, to prevent effusion of blood."[20]
But when the English wouldn't leave peaceably, the Dutch rounded them up,
burned the post to the ground, and then transported their prisoners to New
Amsterdam, whence they were sent back to New Haven.[21]

Despite this blow Lamberton wouldn't give up on his Delaware dreams.
The next year he was back on the river in his pinnace the *Cock*, claiming his
rights to the land he had purchased. He resumed trading for furs, so much as

daring the Dutch or the Swedes to do something about it. This time, however, Lamberton had to contend with Johan Printz, who had become governor of New Sweden early in 1643. A fiery-tempered man of gargantuan proportions, weighing more than four hundred pounds, and called "Big Belly" by the local Indians, Printz had been apprised of the threat posed by the English, and he had been instructed to reassert Swedish control over Varkens Kill.[22] Finding that the English there were in desperate straits, ravaged by disease and unprotected, Printz commandeered the post, adopted some of the English as Swedish subjects, and sent the rest away. To strengthen his grip on the area, Printz then built Fort Elfsborg just below Varkens Kill, outfitting it with eight iron and brass cannon.[23]

When Lamberton arrived and protested that he owned Varkens Kill as well as the land at the mouth of the Schuylkill, Printz took the offensive, inviting Lamberton to Fort Christina, arresting him on charges of inciting the Indians to massacre the Swedes and the Dutch along the river, and of trading for furs without a commission. A court comprised of Swedish, Dutch, and English representatives dismissed the charge of inciting the Indians, but found Lamberton and his men guilty of illegal fur trading. Rather than confiscate the four hundred beavers in Lamberton's possession, the court required him only to pay a double duty on the furs before sending him on his way, warning him that if he returned without permission he would be stripped of his boat and his goods.[24]

Back in New Haven, Lamberton testified before the colonial court about his harsh treatment, calling the Swedish governor "a man very furious and passionate," who cursed freely and reviled "the English of New Haven as runagates."[25] The court in turn elevated Lamberton's case to the commissioners of the recently created United Colonies of New England, a loose confederation between Massachusetts, New Haven, Plymouth, and Connecticut intended to be "a firm and perpetual league of friendship and amity for offence and defense, mutual advice and succor."[26]

There ensued a heated exchange between the commissioners and Printz, in which the commissioners claimed that the Delaware region was English territory and demanded compensation for the injuries suffered by Lamberton, while Printz professed his innocence and claimed that he had acted properly. Printz added—with what may be taken as less than total sincerity—that if the people of New Haven would only present him with a commission from the United Colonies allowing New Haven men to engage in the fur trade along the Delaware, and a copy of the patent that gave the English rights to the area, he would welcome them with open arms. Although New Haven obtained these items, the issue was taken no further at this time.[27]

*N*O SOONER HAD THE DUTCH AND SWEDES HARRIED THE NEW Haven men from the Delaware than another group of Englishmen arrived on the scene, this time from Massachusetts. For decades New Englanders had talked about an almost mythical Lake of the Iroquois—a beaver El Dorado, if you will—which supposedly fed the region's rivers and was its main source of beavers. Since the late 1620s New England explorers had tried to locate the lake, with no success. In the spring of 1644 a group of Massachusetts men tried again, setting their sights on the Delaware, believing that if they followed it to its source they would find what they were after. The men sailed to the Delaware under the leadership of William Aspenwall, carrying letters of introduction from the governor of Massachusetts to the governors of New Netherland and New Sweden requesting liberty to ascend the river, and a commission giving them a twenty-one-year monopoly on the beaver trade at the Lake of the Iroquois.[28]

Aspenwall stopped at New Amsterdam and presented his papers to Kieft, who, after offering a feeble protest, let the expedition pass. When Aspenwall's pinnace came within sight of Fort Elfsborg, the Swedes fired a cannon shot across its bow and then boarded it, forcing the English to "fall down lower" on the river. Aspenwall complained to Printz, who "acknowledged he did ill" then permitted the English to head upriver accompanied by a Swedish vessel, whose job it was to keep an eye on the Englishmen's progress and make sure they didn't trade with the local Indians. Printz's contrition and permission notwithstanding, he didn't trust the English and didn't want them going upriver, fearing that they would cut off New Sweden's fur supply from the north. To forestall this Printz sent a note to the Dutch commander at Fort Nassau asking him to stop Aspenwall's expedition at all costs. Printz needn't have bothered. Immediately after Aspenwall left New Amsterdam, Kieft had sent Fort Nassau orders to "sink the English ship [rather] than . . . let it pass."[29] It wasn't only the Swedes who wanted to protect their precious fur trade.

In the end the English expedition was stopped, ironically not by a rain of cannon shots but by a few too many drafts of liquor. At Fort Nassau the master of the English pinnace "proved such a drunken sot, and so complied with the Dutch and the Swedes" that he refused to proceed. Aspenwall thought briefly about continuing the trip, using the small canoes they had brought along, but jettisoned that idea, worrying that if they left the master behind "he would in his drunkenness have betrayed their goods, etc., to the Dutch." With their voyage a total loss, the Massachusetts men sailed for home. Before leaving the Delaware, however, they suffered one more indignity when the Swedes at Fort Elfsborg forced Aspenwall to pay forty shillings to reimburse them for the cost of the cannon shot they had fired at the English pinnace when it first appeared in the river.[30]

At THE SAME TIME THAT THE DUTCH AND THE SWEDES were beating back the English on the Delaware, the Dutch were also contending with the English invasion from the northeast. The flood of English emigration that had begun in the mid-1630s increased in intensity with the conclusion of the bloody and tragic Pequot War, in 1637, which nearly annihilated the powerful Pequot Indians and opened much of the land in Connecticut and the eastern end of Long Island to colonization.[31] Urged on by politicians back in England, New Englanders were pressed to "put forward their plantations and crowd on, crowding the Dutch out of those places where they have occupied." New towns such as Groton, Stamford, Guilford, Stratford, and Southampton sprang up, "thus making a continuous line of English settlement up to the Dutch boundary, if not, indeed, within it."[32] Because many of these new towns earned part of their keep from the Indian trade, this expansion ate into Dutch profits by absorbing greater supplies of furs. And of all the fur traders who were part of the English invasion, none had a greater impact on the Dutch than William Pynchon, who, since establishing himself in Springfield in 1636, had forged links with the traditional Dutch allies, the Iroquois, and built a mini-fur-trading empire along the Connecticut River that put him on the path to becoming one of the richest men in New England.[33]

By THE MID-1640S THE FUR TRADE WAS STILL ONE OF THE staple commercial enterprises of English and Dutch America, and in many ways its nature hadn't changed much from earlier times. Indians remained the main source of furs, and they either gathered them directly through hunting and trapping, or acted as middlemen, bartering with other

Indians to accumulate pelts, and then bringing them down rivers and overland to the trading posts dotting the countryside. Independent fur traders,
who ventured into the forests and up rivers to trade with the Indians on their
own turf, were also in evidence. Included in this group were the Dutch *boschlopers*, or "runners of the woods."[34] Trading sessions, whether at a post or
in the woods, were preceded by the ritual exchange of presents, and then the
hard negotiating began. The pelts were carefully inspected to assess quality,
and prices were set accordingly.[35] European wares, including beads, hatchets,
mirrors, pots, and cloth, continued to be key trading goods, but wampum was
still king.[36] As Stuyvesant observed, "Wampum is the source and the mother
of the beaver trade . . . without wampum, we cannot obtain beavers from the
savages."[37]

Although the mechanics of the fur trade were in many ways familiar,
dramatic changes had occurred: The use of credit and the bartering of land
had become part of the process. Before the winter hunting season, fur traders
would typically advance the Indians a wide array of goods on credit, with the
expectation that after the hunting season the Indians would pay back their
debts in furs. To ensure that such debts were paid, traders sometimes required
the Indians to put up their land as collateral. While many Indians who had
fallen into debt simply reneged on their deals and perhaps established credit
with another trader, others did indeed turn over their land.[38]

The use of liquor and guns as currencies of exchange increased as well.
Itinerant traders and fishermen had long used wine, brandy, rum, and other
aqua vitae as an invitation and adjunct to negotiating sessions, and Morton
was hardly the first fur trader to capitalize on the Indians' desire for guns. But
by the mid-1640s what had been on the fringe of the fur trade had become
more mainstream, and as time progressed the trade in alcohol and firearms
was an ever-more-omnipresent—and devastating—fixture.

Even as colonial officials railed against the expanding trade in liquor and
guns, colonial traders became ever bolder in trafficking in these items. The
sheer number of laws passed to restrict or eliminate this trade was a testament to governments' failure to do so. Prosecutions for breaking such laws
were few, and governments themselves often exhibited a split personality of
sorts, passing restrictions on the trading of liquor and guns, then rescinding
them under pressure from their constituents, who claimed, accurately, that
such restrictions placed them at a competitive disadvantage with fur traders
who were not similarly encumbered.[39] Roger Williams stands out as one of

the few fur traders to take a moral stand against trading guns to the Indians, commenting, "For myself (as through God's goodness) I have refused the gain of thousands by such a murderous trade."[40]

*T*HE IMPACT OF THE EVOLVING FUR TRADE ON INDIAN SOCIETY was dramatic. As older generations died off they were replaced by new generations who had grown up in a cultural landscape awash in European goods. As a result some ways of life were becoming a thing of the past. This transformation began when the first Europeans visited America to trade for furs, and by the end of the seventeenth century it was widespread. In 1672 Nicolas Denys described the changes he witnessed in the lives of the Indians of Acadia, a description that applies equally to other tribes. "They have abandoned all their own utensils," he said, because the ones they obtained from Europeans in exchange for furs were more convenient. "They still practice the same methods of hunting, but with this difference, however, that in place of arming their arrows and spears with the bones of animals, pointed and sharpened, they arm them today with iron, which is made expressly for sale to them. . . . The musket is used by them more than all other weapons, in their hunting."[41]

As the Indians stopped using the sharpened bones and stones, ceramic pots, and other traditional items, they lost the skills necessary to make them, increasing their dependence on European goods. The significance of this cannot be overemphasized. This cycle of escalating dependency compelled the Indians to ramp up their hunts for beavers and other fur-bearing animals, not only to trade but increasingly just to survive.[42] By the same token the availability of European goods meant that the Indians didn't need to focus as much time and energy on producing things for everyday life, which enabled them, as the historian Daniel K. Richter points out, to spend more time working "with imported tools and materials" to create beautiful decorative items, thus allowing for "a great efflorescence of Native artistic expression."[43] And these were not transient phenomena but hallmarks of the American fur trade for as long as the Indians were involved in it.[44]

The guns the Indians acquired not only affected their mode of hunting but also played a key role in determining the intertribal balance of power. Indians without guns wanted them, and those who had them wanted more. In 1644 the New Netherland Board of Accounts reported that "not only the

Colonists, but also the free traders proceeding from this country, sold for furs in consequence of the great profit, firearms to the Mohawks for full 400 men, with powder and lead; which, being refused to the other tribes when demanded, increased the hatred and the enmity of the latter."[45]

Alcohol had perhaps the most insidious impact on Indian society. As Richter notes, seventeenth-century Indians "drank almost exclusively to get drunk; the European concept of moderate social drinking held little or no attraction." But as many scholars have commented, Indians viewed inebriation differently than did Europeans. On some level Indian alcohol consumption was perceived as a potential pathway to reaching a higher mental plane, akin to "ceremonial inducements of trancelike states, quests for visions, and searches for external sources of spiritual power."[46] Although such metaphysical searches might initially have motivated Indians to drink alcohol, as the fur trade progressed, and the quantity of alcohol being supplied by traders increased, more and more Indians were drinking not to find spiritual salvation but, plainly stated, to get high. Here again Denys provides a vivid description.

> They do not call it drinking unless they become drunk, and do not think they have been drinking unless they fight and are hurt. However, when they set about drinking, their wives remove from their wigwams the guns, axes, the mounted swords [spears], the bows, the arrows, and [every weapon] even their knives, which the Indians carry hung from the neck. They leave nothing with which they can kill one another. . . . The woman carry . . . [the weapons] into the woods, afar off, where they go hide with all their children. After that, they [the men] have a fine time, beating, injuring, and killing one another.[47]

The Indians were hardly unaware of the dangers of alcohol. A Long Island chief pleaded with Peter Stuyvesant in 1642: "You ought not to sell brandy to the Indians to make them crazy, for they are not accustomed to your liquors. Your own people, though used to them, fight with knives and commit fooleries when drunk. We wish you, so as to prevent all mischief, to sell no more fire-water to our braves."[48] Such pleas, however, had virtually no impact. Alcohol became the perfect commodity for fur traders. It was relatively cheap, easy to transport, and, when imbibed by the Indians, often made them more pliable and open to negotiations that benefited the traders' bottom line instead of their own. Alcohol also had another most valuable trait: Whereas the demand for pots, knives, cloth, and other durable goods fluctuated because they were needed only in limited quantities, the demand for alcohol was almost limitless.

Some contemporary observers were not reticent about placing blame for the spread of alcohol in Indian culture. As Daniel Gookin trenchantly wrote, "drunkenness could not be charged upon Indians before the English and other Christian nations, as Dutch, French, and Spaniards, came to dwell in America: which nations, especially the English in New England, have cause to be greatly humbled before God, that they have been, and are instrumental in causing these Indians to commit this great evil and beastly sin."[49] Yet despite the widespread and increasing presence of alcohol in the fur trade, its use was neither universal nor universally destructive. As the historian Peter C. Mancall points out, "Not all Indians drank, and many who did may not have suffered as a result," but still, "The historical record bears vivid witness to the costs of drinking to Indians."[50]

W HEN PETER STUYVESANT ARRIVED IN NEW NETHERLAND in 1647, he was forced to confront the Swedes and the English, whose encroachments to the south and the north were eroding the integrity of the Dutch colony. The Swedish problem, the lesser of the two, took Stuyvesant eight years to resolve.[51] For most of that time he and Printz engaged in a tactical and diplomatic dance of sorts, punctuated by intermittent aggression and chest-thumping, both men motivated by the same fundamental goal— control of the Delaware and its valuable fur trade.

A brusque and humorless man, Stuyvesant had had the lower half of his leg blown off by a cannonball and later replaced by a wooden peg (trimmed with silver bands), earning him the sobriquet "Peg Leg." Not a reticent sort, he was used to making decisions and having them carried out. Had it been entirely up to him he would probably have run the Swedes off immediately, a task that wouldn't have been too difficult since he could muster at least three hundred men to arms, while New Sweden had a population of barely two hundred souls and was only lightly defended. But Stuyvesant was a company man who followed orders, and having been instructed by the Dutch West India Company to be patient with his Swedish neighbors, he remained on cordial if not friendly terms, still maintaining Holland's rights to the river and access to its furs.

With their strategically located forts on the lower Delaware, the Swedes became the gatekeepers for the region's fur trade. They particularly relished harassing and sometimes stopping Dutch ships, confiscating their cargoes. Dutch complaints were either ignored or met with insincere apologies and hollow claims of Swedish desires to live in harmony with the Dutch. When the Swedes reinforced their position at the mouth of the Schuylkill, the Dutch built Fort Beversreede (the road of the beaver) nearby to assert their rights to the area. The Swedes responded by burning some of the buildings the Dutch had just thrown up, and then erecting their own fort almost on top of Fort Beversreede, leading one Dutch officer to write to Stuyvesant that the Swedish fort was "the greatest insult in the world . . . for they have located the house about 12 or 13 feet from our palisades, depriving us thereby of our view of the stream." Another Dutchman professed that Printz had "built there more to mock our lords than to expect that it could realize any profit for him, since there is room enough beside our fort to build twenty such houses."[52] Even if Printz didn't benefit strategically from this bit of brinkmanship New Sweden profited mightily from the fur trade, largely at the expense of the Dutch, which angered Stuyvesant no end.

IN 1651, AS RELATIONS BETWEEN SWEDEN AND HOLLAND WERE deteriorating, and the Dutch became more vocal about Swedish injustices, Stuyvesant decided that he had had enough of New Sweden's "insolence."[53] It was time to bring the Delaware firmly into New Netherland's embrace. With a force of 120 men Stuyvesant marched overland to Fort Nassau, where he met up with eleven ships that he had sent from New Amsterdam, four of which were "well armed." To intimidate the Swedes, Stuyvesant sailed this miniarmada up and down the river accompanied by "drumming and cannonading."[54] Next he invited local Indian chiefs to the fort, bought land from them on the west side of the river, and then led his men to claim their new territory, which lay just below the Swedes' Fort Christina. There the Dutch built Fort Casimir, an impressive edifice just over 120 feet long and half as wide, mounted with twelve cannons.

With Fort Casimir as a base of operations, the Dutch effectively controlled the river, regulating traffic along its length and requiring all traders to pay duties on transported goods. In the face of such overwhelming force, all Printz could do was issue protests, while the Dutch swooped in to absorb much of the region's fur trade. Printz's situation worsened as desertions whittled New Sweden's population to one hundred, forcing the abandonment of all but one of the Swedish forts. Printz had hoped for help from Sweden to counter the Dutch, but year after year there was none. Disgusted, weary, and discredited in the eyes of his own colonists, Printz left New Sweden in the fall of 1653.

The reinforcements and supplies Printz had so desperately wanted finally arrived in May 1654, along with Printz's replacement, Johan Rising, who proceeded to make a major strategic blunder. Learning that Fort Casimir was lightly manned and low on materials, Rising disregarded his orders to leave the Dutch alone and instead attacked the fort, taking it without firing a shot, placing it and some of its defenders under Swedish rule, and renaming it Fort Trinity.[55] When the word of the attack and the "infamous surrender" filtered back to the Dutch West India Company, its enraged directors dispatched the *De Waag* (*The Balance*) with thirty-six guns and two hundred men, to New Amsterdam with orders for Stuyvesant to supplement this force with his own men and "exert every nerve to avenge that injury, not only by restoring affairs to their former situation, but by driving the Swedes from every side of the river."[56]

On September 5, 1655, with seven ships and nearly seven hundred men under his command, Stuyvesant sailed for the Delaware, arriving five days later just above Fort Trinity. Immediately upon landing he sent one of his men to the fort "to claim the direct restitution of our own property."[57] The fort's commandant—warned of the Dutch approach and ordered by Rising to resist any advances—considered the overpowering forces arrayed against him and promptly surrendered.

Stuyvesant now turned his attention to Fort Christina, where Rising was holed up. The Swedish governor endeavored to reason with Stuyvesant and "dissuade him from further hostilities," sending messengers and letters arguing that the Swedes rightfully owned the land, and threatening the Dutch with retaliation should they attack. But Rising's protests went unheeded; Stuyvesant had his orders and he would carry them out. The Swedes had "either to evacuate the country, or to remain there under Dutch protection." If the Swedes wanted to fight, Stuyvesant would give them no quarter.

For more than a week, as communications went back and forth, Rising tried to rally his meager force of thirty men and prepare them for a valiant defense of the fort, but their situation was hopeless. They were almost out of supplies, with barely enough shot and powder to fire off one round each.

Meanwhile the Dutch surrounded the fort and trained multiple batteries on it. They also "pillaged" the Swedes beyond the fort's perimeter, robbing their houses, stripping some of "them to the skin," and killing their livestock.[58]

With desertions increasing and talk of mutiny within the fort, Rising decided "to hold a parley with Stuyvesant" to see if he could change the Dutchman's mind. Rising raised the same issues he had earlier, but Stuyvesant still wouldn't budge, and to drive his determination home he gave Rising twenty-four hours to capitulate or be attacked. Out of options and unwilling to be martyrs for their country, the Swedes unanimously decided to surrender, and they marched out of the fort "with their arms, colors flying, matches lighted, drums beating, and fifes playing; and the Dutch took possession of the fort, hauled down the Swedish flag, and hoisted their own."[59] New Sweden was no more.

*S*TUYVESANT WOULD HAVE LIKED TO DEAL WITH THE NEW Englanders sweeping down on New Netherland from the north in the same way he had dealt with New Sweden. After all, by invading Connecticut and parts of Long Island, the New Englanders had usurped lands that the Dutch claimed as their own, just as the Swedes had done on the Delaware, and this fact alone was enough in Stuyvesant's eyes to merit retaliation. But New England was no minor colony unable to defend itself; it was rather a mighty assemblage of individual colonies whose combined population dwarfed that of the Dutch by more than ten to one.[60] If those colonies joined forces against the Dutch, or even if only one or two of the more powerful colonies took up arms in such a cause, they would easily overrun the Dutch in the same manner that the Dutch had overrun the Swedes. The Dutch West India Company admitted as much when it responded to Stuyvesant's inquires about possible military action against the English colonies by informing him that "war cannot in any event be for our advantage; the New England people are too powerful for us."[61]

With the military option out of the question, Stuyvesant used a strategy of diplomacy and provocation to finally get the New Englanders to the negotiating table in 1650 to resolve boundary disputes and other controversial issues. The most important elements of the resulting Treaty of Hartford as far as the fur trade was concerned were the determination of the northern boundary between the English and the Dutch and the disposition of the Delaware River, in particular the question of whether the New Haven colony had any rights of settlement there. With respect to the northern boundary, the dividing line was drawn essentially where it lay when the negotiations began. Thus the New Englanders would retain all the land they had taken in Connecticut and on Long Island, while Fort Good Hope would remain a Dutch trading post on the Connecticut River, a virtual island surrounded by a sea of English. Although this was a clear loss for the Dutch, in that they permanently gave up rights to land they thought were theirs, it at least stopped the encroachment of the English and thereby enabled New Amsterdam to retain its hold on the valuable fur trade in and around the Hudson.[62]

As for the Delaware the treaty left the Dutch and the New Haven colony "in *status quo prius*, to plead and improve their just interests at Delaware for planting or trading as they shall see cause"[63] —words that didn't solve anything because each side interpreted them differently. This became abundantly clear in 1651, when another contingent of fifty New Haven settlers headed south to the Delaware to claim their land, as they thought they had a right to under the terms of the treaty. Stuyvesant vehemently disagreed, and when the would-be settlers stopped at New Amsterdam, he briefly locked them up and then sent them back to New Haven, warning them not to return. To Stuyvesant "*status quo prius*" clearly meant that the Delaware and its valuable fur trade belonged to the Dutch.[64]

When the New Haven settlers returned and told of their ill treatment, the issue became elevated and was brought before the commissioners of the United Colonies of New England for resolution. The New Haven group wanted their fellow New Englanders to join in an all-out war against the Dutch to vindicate their rights on the Delaware, but the commissioners were not willing to take such drastic action. Instead they promised that if New Haven sent colonists along with 100 to 150 well-armed men to the Delaware, and if they were attacked, then the United Colonies of New England would send soldiers to defend them, as long as New Haven paid the cost of such troops. These terms were too harsh for New Haven, and the issue was dropped.[65]

*T*HE NEXT AND FINAL FLARE-UP BETWEEN THE DUTCH AND THE English over the fur trade began in 1659 when a group of "adventurers" from the Bay Colony obtained a grant to establish a plantation about fifty miles west of Springfield, and between forty to sixty miles south of the Dutch trading post at Fort Orange (which was now surrounded by a town called Beverwijk (beaver town). After visiting the area and selecting a location on Wappinger's Kill, a small tributary of the Hudson just south of present-day Poughkeepsie, New York, the adventurers journeyed to Fort Orange, where they were warmly received. They informed the local Dutch officials that they planned to settle along Wappinger's Kill, as long as it was not within the fort's jurisdiction, and that their prime commercial goal was to supply the fort with cattle. And since traveling overland to Wappinger's Kill from the Boston area was onerous, and not conducive to transporting heavy goods and supplies, the adventurers also asked that they be granted permission to use the Hudson as their highway for shuttling back and forth. The fort's officials "thanked [the adventurers] . . . for their kind offer of friendly intercourse," then told them that they were talking to the wrong people. The fort was "subordinate" to the government of New Netherland, and therefore the adventurers would have to present their request to Stuyvesant and his council.[66]

Before any formal contact had been made Stuyvesant heard of the adventurers' plans and erupted. The adventurers' claim that they only wanted to supply cattle to the Dutch was, he believed, just a ruse. The true purpose, Stuyvesant argued, was "to get into our beaver-trade with their wampum and divert the trade." If the "Boston" men gained a foothold on the Hudson, their presence would strengthen and grow and the Dutch would never be rid of them. "Many hounds are the hare's death," Stuyvesant warned the directors.

To frustrate the Englishmen's designs Stuyvesant proposed that the Dutch strike first by "settling the lands with some good and clever farmers," and providing them with twenty to twenty-five soldiers for protection from the Indians. In order to get this project off the ground quickly, Stuyvesant urged the directors to send over a small contingent of "homeless Polish, Lithuanian, Prussian, Jutlandish or Flemish farmers."[67] If the directors had any doubts about the importance of stopping the English from executing their plan, Stuyvesant reminded them that they had seen this play before, when the English descended on the Connecticut River and rapidly replaced the Dutch and ruined their beaver trade. If the Dutch didn't act now, the Hudson would suffer the same fate.[68]

In December 1659 the directors supported Stuyvesant's decision to purchase land around Wappinger's Kill "in order to make our right [to it] indisputable," and they promised to send farmers as soon as they could. The directors also ordered Stuyvesant to take any steps necessary to forcibly remove the

English should they arrive.[69] And when the directors heard that the English not only had designs on land around Wappinger's Kill, but also on a location on the Mohawk River within a few miles of Fort Orange, they urged Stuyvesant to use force to stop them on both fronts.[70]

Stuyvesant's belief that the English were interested in obtaining beaver, not selling cattle, was confirmed when the General Court of Massachusetts issued the adventurers a twelve-year monopoly to trade for furs and other commodities within fifteen miles of the Hudson. Then the court had the gall to send Stuyvesant a letter admitting that although the proposed settlement at Wappinger's Kill, and the associated right to use the Hudson as a thoroughfare, might "damage . . . your trade and profit," if the Dutch were to oppose the settlement on those grounds that would be "so unbecoming the professors of Christianity that those that do but pretend to common justice & honesty could never allege it seriously without blushing."[71] But of course Stuyvesant did object. He thundered that the Dutch could not let the Massachusetts group establish a trading post on Dutch soil or allow them freely to use the Hudson as a watery highway "without a surrender of [Dutch] . . . honor, reputation, property and blood, their bodies and lives."[72]

Fearing that this bold rejection of English advances would precipitate a military response, and realizing that his forces were no match for those of the Bay Colony, Stuyvesant urgently requested that the directors send a heavily armed frigate to guard the mouth of the Hudson. But before tensions escalated any further, the Restoration in England swept the Stuart monarchy back into power in mid-1661, in the person of Charles II, and due to the changing political landscape, the Massachusetts adventurers' abandoned their plans on the Hudson. Stuyvesant's reprieve from an English invasion, however, would be short lived.

The endgame came in late August 1664, when four English warships, bristling with guns and loaded with soldiers, arrived at the mouth of the Hudson. Charles II, convinced by those around him that now was the time to smash the Dutch trading empire and have England pick up the pieces, had granted his brother James, the Duke of York, a vast expanse of the North American continent, including virtually all of New Netherland. The English warships floating just off New Amsterdam were there to collect James's prize. Although Stuyvesant wanted to fight, he was the only one who did, and under pressure from his peers he surrendered to the overwhelming force arrayed before him.

New Netherland became New York, and Holland's days as an American colonial power were over.[73]

THE EXPULSION OF THE DUTCH INITIATED A NEW PHASE IN THE history of America's fur trade. The English, who had long competed with the Dutch and the French for control of the trade, now faced the French alone. And unlike the Dutch, the French would prove to be much more persistent and dangerous foes.

Adieu to the French

*Benjamin Franklin's warning to the British colonies
in America, printed in 1754, exhorting them to
unite, or "Join," against the French and the
Indians, or "Die." This is widely believed to
be America's first political cartoon.*

WHILE THE ENGLISH, THE DUTCH, AND THE SWEDES WERE battling over the fur trade to the south, to the north the French were struggling to keep their dreams of a fur-based empire alive. From the early 1630s to the early 1660s French merchants and traders veered between optimism and pessimism as New France's fur trade gyrated wildly between great success and utter failure. Things started off encouragingly. In 1633 Samuel de Champlain, the "Father of New France," returned to Quebec as acting governor, with the revitalization of the fur trade as one of his primary goals.[1] But he realized he had a problem. Many decades of hunting in the drainage area of the lower St. Lawrence River had depleted local populations of beaver and other fur-bearing animals. Champlain believed that for the fur trade to thrive New France needed to expand its horizons. From their traditional allies and trading partners the Huron and the Algonquin, the French had heard about the "People of the Sea," whose lands were far to the west and full of beaver. Champlain wanted to contact these mysterious people not only because of the furs they could provide but also because he thought they lived on the edge of the western ocean (the Pacific) and could be Asian. At long last dreams of a Northwest Passage to the Orient might be realized. To head this mission Champlain chose his trusted interpreter, Jean Nicollet.[2]

Nicollet, who first arrived in New France in 1619 when he was about twenty, had become one of Champlain's *truchements*—young men or boys sent out to live among the Indians, learn their language and ways, build stronger ties between the French and the Indians, and encourage the latter to engage in the fur trade. Nicollet spent most of the next fourteen years among the Nipissing, an Algonquian people in the region northeast of Lake Huron, and thus was well suited for the trip Champlain had envisioned. Departing from Quebec in July 1634 and meeting seven Huron escorts along the way, Nicollet proceeded through areas never before seen by Europeans. They canoed through the Straits of Mackinac into Lake Michigan, ending up on the shores of Green Bay at the northeastern boundary between Michigan and Wisconsin.

Nicollet stayed briefly with the Menominee, while he sent one of his Indian companions on a journey south to tell the People of the Sea that he was on his way. They were so thrilled that *Manitouiriniou* (Wonderful Man) was coming to visit that they sent a party to escort him to their village and carry his bags. Still thinking that he might soon be meeting Asians, Nicollet donned "a grand robe of China damask, all strewn with flowers and birds of many colors" to make a good first impression. When Nicollet strode into the village thus attired and gripping two pistols, "the women and children fled at the sight of a man who carried thunder in both hands." Of course Nicollet was nowhere near Asia, and the People of the Sea turned out to be the Winnebago living near the mouth of the Fox River. Word of Nicollet's arrival quickly spread throughout the region, and soon four to five thousand Indians arrived to welcome him, with various chiefs hosting banquets in his honor, one of which served 120 roasted beavers. Nicollet concluded peace treaties with the local tribes, and not long after furs from these western lands began streaming into New France.[3]

In the fall of 1635 Champlain suffered a serious stroke. Paralysis, beginning in his legs, soon spread to his arms. For ten weeks he remained bedridden, but his mind was still sharp. He spent much of this time preparing "a general confession of his entire life," which he gave to his dear friend the Jesuit priest

Charles Lalement. Finally, on Christmas Day 1635, Champlain drew his last breath. All the people of Quebec, along with the many of the Indians he had befriended over the years, turned out for a procession in his honor, followed by his burial at the Church of Notre-Dame-de-la-Recouvrance, to which Champlain had bequeathed much of his worldly possessions.[4]

*D*ESPITE CHAMPLAIN'S HOPES THAT NEW FRANCE WOULD become a functioning, multidimensional colony, it remained little more than a fur-trading outpost with major hubs at Quebec, Montreal, and Trois-Rivières. Even the farmers who came to till the land, and the Jesuit missionaries who came to Christianize the Indians, got swept up in the trade, enticed by the lure of quick profits.

The furs of New France traveled two main routes to market. Men working for the fur-trade monopolies granted by the king waited at their posts for the Indians to arrive in canoes laden with furs brought from the backcountry, whereupon the trading began. Then there were the coureurs de bois (runners of the woods), who, like their Dutch counterparts, the *boschlopers*, were self-employed and went to where the furs were and traded directly with the Indians, often becoming the first Europeans the Indians had ever seen, unwitting ambassadors of Western civilization.

Using the vast and spidery network of streams, rivers, and lakes, the coureurs de bois cut a serpentine path through the landscape of North America. Their main form of transportation was the graceful tapered, cedar-ribbed birchbark canoe, used by the Indians of the north since time immemorial for traveling, hunting, and fighting. This beautifully balanced workhorse, with its neatly stitched skin and seams made watertight with sticky pine gum, was stable and sturdy enough to hold hundreds if not thousands of pounds of people and pelts, yet light enough to be portaged with relative ease. Flat-bottomed and buoyant, and skillfully propelled and maneuvered by powerful sweeps of the broad flat paddles, the birchbark canoe was as serviceable in deep, fast-flowing rivers as it was in shallow, sluggish streams. Made of materials readily available throughout the woods, it could be easily repaired on the fly. So central was the birchbark canoe to the growth of the northern fur trade that it is hard to imagine that trade having succeeded without it.[5]

The coureur de bois, observed the author Bernard DeVoto, was "an Indian with a white man's mind and he lived free . . . pulled the wilderness round [himself] . . . like a robe . . . [and] wore its beauty like a crest."[6] Away for weeks, months, and even years at a time, the coureurs de bois were always bold, often reckless and crude, and expert woodsmen who lived and hunted with the Indians. They were shrewd businessmen, knew how to acquire the best pelts, and loved to have a good time, with raucous singing, dancing, gambling, drinking, and sex being the usual forms of entertainment.[7] They were freelancers par excellence who sold their furs at the French trading posts but did not hesitate to traffic with the Dutch and the English if the price was right.

To some the life of the coureurs de bois verged on the idyllic. As one historian wrote, "They were the most romantic and poetic characters ever known in American frontier life. Their every movement attracts the rosiest coloring of imagination. . . . We catch afar off the thrilling cadences of their choruses, floating over prairie and marsh, echoing from forest and hill, . . . What a rollicking life was this!"[8] Contemporary critics offered harsher assessments. Although the Jesuits usually relied on the coureurs de bois to lead them into the wilderness to set up missions and to trade on their behalf, they still railed against the coureurs de bois' heathenish behavior. The Jesuits were appalled by their liberal use of liquor for personal inebriation and as a means to obtain furs, and they were horrified by their propensity to "go native"—consorting too closely with the Indians, dressing like them, and even taking Indian women as wives. Government officials were frustrated by their unwillingness to settle down and contribute to the growth, permanence, and social fabric of the colony. And the fur-trade monopolies often viewed them as competitors or, worse, turncoats willing to sell their furs to the highest bidder regardless of nationality. Whether seen as romantics, reprobates, rootless wanderers, or simply unwelcome competition, the coureurs de bois remained critically important to the fur trade of New France as long as it lasted.[9]

*A*FTER MANY WILD FLUCTUATIONS NEW FRANCE'S FUR trade recorded its best year ever in 1646, shipping out 168 casks, or more than 33,000 pounds, of pelts, predominantly beaver.[10] But growing violence in the wilderness overshadowed this success. The Iroquois were viciously attacking New France's Indian allies, including its main trading partner, the Huron. As an entry in the *Jesuit Relations* from 1642 relates, "When our Hurons" paddle their canoes to Trois-Rivières or to Quebec to trade their beaver skins, they are less afraid of the turbulent rapids and the precipitous falls they must run, "on which they are frequently wrecked," than they are of the Indians who lurk in the woods. "For every year the Iroquois prepare new ambushes for them, and, if they take them alive, they wreak on them all the cruelty of their tortures."[11]

The attacks were part of a broader conflict called the Beaver Wars, so named because historians originally believed that they were motivated primarily by the Iroquois' need to find new sources of beaver—a need that was created because the beaver populations on the Iroquois land had been devastated by years of hunting. If the Iroquois wanted to continue their economically beneficial fur-trading relationship with the Dutch, they had to find new sources of furs. Inevitably they chose to do so by attacking other Indians and taking the furs they had gathered as well as appropriating their lands.[12] More recent and persuasive scholarship on the Beaver Wars, however, downplays the role of economics and the fur trade. From this perspective the Iroquois's attacks are seen more in the context of mourning wars, which were a traditional means of rebuilding a tribe's strength after many of its members had been killed or died. During the 1630s and early 1640s, a series of smallpox epidemics, likely introduced by fur traders, ripped through the Iroquois nation, cutting its population in half. In mourning for these dead, women demanded that their men raid other tribes to capture replacements for those who had been killed, thereby replenishing the Iroquois' ranks. And in the Beaver Wars that followed the Iroquois tried to do just that.[13]

Whether the Beaver Wars were motivated by economics or mourning, or both, the results were the same. By 1649 the Iroquois had virtually destroyed the Hurons, dispersed its survivors to the west, and in the process brought New France's fur trade to its knees. In subsequent years the range of the Beaver Wars expanded as the Iroquois attacked other Indians, including the Ottawa, the Algonquin, the Petun, the Erie, and the Neutral, further crippling the French-Indian trade.[14] The destructive toll of these wars was captured by an entry in the *Jesuit Relations* of 1653. "Never were there more beavers in our lakes and rivers, but never have there been fewer seen in the warehouses of the country. Before the devastation of the Huron, a hundred canoes used to come to trade, all laden with beaver-skins; the Algonquians brought them from all directions; . . . The Iroquois war dried up all these springs. The beavers are left in peace and in the place of their repose . . . [The Iroquois] are preventing all the trade in beaver skins, which have always been the chief wealth of this country."[15] The dislocation wrought by the Beaver Wars was so bad that by the time the English took over New Netherland from the Dutch, in 1664, New France's fur trade was for all intents and purposes "dead"—although only temporarily.[16]

*N*EW FRANCE'S FUR TRADE EMERGED WITH RESTORED vigor between the mid-1660s and the late 1680s. Part of the reason for this resurgence, ironically, can be traced to the Beaver Wars, which were slowly coming to an end. As the Indians displaced by the Iroquois traveled west, north, and south to the shores of Lakes Michigan and Superior, they met tribes unfamiliar with the fur trade, including the Sioux, Miami, Cree, Fox, and Illinois. These tribes were enamored of the European wares owned by the displaced Indians, and a new trade was born. The Ottawa, whose name literally translates as "traders," exchanged their worn knives, kettles, and cloth for fine beaver robes and pelts provided by the distant tribes, and then took those furs to Montreal, where they were exchanged for European goods, which were in turn used to obtain more furs. Thus the Ottawa became middlemen in a thriving trade, and as the historian Harold A. Innis put it, "The Miamis and the Sioux ceased roasting the beaver for food, and began a search for skins."[17]

Exploration was another reason for the revival of New France's fur trade. Frenchmen whose names now dot America's landscape ventured west and south to claim new lands, establish trading ties with local Indians, and find a water route to the western ocean.[18] Among the first to set out were the Jesuit priest Jacques Marquette and the fur trader Louis Joliet. Lured by tales of a great river—which the Indians called the Meschacebe, or the "Father of Waters"—to the south of the Great Lakes, Marquette and Joliet launched an expedition in the spring of 1673 to see if the tales were true, and to discover into which body of water this great river emptied. With five Indian guides they journeyed in birchbark canoes to Green Bay, ascended the Fox River, portaged to the Wisconsin, and proceeded to its terminus, where they found the Father of Waters, which would later be called the Mississippi.

Although Marquette and Joliet were not the first Europeans to see the Mississippi—that distinction goes to Spanish explorer Hernando de Soto who came upon the river in 1541, near modern-day Memphis, Tennessee—they were the first to map and explore it. Floating downriver, Marquette and Joliet encountered friendly Indians, dined on buffalo, which were plentiful along the riverbanks, and passed the mouths of the Missouri and Ohio rivers. Running low on supplies and convinced that the Mississippi exited in the Gulf of Mexico, and not on the shores of a western ocean or the Atlantic (as some had believed), Marquette and Joliet turned around near the mouth of the Arkansas River and headed back to New France to share the news of their discovery.[19]

René Robert Cavelier de La Salle went Marquette and Joliet one better. In 1682, after many years exploring the Great Lakes region and establishing a series of fur-trading posts, La Salle journeyed down the Mississippi all the way to the Gulf of Mexico. With a flourish, and amid the firing of muskets, La Salle planted a flagpole, raised the royal arms, and claimed the river, and all the lands drained by it and its tributaries, in the name of King Louis XIV. And to honor the king La Salle called the new territory, which one of his party said was "the most beautiful country in the world," Louisiana.[20] While La Salle was traveling south, another Frenchman, Daniel Greysolon, sieur Duluth (originally "Dulhur"), went in the opposite direction, exploring the headwaters of the Mississippi, the shores of Lake Superior, and lands farther north. Along the way Duluth established posts and traded for furs with the Cree and Sioux, earning him the title "king of the *coureurs de bois*."[21]

The discoveries of Marquette, Joliet, La Salle, Duluth, and other less celebrated explorers opened the way for the expansion of New France's fur-trading empire, stretching from the Gulf of St. Lawrence to the Great Lakes region and down to the Gulf of Mexico. New France sent a flood of pelts back to Europe, restoring Paris's preeminence in the production of fashionable furs and hats.[22] Despite this success, New France remained nervous. It had good reason to be, since the English to the north and south threatened its plans for further imperial expansion and, more important, its control of the lucrative fur trade.

*N*EW FRANCE LIKELY WOULDN'T HAVE HAD A PROBLEM with the English to the north if only the French had treated Pierre-Esprit Radisson and Médard Chouart, sieur des Groseilliers, better. While the Beaver Wars were still raging, Radisson and Groseilliers were among the very few coureurs de bois brave enough to pursue their trade and risk being attacked by the Iroquois. When they returned in the late 1650s from an expedition to the Great Lakes with sixty canoes full of pelts, they provided one of the only bright spots in an otherwise dismal time for New France's fur trade.[23] Buoyed by their success Radisson and Groseilliers asked the governor for permission to launch another expedition, which was given, but with so many conditions that the adventurers could not accept them, instead departing on their own terms though the governor expressly forbade them from doing so. Although this expedition was as successful as its predecessor, it had a different outcome. By the time they returned to Quebec in 1663, a new governor was in charge, who decided to enforce the laws intended to clamp down on coureurs de bois for trading without licenses. As a result Radisson and Groseilliers were briefly imprisoned, heavily fined, and forced to hand over most of their furs.

Incensed by such treatment Radisson and Groseilliers journeyed to France and pleaded their case before the king—to no avail. While in Paris they told anyone who would listen about a great body of water (Hudson Bay) far to the north of the Great Lakes that the Indians had spoken of. It was ringed by great rivers populated by an enormous store of fat beavers with luxuriant pelts. If they could only get backing for a northern expedition, Radisson and Groseilliers argued, this rich hunting ground could be claimed for France. But nobody was interested in their plan, either in Paris or back in Quebec, so Radisson and Groseilliers, still committed to their idea, took the only action they felt was left open to them—they set their sights on getting English support.[24]

Radisson and Groseilliers made their way to Boston, where, after a few failed attempts to launch an expedition to Hudson Bay, they met with Sir George Cartwright, vice chamberlain to the king and treasurer of the navy. Intrigued by the Frenchmen's plans, he offered to arrange an audience with King Charles II. Off to London they went, arriving in the fall of 1665 only to find the city in the throes of the bubonic plague that had killed nearly ninety thousand people. Enveloped in the stench of the dead and dying, Cartwright, Radisson, and Groseilliers proceeded by boat up the Thames to their meeting with King Charles, a royal with an insatiable appetite for money, who saw in Hudson Bay an opportunity for great financial gain, and a way of obtaining a competitive edge over the French in the race for North America's furs. He gave Radisson and Groseilliers a weekly allowance of forty shillings and promised that soon they would have a ship to pursue their commercial venture.[25]

Eventually the task of getting the project off the ground was given to the king's cousin Prince Rupert, a dynamo of a man who was already a successful entrepreneur, accomplished artist, celebrated soldier, and noted inventor (who could claim, among other things, to have developed the first torpedo, built a diving bell to retrieve sunken treasure, and introduced the Italian engraving method known as mezzotint to England). Rupert gathered together a company of adventurers whose deep-pocketed subscribers financed a trip to Hudson bay in 1668, which returned the following year with a profitable cargo of beaver and other furs, thereby proving the feasibility of Radisson's and Groseilliers' plan. This was enough to spur further investments in the company, but Rupert's goal was grander than that. He knew that to secure his claim to the Hudson Bay trade he needed a royal monopoly, and on May 2, 1670, he got what he wanted, and then some. With his signature Charles II made Rupert and his partners the "true lords and proprietors" not of only Hudson Bay but also all of the lands whose waters drained into it. This extraordinary real estate transaction, one of the largest in history, gave the newly created Hudson's Bay Company claim to 1.5 million square miles that became known as Rupert's Land, and that encompassed roughly 40 percent of present-day Canada and significant pieces of Minnesota and North Dakota.[26]

By turning its back on Radisson and Groseilliers, New France had fostered the creation of a new and potentially powerful competitor. Indeed the Hudson's Bay Company quickly became a source of great irritation to New France, since the furs they normally received from the Indians were now siphoned off by the company's posts ringing the bay.[27] The upstarts to the north, however, weren't the only Englishmen who kept New France on edge. To the south lay a string of English colonies, also impinging on New France's expanding fur trade.

NEW FRANCE'S BIGGEST COMPETITOR WAS THE NEWLY CREated English colony of New York. With the expulsion of the Dutch in 1664, Fort Orange became Albany, but this hardly changed the commercial character of the old trading post. Many of the Dutch who had made Fort Orange the hub of the North American fur trade remained once the English had taken over. They now swore their allegiance to England's king and continued to profit. The Iroquois, who had long traded with the Dutch, were quick to notice the shifting direction of the winds, and transferred their loyalty to the English. With the Iroquois acting as middlemen for various tribes, bartering English goods for pelts, furs that might otherwise have ended up in New France kept on coming down the Hudson to Albany.

The southern colonies, too, in particular Virginia, Pennsylvania, and the Carolinas, were another threat to New France's fur trade. Capitalizing on the abundance of deer in the region, southern colonists established connections with local Indians and built up a vast trade in deerskins, which were sent to Europe to be processed into shoes, gloves, and other leather goods.[28] The southern colonies also pursued a more traditional fur trade that focused on beavers, raccoons, wolves, muskrat, mink, and black bears, among other animals, but it was far smaller and less economically significant than the deerskin trade.* As the populations of animals along the coast dwindled, southern traders traveled farther inland, ultimately making their way across the Appalachians, bringing them into competition with the French.

Ironically New England, where the English fur trade had begun, was no longer a factor in the growing competition for furs in eastern North America. By the mid- to-late 1600s, and earlier along the coast, the New England colonies, had, with the help of the Indians, run the fur trade into the ground.[29] There simply weren't enough fur-bearing animals left in New England's woods to generate decent profits, and New Englanders' access to furs was limited by competition from other traders and a lack of good water routes to the interior.[30] Even if the New England colonies had wanted to push their trading operations west, they couldn't have, effectively blocked by the huge and rapidly expanding colony of New York.

Although New England's fur trade would continue to sputter along, it was not a force to be reckoned with, nor one that caused New France any concern. And as many historians have pointed out, the withering of New England's fur trade shifted the dynamics for many of the region's Indians, who had depended on that trade as their source for European goods. Without furs to barter the Indians were, as Cronon notes, compelled to "turn to the only major commodity they had left [to trade]: their land."[31] Thus, as the furs disappeared, so too did the Indians' land, piece by piece—a shift that created stresses that fueled regional conflict between the Indians and the English.

The result of all the fur-trading activity along the eastern half of the continent was that by the late 1680s a nearly three-thousand-mile battle line had

---

* The trade in deerskins fed into the leather trade, as opposed to the fur trade, and that is why the extensive American trade in deerskins is not covered in this book.

been drawn from the Gulf of St. Lawrence to the Gulf Coast, with the French and the English on opposite sides. From that point until the middle of the next century, the fur trade would remain a constant source of tension between the two powers, and one that would contribute significantly to the expulsion of the French from the continent during the French and Indian War.

*T*HE FRENCH AND THE ENGLISH HAD BEEN ON A COLLISION course in America since 1611, when an English vessel trading for furs near the Kennebec River captured a French trading vessel, claiming that the latter was trespassing on English territory. The only thing that had really changed by the end of the century was the geographical extent of the conflict. La Salle realized this in 1684, when he urged the French to build on his discoveries and colonize and defend Louisiana before it was too late. "If foreigners anticipate us," wrote La Salle, "they will . . . complete the ruin of New France, which they already hem in through Virginia, Pennsylvania, New England and the Hudson's Bay."[32] The English, too, knew that bold action was needed to outflank the French, evidence of which can be gleaned from a memorial written by a group of Englishmen around 1690 asking for a patent that would give them control over the lands to the west of Maryland, Pennsylvania, and Virginia, all the way to the Pacific coast. "The English by settling [these lands] . . . may without any difficulty perfectly destroy the French commerce with the Indians and secure the [fur] trade wholly to themselves."[33] With the French and the English eyeing lands and opportunities the other had claimed as their own, the question was not if they would come to blows, but when.

The first two such confrontations were King William's War (1689–97) and Queen Anne's War (1702–13). Both of these were offshoots of European wars that preceded them, with the War of the Grand Alliance in Europe giving rise to the former and the War of the Spanish Succession leading to the latter. Although the European wars had nothing to do with the fur trade, when they spilled over to America, control of the fur trade became one of the strategic goals, with the French, the English, and their Indian allies jockeying for advantage. The net result was a wash, however, since virtually all the gains achieved on the ground were relinquished at the negotiating tables.[34]

The Treaty of Utrecht, which ended Queen Anne's War, ushered in a thirty-one-year period of relative peace between the English and French. At the conclusion of the war New France's fur trade lay in ruins. The troubles began in the late 1600s, when French explorers expanded New France's geographical reach, and traders flooded the new lands, returning with canoes overflowing with furs. These traders included the ubiquitous coureurs de bois as well as a newer breed, the voyageurs, who were essentially highly skilled paddles for hire, employed by merchants to travel into the backcountry to trade with the Indians.[35] For a while the coureurs de bois and voyageurs were able to earn rich rewards for their efforts because French furriers and hat makers could use all the furs they could get.

But the wars put a damper on the trade. The French people, heavily taxed to fund the wars, had little money left over for furs. And because France was at war with so many European countries, its access to many of its traditional markets was cut off. As a result the demand for French furs dropped precipitously. Yet the traders still ventured forth and were as productive as ever, and soon the supply of furs far outstripped what the market could bear. By the late 1690s the furs collected annually in New France were four times what was needed in France, and the price for pelts plummeted. The king clamped down on the coureurs de bois and closed western fur trading posts to try to reverse the trend, but the pelts continued to arrive. Excess furs piled up in warehouses, where many of them rotted or were eaten by rats. Small mountains of furs were burned to help reduce the supply, enveloping Montreal in thick black plumes of acrid smoke, which could be seen and smelled for miles around.[36]

By the time the Treaty of Utrecht was signed, most of New France's stockpile of furs had been sold, burned, or become so riddled with holes as to be useless. King Louis XIV and the leaders of New France, convinced that furs were the colony's economic lifeline to the future, reinvigorated the trade. Restrictions on coureurs de bois were lifted, and they were encouraged to gather as many pelts as quickly as they could. Forts and trading posts were strengthened, reestablished, or created anew to protect and extend the fur trade in the Great Lakes region and along the Mississippi and its tributaries. And the increasing number of furs supplied by New France quickly found receptive markets overseas.[37]

*M*EANWHILE THE BRITISH PURSUED A SIMILAR COURSE. After the war Britain enjoyed great prosperity. An upsurge in the demand for beaver hats and furs kept the traders at Hudson Bay and in the American colonies busy. Charleston, South Carolina, became a trading entrepôt. By the 1730s it was annually sending more than two hundred thousand deerskins and many furs to Britain, a veritable flood that generated "more wealth in the colony than indigo, cattle, hogs, lumber, and naval stores combined," leaving rice as the only product in the colony more lucrative than furs.[38] Augusta and Savannah, Georgia, and Columbia, South Carolina, which were started as trading posts, prospered accordingly. Virginia consistently exported around twenty thousand furs, using the taxes levied on such exports to support the College of William and Mary.[39] And during most of the first half of the eighteenth century roughly 20 percent of the value of New York's shipments to Britain came from the sale of furs, creating a new aristocracy of rich New Yorkers. It wasn't just demand from Britain, however, that stimulated the fur trade. A growing hatmaking industry in the colonies, as well as increased colonial consumption of hats, added to the British fur traders' incentive to produce.[40]

The colonies often competed for control of the fur trade, at times violently.[41] But no matter how hostile the colonies were toward one another, they were united against the French. Although Great Britain and France were technically at peace, their American satellites were constantly in conflict along shifting borders extending from the Great Lakes to the Gulf of Mexico.[42] Both sides forged military and trading alliances with the Indians and often encouraged their allies to attack the competition, with the fur traders occasionally participating in the assaults. And as the English and French did their best to encourage the Indians to trade only with them, the Indians played the "French off against the English, using the fur trade as an instrument of their own foreign policy."[43]

In this struggle for furs the British had key advantages, the most important of which were the quality, quantity, and price of their goods. British cloth, kettles, knives, guns, and the like were not only more abundant and in many instances superior to their French counterparts, but also much cheaper, in large part because of heavy taxes the French placed on the fur trade and the higher cost of transporting goods from France.[44] With alcohol, too, the British outcompeted the French, since Indians preferred the more potent British West Indian rum—which they soon began calling "English milk"—to the relatively weak though better-tasting French brandy.[45] Regardless of which "spirituous" drinks were employed, however, the devastating impacts were the same, leading some Indians to call for a halt to the use of firewater altogether.[46] In 1753 Iroquois chief Scarrooyady lodged a complaint with the governor of Pennsylvania that could easily have been made ten, twenty, or thirty years earlier:

> The Rum ruins us. We beg you would prevent its coming such quantities by regulating the Traders. . . . When these Whiskey Traders come, They bring thirty or forty kegs and put them down before us and make us drink, and get all the skins that should go to pay the debts we have contracted for goods bought of the fair traders; by this means we not only ruin ourselves but them too. These wicked whiskey sellers, when they have once got the Indians in liquor, make them sell their very clothes from their backs. In short, if this practice be continued, we must be inevitably ruined.[47]

As had been the case in the prior century, such pleas had little impact, and alcohol remained an integral and free-flowing part of the trade. Simply put, many Indians demanded alcohol as a part of the trade, and traders were more than willing to oblige.[48]

THAT THE FRENCH WERE ABLE TO MAINTAIN THEIR NORTH American fur trade in the face of British competition is a testament to many factors. French traders ventured farther in search of furs, tapping areas and tribes that lay outside the English sphere of activity and influence. French gunpowder was a draw since it was more plentiful, and perhaps the only French commodity of higher quality than the British. To undercut the English the French sometimes increased the amount they paid the Indians for pelts, to the point of eliminating profits or even selling at a loss. The French also often purchased trading goods from the British to improve their competitive stance. And knowing that they could get more money for their pelts from the British, French traders regularly flouted laws against smuggling and sold their furs at British trading posts.

The French also benefited from better overall relations with the Indians. Although neither the French nor the British viewed their Indian allies and trading partners as equals, the French generally treated the Indians, and their way of life, with more respect. This earned the French some measure of loyalty.[49] They were more solicitous and extravagant in giving gifts to the Indians, and many coureurs de bois and voyageurs integrated themselves into

Indian society, further strengthening economic ties. As one British colonist bitterly observed, the French traders "live and marry among them, in short are as one people which last is not commendable but gains their affection . . . but our nation is quite the reverse notion, and will be baffled out of this trade."[50]

Perhaps the most important reason why the French traders looked good to the Indians is that so many British traders looked so bad. As the historian Charles Howard McIlwain wrote, "Most of these [British] traders were the very scum of the earth, and their treatment of the Indians was such as hardly to be suitable for description."[51] The governor of Pennsylvania observed in 1744, "I cannot but be apprehensive that the Indian trade, as it is now carried on, will involve us in some fatal quarrel with the Indians. Our traders, in defiance of the law, carry spirituous liquors among them, and take advantage of their inordinate appetite for it, to cheat them of their skins and their wampum . . . and often to debauch their wives into the bargain."[52] And Benjamin Franklin, that keen observer of human behavior, labeled British fur traders "the most vicious and abandoned wretches of our nation!"[53] Of course French traders were hardly without faults. They also often plied Indians with liquor and abused them in various ways, just not as much as the English did.

Another reason why the French were often viewed more favorably by the Indians had to do with the differences between French and English colonization. New France was still more a glorified fur-trading post than a thriving colony. Altogether there were about sixty thousand Frenchmen in North America, concentrated in Canada and the Great Lakes regions and then spread rather thinly down to the Gulf of Mexico, shadowing the course of the Mississippi. Only a relatively small percentage of them were able to take up arms and defend the colony, making it incumbent upon the French to maintain good relationships with the Indians as a security precaution. The French were also less interested in settlement than they were in maintaining an active fur trade. The main goal, therefore, was to limit the French footprint to a relatively small number of scattered forts and trading posts so that natural habitat could be preserved and the Indians could continue to live on the land and gather furs for French markets. British colonization, in contrast, was much more aggressive and posed more dangers to the Indians. There were more than a million British on the eastern seaboard and they had already shown their eagerness to buy land and evict Indians, with or without their consent, to make way for settlements.[54]

*D*URING THIS PERIOD OF COMPETITION WITH THE BRITISH, the French implemented a two-pronged policy: expanding westward to find new fur-trading opportunities, and consolidating their hold on the lands they already claimed, which meant extending their system of forts and keeping the British from advancing beyond the Appalachians. Westward expansion netted some promising results, including those from the travels of Pierre Gaultier de Varennes, sieur de la Vérendrye, and his sons, which led to increased trade with the Cree and the Assiniboin, the building of new posts as far west as Lake Manitoba, and an expedition in search of the Pacific coast that took one of the sons all the way to the foot of the Rocky Mountains near the Big Horn range.[55] Consolidation, too, proceeded apace, as a growing array of French fur-trading posts stretched from the Gulf of Mexico up through the Mississippi Valley to Canada, the most important of which was Fort Detroit, established by Antoine de La Mothe, sieur de Cadillac, in 1701.[56] On the other hand French policy of stemming the English advance over the Appalachians failed miserably. With each passing year British traders were a more common sight on the western side of the mountains.

While the French were bemoaning the British incursions, the British were growing increasingly concerned about the French. New France's designs on the territory west of the Appalachians angered British colonists for three reasons. First, many of the royal patents establishing the British colonies gave them rights to land stretching from the Atlantic to the Pacific and they argued that that included all the lands occupied by the French.[57] Second, the British believed that their special relationship with the Iroquois confederacy—now the six nations with the addition of the Tuscarora—supported their claim to the disputed lands. After all, the Treaty of Utrecht had declared the Iroquois to be British subjects, and in British eyes this meant that any lands conquered by the Iroquois necessarily became part of the British Empire. A lot therefore turned on how one defined "conquered," and the British chose to do so quite liberally. As the historian Francis Parkman points out, the British "laid claim to every mountain, forest, or prairie where an Iroquois had taken a scalp," and that included most of the "country between the Alleghenies and the Mississippi."[58] Finally, the British didn't want the French to monopolize the fur trade. As Cadwallader Colden, surveyor general of New York, wrote in 1724, New France "extends from the mouth of the river Mississippi, to the mouth of the river St. Lawrence, by which the French plainly show their intention of enclosing the British settlements, and cutting us off from all commerce with the numerous nations of Indians, that are everywhere settled over the vast continent of North America."[59]

For all these reasons the British saw the French as interlopers on British land and not the other way around. And the British colonists feared that should the French succeed in usurping these lands and keeping the British hemmed in on the eastern side of the Appalachians, the colonies would "wither and die for lack of expansion."[60] Thus, for an increasing number of British colonists the solution to the French problem was not continued hostile coexistence, but rather conquest. If the French could be chased from the continent, then the disputed lands and the fur trade would fall into British hands.[61]

*B*Y THE EARLY 1740S IT APPEARED THAT THE LONG PEACE between the French and British in North America was on the verge of shattering. The War of the Austrian Succession (1740–48) had engulfed much of Europe, and Britain and France would soon be dragged into the fray. The war finally spilled over into America in 1744, where it was called King George's War (1744–48). Bloody, dramatic, and long, King George's War nevertheless failed to reduce any of the tensions between the British and the French because the Treaty of Aix-la-Chapelle, which ended the war, restored the *status quo ante bellum*, returning all captured territories to their original owners. Although the war didn't resolve the disputes between the French and the British over contested lands, it had a dramatic impact on the balance of power in the fur trade, which in turn set in motion a series of events that transformed the Ohio Valley into a battlefield and ignited another intercolonial war that resulted in the downfall of New France.[62]

During the war, British victories on land and supremacy at sea virtually halted the supply of goods coming into New France, and without those goods the French found it nearly impossible to compete with the British for the fur trade, especially in the Ohio Valley.[63] British traders, who still had plenty of high quality goods, seized this opening, finding the Indians only too willing to switch allegiances, placing their current commercial interests far above their historical ties to the French. In 1747 Pennsylvania fur trader George Croghan wrote a letter to the provincial secretary of the colony that clearly showed the new dynamic in the valley. "I am just returned from the woods, and have brought a letter, a French scalp, and some wampum, for the governor, from a part of the Six Nation Indians that have their dwelling on the border of Lake Erie. Those Indians were always in the French interest till now, but this spring almost all the Indians in the woods have declared against the French: and I think this will be a fair opportunity, if pursued by some small presents, to have all the French cut off in them parts."[64] As if to prove Croghan's point, a Miami Indian chief called La Demoiselle by the French, frustrated by New France's lack of goods and high prices, turned his back on the French that same year and led his tribe south to the confluence of Lorraine Creek and the Great Miami River, where he established the village of Pickawillany and welcomed the British with open arms. Pennsylvanians, who dubbed La Demoiselle "Old Briton," flocked to the new village, built a rudimentary trading post, and established a thriving fur trade.[65]

*W*ITH THE CONCLUSION OF THE WAR THE FRENCH WERE determined to regain control of the Ohio Valley. Not only was the loss of the fur trade a serious blow, but the valley itself was also a key to the future integrity of New France. As Parkman put it:

> French America had two heads—one among the snows of Canada, and one among the canebrakes of Louisiana; one communicating with the world through the Gulf of St. Lawrence, and the other through the Gulf of Mexico. These vital points were feebly connected by a chain of military posts[.] . . . Midway between Canada and Louisiana lay the valley of the Ohio. If the English should seize it, they would sever the chain of posts, and cut French America asunder. If the French held it, and entrenched them-selves well along its eastern limits, they would shut their rivals between the Alleghenies and the sea, control all the tribes of the West, and turn them, in case of war, against the English borders.[66]

New France's first gambit was to reassert its sovereignty over the Ohio Valley, persuade the Indians to return to the French fold, and warn the British traders to leave the area at once. With these goals in mind Capt. Pierre-Joseph Céloron de Blainville led two hundred French soldiers and thirty Indians into the heart of the valley. At the junctions of key rivers Céloron nailed plates of tin embossed with the arms of France to the largest trees, and planted lead markers in the ground beneath them proclaiming in no uncertain terms that this was French land and that the French had returned to claim what was rightfully theirs.[67] Céloron met with any Indians he could find, including Old Briton, to persuade them to renounce their associations with the British. At a Seneca village he relayed a message from the marquis de la Galissonière, governor of New France. "My children, since I was at war with the English, I have learned that they have seduced you; and not content with corrupting your hearts, have taken advantage of my absence to invade lands which are not theirs, but mine. . . . I will not endure the English on my land. Listen to me, children . . . follow my advice, and the sky will always be calm and clear over your villages." The Indians were quick to tell Céloron that they would renew their allegiance to the French, but Father Bonnecamp, the expedition's chaplain, knew better—"We should all have been satisfied if we had thought them sincere; but nobody doubted that fear had extorted their answer."[68] And although Céloron was able to run off a few of the British traders, some refused to leave. Getting rid of the British, he now realized, was not going to be easy.

At a gathering of representatives from the Iroquois Confederacy, the Miami, Delaware, Shawnee, and Huron convened in 1751 at the Indian village of Logstown, in the vicinity of modern-day Pittsburgh, the French tried once again to reason with the Indians. A French officer, who was half Seneca, named Philippe Thomas Joncaire urged the Indians to banish the British from the valley and instead trade with the French.[69] "The English are much less anxious to take away your peltries," argued Joncaire, "than to become masters of your lands; they labor only to debauch you; you have the weakness to listen to them, and your blindness is so great, that you do not perceive that the very hand that caresses you, will scourge you like negroes and slaves, as soon as it will have got possession of those lands."[70] No sooner had Joncaire sat down than an Iroquois chief stood up to speak: "Fathers, I mean you that call yourselves our fathers, hear what I am going to say to you. You desire we may turn our brothers the English away, and not suffer them to come trade with us again; I now tell you from our hearts we will not, for we ourselves brought them here to trade with us, and they shall live amongst us as long as there is one of us alive."[71] Such repudiation was exactly what the Pennsylvania traders in the audience, including Croghan, wanted to hear. And to strengthen their relationship with the Indians, the Pennsylvanians distributed seven hundred pounds worth of gifts to the Indians.

BUT THE TIDE IN THE VALLEY WAS ABOUT TO TURN IN FAVOR of the French. The leaders of New France had long been calling for the destruction of Pickawillany, viewing the British traders there and Old Briton as the "instigators of revolt [in the Ohio] and the source of all our woes."[72] In June 1752 those leaders got what they were asking for when the French trader Charles-Michel de Langlade and a force of 250 Chippewa and Ottawa sacked Pickawillany, and to celebrate their victory feasted on the roasted flesh of Old Briton.[73] This bold move devastated the British trade in the region and caused many Indians to realign themselves with the French.

The following year Michel-Ange Duquesne de Menneville, marquis Duquesne, the governor general of New France, implemented a plan intended to drive out any remaining British traders and permanently discourage the British from settling in the Ohio. Duquesne's forces built forts at Presqu'isle (now Erie, Pennsylvania), and on the Rivière aux Boeuf (now French Creek), a tributary of the Allegheny River. They also took over and fortified a small British trading post at Venango (now Franklin, Pennsylvania). Duquesne had planned to construct yet another fort at the Forks of the Ohio, where the Allegheny and Monongahela rivers join to form the Ohio, which the French called *la Belle Rivière* (the beautiful river). Of all the forts envisioned by Duquesne, this was the most crucial because the Forks, at the site of modern Pittsburgh, were the strategic key to controlling the Ohio Valley and the gateway to the upper Mississippi. But the realization of Duquesne's vision would have to wait. His men, ill, tired, and low on supplies, were in no condition to press on.[74]

Duquesne's aggressive moves in the Ohio provoked a sharp British response. The French had to be stopped, or the entire Ohio would fall under their control. A contemporary letter to the editor of the *Pennsylvania Gazette*, signed "A Friend to Publick Liberty," made the case for swift action: "There are they who are now, contrary to all justice, invading the English settlements all around. . . . What must inevitably be the consequences if they are permitted to settle and erect forts? I tremble to think;—the loss of liberty, devastation, and ruin;—my heart can speak no more. . . . A branch of trade of no less value than forty thousand pounds per annum (I mean the fur trade) totally cut off . . . if you have any love for your country, rouse at length in its defense, and show by your present conduct that you are not unworthy of the liberty you enjoy."[75] The British home government, alive to the threat, ordered the colonies to resist any French incursions, by force if need be.[76]

Virginia's governor, Robert Dinwiddie, took up the call. Virginia had long claimed rights to the Ohio, which the French were now threatening—incentive enough for Dinwiddie to fight back. But Dinwiddie also had another, more personal reason for wanting the French out of the valley. In 1749 King George II granted a group of prominent Virginians five hundred thousand acres of land in and around the Forks of the Ohio, with the understanding that they would settle and defend the area with a fort. The investors in this Ohio Company were also very eager to exploit the area's fur trade, seeing it as an excellent way to support subsequent settlement. Dinwiddie was one of those investors.[77] The London Board of Trade and Plantations heartily approved of Dinwiddie's aggressive stance, and if he needed further encouragement, he received it in a letter from an Ohio Company agent and fur trader named William Trent. "The eyes of all the Indians are fixed upon you," wrote Trent on August 11, 1753. "You have it now in your power with a small expense to save this whole country for his Majesty, but if the opportunity is missed it will never be in the power of the English to recover it but by a great expense and the united force of all the colonies. . . . [The French] tell the Indians in all their speeches that they will drive the English over the Allegheny Mountains."[78]

Trent could have added that the Indians were not only listening to but believing the French. The Indians respected strength, and they could see that it was the French who were gaining the upper hand in the region. One contemporary Indian chief spoke for many of his peers when he observed that the British were being humiliated by their European foes. "Look at the French, they are men, they are fortifying everywhere. But we are ashamed to say it, you are all like women, bare and open without any fortifications."[79] If the situation were allowed to stand, it would undoubtedly mean the end for British designs on the Ohio.

The governor's first salvo in his effort to turn things around was a letter to the French warning them that they were occupying British land and should leave immediately. To perform the delicate task of delivering the letter Dinwiddie chose his protégé, George Washington, a six-foot-three-inch, twenty-one-year-old major in the Virginia militia, who had plenty of physical strength and ambition, but no real-life military or diplomatic experience.[80] Washington departed Williamsburg on November 1, 1753, and arrived with his party at the French fort at Venango in early December, where he learned that the French commander to whom he must give the letter was upriver at Fort Le Boeuf. Rather than continue his mission right away, Washington accepted a dinner invitation from Venango's hospitable officers, one of whom was Joncaire. As Washington later recalled, the wine flowed freely and "soon banished the restraint which at first appeared in . . . [the French officers'] conversation, and gave a license to their tongues to reveal their sentiments more freely. They told me that it was their absolute design to take possession of the Ohio, and, by G———, they would do it; for that although they were sensible the English could raise two men for their one, yet they knew their motions were too slow and dilatory to prevent any undertaking of theirs."[81] A few days later Washington arrived at Fort Le Boeuf, delivered his letter, and collected the reply. Dinwiddie could hardly have been surprised that the French commander's answer was a polite but firm no.

Impatient to solidify Virginia's and the Ohio Company's claims to the valley, in February 1754 Dinwiddie sent forty-one men, including many carpenters, to the Forks of Ohio to build a fort. Another, much larger force, led by Washington, was supposed to follow soon after, with orders to protect the fort from the French should they be bold enough to attack. But before Washington arrived, disaster struck. On April 17 hundreds of canoes and scores of bateaux, carrying one thousand French troops, and eighteen cannons, descended on the Forks. The Virginians, who were in the midst of constructing their fort, understandably surrendered without a fight. And as soon as they left, the French began building Fort Duquesne on the spot.

Washington was still en route when he received word of France's bloodless victory. He immediately began laying the groundwork for future military operations intended to retake the Forks, clearing paths through the woods and building a camp at Great Meadows. Learning from Indian allies that thirty-five French soldiers were nearby, Washington, believing them to be a war party sent to hunt him down, decided to attack. The short preemptive battle on the morning of May 28 left one Virginian and fourteen French dead. As it turned out, the French soldiers were indeed looking for the British, but not to fight them. The French commander, Joseph Coulon de Villiers de Jumonville, had been sent from Fort Duquesne to deliver a letter to Washington ordering the British to leave the valley or risk incurring the military wrath of the French—ironically enough, a mirror image of the message Washington had delivered to the French just a year earlier.[82]

The shots fired on the morning of May 28 sparked the French and Indian

War in America (1754–63), which would later morph into the Seven Years' War in Europe (1756–63). The details of the war—its bloody engagements, twists and turns, and shifting fortunes along the ravaged frontier—are beyond the scope of this book. What is important, however, is the outcome: The British won and the French lost. The long battle between these two countries for dominance in America was over. British territory now included Canada, and to the south all the land east of the Mississippi with the exception of New Orleans.[83] Many in France took the loss of their North American empire in stride. In 1759 Madame de Pompadour, King Louis XV's mistress, dismissed the news of the fall of Quebec succinctly: "It makes little difference; Canada is useful only to provide me with furs."[84] And the day the Treaty of Paris was signed, Voltaire wrote to a friend, "Permit me to compliment you. I am like the public; I like the peace better than Canada and I think that France can be happy without Quebec."[85] But as glad as some French may have been to be rid of their American holdings, the victors were happier still.[86] For more than a century Britain had been jealous of New France's fur trade and had coveted the fur-rich lands it possessed. Now those lands were British, and the big question was what the British would do with them.

8

Americans Oust the British

*Surrender of Gen. Lord Charles Cornwallis at Yorktown,
October 19, 1781, by Currier & Ives, 1846.*

WHILE TESTIFYING BEFORE THE HOUSE OF COMMONS ON THE
Stamp Act in 1766, Benjamin Franklin argued strenuously that the
French and Indian War had been a British, not an American, war. One of the
main thrusts of his argument centered on the role of the fur trade in precipitating the conflict: "As to the Ohio, the contest there began about your right
of trading in the Indian country. . . . [The French] seized the [British] traders and their goods, which were your manufactures; they took a fort [at the
Forks of the Ohio] which a company of your merchants [the Ohio Company]
. . . had erected there, to secure that trade." Franklin claimed that it was the
British who decided to send troops to take back the fort, and further that the
colonies weren't drawn into the fray until after those troops were defeated.
"The trade with the Indians," he concluded, "though carried on in America,
is not an American Interest. . . . [It] is a British Interest; it is carried on with
British manufactures, for the profit of British merchants and manufacturers;

therefore the war, as it commenced for the defense of territories of the crown (the property of no American) and for the defense of a trade purely British, was really a British war.[1]

Franklin was correct about the fur trade being a British interest supported by British manufactures, but he was uncharacteristically wrong when he claimed that the fur trade was not an American interest as well. He was disingenuous (at the least) in not admitting that the Americans wanted to drive the French out and take control of the fur trade every bit as much as the British did. The Pennsylvania and Virginian fur traders who flooded into the Ohio Valley during the 1740s were American colonists intent on making money, not front men acting on behalf of British merchants. Similarly the Ohio Company was indisputably an American concern, its colonial backers as interested in lining their own pockets as they were in maintaining the vibrancy of the British fur trade. Thus, when the war ended, it is not surprising that many Americans, jubilant at the French ouster, looked forward to expanding the fur trade into the newly conquered lands. But although some expansion did occur, the American fur trade remained in disarray and relatively insignificant up through the mid-1770s. Nevertheless it played a pivotal role in fueling American resentment of the British, which in turn sparked the American Revolution.

The first obstacle to the expansion of America's fur trade was the Indian uprising in the Great Lakes region, or the *pays d'en haut* (upper country), as the French called it. While the official conclusion of the French and Indian War didn't come until the signing of the Treaty of Paris on February 10, 1763, the war in North America ended for all intents and purposes with the fall of Montreal in early September 1760. A few days later Maj. Robert Rogers headed west with an armed contingent to take control of the French forts. Along the way many Indians, anxious to establish peaceful relations with the British so as to reinvigorate the fur trade and renew the flow of trade goods that had been cut off during the war, warmly greeted Rogers, who in turn did nothing to discourage their hopes by promising that soon "all the rivers would flow with rum—that presents from the Great King were to be unlimited—that all sorts of goods were to be in the utmost plenty and so cheap."[2] Rogers's promises, however, were hollow, because Gen. Sir Jeffrey Amherst, the man in charge of administering Britain's new territory, had other plans. He didn't view the Indians as equal trading partners but as savages to be controlled and put in their place. Now that the French were vanquished, Amherst believed that the Indians had no alternative but to barter with the British. He acted as if he had not just the upper hand but also the only hand. He would not treat the Indians with civility or deference; instead he would dictate the terms of the fur trade to the Indians—and those terms were harsh. He eliminated the time-honored tradition of giving gifts to Indians, claiming that they were the equivalent of "purchasing good behavior," and he didn't "think it necessary to give them any presents by way of bribes, for if they do not behave properly they are to be punished."[3] He believed that "the more . . . [the Indians] get the more they ask, and yet are never satisfied." Furthermore he thought that not providing gifts would force the Indians to work harder to gather furs to trade for the goods they wanted, and that such work would keep them from causing any trouble to "His Majesty's Interests." To limit the Indians' capacity to engage in military schemes, Amherst, acting now with colonial presumption, virtually cut off the Indians' supply of ammunition, "since," he argued, "nothing can be so impolitic as to furnish them with the means of accomplishing the evil which is so much Dreaded." But in doing so he also took away their primary means of hunting and procuring food.[4] Finally Amherst outlawed the sale of liquor.

These policies infuriated the Indians; so too did the arrival of colonists and a sizable contingent of British soldiers to man garrisons on the frontier. Seeing their trading position diminished and their lands encroached upon by an occupying force, the Indians cried foul. They complained that the British had conquered the French, but not them. The British therefore had no right to usurp their lands and treat them with such utter contempt.[5]

All that was needed to get the Indians on the warpath against the British was a leader, and they soon found one in the person of Pontiac, an Ottawa chief whose people lived near Detroit. Like many Indians who had formerly been allied with the French, Pontiac was shocked that the British had won, and he assumed that this could have only happened because the Great Father in France, the king, had "fallen asleep." So Pontiac took heart when the Frenchmen traveling through the region, hoping to incite the Indians to attack the British, told him that the king had awakened and would now help the Indians drive off the "red-coated dogs."[6] Pontiac was also impelled by the teachings of Neolin, an Indian dubbed the "Delaware Prophet" by the English, who preached that Indians must sever all connections with the white man to reinvigorate their way of life, recapture their hunting grounds, and achieve spiritual salvation and entry into heaven.[7]

Drawing on his anger over Indian treatment at the hands of the British, his belief that the French would aid his cause, and Neolin's call to action, Pontiac persuaded his tribe and the neighboring Potawatomi and Wyandot to launch an attack on the British at Fort Detroit in May 1763.[8] Although this attack proved unsuccessful, it helped to launch a pan-Indian uprising, and while the French king never did rouse from his long slumber to help his "children" drive off the "red-coated dogs," the Indians nevertheless quickly defeated all but three of the British forts in the Great Lakes region, in the process killing five hundred British soldiers and at least two thousand colonists.[9]

The British responded slowly at first but then with increasing intensity, beating back the Indians in most instances, and being beaten by them in others. In the end, however, it was negotiations and changes in British policies, not fighting, that brought an end to Pontiac's Rebellion. On October 7, 1763, the king issued a proclamation that essentially gave the Indians much of what they wanted. British colonists were banned from settling on any of the lands around the Great Lakes and between the Appalachians and Mississippi, and "and all persons who . . . [had] willfully or inadvertently seated themselves upon" any of those lands were ordered "forthwith to remove themselves from such settlements."[10] A year later the British enlivened Indian spirits even more by rescinding the ban on distributing gifts, liquor, and ammunition.[11]

W HILE THE INDIANS WELCOMED THE PROCLAMATION OF 1763, it shocked and dismayed Americans. They had fought the French and Indian War specifically to expel the French, eager to cross over the Appalachians and inhabit lands that they believed were rightfully theirs. Now that the French were vanquished, the Americans wanted to claim their prize, but the proclamation directed otherwise. In a cruel but, by hindsight, not surprising twist, it dawned on the Americans that the French and British had merely switched places, with the latter becoming the new barrier to westward expansion, revealing that the British hardly wished to relinquish their colonial hegemony. The Americans can hardly be blamed for wondering why they had spilled their blood if all it had accomplished was replacing one obstacle with another.

The British home government viewed things quite differently, as evidenced by a report by Lord Hillsborough, one of the commissioners of the Board of Trade and Plantations, in which he told his peers that the proclamation had two primary goals. The first was to keep the American settlements near the coast so that they would remain subordinate to and dependent on the mother country, and therefore more easily controlled. And the second was to leave the Indians unmolested so as to maximize the benefits of the fur trade. As Lord Hillsborough observed, "the extension of the fur trade depends entirely upon the Indians being undisturbed in the possession of their hunting grounds; that all colonizing does in its nature, and must in its consequences, operate to the prejudice of that branch of commerce. . . . Let the savages enjoy their deserts in quiet. . . . Were they driven from their forests, the peltry trade would decrease."[12] While the proclamation's goals squared with the mercantile theories of the day, which posited that colonies existed to benefit the mother country, this hardly made the terms more palatable. Indeed, for most Americans the Proclamation of 1763 was just another indication of how poorly Britain treated them, how little respect the imperial politicians in London had for American needs, aspirations, and rights. In the coming years the proclamation would stand alongside other examples of Britain's cavalier and reckless management of the colonies, including the Stamp Act, the Sugar Act, and the Townshend Acts, the combination of which would ignite the flames of revolution.

Although the proclamation rattled the American colonists' psyche, it had little practical impact. Even if the British had made a valiant effort to enforce the ban on settlement, they could not stop the vast tide of land-hungry colonists from sweeping west. And sweep they did.[13] As for American fur traders, they viewed the proclamation a bit differently than did the average colonist. The proclamation had not restricted their movement, since one of its goals was to establish an exclusive fur-trading zone where traders were welcome. Thus the proclamation was more of an opportunity than an impediment. Gone was the Indian unrest of the early 1760s, culminating in Pontiac's Rebellion, which had sharply curtailed fur trading in the region, and now it appeared as if the fortunes of the American fur trade would markedly improve.

Despite these heightened expectations, however, the fur trade failed to rebound. Part of the problem was regulatory in nature. Neither the colonies nor the British government could decide on and implement a coherent and efficient set of policies to govern the frontier trade. In the absence of such control, the trade became chaotic, a bit of a free-for-all, with abuses being committed not only by traders on one another but also by traders on the Indians. Another obstacle was diminishing interest in the fur trade as an engine of economic growth. During the French and Indian War the colonial fur trade nearly ground to a halt. After the war the colonial economy was slow to revive, and when it did, fur trading was no longer as dominant as it once had been. In New York, for example, furs comprised roughly 20 percent of the value of New York's shipments to Britain before the war; that number had dropped to less than 5 percent after the war. Increasingly Americans looked beyond the fur trade for places to invest their time and money.[14] A final obstacle to renewed American success was competition in the race for pelts coming from two key groups who also wanted to capitalize on the western trade—on one side were the British who had taken over Canada from the French, and on the other side were the French who operated out of the Spanish-controlled Louisiana territory.

*A*FTER THE FALL OF CANADA A LARGE NUMBER OF SCOT-tish Highlanders and other emigrants from Great Britain settled in the Montreal area and quickly took over the thriving fur trade that had been under French control. The new Montreal traders, or "peddlers," as they were derisively called by the jealous employees of the Hudson's Bay Company, realized that their success hinged on employing people who were the most knowledgeable in the methods of conducting the fur trade, so they promptly hired large numbers of the coureurs de bois and voyageurs who had chosen not to leave Canada despite its change in nationality. With these experts as their vanguard, the Montreal traders, who would later join forces to establish the North West Company, used many of the former French fur-trading posts to the south and west as jumping-off points to pursue the fur trade in the region bounded by the Great Lakes and the Mississippi and Ohio rivers, which is now referred to by historians as the Old Northwest.[15] And "in a short time the flow of peltries that had been accustomed for generations to follow the Saint Lawrence River to Paris was turned aside to find a final harbor in the storage rooms of London and Glasgow."[16]

Meanwhile, French fur traders on the west side of the Mississippi were enjoying great success as well, particularly those from Saint Louis, a town located on the west bank of the Mississippi, just below the confluence of the Missouri River. The history of St. Louis's origins is a bit convoluted. When the Treaty of Paris was signed on February 10, 1763, it appeared that New Orleans and the Louisiana territory would remain in French hands. However, appearances deceived. In 1762, as part of the secret Treaty of Fontainebleau, France ceded these lands to Spain, a measure of thanks for Spanish support in the war, and to keep the area from falling under British control. This secret transfer, however, was not made known to French officials in Louisiana (or the world) until October 1764. Thus, when the Frenchman Pierre Laclède founded St. Louis as a fur-trading post on February 15, 1764, he thought he was doing so under the flag of France. It therefore came as no small shock to him and his fellow French settlers when they learned, communication being so slow in the eighteenth century, in December 1764 that St. Louis was a Spanish, not a French town, and they were now Spanish subjects. Nevertheless Laclède and the settlers decided to stay and make the best of it, rapidly expanding their fur-trading operations up the Missouri, as well as east of the Mississippi and into the Old Northwest, generating as much as five hundred thousand dollars annually in those early years.[17]

Up through the late 1760s and into the early 1770s, the traders from Montreal and St. Louis competed fiercely for furs, and in the process they absorbed most of the trade west of the Appalachians and east of the Mississippi, leaving Americans with very little of the trade to call their own. The situation for the American fur traders worsened when colonial merchants, furious with Britain for foisting new taxes on the colonies, agreed not to import British goods until those taxes were repealed. Since British goods were critical to the fur trade, their disappearance affected the Indians' willingness to trade with the Americans.[18] It is no surprise, then, that the American fur trade was in a pitiable state on the eve of the American Revolution.

Conditions deteriorated even more when Parliament passed the Quebec Act in 1774, which, among other things, placed all the land north of the Ohio and west to the Mississippi—basically the entire Old Northwest—under the control of the governor of Quebec, giving him the right to regulate the region's fur trade. While the Canadians cheered this move, and in fact had lobbied on its behalf, the Americans were incensed, less on account of potential damage to the fur trade than because Parliament had nullified the American colonies' rights to these western lands, which in the case of Virginia, Connecticut, and Massachusetts had been conferred through their original charters.[19] It was the Proclamation of 1763 all over again. In the end, however, the Quebec Act, along with a whole raft of similarly imperious and punitive British laws and resolutions, taxes and pronouncements, finally compelled Americans to pick up their guns and fight for their rights and their sovereignty. Less than a year after the Quebec Act the "shot heard 'round the world" was fired on the out-skirts of Lexington, Massachusetts. The American Revolution had begun.

*T*HE AMERICAN FUR TRADE, MORIBUND ON THE EVE OF THE REV-olution, completely collapsed during it. Although American leaders desperately sought to use the fur trade to forge new alliances with the Indians, they couldn't do so because they were unable to obtain any goods to trade. Independent American fur traders were hamstrung for the same reason. The British fur trade, in contrast, continued during the war much as it had before, generating annual returns on the order of two hundred thousand pounds. Traders from Montreal, Quebec, and the Hudson's Bay Company, liberally supplied with goods from Britain and still in control of all the major trad-ing posts east of the Mississippi, collected furs from Canada, the Great Lakes region, and elsewhere.[20]

When the British prime minister, the arrogant Lord North, learned that Lord Charles Cornwallis had surrendered to George Washington at York-town on October 19, 1781, he moaned "Oh God, it is all over!"[21] Indeed it was. The surrender effectively ended the war and propelled the peace negotiations, resulting in the Treaty of Paris on September 3, 1783. The treaty's preamble painted a picture of postwar amicability intended to repair the fractured rela-tionship between the colonial power and the fledgling nation. Britain and the United States agreed "to forget all past misunderstandings and differences . . . and to establish such a beneficial and satisfactory intercourse between the two countries upon the ground of reciprocal advantages and mutual convenience as may promote and secure to both perpetual peace and harmony."[22]

The treaty, on paper at least, was a boon for the struggling American fur trade. The treaty basically established the current border between Canada and the United States, which extends from the northern reaches of Maine all the way to the Lake of the Woods—located at the intersection of present-day Minnesota and the provinces of Ontario and Manitoba. From there the border ran along the east side of the Mississippi down to the Gulf of Mexico. The Americans thus were left in control of the rich fur country south of the Great Lakes, the region that first the French and then the British had placed off lim-its. The treaty also gave both the United States and Britain unfettered access to the Mississippi, thereby ensuring that fur traders of both countries could make use of this critical thoroughfare. Finally, Britain agreed to evacuate promptly—"with all convenient speed"—its military and fur-trading posts that now lay in American territory. It was a move that should have enabled American fur traders to fill that void and establish themselves as key players in the movement of furs to Europe. The only way in which the American fur trade could have made out better is if Britain had ceded all of Canada, as Benjamin Franklin had asked it to do at the outset of the treaty talks.[23]

Although the American negotiating team had not made the resuscitation of the fur trade one of its primary goals, it was nevertheless pleased with the outcome.[24] A beleaguered John Adams wrote in a letter to his wife, Abigail, that "nothing in life ever cost me so much sleep, or made me so many grey hairs, as the anxiety, I have suffered for these three years. . . . Nobody knows of it: Nobody cares for it. But I shall be rewarded for it, in Heaven I hope." Adams mused that if he had stayed home instead of negotiating the treaty, his "lot in life" would have been far easier, but in the very next sentence he acknowledged that had he chosen that course, America would have been the poorer for it. "Where would have been our cod and haddock, our beaver skins, deer skins and pine trees? Alas all lost, perhaps. Indeed I firmly believe so, in a good conscience."[25]

While American fur traders viewed the peace treaty in a favorable light, Canadian fur traders and their supporters in London clearly did not. They had protested vigorously throughout the negotiations that the British government was giving too much of the valuable fur country to the Americans. John Graves Simcoe, the lieutenant governor of the Upper Province of Canada, ridiculed the "lavish unnecessary concession which induced the negotiators of the treaty with America to lay at her feet the most valuable branch of trade in this country."[26] What really irked so many British observers was that the Americans had outmaneuvered their government, and Prime Minister Lord Shelburne in particular, so easily. One member of the House of Commons tartly observed that Shelburne, "not thinking the naked independence a sufficient proof of his liberality to the United States . . . had clothed it with the warm covering of our fur trade."[27]

Shelburne shot back that his decision to draw the boundary line where he did was based primarily on economics—the most lucrative fur trade was north of the line—and that the cost of maintaining the lands south of the line was not justified by the value of the trade gained by doing so. Shelburne also had another motive. He had bought into the concept of using the peace treaty as a means for Britain to reconcile with America, thereby treating the

Americans as "brethren," and one of the best ways to do so was by drawing the line liberally and giving Americans a share of the fur trade.[28] Certainly bending boundaries a bit was a small price to pay for peace with a new nation that would, not coincidentally, be likely to become the most important market for British goods after the war.

Shelburne's arguments didn't convince his detractors. The most stinging rebuke of Shelburne's purported fire sale came from the Earl of Carlisle. "You had better have ceded all Canada than have given in to this mockery of keeping the two ports of Montreal and Quebec (for they are no other than mere ports without the trade of the interior country) to be supported from this country with much expense." At another point in the debate Carlisle stated, "All Canada is in fact lost to Great Britain. All the country from the Allegheny Mountains to the Mississippi lost. All the forts, settlements, carrying places, towns, inhabitants upon the lakes, lost. The peltry and fur trade lost."[29]

*B*UT ALL WAS NOT "LOST." WORDS ARE NOT ACTIONS, AND it immediately became clear that the concessions afforded the Americans were more apparent than real. It would be thirteen years before the British evacuated the forts and trading posts south of the new border—thereby giving new meaning to the phrase "with all convenient speed." During that time the Americans were virtually shut out of that branch of the fur trade while British traders continued to reap all the benefits. The official reason the British gave for their intransigence was that the Americans had failed to live up to the treaty's provisions that required them to treat Loyalists with respect and repay debts owed to British subjects. There was certainly some merit to these complaints, and there is no doubt they were part of the explanation for the British refusal to budge in the Old Northwest.[30] But the much more important reasons for British actions were that they didn't want to give up the valuable fur trade or abandon the Indians of the region who had fought so valiantly on the side of the British during the war, and therefore deserved some measure of respect and loyalty. And furthermore, if Britain maintained these Indian alliances, then should another war with America commence, the Indians could be counted on once again to stand on Britain's side.

As a result there was a quick change in policy. The British administration that replaced Shelburne's in 1783 decided that protecting Canada's economic foundation and Indian alliances trumped the need to appease the Americans by handling over the posts.[31] In May 1786 Gen. George Washington wrote to his trusted friend and fellow revolutionary the Marquis de Lafayette, voicing his concerns about Britain's double dealing. "The British still occupy our Posts to the Westward," and they have no intention of relinquishing them. "It is indeed evident to me, that they had it in contemplation to do this at the time of the treaty. . . . I have not the smallest doubt but that every secret engine is continually at work to inflame the Indian mind, with a view to keep it at variance with these States, for the purpose of retarding our settlements to the Westward, and depriving us of the fur and peltry trade of that country."[32]

Washington had good reason to be perturbed, and his anger mirrored that of the new nation. The British had utterly disregarded multiple American requests to turn over the posts.[33] From the mid-1780s through the early 1790s, American diplomats vigorously protested British actions. An excellent example of this came in 1791, when U.S. Secretary of State Thomas Jefferson wrote a heated letter to George Hammond, the British minister to America, cogently laying out America's concerns. After noting that the British had failed to withdraw from Forts Michilimackinac, on Lake Michigan; Detroit, on the strait of Lakes Erie and Huron; Erie, on Lake Erie; Niagara and Oswego, on Lake Ontario; Oswegatchie, on the St. Lawrence; and Point au fer and Dutchman's Point, on Lake Champlain, Jefferson argued that the British military had taken control of the entire region and its inhabitants, restricting the movements of United States citizens. As a result Americans had "been intercepted entirely from the commerce of furs with the Indians to the northward, a commerce which had ever been of great importance to the United States, not only for its intrinsic value but as it was a means of cherishing peace with those Indians."[34]

Jefferson's missive didn't generate a satisfactory response, but soon the tide began to turn. Although Americans had just barely survived one war, and were in no position to launch another, talk of a new altercation with Britain had entered the national discussion. Britain's retention of the posts in the Old Northwest, along with a range of other issues, including the British navy's policy of seizing American ships and impressing American sailors, had so infuriated Americans that many of them thought that another war was inevitable. Their first president, George Washington, disagreed. Instead of declaring war Washington sent Supreme Court Justice John Jay to London to see if he could negotiate a settlement that would resolve the differences between the two countries. The resulting "Jay treaty," ratified by the United States in

1795, was successful in averting war, but at a price. On almost every major issue Jay had capitulated to the British position, except one.[35] Under article 2 of the treaty the British agreed to turn over to the United States all its posts in the Old Northwest on or before June 1, 1796, and they did.[36]

The British yielded on the issue of the posts in part for practical reasons. Originally the British had viewed the Indian tribes in the Old Northwest as an insurance policy of sorts. The tribes' strength would, it was assumed, be an effective defense against any American incursions into the area, thereby providing a protective buffer for the posts occupied by the British.[37] For a time the policy held. But after the Congress passed the Northwest Ordinance in 1787, transforming the Old Northwest into the Northwest Territory, Americans settled the area in greater numbers and Britain's insurance policy began to fray at the edges. This migration of Americans angered many Indians, who had not given anyone rights to cede or take their lands. Their anger soon became rage, with renewed Indian attacks on the settlers, precipitating a American military response intended to protect the settlers and make it clear to the Indians that the Northwest Territory was owned by the United States.

At first the Indians had little difficulty thrashing the poorly trained and hapless American forces, and each time the Indians won their confidence was bolstered, and they stepped up their attacks on the settlers. But, in the summer of 1794 the balance of power shifted, when the Indians had to face Revolutionary War hero Gen. "Mad" Anthony Wayne, whom Washington had called out of retirement especially for this mission. Despite his reputation for being somewhat rash, Wayne decided not to rush into battle. He spent more than a year gathering more than three thousand men and drilling them at training camps in the vicinity of Pittsburgh and Cincinnati, preparing them for the final assault. When it finally came, at the Battle of Fallen Timbers near present-day Toledo, Wayne's finely honed fighting force routed the Delaware, Shawnee, and Miami Indians arrayed against it.[38]

As the historian James A. Hanson notes, this battle "proved to be a major watershed for the new republic. The British, depending on the Indian barrier to protect its interests, were embarrassed to discover how easily the Americans had broken the power of the numerous and well-equipped tribes." This near-humiliation, combined with the French Revolution, which put Britain on a war footing, helped convince the British that sacrificing their posts in the Old Northwest was a relatively small price to pay to avoid a new war with the Americans. Furthermore, with the Americans in control of the post, Britain would benefit from the furs the Americans collected. If the Americans wanted to sell their furs they would have to go through London, the world's main portal for pelts and finished fur garments.[39]

There is another, more devious reason that the British were so willing to relinquish the posts and seemingly hand over the area's fur trade to the Americans: They didn't think they were handing it over at all. Article 3 of the Jay treaty gave the British and the Americans reciprocal cross-border fur-trading rights, and the British were confident that by exercising such rights they would be able to maintain their lock on the fur trade in and around the Great Lakes and the Old Northwest. After all, the British had greater resources at their disposal, and stronger ties to the region's Indians.[40]

THE EVACUATION OF THE POSTS COINCIDED WITH AN INCREASE in government intervention in the fur trade. Washington, who became president in 1789, desperately wanted to put an end to the widespread Indian unrest along the western frontier, and one of the ways he felt he could do this was by providing an alternative to the traditional fur trade, which he believed contributed to that unrest. In Washington's eyes, and in the view of many other Americans, fur traders, both domestic and foreign, were rogues who mistreated and cheated the Indians—selling them short and plying them with alcohol—and it was up to the government to counteract their destructive influence by regulating the fur trade, or in his words, establishing "intimate intercourse" that was "calculated to advance the happiness of the Indians, and to attach them firmly to the United States."[41] To that end Washington urged Congress in 1793 "to render tranquility with the savages permanent" by creating government-run posts at which fur trading would "be conducted without fraud, without extortion, with constant and plentiful supplies, with a ready market for the commodities of the Indians, and a stated price for what they give in payment, and receive in exchange."[42] Because the government wouldn't have to make a profit, Washington claimed it could offer the Indians better terms than the traders, with whom the new government posts were intended to compete. And by prohibiting the posts from trading liquor for furs, the government would be protecting the Indians from the ruinous consequences that inevitably resulted from the use of alcohol. Congress finally came around to Washington's way of thinking in 1795, when it created the Office of Indian Trade, which was responsible for establishing fur-trading posts, or factories as they were called, where the Indians were supposed to get a fair deal.[43] According to Hanson, given the Office of Indian Trade's humanitarian focus, "it might be considered the earliest example of federal social welfare legislation" in the United States.[44]

*F*ROM THE END OF THE REVOLUTION TO THE IMPLEMENTA-tion of Jay's treaty, the American fur trade was in the doldrums. Virtually cut off from the trade in the Old Northwest, Americans had to rely largely on the furs provided by the lands in and around the thirteen colonies, which had already been depleted of animals as a result of more than 150 years of intensive hunting. And when Americans could muster a good supply of furs, they had a tough time selling them because furs were not a staple commodity in the impoverished colonies, and American furs were not wholly welcome in postwar London. Even after Jay's treaty officially transferred the posts in the Old Northwest into American hands, and British import barriers loosened, the American fur trade remained relatively inconsequential until the early 1800s. This was due to the small number of American traders, the continued domination of British traders in American territory, faltering European markets, and the insignificant impact of the Office of Indian Trade, which in its first seven years managed to establish just two factories.[45] There was, however, one bright spot for the American fur trade during these troubled years: On the Northwest Coast, where the sleek sea otter swam in the briny blue-green waters of the Pacific Ocean.

PART III

America
Heads West

PREVIOUS PAGE | Louis-Rocky Mountain
Trapper, *by Alfred Jacob Miller, 1837.*

9

"A Perfect Golden Round of Profits"

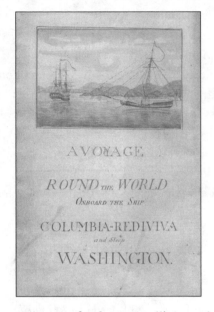

Title page of Robert Haswell's journal,
September 1787–June 1789.

MERICANS IN THE LATE EIGHTEENTH CENTURY HAD only a murky understanding of the West. Once the maps of the day crossed the Mississippi, details became fewer and blank spots multiplied. Over the next century the United States would spread all the way to the Pacific, slowly filling in the map becoming a continental nation. The fur trade played a significant role in this westward movement. America's first foray to the West was in pursuit of sea otter pelts, and it went not overland, but by sea. The credit for providing the earliest impetus for this venture belongs to Capt. James Cook, a taciturn Yorkshireman who became one of the world's most daring explorers.

On the eve of the American Revolution, Cook, whose greatest passion was to go where no Westerner had ever gone before already had two remarkable voyages on his résumé, both circumnavigations of the globe in the Southern Hemisphere.[1] As commander of the *Endeavour* (1768–71) one of his primary tasks was to search for *terra australis incognita*, thought to be a lush, resource-rich continent located near the bottom of the earth. Although Cook didn't find this bountiful land, he did become the first European to chart the entire coastline of New Zealand, and the first to visit southeastern Australia, naming Botany Bay in the process and making contact with the Aborigines.[2]

During Cook's second voyage (1772–75), with the ships *Resolution* and *Adventure* under his command, he once again set out and failed to discover the mythical southern continent. Yet, in pursuing this phantom land, Cook sailed the *Resolution* to within seventy-five miles of Antarctica, and became the first European to cross the Antarctic Circle. Having braved the frigid air and ice-choked waters below the seventy-first parallel, Cook boldly predicted—incorrectly, as it turned out—that because "the risk one runs in exploring a coast in these unknown and icy seas, is so very great, . . . no man will ever venture farther than I have done; and that the lands which may lie to the south will never be explored." If *terra australis incognita* was indeed ever found, Cook averred that it would be "a country doomed by nature never once to feel the warmth of the sun's rays, but to lie buried in everlasting snow and ice."[3]

It was on his third voyage, however, that Cook made his critical contribution to the history of the American fur trade. On July 12, 1776, Cook again sailed from Britain, with 191 men onboard the *Resolution* and the *Discovery*, in yet another in the long line of attempts to find the Northwest Passage to the Orient, spurred on by Parliament's promise of twenty thousand pounds for the first British ship that did so.[4] Rather than search for the passage from the Atlantic side of North America, as most earlier failed expeditions had done, Cook planned to sail to the northern Pacific, where he hoped to find the fabled waterway and follow its course clear through (or around North America), ending up at Hudson Bay.

In mid-January 1778, about eighteen months into the journey, Cook and his men became the first Europeans to visit the Hawaiian Islands, which he named the Sandwich Islands in honor of the Earl of Sandwich, the First Lord of the Admiralty and one of his staunchest supporters. The Hawaiians were dumbfounded by the ships' arrival at the island of Kauai. "In the course of my several voyages," Cook wrote, "I never before met with the natives of any place so much astonished as these people were upon entering a ship. Their eyes were continually flying from object to object; the wildness of their looks and gestures fully expressing their entire ignorance about everything they saw." The Hawaiians were quite welcoming, treating Cook in particular as if he were at a minimum a great chief, and possibly even a god. Wherever he went they threw themselves prostrate to pay their respects to the strange and wondrous visitor. Then, in early February, having loaded the ships with copious amounts of food and water, the *Resolution* and the *Discovery* proceeded on their voyage.[5]

A little more than a month later Cook sighted the coast of present-day Oregon and continued sailing north, anchoring in Nootka Sound on the west coast of Vancouver Island at the end of March. Almost immediately, observed Cook, "a great many canoes, filled with the natives" surrounded the ships, "and a trade commenced betwixt us and them," in which the furs of bears, raccoons, sea otters, and other animals were exchanged for various articles, including knives, buttons, and nails. Cook's men eagerly snapped up the furs to make new clothes to replace their own, in tatters after nearly two years at sea. In the coming months such transactions were repeated multiple times, accumulating fifteen hundred pelts.[6]

Cook spent much of the rest of 1778 vainly searching for the Northwest Passage, and then headed back to the Hawaiian Islands to give his men time to relax, and to stock up on supplies before resuming his explorations. Coming ashore on January 17, 1779, in Kealakekua Bay on the island of Hawaii, Cook and his men were greeted with a joyous celebration. For the next two and a half weeks the British were treated with even more adoration and deference than they had been accorded on their initial visit. When the *Resolution* and the *Discovery* sailed out of Kealakekua Bay in the early hours of February 4, they were escorted by an armada of canoes, a few of which came alongside one of the ships so that the Hawaiians could deliver some hogs and vegetables, a parting gift of friendship.[7]

Four days later, during a powerful gale, the *Resolution's* foremast, already weakened by rot, became dislodged near its base, forcing Cook to head back to Kealakekua for repairs. This time, however, when the British came ashore, the Hawaiians were decidedly cool, then openly hostile. Although the reasons for this dramatic change in attitude, compared with just a week earlier, are the subject of a strident academic debate, the results are not.[8]

Stealing by the Hawaiians soon escalated into altercations with the British, followed by stone throwing, which in turn led Cook to try to reestablish some order through a measured show of force. He went ashore with his lieutenant and nine armed marines to take the king hostage until the Hawaiians returned the *Discovery's* cutter, which had been taken from its mooring. The king agreed to accompany Cook, but as they approached the water's edge one of the king's wives, crying hysterically, begged him not to go; and then two chiefs grabbed the king and "forced him to sit down." All the while the rapidly growing throng of Hawaiians, perhaps three thousand strong, grew more restive. Each time Cook tried to coax the increasingly fearful king to board the boat that would take them to the ship, the two chiefs restrained him. Realizing that forcing the king to come would likely ignite a battle, Cook decided to leave without him. But at that moment news arrived "which gave a fatal turn to the affair."

Earlier in the day two canoes had tried to run the blockade Cook had established in the bay to keep anyone from leaving until the cutter was returned. Cook's men had fired at the fleeing canoes, "killing a chief." As word of the murder spread through the crowd, the Hawaiian men slipped woven "war-mats" over their chests, and armed themselves with stones and spears. One of the men ran up to Cook, gesticulating wildly, threatening to strike. Cook tried to calm him down, but when that failed he fired one of his gun's barrels, loaded with "small-shot." The pellets bounced harmlessly off the man's "war-mat," and the act of firing only further provoked the Hawaiians, who menacingly edged closer and again started throwing rocks.

One of the Hawaiians, dagger in hand, lunged forward, but the marine who was the intended target parried with a well-placed blow of "the butt end of his musket." Cook "fired his second barrel, loaded with ball," killing one of the Hawaiians. While stones rained down on the British, Cook ordered his men to fire and yelled, "Take to the boats." The marines' fire was deadly accurate, but before they could reload the crowd rushed forward "with dreadful shouts and yells." In the melee that ensued, and the mad scramble for the boats, Cook was left behind. As he stood in the surf, urging one of the boats to come get him, he was clubbed and then stabbed in the back. Cook pitched forward into the water, immediately set upon by others who continued the assault, then dragged his body onto the beach where they took turns repeatedly kicking and stabbing him.[9]

Cook's men could scarcely believe the "calamity" that had just occurred. Their commander dead, along with four marines, as well as seventeen Hawaiians (and many more wounded on both sides). The men's grief soon gave way to thoughts of revenge. In the days following Cook's death, the marines went ashore to collect the repaired foremast and gather water. Rock throwing and threatening advances by the Hawaiians elicited a vicious response from the British, who shot and bayoneted perhaps a dozen Hawaiians, set one of the villages ablaze, and even decapitated two natives, parading their heads about on pikes. The crew's tempers grew more inflamed when one of the Hawaiian priests paddled into the bay to deliver a package. Wrapped in a piece of cloth was a ten-pound slab of human flesh. It was from Cook's body, the priest said, claiming that the rest of his body had been burned and that his bones and head were with one of the chiefs. This caused the British to repeat their earlier demand that all of Cook's remains be returned immediately.

On the morning of February 20 a solemn procession of Hawaiians walked down to the beach and deposited presents of sugarcane and fruit near a white flag stuck in the sand. One of the chiefs beckoned to the ships moored just offshore that a boat be sent to pick him up. The chief held in his hands a beautifully wrapped bundle, which he gave the British. It contained the rest of Cook's body, or at least what was left of it, including both of his hands, with the flesh still on; the skull, with the scalp cut off and the facial bones missing; and the thigh and leg bones. The next day Cook's remains were placed in a coffin and consigned to the deep with military honors. With peace restored, the British stayed for another three weeks, during which they charted the rest of the islands. In mid-March the *Resolution* and the *Discovery* departed Hawaii.[10]

NOW UNDER THE COMMAND OF CHARLES CLERKE (WHO would soon die, to be replaced by John Gore), the men visited the Russian settlements on Kamchatka, then continued their fruitless search for the Northwest Passage, and after abandoning that sailed to Canton (Guangzhou), China, to gather supplies for their journey home.[11] It was in that bustling port that they made one of the most valuable discoveries of the entire voyage. In late December 1779, Capt. James King, who had taken over command of the *Discovery*, visited a Chinese merchant to sell twenty sea otter skins. The merchant tried to take advantage of the supposedly naive Briton by offering three hundred dollars for the lot. Although it seemed a large sum on its face, King knew better. During their stop on the Kamchatka Peninsula the British sailors had sold sea otter skins to Russian traders for twice that amount. Thus the hard bargaining began, with King haggling until he received forty dollars per pelt. King soon learned that these already fantastic prices could go even higher. "During our absence [from the ships]," he would later write, "a brisk trade had been carrying on with the Chinese for the sea-otter skins, which had every day been rising in their value," despite the fact that many of the pelts were "spoiled or worn out." One lucky seaman sold his lot of furs for $800, a few especially prime skins fetching $120 apiece.[12] Such huge sums precipitated in the men an almost uncontrollable urge to return immediately to the Northwest Coast to gather more furs, and a near-mutiny ensued. But order was restored, and the *Resolution* and the *Discovery* headed back to Britain, arriving in October 1780. When years later the news of Cook's voyage, in particular the fur sale in Canton, reached the East Coast of the United States it sparked one of the biggest rushes of the American fur trade, a period when the sea otter pelt reigned supreme.

*T*HE SEA OTTER (*ENHYDRA LUTRIS*) IS A REMARKABLE AND exceptionally handsome animal. Related to weasels, mink, skunks, and badgers, it spends virtually its entire life in the ocean, rarely if ever coming ashore.[13] The smallest of marine mammals, reaching nearly five feet and weighing as much as one hundred pounds, sea otters were originally found in a great arc along the Pacific coast, from the Kurile Islands above Japan, north to the Kamchatka Peninsula, across the Bering Sea to the Aleutian Island chain, and then south to Baja California.

The sea otter spends much of its time either floating on its back at the surface or diving deep, up to four minutes at a time, to gather a smorgasbord of delectable morsels to eat, including sea urchins, crabs, and abalones, which it retrieves by either holding them tight in its paws or tucking them into pocketlike folds of skin under its arms. One of the few animals to use tools, the sea otter often consumes its meal by placing a rock on its belly, grabbing the object of its gustatory desire in its paws, and pounding it violently against the rock until the prey's shell is fractured and the succulent meat inside exposed. Abalones, whose bodies are covered by a shell on one side only, do not need to be subjected to this punishing treatment; instead the sea otter digs right in to the mollusks' exposed underside, tearing off big chunks of sweet meat. As for sea urchins, they are approached gingerly, with the sea otter using its dexterous paws to push aside the needle-sharp spines and its mouth to crush the creature's exoskeleton, getting to the soft jellylike animal within.

Playful, curious, and extremely social, sea otters will often leap about and follow one another in the water like seals or dolphins. They will congregate in large groups, or rafts, of up to one hundred individuals, at times interlocking their paws to keep together as they float serenely atop the ocean swells. In warmer climates they will sometimes wrap themselves in the ribbonlike fronds of kelp rising from the bottom, creating an anchor that keeps them from drifting too far while they sleep. With keen senses of sight, hearing, and especially smell, sea otters are ever alert to danger and are quick to evade predators, including killer whales and white sharks.

Arguably the sea otter's most fascinating feature is its fur, which can be brown, reddish brown, or black in the body, and lighter or whitish or silvery about the head. Like the beaver the sea otter has two types of hair: the outer guard hairs and the inner downy underfur. With as many as one million hairs per square inch, sea otter fur is the densest of all mammals', and the most luxurious to the touch.[14] William Sturgis, one of the most famous American sea otter traders, who began voyaging to the Pacific Northwest in the late eighteenth century, opined that it gave him "more pleasure to look at a splendid sea-otter skin, than to examine half the pictures that are stuck up for exhibition, and puffed up by pretended connoisseurs," and that "excepting a beautiful woman and a lovely infant," the sea otter's pelt was the most beautiful natural object in the world.[15]

Unlike many other mammals, the sea otter does not molt. The pelt remains in prime quality throughout the year, with never a season when it is ratty or thin. The fur plays a particularly critical role in thermoregulation. Because the sea otter has no insulating layer of fat, it relies on air bubbles trapped in the underfur to help keep it warm. For that system to work the outer guard hairs must be kept very clean so that they remain waterproof. That is why sea otters spend so much time grooming themselves, and also why they can die of hypothermia or pneumonia if their fur gets dirty or covered with oil. A thick, clean layer of fur, however, is not enough to keep warm. To maintain a constant body temperature in the cold ocean waters the sea otter eats up to 25 percent of its body weight per day to keep its extremely rapid metabolic rate up to speed.[16]

The sea otter's pelt inevitably made it a target of the fur trade. By the time Cook's men arrived in Canton, such pelts had been selling briskly for at least forty years in China, where they were deemed the royal fur, valued more than any other by the rich and powerful, used to trim robes and capes, and to make hats and winter coats.[17] The Japanese were trading sea otter pelts to the Chinese by the early 1700s if not before, but it wasn't until the early 1740s, and the arrival of the Russians, that the sea otter trade became a major entrepreneurial activity.

RUSSIA'S RELENTLESS DRIVE TO THE EAST HAD BEGUN TWO decades earlier when Peter the Great, Russia's most visionary and expansionist czar, called on one of his most trusted naval officers, the Dane Vitus Bering, and ordered him to travel to the farthest eastern reaches of Siberia and then across the ocean to America, with the goal of bringing the North American continent into Russia's embrace. Bering's first expedition lasted five grueling years and ended in failure. Although Peter the Great had died before Bering returned, his successors decided to continue his policy and send Bering forth once again in 1733. Eight and a half years later, after transporting a small army of men and supplies to the Kamchatka coast, building two crude sailing ships, and sailing them nearly two thousand miles to the east, Bering and his men made landfall in America in the middle of July 1741.

Bering's lieutenant, Alexei Chirikov, on board the *St. Paul*, sighted land first in the vicinity of Takinis Bay near what is now Sitka Sound. Three days later he sent ten well-armed men ashore to explore, followed five days later by another group to see what had happened to the first. The mystery was solved a few days later when Tlingit Indians in two canoes paddled within view. Despite the Russians waving white handkerchiefs and motioning for them to come closer, the Tlingit stayed far away from the *St. Paul*. "The fact that the Americans [Indians] did not dare approach our ship," Chirikov concluded, "leads us to believe that they have either killed or detained our men."[18]

Chirikov was now in dire straits. A quarter of his crew had vanished, and with them the only two boats that the *St. Paul* had onboard, meaning that even if Chirikov wanted to send a party ashore to get water or explore somewhere else along the coast, he could not. Stranded on their ship, with only forty-five casks of water in the hold, Chirikov and his men knew they didn't have much time before there was nothing left to drink. With no recourse he sailed his leaking boat back to Kamchatka, losing another twenty-one men to scurvy and other illnesses along the way.[19]

Bering's adventure onboard the *St. Peter* was even more harrowing. He sighted land a day later than Chirikov, a little way southeast of modern Cordova, gazing first upon the jagged towering peaks of Mount St. Elias, which

soared nearly twenty thousand feet into the sky. After four days of coast-
ing to the northwest Bering finally let his men step ashore. One of the first
off the boat was the eighteenth-century German naturalist Georg Wilhelm
Steller, part of the large scientific contingent Bering had brought along at the
behest of the Russian Imperial Academy of Sciences. Steller had hoped to
document exhaustively the wildlife of the region, but within less than a day
Bering announced that the *St. Peter* was heading back, sending Steller into a
rage. "The only reason for this," Steller later wrote, "was stupid obstinacy,
fear of a handful of natives, and pusillanimous homesickness. For ten years
Bering had equipped himself for this great enterprise; the explorations lasted
ten hours!"[20]

The next three months on the *St. Peter* proved a maritime nightmare worthy of Dante's imagination. Rotten food, lack of water, and tempestuous seas
conspired to kill many of the men and nearly destroy the boat. In late October
the *St. Peter* made it to the tip of the Aleutians, a gracefully curving chain of
rugged volcanic islands that stretches roughly twelve hundred miles into the
Pacific. It appeared as if the *St. Peter* might finally make it to Kamchatka. But
neither the ship nor its crew had anything left. The sails were in tatters, the
sixty-year-old Bering was fighting a losing battle against multiple ailments
including scurvy, and his men were barely able to stand, much less run the
ship. On November 4, after most of the men had resigned themselves to a hor-
rendous death, they sighted land. Fleeting hopes that it might be Kamchatka
vanished soon after the crippled ship wrecked on the shore a day or two later.
They had discovered a small group of islands off the Kamchatka coast, which
would later be named the Komandorski, or Commander Islands, in honor of
their commander. And the extinct volcano they were marooned on would
become known as Bering Island.

The emaciated men spent nine months on the island, many of them dying
there, including Bering, who spent his final days partially buried in the sand
in an effort to stay warm and protect himself from the piercing winds. Those
who survived did so because of the sea otters—or sea beavers, as the Russians
called them—that swam in the waters around the island and occasionally
hauled themselves onto the rocks. Despite their infirmities the men were easily able to kill the otters, which provided the main source of food.[21] And the
animals' pelts became a form of currency used as stakes in gambling games.
As the gambling debts mounted, the sea otters' plight worsened. "He who had
totally ruined himself," Steller wrote, "tried to recoup his losses through the

poor sea otters, which were slaughtered without necessity and consideration only for their skins, their meat being thrown away. When this did not suffice, some began to steal the skins from the others, whereby hate, quarrels, and strife were disseminated through all quarters." According to Steller's calculations the men killed at least nine hundred sea otters, far more than would have been necessary if they had been killed for food alone.[22]

Using materials salvaged from the *St. Peter* or found naturally on the island, the survivors built a forty-one-foot boat. Launched in early August 1742, it arrived a few weeks later in Petropavlovsk on Kamchatcka's southeastern shore. The ship was so weighed down that Bering's replacement, Sven Waxell, ordered that the sea otter skins be thrown overboard during the voyage to lighten the load. The men complied, save Fleet Master Sofron Khitrov, who hid his hoard of prime pelts beneath his bunk, and upon landing in Petropavlovsk smuggled them to shore. Unashamedly he began to boast how he would make a fortune selling the furs to the Chinese. It didn't take long for Khitrov's claims that Bering Island and the Aleutians were teeming with sea otters to reach the ears of the *promyshleniki,* the professional hunters who inhabited the eastern reaches of the Russian empire. "As the quest for the black sable had enticed the *promyshleniki* from the Volga over the Urals to Siberia," observed the writer Corey Ford, "so the sea otter was the Golden Fleece which lured these Russian Argonauts across the North Pacific to the Aleutians and Northwest America."[23] The proverbial race was on.

*L*ITTLE MORE THAN BRIGANDS WITH A WELL-DESERVED reputation for using violence to get what they wanted, the *promyshleniki* swept eastward, leaving a path of utter destruction in their wake. Rather than hunt for sea otters on their own, the *promyshleniki* usually forced the natives, or Aleuts, as they dubbed them, to do it for them by taking some of them hostage and threatening their lives unless the remaining members of the tribe returned with pelts. This particularly savage form of extortion worked particularly well for the *promyshleniki,* who were more than willing, and at times almost eager, to slaughter the Aleuts if they disobeyed. When the Aleuts rose up in defiance, bloodbaths ensued. In one particularly gruesome instance, Fedor Solovief, appropriately named the "Terrible Nightingale," attacked Aleuts on Unmak and Unalaska islands in retaliation for earlier

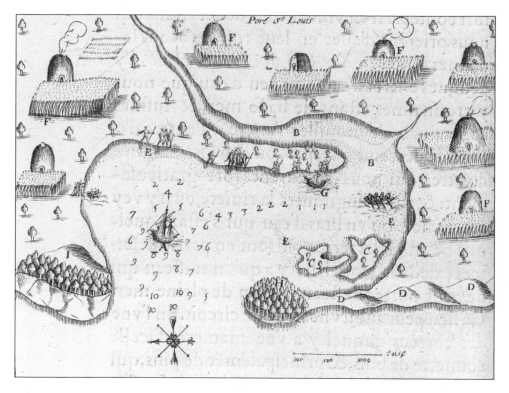

1 | *Samuel de Champlain's map of Plymouth Harbor, 1605.*

2 | *The first sale of furs at Garroway's coffeehouse, London, 1671.*

3 | *Beaver lodge.*

4 | *Birch tree chewed by a beaver.*

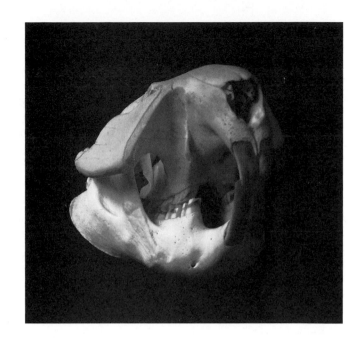

5 | *Beaver skull.*

6 | *Beaver dam near the Red Rock Lakes National Wildlife Refuge, Montana.*

7 | *An assembly line of industrious beavers, employing building techniques never seen in nature, circa 1715.*

8 | *A British engraving from 1839, showing a scene from the beaver-hat-making process.*

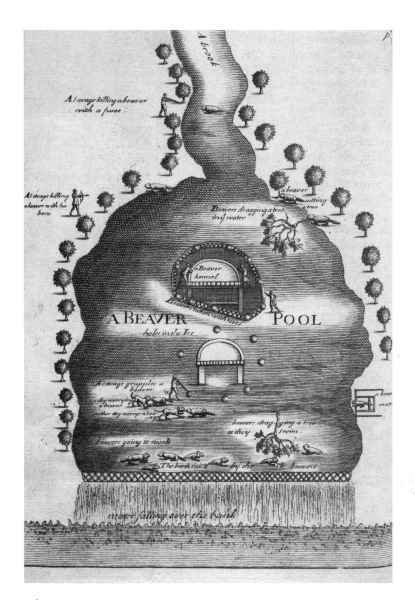

9 | *A drawing from 1703, showing beavers going about their business, as well as various Indian hunting methods.*

10 | *Brass pots used in the fur trade.*

11 | *Benjamin Franklin wearing his marten fur cap.*

12 | *Portrait of John Ledyard by Joseph Swan, 1991.*

13 | *Maquinna, chief of the Yuquot in Nootka Sound, by Suria, circa 1791.*

14 | *A 1799 engraving of a Chinese furrier hawking his wares in Canton, China.*

15 | *Northern fur seal.*

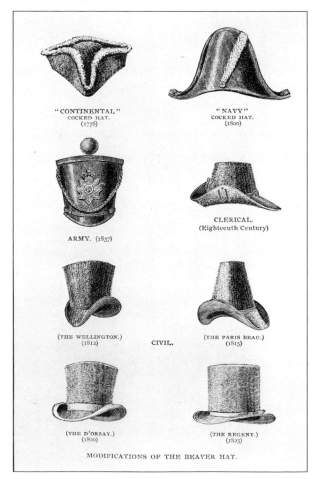

"CONTINENTAL,"
COCKED HAT.
(1776)

"NAVY"
COCKED HAT.
(1800)

ARMY. (1837)

CLERICAL.
(Eighteenth Century)

(THE WELLINGTON.)
(1812)

CIVIL.

(THE PARIS BEAU.)
(1815)

(THE D'ORSAY.)
(1820)

(THE REGENT.)
(1825)

MODIFICATIONS OF THE BEAVER HAT.

17 | *One type of beaver trap.*

18 | *Jim Bridger, between 1860 and 1880.*

19 | *Mountain man James P. Beckwourth.*

20 | *Christopher Houston "Kit" Carson.*

21 | *This is the Museum of the Fur Trade's reconstruction of the James Bordeaux trading post in Chadron, Nebraska. The original post was established in the fall of 1837 by Bordeaux to trade with the Indians and provide the American Fur Company with prime buffalo robes.*

22 | *Bent's Fort, on the Arkansas River, Colorado, 1845. The Bent's Old Fort National Historic Site is a reconstruction of the original fort near La Junta, Colorado, and is operated by the National Park Service.*

23 | *Fur traders in a mackinaw loaded with furs on the Missouri River, being attacked by Indians.*

24 | *Cree chief All Tattooed meets with the traders in the Indians' council room at Fort Union, on the upper Missouri. Drawing by Rudolph Kurz, 1851.*

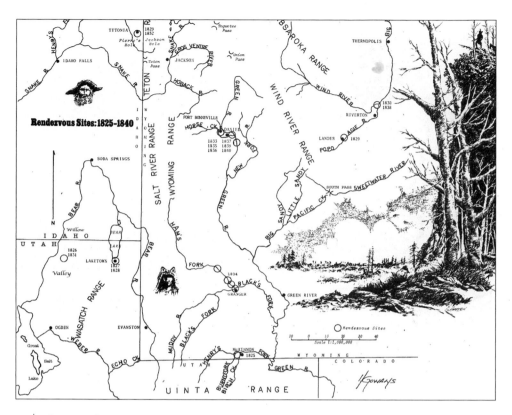

25 | *The sites of the Rocky Mountain rendezvous.*

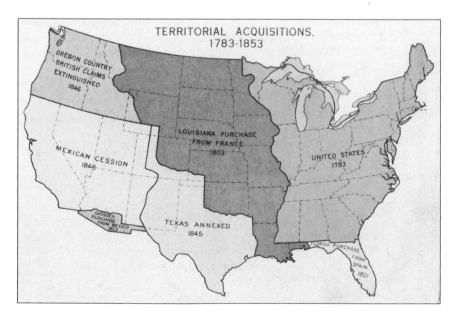

26 | *Map showing the growth of the United States, from the* Atlas of Historical Geography of the United States, *by Charles O. Paullin and John K. Wright, 1932.*

27 | *The oldest known European image of the American buffalo, from Francisco López de Gómara,* La Historia General de las Indias, *1554.*

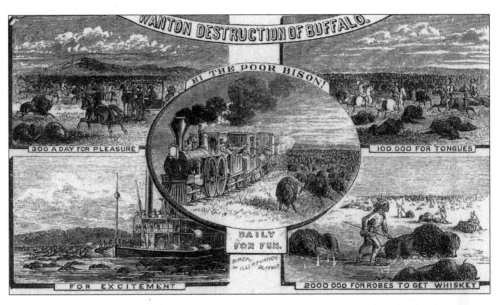

28 | *Image from W. E. Webb,* Buffalo Land, *1872, showing the various ways in which the buffalo were decimated.*

29 | *Fur auction advertisement, late 1800s.*

30 | *Pile of buffalo hides in Dodge City, Kansas; the photograph was taken on April 4, 1874.*

31 | *Fur trader with his wares.*

32 | *Woman in the height of fashion, circa 1906.*

33 | *Sealer with skinned seal carcasses, Pribilof Islands, Alaska, 1892.*

attacks on the *promyshleniki*, and before he was through had murdered nearly three thousand.[24]

The Aleuts used a variety of hunting methods to obtain sea otters for their tormentors. If the tide was out and the otters were up on the rocks, they were clubbed to death. When the otters were in the water, which was nearly all the time, the Aleuts pursued them in one- to three-person skin-covered kayaks called *baidarkas*, which were twelve to twenty one feet long and fewer than two feet wide. In the hands of skilled paddlers this fast and agile watercraft was perfectly suited for the hunt. Sleeping sea otters were approached cautiously and quietly, then dispatched with a bone- or shell-tipped spear. If an otter was awake, the hunters formed a broad circle around the last place the otter had been seen, and waited for it to resurface. They tried to spear it when it did, repeating this procedure until the increasingly winded sea otter was killed. The Aleuts also employed nets, and on occasion set out otter-shaped wooden decoys that were painted black to lure the sea otters into range. And toward the end of the eighteenth century the Russians taught the Aleuts to hunt with guns.[25]

By the time of Cook's ill-fated expedition the sea otter trade had already become a major industry for czarist Russia, where the otter's pelts were referred to as "soft gold." Thousands of Aleuts, driven mercilessly by the *promyshleniki*, killed many hundreds of thousands of sea otters, generating millions of rubles in profits.[26] And at the same time some Russians were already looking to the Alaskan mainland and areas farther to the south to expand their trade.

*A*T THE CLOSE OF THE REVOLUTION, AMERICANS KNEW nothing about the vast sea otter trade with China, but that was all about to change courtesy of John Ledyard, one of the most curious and intriguing characters in early American exploration history. Born in Groton, Connecticut, in 1751, Ledyard had a wandering soul, generating a résumé replete with odd twists and turns. Lasting only a little more than a year at Dartmouth College, he was officially kicked out for failure to pay his bills, but the leaders of the school were not enamored of this "saucy" fellow and his unorthodox ways, and for his part Ledyard disliked the rigid discipline, so the school and the man parted. Rather than travel back to Hartford by road to tell his family the bad news, Ledyard cut down a large pine tree, hollowed it out into a canoe, and paddled it 140 miles down the Connecticut River, becoming the first white man to navigate that span of the waterway. Ledyard floundered about, first failing as a divinity student, then working as a seaman on an American ship transporting mules to the coast of Africa. In 1775 he sailed to London, where he either volunteered for or was impressed into the British army. A short while later he switched to the navy and then, in July 1776, the day after the Declaration of Independence was signed, Ledyard joined Captain Cook's expedition as a corporal on the *Resolution*.[27]

When the expedition returned to London in late 1780, Ledyard was in a quandary. He yearned, like the homesick man he was, to get back to America, but couldn't very well desert the British navy and sail across the ocean without courting certain capture and a quick hanging. He had to wait for the right opportunity to come to him, and it did in the fall of 1781 when he was sent to Long Island onboard a British frigate to fight the Americans. While on shore leave in November the following year, Ledyard bolted for Connecticut, and after convincing the local authorities that, despite his tenure with the British navy, he was a true American, he settled in and wrote his one and only book—*A Journal of Captain Cook's Last Voyage to the Pacific Ocean, and in Quest of a North-West Passage, between Asia and America, Performed in the Years 1776, 1777, 1778, and 1779*—published in 1783.[28]

Ledyard devoted relatively little space in his book to the sea otter trade, noting that "the skins which did not cost the purchaser six pence sterling sold in China for 100 dollars. Neither did we purchase a quarter part of the beaver and other fur skins we might have done, and most certainly should have done had we known of meeting the opportunity of disposing of them to such an astonishing profit."[29] Although the sea otter trade didn't figure prominently in his prose, it quickly became his obsession. His dream was to return to the Pacific Northwest and establish a fur-trading operation selling sea otter pelts to the Chinese. During the expedition Ledyard had met with the Russians on Unalaska Island and learned of their success. If they could carry on a lucrative fur trade, so could he. All he needed was to find backers to supply the ships, men, and materials, and among the first persons he approached was one of the richest men in the country, Philadelphia tycoon and signer of the Declaration of Independence, Robert Morris, who granted Ledyard an audience in June 1783. The two men got along well, and Morris threw himself into the venture, leading Ledyard to write to one of his cousins, "but it is a fact that the Hon'l Robert Morris is disposed to give me a ship to go into the N. Pacific Ocean."[30]

Morris's enthusiasm for Ledyard's plan made sound business sense.

Before the Revolution, Americans received most of their goods from the mother country, paying for them with a range of raw materials. After the war the pipeline to and from Britain was virtually cut off, forcing American merchants to look for new ways to invest their capital and obtain the things their countrymen wanted to buy. Among the items most cherished by Americans were the teas, silks, and porcelains of China that had formerly been provided by the British East India Company, which held the monopoly on the China trade. Now that the Americans were no longer part of the British Empire, they could ignore the company's monopoly and go straight to the source to obtain Chinese goods. The pressing issue facing American merchants, therefore, was precisely what they should trade with China. The Americans knew the Chinese would pay dearly for ginseng, a wild and purportedly medicinal root that grew in the United States. Ginseng alone, however, was a slender thread from which to hang the weight of the entire China trade. American merchants wanted other goods to offer, and sea otter pelts looked to be the perfect addition to their marketing repertoire because they were not only plentiful in the Pacific Northwest but also in great demand in China.[31]

Frustration and then despair slowly replaced Ledyard's initial excitement over the project. The partners Morris had enlisted were a motley crew who did little to keep Ledyard informed as planning progressed, and although they managed to build an impressive ship—the *Empress of China*—their arguments and mistrust of one another fractured relationships and led some of them to withdraw their support. The resulting financial shortfall led to a downsizing of the venture. There would be no stop along the Pacific Northwest to pick up sea otter pelts; instead the ship would sail directly to China with a load of ginseng and other goods to barter. Thus, when the *Empress of China* left the port of New York on February 22, 1784, Ledyard was not on board.

Deeply discouraged but unwilling to give up, Ledyard traveled first to Spain, then to France, ending up in Lorient in September 1784, where he quickly found enthusiastic backers for his fur-trading venture. His new French partners forged ahead but found it impossible to gain a royal commission for their project or permission to sail to China. Then, in August 1785, the king decided to send the explorer Jean-François de Galaup, the comte de La Pérouse, on a voyage to the Pacific. With France focusing so much of its attention and resources on the La Pérouse expedition, Ledyard's partners were simply ignored, and once again his dream was deferred.[32]

Ledyard next went to Paris, where he met American naval hero John Paul

Jones and tried to entice him into his fur-trading scheme. Holding out the prospects of profits of as much as 1,000 percent, Ledyard soon hooked Jones, and together they formed a company and began planning their voyage. Their ship, proposed to be a stout 250 tons, crewed by forty-five French sailors, and with Ledyard as the supercargo, would double Cape Horn, visit the Hawaiian Islands, and then head to the Pacific Northwest to commence trading. Once stocked with furs, the ship would sail to Japan to sell the peltry for gold or other goods, and failing that, continue on to Macao. Then it would be back to France, all in the span of eighteen months. Ledyard evinced no doubts in the basic economics of his business model. "Such precious furs might be bought for a bagatelle," he claimed, "and sold at a market where the venders might fix their own price."[33]

But as might be expected in Ledyard's star-crossed life, his plans began to unravel. One of the investors in the company told Jones that British ships were on their way to the Pacific Northwest, raising the unwelcome specter of competition. Ledyard learned that the *Empress of China* had succeeded, becoming the first American-flagged ship to trade with China, and he and Jones worried that other American ships might soon follow. The only ships Ledyard could find cost three times what he had budgeted. Jones wanted Robert Morris's approval for the voyage, but his assent didn't come. Jones was also somewhat distracted at the time, trying to secure from the French government the prize money he thought he was due as a result of capturing British warships during the American Revolution. The most damaging blow, however, was dealt by the king of Spain, who claimed ownership of pretty much the entire West Coast of America, and had made it clear that the proposed fur-trading expedition would violate Spanish sovereignty. Given that King Louis XVI of France was at the time an ally of Spain, he wasn't about to allow a French ship to threaten that relationship. All these factors combined to kill the project. With this final rejection, Ledyard wrote to a cousin, "Upon the whole I may venture to say that my enterprise with Paul Jones is no more—that I shall inter this hobby at Paris."[34]

W HILE LEDYARD'S PLANS FOUNDERED, OTHERS FORGED ahead, spurred on by the 1784 publication of the official narrative of Cook's expedition to the Pacific. Whereas Ledyard's 1783 account barely touched upon the sea otter trade and its potential profitability, the official narrative gave this topic more extensive attention. Not only did it recount the dynamics of trading activity during the voyage, and the great value of the otter pelts, but it also presented a call to action. Cook observed, "The fur of these animals . . . is certainly softer and finer than that of any others we know of; and therefore the discovery of this part of the continent of North America, where so valuable an article of commerce may be met with, cannot be a matter of indifference." Captain King added, "The advantages that might be derived from a voyage to that part of the American coast, undertaken with commercial views, appear to me of a degree of importance sufficient to call for the attention of the public."[35]

It was King's intention, of course, to capture the attention of the British. He was not disappointed. As early as 1785 the East India Company and the South Sea Company, which held monopolies on British trade in the Pacific and Canton, licensed a few British ships to enter the Northwest trade. Most British merchants, however, preferring to avoid the rigid constraints imposed by government monopolies, sent their ships out of non-British ports under foreign flags, and in that manner more than a half dozen ships were launched by early 1788.[36] But the British were not the only ones who read King's words: So too did the Americans.

*T*HOMAS BULFINCH, AN EMINENT BOSTON PHYSICIAN, hosted a gathering at his mansion on Bowdoin Square in early 1787. Around the roaring fire, the men's conversation soon turned to business, more specifically the prospects for Massachusetts' maritime trade. Relying on Cook's narrative, and to a lesser extent Ledyard's account, Joseph Barrell, a Boston merchant, proposed that they join forces, outfit a couple of ships, and enter the sea otter trade. The logic was particularly compelling because Massachusetts' traders were facing a problem with ginseng. Since the end of the Revolution a growing number of American ships had sailed for China with large amounts of the root to sell. These ships had done well for their owners but in the process had dumped so much ginseng on the Chinese market that the supply outstripped demand. Sending more ginseng was, therefore, a losing proposition. As a result Barrell had little difficulty persuading the small group sitting by Dr. Bulfinch's hearth that sea otter pelts were their best bet if they wanted to continue the China trade. "There is a rich harvest to be reaped," Barrell remarked, "by those who shall first go in."[37]

Duly excited by the prospects for success, the men raised fifty thousand dollars to purchase two ships, the eighty-four-foot and 212-ton *Columbia Rediviva,* and its tender, a forty-foot 90-ton sloop, *Lady Washington,* which were commonly referred to by the sailors themselves as the *Columbia* and the *Washington.* John Kendrick was picked to command the expedition and served as captain of the *Columbia,* while Robert Gray was put in charge of the *Washington.* Barrell ordered three hundred medals struck, in pewter, copper, and silver, with the images of the two ships on one side and the names of the investors on the other. These, the first die-struck medals to be minted in the United States, were, according to the voyage's bill of lading, "to be distributed amongst the Natives on the North West Coast of America, and to commemorate the first American Adventure on the Pacific Ocean."[38]

The two ships left Boston's inner harbor on September 30, 1787, with many merchants and friends and family still onboard. That evening, while they were anchored in the outer harbor at Nantasket Roads, a high-spirited farewell party was held on the *Columbia.* Songs echoed from the main deck, drinks flowed, and before the sailors turned in, their visitors wished them a safe and prosperous voyage.[39] The next morning the ships weighed anchor and began their journey.

The *Columbia* and the *Washington* kept company all the way to the tip of South America, reaching Cape Horn early the next year. Here was a mighty and fearsome obstacle: Many sailors from other countries had met their end in the tempestuous waters off the Cape, and now it was the Americans' turn to run the gauntlet, during late winter, no less. For more than a month the men and their ships battled frigid gales that generated seas of a "mountainous height," which pounded the ships, ripped sails, and at times threatened the bone-weary crews and their vessels with "instant destruction."[40] But they survived, and in mid-April 1788 the *Columbia* and the *Washington* became the first American ships to round the Cape. During the passage, however, the two ships had lost sight of each other, forcing them to continue separately on their voyages to the Northwest.

The *Washington* made better speed, and on August 14 it anchored in Tillamook Bay on the Oregon coast. Salish Indians in dugout canoes visited the ship and commenced trading sea otter skins for knives and axes. A few days later Davis Coolidge and Robert Haswell, the first and second mates, respectively, took a small party ashore. While some men stayed with the boat and others gathered food and water, Coolidge and Haswell visited the local village and watched as the Indians showed off their spear- and arrow-handling skills. They then launched into a war dance, whose gyrations and screaming, Haswell said, "chilled the blood" in his veins.[41]

Marcus Lopez, Captain Gray's Cape Verdean cabin boy, was nearby hauling supplies to the boat, when an Indian grabbed Lopez's cutlass, which he had "carelessly" left in the sand. One of the other crewmen saw what had happened and let out a yell, which brought Coolidge and Haswell running to the spot, only to learn that Lopez had taken off after the Indian. Coolidge, Haswell, and the other man onshore rushed into the woods, and when they rounded a dense clump of trees came upon a harrowing sight. Lopez was in the middle of a throng of Indians, holding the thief by the collar and screaming for help. When the Indians saw the men, they instantly rushed Lopez and "drenched their knives and spears with savage fury in the body of the unfortunate youth," who staggered forward before being felled by a "flight of arrows" in the back.

The three men ran as fast as they could to the boat while arrows and spears assaulted them from every side. They fired on the Indians, hitting a few, yet still they came. As Coolidge and Haswell waded into the water to get to the boat, an arrow struck the third man, who fell disabled, bleeding profusely, into the surf. The two officers, who were themselves slightly injured, managed to drag the third man to the boat, where the others pulled them onboard and began rowing for the sloop. But it wasn't over yet. The Indians jumped into canoes and pursued the men, who continued firing until they reached the *Washington*, whereupon blasts from their sloop's small cannons hastened the Indians' retreat. That night the Indians lit bonfires on the shore, howling wildly as they paraded back and forth in front of the flames. For two days, while Gray waited for favorable conditions to make his departure, the Indians taunted the Americans from the beach and on one occasion approached the sloop in canoes only to be turned back with cannon fire. Then, when the tide was right, the *Washington* sailed out of what the men had dubbed Murderers' Harbor, and by the middle of September the sloop entered Nootka Sound, the expedition's designated rendezvous, to wait for the *Columbia*.

*M*ISERABLE WEATHER PLAGUED THE *COLUMBIA*'S JOURNEY after rounding Cape Horn, greatly damaging the ship and forcing Kendrick to take refuge at Juan Fernandez Island off the Chilean coast for repairs. When the *Columbia* finally limped into Nootka Sound in late September, it had already lost two men to scurvy, and the rest of the crew, suffering from the advanced stages of that disease, were barely able to stand. Kendrick realized that it was too late to start trading, so after his men had regained their strength, he ordered them and the crew of the *Washington* to build houses on the shore of Vancouver Island and settle in for the winter. Between hunting and fishing, the men spent most of their time fashioning iron bars into chisels to trade once warmer weather returned. Haswell took advantage of frequent visits from the Indians to record extensive observations of their physical characteristics and way of life, in addition to compiling a "vocabulary of Nootka Sound," which ran to more than three hundred words. It included many fascinating and melodious entries such as *upsee oop* for "hair," *mooxey* for "rocks," *oona* for "how many," and *shucksheetle* for "to strike."[42]

During the spring and summer of 1789 Kendrick and the *Columbia* stayed in Nootka Sound, while Gray on the *Washington* sailed up and down the coast from the Queen Charlotte Islands to Cape Flattery, and fifty miles up the Strait of Juan de Fuca, trading with the Nootka, Haida, and Salish, and gaining in one transaction two hundred sea otter pelts for one chisel each. Overall, however, the trading was somewhat sluggish. The Americans found out to their chagrin that Indian tastes in trading goods had changed since Cook and Ledyard had visited, and that many of the trading goods they had stocked in Boston, such as Jew's harps, snuff bottles, beads, and combs, were not in as much demand as they had expected.[43]

In July, with supplies running low, Kendrick decided it was time to conclude the trading expedition, divide the pelts, and head to China to sell their cargoes, then return to Boston. Before departing Kendrick switched commands, taking over the *Washington* while putting Gray in charge of the *Columbia*. Kendrick, however, never did make it back to Boston. He grew quite fond of his new ship and his own self-importance, and effectively commandeered the *Washington* for his own use, at one point even selling it to himself in a sham transaction. The rogue freelancer traveled between the Pacific Northwest and China, trading for furs and selling them in Macao. On one voyage he even ventured to Japan, and although he was unable to interest the Japanese in his hold full of sea otter skins, he did become the first known American to visit that "Forbidden Country." During the return leg of his second trip to China, Kendrick stopped in Hawaii, becoming involved in a dispute involving the natives. He threw in his lot with Capt. William Brown of the *Jackal*, ending up on the winning side. Kendrick and Brown, flush with victory, decided to toast each other with a cannon salute, using blanks. Unfortunately for Kendrick one of the *Jackal*'s guns was still loaded, and when the celebratory explosion went off, the cannonball ripped through the side of the *Washington*, wounding several crewmen and splattering Kendrick's head about the cabin. Needless to say the original owners of the *Washington*, who were not happy with Kendrick's behavior, never got any money from their erstwhile expedition leader.[44]

*G*RAY TOOK A DECIDEDLY DIFFERENT PATH. HE STOPPED IN Hawaii before Kendrick, making the *Columbia* the first American vessel to visit the islands. He stayed there for three weeks gathering supplies, including 150 hogs, and taking onboard a native prince named Attoo who wanted to visit America. Gray then sold his pelts in Canton for $21,404.71, but after factoring in port charges, bribes, and the cost of ship repairs, the profits amounted to only about half as much, and they went toward the purchase of nearly twenty-two thousand pounds of tea.[45] Heading west from Canton, Gray rounded the Cape of Good Hope and sailed into Boston on August 9, 1790, giving the *Columbia* the honor of being the first American ship to circumnavigate the globe, logging nearly forty-two thousand miles since leaving Boston three years earlier.

When the *Columbia* came alongside Castle Island, Gray offered a thirteen-gun salute, which was repeated onshore, and then he fired his cannons once again upon mooring in the harbor, causing the "great concourse of citizens assembled on various wharfs . . . [to respond] with three huzzahs and a hearty welcome."[46] The crowd's excitement grew when they learned that a native of "Owyhee" was onboard, and soon they saw Attoo, bedecked in "a helmet of feathers that glittered in the sunlight, and an exquisite cloak of the same yellow and scarlet plumage."[47] Attoo walked behind Gray as the two men paraded to the state house for a meeting with Governor John Hancock, which was followed by a lavish dinner in honor of Gray, his officers, and the *Columbia*'s owners, during which Gray regaled those in attendance with stories from his trip. The *Massachusetts Spy* reported, in orotund phrases that were repeated in many other newspapers, that the country was "indebted" to the *Columbia*'s backers "for this experiment in a branch of commerce before unessayed by Americans," and that the country was "also under obligation to the . . . navigators who have conducted this voyage—whose urbanity and civility have secured the friendship of the aboriginals of the country they visited; and whose honor and intrepidity have commanded the protection and respect of the European *Lords of the Soil*, to the American flag."[48]

Despite the fanfare in Boston, the *Columbia's* investors had plenty to be glum about. Not only had more than half of the tea been damaged in transit, greatly reducing the voyage's relatively meager profits, but also Kendrick and the *Washington* had not returned, and it was beginning to appear that neither ever would. Two of the original investors, greatly discouraged, lost faith and sold their shares in the venture to Gray and a couple of other men. The remaining investors, however, still saw great promise in the *Columbia's* return. It had proved the basic feasibility of the business model Barrell had presented at Bulfinch's fireside back in 1787, and the men believed that, with a little better planning and execution, future voyages would profit handsomely. So confident were they that the *Columbia* was overhauled, refitted, and sent on another voyage to the Northwest less than two months after its return, with Gray at the helm. This trip, which lasted from September 1790 to July 1793, was much more profitable than the first. But it wasn't profits for which the *Columbia's* second voyage would be remembered.

*I*N THE WANING DAYS OF APRIL 1792 THE *COLUMBIA* WAS A little less than fifty miles south of Cape Flattery, along the coast of present-day Washington, when Gray spotted two sails in the distance. They were his majesty's ships the *Discovery* and the *Chatham*, captained by George Vancouver and William Broughton, respectively. Vancouver had been sent to deal with problems the British were having with the Spaniards, to chart the coastline, and to search for the Northwest Passage. Vancouver sent emissaries to meet Gray and gather intelligence about the region, and Gray told them that he had recently "been off the mouth of a river in the latitude of 46° 10', where the outset or reflux was so great as to prevent his entering for nine days."[49] Could this be the almost mythical "Great River of the West" that supposedly led to the Northwest Passage?[50] Vancouver didn't think so. Just a day before encountering the *Columbia*, Vancouver had been in that vicinity, and noticed that "the sea had . . . changed from its natural to river-colored water," but he attributed that to the effects "of some streams falling into the bay," and not the presence of a mighty river. Vancouver thus concluded that "this opening [was not] worthy of more attention."[51] Gray, however, was of a different mind. So, after sailing northwest in the company of the British, he turned the

Columbia around and headed back down the coast. Perhaps, with a bit more persistence, the Great River could be found.

But first a detour. On May 7, off the port bow Gray saw an inlet and went to explore. After crashing through the breakers rolling over the bar at the inlet's mouth, the men of the *Columbia* found themselves in an "excellent harbor," which they called Bulfinch Harbor (now Grays Harbor). Soon canoes full of Indians surrounded the ship, ready to trade. "They appeared to be a savage set," remarked John Boit, the *Columbia's* fifth mate, and were "well armed, every man having his Quiver and Bow slung over his shoulder. . . . [They] viewed us and the Ship with the greatest astonishment." Trading proceeded the next day, but that night, under a full moon, some of the men on the *Columbia* saw canoes approaching and tried to scare them off with cannon shots over their heads. This only set the Indians to whooping and hollering, and when a large canoe with twenty warriors got to within a "1/2 pistol shot of the quarter," the men fired the nine pounder and ten muskets right at them, which "dashed . . . [the canoe] all to pieces, and no doubt killed every soul in her," causing the rest of the canoes to beat a hasty retreat. "I am sorry we was obliged to kill the poor devils," Boit wrote in his log, "but it could not with safety be avoided."[52]

On May 10 Gray continued sailing south, and early the next morning, according to the *Columbia's* official log, he "saw the entrance to our desired port bearing east-south-east, distance six leagues." This time the *Columbia* made a safe passage over the bar and found itself in the middle of "a large river of fresh water," ultimately ascending it to a point some thirty miles from the mouth. It was the river Gray had told Vancouver's emissaries about, which Gray named Columbia's River, in honor of his ship, but which would soon be shortened to the Columbia River.

GOING ASHORE, GRAY CLAIMED THE RIVER AND THE SUR-rounding land for the United States. For eight days the men explored the river and the adjoining coast, and carried on a vibrant trade with the Indians, who greatly impressed Boit. "The Men, at Columbia's River, are strait limbed, fine looking fellows," Boit observed, "and the Women are very pretty. They are all in a state of Nature, except the females, who wear a leaf Apron—perhaps 'twas a fig leaf. But some of our gentlemen, that examined them pretty close, and near, both within and without reported, that it was not a leaf, but a nice wove mat in resemblance!!" Boit also offered his thoughts on the role the Columbia might play in the development of America's fur trade. "This River . . . would be a fine place for to set up a Factory [trading post]. The Indians are very numerous, and appeared very civil . . . we collected 150 Otter, 300 Beaver, and twice the number of other land furs."[53]

By July the *Columbia* was back in Nootka Sound, where Gray and his men were entertained in opulent fashion by Spanish commandant Don Francisco de la Bodega y Quadra, who provided a five-course dinner for fifty-four people, with plates, utensils, and everything else were made of "solid silver." After dinner Gray told his host about his discovery of the Columbia, and even sketched him a map of the area. This transfer of information set off a cascade of events whose reverberations would be felt well into the next century. Soon after Gray left Nootka, Vancouver and Broughton arrived. Bodega told Vancouver about Gray's discovery, and gave him a copy of Gray's map, which caused Vancouver to second-guess his earlier dismissal of the "river-colored water" as not meriting further exploration. Had Gray really discovered the Great River of the West? Vancouver had to see for himself, so off he sailed to the southeast on the *Discovery*, with Broughton on the *Chatham* following close behind.[54]

Upon reaching the mouth of the Columbia, Vancouver decided that there was no safe passage for the *Discovery* across the bar so he left Broughton to investigate while he sailed the *Discovery* to California. Using a complex set of calculations and rationalizations, Broughton concluded mistakenly that Gray had actually never entered the river proper and that therefore his claims of discovery were null and void. To Broughton this provided a brilliant opportunity to stake his own claim, and with that in mind, he ventured nearly one hundred miles upstream, giving proper British names to a number of landmarks along the way, including Mt. Hood, Vancouver Point, Puget's Island, Whidbey's River, and Cape George. To make it official Broughton "took possession of the river, and the country in its vicinity, in His Britannic Majesty's name," and then sailed off to rendezvous with the *Discovery* father down the coast. When Vancouver was briefed on Broughton's actions, he fully concurred, adding that Broughton had "every reason to believe that the subjects of no other civilized nation or state had ever entered this river before. In this opinion he was confirmed by Mr. Gray's sketch, in which it does not appear that Mr. Gray either saw or ever was within five leagues of its entrance." With that bold assertion the stage was set for decades of debates between the United States and Britain over which country had the rights to the region and where the northwestern border of America should be drawn.[55]

*O*N HIS SECOND VOYAGE TO THE PACIFIC NORTHWEST COAST, Gray had company. The *Columbia's* triumphant return to Boston in 1790 inaugurated what the author David Lavender called "the famous three-cornered trade of the Yankees: Massachusetts gimcracks to the Northwest; Northwestern furs to Canton; and Chinese goods on around the world to Boston."[56] The *Columbia's* investors were not the only ones who saw promise in the ship's first voyage. Other American merchants were watching as well, and they rushed to get a share of the business. In 1791 the *Columbia* was one of seven American ships trading in the Pacific Northwest, and for the rest of the decade that number fluctuated between three and six. But during these early years the Americans weren't alone. British, Portuguese, French, Spanish, and Russian ships were also in the area, in search of furs.[57]

By the turn of the century, however, the Pacific Northwest fur trade had become, in the words of the historian Mary Malloy, "an American specialty, almost an American monopoly."[58] Its remarkable record seemed to reflect the economic dynamo that the new nation was becoming. In 1801, of the twenty-three ships on the coast, twenty were American, two were British, and one Russian. America sustained this dominant position until the early 1830s, and the vast majority of American ships hailed from Boston. So great was the Boston influence that the Northwest Coast Indians thought for many years that Boston *was* America, and referred to all citizens of the United States as "Boston Men," in contrast to those coming from Britain, who were called "Kintshautsh (King George) men."[59]

A Virginian by birth, President James Monroe noted that "the habits and ordinary pursuits of the New Englanders qualified them in a peculiar manner for carrying on this trade."[60] New Englanders, and in particular Bostonians, had a well-earned reputation as excellent sailors and navigators, sharp traders, and frugal businessmen. They also were less constrained than some of their competitors, particularly the British, by cumbersome regulations and oversight of their activities. In fact once the "Boston Men" left port they were essentially on their own, and were ordered by the owners to use their judgment and bargaining skills to cut the best deals not only with the Indians but also the merchants in Canton. This freedom to improvise and respond flexibly to whatever situation arose gave them a competitive advantage over their would-be rivals, often producing spectacular results. In some years the Americans transported nearly eighteen thousand sea otter pelts to Canton, and when the sales of those were added to those of the other furs they had on board, profits were astronomical, regularly returning as much as 300 to 500 percent on the original investment in the voyage, and in some instances reaching as high as 2,200 percent.[61] The key to generating such handsome returns was embedded in the nature of the trade. As one early-twentieth-century historian saw it, "The Americans had a perfect golden round of profits: first, the profit on the original cargo of trading goods when exchanged for furs; second, the profit when the furs were transmuted into Chinese goods; and, third, the profit on those goods when they reached America."[62] Despite these profits, however, success was by no means always assured, there being many instances in which impetuous and inexperienced men entered the Pacific Northwest trade with high hopes, only to have them dashed in the end.

*T*HE DYNAMICS OF THE PACIFIC NORTHWEST SEA OTTER TRADE mirrored those of the fur trade on the East Coast. The Indians were savvy negotiators who quickly learned the value of their furs and how best to get the best deal, often by withholding furs until demands were met or playing one trader off against another. In many instances Indian women did the trading, because, as some of the men said, "women could talk with the white men better than they could, and were willing to talk more."[63] European and American goods were readily incorporated into Indian society and used to enhance "material prosperity" and one's standing within the community, although as the geographer James R. Gibson argues, these goods "generally . . . supplemented rather than supplanted Indian products, and served to further, not initiate changes."[64] Alcohol and epidemics tore tribes apart and sent many to an early grave, as did the increased availability and use of guns. And like the eastern trade, the northwestern trade was a source of deadly conflict between whites and Indians. One of the most remarkable examples of such conflict is provided by the case of John R. Jewitt.[65]

Jewitt, nineteen, was living in the port town of Hull, England, in the summer of 1802, when the American ship *Boston* arrived to stock up on goods for a fur-trading expedition to the Pacific Northwest. The *Boston's* captain, John Salter, hired Jewitt's father, a blacksmith, to do some work on the ship, and the two quickly became friends. One day, when young Jewitt visited the *Boston*, Captain Salter invited him to join the crew as the ship's armorer. Jewitt quickly assented, but his father had severe reservations about sending his son halfway around the world, and took some convincing before agreeing to let him go. In early September the *Boston* sailed from Hull with twenty-seven men onboard, including Jewitt, who was extremely excited to start his grand adventure.

Jewitt, who had never before been out of sight of land, soon got over his sea-sickness and focused on working at the ship's forge, repairing muskets and making daggers, knives, and small hatchets. The *Boston* arrived at Nootka Sound on March 12, 1803. The next day Maquinna, the chief of a Yuquot village in nearby Friendly Cove, visited the ship and offered a warm welcome. Jewitt, who had never seen an Indian before, said he was "particularly struck" by Maquinna's appearance, noting that he "was a man of a dignified aspect, about six feet in height and extremely straight and well proportioned. . . . His complexion was of a dark copper hue, though his face, legs, and arms were . . . so covered with red paint, that their natural color could scarcely be perceived. . . . His long black hair, which shone with oil, was fastened in a bunch on the top of his head and strewed or powdered all over with white down. . . . He was dressed in a large mantle or cloak of the black sea otter skin, which reached to his knees."

Salter hadn't expected to obtain furs in this place, but rather merely wanted to replenish the ship's supplies before proceeding farther up the coast; and indeed no fur trading took place. Nevertheless Salter was gracious to the Indians who visited the following week, and after first checking them for hidden arms as a safety precaution, would allow them freely on the ship. One evening Salter had the Indians to dinner, and at its conclusion presented Maquinna a double-barreled fowling gun. The following day Maquinna returned and told Salter that one of the gun's locks had broken and that it was *peshak,* or "bad." "Salter was very much offended at this observation, and considering it as a mark of contempt for his present, he called . . . [Maquinna] a liar, adding other opprobrious terms." Salter grabbed the gun from Maquinna and threw it into the cabin, and then told Jewitt, "John, this fellow has broken this beautiful fowling piece, see if you can mend it." Maquinna took this verbal abuse without uttering a sound, but as Jewitt recalled, it was clear from his "countenance" that the chief was enraged. During the harangue Maquinna repeatedly placed his hand on his throat, then rubbed it on his chest. As Jewitt would later learn, Maquinna did this "to keep down his heart which was rising into his throat and choking him."

Maquinna and other chiefs, along with many men, visited the ship a day later, and Salter let them onboard. Maquinna seemed quite happy as he paraded around wearing a wooden mask over his head and using a whistle to play a tune, which his men seemed to follow along with as they "[sang] and capered about the deck." Salter did not know he was being lured into a trap. Maquinna wanted revenge for being treated so rudely, but attacking the entire ship's complement made him nervous, so his goal was to divide and conquer, which is exactly what he did. Maquinna asked Salter when he intended to leave, and when Salter said the next day, the chief responded, "'You love salmon—much in Friendly Cove, why not go then and catch some?'" Salter thought this was a capital idea, and after dining with Maquinna and the other chiefs onboard, he sent one of the ship's boats and nine crewmen to seine for fish. Now the number of Indians onboard was almost as great as the number of white men. Maquinna was about ready to pounce.

Jewitt was belowdecks when he heard a great commotion up top. He ran up the stairs, but as soon as he thrust his head above the deck, an Indian grabbed him by the hair and yanked him into the air. Jewitt's hair, however, was short and the Indian lost his grip. Seeing his prize slipping away, the Indian swung his ax, hitting Jewitt in the head and sending him hurtling backward onto the deck below, where he lay unconscious, bleeding from a gash in his skull. Nightmarish whooping and hollering awakened Jewitt a short while later. The only reason he remained alive was that Maquinna wanted him that way. The Indian who attacked Jewitt wanted to finish the job but Maquinna ordered him to stop because the chief thought that Jewitt's skills as the ship's armorer could be useful to the tribe. Soon after Jewitt came to, Maquinna summoned him to the main deck, where six naked, blood-drenched warriors surrounded him, with daggers raised ready to strike. Maquinna stood before Jewitt and said, "'John—I speak—you no say no—You say no—daggers come!'" Maquinna asked Jewitt if he would be willing to become his slave, not only to fight alongside the chief in future battles, but also to repair his muskets and make knives and other arms for him. Jewitt assented and then was taken to the quarterdeck, where he beheld what he called "the most horrid sight . . . ever my eyes witnessed—the heads of our unfortunate Captain and his crew . . . all arranged in a line." Jewitt noticed that one of the crew was missing from this macabre display, John Thompson, the *Boston*'s sailmaker, whom the Indians found the next day. They wanted to kill him, too, but Jewitt was able to save his life by quick thinking, claiming that the older man was actually his father.

Just four days after the massacre two ships appeared in Friendly Cove, but before they got too close to shore, the Indians fired on them with their newly acquired muskets and blunderbusses, and after firing back a few times, the ships sailed away. Thus began more than two years of captivity, during which Jewitt was treated quite well by his captors, yet he never stopped hoping that another ship would arrive and set him free. To hasten that day Jewitt wrote sixteen letters on paper salvaged from the ship, telling of his plight and pleading to be rescued. He gave these letters to visiting Indians, asking that they deliver them to any white men they saw. But no ships appeared. Word of the massacre had spread, and ships scrupulously avoided the area.

In the summer of 1805 Jewitt's savior arrived. One of his letters had made it into the hands of Sam Hill, the captain of the brig *Lydia*, a fur-trading ship out of Boston. On July 19 Hill sailed into Friendly Cove, signaling with three cannon shots that he wanted to trade with the Indians. Maquinna was greatly excited. After two years with no fur trading, the white men had finally returned. But how should he handle this golden opportunity? Wouldn't the men on the ship be very angry over the fate of the *Boston's* crew and the imprisonment of Jewitt and Thompson? Finally Maquinna devised a plan. He would visit the ship, but only if Jewitt would write him an introductory letter, telling the ship's captain that Maquinna had treated Jewitt and Thompson "kindly," a move the chief hoped would assure a favorable reception. Jewitt readily agreed, but believing that this would be his "only chance of regaining [his] . . . freedom," he wrote a letter that was quite different from the one Maquinna had in mind.

To Captain _____ ,
            of the Brig _____
                Nootka, July 19, 1805.

SIR,
    THE bearer of this letter is the Indian king by the name of Maquinna. He was the instigator of the capture the ship Boston, *of Boston in North America, John Salter captain, and of the murder of twenty-five men of her crew, the two only survivors being now on shore—Wherefore I hope you will take care to confine him according to his merits, putting in your dead lights, and keeping so good a watch over him, that he cannot escape from you. By so doing we shall be able to obtain our release in the course of a few hours.*

    JOHN R. JEWITT,
        Armourer of the Boston, *for himself and*
    JOHN THOMPSON,
        Sail-maker of said ship.

Maquinna grilled Jewitt on the letter's contents line by line, as Jewitt, feeling as if this "destiny was suspended on the slightest thread," struggled to maintain his composure, finally convincing the suspicious chief that the message was as he wished. Telling his followers not to worry because "John no lie," Maquinna climbed into one of his war canoes, and was paddled out to the *Lydia*, where Jewitt's plan worked flawlessly. Upon reading the letter Hill had Maquinna placed in irons, and told him he would remain a prisoner until the two men on shore were released. When the Indians realized what had happened, they worked themselves into a frenzy, running back and forth along the shore like "so many lunatics, scratching their faces, and tearing the hair in handfuls from their heads." Some rushed Jewitt threatening to cut him into "pieces no bigger than their thumb nails." Jewitt remained calm, telling them, "kill me . . . if it is your wish, throwing open the bear skin which I wore, here is my breast, I am only one among so many, and can make no resistance, but unless you wish to see your king hanging by his neck to that pole, pointing to the yard arm of the brig, and the sailors firing at him with bullets, you will not do it." And they didn't.

After much debating Jewitt told the Indians that the best plan would be for them to trade him and Thompson for Maquinna's release, to which they agreed. When the two white men, however, finally got onboard the *Lydia*, and Hill learned the full extent of their story, he wanted to execute Maquinna, but Jewitt rose to defend the old chief. He argued "that Maquinna's conduct in taking our ship, arose from an insult that he thought he had received from captain Salter, and from the unjustifiable conduct of some masters of vessels, who had [visited the coast in prior years, and] robbed him, and without provocation, killed a number of his people." Finally Jewitt said that if Hill killed Maquinna, his warriors would exact revenge on the next American ship to enter this cove, and more men would be killed. Convinced, Hill set Maquinna free, and Jewitt began his long journey home.

*T*HE EVENTS SURROUNDING THE *BOSTON* AND, IN PARTICULAR, the Indians' attack on the crew must be viewed more broadly to be fully understood. As the author Hilary Stewart notes, "Certainly [the attack] . . . was triggered by an insult to the high-ranking Maquinna, . . . but behind the deed also lay a buildup of injustices and mistreatment of the native people by intolerant and greedy white traders."[66] In pleading with Hill to spare Maquinna's life, Jewitt alluded to such mistreatment, a point which he made more forcefully on another occasion. "I have no doubt," wrote Jewitt, "that many of the melancholy disasters [along the Pacific Northwest coast] have principally arisen from the imprudent conduct of some of the captains and crews of the ships employed in this trade, in exasperating [the natives] by insulting, . . . plundering, and even killing them on slight grounds. This, as nothing is more sacred with a savage than their principle of revenge, . . . induces them to wreak their vengeance upon the first vessel or boat's crew that offers, making the innocent too frequently suffer for the wrongs of the guilty."[67]

In fact the history of the Pacific Northwest coast fur trade is littered with examples of white men, and certainly not just Americans, behaving atrociously and brutalizing the local Indians. Sturgis, whose brother was killed by Indians on the coast, looked back on his many years in the northwestern trade, and concluded that the Indians were often the "victims of injustice, cruelty, and oppression, and of a policy that seems to recognize *power* as the sole standard of *right*."[68] Sturgis once told a genteel audience in Boston: "Should I recount all the lawless & brutal acts of white men upon the coast you would think that those who visited it had lost the usual attributes of humanity, and such indeed seemed to be the fact." The wise old ship's captain placed the blame for this mainly on the degraded character of the men on these voyages, who "considered" the Indians "little better than brutes," and "finding themselves beyond the pale of civilization and accountable to no one, pursued their object without scruple as to means, and indulged in every brutal propensity without the slightest restraint."[69] Gibson posits another potential reason why traders on the coast so frequently acted with such cruelty. "Perhaps because they were 'transient traders,'" who usually made but one voyage to the coast, "they were wont to treat the Natives more callously and brutally than if, like the land fur traders, they had to live among them permanently."[70] The coastal traders also often had the option of making a quick escape by sea, which no doubt encouraged the tendency to strike, plunder, and flee.

Of course not all northwestern fur traders treated the Indians so horrifically. Many trading sessions were civil, and both sides involved perceived the trades to be fair or at least acceptable. But over time problems multiplied. And for every case like Jewitt's, in which the Indians were the instigators of violence, there were more in which it was the other way around. Similarly, although there were many instances in which the Indians stole from the traders and tried to cheat them in their dealings, it was certainly more common for the traders to try to cheat the Indians and take their furs by force.[71] As Sturgis commented, the Indians were "more 'sinned against' than 'sinning.' "[72]

AMERICAN PROFITS IN THE FUR TRADE WITH CHINA didn't rely solely on the sale of sea otter pelts from the Pacific Northwest. There were other sources of income. One of the most unusual arose from a unique partnership between the Americans and the Russians. In early October 1803 Joseph O'Cain, the captain of the *O'Cain* out of Boston, arrived at Kodiak Island off the Alaskan coast with a proposition for Alexander A. Baranov, the chief manager of the Russian American Company, an entity created by the Russian emperor Paul I to control his country's economic activities in America, including the fur trade. O'Cain told Baranov that the California coast was teeming with sea otters, and all that was needed to get their valuable pelts was hunters who could kill them. If Baranov would provide him with a brigade of Aleuts and a small fleet of *baidarkas*, O'Cain promised to get those pelts and share them with the Russians.

Baranov was intrigued. The Russian sea otter trade had been a bit anemic lately, making O'Cain's proposal especially attractive, and Baranov had no compunction about forcibly sending Aleuts, whom he considered no better than chattel, to these distant lands. Also, the Russians were quite interested in getting a foothold in California, and through this venture Baranov might glean valuable information that could contribute to that end. The deal struck, O'Cain left Kodiak at the end of October with forty Aleuts, twenty *baidarkas*, and one Russian overseer on board, proceeding to San Quentin Bay in Baja California. Living up to their reputation, the Aleuts had soon killed eleven hundred sea otters. O'Cain bought another seven hundred otter pelts from Spanish priests in the area, and in June 1804 returned to Kodiak to give Baranov his share, then sailed for Canton to dispose of the rest.[73]

This general arrangement, in which Baranov supplied Aleuts and *baidarkas*, and various Americans provided ships and transportation, lasted nearly ten years, and yielded the Russians more than eight thousand pelts, and the Americans an equal or perhaps even greater amount.[74] But that wasn't the end of the story. The Russians had learned enough about the California coast to know that they wanted a permanent settlement in the region, which would enable them to farm the fertile valleys and send much needed food to their agriculturally barren outposts in Alaska. Not only that, but by transplanting Aleuts to California the Russians could pick up where the Americans left off in the hunt for sea otters.

With these goals in mind the Russians established a trading post at Bodega Bay in 1812, about fifty miles northwest of San Francisco, and a fort about twenty miles farther up the coast, which they named Fort Ross, a diminutive of *Rossiya* (for "Russia"). Twenty-five Russians and eighty Aleuts with their *baidarkas* were imported to man the operations. While the farming was a bust, with the Russians barely able to feed themselves, the hunt fared better. Some weeks as many as eight hundred otters were killed, and during one incredibly successful season Aleuts working the waters around the Farallon Islands and along the coast, netted nearly eighty thousand pelts. But no bounty of this magnitude could last. By the early 1820s local sea otter populations were virtually wiped out.[75] Despite their declining fortunes the Russians remained at Fort Ross until December 1841, when, harried by both the Spaniards and the Americans, they sold it to a German-born immigrant of Swiss descent, John Augustus Sutter, who would gain international fame in 1848 when gold was discovered at the site of his sawmill in Coloma, California, setting off America's first gold rush.[76]

*I*N ADDITION TO SEA OTTER SKINS, AMERICANS ALSO SOLD THE pelts of fur seals to the Chinese. Even before the *Columbia* and the *Washington* left port, the *United States,* out of Nantucket, arrived in New York in 1786 with thirteen thousand fur seal skins, which were then shipped to Canton, signaling the beginning of America's sealing industry. Over the next thirty-five years, the fur seal trade expanded tremendously, as an increasing number of ships rushed to Canton where they could sell the pelts for an average of about one dollar to Chinese merchants who transformed them into various garments.[77]

Sealers traveled the world over in search of fur seals, which was actually a generic name applied to a number of species of seal to distinguish them from the so-called hair seals, including sea lions, whose pelts were not as plush and therefore less desirable. Sealers didn't rely on natives to kill and prepare the animals; rather they did it themselves, visiting the islands and coasts where the animals congregated, then clubbing and stabbing them to death before stripping them of their skin. The scope of carnage was almost beyond belief.

Single voyages could net more than 100,000 pelts, and all told many millions of fur seals were slaughtered and brought to market.[78]

BY THE EARLY 1820S THE AMERICAN SEA OTTER TRADE WAS IN its death throes. Instead of sending nearly eighteen thousand pelts to Canton annually, the Americans were shipping barely a fifth of that amount. A decade later that had dwindled to just three hundred, leading a prominent American sea otter merchant to inform one of his captains in 1832 that "I shall not make any outfit this season, the trade appears fairly run out."[79] Although some preferred to blame competition from Russian and English traders for their predicament, the root cause was clear—the sea otter had been hunted nearly to extinction, not only in the Pacific Northwest, but all along the coast, from California to Alaska. Not prolific breeders to begin with, sea otters didn't have chance against human avarice.

The American fur seal industry followed a similar trajectory. Rookery after rookery was destroyed as American sealers, joined by those of other nations, raced around the world to find, club, stab, and skin as many seals as they could. The scene that whaling captain Benjamin Morrell found when he visited the Auckland Islands was an all-too-familiar one. "Although . . . [these islands] once abounded with numerous herds of [seals], . . . the American and English seamen engaged in this business have made such clean work of it as scarcely to leave a breed; at all events, there was not one fur-seal to be found on the 4th of January, 1830."[80]

In 1843 the British consul in Canton provided a requiem of sorts for America's once-thriving sea otter and fur seal trade with Asia. "Twenty years ago the fur trade (which was almost entirely in the hands of the Americans) carried on with China amounted to upwards of 1,000,000 dollars annually. But, owing to the indiscriminate slaughter of the animals of the chase, it has dwindled away so much as to be no longer worth pursuing, and, indeed, during these last two or three years no skins or furs whatever have been imported into China."[81] This era was over, and American merchants who had been invested in the maritime fur trade found other outlets for their capital, including whaling and transporting cattle hides for the leather trade.

---

*W*HILE THE "BOSTON MEN" WERE SAILING TO THE PACIFIC Northwest for sea otters, and the sons of Stonington, New London, New York City, and elsewhere were sailing far and wide pursuing seals, the American fur trade branched out in another direction. With Meriwether Lewis and William Clark leading the way, American fur traders began their long march into the heart of the continent, and ultimately clear across it to the Pacific.

— 10 —

Up the Missouri

Meriwether Lewis and William Clark holding a council with the Indians.

WHEN PRESIDENT THOMAS JEFFERSON ANNOUNCED ON JULY 4, 1803, that the United States had purchased the Louisiana Territory from France, doubling the size of the country, the American march to the Pacific was given an enormous boost. Soon thereafter Lewis and Clark led the Corps of Discovery on their voyage of exploration from St. Louis up the Missouri River, over the Rocky Mountains, down to the mouth of the Columbia River on the Pacific Ocean, and then back again. Lewis and Clark's reports of the phenomenal fur riches of these new lands spurred the expansion of America's fur trade, as trappers followed in the explorers' wake.

The seeds of this expedition were, in fact, sown in the early 1750s when Jefferson was still a boy in colonial Virginia, surrounded by men who believed that America's future lay to the west. Among them was Jefferson's father, Peter, a prosperous farmer, surveyor, and occasional "explorer of the wilderness," who as a member of the Loyal Land Company had an ownership stake in nearly one million acres located west of the Appalachians.[1] Also influential were two of Jefferson's neighbors, the Reverend James Maury and

Dr. Thomas Walker. One of Jefferson's most important teachers, Maury possessed a keen understanding of geopolitics, while Walker had planned to lead an expedition to determine if the Missouri River provided a water route to the Pacific, a journey that was aborted when the French and Indian War intervened. These men helped to shape Jefferson's mind and imbued him with an enduring fascination with the West, which intensified throughout his life.[2]

Jefferson's view of the West matured and became more strategic with the conclusion of the American Revolution. No longer was the West merely an extension of the British Empire; instead he now saw it as of vital importance to his new country. That is why less than a month after the end of the war Jefferson wrote to Gen. George Rogers Clark, the famed "conqueror of the Old Northwest," informing him that the British were planning to explore the "country from the Mississippi to California," with a possible eye toward colonization. Jefferson asked Rogers if he might be interested in leading a competing expedition.[3] Clark thought this a good idea but declined citing financial constraints: "Your proposition . . . would be extremely agreeable to me could I afford it, but I have lately discovered that I knew nothing of the lucrative policy of the world[,] supposing my duty required every attention and sacrifice to the public interest." In other words his patriotism had impoverished him, forcing him to focus on earning a living.[4]

Although the British expedition Jefferson feared failed to materialize, he soon had reason to worry anew. In 1785, while residing in Paris as America's minister to France, he heard of Louis XVI's plans to send La Pérouse to the Pacific Northwest to gather scientific information and search for the Northwest Passage. But the materials that had been gathered for La Pérouse's voyage, as well as other information he had received, persuaded Jefferson that the French had "some other design: perhaps that of colonizing on the western coast of America; or, it may be, only to establish one or more factories there, for the fur trade."[5] In the end, however, La Pérouse did neither, instead spending his time exploring and mapping large swaths of the western coastline, and obtaining furs along the way, which he ultimately sold in China.[6]

Jefferson was especially troubled by Britain and France's interest in the West because it threatened his evolving vision for America. More than fifty years before the term "Manifest Destiny" was coined, Jefferson had already internalized the basic tenets of this radical notion.[7] Like the men who influenced him in his youth, Jefferson believed that America, or at least American influence, was destined to spread westward across the continent. "Our confederacy must be viewed as the nest from which all America, North & South is to be peopled," he wrote in 1786. As for the European powers that currently laid claim to the West, Jefferson was confident that eventually they would be shouldered aside. With Spain, for example, which at the time controlled the Louisiana Territory, Jefferson greatest concern was not that Spain would be an obstacle to America's westward expansion, but rather that the Spaniards would be "too feeble to hold [on to the territory] . . . till our population can be sufficiently advanced to gain it from them piece by piece."[8]

Jefferson's expansive view of America's future was hardly unique. A contemporary American geography book written by Jedidiah Morse, a minister of the Congregational church in Charlestown, Massachusetts, made the case even more strongly:

> We cannot but anticipate the period, as not far distant, when the American Empire will comprehend millions of souls, west of the Mississippi. Judging upon probable grounds, the Mississippi was never designed as the western boundary of the American Empire. The God of nature never intended that some of the best parts of his earth should be inhabited by the subjects of a monarch 4,000 miles from them. And may we not venture to predict, that, when the rights of mankind shall be more fully known, and the knowledge of them is fast increasing both in Europe and America, the power of European potentates will be confined to Europe, and their present American dominions become like the United States, free, sovereign and independent empires.[9]

*J*EFFERSON'S EVOLVING PHILOSOPHY OF AMERICAN EXPAN-sionism, combined with his growing fears that Britain or France might colonize the West or absorb the fur trade in those regions, only intensified his desire to stake America's claims to the area first. Thus, when John Ledyard arrived in Paris intent on fulfilling his dream of sailing to the Pacific Northwest, Jefferson was only too happy to welcome him and propose that he consider another type of journey to America. "In 1786," Jefferson later recounted, "while at Paris I became acquainted with John Ledyard of Connecticut, a man of genius, of some science, and of fearless courage, & enterprise." Since Ledyard's hopes of establishing a fur-trading post in the Pacific Northwest had been dashed, Jefferson "suggested to him the enterprise of

exploring the western part of our continent, by passing through St. Petersburg to Kamchatka, and procuring a passage thence in some of the Russian
vessels to Nootka Sound, whence he might make his way across the continent
to America."[10]

Ledyard, who had already been thinking along the same lines, readily
agreed to proceed with the expedition, whereupon Jefferson contacted Russian empress Catherine II, asking her to grant his new protégé permission
to pass through her country. Even after the empress refused, Ledyard began
his journey, hoping that once he made it to St. Petersburg and spoke with
the empress he could persuade her of the merits of his plan and thereby gain
her blessing to carry on. As with so many of Ledyard's plans, this one, too,
quickly unraveled.

He arrived in St. Petersburg only to find that Catherine was away tour-
ing the Crimea. Undeterred, he continued east, much to the consternation of
Catherine, who, upon returning to St. Petersburg in July 1787 and learning
of Ledyard's audacity, issued orders for his arrest and deportation. Not about
to let a mere American defy her, and doubting that Ledyard was interested
just in exploring America, the empress believed he would seek to establish
fur-trading operations on the Pacific Northwest coast, a move that would
compete with the Russian fur traders in Alaska. Catherine's forces caught up
with Ledyard in late January 1788, and by the middle of March he was unceremoniously dumped in Poland, whence he made his way to London, arriving
at the end of May.[11]

*D*ISCOURAGED BUT NOT DISHEARTENED BY LEDYARD'S
failure, Jefferson looked for another opportunity to launch a western expedition. As further inspiration for his efforts, Jefferson pointed to the
spectacular voyage of the *Columbia*, which had triumphantly returned to Boston in 1790 from its fur-trading venture in the Pacific Northwest. No further
proof of the West's importance to America was needed. By late 1792, Jefferson had convinced the American Philosophical Society to "set on foot a
subscription to engage some competent person to explore [the West] . . . by
ascending the Missouri, crossing the Stony [Rocky] mountains, and descending the nearest river to the Pacific."[12] Within a few months the society had
raised a considerable amount from a group of illustrious supporters, including
George Washington and Alexander Hamilton, and had chosen the French

botanist André Michaux to lead the expedition. Jefferson's instructed Michaux that "the chief objects of your journey are to find the shortest and most convenient route of communication between the United States and the Pacific ocean, . . . and to learn such particulars as can be obtained of the country through which it passes, its productions, inhabitants, and other interesting circumstances."[13] Unfortunately the only thing that Jefferson and the society learned from Michaux was that he was a spy whose mission was to incite the French inhabitants of Louisiana to rebel against their Spanish overlords. And with that intelligence the expedition was halted, and Michaux, who had barely reached Kentucky, was recalled forthwith by the red-faced French minister at Jefferson's request.[14]

Three times Jefferson had tried to launch a western expedition; three times his hopes had been dashed. His fourth attempt, however, was a brilliant success.

*T*HOMAS JEFFERSON BECAME THE THIRD PRESIDENT OF THE United States on March 4, 1801. In the nearly ten years since the Michaux debacle, Jefferson hadn't lost interest in western exploration, but pursuing that goal was not foremost on his mind upon entering office. That changed in the summer of 1802, when a package arrived at Monticello, Jefferson's Virginia mountaintop plantation, containing a recently published book, *Voyages from Montreal Through the Continent of North America to the Frozen and Pacific Oceans in 1789 and 1793, With an Account of the Rise and State of the Fur Trade.* Written by Alexander Mackenzie, a daring and determined Scotsman, the book recounted two trips he took while in the employ of the North West Company, which at the time was fighting an epic battle with its archcompetitor, the Hudson's Bay Company, for control of the Canadian fur trade.[15]

It was the second trip in 1793 that captured Jefferson's attention. That was when Mackenzie's party reached the Pacific, in the vicinity of the Dean Channel along the central coast of present-day British Columbia, thus becoming the first Europeans to traverse the continent north of Mexico. To commemorate his tremendous achievement, Mackenzie mixed together vermilion and bear grease and used the resulting red paint to write the following inscription on a broad flat rock near the water's edge: "Alexander Mackenzie, from Canada, by land, the twenty-second of July, one thousand seven hundred and ninety-three."[16]

Those words shook Jefferson to the core. By crossing the continent and pointing the way west, Mackenzie had realized Jefferson's dreams. To make matters worse Mackenzie implored his countrymen to take advantage of his pathbreaking voyage by colonizing the Pacific Coast and expanding *Britain's* commercial empire. Mackenzie argued:"By opening this intercourse between the Atlantic and Pacific Oceans, and forming regular establishments through the interior, and at both extremes, as well as along the coasts and islands, the entire command of the fur trade of North America might be obtained, from latitude 48 North to the pole, except that portion of it which the Russians have in the Pacific [Alaska]. To this may be added the fishing in both seas, and the markets of the four quarters of the globe."[17]

Jefferson viewed Mackenzie's feat and his call to action as a direct threat to American interests. America's future still lay in the West, he believed, and as a result it was imperative that America respond to Mackenzie's challenge with a sally of its own. Jefferson set the wheels in motion on January 18, 1803, by sending a "confidential message" to Congress in which he asked for $2,500 to send a party of men up the Missouri River "and even to the Western Ocean [the Pacific]." The expedition's main goal was to lay the groundwork for the commercial exploitation of the region's furs, and Jefferson used that economic hook to try to persuade a skeptical Congress to fund the plan. He pointed out that the Indians along the Missouri were currently engaged in a profitable fur trade with Canada, which was "carried on in a high latitude, through an infinite number of portages and lakes, shut up by ice through a long season." But, he added, that trade "could bear no competition with that of the Missouri, traversing a moderate climate, offering according to the best accounts, a continued navigation from its source, and possibly with a single portage [enabling our fur traders to travel] from the Western Ocean . . . [to] the Atlantic."[18]

As the historian Stephen Ambrose noted, "Those congressman who were listening hard got the clear message: we can steal the fur trade from the British."[19] A subsidiary goal—although scarcely less important to Jefferson—was to "advance the geographical [and scientific] knowledge of" the continent.[20] And the expedition's final aim, unstated but clearly understood, was to gather intelligence and foster alliances with the Indians so that the United States would be well positioned to extend its domain westward into lands controlled by other countries when the time was right.[21]

Ever the astute politician, Jefferson also viewed the expedition as a means of getting Congress to support one of his proposed Indian policies. "The

Indian tribes residing within the limits of the United States," Jefferson noted at the outset of his confidential message, were "growing more and more uneasy at the constant diminution of the territory they occupy, although effected by their own voluntary sales," and increasingly refusing to sell their land. In Jefferson's eyes this was a serious concern because the rapidly growing American population needed new territory, and since much of that territory belonged to the Indians, if they didn't sell their land, American settlers would have nowhere to go—unless of course the Indians were forcibly evicted, a path Jefferson preferred to avoid.

Jefferson urged Congress to put in place two measures that would open up Indian lands to settlement. The first was "to encourage" them to become farmers, which would supposedly prove that agriculture was a better way of life than hunting and lead them to sell their "extensive and uncultivated wilds" as a "means of improving their farms and of increasing their domestic comforts." The second measure was to expand the number of government trading posts. This would, Jefferson argued, drive out unscrupulous private fur traders, who tried to turn the Indians against the government, and show the Indians "the wisdom of exchanging what they can spare and we want [land], for what we can spare and they want [trade goods]. In leading [the Indians] thus to agriculture, to manufacturers, and civilization; in bringing together their and our settlements, and in preparing them ultimately to participate in the benefits of our government, I trust and believe we are acting for their greatest good."[22]

Although Jefferson didn't mention it in his confidential message, he believed that a key link between expanding the influence of government factories and getting at the Indians' land was debt. Writing to William Henry Harrison, governor of the Indiana Territory, Jefferson noted that the Indians who came to the factories would want more goods than they could pay for in furs, and the factories would gladly give them those goods on credit. The government, he continued, would "be glad to see the good and influential individuals among them run in debt, because we observe that when these debts get beyond what the individuals can pay, they become willing to lop them off by a cession of lands."[23]

Jefferson realized that some congressmen might find it difficult to vote in favor of an increase in government factories since they would compete with private fur traders who also happened to be constituents. The solution to this potential problem, he believed, was the expedition itself, adding that any business that fur traders might lose in this manner could be more than offset by profits they would gain from the new fur-trading opportunities that would result from the expedition.[24] Jefferson's arguments ultimately persuaded Congress to support both the expansion of the factory system and the launching of the expedition.

The president's message to Congress was confidential because he recognized that it had potentially explosive international implications. The lands the expedition would be traversing belonged to or were claimed by other nations, the most important being France, whose leader, Napoleon Bonaparte, had recently taken back control of the Louisiana Territory from Spain as the result of the Treaty of San Ildefonso. Neither France nor Britain, whose traders had penetrated deep into Louisiana and the Pacific Northwest, would take kindly to an American expedition designed to wrest control of the fur trade and possibly spread the seeds of dissension among the Indians in order to hasten the transfer of the West into American hands. So instead of trumpeting the actual goals of the expedition, Jefferson concealed his true intentions. The expedition was presented to the world at large as nothing more than a "literary pursuit" intended to increase knowledge about the West. But the Europeans were not so easily fooled: They knew that literary goals were the last thing that the Americans had in mind.[25]

J EFFERSON SELECTED HIS PERSONAL SECRETARY AND fellow Virginian, twenty-eight-year-old army captain Meriwether Lewis, to lead the expedition. Interestingly enough, when Lewis asked Jefferson to pick him to lead the American Philosophical Society's western expedition in 1792, Jefferson had declined, instead giving that position to the ultimately disappointing Michaux. Much had changed in the intervening years. Brimming with a decade's worth of experience and maturity, Lewis not only qualified for the job but was also the only man Jefferson considered. Lewis in turn chose thirty-two-year-old army captain William Clark to be the cocaptain of the expedition. These two explorers gathered around them thirty-one additional men, and one Newfoundland dog named Seaman, who would constitute the central elements of the Corps of Discovery.[26]

Jefferson's instructions for Lewis were quite detailed. "The object of your mission," Jefferson explained, "is to explore the Missouri river, and such principal streams of it, as, by its course and communication with the waters of the

Pacific Ocean, whether the Columbia, Oregon, Colorado, or any other river, may offer the most direct and practicable water-communication across the continent, for the purposes of commerce." Along the way Lewis was to become familiar with the Indians he encountered, learning, among other things, the extent of their possessions, their relations with other tribes, and their laws and customs. Lewis was also to pay particular attention to the "articles of commerce" the Indians could supply, such as furs, and what goods they would like to receive in exchange. A renaissance man who embraced science and precise detail, Jefferson instructed Lewis to document climate, geographic features, mineral resources, and the flora and fauna. "In all your intercourse with the natives," Jefferson continued, "treat them in the most friendly and conciliatory manner which their own conduct will admit; allay all jealousies as to the object of your journey; satisfy them of its innocence; make them acquainted with the position, extent, character, peaceable and commercial dispositions of the United States; of our wish to be neighborly, friendly, and useful to them, and of our dispositions to a commercial intercourse with them." And if Lewis and the Corps of Discovery were to make it to the Pacific, they were to determine "whether the furs of those parts may not be collected as advantageously at the head of the Missouri . . . as at Nootka Sound, or any other point of that coast; and [whether] that trade [could] be consequently conducted through the Missouri and United States more beneficially than by the circumnavigation now practiced." In other words, if Pacific Coast furs could be transported east via the Missouri, and trading goods could be transported west along the same path, this would save American merchants the expense of having to send ships around Cape Horn to deliver goods and pick up furs.[27]

As Lewis prepared to depart from Washington, momentous news arrived in the capital. The Washington-based *National Intelligencer* announced on July 4, 1803, that the United States had purchased the Louisiana Territory from Napoleon for $15 million—arguably the most consequential real estate deal in history.[28] The transaction completely changed the nature of the expedition. Instead of traveling through another country's territory, the Corps of Discovery would now be traversing America's newest addition for much of their trip, though for just how much was not exactly known because nobody was quite sure how far the Louisiana Territory extended. As Jefferson later commented, the purchase "increased infinitely the interest we felt in the expedition, and lessened the apprehensions of interruption from other powers."[29] It also meant that Lewis and Clark would have the added responsibility of informing the Indians they encountered that the Louisiana Territory was part of the United States, that they were now the "children" of the "Great Father" in Washington.

*I*N MAY 1804 THE CORPS OF DISCOVERY BEGAN ITS JOURNEY UP the Missouri. Eighteen months later, having covered a little more than four thousand miles of some of the most spectacular and unforgiving terrain in the world, the captains and their men finally arrived at the mouth of the Columbia on the shores of the Pacific. The exhilarating arrival buoyed everyone's spirits, not the least those of Clark, who wrote in his journal, "Ocean in view! O! The Joy."[30] A few weeks later Clark carved the following words into the bark of a large pine tree: "Cap' William Clark December 3rd 1805. By Land. U. States. in 1804–1805."[31]

It is not unreasonable to imagine that in mimicking Mackenzie's inscription, Clark was not only paying homage to Mackenzie but also making a proud statement of his own—as in, We did it too. Jefferson had instructed Lewis that upon arriving on the coast he should endeavor to look for "vessels of any nation," and if possible send two of his men along with his notes back by sea; and if Lewis thought that a return journey overland by the rest of the corps was too dangerous to attempt, he should try to have the entire party return by ship. But the corps encountered no vessels and instead settled in for the winter a few miles up one of the Columbia's tributaries, where they built a small, palisaded enclosure christened Fort Clatsop.[32]

Lewis and Clark bid their "final adieu to Fort Clatsop" on March 23, 1806, and began their long march back east, arriving in St. Louis on September 23. After nearly two and a half years the epic journey was over. The results were spectacular. Lewis and Clark had established friendly relations with many Indian nations, and gathered detailed information on their numbers, customs, alliances, and general way of life. The expedition had collected hundreds of animal and plant specimens, many new to science. Lewis and Clark's detailed topographical notes and sketches provided the basis for the first detailed map of the overland pathway to the Pacific. And throughout the journey, the cocaptains never lost sight of the expedition's main goal, documenting the commercial potential of the West. As a result their journals contain numerous references to furs and the opportunities for trade. In an entry for the winter of 1804–5, for example, Lewis noted that the area surrounding the Yellowstone River abounded "in animals of the fur kind," and he asserted that establishing a trading post at the mouth of the river would lead to a "most lucrative fur trade," keeping the British North West Company from expanding its fur-trading operations in the area.[33]

*D*ESPITE ITS MANY SUCCESSES, THE EXPEDITION HAD failed in one key respect. It had been Jefferson's hope that Lewis and Clark would find an all-water route from the Missouri to the Pacific, which could be used as a highway for the fur trade. Unfortunately for Jefferson the Rocky Mountains loomed as a soaring hindrance, and in his official report to the president, Lewis gave him the bad news. Lewis described the difficult but manageable portage between the Missouri and the Columbia, which ran for 340 miles, 140 of which were "over tremendous mountains which for 60 miles are covered with eternal snows."[34] As Ambrose observed, "With those words, Lewis put an end to the search for the Northwest Passage."[35]

Still, that was only a minor problem as far as Lewis was concerned, who told Jefferson that he and Clark viewed the "passage across the continent as affording immense advantages to the fur trade." The Missouri and its tributaries had more beavers and otters "than any other streams on earth," he claimed, and all the furs that were gathered there could be transported to the mouth of the Columbia for shipment to China, faster than the British could get their furs to market. And Lewis did not leave the fur resources of the Columbia out of his calculations, noting that, although this river and its tributaries lacked the huge beaver population of the Missouri, "it is by no means despicable in this respect and would furnish a profitable fur trade." Lewis's grand scheme comes into view: "If the government will only aid," he concluded, "even in a very limited manner, the enterprise of her citizens I am fully convinced that we shall shortly derive the benefits of a most lucrative trade from this source, and in the course of 10 or 12 years a tour across the continent by this route will be undertaken with as little concern as a voyage across the Atlantic is at present."[36]

*T*HE RETURN OF THE CORPS LAUNCHED AN EVER-WIDENING celebration of America's new heroes. Two days after arriving in St. Louis, Lewis and Clark were feted by the town's leading citizens with a "splendid dinner" and ball at Christy's Inn, which was, according to a contemporary newspaper account, "an honorable testimony of the respect entertained for those characters who are willing to encounter fatigue and hunger for the benefit of their fellow citizens." The alcohol flowed, as did the toasts. Glasses were raised to "the memory of Christopher Columbus—may those who imitate his hardihood, perseverance and merit, never have, like him, to encounter public ingratitude"; "the Missouri—Under the auspices of America, may it prove a vehicle of wealth to all the nations of the world", and to "the commerce of the United States—the basis for the political elevation of America."[37]

While word of the journey's end slowly made its way to the nation's newspapers, the residents of St. Louis had a firsthand chance to ask the explorers about their trip. One topic in particular quickly became the focus of attention—furs and the opportunities for exploiting them on the Missouri and beyond. Jean-Pierre Chouteau, a member of St. Louis's first family and one of the city's most prominent fur traders, sumptuously hosted Lewis and Clark at his home and eagerly questioned his guests about what they had seen. Other members of the corps fanned throughout the town, and were pumped for similar information. According to the author Arlen J. Large, "this kind of unrecorded talk—campfire bull sessions, barroom yarns, refined after-dinner conversation over cognac and cigars . . . sparked the initial exploitation of the expedition's findings. The first follow-up wave of fur-business exploration that spread across the west was due more to post-expedition gossip and gab than any written documents."[38]

But it is important to place this "wave" in its proper perspective. The Lewis and Clark expedition didn't launch the western fur trade.[39] St. Louis had been a major fur trade hub since 1764, and from at least that point forward French, Spanish, and then American fur traders had been heading up the Missouri. And of course Lewis and Clark had seen plenty of evidence that the fur trade had preceded them in their travels. Many of the Indians they encountered already possessed European and American goods they had received in exchange for furs, and the corps crossed paths with fur traders on a number of occasions.

Although the expedition can't be credited with sparking the western fur trade, it did propel it forward. The detailed information about the physical and natural geography of the lands explored by the expedition, especially those surrounding the upper Missouri and beyond, excited and inspired St. Louis fur traders, one in particular being Manuel Lisa.

ORN TO SPANISH PARENTS IN NEW ORLEANS ON SEPTEM-
ber 8, 1772, Lisa arrived in St. Louis in the late 1790s, quickly establishing himself as one of the towns leading fur traders, providing the Chouteau family with its most serious competition.[40] To his legions of detractors
Lisa was an exceedingly aggressive businessman with an abrasive personality
who believed that the ends justified the means. He was, in short, not to be
trusted. One of Lisa's employees claimed that his men "thoroughly detested
and despised [him], both for his acts and his reputation. There were many
tales afloat concerning villainies said to have been perpetrated by him on the
frontiers. These may have been wholly false or greatly exaggerated, but in his
looks there was no deception. Rascality sat on every feature of his dark com-
plexioned, Mexican face—gleamed from his black Spanish, eyes, and seemed
enthroned in a forehead 'villainous low.' "[41] And when Meriwether Lewis had
to deal with Lisa to obtain supplies for the expedition, the normally restrained
captain could barely contain his anger with the Spaniard and his partner,
Francis Benoit. "Damn Manuel [Lisa] and triply damn Mr. B[enoit]," wrote
Lewis to Clark. "They give me more vexation and trouble than their lives
are worth. I have dealt very plainly with these gentlemen, [and] in short have
come to an open rupture with them; I think them both great scoundrels."[42]

But Lisa also has his admirers, among them the fur trade historian Hiram
Chittenden, who said of him, "In boldness of enterprise, persistency of purpose, and in restless energy, he was a fair representative of the Spaniard of the
days of Cortez. He was a man of great ability, a masterly judge of men, thoroughly experienced in the Indian trade and native customs, intensely active in
his work, yet withal a perfect enigma of character which his contemporaries
were never able to solve." Chittenden added that even if Lisa was "unscrupulous in the means he employed to promote his own interests . . . the only difference between him and his detractors is that he was too sharp for them and
succeeded where they failed."[43]

In the spring of 1807, a half year after Lewis and Clark's triumphant
return, Lisa departed from St. Louis with fifty to sixty men under his command, including a few former members of the Corps of Discovery. Using
keelboats to haul goods to barter with the Indians, the party ascended the
Missouri. Going upriver on any type of vessel was difficult, but doing so in
a keelboat—basically a floating barge from fifty to seventy-five feet long,
eight to eighteen feet wide, and loaded down with twenty to thirty tons of

cargo—was a truly daunting task. The real challenge came from the river itself, the longest in the United States, stretching for nearly 2,600 miles. Its rapids and eddies, twists and turns, treacherous shifting shoals, and hidden snags lying just beneath the roiling surface make the Missouri—nicknamed the Big Muddy because of its silt-laden waters—one most dangerous and unpredictable rivers in the world.[44] When Marquette passed by the Missouri's mouth on his way down the Mississippi in 1673, the experience unnerved him. "As we were . . . sailing gently down a beautiful, still, clear water," the good Father wrote, "we heard the noise of a rapid into which we were about to fall. I have seen nothing more frightful; a mass of large trees, entire, with branches, real floating islands, came rushing from the mouth of the river Pekitanoui [the Indian name for the Missouri] so impetuously, that we could not, without great danger, expose ourselves to pass across. The agitation was so great that the water was all muddy and could not get clear."[45]

If there was any man equal to the Missouri, it was Lisa. He knew from hard experience how to guide a cumbersome keelboat, having learned this skill by navigating such craft on the Mississippi and up the lower reaches of the Big Muddy. The strategies he and other rivermen employed depended on the conditions. When the current was swift and the boat could get close to shore, which was most of the time, cordelling was employed, in which twenty to forty men walked along the riverbank pulling a towline up to a thousand feet long. This was particularly grueling work since, with few paths or clear stretches, the men were often forced to fight their way past dense tangles of trees and underbrush, traverse sheer and crumbling bluffs, and trudge through thick mud at the water's edge. When an obstruction made progress along the bank impossible, keelboaters resorted to another form of cordelling called warping, in which a few men would row past the obstacle in a skiff and tie one end of a rope to a sturdy tree. Since the other end of the rope was still onboard, the boat would be pulled ahead when the men drew in the line. When sandbars kept the keelboat too far from shore or the riverbank was totally impassable, cordelling had to be abandoned in favor of poling. Eight to ten men would array themselves in a line on either side of the boat near the bow, and each of them would thrust a long poles into the water, pointing downstream, until the end hit bottom. Leaning hard against the rounded tops of the poles, the men began walking aft until the lead man could go no farther, whereupon all the men lifted their poles out of the water, walked to the bow, and repeated the cycle, mindful to get back into position as quickly as possible so as to maintain forward momentum. If the water was too deep for poling and the current was slight, the men would row. And in rare instances, on long relatively straight stretches of river, when the winds were favorable and strong enough to counter the current, the men had the luxury of sailing the keelboat.[46]

Using all these variants of keelboat locomotion, Lisa and his men made slow but steady progress. Near the junction of the Missouri and Platte rivers, just below present-day Omaha, Nebraska, Lisa got an unexpected gift when he encountered a lone white man traveling downriver in a canoe. It was John Colter, a former member of the Corps of Discovery, who had left the expedition in its final stage to trap for beaver along the upper Missouri. Lisa saw Colter as the perfect addition to his team, since he had just come from where Lisa's party was heading, and after some quick negotiations Colter signed on.[47]

Lisa proceeded to the junction of the Missouri and the Yellowstone rivers, and then headed up the latter until reaching the Bighorn River in October, where the expedition stopped and Lisa took fur trading in a new direction. Americans had traditionally relied on the Indians to bring the furs to them, and Lisa did the same—up to a point. From his earlier travels and from information received from other fur traders, as well as Lewis and Clark, Lisa knew that the Plains Indians weren't interested in or skilled at hunting for beavers. As one Canadian trader observed in 1805, "Beavers are plentiful, but the Indians [of the upper Missouri] will not take the trouble of attending to them. They often remarked to me that they would think it a pleasure to supply us with beavers if they could be secured the same as buffaloes by a chase on horseback, but they considered the operation of searching for them in the bowels of the earth, to satisfy the avarice of the whites, not only troublesome, but very degrading."[48]

Given this dynamic, Lisa knew that a strategy that relied on the Indians alone was destined to fail. So he implemented an approach that had never been tried before. He not only traded with the Indians when they had furs to barter, but he also sent his own trappers into the countryside to bring in the beavers. Each of the men Lisa hired was given an outfit that consisted of all the items needed to survive and work in the wilderness, including a rifle, a horse or mule, and a sack filled with six to eight steel traps, each of which were handwrought by blacksmiths and could cost as much as six dollars apiece. Of these items the trap was the most important because it was the tool that caught the beavers.

*T*HERE WAS A GREAT VARIETY OF TRAPS, BUT THEY ALL USED the same basic mechanism to catch their intended victims. The trap's semicircular or squared-off jaws, usually flat-edged but sometimes studded with teeth, were spread wide open, and in the process the two thick, elbow-shaped bands of steel that served as the trap's spring mechanism were compressed and held in place under great tension by a metal rod, called a dog. The dog was connected to a flat sheet of metal called the pan, and when the beaver stepped on the pan, the dog released and the jaws snapped shut with tremendous force on the beaver's foot or lower leg. To get the beaver to make that fateful step, the trapper employed deception and a sneak attack. First, he placed the trap—set and ready to spring—in four to five inches of water near the edge of a beaver pond. Next, the trap's chain, which could be up to five feet long, was attached to a wooden stake pounded into the bottom of the pond in deeper water. Then the trapper took a short twig, frayed at one end, and dipped that end into a horn bottle of what he called "medicine," which was a pungent mixture of castoreum and other ingredients, such as spices, gum of camphor, and juniper oil. There were scores, if not hundreds, of different "medicine" recipes, which the trappers swore by and would not divulge lest the competition gain the upper hand. With this aromatic lure ready to go, the trapper planted the other end of the twig in the mud along the edge of the pond, just inches above the waterline and only a foot away from the trap. When the curious beaver came out of the water to inspect the lure, it would step on the pan, releasing the pent-up power of the springs, and be caught in the trap's jaws. When the trap grabbed hold of the paw only, the beaver could gnaw it off and free itself. However, if the hold was higher on the leg, there was no escape. The panicked animal would often dive for deeper water only to have its flight arrested because the trap was tethered to the stake. The beaver would struggle mightily but in the end it would drown, being pulled under by the weight of the trap and chain.[49]

In addition to their wages, the trappers hired by Lisa received a portion of the profits earned from the pelts they secured, an incentive that served as a successful motivational tool. And Lisa added yet another innovation to the mix when he built a fort at the confluence of the Yellowstone and the Bighorn—first called Fort Raymond, after Lisa's son, and later Fort Manuel or Fort Lisa—which was not only the first trading post built on the upper Missouri but also the first building erected in Montana. To Lisa's men the fort was a place to offload pelts, resupply, recuperate, and seek protection in case of Indian attacks. To the Indians it was a bartering station where they could obtain desired goods, and to Lisa it provided a convenient and central location where he could deposit the materials his men needed and gather furs for transport back to St. Louis.[50]

SOON AFTER ESTABLISHING FORT MANUEL, LISA SENT Colter on a reconnaissance trip to forge trading relations with area Indians and locate the best places for trapping. Colter did that and more. He cut a serpentine path five hundred miles through uncharted territory in present-day Montana, Wyoming, and Idaho, hiking alone over treacherous mountains, through deep and winding valleys, and along meandering riverbeds during some of the worst winter months with a thirty-pound pack on his back and just enough clothes to keep from freezing to death.[51] As a result Colter became, in Chittenden's words, "the first explorer of the valley of the Bighorn river; the first to cross the passes at the head of Wind river and see the headwaters of the Colorado of the West; the first to see the Teton mountains, Jackson Hole, Pierre's Hole, and the sources of the Snake river; and most important of all, the first to pass through that singular region which has since become known throughout the world as the Yellowstone Wonderland."[52]

In large part because Colter didn't write anything down—and what information he shared was vague enough to give generations of academics and armchair historians plenty of ammunition—there have been maddeningly inconclusive debates over the precise scope of his journey.[53] Many have questioned whether he traversed what is now Yellowstone National Park, and wondered about the veracity of his claims to have visited a place that had towering geysers, sulfurous tar pits, and flames issuing from fissures in the earth, a seemingly devilish suite of natural features that led trappers to call the area "Colter's Hell."[54] But even if some of the claims about Colter's trek are false, it was still without a doubt one of the most impressive solo journeys in American exploration history.[55]

WHILE COLTER WAS AWAY LISA'S STRATEGY WORKED BEAUtifully. His men trapped in the streams and rivers around Fort Manuel, while Indians visited the fort with furs to trade. Part of Lisa's success was attributable to his keen understanding of and respect for his Indian customers.

Commenting later in his career on his striking ability to maintain friendly relations with a great variety of tribes—a skill even his enemies admired— Lisa said, "I appear as a benefactor, not as a pillager of the Indian. . . . My blacksmiths work incessantly for them, charging nothing. I lend them traps, only demanding a preference in their trade. My establishments are the refuge of the weak, and of the old men no longer able to follow their lodges; and by these means I have acquired the confidence and friendship of the natives and the consequent choice of their trade"[56]

The collected furs were bundled together into packs of sixty to eighty, and in the summer of 1808 Lisa took them to St. Louis, where the pelts sold for as much as four dollars each. Lisa's triumphant return and the promise of money generated great excitement in the bustling frontier town of one thousand, encouraging a small group of local business leaders with capital and connections to join Lisa to establish the Missouri Fur Company, whose goal was to exploit the upper Missouri fur trade as far as the Rocky Mountains.[57] Stockholders included two members of the Chouteau family, Andrew Henry, Reuben Lewis (Meriwether's brother), Pierre Menard, and William Clark, who saw this investment as a way to profit from the hard-won intelligence he had collected on his epic western journey. The launch of this enterprise caught the attention of the *Missouri Gazette*, which wrote that the company "has every prospect of becoming a source of incalculable advantage not only to the individuals engaged but to the community at large."[58]

The company's expedition left St. Louis in spring 1809, and come fall Lisa's men were trapping for beaver in the vicinity of Fort Manuel. The trapping was good for the balance of 1809 into the following year, when Menard and Henry lead a group of men to the headwaters of the Missouri, the so-called Three Forks area at the confluence of the Jefferson, Madison, and Gallatin rivers where they built a new post. This was prime, virgin territory, and there were furs aplenty, to the point that the men thought they might be able to secure as many as three hundred packs, or up to 24,000 beaver pelts, in their first season. But before that vision could be realized, the Blackfeet Indians attacked, fueled by an intense anger toward the Americans.[59]

*T*HE RELATIONSHIP BETWEEN THE BLACKFEET INDIANS AND Americans suffered its first blow at the end of July 1806, when Lewis and three of his men were riding alongside Two Medicine Creek, not far from the headwaters of the Marias River. Out of the corner of his eye Lewis noticed about thirty horses and a few Indians on a ridge a mile away. Deciding that fleeing would only "invite pursuit," Lewis approached the Indians, holding out his hand and "beckoning" them to come meet him, which, after some hesitation they did. The eight Indians were Piegans, one of the Blackfeet tribes. Lewis was wary of the Indians' intentions, and told his men to be on guard. Nevertheless, with darkness coming on and believing that his men could hold their own against any attack, Lewis invited the Indians to "encamp together."

Lewis and his men took turns on watch throughout the night, fearing that the Indians might rob them if given the chance. Early the next morning, while three of the men were still asleep, the Indians gathered around the fire when one of them noticed that the man on watch, Joseph Field, had, as Lewis wrote in his journal, "carelessly laid his gun down behind him near where his brother [Reuben] was sleeping." The Indians pounced on this opportunity, grabbing Joseph's gun as well as Reuben's, then lunging forward to take Lewis's gun and the gun of the fourth man in the party, George Drouillard. Joseph yelled to Reuben, who jumped up, and both of them ran after one of the thieves, overtaking him within about sixty yards and wrenching their rifles from his hands. Reuben thrust his knife into the chest of the Indian, who staggered before collapsing to the ground. Meanwhile the commotion roused Drouillard, who screamed at one of the Indians, "Damn you let go [of] my gun," and then wrestled it free. Drouillard's outburst in turn woke up Lewis, who saw that yet another Indian was making off with his rifle. Lewis raced after the Indian, and when he caught up, he leveled his pistol at the Indian's head, "persuading" him to drop the rifle.

Now that Lewis and his men had retrieved their guns, they turned their attention to keeping the Indians from taking their horses. Lewis cornered two of the Indians in a box canyon, raised his gun, and threatened to shoot them if they didn't give back his horse. One of the Indians jumped behind a rock, but the other, still armed, wheeled around and Lewis shot him in the belly. The Indian fell to his knees, propped himself up on his right elbow, returned fire, and then crawled behind the rock, where he later died. Although the Indian missed, the shot came so close to Lewis's bare head that the captain claimed that he "felt the wind of his bullet very distinctly." Having left his shot pouch behind, Lewis was unable to reload, so he hurried back to camp and organized his men to leave the area. But before doing so, Lewis decided to make a statement. One of the Indians who lay dead next to the camp still had around his neck the Jefferson Peace Medal Lewis had given him the night before, as a token of friendship from the "Great Father" in Washington. Lewis left it there so that any other Indians who came across this grisly scene would "be informed who we were."[60]

This violent clash, leaving two Piegans dead, initiated the long era of animosity between the Blackfeet and the Americans. Two issues came into play. First was the deaths themselves, which led the Indians to call for revenge. Second, and more important, was the information that the surviving Piegans brought back to their tribe. Around the campfire Lewis had told the Indians that the United States wanted peace with all the Indian tribes. He informed them that the United States had not only signed a peace treaty with the Shoshone and the Nez Percé, foes of the Blackfeet, but had also agreed to supply those two tribes with trade goods, including guns. To the Blackfeet the message was clear—the Americans were planning on trading with and arming their enemies, and that meant the Americans were enemies too.[61]

Another clash two years later aggravated an already tense situation. In the early spring of 1808 Lisa sent Colter on a mission to escort Crow and Flathead Indians to Fort Manuel to trade. During the trip a huge band of Blackfeet appeared and attacked. Although Colter didn't want to fight, he had little choice but to defend himself, and started shooting at the fast-approaching Indians. Wounded in the leg, Colter crawled into a thicket, from which he continued to fire with deadly accuracy. After sustaining serious casualties the Blackfeet retreated. One image, however, remained indelibly seared in their minds—that of Colter fighting shoulder to shoulder with their enemies the Crow. It gave the Blackfeet yet another reason to hate Americans.[62]

Later in 1808 Colter experienced this hatred firsthand, when he and John Potts, another former member of the Corps of Discovery, were trapping beaver in the Three Forks area. Being in Blackfeet territory, they knew they were potentially in danger. Accordingly they set their traps at night and remained hidden during the day. Early one morning while checking their traps on the river, they heard a thundering roar off in the distance, just beyond the lip of one of the bluffs rising up from the river's edge. Colter thought it was a large group of Indians. He wanted to leave the river immediately, but Potts called him a coward, claiming the noise to be nothing more than a herd of buffalo, and they continued on their rounds.

A few minutes later Colter's fears were realized when five or six hundred

Blackfeet appeared on either bank. The Indians waved at the men to come ashore. With no escape possible, Colter and Potts complied, paddling their canoe into the shallows. As soon as the canoe came to rest, an Indian stripped Potts of his rifle, whereupon Colter jumped out of the canoe, yanked the gun free, and returned it to Potts, who immediately pushed off in the canoe. Potts hadn't drifted more than a few feet downstream before an arrow pierced him. "Colter, I am wounded," he yelled. Potts ignored Colter's plea for him to paddle back to shore, and instead shot one of the Indians dead. A barrage of arrows whizzed through the air, and Potts was, in Colter's words, "made a riddle of."

The Indians grabbed Colter and stripped him naked. Having learned a respectable amount of the Blackfoot language from his time with the Crow, Colter now listened as the Indians debated what to do with their prize. Their first impulse was to use him for target practice, but then the chief intervened with a better idea. He gripped Colter's shoulder and "asked him if he could run fast." Colter knew what was in store—a race to the death—so he responded that he was a very slow runner, even though the exact opposite was true. The chief, no doubt thinking this should be over quickly, took Colter about three hundred to four hundred yards off and then told him to "save himself if he could."

As soon as Colter began running, he heard the Indians' fierce cries, and the hunt was on. His only hope, he thought, was to make it to the fork of the Jefferson River about six miles away. Propelled by intense fear and the rush of adrenaline, Colter ignored the pain in his feet as his bare soles were cut and punctured by sharp-edged stones and the spines of prickly pear. His exertions were such that blood vessels in his nose ruptured, sending a crimson stream down the front of his body. Nearly halfway to the river, Colter glanced behind to check on his pursuers. Much to his surprise he had outpaced all of them, except one fleet warrior, who, spear in hand, was barely one hundred yards away. A mile from the river, with the lone Indian now just twenty yards away and closing in, Colter realized that his only chance was to confront his attacker and throw him off guard. With that Colter abruptly stopped, spun around, and spread his arms wide, ready to fend off any impending blow. The Indian, startled by Colter's sudden action, tried to pull up and at the same time throw his spear, but stumbled, jamming the spear into the ground and breaking it in two. Colter leaped forward, grabbed the pointed half of the spear, and stabbed the prostrate Indian, then continued his headlong dash to the river.

When the other Indians came upon the grisly scene of their wounded fellow they let out "a hideous yell" and redoubled their efforts to catch their prey.

Colter soon gained the river's edge, and seeing a large raft of driftwood near the bank, he dived under the tangle of branches, finding a spot where he could just peek his head out of the water yet still be concealed from view. A few moments later the Indians arrived, yelling, Colter recalled, "like so many devils." For hours they tramped up and down both sides of the river and even on top of Colter's hiding place, but they didn't find him. Finally, once the sounds of the Indians had abated, and under the cloak of night, Colter left the protection of the raft, swimming slowly and silently downstream in the darkness before hauling himself out on the riverbank. Although Colter had eluded the Indians, he still faced equally hostile foes—the broiling sun, frigid nights, and the threat of starvation—as he headed toward Fort Manuel, nearly 250 miles away. Subsisting entirely on the succulent roots of the prairie turnip, or breadroot, Colter hiked for seven days, arriving emaciated and nearly dead at the fort, where he was nursed back to health.[63]

G IVEN THIS RECENT AND VIOLENT HISTORY BETWEEN THE Blackfeet and Americans, it was not surprising that Menard and Henry's trading post at the Three Forks soon came under attack. On April 12, 1810, only a short time after Menard and Henry's arrival, five of their trappers were killed by a roving band of Blackfeet. This forced the trappers to change their operations to protect themselves. Most of them remained at the post in a defensive posture while small groups ventured out to tend the traps, being mindful to stay close together. One who disregarded the danger was Drouillard, saying at one point that he was "too much of an Indian to be caught by Indians." Despite the protest of his peers, Drouillard began setting beaver traps far away from the post and tending to them on his own. Each full trap emboldened him to go farther upriver. But on his third day out he didn't return, and neither did two others who had gone hunting for food. The rest of the trappers searched for the missing men and first found the two hunters, whose bodies were "pierced with lances, arrows, and bullets and lying near each other." A short distance away was Drouillard, who was "mangled in a horrible manner; his head . . . cut off, his entrails torn out, and his body hacked to pieces."[64]

Indian attacks continued and the death toll rose, causing Menard and

Henry to abandon the Three Forks post in the summer and fall of 1810, Menard returning to St. Louis with the accumulated furs, and Henry heading south over the continental divide to the north fork of the Snake River, where he set up a small trading post and in the process became the first American fur trader to operate west of the Rockies. Adding to the Missouri Fur Company's woes was a major fire that consumed fifteen thousand dollars worth of furs, and a precipitous decline in the price paid for beaver pelts, falling from four dollar to two dollars and fifty cents per pound.[65] In the midst of these troubling times for the company, Lisa, its fearless leader, found himself facing off against yet another and particularly powerful foe—John Jacob Astor, the nation's most prosperous fur trader.

—11—

Astoria

Astoria in 1813.

IN THE PICTURESQUE HAMLET OF WALLDORF, GERMANY, NEAR the northern edge of the Black Forest, Maria Magdalena Astor gave birth on July 17, 1763, to Johann Jakob, her sixth child and fifth son (the first son died in infancy). The father, Jakob Astor, was a man of limited education and narrow horizons who worked hard and ran the most prosperous butcher shop in the area, although he was by no means wealthy. After Maria died when young Johann was three, his father remarried and in relatively short order he and his new wife added another six children to the already over-crowded Astor home.

Jakob had high hopes that his sons would join the family business, but one by one they disappointed him. George Peter, the oldest, was the first to go, heading to London in the early 1770s, where he made a name for himself as a maker of fine musical instruments. The second oldest, Johann Heinrich, then joined the German army as a cook and was shipped off to America in 1775 as part of a Hessian mercenary force hired by Britain's King George III to fight the rebels. It wasn't long though before Johann Heinrich, who by this time had changed his name to Henry, decided that his future lay in America, and after the Battle of Long Island in the summer of 1776, he deserted his regiment and opened a butcher's stall in Fly Market, at the intersection of Maiden Lane and Pearl Street near the East River in New York.[1] The third oldest son, Johann Melchior, settled near Koblenz, where he ran a school and became a tenant farmer on a local prince's land. Next it was Johann Jakob's turn to pursue his own course. While he excelled as a butcher in his father's shop, he was also a gifted student with unbridled confidence, who from an early age believed he was destined for great success far beyond the borders of his sleepy hometown. The letters from George and Henry, which painted pictures of unlimited opportunity in their adopted cities, only heightened Johann Jakob's desire to leave.[2]

Johann Jakob first discussed the idea of leaving with his pastor and Valentine Jeune, his beloved teacher. They knew Walldorf was too small to contain Johann Jakob's talents and ambitions, but they thought that going straight to New York was unwise. America was in the throes of the revolution, and although Henry had successfully established himself, that didn't mean Johann Jakob would have the same luck, especially since attempting to launch one's career in the middle of a war zone seemed risky at best. Instead Jeune and the pastor encouraged Johann Jakob to go to London, where he could work for George, learn to speak proper English, and then, when the situation in America resolved itself, immigrate to New York.

The biggest obstacle to carrying out this plan was Johann Jakob's father, and Jeune and the pastor kindly offered to broach the subject with him on the young man's behalf. Not surprisingly Johann Jakob's father was adamantly opposed to the idea. He didn't want to lose a fourth son, especially one so skilled with a knife and good with numbers—who, then, would take over the shop? Finally, however, after months of heated discussions, Jakob relented and gave his son permission to go. Just two months shy of his seventeenth birthday, in May 1779 Johann Jakob waved good-bye to Walldorf forever.

As the familiar story goes, Johann Jakob walked to the Rhine, made his way to Holland as a deckhand on a timber barge heading downriver, then hopped a ship to London, where he immediately began working in George's musical instrument factory. Four years later, after anglicizing his name to John Jacob, learning the language, and honing his skills as a salesman, John was ready for America. His brother Henry had become a prosperous butcher in New York, and his letters to John were brimming with optimism—all one needed to succeed in this new land was intelligence and a strong work ethic, both of which John possessed in abundance. So in November 1783, less than two months after the Treaty of Paris officially ended the war, John booked a berth in steerage on the *North Carolina*, bound for America, and began his voyage across the Atlantic with just five pounds in his pocket. Packed in his luggage was a small consignment of flutes, the sale of which he hoped would launch his American adventure.

It was on this ship that Astor's education in furs began. A few of the first-class passengers happened to be employees of the mighty Hudson's Bay Company, the largest and most powerful fur-trading operation in the world. Astor overheard these men talking shop on their occasional rambles beyond the confines of the first-class decks, and he was intrigued by their animated conversation. His interest was piqued further by a fellow German traveling in steerage, who had been a fur merchant in America since before the war and was eager to answer Astor's many questions. Most exciting of all was the intelligence that the furs obtained from the Indians for trifling amounts of goods could be sold at a tremendous profit in New York or London.

By the time the *North Carolina* reached coast of Virginia in mid-January, the frigid grip of a particularly cold winter had choked the lower reaches of Chesapeake Bay with ice. For about a week the captain slowly sailed the ship up the bay, gingerly steering his way through the constantly shifting, sharp-edged floes, which often came dangerously close to the hull. Then, just when Baltimore Harbor hove into view, the temperature plummeted and the ice closed in, immobilizing the ship tantalizingly close to the shore. Frugal and in no particular hurry, Astor opted to stay on board, since according to the terms of his ticket the ship's owners had to provide food and lodging until the trip was over. More than a month passed while Astor watched many of his fellow passengers lower themselves to the frozen surface of the bay and drag their belongings to land. Then, with the food onboard running low, Astor did likewise and caught a coach that deposited him in downtown Baltimore on March 24 or 25. That same day, while walking up Market Street, Astor met Nicholas Tuschdy, a Swiss shopkeeper, who invited him into his house for a drink and offered to display some of Astor's flutes in his shop. A few of them sold, and within a month's time Astor had saved enough money to buy passage to his ultimate destination, New York.[3]

Having not seen him for nine years, Henry heartily welcomed his younger brother and offered to put him to work at Fly Market cutting meat, but John had no interest in re-creating his life in Germany, and instead took a job peddling cakes, cookies, and rolls baked by one of Henry's friends. This gave him a chance to learn his way around New York, at the time a relatively compact and impoverished city that was still digging its way out of the rubble of seven years of war and occupation. While he hawked pastries Astor never forgot the informal education he received onboard the *North Carolina*, and during the summer of 1784 he decided to see if the stories he had heard about furs were true. To find out he knew he would have to learn more about the trade, so he went to work for a Quaker fur dealer named Robert Browne, beating furs to keep them free of moths, a job for which he received two dollars per week as well as room and board.[4]

Astor, ever the diligent and conscientious employee, readily absorbed everything Browne taught him. Then, on his own time, at night and on weekends, Astor took his education one step farther. He scoured the city's docks, looking for river men or Indians who had furs to sell, and then bought them using the savings from his job as well as the proceeds from any instruments he had sold. Within a year Astor sailed to London with a sizable number of pelts, which he sold for a handsome profit. He picked up more flutes from his brother, persuaded two London piano makers to appoint him their sole American agent, and then returned to New York. Henry was right; America was the land of opportunity, and John was eager to build on his success.[5]

Astor continued working for Browne during the day and peddling instruments and furs on the side, but circumstances were changing, and he was ready to head in a new direction. In September 1785, Astor married Sarah Todd, who brought a dowry of three hundred dollars along with a self-confidence to match her husband's and an equally strong entrepreneurial drive. With her encouragement and support, Astor struck out on his own in the late 1780s, opening an instrument shop at 81 Pearl Street and also getting more deeply involved with furs.[6] The instrument business prospered, but furs were foremost on Astor's mind, and increasingly they took up most of his time and energy. He went on long, arduous, and at times dangerous trips to the backwoods of upstate New York, Pennsylvania, and New Jersey, lugging a sixty-pound backpack and trading with trappers, Indians, and other traders for furs, and then bringing them back to New York for sale or export. He forged strong ties with merchants in Montreal and arranged for joint shipments of furs to Europe, while establishing trading depots at Albany, Schenectady,

Fort Schuyler (Utica), and in the Catskills, which became magnets for anyone who had fur to sell.

With beaver selling for twenty shillings per pound or more, the profits accumulated, and Astor saw the promise of an even brighter future. He boldly predicted that when the British finally handed over the disputed fur trading-posts along the northern frontier, "then . . . I will make my fortune in the fur trade."[7] And he was right. After the Jay treaty transferred the posts to the Americans, Astor expanded his operations, and by 1800 he was reportedly worth $250,000, most of which came from the sale of furs.[8] His success was all the more remarkable, coming at a time when the continental fur trade in America was at a relatively low ebb—indeed, at the beginning of the nineteenth century the only other American fur traders who were generating impressive profits were the "Boston Men" trading for furs in the Pacific Northwest and sending them to China. Astor was well aware of their success, and in 1800 he joined with three other merchants to send the *Severn* to Canton, loaded with furs. Its return cargo of satin, silk, tea, and porcelain generated hefty profits, which Astor supplemented in subsequent years by assuming sole ownership of the *Severn* and adding two other ships to his growing China fleet.[9]

*N*OT ONE TO LET HIS MONEY SIT IDLE, ASTOR PLOWED HIS growing profits from the fur trade into real estate. His first purchase came in 1789, when he bought two lots of land on Bowery Lane for a little more than six hundred dollars; an impressive amount when one considers that Astor's fellow countrymen were earning an average of about one dollar per day. At about this time, as legend has it, some splendidly lavish row houses were built on Broadway, which had the whole city talking. While walking by them one day, Astor supposedly remarked, "I'll build . . . a greater house than any of these, and on this very street." Whether or not he actually uttered these words, he nevertheless followed through on the promise, after a fashion. In 1802, for the grand sum of $27,500, Astor purchased 223 Broadway, the spacious home of Rufus King, New York's first senator. Thirty-four years later Astor tore down the house and all the others on that block to build an even more imposing edifice—the six-story, 309-room, granite-faced Astor House, which quickly became one of the most fashionable hotels in the city.[10]

Over the years many of Astor's associates ridiculed his real estate transactions, especially those in which he acquired empty land well beyond the city proper. They said he had wasted his money on dirt and trees, but when the city expanded right up to the edge of Astor's holdings, he sold or rented his "worthless" land for enormous sums—including all of what would one day become Times Square. When he was very old, Astor was asked if he had accumulated an excessive amount of real estate, to which he replied, "Could I begin life again, knowing what I now know, and had money to invest, I would buy every foot of land on the Island of Manhattan."[11]

When Astor purchased the King house on Broadway, however, real estate was not yet his primary interest, nor his primary source of income, although in later years it would become both. In the early 1800s Astor, already one of the richest men in the country and on the verge of becoming a millionaire, was first and foremost a fur dealer—the most successful one in the United States, if not the world.[12] Unwilling to sit on his laurels or his growing fortune, he was looking for ways to expand his operations and earn more. And soon after Lewis and Clark returned from their epic journey, Astor's gaze shifted westward.

WHILE MANUEL LISA WAS LAUNCHING HIS FIRST FORAY UP the Missouri in the spring of 1807, Astor was busy formulating a plan, the implementation of which was designed to give him a virtual monopoly of the fur trade west of the Mississippi all the way to the Pacific. The plan was bold in conception and sweeping in scope. He would build a series of trading posts along the Missouri, shadowing the trail of Lewis and Clark, up to and over the continental divide, then along the Columbia to the ocean. Furs gathered to the east of the divide, from throughout the Missouri drainage basin, would be transported to St. Louis or New Orleans and ultimately to markets in New York and Europe, while furs collected on the western side would be brought to the shores of the Pacific and then shipped to China, where they would be traded for silk, spices, tea, and porcelain, which would be sent to New York for domestic and overseas sale. As the anchor of his trading empire in the West, Astor envisioned establishing a post at the mouth of the Columbia River, which would be the portal for the distribution of furs flowing in from the countryside. To carry out his designs, Astor incorporated the American Fur Company on April 6, 1808, with a capital stock of one million dollars.

Astor faced few obstacles in forging ahead with his scheme. He had the money to hire as many people as he needed, and to outfit them with the best supplies and materials. And the federal government, while keenly interested in western development, had no policy regarding private ventures in that quarter and would not stand in Astor's way. But before beginning his march to the West, Astor wanted President Jefferson to sanction or at least approve of his new enterprise. Such "approbation" would give him an advantage over the competition and might come in handy should any problems arise. Getting the president's support, however, would not be easy. Astor knew that if he told the truth—that his interests were purely commercial and that he wanted to monopolize the western fur trade for his own personal gain—Jefferson would likely decline. After all, monopolistic ambitions and great concentrations of wealth were not currently in fashion, and Jefferson's view of western development encompassed more than just expanding the opportunities for trade. So, according to the biographer John Upton Terrell, Astor lied. Astor presented the American Fur Company as being an organization composed of many key investors, when in reality it was almost entirely under his control. He claimed that his goal was to improve relations with the Indians and pave the way for peaceful settlement of the West, when his primary interest was making more money from furs. And he averred that his operations would save government resources because they would obviate the need for the establishment of more fur factories, when all he really wanted was to avoid government competition.[13]

To this litany of mistruths, or at least lies by omission, Astor added one undeniable fact—the Canadians were thrashing the Americans in the race for furs out West. Although article 3 of the Jay treaty gave the Canadians and Americans reciprocal fur-trading rights across the border in and around the Great Lakes region and the Old Northwest, the Americans were not at all sure that these rights extended to the lands of the Louisiana Purchase; the problem was, the Canadians were sure they did, and Canadian trappers and traders annually had been taking hundreds of thousands of dollars' worth of "American" furs from the lands west of the Mississippi out to the Missouri and bringing them to Montreal for sale.[14] Astor rightly argued that this traffic amounted to a cross-border flow of profits. He claimed that America was the poorer for it because American trappers and traders were losing out on sales, and American consumers were paying more for their furs because, to meet growing demand, merchants like Astor had to buy furs from Montreal at inflated prices. Invoking the early-nineteenth-century jingoism of his adopted land, Astor maintained that America's furs should be controlled and sold by Americans; if his plan worked, that would be the case.[15]

Astor relied on all these factors in making his pitch to Jefferson, and the president gave his blessing to the enterprise in a letter to Astor in early April 1808. "I learn with great satisfaction the disposition of our merchants to form into companies for undertaking the Indian trade within our own territories. . . . In order to get the whole of this business passed into the hands of our own citizens, . . . every reasonable patronage and facility in the power of the Executive will be afforded."[16]

W ITH THE FEDERAL GOVERNMENT ONBOARD, ASTOR SHIFTED into high gear. To spearhead the establishment of a fur-trading post at the mouth of the Columbia, he created a subsidiary of the American Fur Company and called it the Pacific Fur Company. The latter was charged with sponsoring two expeditions—one by sea and the other by land. A ship with an assortment of managers, clerks, and fur traders, as well as necessary trading goods, stores, and armaments would be sent around Cape Horn to lay the groundwork for the fortified post at the mouth of the Columbia, while another equally varied group would follow Lewis and Clark's path and then meet up with the shipborne contingent.

Astor knew that once the Canadians found out about his plans for the Pacific Fur Company they would be incensed; after all, they were equally interested in exploiting the furs beyond the Rockies, and didn't want to be crowded out by the Americans. So, ever the pragmatist, Astor decided to invite the Canadians in, even though such a move appeared to run counter to his implied promise to Jefferson that his venture would place the trade entirely in American hands. Realizing that unbridled competition for western furs would be damaging to both his interests and the Canadians', Astor proposed that they join forces, offering his chief Canadian competitor, the North West Company, the opportunity to buy a one-third interest in the Pacific Fur Company. The North West Company, however, wasn't biting. It wanted the far-western fur trade all to itself. While this rejection frustrated Astor, it also redoubled his resolve to get his post up and running before the Canadians established themselves on the coast.

Although the Pacific Fur Company was not going to be part owned by a Canadian company, Astor still wanted Canadians to be intimately involved in its operations. Astor had long worked with and bought from Canadian fur traders and agents, whom he believed were the best in the business. Since he wanted to do everything to ensure the success of his enterprise, he set about hiring numerous Canadians, many of whom were disgruntled North West Company employees, and giving them minority partnership stakes in the Pacific Fur Company. Among those brought on in this manner were Alexander McKay, Duncan McDougall, David Stuart, and Donald Mackenzie, and to their ranks were added a corps of French Canadian voyageurs, as well as a few Canadian clerks. To round out the Pacific Fur Company's forces, which ultimately exceeded 140 men, Astor also hired quite a few American fur traders, agents, and clerks, but to make it clear that this was an American operation, he appointed Wilson Price Hunt, a New-Jersey born merchant, to serve both as the leader of the overland expedition and Astor's chief representative and agent at the planned western post. Astor provided $400,000 to cover the expenses of this massive operation.[17]

*A*STOR'S SHIP THE *TONQUIN* WAS READYING FOR ITS voyage to the Columbia in early September 1810. It was a fast, sturdy, and relatively new ship, ninety-four feet long, twenty-five feet wide, twelve feet deep, mounted with ten guns, and rated at 269 tons burden. To its crew of twenty-one were added thirty-three employees of the Pacific Fur Company, including four of the partners—McKay, McDougall, Stuart, and Stuart's nephew, Robert. The captain of the ship was a highly decorated and respected navy lieutenant named Jonathan Thorn, who had been granted a furlough from the navy to command this voyage.[18] And command is exactly what he planned to do. Gabriel Franchère, one of the clerks who sailed on *Tonquin*, later wrote that Thorn was "a strict disciplinarian, of a quick and passionate temper, accustomed to exact obedience, considering nothing but duty, and giving himself no troubles about the murmurs of his crew, taking counsel of nobody, and following Mr. Astor's instructions to the letter. Such was the man who had been appointed to command our ship."[19] While some of these traits had no doubt served Thorn well in the navy, onboard the *Tonquin* they became a recipe for disaster.

As the *Tonquin*'s departure date approached, Astor grew increasingly worried about the safety of his ship. Tensions between the United States and

Great Britain, which would soon erupt in the War of 1812, were on the rise. Astor had heard a rumor that a British warship had been dispatched from Halifax, perhaps at the urging of the North West Company, to stop the *Tonquin*, impress all of its British passengers, and thereby put an end to the expedition. To counter this perceived plot, Astor asked the commodore of the navy stationed in New York to provide an escort for the *Tonquin* so it could safely clear the coast. The commodore obliged, and placed "Old Ironsides," the U.S. frigate *Constitution*, at Astor's service.

The day before the *Tonquin* was scheduled to leave, Astor handed his partners a letter outlining what he expected of them and how they were to comport themselves during and after the voyage. He asked them to try their best to encourage "harmony and unanimity," and to discuss major decisions with the entire company and resolve any differences by a majority vote. Since so much of the expedition's ultimate success would depend on cordial or at least civil relations with the local Indians, who would be supplying most of the furs, Astor gave special attention to this issue, directing his representatives to conduct themselves in such a manner as to win over the Indians. "If you find them kind, as I hope you will, be so to them. If otherwise, act with caution and forbearance, and convince them that you come as friends." Astor furthermore warned Thorn "to be particularly careful on the coast, and not rely too much on the friendly disposition of the natives. All accidents which have as yet happened there arose from too much confidence in the Indians."[20]

THE *CONSTITUTION* ESCORTED THE HEAVILY LADEN *TONQUIN* out of New York Harbor on September 8, 1810, and with no British warship in the offing, Astor's ship was sent on its way. The troubles began almost immediately. Used to barking orders and having them instantly obeyed, Thorn quickly came to despise his passengers, whom he viewed as landlubbers and dandies. He didn't like the familiarity and lack of discipline onboard, or the voyageurs' boisterous behavior and propensity to break into song. Deriding the incessant note taking of some of the clerks, he found their "literary pretensions" and intention to publish tales of the voyage contemptible. Thorn was particularly disgusted with the partners' complaints about the food, which the captain believed was more than adequate, including an array of fresh and smoked meats. "When thwarted in their cravings for delicacies," Thorn commented, "they would exclaim that it was d———d hard they could not live as they pleased upon their own property, being on board their own ship, freighted with their own merchandise. And these are the fine fellows who made such boast that they could 'eat dogs.'" Thorn questioned the partners' masculinity and vowed never to ship out with them again "without having Fly-market on the forecastle, Covent-garden on the poop, and a cool spring from Canada in the maintop." And as for the clerks and laborers on board, Thorn labeled them the "most helpless, worthless beings 'that ever broke sea biscuit.'"[21]

Thorn's passengers, in turn, chafed under the military discipline he tried to impose on the ship. The partners were incensed with Thorn's imperious manner, since they viewed themselves as being his masters instead of the other way around. The voyageurs didn't like being chastised for singing, nor did they, the clerks, or the partners appreciate Thorn's demands that they clean their living quarters, exercise on the main deck, and extinguish all lamps at eight o'clock. When Thorn warned the partners that he would clap them in irons if they continued what he perceived to be disrespectful behavior, McDougall grabbed his pistol and threatened the captain with death if he ever carried out such a threat. McKay's concerns about the captain led him to write in his journal, "I fear we are in the hands of a maniac."[22]

No single event better exemplifies the poisonous atmosphere on the *Tonquin* than its stopover at the Falkland Islands. On December 4, 1810, crewmen—accompanied by some of the passengers who wanted to explore the island for "curiosities"—were sent ashore to fill the water casks. Although Thorn had warned them not to wander too far and to return to the ship promptly when the gun was fired, when that signal came they ignored it and didn't reboard the ship until some hours later, when they were greeted with great hostility by the infuriated captain. The *Tonquin* stopped again at another part of the Falklands on December 7, to make repairs to the ship. For four days the *Tonquin* lay at anchor, while most of the partners and a few clerks set up a tent on the nearby island and spent their time killing penguins, geese, ducks, and seals, and searching the island for the remains of French and English habitation. On the morning of December 11, McKay and David Stuart were on the far side of the island looking for game while a small group was gathering grass for the hogs and others were carving new wooden headstones to replace the worn ones that stood at the head of the graves of two long-dead Englishmen.

With the repairs completed and additional water supplies taken on, Thorn gave the order to fire one of the guns. Soon everyone but McKay and Stuart had returned to the beach, where the small boat that had taken them ashore was hauled up on the sand, and where they waited for the two partners to appear. Thorn, however, was in no mood for waiting. This was the second time his passengers had disregarded his plea, and he had had enough. He ordered the anchor weighed and the sails unfurled.

By the time McKay and Stuart arrived at the beach, the *Tonquin* was already receding from view. Dumbfounded and horrified, the eight men jumped into the boat and began rowing furiously toward the departing ship. The ship's passengers pleaded with Thorn to turn around, and one even brandished a gun and threatened to blow the captain's brains out, but he would not relent. For three and a half hours the eight men rowed into the open ocean, and only a shifting wind, which slowed the *Tonquin*'s progress, enabled them to overtake the ship and clamber back onboard.[23] Later writing to Astor about this event, Thorn claimed: "Had the wind (unfortunately) not hauled ahead soon after leaving the harbor's mouth, I should positively have left them; and, indeed, I cannot but think it an unfortunate circumstance for you that it so happened, for the first loss in this instance would, in my opinion, have proved the best, as they seem to have no idea of the value of property, nor any apparent regard for your interest, although interwoven with their own."[24]

*A*FTER A TYPICALLY BRUISING TRIP AROUND CAPE HORN, the *Tonquin* arrived at "Owyhee" on February 11, 1811. The layover lasted a little more than two weeks, and did nothing to elevate Thorn's abysmal estimation of his passengers. "To enumerate the thousand instances of ignorance, filth, etc.," Thorn wrote to Astor, "or to particularize all the frantic gambols that are daily practiced, would require volumes."[25] Still, some critical business was done. The *Tonquin*'s supplies were replenished, and twenty-two islanders were hired, half of whom were slated to service the ship, while the rest were to work for the company. With that the ship left Hawaii and reached the mouth of the Columbia on March 22, 1811.

A less cocksure man would have trembled at the sight of the treacherous, churning waters of the Columbia rushing into the sea, and would have reconsidered his course of action. But Thorn was not that man, and he ordered the first mate along with four men, three of whom were "Canadian lads unacquainted with sea service," into a whaleboat to find a way over the sandbars, which had breakers crashing all around and standing waves rising ominously toward the sky. The first mate protested that this was a deadly gambit since he was being "sent off without seamen to man [his] . . . boat, in boisterous weather, and on the most dangerous part of the Northwest Coast."[26] Thorn, enraged by the mate's temerity, told him that "if you are afraid of water, you should have remained in Boston"; then he thundered, "I command here . . . do not be a coward. Put off!"[27]

The partners pleaded with Thorn to rescind his orders, but he ignored their entreaties, swearing that a "combination was formed to frustrate his designs." Realizing that he had no choice but to obey, the tearful first mate faced the partners and said, "My uncle was drowned here not many years ago, and I am now going to lay my bones with his. Farewell, my friends! We will perhaps meet again in the next world."[28] No sooner had they pushed off than the churning waters tossed the boat about like a cork on the waves, spinning it around, hurtling it over crests and into deep troughs, and threatening to swamp or overturn it at any moment. Less than one hundred yards from the ship, the men and the boat disappeared from view, never to be seen again.

Although Thorn was shaken he was unbowed, and over the next few days he sent repeated forays to find a safe passage over the sandbars and into the broad and relatively quiet waters beyond. Three more men were lost, but finally the *Tonquin* made it across and anchored in Baker Bay near midnight on March 24. Reflecting on the disasters that had just occurred, Franchère commented: "This loss of eight of our number, in two days, before we had set foot on shore, was a bad augury, and was sensibly felt by all of us. . . . We had left New York, for the most part strangers to one another; but arrived at the river Columbia we were all friends, and regarded each other almost as brothers. . . . The preceding days had been days of apprehension and of uneasiness; this was one of sorrow and mourning."[29]

The immediate task at hand was to find a location for the post. After searching the lower reaches of the river estuary, and various coves and harbors, the partners selected Point George (now Smith Point) on the south shore of the Columbia right next to Youngs Bay. By the second week of April the men were busy with the backbreaking work of clearing the ground for and building the structures of what would be christened Fort Astoria, in honor of their employer. As the fort took shape Chinook and Clatsop Indians began their daily visits, bearing food and furs to trade, and sometimes just reconnoitering. Thorn, impatient to follow his instructions and take the *Tonquin* north on a trading expedition, finally embarked in early June, taking with him twenty- three men, including McKay who was to be the supercargo, and an Indian interpreter named Lamazu, who was engaged to join the trip along the way. Just before leaving Astoria, Thorn had gotten into a disagreement with his second mate, and ordered him to stay behind. McKay, alarmed by this turn of events, took one of the clerks aside before departing and whispered, "You see how unfortunate we are: the captain, in one of his frantic fits, has now discharged the only officer on board. If you ever see us safe back, it will be a miracle."[30]

THE *TONQUIN* ANCHORED IN CLAYOQUOT SOUND, ON THE southwestern side of Vancouver Island.[31] The local Indians were cordial at first, warmly welcoming McKay and some others onboard into their village, and giving McKay a plush bed of beautiful otter skins to sleep on at night. At the same time Indians paddled out to the ship to trade furs. All was going well until, true to form, Thorn's imperiousness got the best of him. When the tribal chief badgered Thorn to accept a particularly hard bargain, Thorn grabbed a rolled-up sea otter pelt from the chief's hands and smacked him in the face with it. Seething, the chief and his warriors departed, but they did not forget about the incident; instead they planned revenge.

A few days later the Indians returned to the *Tonquin*, seemingly peaceful and ready to trade. The crew allowed multiple canoes to offload, and soon the ship's deck was swarming with Indians, each of whom was holding a bundle of otter pelts. The sheer number of natives unnerved some of the crew, who ran to inform Thorn and McKay. When the two made it to the poop deck, Lamazu told them that he thought "some evil design was on foot," and although McKay had similar suspicions, Thorn discounted their concerns, claiming, "that with the firearms on board, there was no reason to fear even a greater number of Indians."[32] Apparently Thorn forgot or simply disregarded Astor's stern warning to not "admit more than a few [natives] on board . . . [the] ship at a time."[33] But as the throng of Indians on and around the ship continued to swell, even Thorn grew alarmed. He abruptly ordered the Indians off the ship and told his men to weigh anchor and set the sails, but it was too late. With a cue from their chief, the Indians attacked, wielding knives and war clubs they had hidden in their bundles of furs.

McKay, the first to die, was clubbed in the head and tossed alive over the side into a canoe full of Indian women, who finished him off with their paddles. Thorn, who had failed to bring his pistol from below, put up a valiant fight using a pocketknife, but after killing two of his assailants, he too was overwhelmed. Within five minutes the slaughter was nearly complete, and only five crewmen remained, one of whom was severely wounded. They withdrew to the lower deck, grabbed guns, and began shooting up the companionway, sending the Indians over the railings. The crewmen then ran to main deck and continued shooting as the Indians furiously paddled to shore.

That night the wounded crewman, realizing that he wasn't going to survive, and wanting revenge, stayed behind while the others escaped on a whaleboat. The next morning when the Indians returned, the crewman was ready. Not seeing anyone onboard, the Indians, cautiously at first and then in increasing numbers, climbed over the rails and up into the rigging until there were hundreds on the ship. At that moment the crewman lit the nine thousand pounds of gunpowder in the ship's magazine, and in an instant the *Tonquin* was blown apart, sending "arms, legs, heads and bodies, flying in every direction."[34] All told more than two hundred Indians were killed along with the crewman. The four men in the whaleboat didn't fare any better. They were finally caught by the Indians and tortured to death. The only survivor from the *Tonquin* was Lamazu, who had made it to shore during the initial melee and became a prisoner of the local tribe.

THE ASTORIANS WHO REMAINED AT THE MOUTH OF THE COLUMbia expected the *Tonquin* to return from its northern trading venture in three months' time. But as early as July word of the disaster began filtering back to the fort, and by late August the increasingly detailed reports from various Indians confirmed that the *Tonquin* and its crew were gone, with the final proof coming in early October when Lamazu, freed by his captors, told the Astorians what had happened. The Astorians were deeply depressed over the tragedy, which had greatly diminished their numbers and left them bereft of many goods and supplies that had been blown up along with the ship. But they were also on guard. As news of the *Tonquin* spread, many Indians became furious about the explosion and emboldened about the prospects of overpowering the white men, whose forces were now much reduced. The Astorians knew something was wrong when the Indians began withdrawing from the area and then stopped coming to the fort. Then, as rumors swirled of a planned Indian attack, the Astorians began enhancing the fort's defenses and performing daily drills to familiarize themselves with the use of their weapons. But McDougall, the man in charge at Astoria, realized that his small band was no match for the Indians should they stage an assault, so he staged an assault of his own—a psychological one.

McDougall invited the local chiefs to a meeting. Once they were sitting around a fire, McDougall reached into his pocket and produced a small vial. "The white men among you," said McDougall, "are few in number, it is true, but they are mighty in medicine. . . . In this bottle I hold the smallpox, safely corked up; I have but to draw the cork, and let loose the pestilence, to sweep man, woman, and child from the face of the earth!" Smallpox introduced by fur traders had ravaged the coastal Indians years earlier, and the prospect of its return terrified them. With McDougall's threat hanging over them, the chiefs promised to leave the white men alone, and thus an uneasy truce was achieved.[35]

Despite the disasters that had befallen the Astorians thus far, there was some cause for optimism. They were slowly transforming Astoria into a true fort. They built a warehouse, some dwellings, and a high picket fence, all of which formed an enclosure 90 by 120 feet, palisaded at the front and rear, and with a small cannon mounted at each corner. Using the seeds and root stocks they had brought with them, they planted a sizable garden, which was soon producing a healthy crop of potatoes and turnips, with one of the latter weighing an astonishing fifteen pounds. They used prefabricated materials that had been stowed on the *Tonquin* to build a small schooner—the first American ship ever constructed on the West Coast—and named it *Dolly* after Astor's daughter Dorothea. They had begun trading with the local Indians, and were already sending expeditions upriver to establish new posts. Thus the Astorians appeared to be on their way to establishing the fur-trading entrepôt that Astor had envisioned. But during their raucous celebrations to usher in the new year, 1812, one question was greatly troubling them—what had become of the overland expedition, which was already long overdue?[36]

ON SEPTEMBER 3, 1810, JUST A FEW DAYS BEFORE THE *TONQUIN* left New York Harbor, Pacific Fur Company partners Hunt and Mackenzie arrived in St. Louis, the jumping-off point for the overland expedition. With a large contingent of Canadian voyageurs already in their employ, they still needed more manpower before they could begin the arduous expedition. Although Astor was the most successful fur trader in America, St. Louis was still the fur-trading capital of the country, and plenty of local fur merchants and traders cast a wary eye on Astor's ambition to lay claim to the western trade. None, though, were more antagonistic than Manuel Lisa, who viewed Astor's operation as a most dangerous competitor to his beloved and beleaguered Missouri Fur Company. At every turn Lisa tried to frustrate Hunt's efforts to recruit men and gather additional supplies. While Hunt was ultimately able to get what he needed, it took him, due to Lisa's meddling, much longer than expected, leaving him woefully behind schedule. With winter fast approaching, Hunt's full-scale assault on the Missouri would have to wait until the following year. But overwintering in St. Louis was far too expensive for such a large outfit, so on October 21, Hunt led his men, some sixty strong, on three boats about five hundred miles up the Missouri to its junction with the Nodaway, where he established winter quarters just as the ice was beginning to make river travel impossible.[37]

Hunt still needed more men, especially a Sioux interpreter and more hunters, and on January 1, 1811, he headed back to St. Louis to get them, arriving toward the end of the month. During Hunt's absence Lisa had been busy. He had persuaded the partners in the Missouri Fur Company to launch an expedition up the Missouri, with two goals in mind: first, to see if they could find out what happened to Andrew Henry, who had abandoned the Three Forks in the fall of 1810 and hadn't been heard from since; and second, to monitor Hunt's expedition to keep it from taking business away from them. Thus, when Hunt got to St. Louis he was immediately forced to compete with Lisa for the best available men. Nowhere was this competition fiercer than for Pierre Dorion, Jr., the Sioux interpreter, because there was really only one person in this bustling frontier town who knew the language.

Dorion was the son of a Sioux mother and Pierre Dorion, "a shrewd, hard-twisted, semiliterate half-breed" who had served as a trapper and the Sioux interpreter for Lewis and Clark.[38] Dorion Senior had spent the better part of twenty years among the Yankton Sioux, and that is where his son had become fluent in their language—a fluency that brought Hunt to Dorion's door with an offer to join the overland expedition. But, as Hunt soon discovered, Lisa would not let Dorion go without a fight.

Just a year earlier, on his trip up the Missouri, Lisa had employed Dorion as an interpreter to help him through the notoriously unpredictable and at times dangerous bands of Teton Sioux who controlled the traffic along major sections of the river and required tribute before letting traders pass. While Dorion's interpreting skills served Lisa well, his drinking got him into trouble. At Lisa's Fort Mandan, Dorion freely indulged his love of whiskey, and since it was selling for ten dollars per quart at the company store, he quickly accumulated a hefty tab, which put him ever deeper into debt with his boss. When Lisa learned that Dorion was thinking of signing with Hunt, he became understandably furious. He did everything in his power to keep Dorion from joining the competition, including using the massive debt he had accrued as a cudgel to force Dorion to remain loyal. But it appears that this ploy only served to inflame Dorion's passions against Lisa, and after two weeks of hard bargaining Dorion decided to throw his lot with Hunt (no doubt the lavish three hundred dollars per year salary Hunt offered made Dorion's decision much easier).[39] One of the terms of Dorion's employment was that he would be allowed to take along his wife, an Iowa Indian named Marie, and their two sons, who were four and two at the time.

With Dorion and his family, as well as about a dozen other men, Hunt left St. Louis on March 12 to head back to the Nodaway camp. But Lisa remained determined to hold on to Dorion. The day after Hunt's party started upriver, Lisa obtained warrant for Dorion's arrest to force him to pay his liquor debt. Among those who heard about the warrant were John Bradbury and Thomas Nuttall, English naturalists specializing in botany who had recently signed on to join Hunt's expedition, not to work for Astor but as a means to ascend the Missouri and collect specimens. Bradbury and Nuttall had stayed in St. Louis an extra day to wait for the next mail delivery. Late that evening they were tipped off about the warrant, and also learned that officials were being dispatched the next day to bring Dorion back to face charges. To protect Dorion from capture, Bradbury and Nuttall stole out of St. Louis at two in the morning and headed upriver to get to Hunt's group before they reached St. Charles, where the officials planned to make their arrest. The two botanists caught up with Hunt just in time, and their warning sent Dorion and his family into the secure cover of the woods, where they stayed for a couple of days before rejoining the expedition just beyond St. Charles.[40]

A FEW DAYS LATER, AT THE TOWN OF LA CHARRETTE, Hunt spied an old man with a shock of white hair standing at the river's edge. He casually said to Bradbury, "That's Daniel Boone, the discoverer of Kentucky." Since Bradbury had a letter of introduction from Boone's nephew, he went ashore to speak with the famed hunter, trapper, and explorer. Boone told Bradbury that he was eighty-four years old—although he was only an entirely respectable seventy-seven—and that he had just returned from a hunting trip that yielded nearly sixty beaver pelts. After the two men parted Bradbury caught up with Hunt's boat, and the next day he, along with Hunt, visited another larger-than-life western figure, John Colter, the erstwhile member of the Corps of Discovery who had become one of Lisa's trappers.

Bradbury was on the lookout for Colter because back in St. Louis, William Clark had told him that Colter was in the area and might be able to point the young naturalist to "the place on the Missouri where the skeleton of a fish, above forty feet long, had been found." So when Hunt's group reached Boeuf Creek, and heard from a local man that Colter lived only a mile away, a meeting was quickly arranged. Although Colter knew nothing about the monster fish, he knew a great deal about western travel, and he stayed with Hunt's group for many miles, eagerly sharing his knowledge. Colter, said Bradbury, "seemed to have a strong inclination to accompany the expedition; but having been lately married, he reluctantly took leave of us."[41]

Over the next few weeks Hunt's group slowly progressed up the Missouri, battling torrential rain, strong currents, and many downed trees, which had fallen across the river after the banks beneath them gave way. By early April they had covered 240 miles, and as far as Hunt knew, his little flotilla was the only one on the river. But it wasn't: Hunt was being followed.

*A*S SOON AS HUNT LEFT ST. LOUIS, LISA STEPPED UP HIS efforts to get his own expedition under way, and finally on April 2, under sunny skies, he set off from St. Charles onboard a keelboat said to be "the best that ever ascended" the river.[42] Lisa wanted to catch up to Hunt not only to make sure he didn't steal any of the fur trade, but also because Lisa was fearful of being robbed by "the Teton Sioux," known as the "pirates of the Missouri."[43] Lisa thought that if he could join with Hunt's party before they reached the Sioux, together they would present a defense so formidable that the Indians would not attack. Thus began what some have called the greatest keelboat race ever, even though it was more pursuit than race.[44]

Lisa faced an almost insurmountable task. Hunt had a twenty-one-day head start and was more than two hundred miles upriver. But Lisa prided himself on clobbering his competitors, once telling William Clark that "I put into my operations great activity. I go a great distance while some are considering whether they will go today or tomorrow."[45] In this case, however, Lisa would have to wait until the next day before truly getting under way. Within hours of shoving off in his keelboat, and just a few miles above St. Charles, he was forced to put to shore because much of his crew of twenty-five was missing. The night before, his men, composed mainly of French Canadians and Creoles, had celebrated their departure by getting rip-roaring drunk. Many of them had yet to return to the boat. The men were in such "high glee from the liquor" that Lisa knew it was no use trying to round them up that day, so instead he let them "take their swing" and have one more night of reckless abandon. By two o'clock the next afternoon, all the men had straggled back to the boat and slept off their hangovers. The chase was on.[46]

Lisa pushed his men at a tremendous pace, leading by example. "He is," noted Henry Marie Brackenridge, an adventurous lawyer and writer who had joined Lisa's party, "at one moment at the helm, at another with the grappling iron at the bow, and often with a pole, assisting the hands in impelling the barge." They sailed, poled, and pulled their way up the rapidly rising river, swollen with spring rains, through raging currents and vicious eddies, over sandbars and submerged trees whose branches grazed the keelboat's hull, and past bloated buffalo corpses bobbing rhythmically in the water. Beyond the riverbanks the landscape, awakening from its winter slumber and cast in pastel hues of green and yellow, slowly rolled by. Oceans of grass swayed gently in the breeze. Magnificent stands of hickory, oak, cottonwood, and ash, as well as gently sloping hills and craggy limestone cliffs, could be seen in either direction. And with each mile the white man's mark on the land grew ever fainter until it virtually disappeared.

When Hunt broke up the Nodaway winter camp, about six weeks after leaving St. Louis, and headed upriver in four boats, Lisa was a little more than two hundred miles behind. Six days later, on April 27, some fur traders on the river told Lisa that Hunt was only five days ahead, news that greatly "animated" the party. But their optimism didn't last long. The men were growing weary and irritable. On May 4 some of them complained to Brackenridge, "It is impossible for us to persevere any longer in this unceasing toil, this overstrained exertion, which wears us down. We are not permitted a moment's repose; scarcely is time allowed us to eat, or to smoke our pipes. We can stand it no longer, human nature cannot bear it . . . [Lisa] has no pity on us." Still they slogged on, propelled forward by the indomitable force of the man who brooked neither pain nor exhaustion.

A couple of weeks later two fur traders descending the Missouri gave Lisa disquieting news. Hunt was still four days ahead of him, and rapidly approaching Sioux territory. To halt Hunt's progress Lisa sent one of his men and a hired Indian to take a letter overland to Hunt, asking him to wait until Lisa arrived, hoping that they might join forces. On May 24 the letter reached Hunt at the Poncas village, below the mouth of the Niobrara River. Although Hunt didn't trust Lisa and had no intention of waiting, he sent word back agreeing to do so, hoping that this ruse would encourage Lisa to slow down. Then, two days later, just as Hunt was planning to continue upriver, three trappers arrived and changed the trajectory of the expedition.[47]

Edward Robinson, John Hoback, and Jacob Reznor had been trapping with Henry on the Snake River and now were heading back to Kentucky. "But," as Bradbury commented, "on seeing us, [their] families, plantations, and all vanished; they agreed to join us, and turned their canoes adrift."[48] These three men had traveled extensively throughout the lands Hunt was about to enter, and in sharing their geographic knowledge they prompted Hunt to alter his course.

During the planning stage for the overland trek, Astor had expected his men to follow the path blazed by Lewis and Clark—up the Missouri, across the Rockies, and down the Columbia. But after discussing this scenario with various explorers, Hunt had decided to take a more southerly and suppos-edly quicker path to the Pacific, down the Yellowstone and across the moun-tains, which would also keep them farther from hostile Indians in the north, especially the Blackfeet. Upon hearing this Robinson, Hoback, and Reznor urged Hunt to shift his plans once again. Instead of taking the Yellowstone, they argued, the quickest and safest course was to abandon their boats at the Arikara villages, just above the Grand River near the northern border of present-day South Dakota, and obtain horses to travel overland through the mountains and then to the headwaters of the Columbia. Thus convinced, Hunt's group left the Poncas village midday on May 26, heading toward the Arikara.[49]

The following day Lisa arrived at the Poncas village, only to discover he had been duped. Enraged, he pushed his men to redouble their efforts to catch up, often working them through the night. During one particularly auspicious twenty-four-hour period they managed to cover seventy-five miles. But try as he might, Lisa couldn't catch Hunt before entering the Sioux country, and both he and Hunt had tense run-ins with these Indians yet came through unscathed.

The race ended one week later. It had taken Lisa sixty-one days to travel eleven hundred miles, averaging a staggering eighteen miles per day, and finally he had Hunt in his sights. Thinly veiled hostility and mutual suspicion between the two expeditions made their meeting less than amicable. Nevertheless they agreed to travel together. But only two days after they met, while the expeditions were camped by the side of the river, a fight nearly broke out. Lisa, still furious at Dorion's failure to pay his whiskey debt and his decision to sign on with Hunt, angrily confronted the interpreter; Dorion responded in kind, and then the two parted. Later on, when Lisa walked by Dorion's tent, the interpreter jumped out and repeatedly punched his erstwhile employer. With tempers raging, the two prepared to face off in a duel, and only through the coolheaded intervention of Brackenridge and Bradbury was this clash avoided.[50]

Lisa and Hunt arrived at the Arikara villages on June 12. Although Hunt wanted to leave as soon as possible, obtaining horses for his expedition of sixty-five proved exceptionally difficult. It wasn't until July 18, through trades with the Indians and Lisa, who brought in horses from his fort farther upriver, that Hunt was able to collect eighty-two animals, far fewer than he wanted. Over the next few months Hunt's party, many of whom were on foot while the horses carried the supplies, traveled west through present-day South Dakota and Wyoming, to the junction of the Hoback and Snake rivers, arriving there on September 26. Four men were left behind to trap in the area, while the rest of the expedition continued over the Teton Pass to Henry's Fort on the north fork of the Snake River.

Weary and bruised from their long, punishing journey over rocky terrain, through dense forests, and across windswept plains, Hunt's group looked upon the river as a possible answer to their prayers, thinking that it might take them to the Columbia and then to their final destination. It is clear Hunt thought so, for on October 19, his party, minus five men who stayed behind to trap beaver, boarded fifteen canoes hewn from nearby trees and pushed off into the river, leaving the horses behind in the care of two Shoshone Indians.[51]

*T*HE RIVER LOOKED PROMISING AT FIRST. THE FLOTILLA WAS making excellent time, propelled swiftly forward by the current, but then the true nature of the Snake revealed itself. Treacherous rapids and boiling eddies flipped a couple of the canoes, resulting in the loss of valuable cargo. Still, the intrepid band of explorers proceeded on what the voyageurs now called *la maudite rivière enragée*, or "the accursed mad river," portaging around particularly nasty patches of whitewater and paddling when they could.[52] Nearly 350 miles into their river journey, a canoe smashed against the rocks and one of the voyageurs drowned. They had reached a nightmarish stretch of the river dubbed Caldron Linn, described by a later traveler as an area "where the whole body of the river is confined between two ledges of rock somewhat less than 40 feet apart, and here indeed its terrific appearance beggars all description—Hecate's caldron was never half so agitated when vomiting even the most diabolical spells."[53]

It was no use continuing on the river. With food running out and the cold weather coming on, Hunt decided that their luck might improve if they split up into groups and struck out for the Pacific. The travails of these three parties make for bitter reading. Along riverbanks, across desert plains, and over mountains they trudged though snow and biting winds. They had little or no food, at times being reduced to gnawing on their moccasins and eating roasted strips of beaver skin for sustenance. At one point, while hiking along high cliffs lining the Snake River, two of the parties were unable to descend to the river because the slopes were too steep, and as a result they could not obtain water to slake their thirst, forcing them to drink their own urine. No part of their story is more amazing than that of Marie Dorion. Caring for her two- and four-year-old sons, while many months pregnant herself, she never complained. On December 30, not long after crossing an icy stream, she gave birth to a child, only to have it die in her arms eight days later. Marie's stoic fortitude gained her the admiration of her fellow travelers, and according to Hunt she was "as brave as any among" us.[54]

The first group managed to straggle into Astoria on January 18, 1812, followed on February 15 by Hunt's party and then later in May by the final group—and miraculously only three men had been lost. Although Hunt's arrival merited a celebration, replete with roasted beaver, "a genial allowance of grog," and a "grand dance," the revitalized Astorians quickly got back to work.[55] Having already established a trading outpost at the junction of the

Okanagon and Columbia rivers, they planned others. By late spring Astoria was showing signs of success, having obtained 3,500 pelts from the Indians, mostly beaver, with a smattering of sea otter, squirrel, and fox. On May 11 Astor's ship *Beaver* finally arrived with much-needed supplies and personnel, and the Astorians' spirits rose even further. It appeared that despite all the misfortune thus far, Astor's plan was going to work after all.[56]

Meanwhile, back in New York, Astor learned the *Tonquin*'s fate in the winter of 1812. He took the news calmly, even stoically, as was his temperament. When a friend expressed amazement at his lack of emotion, Astor responded, "What would you have me do? Would you have me stay at home and weep for what I cannot help?"[57] Astor had succeeded so brilliantly because he was determined to surmount obstacles instead of being stopped by them, and that is what he intended to do now. There was, however, one particularly enormous obstacle that Astor had never had to contend with before—war.

*P*RESIDENT JAMES MONROE DECLARED WAR ON GREAT BRITain on June 18, 1812. While the impressments of American seamen, along with punitive British restrictions on seaborne trade are usually cited as the primary causes of the war, the fur trade also needs to be given its due. In the years leading up to the war, the failure to enforce fully the terms of the Jay treaty contributed to rising tensions between Canadians and American fur traders. The Canadians, still seething over the concessions made by the treaty, acted as if they owned the fur trade throughout the Old Northwest as well as parts of the Louisiana Territory, extending their trading networks deep into those areas. No wonder, then, that the Canadians became incensed when American competitors continued showing up on the scene—so incensed, in fact, that the Canadians were among the strongest advocates for war, hoping that they could reclaim the valuable fur lands that the Jay treaty had, at least on paper, given away.

Many American fur traders were equally aggrieved by the Canadians' imperious behavior. They, too, added their voice to the chorus calling for war, hoping that it might finally gain them unfettered access to the western lands they thought they had already won.[58] And behind the dispute between fur traders, yet inevitably entwined with it, was the broader and more momentous issue of Indian relations. The British were making alliances with the Indians. They armed some of the western tribes in an effort to stem the advancing tide of Americans, an end that would also, of course, benefit the Canadian fur trade. Some of those Indians, in turn, used their newly acquired arms to attack American settlements, and many Americans were convinced that the British were instigating those attacks. Such behavior, even more than any concerns about access to furs, inflamed the anger of the frontier states and only intensified to the drumbeat for war.[59]

Astor, too, was upset that the Canadians were taking American furs. But he opposed the war because he knew that it would not only cut off his supply of British goods, which were so important to the Indian trade, but also keep his furs from getting to Great Britain. Once the war came, however, Astor didn't bemoan his predicament; rather he focused his energies on saving Astoria. By late 1812 Astor was hearing through back channels that the North West Company was urging the British government to destroy Astoria, and that if the government failed to act, the company was prepared to take matters into its own hands. To avoid either outcome, Astor wrote to James Monroe, then secretary of state, in February 1813, apprising him of the situation and asking that the United States government send "forty or fifty men" to Astoria, who could, "with the aid of the men already there, repel any [British] force." To make his request more compelling, Astor implied that if America wanted to claim the country in and around Astoria, it would be well served to save the "infant establishment" from being overrun. And finally Astor promised that he would send his own additional reinforcements as soon as possible.[60]

Monroe ignored Astor's plea, frustrating but not deterring the fur tycoon. If the government wasn't going to do anything, he, a financial titan by this time, would. Astor knew that with the onset of hostilities, British men-of-war would be cruising the oceans to capture any American ship that dared leave port, but he was not so easily cowed. His Astorians were in jeopardy, and he was going to help them, the British navy be damned. So Astor outfitted the *Lark*, a stout merchantman, and sent it to Astoria in March of 1813 to resupply the outpost, collect the warehoused furs, and then sell them in China. In the end, however, it wasn't the British navy but a fierce hurricane off Hawaii that terminated the *Lark*'s mission, leaving the ship wrecked and five men dead.

A few weeks after the *Lark* sailed, Astor learned that the North West Company had sent another memorial to the British government asking for aid in destroying Astoria, and further that the government had responded favorably by sending ships to carry out the plan. With this alarming information, Astor wrote to Monroe once again, warning him of the impeding blow. This time the response was swift. President Madison ordered the frigate *Adams*, docked in New York, into action to protect Astoria, and while this ship was being readied, Astor began fitting out his own merchant ship to accompany the *Adams* and resupply the fort.

At this time Astor received information from the Astorians that buoyed his spirits. A small contingent, headed by Robert Stuart, had been dispatched from Astoria in June 1812, to travel east and update Astor on the post's progress. They arrived in St. Louis on April 30, 1813, after an amazing cross-country trek. The *Missouri Gazette* trumpeted their return, focusing particular attention on the route taken: "By information received from these gentlemen, it appears that a journey across the continent of North America, might be performed with a wagon, there being no obstruction in the whole route that any person would dare to call a mountain." Not only that, but Stuart's route appeared to be largely devoid of Indians, who might "interrupt" the trip. As a result this new route was claimed to be much better than the more northerly route to the Pacific taken by Lewis and Clark, which posed "almost insurmountable barriers."[61]

Although neither the newspaper nor its readers could know it at the time, Stuart's route, with one minor alteration, would become one of the most storied paths in American history. As the historian William H. Goetzmann observed, "With the exception of the detour to Jackson Hole, [Stuart's group] . . . had located and traversed what became the Oregon Trail. The most important features they had discovered were the South Pass across the mountains around the southeast end of the Wind River Mountains, and the Sweetwater River route to the Platte, which they followed across the plains. The South Pass became the 'great gate' through which hundreds of thousands of immigrants poured on their way west."[62]

Astor was less interested in the route than in finding out what was happening in Astoria. Before Stuart's return the only thing he knew for sure was that the *Tonquin* had been blown up and its crew massacred. In contrast the letter that Stuart sent to Astor immediately upon arriving in St. Louis, painted a "flattering" picture of the progress at the mouth of the Columbia, which Astor claimed made him "ready to fall upon my knees in a transport of gratitude."[63] But his joy proved fleeting. Just as the *Adams* and Astor's merchant ship were ready to depart, the exigencies of war intervened. Cmdr. Isaac Chauncy, whose small squadron was harassing the British on Lake Ontario, called for more men, which included the crew of the *Adams*. This resulted in the frigate being laid up along the docks of New York, thus dashing Astor's hopes of reinforcing and resupplying Astoria. This crushing blow was bad enough, but if Astor knew what was taking place a continent away he would have been even more depressed.

WHEN ASTOR'S SUPPLY SHIP, THE *BEAVER*, DEPARTED ASTORIA in August 1812, with Hunt onboard, the plan had been for it to go to the Russian fur-trading post at Sitka, trade for furs, and then return to Astoria within a few months' time. Instead, Hunt didn't return for an entire year. This lengthy delay resulted from a disastrous comedy of errors. When Hunt arrived in Sitka, the Russians had no furs on hand, and Hunt was told to go to the Pribilof Islands to get them. Hunt did, and along the way the *Beaver* was nearly demolished in a storm. Hunt wanted to head back to Astoria, then go on to Canton to sell the furs, but since winter was fast approaching, he thought the heavily damaged *Beaver* might not survive the stormy seas off the Northwest Coast, so Hunt took the *Beaver* to Hawaii for repairs. After the repairs were completed, Hunt ordered the captain, Cornelius Sowle, to go to Canton to sell the furs, while Hunt waited in Hawaii for one of Astor's resupply ships to take him back to Astoria. When Sowle arrived in Canton, a letter from Astor was waiting for him. It told of the outbreak of war and ordered Sowle to set sail immediately so that he could share that vital intelligence with the Astorians. Sowle wrote to Astor that he would do no such thing, and instead planned to stay in Canton until peace was declared.

Meanwhile Hunt faced a different problem. He desperately wanted to get back to Astoria, but remained stranded in Hawaii because Astor's resupply ship never showed up. It wasn't until June 20, 1813, that the *Albatross* arrived at Hawaii, bearing the first news of the war to reach the islands, information that made Hunt even more determined to get back to Astoria. So he chartered *Albatross* for two thousand dollars, loaded it with food and other goods, and sailed with it across the Pacific, arriving at the mouth of the Columbia on August 20, 1813. As he soon discovered, Astoria had not fared well during his yearlong absence.[64]

THROUGHOUT THE FALL AND WINTER OF 1812 THE ASTORIANS had waited in vain for the *Beaver*'s return. A gloom had settled over the fort, as McDougall, who was in charge in Hunt's absence, and the others began to fear that the ship had been lost at sea or attacked by Indians. Then, at the end of January 1813, John George McTavish, a partner of the North West Company, who was trading in the area, informed the Astorians not only that war had broken out but also that, come March, a British naval ship would arrive on the coast to take over Astoria, and that McTavish and his men were supposed to be on hand to meet the ship.[65]

With the *Beaver* apparently never coming back and there being no expectation that the U.S. Navy would come to the aid of Astoria, McDougall and Mackenzie decided to abandon the post and return to St. Louis. As they began preparing to leave, McTavish and his men arrived. Since it was early April, McTavish expected to see the British naval ship already in control of the post, but the ship wasn't there. So McTavish, who was cordially greeted by his fellow Canadians McDougall and Mackenzie, stayed in Astoria waiting patiently for the ship to arrive. Months passed, and still no ship.

In late June, McDougall called a meeting of all the partners, and although some of them argued strenuously against abandoning Astoria, in the end all agreed it was the best available option.[66] By the time this decision had been reached, however, it was too late in the year to begin a trek over the Rockies, so McDougall and McTavish cut a deal. They would both remain in the area, split the fur trade between them, and then, the following spring, the Americans would leave. With this agreement McTavish and his men headed to their post in Spokane, while the Astorians stayed put.

Then, on August 20, the *Albatross* hove into view. Hunt, alarmed by the Astorians' dealings, wanted to reverse the decision to abandon the post but couldn't because the other partners would not change their minds. Still, there were Mr. Astor's interests to be considered, and Hunt decided that the best he could do on that account was to get a ship to transport Astoria's furs to Canton so that some profit from the venture could be realized. The *Albatross*, the most likely candidate, could not make the voyage because it was already engaged to go to the Marquesas Islands in the South Pacific, and then head to Hawaii. Undaunted, Hunt departed on the *Albatross*, and when it finally pulled into Hawaii four months later, Hunt hired a brig called the *Pedlar* and left for Astoria on January 22, 1814.[67]

*W*HILE HUNT WAS TRAVERSING THE PACIFIC IN SEARCH OF Astoria's salvation, the British arrived in force. The first wave came in early October 1813, when ten canoes carrying McTavish and seventy-four men from the North West Company pulled up in front of Astoria. McTavish informed the Astorians that a British warship would soon be there, and that its orders were to "annihilate" the American post. After letting this sink in McTavish bought Astoria's entire supply of furs and trade goods for a fraction of what they were worth.[68] As part of the sale the Astorians were given the option of joining the North West Company, or, if they chose not to, they would be afforded safe passage east, back to American territory.

The second and final wave of British forces arrived on the *Racoon*, captained by William Black, at the mouth of the Columbia on November 30. Black, who had been eagerly anticipating his triumphant capture of Fort Astoria, was deeply disappointed when he discovered that the North West Company had already purchased his prize. In fact it wasn't much of a prize at all. "Is this the fort about which I have heard so much?" Black queried. "Damn me, but I'd batter it down in two hours with a four pounder!"[69] Nevertheless, on December 13, Black formally took control of Fort Astoria and renamed it Fort George.

By the time Hunt arrived back at Astoria on February 28, 1814, it was too late for him to do much of anything. The sale had been made, and many of the Canadians whom Astor had employed had by now switched allegiance to the North West Company, including McDougall, who had signed on as a partner. Hunt tried to retrieve the furs, but the only deal McDougall offered was to sell them for a much-inflated price, which Hunt was unwilling to match. After recovering the Pacific Fur Company's notebooks, Hunt boarded the *Pedlar* on April 3 and sailed for New York. Then next day those Astorians who had not joined the North West Company—ninety in number—headed out in ten canoes up the Columbia, beginning their journey back east.[70]

*O*N APRIL 17 THE DEPARTING ASTORIANS WERE NOT FAR FROM the mouth of the Walla Walla River when three Indian canoes pushed off from the shore and gave chase. The Astorians, unsure of their pursuers' intentions, continued paddling, but then they heard a child's voice screaming in French, imploring them to stop, which they did, making for the nearest bank. When the Indians pulled in, the Astorians recognized three of the passengers in one of the canoes. It was Marie Dorion, the wife of the interpreter, Pierre Dorion, and her two boys. She had a tragic tale to tell.

During the summer of 1813 John Reed, one of Astoria's clerks, led a party to the Snake River to trap beaver. He took with him six men, including Pierre Dorion, who, as was his custom, was joined by his wife and children. In the fall one of the men died after being thrown from a horse, and another deserted. But soon thereafter the ranks of Reed's party swelled with the arrival of Robinson, Hoback, and Reznor, who had been trapping in the area. As winter approached, the party split up. Reed built a log cabin on the Snake, where he and four men remained. The rest—a Canadian named Gilles Le Clerc, along with Reznor, Dorion, and Dorion's family—traveled for five days to a spot that was known to be rich with beaver, where they built a hut. There the men spent the days trapping, while Marie and her two boys stayed at the hut, dressing the skins the men brought in and preparing their meals.

One day in early January 1814, Le Clerc arrived at the hut, bloodied and barely able to stand. Just before dying he told Marie that Indians had attacked him and the others, and that her husband and Reznor were dead. Fearing that the Indians would soon come for her, Marie grabbed some provisions, bundled up her boys, and placed them on one horse while she mounted another. She headed for Reed's cabin on the Snake, hoping to warn him that he was in danger. But she was too late. The cabin was deserted, and the blood-spattered ground was proof enough that Reed and the others had been killed.

Marie immediately headed northwest, toward the Columbia, but the deep snow in the Blue Mountains was impassable. Marie knew that her only chance was to try to survive until the weather turned. So she and her boys hunkered down in a shallow ravine, where they hollowed out a snow cave and pieced together a crude shelter out of bark, branches, twigs, and covered it with the few animal skins she had brought with her. The two horses were soon sacrificed for food, and their skins were added to the shelter to provide more protection from the biting cold.

By mid-March, her food nearly gone and the snows starting to melt, Marie led her boys over the mountains to the Columbia, where the Walla Walla Indians took them in. Marie knew that the Astorians had planned to head back home in the spring, so she waited, hoping that their canoes would soon pass by, which they did on April 17, when the cries of one her boys led to their reunion. The Astorians gave the Indians some presents "to repay their care and pains," and then took Marie and her boys to a nearby Canadian fur-trading post before continuing on their journey.[71]

*T*HE *NEW-YORK GAZETTE AND GENERAL ADVERTISER* PROVIDED a terse obituary for Astoria on November 12, 1814, noting, "The firm of the Pacific Fur Company is dissolved." A few months earlier, when Astor first began getting reports telling of the enormity of what had happened to his "infant establishment," he wrote to a colleague, "Was there ever an undertaking of more merit, of more honor and more enterprising, attended with a greater variety of misfortune?"[72] Astor's sense of loss was made bitterer by what he perceived to be McDougall's treachery. Astor was convinced that McDougall had colluded with the North West Company men and as a result had sold out too cheaply, and that for his duplicity he was richly rewarded by being offered a partnership stake in the company.[73] McDougall vehemently denied these charges, claiming that given the powerful forces arrayed against him, he had gotten Astor the best deal possible. Whether Astor or McDougall was correct, Astoria was now in Canadian hands. Nevertheless Astor was not ready to let it go. "While I breathe & so long as I have a dollar to spend," Astor wrote to one of his former partners, "I'll pursue a course to have our injuries repaired. . . . We have been sold, but I do not despond."[74]

*T*HE TREATY OF GHENT, ENDING THE WAR OF 1812, WAS SIGNED on December 24, 1814. Article 1 of the treaty required that "All territory, places, and possessions whatsoever taken by either party from the other during the war . . . shall be restored without delay."[75] Astor took this as good news, writing to his nephew in March 1815, "By the peace we shall have a right to Columbia River & I rather think, that I shall again engage in that business."[76] But the debate between the United States and Great Britain over the status of Astoria dragged on for years. The Americans, with Astor pushing behind the scenes, argued that Astoria had been captured as a prize of war by Captain Black and therefore must be returned. The British, however, claimed that the sale of Astoria, which had taken place prior to Black's arrival, meant that the Canadians were entitled to the post.

By late 1817 it looked as if Astor's wish was finally going to be fulfilled. That is when President James Monroe sent the USS *Ontario* to the mouth of the Columbia "to assert the claim of the United States to the sovereignty of the adjacent country, in a friendly and peaceable manner, and without the employment of force."[77] As a courtesy Monroe sent Astor a letter informing him of the voyage and its purpose. This news, however, did not bring Astor any joy.

He had already determined not to reestablish Astoria, because the government had refused his request to deploy military troops to protect the post. Without such protection Astor didn't think that his traders would be able to stand up to the Canadian traders in the area, who had already shown in their dealings with one another a willingness to resort to violence to secure their access to furs. In other words, even if the U.S. government asserted its claim of sovereignty to the area, Astor wasn't coming back. Instead he would focus his energies on other ventures.[78]

The intricacies of the diplomatic ballet between the United States and Great Britain, which ensued after the *Ontario* left on its mission, are irrelevant here. In the end the two parties concluded that Astoria should be restored to the United States, and on October 6, 1818, the Union Jack flying above Fort George was lowered, and replaced with the Stars and Stripes. But this restoration was merely symbolic. The employees of the North West Company were allowed to remain in the fort, and less than two weeks later the Canadians received the equivalent of a long-term lease to the post when Great Britain and the United States signed the Convention of 1818, in which it was agreed that "all territories and their waters, claimed by either power, west of the Rocky Mountains, should be free and open to the vessels, citizens, and subjects, of both for the space of ten years."[79] The Canadians, who quickly rehoisted the Union Jack after the American envoy had left, weren't going anywhere.

Although Astor's Fort Astoria was a failure, it would later gain a measure of immortality and fame through the publication in 1836 of Washington Irving's *Astoria: or, Enterprise Beyond the Rocky Mountains*. Irving, already one of the most famous American writers of the day, and author of the wildly popular short stories, "The Legend of Sleepy Hollow" and "Rip Van Winkle," was one of Astor's friends. When Astor suggested to Irving that he write a history of the Astorian enterprise, he got right to work. "It occurred to me," Irving wrote in the introduction to the book, "that a work of this kind might comprise a variety of those curious details, so interesting to me, illustrative of the fur trade; of its remote and adventurous enterprises, and of the various people, and tribes, and castes, and characters, civilized and savage, affected by its operations."[80] While it is reasonable to assume that Irving's friendship with Astor influenced his interpretation much to Astor's advantage, *Astoria* nevertheless provided its many readers with a fascinating depiction of one of the most memorable passages in the entire history of the American fur trade.

*T*HE WAR OF 1812 WASN'T A COMPLETE DISASTER FOR ASTOR. While it crushed his aspirations in the Pacific Northwest, he still managed to get a few of his ships loaded with furs off to Europe and China. Other American fur traders were not so resourceful, and as a result their businesses greatly diminished. After the war Astor, with the deepest pockets and a fervent desire to control as much of the fur trade as possible, was the first into the field, and he quickly expanded his operations in the Old Northwest, hiring a small army of traders and establishing new posts. His efforts were given an enormous boost on April 29, 1816, when Congress passed an act for which he—ironically, as an immigrant himself—lobbied, excluding foreigners from participating in the fur trade in the United States unless they were employed by American traders.

Astor's position was further strengthened by the Convention of 1818, which established the forty-ninth parallel from Lake of the Woods, in present-day northern Minnesota, to the Rocky Mountains as the northern border of the United States. Astor used these new political realities to tighten his grip on the trade in and around the Great Lakes and the upper Mississippi. He bought out the Canadian fur-trading companies that had been operating in United States territories south of the forty-ninth parallel, and then hired hundreds of suddenly unemployed British traders and French voyageurs to work for him. From hubs at Mackinac and Detroit, Astor's small army of trading brigades, consisting of scores of men and from five to twenty bateaux overflowing with goods, ranged throughout the region. As a result Astor's American Fur Company became unimaginably lucrative, bringing in hundreds of thousands of dollars annually. And driving much of Astor's success was the revitalization of European and American markets after the war, and the resurgence of beaver hats, along with other furs, once again valued for the comfort and social distinction they provided discriminating consumers.[81]

While Astor was dominating the fur trade of the Old Northwest, the St. Louis traders were having a more difficult time rebounding from the ravages of war. Lacking the extraordinary financial resources and commercial connections that Astor possessed, the St. Louis traders only haltingly reestablished their presence on the Missouri. Even the redoubtable Lisa faced obstacles resurrecting his beloved Missouri Fur Company, and when he died on August 12, 1820, his company was still relatively small. Nevertheless there was little doubt that the Missouri was going to play a major role in the future of America's fur trade. By virtue of the discoveries of Lewis and Clark and the ventures of Lisa and other fur traders, everyone knew that the Missouri was teeming with beavers. And in 1822 one man decided he was going to get them.

—12—

Mountain Men

An Old-Time Mountain Man with His
Ponies, *by Frederic Remington, 1888.*

WILLIAM HENRY ASHLEY WAS IN FINANCIAL FREEFALL BY the early 1820s. Some two decades earlier, as a young man, he left Virginia, settling in Ste. Genevieve, a small French community on the banks of the Mississippi, about fifty miles south of St. Louis. Over the years Ashley had manufactured gunpowder, mined lead, speculated in real estate, and joined the militia—rising to the rank of brigadier general. He had even been elected lieutenant governor of the Missouri Territory, on the eve of its becoming a state in 1821. But Ashley's expenditures often outpaced his income, and some of his investments went bust, leaving him deeply in debt. Ashley's financial problems were especially serious because he had finally decided to pursue a career in politics, and, even in the early nineteenth century, a prospective politician needed considerable capital. The question was where it would come from. Ashley turned to furs. Despite his financial predicament, he had a solid reputation, which he used to secure the funds to launch a fur-trading company with Andrew Henry, a man Ashley had been friends with as far back as 1804, when they were partners in a mining operation.[1]

Ashley placed the following advertisement in the *Missouri Gazette & Public Advertiser* on February 13, 1822: "To enterprising young men. The subscriber wishes to engage ONE HUNDRED MEN to ascend the Missouri River to its source, there to be employed for one, two, or three years—For the particulars enquire of Major Andrew Henry, near the lead mines in the county of Washington, (who will ascend with, and command the party) or to the subscriber near St. Louis."[2] Although the ad didn't mention the nature of the employment, anyone who read it would know it involved the fur trade. After all, next to New York City, St. Louis was the nation's most important fur-trading hub. Henry, who had earned his bona fides as one of Lisa's partners in the Missouri Fur Company, was already a legendary figure in the trade. And the only thing of value that could lure "enterprising young men" to leave home and "ascend the Missouri" for years at a time was the prospect of riches in the form of lustrous beaver pelts. Also, since Ashley and Henry had been planning the expedition for months, rumors of its purpose had been circulating among would-be adventurers for some time.[3]

In short order 150 men signed on, many of them already trappers. A gentleman who had done much of the recruiting for Ashley, in "grog shops and other sinks of degradation," said he could not offer a good description of the crew thus assembled, but remarked that "a Falstaff's battalion was genteel in comparison."[4] The terms of their employment were unique. Instead of being *engagés* (salaried employees), these men were to be paid solely in furs. In exchange for providing the trappers with outfits, the company expected the men to help build and defend trading posts and turn over half the furs they collected, with the other half being their compensation.[5]

By early April the expedition was on its way upriver to a region reputed to "possess a wealth of furs not surpassed by the mines of Peru."[6] One of the most influential newspapers of the day, the Baltimore-based *Niles' Weekly Register*, reflected on the expedition's departure, noting that the men "are described to be of vigorous and masculine appearance, well armed, and prepared for a three years' tour through this almost unknown and savage country. . . . If they are successful, [the expedition] will not only be very profitable to themselves, but a great national benefit, in laying the foundation for an extensive fur trade, and proving to the effeminate sons who remain at home, that activity is the true source of wealth and greatness."[7]

High hopes notwithstanding, the company's first two years were marked by tragedy and failure. Ten thousand dollars' worth of supplies were lost when a keelboat sank to the muddy bottom of the Missouri. Attacks by the Blackfeet and Arikara killed more than twenty men, and perhaps as many or more deserted. Although a fort had been established at the mouth of the Yellowstone, and trapping parties had fanned out in various directions, the haul of beaver was nothing close to what had been expected. By late 1824 the company's prospects were bleak, as were Ashley's. Between trips to resupply his men, Ashley had lost his bid to become governor, his line of credit had been drastically depleted, and worst of all, Henry, the company's most skilled trapper and leader, announced his retirement, leaving Ashley to soldier on alone. Rather than give up, Ashley, ever an optimist, branched out in a new direction. One of the company's trapping parties had traveled over the continental divide at South Pass to the Green River Valley, where they found a bonanza of beaver. When word of this find reached Ashley in the summer of 1824, he decided to forsake the upper Missouri and head into the Rockies.[8]

Later that fall Ashley led a supply train and twenty-five trappers out of Fort Atkinson, at the eastern edge of present-day Nebraska, heading toward the Green River valley. The journey was plagued by brutal cold, slicing winds, a scarcity of firewood, and snows so deep that at times the only way the men could advance was to follow the paths made by wandering buffalo herds. But with the kindly assistance of local Pawnee, who not only offered the party valuable advice on the best trails to take but also sold them horses to replace those that had died, Ashley and his men arrived in the valley on April 19, 1825.[9]

He split his men into small groups and sent them into the mountains to trap beaver. Before they departed Ashley told them that they were to rendezvous that July at a location along the Green, which he would select. They would know where to go because he would leave markers for them to follow. As planned, the rendezvous took place on July 1, on Henry's Fork about twenty miles from its junction with the Green.[10] Ashley surveyed the 120 men gathered before him—including 29 who had defected from the Hudson's Bay Company—with a measure of pride. They had, he observed, "been scattered over the territory west of the mountains in small detachments from the 38th to the 44th degree of latitude, and the only injury" they had sustained was the loss of seventeen horses, stolen by a band of Crow, and the death of one man who had been killed "on the headwaters of the Rio Colorado, by a party of Indians unknown."[11] Ashley resupplied his men, collected his furs, and headed back east on July 2 with a small group, while the rest of his men remained in the mountains to continue trapping. He arrived back in St. Louis with roughly one hundred packs of beaver valued at fifty thousand dollars (each pack included sixty pelts and weighed about one-hundred pounds).

Flush with this success Ashley led another supply train back into the mountains the following summer, meeting his men at the second rendezvous, which was held at the south end of the Cache Valley, near present-day Logan, Utah. This gathering was even more profitable than the first, with Ashley returning to St. Louis with about 125 packs worth sixty thousand dollars. Having reclaimed his solvency and built up a sizable campaign war chest, Ashley sold his interest in the company to three of his best trappers, Jedediah Smith, David Jackson, and William Sublette. Ashley continued in the fur business as a supplier of trading goods to his former company, but he was already switching gears, settling into married life in his St. Louis mansion and turning most of his attention to his first love, politics. Finally, in 1831, after Missouri congressman Spencer Pettis was killed in a duel, Ashley got his chance, winning election to the vacant seat, which he held for two more terms.[12]

Although Ashley's tenure as the leader of his company was relatively brief, he is properly considered a giant in the history of the fur trade. The rendezvous system, whereby men stayed in or near the Rockies year round and met each summer at predetermined locations to sell their furs and purchase supplies from company representatives, remained a fixture of the Rocky Mountain trade until 1840. The overland trail the companies used to supply these annual gatherings spanned more than one thousand miles. Beginning at various jumping-off points in western Missouri, including Westport, Independence, and St. Joseph, the trail traced a path along the Missouri, Platte, North Platte, and Sweetwater rivers, and then over the gently rolling South Pass, into the Green River valley, and beyond.[13] All the rendezvous were held west of the continental divide, with most being located in present-day Wyoming, and a smaller number in Utah and Idaho. Hundreds and at times more than a thousand people gathered at the rendezvous, including trappers, clerks, fur company officials, and Indians intent on trade, creating transient villages that lasted days, weeks, or sometimes more than a month. The men who stayed in the wilderness year after year and attended the rendezvous became known as mountain men, a unique breed who were in form and function distantly related to the French coureurs de bois and the Dutch *boschlopers*, and directly descended from trappers such as Colter, Drouillard, Robinson, Hoback, and Reznor.[14]

*M*OUNTAIN MEN WERE EITHER HIRED BY ONE OF THE many fur companies operating in the Rockies, or they were free trappers.[15] Akin to an indentured servant, the hired trapper was paid a set wage and outfitted by the company. In return he performed the chores required to maintain the trappers' camp, and was obliged to bring his employer as many beaver pelts as possible. There were also free trappers who received their outfit from the company but no wages, and were required to sell their pelts to the company at a predetermined price. But the most storied characters in the trapper's fraternity were the truly free trappers who set their own course, answering to nobody. As the mountain man Joseph Meek observed, the "genuine free trapper regarded himself as greatly the superior of either of the foregoing classes. He had his own horses and accoutrements, arms and ammunition. He took what route he thought fit, hunted and trapped when and where he chose; traded with the Indians; sold his furs to whoever offered highest for them; dressed flauntingly, and generally had an Indian wife and half-breed children."[16]

Between 1825 and 1840, the span that most historians define as the era of the mountain men, there were likely no more than three thousand men who pursued this trade.[17] Most of them where relatively young, in their late teens, twenties, or thirties, and hailed from Missouri, Kentucky, Virginia, and Canada, while a smaller number came from other areas throughout the United States. Mountain men were overwhelmingly white, but there were also some Indians, black men, and métis, the latter of which were descendants of European and French Canadian fathers and Indian mothers—métis being the French word for a person of mixed blood.[18] Often bred away from cities and towns, in relatively unsettled areas where homesteaders and farmers labored to eke out a subsistence living, mountain men were usually quite familiar with the perils and promise of life on the edge of the wild. Forced to confront a lawless world, where violence lurked at every bend, they were skilled in the use of guns and horses. And because their success depended almost entirely on their own initiative, they were exceedingly self-reliant and resourceful.

Their harsh lifestyle notwithstanding, more than 80 percent of mountain men were married, and roughly 33 percent married Indian women, occasionally more than one at a time.[19] The marriages to Indians—or "country marriages," as they were called—were usually the result of trades in which the mountain man offered the bride-to-be's father an array of goods, or perhaps a horse, in exchange for his daughter. The western artist Alfred Jacob Miller described one such deal in which the trapper paid a total of six hundred dollars in the "legal tender of . . . [the] region," including "guns $100 each, blankets $40 each, red flannel $20 per yard, alcohol $64 per gallon," as well as tobacco, beads, and other items at varying rates.[20] Once the exchange was made, the Indian wife became, as another contemporary observer noted, "the absolute personal property of the enamored jockey, subject to be re-sold whenever the state of the market and his own affection will allow."[21]

Despite the rather cold mercantile nature of these unions and the treatment of Indian women as chattel, often country marriages were strong and caring, lasting for many years and producing multiple children. More than just providing companionship and offspring, Indian wives were critical to their husbands' success, serving as translators and guides, preparing food, dressing the pelts for trade, and helping to manage the camps that mountain men used as home base during their forays into the wilderness. And these marriages created strong bonds between the mountain men and their wives' tribes, which smoothed the way for trade and military alliances.[22]

Formal education was not a prerequisite for life in the mountains, and a significant number of mountain men had little or no schooling, yet for the most part they were far from ignorant. There were some who brought books with them into the wilderness and kept extensive and well-written journals, a number of which were published.[23] One trapper, whose reading material included Shakespeare, Byron, and various works on geology, chemistry, and philosophy, fondly recalled the "long winter evenings" when the men would gather in one of the larger lodges and convene "The Rocky Mountain College," where they would debate the issues of the day.[24] Another trapper claimed that he and his peers "had an abundance of reading matter with us; old mountain men were all great readers. It was always amusing to me to hear people from the East speak of old mountaineers as semi-barbarians, when as a general rule they were the peers of the Easterners in general knowledge."[25]

Various motivations lured men into the mountains to trap. Some were looking for adventure, others wanted to escape from the strictures of civilization or were unable to find another line of work, and no doubt a few were eager to outrun the law. But there was one motivation that virtually all mountain men had in common—they wanted to earn a living, and if possible a good one; they were, as one historian put it, "expectant capitalists."[26] As the mountain man Zenas Leonard commented, "When we first embarked in this business it was with the expectation that to ensure a fortune in the fur trade only required a little perseverance and industry."[27] No matter what had brought them to the mountains, many mountain men fell in love with the freedom and untrammeled beauty of their new life, preferred it greatly to the stultifying lives they had left behind, and as a result never left the West.[28]

RUFUS B. SAGE, WHO SPENT THREE YEARS TRAVELING with mountain men, concluded that "a genuine mountaineer is a problem hard to solve. He seems a kind of *sui genus,* an oddity, both in dress, language, and appearance, from the rest of mankind. . . . His skin, from constant exposure," was deeply tanned, "and his features and physical structure attain a rough and hardy cast." Often his hair was long and unkempt, and his face covered with a bushy beard and mustache, but many mountain men took their grooming quite seriously, cutting their hair regularly and having only a well-trimmed mustache or no facial hair at all.[29] When the trapper first ventured west, he brought with him clothes made of wool or cotton, and after those wore out he exchanged them for typical buckskin garments, which were made not only from male deer but also from buffalo, elk, otters, and antelope. Even when buckskin was the mountain man's main covering, he would often supplement it with cloth undershirts or coats purchased at the rendezvous. A crude wool or leather hat adorned the mountain man's head, leather moccasins covered his feet, and a leather belt cinched around his waist held his knife and pistols. His bullet pouch, powder horn, and bullet-making tools were thrown over his shoulder, along with the felicitously named "possibles bag," which held, among other items, flints, pipes, tobacco, razors, and a container of bear-grease pomade to slick back his hair. Many mountain men also owned a large pouch similar to a present-day expandable file or suitcase, called a parfleche, which was made of rawhide and could carry dried meat and extra clothes and moccasins. And the picture of the fully equipped mountain man would not be complete without a rifle slung across the saddle or resting comfortably in his hands, a sack of beaver traps, an epishemore, which was a blanket or buffalo robe used as a cushion under a saddle and as bedding at night, and a trusty, sure-footed horse or mule ready to take the mountain man wherever he wanted to go.[30]

Contrary to the romanticized image of the lone trapper, mountain men rarely traveled singly, but instead formed brigades of up to sixty men, which provided not only safety in numbers but also camaraderie. The mountain man's year followed a fairly routine pattern. The fall months up until the rivers froze over were spent catching beaver, during which time the men would spread out, usually in pairs, from the brigade's base camp to trap the area's waterways.[31] As the cold set in the men gathered together at their winter quarters. This was when, Meek wrote, "the mountain-man 'lived fat' and enjoyed life: a season of plenty, of relaxation, of amusement, of acquaintanceship with all the company, of gayety, and of 'busy idleness.' Through the day, hunting parties were coming and going, men were cooking, drying meat, making moccasins, cleaning their arms, wrestling, [and] playing games. . . . With their Indian allies, their native wives, and numerous children, the mountaineers' camp was a motley assemblage."[32] When the warmer weather returned, and the rivers were running free once again, the mountain men fanned out to trap. And then, come summer, it was on to the rendezvous.

Before arriving at the rendezvous the mountain men first visited what they called caches, underground hiding places, to retrieve their belongings. These buried vaults were necessary during the trapping season when the sheer bulk of the furs and other materials the mountain man had collected were too great to be carried in tow. The caches solved this problem by serving as a kind of temporary Rocky Mountain storage container, whose construction required considerable skill. The first challenge involved selecting a dry place, and then the men would start digging. The conical chamber, as deep as seven feet, was lined with grass and twigs. The trappers filled it full of furs and other supplies and then covered it over, great care being taken to return the ground to its former appearance so that nobody else would know the location.[33]

Various western geographic features with "cache" in their name, including rivers, streams, junctions, valleys, and mountains, got that appellation because they were favorite places for mountain men to dig these vaults. But in the case of Cache Valley, Utah, there was also a more macabre reason. In the early 1830s some mountain men were preparing a cache in this area, which was then known as Willow Valley. When the excavation was nearly completed, a wall of the chamber collapsed, burying one of the men alive. As the mountain man Warren Angus Ferris later recalled, the man's companions "*believed* him to have been instantly killed, *knew* him to be well buried, and the cache destroyed, and therefore left him unknelled, uncoffined, ne'er to rise, till Gabriel's trumpet shakes the skies, and accomplished their object elsewhere. It was a heartless, cruel procedure, but serves to show how lightly human life is held in these distant wilds."[34] Thus Willow Valley became Cache Valley. Despite the best efforts of their builders, caches were sometimes ruined due to water seepage, dug up by animals, or ransacked by Indians or fellow trappers. And many caches, so meticulously constructed and well concealed, were never exhumed, either because the trapper forgot where he had hidden his handiwork or died without revealing its location to anyone alse.[35]

THE SUMMER RENDEZVOUS WAS THE HIGH POINT OF THE MOUNtain man's year. The main order of business was settling accounts. The trappers traded beaver pelts, also referred to as "hairy bank notes," to the fur company representatives to obtain the supplies and equipment they would need until the next rendezvous. They also bartered pelts for liquid amusement, usually in the form of whiskey. And the mountain men who were married to Indian women, often called "squaw men," would spend some of their earnings, and at times a not inconsiderable amount, on their wives to keep them properly outfitted and adorned. As one mountain man observed, "No sooner does an Indian belle experience this promotion [to becoming the wife of a free trapper], than all her notions at once rise and expand to the dignity of her situation; and the purse of her lover, and his credit into the bargain, are tasked to the utmost to fit her out in becoming style. The wife of a free trapper to be equipped and arrayed like any ordinary and undistinguished squaw? Perish the groveling thought!"[36] As rugged and individualistic as these trappers were, they came to measure their status, much as fussier East Coast businessmen did, at least in part through the appearance of their wives, so that a trapper's wife could conceivably own a fine horse and saddle, ornate jewelry, and an intricately woven, beautifully colored robe.

Having spent so much time in the mountains trapping beaver and hunkering down through the frigid winter months, the mountain men used the rendezvous as an opportunity to reconnect with old friends, make new acquaintances, share information about the mountains, and tell tall tales. They played games, sought sex with compliant Indian women, drank heavily, and generally had a wild time.[37] A participant at the 1826 rendezvous described the scene. The company's supply train arrived, "well laden with goods and all things necessary for the mountaineers and the Indian trade. It may well be supposed that the arrival of such a vast amount of luxuries from the East did not pass off without a general celebration. Mirth, songs, dancing, shouting, trading, running, jumping, singing, racing, target-shooting, yarns, frolic, with all sorts of extravagances that white men or Indians could invent, were freely indulged in. The unpacking of the *medicine water* contributed not a little to the heightening of our festivities."[38]

The rendezvous, especially in later years, frequently dissolved into drunken revels, which left many a mountain man financially hobbled, as the following contemporary account demonstrates:

> The trappers drop in singly and in small bands, bringing their packs of beaver to this mountain market, not infrequently to the value of a thousand dollars each, the produce of one hunt. The dissipation of the "rendezvous," however, soon turns the trapper's pocket inside out. The goods brought by the traders, although of the most inferior quality, are sold at enormous prices. . . . The rendezvous is one continued scene of drunkenness, gambling, and brawling and fighting, as long as the money and credit of the trappers last. . . . [The trappers play cards, and] the stakes are "beaver," which here is current coin; and when the fur is gone, their horses, mules, rifles, and shirts, hunting-packs, and *breeches*, are staked. Daring gamblers make the rounds of the camp, challenging each other to play for the trapper's highest stake—his horse, his squaw (if he have one), and, as once happened, his scalp. There goes "hos and beaver!" is the mountain expression when any great loss is sustained; and, sooner or later, "hos and beaver" invariably find their way into the insatiable pockets of the traders. A trapper often squanders the produce of his hunt, amounting to hundreds of dollars, in a couple of hours; and, supplied on credit with another equipment, leaves the rendezvous for another expedition, which has the same result time after time.[39]

This was one of the cruelest truths of the mountain man's career; namely that the originally optimistic "expectant capitalist" was more often than not left with little or nothing to show for all his hard work. Although a few mountain men managed to avoid the pitfalls of the rendezvous and saved their money, they were the exception to the rule. As Leonard commented, "Scarcely one man in ten, of those employed in this country ever think of saving a single dollar of their earnings, but spend it as fast as they can see an object to spend it for. They care not what may come to pass tomorrow—but think only of enjoying the present moment."[40] For the most part the only people who got rich were the fur company owners who supplied the goods and alcohol at inflated rates, called "mountain prices," that generated profits approaching 2,000 percent.[41]

*I*N PURSUIT OF BEAVER THE MOUNTAIN MEN ROAMED THROUGH-out the Rockies, from the upper reaches of present-day Montana and Idaho, down through Wyoming, Utah, and Colorado. They also made forays well beyond the Rockies, to the south and west, into Arizona, New Mexico, Nevada, California, Oregon, and Washington. Often they were the first white men to tread this ground, preceded only by Indians.[42] And it is for these journeys that many mountain men are best remembered. One of the most widely traveled of these men was Jedediah Strong Smith, whom Goetzmann called "one of the greatest of all American explorers."[43]

Smith was born in Bainbridge, New York, on January 6, 1799, but by the time he reached his late teens, his family had moved to Erie County, Pennsylvania, and then on to Ashland County, Ohio. Smith, or "Diah" as his family called him, was a serious, curious boy who spent much of his time hunting in the woods. Legend has it that when Smith was around sixteen, a family friend gave him a copy of the recently published history of Lewis and Clark's expedition, which captured his imagination and sparked his interest in the West. But even if the tale is apocryphal, Smith's gaze turned in that direction nonetheless.[44] Like many other young men of the day Smith viewed the West as a place teeming with possibilities.

In the spring of 1821 Smith, now six feet tall, lean, with brown hair and penetrating blue eyes, left home and made his way to St. Louis, where in 1822 he signed on as one of Ashley's men heading up the Missouri.[45] Smith launched his career with definite goals in mind. "I started into the mountains," he wrote, "with the determination of becoming a first-rate hunter, of making myself thoroughly acquainted with the character and habits of the Indians, of tracing out the sources of the Columbia River and following it to its mouth; and of making the whole profitable to me."[46]

Smith's first major discovery—or, more accurately, rediscovery—was finding the South Pass through the Rockies. Robert Stuart and his fellow Astorians had been the first whites to discover the pass back in late 1812, when they crossed it heading back east to St. Louis from the mouth of the Columbia. Although the press at the time trumpeted the great value of the pass as low, relatively flat, and easily traveled path through the mountains, the discovery was soon forgotten. It wasn't until 1824, when Smith, heading a detachment of Ashley's men, rediscovered the South Pass that its importance came to be recognized, and from then on mountain men used it as their portal through the Rockies, just as American settlers heading west would do in the coming years.

Smith's most impressive journey was prompted in part by the discovery of another Ashley man, Jim Bridger, who was every bit as tough and daring as Smith. In the fall of 1824 Bridger, scouting the area in advance of his trapping party, came upon the Great Salt Lake—he is usually acknowledged as being the first white man to see this briny remnant of a truly enormous freshwater lake that covered much of present-day Utah, and slivers of Idaho and Nevada, 14,000 to 32,000 years ago.[47] Bridger went to the edge of the lake, took a sip of its water, and returned to the rest of his party, telling them that he had found an arm of the Pacific Ocean. This news piqued Smith's interest. To determine what lay beyond the lake to the southwest, on August 22, 1826, he and fifteen of his men headed into the unknown.[48] "I wanted to be the first," Smith said, "to view a country on which the eyes of a white man had never gazed and to follow the course of rivers that run through a new land."[49] But exploration wasn't his only goal. His business was beaver, and he hoped that the new lands he was about to traverse would be teeming with them.

On the first leg of his journey Smith traded with the Ute in the present-day Utah and San Pete Valleys, then went south along the Sevier and Virgin rivers, past the precipitous peaks of present-day Zion National Park, to the Colorado River, and finally through the rugged Black Mountains down into the broad Mojave Valley, where he remained with the Mojave Indians for a couple of weeks to give his men time to recuperate. After learning from the Indians that Mexican settlements in California were about ten days' ride, Smith headed west, hoping that he would be able to purchase much-needed supplies from the Mexicans, and then head north for beaver.

The journey took sixteen days, fifteen of which were spent crossing the parched Mojave Desert. They walked and rode through a shifting landscape of wind-carved dunes, salt-encrusted sand flats, cacti, creosote bushes, and Joshua trees, punctuated—all too rarely, it seemed to the men—by solitary oases of cottonwoods and fan palms stretching skyward. The Mojave River, Smith found, had the unsettling characteristic of periodically disappearing beneath the sand only to resurface at some distant point—which led him to call it the Inconstant River. Finally, on November 26, the party climbed over the San Bernardino Mountains and dropped into a fertile valley, where they were warmly welcomed by the Franciscan padre who ran the Mission San Gabriel. Smith composed a letter to José Maria Echeandía, the region's governor, asking permission to purchase supplies and head up the coast to the bay at San Francisco, at which point he said he planned to head east over the mountains, back to the Great Salt Lake. Echeandía responded by summoning Smith to San Diego, about ninety miles south of the mission.

Smith arrived on horseback, whereupon the tall, gaunt, and humorless governor questioned him civilly but with a probing intensity. Echeandía was wary of the Americans. He had long been acquainted with American ships doing business along the coast, but he had never heard of Americans traveling by land to his domain, and he was understandably not sure what to make of their claims that they were there only there to gather supplies and hunt for beaver. For a month Echeandía couldn't decide what to do with these strange visitors—lock them up as spies, haul them off to Mexico City for interrogation, or let them go on their way.

While Smith was waiting for the governor's response, he spent some time with a Boston ship captain named William Cunningham, who was quite surprised to see him. "There has arrived at this place," Cunningham later wrote, "Capt. Jedediah S. Smith, with a company of hunters from St. Louis on the Missouri. . . . Does it not seem incredible that a party of . . . men, depending entirely upon their rifles and traps for subsistence, will explore this vast continent and call themselves happy when they can obtain the tail of a Beaver to dine upon?"[50] By that measure, however, Smith was not a happy man. So far the trip from the Great Salt Lake had been a bust. If only Echeandía would let him continue on, perhaps he would find beaver to the north.

Finally, in late December 1826, as winter descended on the coast, the governor told Smith he could go, but he and his men had to leave California the way they had come. Echeandía didn't want them seeing any more of his domain than they already had. Smith sailed with Captain Cunningham up the coast to rejoin his party. After gathering fresh supplies and horses, Smith traveled back over the San Bernardino Mountains and then, disregarding the governor's orders, headed northwest into the San Joaquin Valley along the western foothills of Sierra Nevada, trapping along the way.

By early May the men had caught a respectable amount of beaver, and Smith knew that if they were to make it back to the summer rendezvous in time they would have to head back east immediately. But the towering Sierra Nevada stood in the way.[51] Nearly forty-five years later, as he was coming to the end of his first summer hiking through the Sierra Nevada, a young John Muir reflected affectionately in his journal on these majestic mountains, which would play such a critical role in his life. "Here ends my forever memorable first High Sierra excursion. I have crossed the Range of Light, surely the brightest and best of all the Lord has built; and rejoicing in its glory, I gladly, gratefully, hopefully pray I may see it again."[52] Smith's introduction to the Sierra Nevada, by contrast, was perhaps as memorable but not nearly as pleasant.

Smith's first attempt to get over the mountains was pure misery. Following the course of the boulder-strewn canyon of the American River, facing high water on one side, freezing temperatures, deep snow every step of the way, and more of it falling from the sky daily, Smith's men quickly became discouraged as they battled exhaustion and hypothermia and watched five of their horses die. After sixty miles of this, and with conditions worsening, Smith turned back. He retraced his steps, then headed southeast to the banks of the Stanislaus River. There he left most of the party and the furs behind, while he and two of his best men attacked the mountains again. His plan was to make it to the rendezvous and then return for the others.

With seven horses and two mules loaded with hay and food, Smith's small expeditionary force headed out along the Stanislaus on May 20. They shadowed the river for a while, then turned away into the thickly forested foothills. Slowly the stands of pine and fir thinned out, and within a week's time they reached the rocky summit of the mountains near present-day Ebbetts Pass.[53] Although the ice-encrusted snow was up to eight feet deep in places, the strengthening rays of the sun had compacted it enough so that Smith and his men were able to get by without much difficulty. And when they emerged from the mountains into the arid valley beyond, they were fatigued but in relatively good shape, having lost two horses and one mule. Although this trial was arduous enough, the hardest was yet to come.

Over the next month, they traversed the Great Basin, running across

Nevada. According to Smith, "High rocky hills afford the only relief to the desolate waste. . . . And the intervals between are sand barren plains." Since water was extremely scarce, the men buried themselves in the sand to cool off, and when food ran out, some of the five remaining horses were sacrificed. Then, just after the start of summer, on June 27, Smith wrote, "I saw an expanse of water extending far to the north and east. The Salt Lake a joyful sight was spread before us."[54]

Smith and his men, who were by this point "mere skeletons," made it to the rendezvous on Bear Lake a week later. "My arrival caused a considerable bustle in camp," Smith observed, "for myself and party had been given up as lost. A small cannon brought up from St. Louis was loaded and fired for a salute."[55] In making their transit Smith and his men were the first Americans to travel overland through the Southwest to California, and the first known whites to pass over the Sierra Nevada and cross the Great Basin. After spending ten days at the rendezvous, Smith, true to his word, set out with another party to pick up the men and the pelts he had left behind in California. Since he didn't think this party, loaded with supplies and baggage, could survive the unforgiving "Sand Plain" that was the Great Basin, he decided to follow the route that had brought him to California in the first place.[56]

WHEN SMITH ARRIVED AT THE MOJAVE VALLEY, HE STOPPED to trade for supplies with the same Indians who had been so welcoming the year before. The Mojave were friendly and the trading went well, but it was all a show. Not long after Smith had left the Mojave villages on his first trek to California in 1826, another group of trappers had fought with the Mojave and killed a few. This left the Mojave eager for revenge, and they saw Smith's arrival as an ideal opportunity to exact it. In mid-August, as Smith's party headed out, the Mojave were watching for their chance to strike, which came when the trappers began crossing the Colorado River.

While Smith and his men were in the middle of the river, the Mojave attacked the rest of the party waiting to cross, killing ten men and taking two Indian women prisoner. Smith and the remaining eight men, one of whom had been wounded, hurried to the opposite bank where they spread out their supplies, hoping that the Indians would stop to fight over the spoils rather than begin their pursuit. But the Indians came on, and by the time the fleeing trappers had made it a half a mile from the river, the Indians were fast approaching. Thinking tactically, Smith led his men back to the river so they could defend themselves from the cover of a grove of cottonwood trees. "With our knives," Smith later recalled, "we lopped down the small trees in such manner as to clear a place in which to stand while the fallen poles formed a slight breastwork. We then fastened our butcher knives with cords to the end of the light poles so as to form a tolerable lance, and thus poorly prepared we waited the approach of our unmerciful enemies. . . . It was a fearful time."

Smith's men had only five guns among them, and hundreds of Mojave were rapidly approaching. When a few of the Indians came within range, Smith ordered two of his men to fire, killing two Indians and wounding another. "Upon this the Indians ran off like frightened sheep and we were released from the apprehension of immediate death."[57] Horseless, and with only fifteen pounds of meat and precious few other goods, Smith's group headed west. Along the way they purchased horses from various Indians, and after another grueling trek through the desert and over the mountains, Smith was reunited with the party he had left behind on the Stanislaus.

Over the next three months Smith was caught in the grip of Mexican bureaucracy, as his former nemesis, Governor Echeandía, grilled him repeatedly about why he had returned and what his intentions were. Finally, as 1827 was coming to a close, Smith's party of twenty men and more than three hundred horses and mules was granted permission to leave, and it headed north. Seven months later the party reached the Umpqua River near present-day Reedsport, Oregon. They set up camp, and soon the Kuitsh (or Lower Umpqua) Indians came to trade. In the middle of July, Smith, two of his men, and an Indian guide canoed up the Umpqua River to find a suitable place to cross. Before departing Smith warned the men staying in camp to be vigilant, especially since just days earlier the trappers had violently clashed with the Indians.

When the reconnaissance party returned later that same day and approached the camp, Smith noticed that it was alarmingly quiet. As if on cue the Indian guide grabbed Smith's gun and plunged into the water, while the Indians who had been hiding onshore attacked. Smith and his two companions paddled furiously to the opposite bank, leaped from the canoe, and escaped into the woods, sure that everyone in the camp had been slaughtered. A little more than three weeks later, Smith and his men arrived at the Hudson's Bay Company's Fort Vancouver trading post on the Columbia. They were treated hospitably by their hosts and reunited with Harrison Rogers, the only one of

34 | American Beaver, *by John James Audubon, 1843.*

35 | The Ambassadors, *by Hans Holbein the Younger, 1533. The gentlemen's fine furs reflect their wealth and power.*

36 | *Johan "Big Belly" Printz, governor of New Sweden, by Caroline West van Helden, 1921.*

37 | *This 1685 version of a map created about 1650 shows New Netherland and much of the northeastern coast of America at midcentury. The inset at the lower right offers a view of New Amsterdam.*

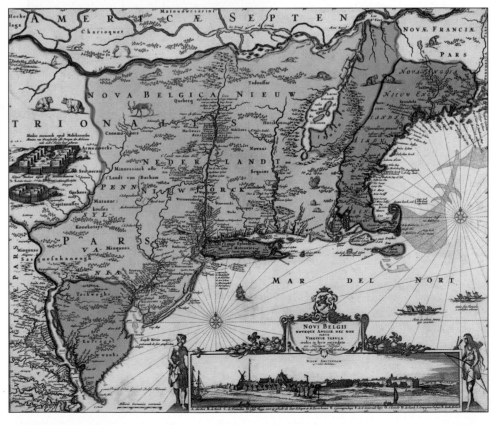

38 | Radisson and Groseilliers, *by Frederic Remington, 1905.*

39 | *Early seventeenth-century Italian "chevron" bead traded to the Iroquois in New York.*

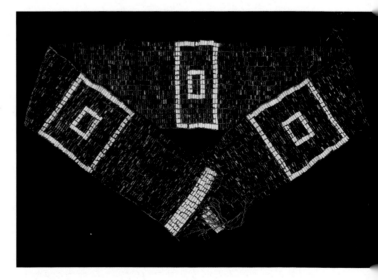

40 | *Algonquian wampum belt, eighteenth century.*

41 | *Beaver hunting, 1782. Many early writers mistakenly assumed that beaver lodges were composed of many individual compartments, which housed scores, if not hundreds, of beavers.*

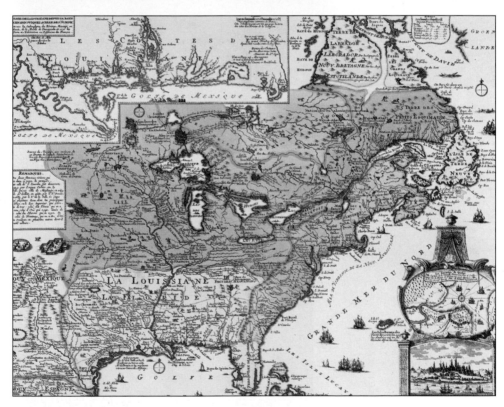

42 | *This French map, circa 1720, shows why France and Great Britain were on a collision course in the New World. French territory is shown as pink and yellow, extending from the St. Lawrence Valley in the northeast all the way down to Louisiana and the Gulf of Mexico (the inset at the upper left shows a close-up of the Gulf Coast). British territory is shown as green, hugging the coast from Newfoundland to the edge of Florida, and also surrounding Hudson Bay at the top-center of the map.*

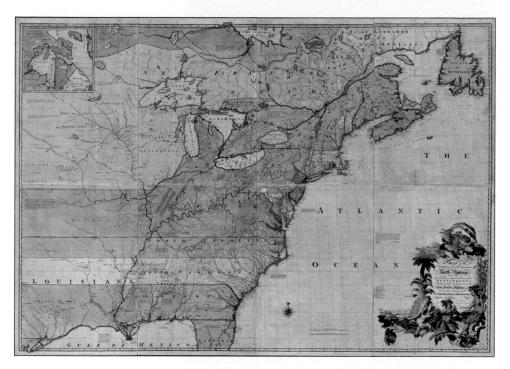

43 | *A map of the British and French dominions in North America, by John Mitchell, 1755, which vividly shows that the American colonies believed their western borders extended well beyond the Mississippi.*

44 | Voyageurs at Dawn, *by Frances Anne Hopkins, 1871.*

45 | *Thomas Jefferson wearing a fur-lined coat, reproduction of an 1805 painting by Rembrandt Peale.*

46 | Sea Otter, *by John Woodhouse Audubon, 1845–47.*

47 | A Man of Nootka Sound, *by John Webber, 1778.*

48 | *Aleut in* baidarka, *off St. Paul, Pribilof Islands, Alaska.*

49 | *Advertisement for a hat and fur store, 1840.*

50 | *Meriwether Lewis, by Charles Willson Peale (from life), 1807–8.*

51 | *William Clark, by Charles Willson Peale (from life), 1807–8.*

52 | *Two Ottawa chiefs, adorned in fur trade goods, including silver brooches and armbands. Early 1800s painting by an unknown artist.*

53 | *Métis man and his two wives, adorned in fur-trade goods, including beads, cloth blankets, and shawls. Painting by Peter Rindisbacher, 1825–26.*

54 | *Manuel Lisa, by an unknown artist, 1818.*

55 | *Jedediah Smith, by Ruth Senf Framberg, 1940.*

56 | *The Astor Medal produced by the American Fur Company (front and back).*

57 | The Steamer Yellowstone, *by Karl Bodmer, 1839.*

58 | Rendezvous near Green River, *by Alfred Jacob Miller, 1867.*

59 | Fort Laramie in 1837, *by Alfred Jacob Miller, 1867. Built in 1834 as a fur-trading post, it is now a National Historic Site in Wyoming, operated by the National Park Service.*

60 | Fur Traders Descending the Missouri, *by George Caleb Bingham, 1845.*

61 | The
Trapper's Bride,
*by Alfred Jacob
Miller, 1858–59.*

62 | Trapping Beaver, *by Alfred Jacob Miller, 1858–60.*

63 | Buffalo Bull, Grazing, *by George Catlin, 1845.*

64 | Winter Morning in the Country, *by Currier & Ives, 1873. The people in the sleigh are kept warm by two thick buffalo robes across their laps.*

65 | The Last of the Buffalo, *by Albert Bierstadt, 1888.*

Smith's men to make it out of the camp alive. Rogers said that despite Smith's warning, the men in camp had let down their guard when the Kuitsh came to trade on the morning of July 14, and as soon as the Indians saw they had the advantage they turned on the trappers, hacking fifteen of them to pieces. Smith's group stayed at Fort Vancouver through the winter, and come spring headed back to the Rockies. Although Smith suffered grievous losses, both human and material, on the trip up the coast, it enabled him to add another distinction to his already illustrious career: He and his companions were the first-known white men to travel by land from California to the Columbia.[58]

Grueling, extensive, and dangerous expeditions were typical of Smith's entire career as a mountain man. He was driven not only by the desire to find beaver and explore new lands but also by his devotion to those he left behind. "It is, that I may be able to help those [of the family] who stand in need," Smith wrote in a letter to his brother, "that I face every danger—It is for this that I traverse the mountains covered with eternal snow—it is for this that I pass over the Sandy Plains in heat of summer, thirsting for water, and am well pleased if I can find a shade, instead of water, where I may cool my overheated body—it is for this that I go for days without eating, & am pretty well satisfied if I can gather a few roots, a few snails, or, much better satisfied if we can afford our selves a piece of horse flesh, or a fine roasted dog, and, most of all, it is for this that I deprive myself of the privilege of society and the satisfaction of conversation with my friends!"[59]

*J*OSEPH REDDEFORD WALKER WAS ANOTHER GREAT MOUN-tain man—explorer.[60] Born in Roane County, Tennessee, on December 13, 1798, Walker grew to be a veritable mountain of a man, at six feet four inches and more than two hundred pounds. He trapped and traded out west during the 1820s and early 1830s, and served a stint as sheriff of Jackson County, Missouri. In 1831 he signed on to be a top aide to Benjamin Louis Eulalie de Bonneville, an army captain who had been granted a two-year leave of absence from military service to pursue the fur trade and to explore the Far West, gathering information about its geography, topography, natural history, as well as learning about the strength and distribution of the region's Indian tribes. With these goals in mind, Bonneville sent Walker on an expedition in the summer of 1833 to travel to California and the Pacific Ocean. According to Zenas Leonard, Walker's clerk on this trip, "Mr. Walker was a man well calculated to undertake a business of this kind. He was well hardened to the hardships of the wilderness—understood the character of the Indians very well—was kind and affable to his men, but at the same time at liberty to command without giving offence,—and to explore unknown regions was his chief delight."[61]

Walker, along with forty men, left the Green River rendezvous on July 24 and headed to the west side of the Great Salt Lake where they added another twenty free trappers to their ranks, and killed enough buffalo to lay in sixty pounds of dried meat per man for the journey. Continuing on their "westerly course," the party entered into "the most extensive & barren plains" Leonard had ever seen—the Great Basin. Here they followed the Humboldt River, which they labeled the "Barren River," because one could "travel for many days on [its] . . . banks . . . without finding a stick large enough to make a walking cane." Along the river Walker's party encountered many Paiute or Digger Indians, who harassed the men by stealing their beaver traps and other supplies. Some of the men urged Walker to retaliate for such thievery, but he counseled restraint. Nevertheless in subsequent days a few of the men took matters into their own hands, killing as many as six Indians. Although the men tried to prevent Walker from learning of the murders, he did, immediately ordering that these acts be stopped. But that was not the end of it. Word of the atrocities had spread, and by the time the party reached the lake and marshes of the Humboldt Sink, into which the river ran, the local Indians were bent on revenge.

Soon after the men set up camp on the shore of the lake, as many as nine hundred Indians surrounded them. Immediately perceiving that their intentions were not of a salutary nature, Walker ordered his men to secure the horses and build a breastworks behind which they could make a stand. After Walker refused to let Indian emissaries into his camp, and the Indians refused to meet him halfway between the breastworks and where they were gathered, a group of Indians approached and indicated that they would come over anyway. Using sign language, Walker's men warned them to stay away or be killed. And to drive the point home the men shot a couple of ducks floating on the lake nearby. "The ducks were killed," recalled Leonard, "which astonished the Indians a good deal, though not so much as the noise of the guns—which caused them to fall flat to the ground. After this they put up a beaver skin on a bank for us to shoot at for their gratification—when they left us for the night."

After Walker's party broke camp the next day, a group of eighty to one hundred Indians approached them in a "saucy and bold" manner. Walker "gave orders for the charge, saying that there was nothing equal to a good start in such a case." After the brief but intense melee, thirty-nine Indians lay dead, and the rest scattered. In writing about this tragic fight at a later date, Leonard defended the slaughter. "The severity with which we dealt with these Indians may be revolting to the heart of the philanthropist; but the circumstances of the case altogether atones for the cruelty. It must be borne in mind, that we were far removed from the hope of any succor in case we were surrounded, and that the country we were in was swarming with hostile savages, sufficiently numerous to devour us. Our object was to strike a decisive blow. This we did—even to a greater extent than we had intended."[62]

By the second week of October, Walker's party reached the eastern foothills of the Sierra Nevada, which were blanketed in the brilliant golds, reds, and oranges of fall. Exactly where they crossed the mountains is not entirely clear, but it appears that they followed the course of the Walker River (named later in Walker's honor). They went over the nearly eleven-thousand-foot-high Mono Pass, traveled along the granite ridge separating the Merced and the Tuolumne rivers, and then descended from the mountains into the San Joaquin Valley by the end of the month.[63] During this transit Walker's men became the first known white men to see parts of what would one day become Yosemite National Park, and they marveled at the stately sequoias that towered far over their heads, and some of whose trunks measured more than one hundred feet in circumference near their base.[64] Vast fields of deep snow and steep slopes slowed their progress to a crawl, and with their food exhausted and no game to be found in the mountains, the men were forced to kill seventeen of their horses for meat. The conditions were so bad that some of the party wanted to turn back, and the only way that Walker could keep them from deserting was to confiscate their ammunition and horses.

Once out of the mountains the party continued west. One night, as the men were setting up camp along the lower reaches of the San Joaquin, they heard a booming noise in the distance that sounded like thunder. While some of the men grew alarmed, thinking that an earthquake would soon swallow them up, Walker calmed their fears, telling them that it was not the earth that was rumbling but waves crashing on the shores of the Pacific. This bolstered the men's spirits, realizing that they were so close to their destination. A few days later they reached the upper parts of San Francisco Bay, along whose edge they found many Indians fishing, who evinced little interest in the new arrivals. Soon after, on November 20, the party made it to the shores of the Pacific. Walker and his men were not only awed by the enormity and power of the ocean, but they were also surprised to see a ship in the distance.

To get the ship's attention Walker's men tied white blankets to a stick and waved them back and forth. As the ship approached the men's surprise turned to great joy and excitement as they "beheld the broad stripes and bright stars of the American flag waiving majestically in the air at the masthead." It was the *Lagoda* out of Boston, on the coast trading with the Spanish for cowhides to be used in the manufacture of leather. The *Lagoda*'s captain, John Bradshaw, sent one of his boats to shore to see who these strange men were, and when he discovered that they were American too, he ordered the cannons fired as a welcoming salute and invited the men onboard for a celebratory feast to honor this most unusual and unexpected meeting. Walker's men quaffed cognac and ate the first bread, cheese, and butter they had seen in years. The next day the feast continued onshore, where the sailors eagerly consumed "the harder fare of the trapper and hunter," especially fresh meat, which was far superior to the salted meat they had been eating during most of their voyage.[65]

Bradshaw told Walker what he knew of the region and recommended that he go to the capital at Monterey and introduce himself to the Mexican governor of the province. Walker arrived at the end of November, and found the capital to be a town of thirty to forty houses, one church, a small fort, and a jail that also served as the governor's office. Monterey was perched on the edge of a magnificent bay, deep and broad, and ships sailing the coast often stopped there to trade and purchase supplies. Indeed some of the people in town had grown rich trading cowhides and furs of all types, including beaver and otter, with the ships that anchored in the bay.

The governor warmly welcomed Walker and gave the Americans permission to remain in the area through the winter, during which they were given free passage throughout the country. They were allowed to hunt for game and trade with the locals but not to trap or trade for beaver on Indian lands—this last admonition because the governor was concerned that the Americans might somehow abuse the Indians, whom the Spanish held in high regard. Over the next two and half months Walker and his men traveled widely in the vicinity of Monterey and were treated well by the Spanish and the Indians, who were as eager to learn about the Americans as the Americans were to learn about them.[66]

At one point the Americans watched a group of Spaniards engage in bullbaiting. A common local form of entertainment, it began with betting on which rider would be first to get a lariat around the neck or horns of a bull in a nearby herd. Once the first rope was placed, the rest of the men helped subdue the bull and drag it to a holding pen. The losers had a chance to recoup their losses by setting out to hunt a grizzly bear, looping lariats around its legs, and dragging it till it tired, after which it was tied up and taken to a spot just outside the pen holding the bull—the winnings going to the man who first lassoed the grizzly.

During the next stage the bull was jabbed repeatedly with long sticks, nails affixed to the ends. When the bull was sufficiently enraged, the bear was let loose in the pen and wagers made as to which animal would emerge victorious. (Although the bear would most likely dispatch the bull rather easily out in the open, in the small pen the bull often won, chasing and goring the bear multiple times.) If the bear won, it would be freed; if the bull "won," final bets were placed—this time on whether a man could enter the pen, touch a specific part of the bull, and emerge unscathed. (The man was allowed to throw a blanket over the bull's head to blind it temporarily. Having touched the chosen spot, he had to grab the blanket and escape the pen.) The successful contestant won the wager for those who bet on him, and got a cut of the winnings. The unsuccessful ones, however, lost not only the bet but sometimes their lives.[67]

Rested and reprovisioned, Walker's party left Monterey in the middle of February 1834, beginning their journey back to the Rockies. Six men, however, opted to stay behind. All of them were carpenters or other craftsmen who were smitten with California but, more important, saw an opportunity to profit by their own handiwork. During their brief sojourn in the area these men learned that competent craftsmen were in short supply, and high-quality finished products were correspondingly in great demand. Two of the men had built a wooden windmill, which they sold for $110, and others had made tables that were fetching from eight to ten dollars a piece. "The parting scene between the company and these six men," was, according to Leonard, "the most melancholy separation we had undergone since" the journey began. On other occasions trappers had left the party, but it was assumed they might meet up again someday, back east. These six men, however, planned to permanently settle in California, and never return to the States.[68]

Instead of going over the Sierra Nevada the torturous way he had come,

Walker headed south and led his men through what would one day be called Walker's Pass, a "low, easy gateway through" the southern portion of the mountains.[69] From there they headed north to the Humboldt Sink, where they had another fight with the Paiute, killing fourteen. Then they struck out along the Humboldt River to its source, traveled overland to the Snake River, and then on to the Bear River, where they met up with Bonneville in the middle of July. Walker and his men didn't catch many beaver while they were away, but their trip was noteworthy for other reasons. They were only the second known white men, after Smith and his party, to cross the Sierra Nevada, and the first to do so going from east to west. And much of the trail that Walker blazed would later become part of the famed California trail that would one day be used by waves of Americans heading for California.

THE VAST SPRAWL OF VIRGIN BEAUTY AWED EVEN THE HARD-ened unsentimental mountain men as they made thousands of journeys over the virtually unexplored western terrain, and their accounts helped fuel the imaginations of painters, writers, and hundreds of thousands of prospective settlers back east. In fact these early accounts contributed to America's expanding consciousness of the grandeur of the western frontier. The mountain man Warren Ferris, for example, recorded the following rhapsodic observation from a "high mound" in the shadow of the Wind River Range, not far from present-day Pinedale, Wyoming. "Immense herds of bison were seen in every direction galloping over the prairie, like vast squadrons of cavalry performing their accustomed evolutions. . . . Detachments passing and repassing, from one point to another, at full speed; . . . and all rushing on, till forms and numbers disappear in the dust and distance, and nothing remains visible of the long black lines but dark clouds slowly sweeping over the distant plains."[70] One cold February night another mountain man, Osborne Russell, camped on an exposed ledge high above the Great Salt Lake. "The air was calm, serene and cold," he wrote, "and the stars shone with an uncommon brightness." When he awoke around midnight, he looked over the precipice into "the dark abyss, silent as the night of death." His main reason for choosing such a precarious perch "was to take a view of the lake when the sun rose in the morning."[71] And while traveling through a ravine near Laramie, Wyoming, Leonard said he "was struck with the rough and picturesque appearance of the adjacent hills." Huge, "somber" black-and-gray boulders, a veritable "avalanche of rocks," jutted out menacingly from the slopes at odd angles, seemingly on the verge of tumbling down on the men below. "If Dante had designed to picture in one of his circles, the Hell of Stones, he might have taken this scene for his model." But Leonard was quick to point out that this "frightful" scene was just one of many that might be encountered. "An hour's travel would present another of a very different character," both "beautiful and enchanting."[72]

$\mathcal{T}$O SURVIVE THEIR ARDUOUS JOURNEYS, THE MOUNTAIN MEN ate large quantities of high-energy food, in that time that meant upwards of ten pounds of meat a day.[73] Given their options, they could little afford to be picky. A common saying among mountain men was "meat's meat," and although preferences ran to buffalo, elk, venison, lynx, beaver tail, and, if they were lucky, mountain lion, they would also eat anything else they could shoot or trap, right down to snakes and lizards. In times of desperation they would even eat their horses or mules.[74]

Mountain men eagerly consumed many parts of the animals they killed. With the buffalo, for example, they ate the hump rib, the tenderloins, the tongue, the heart, the testicles ("prairie oysters"), and the marrow, which was referred to as "trapper's butter."[75] They slit the buffalo's jugular and drank the warm blood that dripped out, which some claimed tasted like milk. They took the coiled intestines, or *boudin*, squeezed out its contents, slowly roasted it over a fire, and ate it by the yard. They cut the liver from the freshly killed carcass and drizzled it to taste with bile from the gall bladder.[76] From either side of the buffalo's spine, mountain men stripped the thick, wide layer of fat, called *dépouille*, which they slathered in hot grease, smoked for the better part of a day, and used in place of bread; it was, claimed one mountain man, "tender and sweet and very nourishing . . . superior to any bread that was ever made."[77] So bountiful and nutritious was the buffalo that it became the mountain man's single most important source of food. As one trapper proclaimed, buffalo "alone will cure dyspepsia, prevent consumption, amend a broken constitution, put flesh upon the bones of a *skeleton*, and *restore a dead man again to life*!"[78]

The meat was boiled, roasted, or smoked over a fire and consumed right away or made into dried meat, something the Plains Indians had been eating for centuries, which the mountain men called "jirk," a term derived from *charqui*, the Spanish word for "dried meat" (the more familiar term, "jerky," didn't come into use until well after the era of the mountain men had ended). Usually made from buffalo meat, jirk would be cut into thin strips, scored, and sometimes smoked for flavor, and then placed on elevated wooden racks to keep it away from the mouths of hungry animals who prowled the camps, lured by the savory smells wafting through the air. After a few days drying in the mountain air, the jirk was ready to eat or be packed and taken on the trail.[79] Pemmican was made by taking the jirk and pulverizing it "to the consistency of mince meat" or sometimes powder, then mixing it with fat, and adding wild berries for sweetness. Jirk and pemmican provided mountain men with a concentrated high-calorie, high-protein food that was easy to transport and lasted for years.[80]

While the mountain man's diet leaned heavily toward meat and fat— indeed, so much fat that trappers were said to "shed rain like an otter, and stand cold like a polar bear"—they did, of course, eat other things, including berries, corn, goose and crow eggs, and wild onions and lettuce. When food was scarce, even a beaver pelt or a pair of moccasins might be on the menu.[81] As for seasoning, the well-stocked mountain man would have spices stashed in his possibles bag, while others not so fortunate had to make due without, which wasn't as bad as it seemed, especially since trappers proclaimed that hunger was "a capital sauce."[82] For drink, in addition to water, coffee, and tea, there was often some type of alcoholic libation, ranging from generic whiskey to more unusual concoctions such as "shrub" and "metheglin," which were honey- or sugar-sweetened wines or liquors with pieces of fruit added for flavor.[83] And after the meal the mountain men often relaxed by lighting their pipes and smoking tobacco, or if there was none to be had, they might use *kinnick-kinnick*, a mildly narcotic Indian substitute made from the dried and pulverized inner bark of willows and other trees.[84]

Away from East Coast civilization for years at a time, the mountain men slowly developed their own special language, a trapper's dialect of sorts, which Chittenden described as a "strange medley of English, French, and Spanish and as distant from grammatical and literary propriety as it is possible to conceive."[85] To this were added Indian words as well as a sign language drawn largely from local tribes.[86] As a result a visitor from the East, overhearing mountain men converse, might have little or no idea what was being said. If he wasn't sufficiently mystified by, say, "epishemore" or "parfleche," he could scratch his head at such "mountain-man-isms" as "plew" (a particularly fine beaver pelt), "painter" (panther), "bushway" (boss, from "bourgeois"), and "shinin times" (special or memorable experiences, from "Shining Mountains," which is what both the Indians and the trappers called the Rockies). Similar frustration could arise from the lack of a dictionary covering terms like "hivernants" (men who had made it through at least one winter in the mountains and earned the right to look down on "greenhorns," or newcomers), "death dust" (good gunpowder), and "Ol Virginny" or "honeydew" (tobacco).[87]

ONE TOPIC THAT MOUNTAIN MEN OFTEN DISCUSSED WAS what they sometimes called "Old Ephraim," or the grizzly bear (*Ursus arctos horribilis*), the monarch of the mountains.[88] During their travels mountain men faced many mortal dangers, but the grizzly was one of the most feared. Although mountain men possessed respect, if not awe, for the grizzly, this didn't stop them from hunting them with a vengeance. Killing a grizzly not only provided valuable and tasty meat, but it was also considered a "signal honor" among the fraternity of mountain men.[89] But there were times—and judging by the number of campfire tales, quite a few—when the hunter became the hunted, and no story is more famous than that of Hugh Glass.[90]

Glass's early history is murky to say the least. According to some accounts, before entering the fur trade he was a pirate with Jean Lafitte in the Gulf of Mexico and a captive of some Pawnee, whose chief was so impressed with Glass's bravery and spirit in the face of danger that he adopted him as a son.[91] However he got there, in September 1823 Glass was part of a small group of men, led by Andrew Henry, heading for the Yellowstone River. As one of the party's hunters he was sent ahead to procure food, when he came upon a female grizzly and her cubs. The mother, who likely had heard or smelled Glass coming, was crouching behind a bush. She suddenly reared up no more than three yards from where the shocked hunter was standing, and before Glass could "set his triggers" or beat a hasty retreat, the bear lunged at him, grabbing him by the throat and shoulder. She raised him into the air, threw him down on the ground, bit off a chunk of his flesh, and turned to feed it to her cubs. Glass tried to escape but was attacked again, this time receiving deep gashes in his left arm and the back of his head. While the mother was thus engaged, her cubs prepared to enter the fray, but Glass's hunting partner arrived and arrested their attention. One of the cubs chased the second hunter, but before it got too close, the hunter wheeled about and shot it dead, or as he later said, "I burst the varmint." By this time the rest of Henry's men appeared on the scene and immediately trained their rifles upon the mother bear, who was standing over Glass, and killed her with a volley of well-aimed shots.

Glass was in dire straits, bleeding profusely, his body battered and bruised, and in excruciating pain. Henry had to decide quickly what to do because they were in the midst of hostile Indian territory, and the party's safety required that they keep moving. Since they were hundreds of miles from the closest trading post, there was no way to get any sort of medical attention, and given the severity of Glass's wounds, Henry was convinced that moving him would be fatal. Leaving Glass behind wasn't an acceptable option, so Henry offered a handsome reward to anyone who would stay with the wounded man until he died or regained enough of his strength to soldier on. Two men stepped forward.[92] Day after day they watched over Glass, no doubt fully expecting him to expire at any moment. But on the fifth day of their vigil, the two guardians decided they had had enough. Whether they thought Glass would never recover, or had simply had lost patience, they took off, taking Glass's rifle and other belongings with them, leaving him nothing but the bloodied and tattered clothes he was wearing. The two men lied when they caught up with the rest of their party, saying that Glass had died and that they had given him a proper burial.

As Mark Twain would quip some seventy years later, "The report of my death was an exaggeration," so it was with Glass.[93] For ten more days he stayed where the two men had left him, surviving on berries and the water from a nearby spring. Then, with some of his strength returning, he began walking toward the Missouri and a trading post about 350 miles distant. Along the way he foraged for food, and at one point came upon a band of wolves who had killed a buffalo calf. Scaring them off before they had cleaned the carcass, he was able to garner himself a bit of meat. Glass finally made it to the post, but he didn't stay long because by this time he had decided to exact revenge upon the two men and get his belongings back, especially his beloved rifle. Over the next few months Glass had more adventures, including a narrow escape from a band of Indians, as he continued his search for those who had left him for dead. Glass tracked down one of them at a military fort on the Missouri only to find that he was now an enlisted man. Glass couldn't very well attack a soldier, but still got some satisfaction when the commanding officer, moved by his story, ordered the soldier to return the trapper's rifle. This apparently "appeased the wrath of Hugh Glass," for he dropped the matter and never did confront the other man. Glass's real-life tale was so fantastical, as if plucked from mythology, that his survival and recovery almost immediately became the stuff of great nineteenth-century legend.

*F*AR MORE DANGEROUS TO MOUNTAIN MEN THAN GRIZ-zlies were Indians, but not all Indians, of course. As a result of marriages, trading connections, and other factors, mountain men by and large got along well with many of the Indians they encountered, or at least avoided physical confrontations.[94] If mountain men needed any more motivation to be civil to the Indians, all they had to do was take stock of their exposed situation. In those uncharted lands, far from settlements or military protection of any kind, Indians greatly outnumbered the white man. Even with normally friendly Indians, however, there were instances in which misunderstandings arose, tempers flared, and violence erupted. Then there were some Indians who were consistently hostile to the mountain men, including the Blackfeet, whose anger at the encroachment of white trappers and explorers had not abated since the days of Lewis and Clark. But the most dangerous and persistent foes of the mountain men were the Atsina, or Gros Ventre, of the prairies, who were close allies of the Blackfeet. Whenever mountain men and the Atsina crossed paths, tensions rose and fights often ensued.

Such encounters are too numerous to list, but the most prominent took place in 1832 just as the rendezvous at Pierre's Hole, on the western edge of the sky-piercing Tetons, was breaking up.[95] On July 17 Milton Sublette, William's brother, and fourteen of his men, along with two other small groups of trappers, left the rendezvous heading in a southeasterly direction toward the Snake River. About eight miles into their journey, while still in the valley of Pierre's Hole, the men camped for the night. The next morning, just as the men were about the leave, they noticed in the distance a large group of people issuing from a mountain pass. At first the mountain men thought it might be a party of fellow trappers, but when one of the men looked through his spyglass he announced that they were Indians and were rapidly sweeping down onto the valley floor with two columns of horsemen leading the way. Soon the mountain men could hear yelling, and they realized it was a band of the dreaded Atsina, an entire village on the move with women, children, and horses in tow.[96] Two men rode out to meet the Indians, both of whom had a score to settle. One was Antoine Godin, a métis trapper with Sublette's brigade, whose Iroquois father had been slaughtered by the Atsina during an earlier fight in the mountains; the other, a Flathead Indian chief who hated the Atsina for the attacks they had made on his tribe.

Seeing these emissaries come forward, the Atsina sent forward a small party of their own, headed by one of their chiefs, who was unarmed and approached holding a peace pipe in his hand. But Godin and the Flathead were not interested in peace, nor talking for that matter, and when they came face-to-face with the Atsina chief they launched their assault. As soon as the chief extended his hand in what appeared to be a conciliatory gesture, Godin grabbed it and yelled, "Fire!" whereupon the Flathead raised his rifle and shot the chief, who fell lifelessly to ground.[97] Godin then tore the chief's scarlet robe off his body and raced wildly back to his fellow mountain men, hollering triumphantly all the way, with his trophy fluttering in the wind. The bloody gauntlet had been thrown down.

Quickly surveying the area to find the best place to make a stand, the Atsina raced into a nearby grove of willow and cottonwood trees on the edge of a swamp and surrounded by a dense thicket of bushes and vines. While the warriors took up stations at the grove's edge and fired at the mountain men, who had positioned themselves in a ravine not far away, the Atsina women retreated into the center of the grove where they dug a trench, mounded the dirt, and covered the mound with a tangle of logs and branches. The Atsina had the numbers and the superior position, and the mountain men knew that if they were to prevail they needed reinforcements. A messenger rode back to the site of the rendezvous, where he rallied the trappers and Indians who had yet to break camp. Now a sizable group of mountain men, accompanied by Nez Percé and Flathead, galloped into battle, with William Sublette, leading the way.

When the Atsina saw the new arrivals stream into the valley, their calculus changed. Rather than outnumbering their enemies, they were now outnumbered. As thoughts of offensive action disappeared, the Atsina retreated to their makeshift fort within the grove and prepared to defend themselves. The mountain men quickly discovered that it was nearly impossible to get off good shots because the Indians were so well protected behind the brush, trees, and breastworks they had built. Anytime the trappers and their allies approached, they were exposed, and a few of them were shot. Despite the risks William Sublette decided to end this siege by overrunning the fort—a deadly gambit for sure, but soon he and a group of roughly thirty mountain men and Indians were crawling forward, rifles at the ready. Some of the men "made their wills as they went, feeling that they were upon perilous business." But even this determined attack was unsuccessful, and the casualties on both sides mounted, one of them attributed to inebriation. Before the mountain men entered the fight, they passed around the whiskey to give them an added dose of courage, or perhaps just to deaden their fear. One of these men, who had taken too large a swig, became sufficiently convinced of his own invincibility to crawl up to the edge of the Indian fort and peer over the top. "He paid for his temerity," observed one of his fellows, "when he received two bullets in his forehead."[98]

Finally Sublette, who had been shot in the shoulder, decided to set fire to the fort and burn the Indians into the open. Before he could carry out this plan, however, some of the mountain men's Indian allies pleaded that this drastic step not be taken, because once the fighting was over they hoped to plunder the Atsina's possessions. Sublette relented, and as he was considering his next move, the situation changed dramatically. During a lull in the fighting one of the Atsina chiefs yelled to his attackers that although they might win this battle, they would lose in the end. There were hundreds of Atsina not far away, he claimed, and when they arrived they would extract revenge. The chief spoke in his native tongue, and by the time his speech had been translated, the message became garbled to the point that the mountain men believed that the promised phalanx of Atsina were not bearing down on them but were instead going to attack the rendezvous.

Fearing that the skeleton force left behind at the rendezvous would be unable to defend themselves, the mountain men and their allies rushed back down the valley on horseback, leaving behind a small group of men to keep an eye on the fort. When they arrived at the rendezvous, they discovered that they had been mistaken, but it was too late to retrace their steps, so they camped for the night.

The next morning, when the mountain men returned to the site of the battle, they were shocked. Under the cover of darkness, and without any of the men on guard hearing a thing, the Atsina had made their escape. According to one of the participants, Joseph Meek, "on making this discovery there was much chagrin among the white trappers, and much lamentation among the Indian allies, who had abandoned the burning of the fort expressly to save for themselves the fine blankets and other goods of their hereditary foes." A macabre scene greeted the mountain men inside the fort. Ten Atsina lay dead along with more than thirty of their horses. Others must have been taken away during the escape, since the Atsina later claimed that they lost twenty-six men that day. As for the mountain men, their losses stood at six killed and six wounded, with similar numbers for their Indian allies.

How many mountain men lost their lives as a result of Indian attacks, encounters with grizzly bears, exposure to the elements, or injuries will never be known. One estimate for men employed by two of the main fur-trapping companies, and only for the years 1822–29, puts the number who died of other than natural causes at seventy. Another source claims that on average one mountain man died per week, and yet another puts the number of men killed by Indians alone at ten to twenty annually between 1825 and 1830.[99] Whatever the true tally, when one factors in all the various companies involved and the nearly twenty years over which the main era of the mountain man spanned, there is no doubt that the death toll was in the low to mid-hundreds, and considering that no more than three thousand men ever made their living as mountain men, such numbers add up to a truly astonishing death rate.

The lives of mountain men fascinated their contemporaries, as evidenced by the large number of articles and books on that topic published during the early to mid-nineteenth century. This keen national interest, if not obsession, with mountain men, gave rise to a myriad of stereotypes, two of which were particularly pervasive. One viewed the mountain man as the romantic hero, who ventured boldly and even joyfully into the uncharted wilderness, and who relied on his strength, resourcefulness, and courage to confront and in many cases surmount manifold obstacles. The other stereotype painted the mountain man's life in much darker hues, as a daring and brave individual but also one who had turned his back on civilization. Such a renegade, it was believed, abandoned all moral constraints to pursue a licentious, lawless life, which physically and mentally transformed him into little more than a savage. Perhaps the best example of the first stereotype comes from the pen of Washington Irving. In his 1837 best seller, *The*

Adventures of Captain Bonneville, Or Scenes Beyond the Rocky Mountains of the Far West, he offered this almost rapturous depiction of the mountain man:

> It is difficult to do justice to the courage, fortitude, and perseverance of the pioneers of the fur trade, who conducted these early expeditions, and first broke their way through a wilderness where every thing was calculated to deter and dismay them. . . . They knew nothing of the country beyond the verge of their horizon, and had to gather information as they wandered. . . . There is, perhaps, no class of men on the face of the earth, who lead a life of more continued exertion, peril, and excitement, or are more enamored of their occupation, than the free trappers of the West. . . . His passionate excitement at times resembles a mania. In vain may the most cruel and vigilant savages beset his path; in vain may rocks, and precipices, and wintry torrents oppose his progress; let but a single track of a beaver meet his eye, and he forgets all dangers and defies all difficulties. . . . Such is the mountaineer, the hardy trapper of the West; and such as we have slightly sketched it, is the wild, Robin Hood kind of life, with all its strange and motley populace, now existing in full vigor among the Rocky Mountains.[100]

For insights into the less adulatory stereotype, consider the characterization by George F. Ruxton, a British army lieutenant and adventurer who spent a few months traveling through the Rockies in 1847:

> The trappers of the Rocky Mountains belong to a "genus" more approximating to the primitive savage than perhaps any other class of civilized man. Their lives being spent in the remote wilderness of the mountains, with no other companion than Nature herself, their habits and character assume a most singular cast of simplicity mingled with ferocity. . . . Constantly exposed to perils of all kinds, they become callous to any feeling of danger, and destroy human as well as animal life with as little scruple and as freely as they expose their own. Of laws, human or divine, they neither know nor care to know. Their wish is their law . . . people fond of giving hard names call them revengeful, bloodthirsty, drunkards . . . [and] gamblers. . . . I *have* met honest mountain men. Their animal qualities, however, are undeniable. . . . They are just what uncivilized white man might be supposed to be in a brute state, depending upon his instinct for the support of life.[101]

Many historians have analyzed these and other mountain-man stereo-types, documenting their strengths and weaknesses and arguing over whether they provide useful generalizations or useless oversimplifications.[102] Suffice it to say that no single stereotype can capture the complexity and variation that existed within the fraternity of mountain men. For example, the two contrast-ing stereotypes just discussed—the romantic hero versus the misanthropic savage—both have features that ring true, at least some of the time for some mountain men.

*T*HE FUR TRADE OF THE NORTHERN AND CENTRAL ROCKY MOUN-tains, which revolved around the annual rendezvous, was a signifi-cant part of America's fur trade in the 1820s and 1830s, but it was hardly the only part. Even before Ashley placed his ad for "enterprising young men" in the *Missouri Gazette*, the American fur trade was heading in two other direc-tions, spearheaded by the trappers in the Far Southwest, and the indomitable Astor nearly everywhere else.

—13—

Taos Trappers and Astor's Empire

John Jacob Astor.

*I*N THE EARLY 1800S MERCHANTS ALONG AMERICA'S WESTERN frontier grew increasingly interested in tapping the riches of Santa Fe, the nearly two-hundred-year-old capital of New Mexico and one of the main outposts of the Spanish empire in North America (or New Spain, as it was called). For many years Americans had heard rumors about Santa Fe's wealth and its great potential as a trading hub, which were fed by the shadowy tales of the few travelers who had ventured there. One of the first Americans to try to corroborate these rumors was William Morrison, a merchant from Kaskaskia in the Illinois Territory. Outfitting a French Creole named Baptiste La Lande with two thousand dollars' worth of goods, Morrison sent him in 1804 to Santa Fe to trade for whatever items might turn a profit. La Lande, however, proved to be an exceedingly poor choice for the job. Soon after arriving in Santa Fe, he successfully traded his goods, but rather than head back to Kaskaskia with Morrison's profits, he decided to make Santa Fe his new home. Exactly what caused La Lande so easily to shed his responsibilities is not clear, but it seems that his dalliances with Mexican women proved irresistible and quashed any thoughts he had of leaving.

In subsequent years many other Americans headed to Santa Fe to establish trading relations, and almost all of them failed because of determined opposition from the Spanish government. As a result of France's takeover of the Louisiana Territory, and Jefferson's subsequent purchase of those lands, New Spain's reach had already been dramatically diminished. Spain, a fast-fading power on the world stage, didn't want to lose any more of its hold on the region, and it viewed any American incursions with alarm. Even commercial expeditions, which would ostensibly benefit Spanish and American traders alike, had to be stopped. Such trade would not only threaten New Spain's profitable monopoly on the supply of goods within its domain, but it might also generate interest in Spanish land and inflame America's expansionist ambitions. It was not surprising, then, that Spanish policy was predicated on keeping all foreigners out, by force if necessary. This policy didn't apply only to traders but also to American trappers who were increasingly searching for beaver in the mountains and rivers to the north and east of Santa Fe, lands also claimed by Spain. Thus any Americans traveling to the southwest in the early 1800s did so at considerable risk. More than a few of them were stripped of their belongings and thrown in jail, or sent back from whence they came at gun point.[1]

The experience of a small group of men from St. Louis, who had been trapping beaver near the headwaters of the Arkansas River and trading for pelts with the Arapaho in 1817, proved particularly noteworthy. Rounded up by Spanish troops who claimed that the men were trespassing on Spanish territory and hauled to Santa Fe, they were berated by the governor, who told them that if they weren't careful they would have their "brains blown up." He confiscated thirty thousand dollars' worth of pelts and other supplies and had the Americans clapped in irons and thrown into a dungeon for forty-eight days. At the end of their confinement the men were brought before a court-martial and were, as one of them later recounted, "forced to kneel down . . . [and] kiss the unjust and iniquitous sentence that deprived harmless and inoffensive men of all they possessed—the fruits of two years' labor and perils." The governor then gave the men broken-down horses and sent them back to St. Louis, warning them never to return.[2]

The situation changed dramatically in 1821, when Mexico successfully achieved its independence from Spain. With their oppressive Spanish overlords gone, Mexican officials acted quickly to establish trading relations with their American neighbors. An announcement from the central government in Mexico City proclaimed that, "With respect to foreign nations, we shall maintain harmony with all, commercial relations, and whatever else may be appropriate."[3] This shift promised to be a boon for the people of Santa Fe: No longer would they be required to pay exorbitant prices for the limited suite of goods and supplies sold by Spanish merchants operating out of towns and cities far to the south. Now they could benefit from American trade, and they had high expectations that a great variety of cheap and high-quality goods would soon become available.

The first American to take advantage of this liberalization was William Becknell, a former military officer and Missourian who had held a number of jobs, including digging for salt and running a ferry. Hit hard by the Panic of 1819, he was having trouble paying his mounting debts when he latched on to the idea of regaining his solvency by trading in Santa Fe. On June 25, 1821, after hearing that Mexico had declared its independence, he placed an ad in the *Missouri Intelligencer* to recruit men "to go westward for the purpose of trading for horses and mules, and catching wild animals of every description."[4]

Perhaps as many as twenty-five men answered the call, and they began their journey on August 4. In mid November they reached Santa Fe, where they learned that the revolution had been a success and Mexico was now its own country. The trading went very well, and the provincial governor told Becknell that it was his "desire that the Americans would keep up an intercourse with" New Mexico.[5] When Becknell returned to Franklin, Missouri, in late January 1822, he amazed onlookers by cutting open rawhide packages bulging with silver dollars, letting the shiny coins tumble out on to the stone pavement below, where they bounced in every direction. Becknell told his fellow Missourians that the Santa Fe trade was "very profitable, money and mules are plentiful"—so profitable, in fact, that in the spring Becknell returned to Santa Fe with men and wagons carrying three thousand dollars' worth of goods.[6] His second trip reaped a spectacular bonanza, realizing profits of roughly sixty thousand dollars. At the same time he pioneered a direct and level route from Missouri to the New Mexican capital, suitable for wagon trains, for which he became known as the "Father of the Santa Fe Trail."[7]

Others followed in Becknell's wake, and the Santa Fe Trail quickly became a well-traveled thoroughfare. Parties departed from Franklin, then picked up the main trail in Independence, Missouri, and headed about eight hundred miles in a roughly diagonal line across present-day Kansas, a little sliver of southeastern Colorado, the northwest corner of the Oklahoma panhandle, and on through northeastern New Mexico to Santa Fe. It was not a trail for the faint of heart. In addition to traversing the territory of occasionally hostile Indians, including the Osage, the Pawnee, and the Comanche, it included some very difficult terrain, the most challenging of which was Cimarron Desert in southwestern Kansas, a high, flat, and perpetually parched plain more than fifty miles long, where water—if it could be found at all—usually lay in deep hollows or maddeningly hidden in dry riverbeds, inches or feet beneath the rock-hard sand. During Becknell's first transit across the desert he and his men became severely dehydrated and were forced to slake their thirst by cutting off the ears of their mules to drink their blood, and also killing a buffalo, slicing open its stomach, and drinking the greenish, watery liquid within, which they claimed "was an exquisite delight."[8]

A contemporary Missouri newspaper commenting on those who dared to travel the Santa Fe Trail observed:

> The extent of country which the caravans traverse, the long journeys they have to make, the rivers and morasses to cross, the prairies, the forests and all but African deserts to penetrate—require the most steel-formed constitutions and the most energetic minds. The accounts of these inland expeditions remind one of the caravans of the East. . . . The dangers which both encounter—the caravan of the East and that of the West—are equally numerous and equally alarming. Men of high chivalric and somewhat romantic natures are requisite for both.[9]*

The American parties that headed out over the Santa Fe Trail had two goals in mind. They brought with them all manner of goods, including tobacco, buttons, knives, shoes, drugs, fruits, rice, and even spermaceti candles, to trade with the New Mexicans for silver coins, livestock, cloth, and other salable items.[10] But the Americans also came to trap for furs, and the

---

* There were really two main routes of the Santa Fe Trail. The one discussed in the text above, is the Cimarron route, used by the vast majority of traders, trappers, and travelers, and the one for which Becknell earned his nickname. There was also the Mountain route, which broke off from the Cimarron route a little beyond present-day Cimarron, Kansas, and followed the Arkansas River to present-day La Junta, Colorado, where it headed to the southwest through the Raton Pass, on the eastern side of the Sangre de Cristos, and then continued to Santa Fe. The Mountain route, also pioneered by Becknell, was longer and less suitable for wagons than the Cimarron, but it had more places to get water and was less susceptible to Indian attacks.

trapping exceeded expectations because the rivers and streams in New Mexico were full of beaver because they had never been trapped before.[11] The New Mexicans had ignored the beavers in their own backyard in large part because there was little need for warm furs or felt hats in such a hot climate, so there wasn't much of a market for beaver in the province or anywhere else in New Spain. This was compounded by the fact that New Mexicans were not skilled in the art of trapping beaver or preparing their pelts. In contrast there was a thriving New Mexican trade in the coarser furs, such as deer, elk, and buffalo, whose skins were tanned into leather products, including coats, shirts, saddles, and even canvases for the religious paintings that adorned the austere adobe churches dotting New Mexican landscape.[12]

As word about the beaver windfall in New Mexico spread, an increasing number of American traders and trappers headed west along the Santa Fe Trail. Most of them used Taos, a small town situated in the mountains to the northeast of Santa Fe, as their base of operations. From there they traded their goods and also fanned out into the countryside to trap beaver and then send the pelts on wagons back to St. Louis for sale. Some of the early returns were quite impressive, as Becknell demonstrated in 1824, when he and his partners brought back $10,000 in furs and $180,000 in silver coins.[13] The Americans' growing success soon caught the disapproving eye of the new governor, who understandably viewed each wagonload of furs that left his province as money lost. To address this perceived imbalance the governor passed a law in 1824 restricting trapping privileges to New Mexican citizens. This, however, didn't stop the Americans from taking furs out of the province, because enforcement was limited and there were many ways to circumvent the law. These included becoming a Mexican citizen to obtain a license to trap, hiring "Mexican surrogates to obtain a license," bribing officials to look the other way, or running the risk of being caught.[14] So relentless were the trappers that the law was essentially useless. In fact, "During the first fifteen years of the overland commerce [on the Santa Fe Trail] practically every returning caravan had considerable quantities of fur."[15] In 1831, for example, two Taos traders brought pelts to St. Louis worth a combined total of $50,000.[16]

*T*HE AMERICAN FUR TRADE IN THE SOUTHWEST EVOLVED TO survive. As the number of trappers grew, they had to expand their search for beaver in ever-widening arcs as the areas closest to Taos were trapped out. Later the streams and rivers of the Rio Grande and Pecos valleys were picked clean, forcing the trappers to head north and west, into the present-day states of Colorado, Utah, Arizona, Nevada, and California. They followed the great southwestern rivers, such as the Colorado and the Gila, which course through steep, winding, colorful canyons that the rivers themselves have carved out of the earth's rocky crust.[17] They traversed the region's magnificent mountains, fertile valleys, and scorching deserts, becoming experts on southwestern geography.

And virtually everywhere the Taos trappers went, they were on Mexican soil. Before Mexico achieved its independence, then–U.S. Secretary of State John Quincy Adams and the Spanish minister to the United States, Don Luis de Onis, signed a treaty—on February 22, 1819—establishing the boundaries between American and Spanish territory. Spain ceded Florida to the United States, gave up its claims to the Northwest Territory above the forty-second parallel, and agreed on the location of the border between the Louisiana Territory and New Spain. As a result New Spain was left with all of present-day California, Nevada, Utah, New Mexico, Arizona, and Texas, as well as parts of Oklahoma, Kansas, Colorado, and Wyoming. And when Mexico revolted and kicked the Spanish out, it took control of this territory, thereby making the Taos trappers visitors in a foreign land.

*T*HE TAOS TRAPPERS HAD MUCH IN COMMON WITH THE MOUN-tain men. Beaver was their main target, and although the pelts of beavers in the arid Southwest were inferior to those caught farther north—being lighter in color and thinner—they still commanded good prices back east. Taos trappers' journeys rivaled those of the mountain men. Taos trappers faced many of the same dangers and they had a fondness for liquor, their usual drink being "Taos lightning," an explosively powerful concoction made from distilled wheat. And many Taos trappers married local women, including Mexicans and Indians, and after the men's trapping days were through, a considerable number of them remained in the Southwest.

There were, however, a number of differences between the mountain men and those involved in the Taos trade. For one thing the fur trade of the Southwest was much smaller. While at the height of the mountain man era there might have been as many as one thousand mountain men, the number of trappers in the southwest was at most in the low hundreds. No large fur companies organized the trade; rather the Taos trappers usually operated in small, loosely connected groups of free trappers. Instead of rendezvousing in the mountains, most of them used Taos as their rendezvous point. And because southwestern trappers spent their time in Taos or other Mexican settlements when they weren't trapping, it was not unusual for them to supplement their income by taking on additional jobs, such as working in the mines, farming, or ranching.[18]

The geographic divisions between the mountain men and the Taos trappers were not always precise. Many of the former trapped in the Southwest, just as many of the Taos trappers ventured well to the North, into the central and northern Rockies, and even participated in the rendezvous before heading back to New Mexico. And then there were some men who drifted from one fur trade culture to the other, as was the case for Christopher Houston Carson, who started out as a Taos trapper, then became a mountain man.

*C*ARSON WAS BORN IN MADISON COUNTY, KENTUCKY IN 1809, but within a year his family, who affectionately called him "Kit," moved west to an unsettled area not far from the Missouri River, which had been purchased by Daniel Boone's sons years earlier, and was called "Boone's Lick" on account of the local salt deposits. Carson was a small, surprisingly strong boy with deep blue eyes, who talked little and manifested a cool confidence and a keen intellect. His formal education, however, came to abrupt end at age eight, when his father died and he was forced to take on the responsibilities of providing for his family. In 1822 Carson's mother married a man he didn't respect, and as the friction between them grew, his stepfather decided to get Kit out of the house. Thus at fourteen Carson was apprenticed to David Workman, a saddler in nearby Franklin. Carson thoroughly disliked the work, so much so that in August 1826 he ran off to Independence and joined a caravan heading to Santa Fe, hoping to see "different countries," and find out if there was any truth to the exciting stories he had heard about the opportunities out west.[19]

After arriving at the end of the Santa Fe Trail, Carson headed to Taos, and over the next couple of years he learned Spanish and earned his keep through various jobs, including working as a teamster at the Santa Rita copper mines in southwestern New Mexico, an interpreter, and a cook for Ewing Young, who ran a store in Taos that supplied trappers. But Young was also a trapper himself, who had arrived in New Mexico in 1822 as part of Becknell's second expedition to the area. By the time Carson came to work for him, Young had already become one of the most famous trappers in the Southwest, known as much for his success and honesty as for his fights with Indians. And in August 1829 Carson joined Young on a trapping expedition heading to California.[20]

Over the next eighteen months, as Young's party traveled to San Francisco and back, Carson became a skilled trapper. Upon returning to Taos in the spring of 1831, he received several hundred dollars as his share of the profits. "We passed the time gloriously," recalled Carson, "spending our money freely, never thinking that our lives had been risked in gaining it. Our only idea was to . . . have as much pleasure and enjoyment as the country could afford. Trappers and sailors are similar in regard to money that they earn so dearly, being daily in danger of losing their lives. But when the voyage has been made and they have received their pay, they think not of the hardships and dangers through which they have passed, but spend all they have and are then ready for another trip."[21]

Carson's next trip began in the fall of 1831, but this time he headed north and trapped for two years throughout a broad swath of the Rockies, from Colorado to Idaho. Although he returned to Taos in October 1833 to sell his beaver, he quickly headed north again, where he remained a mountain man for the next seven years, further honing his hunting, trapping, and survival skills, and getting into many vicious confrontations with Indians, which burnished his already growing reputation as "heroic" Indian fighter.

ONE OF THE MOST FAMOUS EVENTS OF CARSON'S LIFE IN THE mountains was his fight with Joseph Chouinard, a French Canadian trapper.[22] Chouinard, a large and unusually strong man, was widely known as the "great bully of the mountains," who "made a practice of whipping every man that he was displeased with—and that was nearly all."[23] At the 1835 rendezvous at Green River, he did his best to live up to his reputation. After getting drunk Chouinard beat up two or three fellow Frenchmen, and then announced that he was eager to pummel Americans, and would gladly "take a switch and switch them." When Carson—a man who preferred action to words and humility to arrogance—heard these boasts, he bristled with anger, especially since he already held Chouinard in contempt since they were both competing for the affections of Singing Grass, a comely Arapaho who was also at the rendezvous.

The Frenchman's taunts sent Carson over the edge. "I did not like such talk from any man," Carson recalled, "so I told him that I was the worst American in camp," and further that "there were many who could thrash him but for the fact that they were afraid," and if he didn't stop making threats, "I would rip his guts." Carson's willingness to stand up to Chouinard was all the more impressive because of the disparity in their size. While Chouinard was a bear of a man, Carson was just five feet four inches tall and slight of build. When William Tecumseh Sherman, who would later gain fame as a Union general in the Civil War, met the already legendary Carson in 1848, he was shocked "at beholding a small, stoop-shouldered man, with reddish hair, freckled face, soft blue eyes, and nothing to indicate extraordinary courage or daring."[24] As Carson proved throughout his career, looks can be very deceptive.

Chouinard said nothing to Carson, but instead went for his rifle, mounted his horse, and rode it to the edge of the camp, where a crowd was gathering to see what would happen next. Taking this as a challenge, Carson grabbed the first gun he could find—a pistol—jumped on his steed, and galloped toward Chouinard, pulling up so close to the Frenchman that their "horses were touching." Carson demanded to know if Chouinard intended to shoot him. Although the hulking giant said no, his actions belied his words. He raised his rifle in Carson's direction. Both men fired at exactly the same instant, so that "all present said that but one report was heard." Carson's bullet ripped through Chouinard's arm, but the Frenchman delivered only a glancing blow. His rifle was so close to Carson's head when it discharged that the hot powder leaving the muzzle singed Carson's left eye, while the bullet gouged a sliver of flesh from beneath his ear, leaving him scarred for life. "During the remainder of our stay in camp," Carson later recalled with his characteristic brevity, "we had no more bother with this French bully." Carson vanquished Chouinard not only on the field of battle but also in his amatory ventures: Within a year's time Carson had won Singing Grass's hand in marriage, after paying her father, Running Around, three mules and a gun.[25]

WHILE CARSON WENT FROM BEING A TAOS TRAPPER TO A mountain man, some men did the reverse. Such was the case for Jedediah Smith, David Jackson, and William Sublette, the three men who bought out Ashley in 1826, and ran their own fur-trading company in the mountains for the next four years. Taking stock of their situation at the 1830 rendezvous at Wind River, the partners decided they had had enough of the business. Since 1826 they had lost more than forty men and more than $40,000 in equipment, horses, mules, traps, and furs. Heading into the rendezvous they were "barely solvent," and although that year's catch was an excellent one, which would sell for nearly $85,000 back in St. Louis and put them firmly in the black, they were not confident about the direction of the mountain trade. Increasing competition, the growing scarcity of beaver, and the rising cost of supplying and paying their men made them nervous.[26] They also wanted to go home and spend time with their friends and family. So, the three partners sold their company to five other mountain men—Thomas Fitzpatrick, Jim Bridger, Milton Sublette, Henry Fraeb, and Jean Baptiste Gervais—who created the Rocky Mountain Fur Company.[27]

After Smith, Jackson, and Sublette arrived back in St. Louis in early October 1830, they went their separate ways. Soon, however, Sublette and Jackson got the itch to get back into business, but instead of returning to the mountains they set their sights on Santa Fe, where they planned to get their share of the growing "commerce of the prairies."[28] When Smith heard about these plans, he was intrigued. Although he had sworn off the Rocky Mountain trade, Santa Fe offered a new adventure, and by early 1831 the partnership was reconstituted. In late April their party of eighty-three men and twenty-four wagons set off on the Santa Fe Trail.[29]

Disasters mounted as the caravan proceeded to the new beaver mecca in the Southwest. Within the first three hundred miles of the journey, the party was forced to fire their six-pound cannon to fend off an attack by several hundred mounted Indians. They then lost a man who dropped back to hunt antelope and was set upon by a small band of Pawnee. Having launched their assault on the broiling plain during a particularly dry spell, the Cimarron Desert proved their biggest challenge. The trail blazed by earlier wagon trains, difficult to discern even under good conditions, was virtually obliterated by the tracks of wandering buffalo herds. The few water holes the men passed were dry, their surfaces "deeply cracked by the withering air and the scorching rays of the sun."[30] In late May, after nearly three days without anything to drink, the men and their animals were near death, their only hope to find water. In their search Smith and Thomas Fitzpatrick rode ahead of the caravan. The first water hole they reached was empty, and Smith left Fitzpatrick there to dig deeper while he continued on. When he reached the dry bed of the Cimarron River, Smith began digging and soon water collected at the surface.

What Smith did not know was that twenty or so Comanche were in the area hunting buffalo. They had kept themselves concealed as Smith rode up, and now approached. As soon as Smith saw the Indians about a half mile off, he realized it was too late to flee. He mounted his horse and rode up to them with his rifle at the ready, hoping that a show of confidence might spare his life. Smith signaled to the Indians to stop when they were just a few yards away, and they did. The Indians then tried to spook Smith's horse so that it would wheel about, allowing them to shoot him in the back. When the horse finally spun around, one of the Indians sent a bullet into Smith's left shoulder, nearly knocking him to the ground. But Smith managed to turn on his attackers, level his rifle, and get off one round, killing the chief and wounding one of his warriors. Before Smith could raise his pistols, the Comanche rushed in and lanced him to death.[31]

The rest of the caravan, unaware of Smith's demise, found water, and hadn't gotten much farther along the trail before a menacing party of fifteen hundred Gros Ventre descended on them. The wagons quickly circled, and the men dug in and prepared to defend themselves, but before any fighting commenced, Sublette negotiated a truce, and the caravan continued, reaching Santa Fe a couple of weeks later. There Smith's partners got the shocking news of his death. Mexican traders who had heard the story of Smith's final moments from the Comanche warriors who had killed him told Sublette and Jackson what had happened. It was hard for them to believe that Smith, a man who had survived so many mortal dangers in his storied life, was dead at the age of thirty-two. Their sorrow was considerable: They had lost not only an associate but a close friend.

Sublette and Jackson did well for themselves in Santa Fe. They traded for fifty-five packs of beaver and eight hundred buffalo robes, the latter of which were of growing importance in the domestic fur trade back east, where they were manufactured into coats and sold as sleigh blankets. Despite their initial success, the two men's tenure in the southwestern fur trade was brief. Before the summer was out they dissolved their partnership, with Jackson venturing to California to enter the mule trade, and Sublette returning to St. Louis and ultimately finding his way back to the Rockies to resume his career as a mountain man.[32]

———

*W*HILE THE SOUTHWESTERN FUR TRADE WAS GETTING OFF the ground, John Jacob Astor, already the single most powerful fur trader in the United States, was looking to expand the reach of his New York–based behemoth, the American Fur Company. By the early 1820s Astor had further strengthened his hold on the fur trade around the Great Lakes and the upper Mississippi, where his able partners and former Astorians, Ramsey Crooks and Robert Stuart, ran the company's Northern Department and managed to thrash the competition into irrelevance. Never one to rest on his laurels, Astor had also begun to make inroads in St. Louis, where the local fur-trading elite had for many years eyed him with jealousy if not dread. They viewed the evolving fur trade on the upper Missouri as their domain, and they did not want Astor as a competitor, realizing full well that his expansion onto their turf would be impossible to prevent.

Astor's initial foray into the Missouri trade came in 1816, when he used his superior access to high-quality goods and his deep pockets to sign deals with two St. Louis firms, locking them into a trading arrangement in which he would supply them with goods and they would sell him their furs. But this was just a first step. Despite the Astoria debacle, Astor had never given up on his goal of establishing a series of fur-trading posts all the way up the Missouri, and thereby controlling the fur trade of that region, and even beyond into the Rockies. With that goal in mind, he opened a store and a warehouse in St. Louis in the spring of 1822, and created the American Fur Company's Western Department, which was to orchestrate his expansion upriver. While Astor, the grand tactician, was considering his next moves, he received news he had been longing to hear—the United States government had finally decided to dismantle its factory system.

*S*INCE ITS INCEPTION IN 1795 THE FACTORY SYSTEM HAD expanded to twelve trading posts on the eve of the War of 1812, but by the end of the decade there were only eight posts left, all but one of which were located east of the Mississippi.[33] The system's supporters, who accused the private traders of cheating the Indians and debauching them with liquor, had hoped that the factories would drive the traders out of business. The factories were also supposed to create strong bonds between the Indians and the government, eliminate Indian aggression on the frontier, and civilize and Christianize the supposedly savage Indians, ultimately leading them to give up their way of life and merge into the American mainstream.[34] By all these measures, the factory system failed, and with the aid of hindsight it is clear that it was doomed from the start.

In creating the system the government made a critical mistake in continuing to license private fur traders, thus ensuring that the traders would compete with the factories. This was a serious problem because the factories were not designed to beat the competition. As it turned out, most of the factors who manned the government trading posts were retired military or ex-political appointees, who had little or no understanding of the dynamics of the fur trade or the nature of their clientele—the Indians. The factors, in effect enjoying sinecures of one sort or another, were paid a salary and they didn't venture from their comfortable living quarters at the posts but rather waited for the Indians to arrive with furs. Controlled by the federal government, their salaries were the same regardless of the number of furs purchased, so there was no incentive to expand the business. They knew nothing or cared little about the proper grading or handling of furs, and as a result many of the furs they bought were of poor quality, and their shipments often arrived back east in a pitiable state. The factors were not permitted to offer presents, a long-standing and well-accepted feature of the Indian trade. Even though the government didn't have to make a profit and could therefore provide relatively cheap goods, the factories relied primarily on American-made goods, which were of inferior quality to the British goods that the Indians preferred. Even when an American product might have sufficed, it was often supplied in an unsuitable form, one example being silver. The Indians wanted thin pieces of silver to fashion into jewelry, but the American silversmiths who were contracted to supply silver by the pound, sent thick, heavy bars since they were cheaper and less time-consuming to make. Because those bars were less desirable than thinner pieces of silver, the Indians refused to pay the price the factors demanded. Thus the bars sat in the warehouse unsold. Finally, by prohibiting the sale of alcohol, the government took out of the factors' hands one of the items that the Indians desired most. It is no wonder that the factories were at a competitive disadvantage compared to private traders, who traveled widely to obtain furs, offered presents, provided high-quality British goods and plenty of alcohol, knew how to grade and protect furs, received pay based on performance, and were very familiar with the Indian way of life, often marrying into key tribes, thereby creating ties that facilitated commerce.[35]

It is hardly surprising that the Indians looked down on the factories, expressing "contempt [for] a government that turned trader."[36] Still, many Indians went to the factories, often selling them their worst furs for high prices—since the factors didn't realize they were being duped—while saving their best furs for the private traders. The weak ties the factors forged with their customers did nothing to further the government's goal of developing a strong relationship with the Indians. Indeed, during the War of 1812, most of the tribes living near the factories fought alongside the British and eagerly attacked the factories with which they had formerly traded. As for the larger goal of "civilizing" and Christianizing the Indians and thereby merging them into the American mainstream, the factories fared no better.[37]

Despite its flawed design, the factory system absorbed enough of the fur trade to anger private traders, who viewed every pelt that went to the government as lost profits. As a result Astor and his main competitors in St. Louis teamed up after the end of the War of 1812 to launch an all-out assault on their common enemy. Astor spearheaded the attack, using his political influence and money to good advantage. Crooks was sent repeatedly to Washington to lobby on behalf of abolishing the factories, pointing out all their defects while at the same time discounting any criticism of the American Fur Company, or fur traders in general. A barrage of newspaper articles, editorials, and formal petitions, urging the federal government to take action on this critical issue, supplemented this campaign. And many politicians, especially from frontier states and territories, jumped on the antifactory bandwagon.

Its poor track record notwithstanding, the factory system had supporters, many of whom believed that the biggest defect of all was the one that had been there from the beginning—competition from private traders. "Let the government take the trade into their own hands," argued Maj. Thomas Biddle, who in 1819 had completed an important study of the Indian trade: "Let the agents be honest, capable, and zealous; let their factories be established, not only where troops may be stationed, but at all points convenient for trading with the Indians; let certain prices be fixed, and let the compensation of the factors depend upon the value of the furs they obtain; let their accounts be rigidly inspected. The Indians would then be completely within the influence of the government [and it wouldn't be necessary] to debauch the Indians with whiskey."[38]

The debate over the factory system sputtered and flared until early 1822, when Senator Thomas Hart Benton struck the final blow. A lawyer and former newspaperman, Benton was a rising political star in the Missouri Territory when he began railing against the factory system. Now, as one of the first senators of the newly created state of Missouri, and the chairman of the Senate Committee on Indian Affairs, he drafted legislation to shut down the system once and for all. Benton's zeal was no doubt stoked by Astor's decision to hire him as an advocate on the American Fur Company's behalf.[39] The bill sailed through Congress and became law on May 6, 1822. An enthused Crooks wrote to Benton to congratulate him on his victory: "The result is the best possible proof of the value to the country of talents, intelligence, and perseverance, and you deserve the unqualified thanks of the community for destroying the pious monster."[40] Astor, too, was quite happy, or at least as happy as his usually dour personality allowed him to be. With the factories out of the way, he could focus more of his attention on gaining control of the Missouri fur trade.

ONE OF ASTOR'S BIOGRAPHERS, JOHN UPTON TERRELL, claimed:

> Astor had more resources, money, brains, affiliations, political power than all the other St. Louis traders combined. He had agents in Europe who purchased manufactured goods for him at the lowest possible cost, directly from the factories. He was the largest fur dealer in the world, associated with the best houses of England, France, Germany, Belgium, and other countries. His own ships carried his furs across the seas and returned with his merchandise. Astor could put British goods on the waterfront of St. Louis at a lower cost than could any other merchant.[41]

Although Terrell was too harsh on the intelligence of the St. Louis crowd, the rest of what he says rings true. Astor was a colossal, almost unstoppable force, and once he set his sights on a goal, it was unwise to bet against his achieving it.

Unlike the Rocky Mountain and the Taos trade, the Missouri fur trade as it evolved now relied mostly on the Indians for labor. They were the ones who killed the animals, prepared the pelts, and then traded them to the fur company representatives, who would either travel to the Indian villages to collect the furs or wait at one of the company's permanent or temporary posts along the river for the Indians to arrive. Thus a company's success turned on its ability to establish trading relationships with the various tribes. Astor dispatched his men upriver to build posts and forge such ties, but in many cases they found other companies already on the scene. When this happened Astor did not hesitate or back down; instead he proceeded to crush, purchase, or absorb the competition. If the companies were small and poorly financed, teetering on the edge of solvency, Astor's men simply moved into their areas of operation and outbid them for the available furs by giving the Indians better merchandise at a lower price, and liquor in copious amounts. With his deep pockets, Astor could afford to pay any price. As a result the Indians soon sent all their furs Astor's way, while his erstwhile competitors died as a result of economic strangulation. For larger companies, who could not be vanquished so easily, Astor used one of two approaches. If he could buy them outright for a reasonable price, he would. But if the company's owners preferred to be his partners, he readily acceded because the exclusive agreements Astor struck with such companies essentially made them wholly-owned subsidiaries of the American Fur Company.[42]

Using whatever strategy best suited the situation, Astor marched up the Missouri during the mid- to late 1820s, and by the end of the decade the entire river had become, "in so far as the fur trade was concerned," his "private creek."[43] He had bested, engulfed, or elbowed aside all of the other firms, including Stone, Bostwick & Company, Menard & Valle, Bernard Pratte & Company, and the Columbia Fur Company, the last proving to be Astor's most important acquisition.[44] With it came seven significant posts on the Missouri, including ones located at Council Bluffs in Iowa and near the Mandan villages in North Dakota. The Columbia Fur Company's trade, most of it in buffalo robes, earned it in some years as much as two hundred thousand dollars in gross profits, an impressive amount that Astor hoped to increase. Particularly helpful to Astor was Kenneth McKenzie, a Scotsman by birth, who had risen to become president of the Columbia Fur Company.[45] In 1827, Astor appointed him as head of the new Upper Missouri Outfit of the American Fur Company's Western Department, with the responsibility for the trade on the Missouri above its junction with the Big Sioux.

McKenzie, a confident man who was very impressed with himself, was fond of wearing fancy military uniforms and parading about in front of his men as if he were Caesar or Napoleon. At one point he imported a custom-made suit of armor from Europe, although there is no record that he wore it. Despite McKenzie's foppishness, Astor's decision to pick him to lead the company's westward expansion proved to be a masterstroke, for behind his outsize ego lay a man of uncommon ability, boldness, and enterprise, not unlike his German immigrant boss. McKenzie, dubbed "King of the Missouri," lorded over his domain from his headquarters at Fort Union, the largest and most important of all the American Fur Company posts in the region, located just above the junction of the Yellowstone and Missouri rivers. From this perch he orchestrated the expansion of Astor's empire in a number of critical ways.[46]

*E*AGER TO MAKE INROADS INTO THE ROCKY MOUNTAIN TRADE, in 1828 Astor gave McKenzie the task of leading the charge. That fall McKenzie sent Étienne Provost, a former Ashley man, into the mountains to tell the free trappers that the Western Department of the American Fur Company was open for business and would offer competitive prices for their furs. Soon thereafter the already legendary Hugh Glass showed up at McKenzie's door, representing a number of free trappers who didn't want to travel to the company's posts on the Missouri but wanted the company to come to the rendezvous. The number of firms supplying goods to the mountain men had been declining, and the prices the mountain men had to pay for those goods had been on the rise. Glass and his fellows hoped that if the American Fur Company entered the trade, competition would increase and prices would drop. This was all the coaxing McKenzie needed, and in 1829 the American Fur Company, at McKenzie's urging, sent a party of trappers and goods into the mountains. Astor had finally entered the Rocky Mountain trade.[47]

*W*HILE MCKENZIE WAS EXPANDING TO THE ROCKIES HE WAS also wondering how to open up another potentially profitable area of trade. American fur trappers had for decades longed to get their hands on the beavers that swam in the streams and rivers running throughout Blackfoot territory. Those areas, however, located primarily in the northwestern parts of present-day Montana on the eastern slopes of the Rockies, were essentially off limits due to the enmity of the Blackfeet. Although the Blackfeet were willing to trade furs with the Hudson's Bay Company, Americans were not welcome. McKenzie viewed the Blackfeet's land as an unfathomable opportunity, but he feared that if he sent his trappers there, they would risk getting killed.

In the fall of 1830 a grizzled trapper named Jacob Berger arrived at Fort

Union and presented McKenzie with a possible solution to his problem. A trapper for at least twenty years, during most of which he had been an employee of the Hudson's Bay Company at one of its forts on the edge of Blackfoot country, Berger had traded with the Blackfeet, become fluent in their language, and friendly with many of the tribes. Exactly why he chose to leave his former employer and wander into the American post remains unknown. Perhaps he had had a falling-out with his superiors at the Hudson's Bay Company, or he was just curious to see what the Americans were up to. Whatever the reason, when McKenzie learned of Berger's unusual skills and connections, he did not hesitate to take advantage of them. He asked Berger if he was willing to visit the Blackfeet as an emissary to encourage them to open trade relations with the Americans. Berger consented and headed west with four of McKenzie's men.

The quintet traveled on horseback for four weeks without seeing a single Indian. At all times Berger kept an American flag unfurled at the head of their column to let anyone who might be watching know who they were. Although McKenzie's men had volunteered to join Berger's quest, they grew increasingly apprehensive with each passing day. The Blackfeet had killed many Americans, and their bellicose reputation preceded them. Alone on the trails in foreign territory, the men's fears began to overwhelm them, when they finally found a large camp of Blackfeet a short distance above the mouth of the Marias River. The four men were eager to flee, but Berger reassured them, despite their terror that they would become flesh for the Indians' abattoir.[48] As soon as the Indians saw the men approaching, mounted warriors raced toward them. Berger ordered his party to stop and then rode out to meet the Indians, who themselves had halted, unsure what to make of the lone flag bearer boldly advancing in their direction. After a few tense moments Berger called out his name, and the Indians rushed forward to welcome their old friend, shaking his hand and patting him on the back.

During the feasts and discussions that followed, Berger persuaded a few of the chiefs, along with about forty of their warriors, to visit McKenzie at Fort Union, where they negotiated a historic peace treaty in the summer of 1831.[49] Soon thereafter McKenzie built a trading post in the heart of Blackfoot territory, near the junction of the Marias and Missouri rivers. It was called Fort Piegan in honor of the Blackfoot tribe that had negotiated the peace. When that fort burned down, another was built about six miles farther up the Marias and named Fort McKenzie. This relationship with the Blackfeet was a boon to the American Fur Company, which benefited from the thousands of beaver pelts the Indians provided.[50]

*M*CKENZIE'S GREATEST INNOVATION LAY NOT IN HIS trading or diplomatic skills, however, but in his understanding of river travel. Getting supplies to the fur-trading posts on the upper Missouri in the 1820s was a tedious affair. Heavily laden keelboats ponderously made the trip employing a combination of poling, cordelling, and sailing. McKenzie had another vision: What about using a steamboat to navigate upriver?

The first steamboat arrived in St. Louis in 1817, when the *Pike* moored in the Mississippi at the city's edge. Two years later the *Missouri Gazette* wrote that when the *Pike* steamed into view, "We hailed it as the day of small things, but the glorious consummation of all our wishes is daily arriving. Already we have seen during the present season at our shores five steamboats, and several more expected. Who could or would have dared conjecture, that in 1819, we would witness the arrival of a steamboat from Philadelphia or New York? And yet, such is the fact!"[51] To an early-nineteenth-century American the steamboat must have seemed as thrilling as the airplane would to early-twentieth-century Americans. The effect on commerce was meteoric.

As impressive as the steamboats were, it was almost universally believed that the fickle nature of the mighty Missouri would bar their navigating beyond Council Bluffs. McKenzie didn't agree. He saw steamboats as a way to revolutionize the fur trade, and in the late 1820s he began urging Pierre Chouteau, Jr., the head of the Western Department, to encourage Astor to take a risk and build the company's first steamboat. Chouteau was finally convinced of the value of this project, and in the summer of 1830 he wrote to Astor, pointing out the benefits of steamboat traffic. He noted the speed of getting goods to the posts and furs back down, as well as the fact that fewer men would be needed to do the job. Astor agreed. A shipbuilder in Louisville was hired, and in early 1831 the *Yellowstone*, costing nearly ten thousand dollars to complete, paddled its way to St. Louis ready for service. It was a grand boat, 130 feet long, 20 feet wide, with three decks above the waterline, multiple berths, two smokestacks up front, and an 18-foot-wide paddle wheel on the side. It rode high in the water, drawing just 5.5 feet when carrying the maximum load of seventy-five tons.[52]

The *Yellowstone* appeared equal to the task of taking on the Missouri, but its maiden voyage was disappointing. After leaving St. Louis on April 16, 1831, the *Yellowstone* got mired in the mud a little more than a month later, not far above the junction of the Missouri and the Niobrara rivers. Keelboats sent down from Fort Tecumseh, near the mouth of the Teton River, lightened the *Yellowstone's* load enough so that the steamer was able to refloat itself and make it to the fort, where the rest of its goods were taken to shore. Then the boat was filled with a "cargo of buffalo robes, furs, and peltries, besides ten thousand pounds of buffalo tongues," before heading back to St. Louis.[53]

Although the *Yellowstone* had ventured higher up the Missouri than any other steamboat before it, McKenzie was convinced it could go higher still. One year later, in June 1832, the *Yellowstone* made it all the way to Fort Union, and then returned to St. Louis by early July, traveling an average of one hundred miles per day on its way downriver. Crooks, writing to Chouteau, knew full well the significance of this event. "I congratulate you most cordially on your perseverance and ultimate success in reaching the Yellowstone by *steam* . . . You have brought the Falls of the Missouri as near, comparatively, as was the River Platte in my younger days." The *Yellowstone's* trip had reverberations that went far beyond the United States. Astor sent a letter from France also congratulating Chouteau, and telling him, "Your voyage in the *Yellowstone* attracted much attention in Europe, and has been noted in all the papers here." But the *Yellowstone's* most important impact, at least as far as the American Fur Company was concerned, was that it greatly improved the company's competitiveness, especially with respect to the Canadians who were still trading with Indians south of the forty-ninth parallel, and thereby taking a significant number of furs out of the country. "Many of the Indians who had been in the habit of trading with the Hudson's Bay Company," wrote the *Missouri Republican*, "declared that the company could no longer compete with the Americans, and concluded thereafter to bring all their skins to the latter; and said, that the British might turn out their dogs and burn their sledges, as they would no longer be useful while the *Fire Boat* walked on the waters."[54]

*S*UCCESS OF ASTOR'S WESTERN DEPARTMENT ON THE MIS-souri, and increasingly in the Rockies, mirrored that of his Northern Department. The virtual monopoly he established around the Great Lakes, and along the northern Mississippi after the British were expelled in 1816, only grew stronger during the 1820s and early 1830s. With Crooks at the helm Astor's men fanned out through the present-day states of Minnesota, Wisconsin, Illinois, Indiana, Michigan, Ohio, and Iowa, bringing virtually every tribe in the area into the vast trading network that funneled furs to one of the Northern Department's many posts, including ones at the sites of present-day Minneapolis–St. Paul, Duluth, Chicago, Milwaukee, and Detroit. The Ojibwa, the Sauk, the Fox, the Kickapoo, and other tribes scoured the countryside not only for beaver but also for any other animals whose furs could command a decent price, including raccoon, river otters, muskrat, fox, and rabbits. The Northern Department also purchased furs from free trappers and traders who operated throughout the region. Once all the furs were collected at the company posts, most were transported to St. Louis, where they were unpacked, counted, graded, weighed, and repacked into bales, then sent by steamboat down to New Orleans, and transferred to vessels that took them to New York City, where they entered the domestic and international markets. When the Erie Canal opened in 1825, a significant portion of the Northern Department's furs made it to New York via that route.[55]

Wherever Astor's men operated, many of the individuals with whom they worked were métis. In those places as well as throughout the Pacific Northwest, métis were an integral part of the fur trade, acting as traders, trappers, and intermediaries between white fur traders and Indian suppliers. Thus, in many ways, Astor's men and other fur traders benefited from the distinct métis communities that had developed along with the spread of fur trade in the seventeenth, eighteenth, and early nineteenth centuries, as coureurs de bois, voyageurs, and employees of fur-trading companies entered into country marriages and settled down.[56]

*A*S THE WESTERN DEPARTMENT EXTENDED ITS REACH UP the Missouri and into the Rockies, and the Northern Department consolidated its hold on its domain, the one constant was the liberal use of alcohol. And it wasn't only Astor's men who were guilty of this: All his competitors relied on intoxicating spirits to help steer furs in their direction. A variety of federal laws aimed at protecting the Indians by banning the importation of liquor into Indian country failed miserably. The first of these had an exception for liquor imported solely for the use of fur company employees, which of course led the companies to claim many more people on their payroll than was actually the case. Even when a law was passed that eliminated the employee exception and banned all alcohol imports outright, it failed as well. Enforcement was limited, and fur companies routinely stymied government agents' efforts to intercept alcohol by adopting creative smuggling techniques to transport the contraband upriver and into the mountains. And when the government did manage to confiscate enough liquor to hamper the trade, some traders decided to produce what they needed, using stills to make moonshine.

A few fur company owners, including Astor, publicly decried the use of alcohol and its impact on the Indians, but their main concern was not for the Indians' well-being but rather that drunk Indians were not as effective in gathering furs. Even so the owners never went so far as to stop the practice of supplying liquor to the Indians or to throw their support behind efforts to adequately enforce the laws on the books. The common refrain was, If we don't give the Indians alcohol, some other company will, and they will absorb the trade, leaving us with nothing. This argument applied not just to American companies but also to the Hudson's Bay Company, which used alcohol as a means of luring Indians on the upper Missouri to cross the border into Canada and bring their furs to British trading posts. It is not surprising, therefore, that during the 1820s and early 1830s the amount of alcohol traded to the Indians dramatically increased.[57]

Although there is no doubt that alcohol played a crucial and damaging role in the fur trade of this era, it is important to place its use in perspective. Virtually all the people who wrote about the fur trade and its impact on the Indians were white, and they often spoke of the Indians as if they were a monolithic group. Most of these accounts depict Indians as wanting alcohol more than anything else. Because of their supposedly uncontrollable lust for liquor, trading sessions devolved into drunken revels during which Indians became incapable of looking out for their own best interests. An example of this type of one-size-fits-all mentality can be seen in a comment Biddle made in 1819. "So violent is the attachment of the Indian for it [alcohol] that he who gives most is sure to obtain the furs, while should any one attempt to trade without it he is sure of losing ground with his antagonist. No bargain is ever made without it."[58] The truth is that not all Indians participated in the fur trade, not all who did drank alcohol, and even those who drank didn't necessarily do so to the point that conniving traders were able to swindle them out of their furs. In many instances trading sessions were rather routine and the Indians were not easy marks. As William Clark, the former explorer and superintendent of Indian affairs at St. Louis, wrote in 1828, "Contrary to the opinion generally entertained, they [Indians] are good judges of the articles which are offered to them. The trade is not that system of fraud which many suppose."[59] Just as the stereotypes of mountain men fail to capture the great variability of individuals in that trade, so too do the stereotypes of Indians as drunken victims—while many were, many were not.[60]

ASTOR'S GREAT SUCCESS IN THE FUR TRADE WAS BUILT NOT only on a liberal use of alcohol but also on a system that ensured that he made a healthy profit at nearly every step of the trading process.[61] A key part of this system was his ability to squeeze those at the bottom of the supply chain. Like virtually every other fur-trading company, the American Fur Company did its best to sell its goods dear and purchase furs for as little as possible. This placed the Indians in an exceedingly uncomfortable position. When there were competing traders in the area, the Indians could drive a better bargain for their furs by playing one competitor off against another. As the American Fur Company came to dominate, this option was increasingly foreclosed. As one keen observer of the company's operations in the early 1830s noted, "The Sauk and Fox Indians, whose present population exceeds six thousand souls . . . are compelled to take goods, etc., of the [American Fur Company] traders at their very high prices, because they cannot do without them, for if the traders do not supply their necessary wants and enable them to support themselves, they would literally starve."[62]

It wasn't only the Indians who got squeezed. The American Fur Company drove hard bargains when purchasing furs from independent traders, and it also maximized its profits by minimizing the salaries it paid to its own traders, and forcing them to purchase their outfits and supplies from company posts at grossly inflated prices. Just like the mountain men, the traders who worked for the American Fur Company's Northern and Western Departments rarely made much money, and more often than not found themselves in debt to their employer.[63] In return for such paltry wages, these traders often made a terrible sacrifice. As Secretary of War Lewis Cass reported to President Andrew Jackson in 1832, "The general course of the trade itself, is laborious and dangerous, full of exposure and privations, and leading to premature exhaustion and disability. Few of those engaged in it reach an advanced stage of life, and still fewer preserve an unbroken constitution. The labor is excessive, subsistence scanty and precarious; and the Indians are ever liable to sudden and violent paroxysms of passions, in which they spare neither friend nor foe."[64]

Considering that the American Fur Company engaged in thousands of profitable transactions over the years, it is easy to see why Astor made a fortune in furs.[65] And Astor's success as well as his company's actions certainly bred contempt. As Chittenden observed, "It is difficult to exaggerate the state of affairs which at times prevailed. 'The company,' by which is always meant the American Fur Company, was thoroughly hated even by its own servants. Throughout its career it was an object of popular execration, as all grasping monopolies are." At another point Chittenden added that, "to the average individual the American Fur Company was . . . determined to rule or ruin, and hence it was thoroughly hated even by those who respected its power."[66] Gen. Zachary Taylor, who would later become president of the United States, declared in 1830 that "the American Fur Company in the aggregate [were] . . . the greatest scoundrels the world ever knew."[67]

*B*Y THE EARLY 1830S ONLY ITS ENORMOUS SUCCESS—ENABLED by the manifold resources at Astor's command—set the American Fur Company apart from its principal competitors. By this time, too, the fur trade spanned vast areas of the young United States, killing huge numbers of animals and employing thousands of individuals (some of whom became comfortable, and a few, like Astor, exceedingly rich). Nevertheless, despite its great scope the fur trade was not a major American industry—in 1833, for example, the roughly eight hundred thousand dollars' worth of furs shipped overseas represented less than 2 percent of the country's exports. (Its economic impact was more significant only in places like St. Louis and New York City, where the fur trade had a strong presence.)[68]

For more than two centuries the beaver had played—symbolically if not always economically—the starring role in the drama of the fur trade. But at that very moment the fur trade was moving in a new direction. Within less than a decade the era of the beaver would be over.

—14—

Fall of the Beaver

Beaver Hut on the Missouri, *by Karl Bodmer,*
1840–43.

LWAYS EAGER TO BEST THE COMPETITION, KENNETH
McKenzie floated an idea up the American Fur Company chain
of command in 1831. Why not create a medal to give the Indians in the name
of the president of the United States? The Jefferson medals given out by Lewis
and Clark, as well as the medals distributed by the Hudson's Bay Company
had been well received and much appreciated by the Indians, who saw these
presents as an integral part of building trading relationships. If the American
Fur Company had its own medals to bestow, McKenzie thought, they might
help the company strengthen their ties with the Indians on the upper Missouri, especially the Blackfeet, with whom McKenzie had just concluded a
treaty of peace.[1]

Astor consented, but there remained a small problem. Making medals to
distribute to the Indians on behalf of the president was a government function,
not something to be undertaken by a private enterprise. The American Fur
Company skirted this difficulty by calling the objects ornaments, not medals,
clarifying that they would be presented on behalf of Astor, not the United

States government. That satisfied the War Department, and soon a diemaker began producing the ornaments, which everyone called medals anyway. They were quite impressive. Struck in silver, copper, and aluminum, and sometimes gilded, the medals showed, not surprisingly, Astor's likeness in profile on the front, surrounded by the words, "President of the American Fur Company." The reverse had two calumets (peace pipes) and two tomahawks crossing each other, creating a frame for a pair of clasped hands encircled by "Peace and Friendship." The outer edge on the reverse bore the words "Fort Union" and "U.M.O." for the Upper Missouri Outfit. It appeared as if the American Fur Company's empire was almost a government unto itself, with Astor as its ruler. His reign, however, was quickly drawing to a close.[2]

Astor began considering the possibility of retiring from the fur trade in 1825, when he confided to Crooks, "with regard as to whether I continue in the trade I really cannot now tell."[3] Throughout the balance of the decade and into the next, Astor occasionally broached the subject, but his lieutenants thought it was mere talk. In 1830, when a rumor surfaced that Astor's departure was imminent, Robert Stuart wrote to another fur trader, "Pray give yourself no concern about Mr. Astor's retiring . . . my opinion is that he will never retire *until he is called*."[4] Even after Astor had begun negotiations in 1833 to sell his stake in the American Fur Company, Crooks, who referred to Astor as "*de notre estimable grand-papa*," told Pierre Chouteau that "the business seems to [Astor] . . . like an only child and he can not muster courage to part with it."[5] But courage he had, and by June 1, 1834, Astor had sold the American Fur Company's Northern Department to Crooks, and the Western Department to Pratte, Chouteau and Company of St. Louis, both of which would, confusingly, continue to be referred to as the American Fur Company.[6] Furs had launched Astor's career and helped to make his fortune. It was time for him to move on.

*S*EVERAL FACTORS PRECIPITATED ASTOR'S DRAMATIC DECI- sion to divest. Part of it had to do with his concerns about the future viability of the fur trade. In the best of times fur trading remained a tricky business, subject to the vagaries of fashion, fluctuations in supply, and shifting economic conditions. The early 1830s was a particularly volatile period. In 1832 prices for beaver began falling. Astor, who was in France at the time, placed at least some of the blame for this on changing styles. In a letter he sent to Chouteau in August 1832, he observed, "I very much fear beaver will not sell well very soon unless very fine. It appears that they make hats of silk in place of beaver."[7] Astor also worried about the impact of another substitute for beaver—the nutria pelts from South America, which were being imported into Europe in large numbers.[8] Nutria was much cheaper than beaver, and its hair, although inferior in quality to that of beaver could easily be made into felt hats. The cholera epidemic then enveloping much of the world was yet one more reason for beaver's decline, since it was believed that the contagion could be spread by contaminated clothing, including furs. Instead of buying new furs many people were burning or throwing out the ones they had.[9] These were gloomy times indeed for the house of Astor. In October 1832 William Backhouse Astor, John Jacob's second son and partner in the business, told Chouteau that "a loss must be sustained by the holders of beaver," and as a result he was to stop buying pelts. By January 1833 the price paid in New York for beaver from the Rockies dropped 33 percent to four dollars per pound, and the less desirable beaver coming from Santa Fe couldn't be sold for any price. Reflecting on the situation William commented that, "this is our very dullest business season."[10]

The deteriorating beaver market certainly strongly influenced Astor's decision to abandon the fur trade, but there were other reasons. The original twenty-five-year charter for the American Fur Company expired in 1833, creating a convenient point for exiting the company. Passing control of the company to his son was not an option, since William had no interest in taking over the reins from his father. He preferred to focus his time on real estate, especially given the explosive growth that American cities were experiencing as urbanization began to alter the American landscape. But perhaps the most important factor leading Astor to sever his ties was his health. Seventy years old and increasingly infirm, Astor returned to New York in April 1834 from a two-year sojourn in Paris, where he had been ill for much of the time. A month later he wrote a sorrowful letter to former Astorian Wilson Hunt, in which he complained, "While absent I lost wife, brother, daughter, sister, grandchildren and many friends and I expect to follow very soon."[11]

As it turned out Astor was wrong. He lived for another fourteen years, adding enormously to his fortune through shrewd investing in real estate and other concerns. Then, on March 29, 1848, just shy of his eighty-fifth birthday, John Jacob Astor, who had been dubbed "the Napoleon of commerce," died at Hellgate, his mansion on the Upper East Side of New York City overlooking the East River.[12] His close friend and business associate Philip Hone wrote in his diary that day, "John Jacob Astor died this morning . . . the material of life exhausted, the machinery worn out, the lamp extinguished for want of oil. Bowed down with bodily infirmity for a long time, he has gone at last, and left reluctantly his unbounded wealth. His property is estimated at $20,000,000, some judicious persons say $30,000,000; but, at any rate, he was the richest man in the United States. . . . The fur trade was the philosopher's stone of this modern Croesus; beaver-skins and muskrats furnished the oil for the supply of Aladdin's lamp. . . . All he touched turned to gold, and it seemed as if fortune delighted in erecting him a monument of her unerring potency."[13]

*A*STOR'S CONCERN ABOUT BEAVER HAD BEEN PRESCIENT. In fact, by 1840 beaver pelts were a relatively insignificant part of the American fur trade. Many have argued that the main reason for this was the introduction of the silk hat, and second the rising use of nutria in place of beaver—the very things that Astor pointed out in 1832.[14] In February 1836 Crooks in fact wrote a letter to Pratte, Chouteau and Company, stating, "Nutria can now be had at about half the price it brought a year since, and the silk hat gives up such a vigorous competition, that beaver cannot possibly rise in value." Five months later he added, "Nutria has diminished the consumption of beaver so much, that we fear a decline in the price of [beaver] must be submitted to."[15] Crooks's predictions notwithstanding, the traditional argument about the impact of silk and nutria is exaggerated.[16] Although these two competitors did take market share away from the beaver trade, they did not cripple it. Even the Panic of 1837, which ripped through the American economy and depressed fur prices, did not deliver a knockout blow to the trade. Indeed, after the lows of the early 1830s, the price for beaver pelts fluctuated in subsequent years, and the market for beaver—not only for hats, but also for trimming and lining coats and making gloves—remained relatively strong. To understand why the American beaver trade was in such bad straits by the end of the decade, one needs to focus less on competition from silk and nutria or the Panic of 1837, and more on the beaver itself.

In 1834 the *American Journal of Science* revealed some depressing news. "It appears that the fur trade must henceforth decline. . . . In North America, the animals are slowly decreasing, from the persevering efforts and the indiscriminate slaughter practiced by hunters, and by the appropriation to the uses of man of those forests and rivers which have afforded them food and protection. They recede . . . before the tide of civilization."[17] In many ways this was a very old story. Throughout history the advance of humans and their rapacious hunt for pelts had inevitably led to the decline in animal populations. And although the *Journal* was too sweeping in its claim that "the fur trade" as a whole "must henceforth decline," it was absolutely correct when it came to the beaver trade in America.

The beaver's plight was nothing new. The American naturalist John D. Godman had warned in 1826 that the unrelenting war on the beaver would eventually, and tragically, lead to its extinction. "A few individuals may," he conceded, "for a time, elude the immediate violence of persecution, and like the degraded descendants of the aboriginals of the soil, be occasionally exhibited as melancholy mementos of tribes long previously whelmed in the fathomless gulf of avarice."[18]

The 1830s witnessed an acceleration of the trend. The number of beaver coming from the Southwest rapidly declined, and the Taos trappers felt the pinch. In 1834 Ewing Young commented, "I am not catching much beaver but doing the best I can," and each year the wagons heading over the Santa Fe trail to St. Louis carried fewer pelts.[19] In 1831 fur trapper William Gordon noted that, "The furs are diminishing, and this diminution is general and extensive. The beaver may be considered as extinguished . . . [east] of the Rocky Mountains; for, though few beavers may be taken, yet they are not an object for any large investment."[20] Nowhere was this trend more evident than in the Rocky Mountain fur trade, whose lifeblood was the beaver pelt.

A government report predicted in 1832 that the beaver trade in the Rockies was unsustainable. The mountain men "occasion an immense destruction of the animals. . . . This state of things will, before many years, lead to the entire destruction of the beaver, even in those remote regions, which have, till recently, been inaccessible to our citizens."[21] At the Green River rendezvous in 1837 the mountain man Doc Newell ruefully commented, "Times is getting hard all over this part of the country, beaver scarce and low all peltries are on the decline."[22] And in 1839 Frederick Wislizenus, a German doctor who was traveling through the mountains, stopped at the Green River rendezvous and recorded this doleful observation on the proceedings. "Formerly single trappers on such occasions have often wasted a thousand dollars. But the days of their glory seem to be past, for constant hunting has very much reduced the number of beavers. This diminution in the beaver catch made itself noticeable at this year's rendezvous in the quieter behavior of the trappers. There was little drinking of spirits, and almost no gambling."[23] The blame, of course, fell largely on the mountain men, for they were the ones who had hunted without restraint. But there was another very important player whose impact cannot be overlooked—the Hudson's Bay Company, whose trappers helped to devastate the beaver populations of the Far West.

W HEN THE UNITED STATES AND GREAT BRITAIN SIGNED THE Convention of 1818, they extended the boundary between the United States and Canada along the forty-ninth parallel as far as the Rockies, and also grudgingly agreed to share all the land and waters "claimed by either power, west of the Rocky Mountains" for a period of ten years. This huge region, which was dubbed the Oregon Territory, ran from the top of California, or the forty-second parallel, all the way up to the southern tip of Alaska at latitude 54°40'. The territory was not really America's and Britain's to share. At the time both Spain and Russia had claims to the territory. But Spain dropped its claim in 1819, and Russia followed suit five years later, leaving the Americans and the British to fight over the disputed lands.[24]

This diplomatic battle raged almost incessantly for many years. The fracas was quite complicated, both legally and strategically, but it boiled down to the fact that the United States and Great Britain each argued that they owned the Oregon Territory. The Americans bolstered their position by pointing to a number of key events, most of them associated with the history of the fur trade, that purportedly proved their claim. This included Gray's voyage and the discovery of the Columbia River in 1793, Lewis and Clark's expedition and the construction of Fort Clatsop, the establishment of Astoria, and even the Louisiana Purchase, which some argued extended America's domain to the Pacific. The British countered with their own list, which highlighted, among other things, Sir Francis Drake's voyage to the West Coast of America in the 1500s (although how far north he reached is unclear), Cook's voyage to the Pacific Northwest in 1778, Vancouver's "discovery" of the Columbia a few months after Gray, and the British purchase and occupation of Astoria in 1816. It was because the British and the Americans couldn't agree whose claims were stronger that they decided on the sharing arrangement embodied in the Convention of 1818.

Although both sides claimed all of the Oregon Territory, from the forty-second parallel up to 54°40', the dispute was actually much narrower. Indeed, during the negotiations for the Convention of 1818, as well as subsequent negotiations in the early 1820s, the United States offered to set the boundary between the two countries at the forty-ninth parallel, all the way to the Pacific Coast. The British responded with a counterproposal, which would set the boundary at the forty-ninth parallel until it reached the Columbia, at which point the boundary line would follow the course of the river to the sea—effectively ceding all of what is now western Washington State to Canada. Thus the real sticking point was the contested area that lay between the forty-ninth parallel to the north and the Columbia to the south. Since the two countries couldn't agree what to do about that area, they decided when the Convention of 1818 was up for renegotiation in 1827 to continue the sharing agreement indefinitely.

The failure of the United States and Great Britain to set a boundary created a strategic opportunity for the Hudson's Bay Company, which had merged with its former rival, the North West Company, in 1821. The company wanted the contested area not only because it was a productive fur region where the company had established posts but also because it wanted to capitalize on the Columbia's access to the ocean. The best way to make sure that this happened, the company's governor, George Simpson believed, was to create a "fur desert" south and east of the Columbia river, a sort of "beaver-free buffer zone" that would dissuade the American trappers from expanding into the Northwest, the theory being that where trappers go, settlers are sure to follow.[25] As Simpson argued, "The greatest and best protection we can have from opposition is keeping the country closely hunted as the first step that the American government will take towards colonization is through their Indian traders and if the country becomes exhausted in fur bearing animals they can have no inducement to proceed hither."[26] And because every beaver the company took would add to its bottom line, "the territorial strategy of the governor was," as the historian Frederick Merk observed, "a masterly combination of profit and empire. The contested north side of the Columbia was to be insulated against American competition. The lost south side was to be the insulator."[27]

This "scorched-earth" campaign provided a sharp contrast with what the Hudson's Bay Company did on its own territory farther to the north, where it implemented a policy based on quotas, which limited hunting so as to ensure the sustainability of the harvest.[28] Streams were not denuded of beaver but rather were trapped on a rotating basis so as to leave behind enough animals to reproduce and repopulate the area. One year of trapping would be followed by two years during which the beavers were undisturbed.[29] Although enforcement was difficult, there is no doubt that this policy contributed to the Hudson's Bay Company's consistent track record of killing large numbers of beaver year after year.[30] Conservation, however, was the last thing on the company's mind when it came to dealing with the Americans.

*D*URING THE 1820S AND 1830S, THE HUDSON'S BAY COMPANY sent forth trapping brigades to hunt for beaver south and east of the Columbia.[31] The most famous and consequential of these expeditions were headed by Peter Skene Ogden, a bulldog of a man who had an iron will and stamina to match it.[32] The son of American parents but a Canadian by birth, Ogden was thirty years old when the first expedition departed in 1824, and over the next six years he led five more expeditions, and in the process explored as much if not more of the West than Jedediah Smith, ranging throughout parts of present-day eastern Washington and Oregon, as well as much of Idaho, Utah, Nevada, and California.[33] He was the first white man to see the Humboldt River, which he called the "Unknown," and the first to travel the Far West from north to south.[34] Ogden crossed paths with his American competitors on occasion, and usually these meetings were guarded but civil.[35]

An encounter on May 22, 1825, proved more fractious. Ogden was camped on the Weber River, to the east of the Great Salt Lake, when two men who had deserted from the Hudson's Bay Company arrived with disturbing information—"the whole country [was] overrun with Americans." Ogden knew that could only mean trouble, and that night he wrote in his journal, "Americans & Canadians all in pursuit of the same object"—beaver.[36] Things took a turn for the worse the next day, when a group of twenty-five American trappers with "colors flying" rode to within one hundred yards of Ogden's camp and set up a camp of their own. This was no social call. The Americans were visibly upset. They thought the British were trespassing on American land and shouldn't be taking *American* beaver. They had heard that the British were in the habit of raising the Union Jack above their camps at night, which they perceived as an "insult to the United States."[37] The Americans had also been angered by tales from Hudson's Bay Company deserters, who said the company had treated them poorly, charged them high prices for goods, and paid them next to nothing for their furs.[38]

After the Americans settled in, their leader, Johnson Gardner, a free trapper who had come west with Ashley, marched over to Ogden and told him none too politely that he and his men were on American territory. They had better leave, he warned, and soon. Gardner also offered Ogden's men a deal: If they wanted to join the Americans, and bring with them any furs they had trapped, Gardner would welcome them and fight for their freedom if necessary. To encourage them to desert, Gardner assured the trappers that the prices they could get from American traders were at least eight times greater than what the Hudson's Bay Company paid.

Gardner let his offer marinate overnight, and the next morning he renewed his verbal offensive. "Do you know in whose country you are?" Gardner bellowed at Ogden. Thinking that he was still in the Oregon Territory, Ogden responded that he didn't because Great Britain and the United States had yet to decide who owned it, and in the meantime both countries had equal rights to the region. He was wrong, yelled Gardner. Great Britain had "ceded" the territory to the United States, and therefore Ogden and his men "had no license to trap or trade" in the area, and they should "return from whence . . . [they] came." Ogden coolly replied that he would leave only after he had "received orders from the British government" to do so. Hearing this, Gardner snarled, "Remain at your peril," and then stormed off.[39] Of course Gardner was mistaken about the status of the Oregon Territory, and both men were wrong about their location. Their argument had taken place, in fact, in Utah, below the forty-second parallel, and therefore they were trespassers on Mexican land.[40]

Gardner's deal ultimately proved persuasive. Many of Ogden's men were upset about how they had been treated, and twenty-three of them deserted to the American side, taking with them seven hundred beaver pelts.[41] Considerable pushing, shoving, and cursing attended this mass exodus, and armed violence was only narrowly averted. "Here I am," Ogden confided in his journal on May 26, "surrounded on all sides by enemies and our expectations and hopes blasted for returns this year. To remain in this quarter any longer would merely be to trap beaver for the Americans, for I seriously apprehend there are still more of the trappers who would willingly join them" to take advantage of the good prices they could get for their pelts.[42] When the disconsolate Ogden returned from this trip, his bosses took stock of the situation and changed their policy. From then on the Hudson's Bay Company would meet or beat the prices offered by the Americans to avoid any more defections. The strategy worked. Ogden was able to maintain his brigades, and on most of his subsequent trips he returned loaded with beaver.[43]

The success of the Hudson's Bay Company expeditions infuriated the Americans, who bitterly complained that the Canadian trappers were taking most of the beaver west of the Rockies.[44] In a letter to Senator Benton, Ashley reported that Ogden had boasted "rather exultantly" that in the Snake Valley region alone—an area that included parts of present-day eastern Washington and Oregon, and much of Idaho—he and his men had in the span of two or three years taken 85,000 beaver, worth roughly six hundred thousand dollars.[45] As early as 1830 Smith, Jackson, and Sublette worried that "this territory, being trapped by both parties [the Americans and the British], is nearly exhausted of beavers; and unless the British can be stopped, will soon be entirely exhausted, and no place left within the United States where beaver fur in any quantity can be obtained."[46] The Hudson's Bay Company's success not only infuriated the Americans, it also helped to put an end to the rendezvous.

*T*HE 1840 GREEN RIVER RENDEZVOUS HAD AN UNUSUAL PARTIC-
ipant, the Roman Catholic priest Pierre-Jean De Smet, who had traveled out with that year's supply train to perform missionary work in the West. A genial man with an easy laugh, who once claimed that "no bitterness towards any one whomsoever ever entered my heart," De Smet chose Sunday, July 5, to perform a mass for the assembled throng.[47] "The altar was placed on an elevation," De Smet recalled, "and surrounded with boughs and garlands of flowers; I addressed the congregation in French and in English, and spoke also by an interpreter to the Flathead and Snake Indians. It was a spectacle truly moving . . . to behold an assembly composed of so many different nations, who all assisted at our holy mysteries with great satisfaction—The Canadians sung hymns in French and Latin, and the Indians in their native tongue."[48] What De Smet failed to apprehend was that his mass also served as a requiem of sorts. This would be the last rendezvous ever held.[49] It wasn't a sudden death. The rendezvous system had been in decline for years. As the number of beaver diminished, so too did the financial incentive to bring expensive supply caravans into the mountains. The year 1840 was especially

bad. As Newell commented, "Times was certainly hard no beaver and every thing dull." So Pierre Chouteau, whose company had been the main supplier of goods to the rendezvous, decided not to return to the mountains the following year. And just like that it was over.[50]

For most mountain men the end of the rendezvous meant the end of their lives as trappers. This denouement was beautifully captured by a conversation that Meek had with Newell after the last rendezvous broke up, paraphrased by Meek's biographer as follows: " 'Come,' said Newell to Meek, 'we are done with this life in the mountains—done with wading in beaver-dams, and freezing or starving alternately—done with Indian trading and Indian fighting. The fur trade is dead in the Rocky Mountains, and it is no place for us now, if ever it was. We are young yet, and have life before us. We cannot waste it here; we cannot or will not return to the States. Let us go down to the Willamette and take farms.' "[51]

Some mountain men, however, were not ready to give up their way of life, and after the last rendezvous they continued to trap, overwinter in the mountains, and bring their furs to one of the numerous trading posts on the Missouri, the Arkansas, and the Platte rivers, which had been built during the 1830s and had long been frequented by mountain men who chose to bypass the rendezvous. Eventually, though, the number of mountain men dwindled along with the number of furs they brought in, until by the late 1840s there were almost no mountain men left. And with that, one of the American fur trade's most colorful periods came to an end, as the mountain men slowly faded into history, their exploits left to reverberate through the years.

*A*LTHOUGH THE MOUNTAIN MEN'S TIME ON THE NATIONAL stage was relatively brief, their impact on the course of American history was significant, especially in the realm of exploration and opening up the West to settlement.[52] The mountain men's contemporaries recognized this. "These daring men secure to us the fur trade," the author and banker James Hall wrote in 1848, "while they explore the unknown regions beyond our borders, and are the pioneers in the expansion of our territory."[53] A half century later Hiram Chittenden echoed a similar theme. "It was the trader and trapper who first explored and established the routes of travel which are now, and always will be, the avenues of commerce in that region. *They were the 'pathfinders' of the West.*"[54]

Much of what the mountain men discovered, however, was lost to posterity because the vast majority of them didn't transfer their accumulated geographic knowledge to the written page, nor did they prepare maps illuminating the Far West. Instead, they took most of what they knew with them to their grave. Jedediah Smith provides the saddest case of such a missed opportunity. He had planned to publish a journal and maps based on his encyclopedic knowledge of the West, but put off doing so until after his trip to Santa Fe, and when the Comanche killed him along the Cimarron River, his plan died too. But enough information from the mountain men, including Smith, did get back east to generate a real and growing interest in the West. The information traveled many paths. The mountain men who returned to St. Louis and other cities and towns shared their stories with friends, local officials, and, most important, journalists who found their tales of discovery compelling copy. In early September 1826 the *Missouri Herald and St. Louis Advertiser* told its readers that:

> The recent expedition of general Ashley to the country west of the Rocky Mountains has been productive of information on subjects of no small interest to the people of the union. It has proved, that overland expeditions, in large bodies, may be made to that remote region, without the necessity of transporting provisions for man or beast. . . . The whole route lay through a level and open country, better for carriages than any turnpike road in the United States—Wagons and carriages could go with ease as far as general Ashley went.[55]

According to Goetzmann it was in this way that "Ashley and his men had begun to point the way West for American emigrants as well as fur traders."[56]

Mountain men also contributed to the government's increasing interest in the West through formal written reports that they sent back east. The information they provided not only gave officials a much improved understanding of the geography and Indians of the region, but it also highlighted the ease with which wagon trains could travel not just to the Rockies, but all the way to the west coast, where the land, the mountain men claimed, was fantastically fertile, providing an excellent foundation for American settlement. But such settlement, the mountain men warned, would not happen unless the government took steps to overturn the Convention of 1818, thereby ousting the British from those parts of the Pacific Northwest claimed by the United States.

And the mountain men were not shy about urging their government to act quickly to force out the British.[57]

Contemporary books about and by mountain men added to the America's fascination with the West and the evolving view that those distant lands would one day be part of the United States. The most famous of these was Washington Irving's *The Adventures of Captain Bonneville*, in which he painted an alluring picture of the Willamette and Des Chutes River valleys in present-day Oregon. "These valleys must form the grand points of commencement of the future settlement of the country; but there must be many such enfolded in the embraces of these lower ranges of mountains which, though at present they lie waste and uninhabited, and to the eye of the trader and trapper present but barren wastes, would, in the hands of skilful agriculturists and husbandmen, soon assume a different aspect, and teem with waving crops, or be covered with flocks and herds."[58] Zenas Leonard's own book, which came out two years after Irving's, clearly showed that some of the trappers had what Goetzmann called a " 'public' or nationalistic view of the Far West," seeing it as more than just a place to catch beaver.[59] On his expedition with Walker to California, Leonard stood on the edge of San Francisco Bay in late 1833 and mused about what the future might have in store. "Most of this vast waste of territory belongs to the Republic of the United States," Leonard rather presumptuously and prematurely claimed. "Our government should be vigilant. She should assert her claim by taking possession of the whole territory as soon as possible—for we have good reason to suppose that the territory *west* of the mountains [the Rockies] will some day be equally as important to the nation as that on the *east*."[60]

Even after the mountain men left the trapping life behind, however, their influence on settlement continued. Many of them served as guides for expeditions, including Joseph Walker and Kit Carson, who used their intimate familiarity with the West to help John C. Frémont, "the Great Pathfinder," map the trails that innumerable emigrants would follow in their wagon trains across the continent. Mountain men led the settlers westward over the Oregon Trail, and a few, such as Jim Bridger, set up trading posts along the way to supply the emigrants during their journey. Finally, after retiring from trapping, most mountain men didn't head back east but instead, like Meek and Newell, went west, becoming settlers themselves and contributing mightily to the survival and strength of the American outposts on the western frontier.[61]

*T*HUS, IN THE END, THE HUDSON'S BAY COMPANY'S GRAND PLAN failed miserably. Simpson had hoped that by creating a "fur desert" south and east of the Columbia River, he could keep the American fur trappers out, and by doing so keep the settlers away. Although the desert created by Simpson's men did help to stave off the American fur trade in the area, it did nothing to stop the settlers from coming in. And ironically, it was the mountain men themselves who helped usher in the very settlement that Simpson feared. Through their discoveries, writings, and service as guides, the mountain men played a significant role in making the West a destination for thousands of Americans from the late 1830s to the mid-1840s. And this vast procession of settlers, in turn, was part of the reason why Britain decided to give up its claim to the land between the Columbia River and the forty-ninth parallel—the very land that Simpson tried so hard to secure.

During the 1844 presidential campaign, the Democratic candidate James K. Polk promised to reoccupy Oregon. And when he got into office he set his sights on establishing a permanent border between the United States and Great Britain in the Pacific Northwest. His battle cry, "Fifty-four Forty or Fight!" was meant to scare Britain into thinking that he would take the Oregon Territory all the way to the southern boundary of Russian Alaska, by force if necessary. But this position was essentially bluster, aimed primarily at the extremists in his party. As a result of its annexation of Texas in 1845, the United States was on the verge of war with Mexico, and the last thing Polk wanted to do was start another war with Britain. So he let the British know he was willing to negotiate setting the border at the forty-ninth parallel— the same line the United States had proposed many times before. Although Britain initially rejected the deal, it quickly decided that it would rather be on good terms with the United States, a major trading partner, than fight to retain its hold on land that was mainly of interest to the Hudson's Bay Company instead of the British government.[62] There were, after all, plenty of beaver north of the forty-ninth parallel for the company to trap, and getting into a war to protect the company's hold on a relatively small part of its enormous domain seemed particularly imprudent, especially since Britain had more pressing political and military problems back home. Finally, the British could see that American settlers, who had already pushed the population of the Willamette Valley past six thousand, were going to continue coming west in large numbers and would inevitably spread north well beyond the Columbia. These tangible facts only added to Britain's desire to compromise, and on June 15, 1846, it signed a treaty with the United States that set the border at the forty-ninth parallel, and also gave Britain Vancouver Island, part of which fell below the line.[63]

*W*HILE BEAVER POPULATIONS IN THE SOUTHWEST, ON THE upper Missouri, and in the Rockies dwindled, and the mountain men slowly disappeared, the American fur trade, ever adaptable, headed in new directions. For many years buffalo robes coming from the West had been an important part of the trade, and now they took center stage.

—15—

The Last Robe

The Last Buffalo, *by Thomas Nast,*
Harper's Weekly, *June 6, 1874. The
cartoon's caption reads, "Don't shoot, my
good fellow! Here, take my 'robe,' save
your ammunition, and let me go in peace."*

THE AMERICAN BISON (*BISON BISON*), OR BUFFALO AS IT IS MORE
commonly called, is the largest land animal in North America. It is a
magnificent beast.[1] The adult male, or bull, weighs as much as two thousand
pounds, and sports a pair of jet black horns and a bushy goatee on its massive
battering ram of a head. At its hump it is five and a half to six feet tall, and
up to nine feet long from its muzzle to the base of its tail. The front half of
its body—broad, powerfully muscled, and covered in a thick coat of woolly
hair—is attached to a rear end so slender that it looks almost petite in comparison. The adult female, or cow, is far more diminutive than the bull, being
about five feet tall at the hump, up to six and a half feet long, and approaching
twelve hundred pounds.[2]

Before Europeans arrived in North America, buffalo ranged over
roughly one-third of the continent, from the western slopes of the Rockies

to the eastern foothills of the Appalachians, and nearly to the coast in some mid-Atlantic states. On a north-south axis, buffalo could be found from New York to Florida, and from the Great Slave Lake in the Northwest Territories of Canada to northern Mexico.[3] Nobody knows how many buffalo there were at this time, but estimates abound. The most defensible are in the neighborhood of thirty million, while others go as high as seventy-five million or more.[4] What the actual number may have been, it is an uncontestable and tragic fact that by the end of the nineteenth century this mighty animal, the "monarch of the prairies," was on the verge of extinction. Many causes contributed to this sad result, but the excessive trade in buffalo robes was among the most significant.

Around 1521, while he was in the midst of ravaging the Aztec empire, the conquistador Hernán Cortés became the first European to see a buffalo. According to the seventeenth-century Spanish historian Antonio de Solís, it was during a visit to the menagerie of the former Aztec ruler Montezuma that Cortés saw the "Mexican bull," as he called it. Its ungainly, even bellicose appearance must have startled these Europeans. De Solís referred to the buffalo as "the greatest rarity . . . a wonderful composition of diverse Animals. It has crooked shoulders, with a bunch on its back like a Camel; its flanks dry, its tail large, and its neck covered with hair like a Lion. It is cloven-footed, its head armed like that of a Bull, which it resembles in fierceness, with no less strength and agility."[5]

A decade later the Spanish explorer Álvar Núñez Cabeza de Vaca, whose surname means "head of a cow," became the first European to see a buffalo in the wild, somewhere in present-day Texas. "I have seen them three or four times and eaten them," Cabeza de Vaca noted. "They have two small horns, like Moorish cattle, and very long hair, like a fine blanket made from the wool of merino sheep. Some are brownish and others black. . . . From the small ones the Indians make blankets to cover themselves, and from the large ones they make shoes and shields. . . . All along their range, through the valleys where they roam, people who live near there descend to live off them, and take inland a great quantity of their hides."[6] The first Englishmen known to have seen a buffalo was Thomas Argall, who landed on the Virginia coast in 1612, in the vicinity of the Potomac River, and marched inland many miles, whereupon he found a "great store of Cattle as big as Kine [oxen]."[7]

HE TRADE IN BUFFALO ROBES BETWEEN EUROPEANS AND Indians began many years after these encounters. As Spain extended its reach into New Mexico in the late 1500s, relationships were established with various tribes, including the Pueblo, the Comanche, and the Apache. At periodic trade fairs the Spaniards exchanged European goods and horses with the Indians for meat, human slaves to work the mines, and all sorts of skins, including buffalo robes. Some of these robes were beautifully painted for decorative purposes, and others were used as rugs or bedding.[8] French fur traders who later came down through the Ohio Valley to the Mississippi in the 1700s often returned home with buffalo robes, while the Spanish and French traders who used St. Louis as their base did the same. Toward the end of the eighteenth century even a few Americans were trading in buffalo skins. Traveling through western Pennsylvania in 1806, Thomas Ashe encountered an "old man, one of the first settlers in this country," who told him that during his first two years in the area, when the buffalo were fairly common, he and his friends had "killed from six to seven hundred of these noble creatures, merely for the sake of the skins, which to them were worth only two shillings each."[9]

The American trade in buffalo robes didn't really take off until after the War of 1812. By this time the relatively small herds of buffalo east of the Mississippi had been decimated, as a result of being hunted for their meat or having their habitat appropriated by settlers. The region's Indians waxed elegiac about a world they once knew, which had vanished. In 1827 Shabonee, chief of the Potawatomi in Illinois, recalled that in his youth he had "seen large herds of buffalo on these prairies, and elk were found in every grove, but they are here no more, having gone towards the setting sun. For hundreds of miles no white man lived, but now trading posts and settlers are found here and there throughout the country, and in a few years the smoke from their cabins will be seen to ascend from every grove, and the prairie covered with their cornfields."[10] Beyond the Mississippi, however, the story was different. Vast herds of buffalo still stretched to the horizon, especially on the Great Plains, that huge swath of land that reaches from Canada to Mexico, and from the foothills of the Rockies in the west to the ninety-eighth meridian, or a little beyond that point at places in the east (the latter can be envisioned roughly as a line extending from the eastern border of North Dakota down to the middle of Texas).

The buffalo of the Great Plains not only ruled the land, they were also central to the lives of the area's Indians. In the annals of human history there has perhaps never been another animal that has proved more integral to the cultural, spiritual, or economic fabric of a people than the buffalo was to the Plains Indians, which included more than twenty tribes, among them the Comanche, Apache, Blackfeet, Crow, Kiowa, Sioux, Mandan, Hidatsa, and Pawnee. As Thomas Mails put it: "If God was the creator and overseer of life, if the morning star, the moon, and Mother Earth combined their talents to give birth and hope to the Indian, if the sun was dispatcher of wisdom and warmth, then the buffalo was the tangible and immediate proof of them all, for out of the buffalo came almost everything necessary to daily life."[11]

There wasn't a single part of the buffalo that the Plains Indians wasted. The tanned hide was used to make winter robes, shirts, cradles, tipi covers, and pipe bags; rawhide was fashioned into moccasin soles, rattles, shields, and saddles; the hair filled pillows, adorned headdresses, and was braided into rope; the tail became a whip or fly brush; the horns were transformed into cups, spoons, powder horns, and ladles; and all the meat and most of the organs were eaten, with the tongue being the greatest delicacy of all. The bladder was transformed into quill pouches, or, when attached to a hollow bone from a bird or a de-pithed twig, it became a syringe, while the contents of the stomach were used to cure skin diseases, and the stomach lining became buckets, canteens, or cooking vessels. Bones were turned into knives, arrowheads, war clubs, skin scrapers, and dice, and the hip-bones' porous core was used to suck up pigments and apply them like a brush. The hooves, muzzle, eyes, hide shavings, cartilage, and even the penis were simmered in a pot to make a sticky stew that was clarified into glue, which bound feathers and points to arrows, and was eaten by certain tribes as a chewy treat. Buffalo teeth ornamented dresses and dangled from necklaces. Dried tendons were pulled apart into strands that became thread for sewing clothes. Indeed, nothing was neglected: The dried scrotum, filled with pebbles, became a rattle; buffalo dung or chips were burned for fuel or crumbled and sprinkled on tobacco to help ignite the mixture and add a unique aroma; the brains, mashed and spread on the hide, were used in the tanning process; the skull was a treasured ceremonial object; and even the hairballs the buffalo occasionally coughed up were used in rituals to "call" the buffalo to appear."[12]

*T*HE FUR TRADERS WHO FOLLOWED IN LEWIS AND CLARK'S WAKE and snaked their way up the Missouri, like those who traveled the Santa Fe Trail, came primarily looking for beaver, but they also bartered for buffalo robes. And just as with the beaver, the buffalo robe trade was governed by the fashions of the day. As one writer in 1821 observed, "The [buffalo] skin dressed with the hair on . . . constitutes those durable and often beautiful sleigh-robes which are now in such universal use in the United States and [Canada]."[13] Robes also were used to make exceedingly warm winter coats and bedding.[14] According to one government estimate between 1815 and 1830 fur traders along the Missouri and in the Southwest annually brought an average of 26,000 buffalo robes to St. Louis, where they sold for three dollars a piece.[15]

In the eyes of the robe trade, all buffaloes were not equal. The robes of adult bulls over three years old were rarely traded since their skin was too thick and heavy to be made into a lightweight robe, and the hair was usually quite coarse and generally of poor quality. Old bull robes, instead, were often cut down to size and made into boots with the hair on the inside, which were, as one customer noted, "absurdly large and uncouth, but very warm."[16] The robes of younger males proved more attractive, and were regularly traded because the skin was thinner and the hair of finer quality. The best robes, however, came from the cows, whose skin was thin and whose coat was relatively full and plush regardless of the animal's age. This preference for cows and young males had the deleterious side affect of diminishing the reproductive potential of the herds, thereby amplifying the fur trade's devastating impact on the buffalo's survival.

Most robes were a variation of brown in color and had fairly coarse woolly hair, but a small number were especially esteemed and commanded the highest prices because of their unusual character. The "beaver robe" had particularly fine, soft wavy hair and was similar in color to a beaver pelt. The "blue robe" also had a fine coat, with a bluish cast. The "black and tan robe" was black throughout much of the body, but a lighter tan or reddish on the flanks, near the muzzle, and inside the forelegs. And the "buckskin robe" was either white or more of a dirty cream in color. Many Indians attributed great sacred and spiritual powers to these white buffalo robes, viewing them as "big medicine." Finding a white buffalo was an extremely rare event, with fewer than a dozen instances on record.[17]

----

*I*N THESE EARLY YEARS THE BUFFALO ROBE TRADE WAS ENTIRELY dependent on Indian labor. The men usually hunted buffalo during the winter months, when the hair on the robes was thickest, although spring and fall hunts took place as well. One of the oldest hunting methods was stampeding the buffalo off a cliff, or "jump." Another method was to herd the buffalo into a corral, or *piskun* as it was called, where they could be shot with arrows.[18] Some Indians on horseback used the "surround" technique, in which they encircled a herd, forcing it into an ever-tighter bunch, and then sent their arrows and spears into the panicked mass of animals until none were left standing. Perhaps the most common but challenging means of killing the buffalo was called "running buffalo," where an Indian would dash into a herd on his best "buffalo horse," pick out his target, and kill it with an arrow or spear aimed at its vital organs. While there was a thrilling aspect—the excitement of the chase—to this last method, there was also considerable risk. According to one observer, "The danger is not so much from the buffalo, which rarely makes an effort to injure his pursuer, as from the fact that neither man nor horse can see the ground, which may be rough and broken or perforated with prairie dog or gopher holes. This danger [of the horse falling and the rider being trampled] is so imminent that a man who runs into a herd of buffalo may be said to take his life in his hand."[19]

The grueling and time-consuming job of processing the robes was left to the women. The first step was to stretch the hide and pin it taut with pegs driven into the ground. Then a sharp bone or metal instrument was employed to scrape the hide free of meat. For a day or more the women would rub the hide with the smashed brains of a deer or buffalo, or with liver or fat. This greasy paste was left on the hide up to three days, to soak in and soften the skin. Next the hide was slowly dried near a low fire, and constantly beaten and rubbed to make it "uniformly soft and pliable." As soon as the hide was dry the women would begin rubbing it once again, this time "around a taut horsehair rope or braided leather to make it smooth." Finally a stone, commonly pumice, was used to polish the hide. Since one woman could only tan about ten robes a year, some Indian tribes increased production by raiding other tribes and abducting females, putting them to work as slaves. Taking multiple wives was yet another means of expanding production.[20]

*T*HE ROBE TRADE GREATLY EXPANDED IN THE 1830S WITH THE arrival of steamboats on the upper Missouri, which facilitated the traffic of trading goods and robes. Before being sent downriver, the robes were folded fur-side in, stacked into packs of ten, and placed in a wooden press that squeezed them into a tight bundle weighing about one hundred pounds, which was then tied with hemp or rawhide cords. When there were more robes than the steamboats could handle, flat-bottomed wooden boats called mackinaws were also employed, which could hold up to fifteen tons of robes. Piloted downstream by four oarsmen and one steersman at a rate of some one hundred miles per day, the mackinaws were broken up for kindling upon their arrival in St. Louis.[21]

The steamboat facilitated not only the fur trade but also the transmission of disease. Fur traders operating on the northern plains during the early 1800s had spread disease among the Indians before, with devastating effects, but the smallpox epidemic that hit the upper Missouri in the summer of 1837 had particularly horrific consequences.[22] The primary vector of the disease was the American Fur Company's steamboat *St. Peter's*, which was heading to Fort Union to deliver goods and supplies. Onboard were passengers who had come down with smallpox during the trip. Company employees tried to keep Indians away from the boat as it stopped at Fort Mandan, but the Indians thought the traders were just trying to cheat them out of their goods, and at least one Indian came on board and stole an infected blanket. With dying people onboard, the *St. Peter's* continued on to Fort Union, where a botched effort to inoculate only served to spread the disease. When the Assiniboin came to the fort with their buffalo robes, the men inside tried to keep them out, but again the Indians would not be dissuaded from pursuing their trade, and after entering the fort were soon stricken with the disease. The company men continued to trade with the Indians, and they also sent some of their goods farther up the Missouri and the Yellowstone to other posts, where additional trading took place.

Like a wildfire raging through a drought-stricken forest, the disease quickly spread not only throughout the tribes that had direct contact with the traders but also to other ones as well. Six tribes were hit the hardest— the Mandan, Minataree, Arikara, Sioux, Assiniboin, and Blackfeet—losing a combined total of a little more than seventeen thousand men, women, and children.[23] In November 1837, a few months after the epidemic had run its course, an observer at Fort Union described the horrific results. "In whatever direction you turn nothing but sad wrecks of mortality meet the eye; lodges standing on every hill, but not a streak of smoke rising from them. Not a sound can be heard to break the awful stillness, save the ominous croak of ravens and the mournful howl of wolves, fattening on the human carcasses that lie strewed around. It seems as if the very genius of desolation had stalked through the prairies and wreaked his vengeance on everything bearing the shape of humanity."[24] Those whose lives were spared faced unimaginable physical and psychological damage. Another contemporary reported: "Many of the handsome Arikaras, who had recovered, seeing the disfiguration of their features, committed suicide, some by throwing themselves from rocks, others by stabbing and shooting. The prairie has become a graveyard; its wild flowers bloom over the sepulchers of Indians. The atmosphere, for miles, is poisoned by the stench of the hundreds of carcasses unburied. The women and children are wandering in groups, without food, or howling over the dead. The men are flying in every direction. The proud, warlike, and noble-looking Blackfeet are no more."[25]

So voracious was the demand for robes that even an epidemic of this magnitude failed to stop the trade. The Assiniboin, who had lost more than half their number to the disease, actually brought the usual amount of robes to Fort Union in the spring of 1838. When Charles Larpenteur, one of the company traders, asked them "how it happened that there were so many robes brought in," they said "laughingly that they expected to die soon, and wanted to have a frolic [by trading robes for alcohol] till the end came."[26]

WHILE THE BUFFALO ROBE TRADE THRIVED ON THE UPPER Missouri, it was also doing well in the Southwest, where Bent's Fort, built in 1833–34, was the busiest trading post in the region. Although it handled plenty of beaver pelts and other furs, the fort, on the Arkansas River near present-day La Junta, Colorado, focused mainly on the robe trade. The same year that the ninety thousand robes were wending their way down the Missouri, roughly fifteen thousand robes were sent on wagons over the mountain route of the Santa Fe Trail from Bent's Fort to St. Louis.[27] Part of Bent's Fort's success was due to the marriage of William Bent, one of the fort's founders, to a Cheyenne named Owl Woman—a marital bond that helped to secure the fort's commercial connection with that tribe.[28]

From the late 1830s through the 1860s, an average of ninety to one hundred thousand buffalo robes were sent to St. Louis annually, with smaller numbers arriving at other trading hubs, including St. Paul, Minnesota.[29] These robes, which might wholesale for four to ten dollars, could retail for twenty-five up to fifty dollars for ones of exceptionally high quality.[30] Unlike beaver pelts, which sold very well in Europe, buffalo robes were purchased almost entirely by Americans or Canadians. When Ramsay Crooks had tried to interest the Europeans in purchasing buffalo robe, he had limited success, since the cost of transporting the bulky robes overseas made them too expensive to compete effectively with locally produced and equally warm sheepskin garments.[31]

*T*HROUGHOUT THIS PERIOD THE ROBE TRADE WAS ONLY ONE OF many factors pressuring the buffalo population. Indians took perhaps as many as half a million buffalo per year "for subsistence and intertribal trade."[32] The métis living along the Red River in Manitoba conducted buffalo hunts of extraordinary proportions in western Manitoba, Saskatchewan, Montana, the Dakotas, and even northern Minnesota, in which they killed perhaps as many as fifty thousand animals annually, mainly for their meat.[33] Each year fur traders, farmers, and settlers killed tens of thousands, if not hundreds of thousands, of buffalo for food, sport, or by displacing the buffalo's habitat with crops, livestock, and expanding towns.[34] And because the steamboats required so much wood to run, and the mackinaw boats so much wood to build, they contributed to deforestation along the Missouri, which in turn diminished the land's carrying capacity and its ability to support the herds. Many environmental factors, too, such as drought, disease, blizzards, fires, and predation, played a significant role in determining the buffalo's fate.[35]

Despite all these pressures, there were still huge numbers of buffalo out west. In June 1839, while traveling on the Santa Fe Trail through Kansas, Thomas Farnham found himself surrounded by an enormous herd. "The buffalo during the last three days had covered the whole country so completely," he wrote, "that it appeared oftentimes extremely dangerous even for the immense cavalcade of the Santa Fe traders to attempt to break its way through them. We traveled at the rate of fifteen miles a day. The length of sight on either side of the trail, 15 miles; on both sides, 30 miles:—$15 \times 3 = 45 \times 30 = 1,350$ square miles of country, so thickly covered with these noble animals, that when viewed from a height, it scarcely afforded a sight of a square league of its surface."[36] Twenty years later in the same area, another writer claimed: "I have indeed traveled through buffaloes along the Arkansas river for 200 miles, almost one continuous herd, as close together as it is customary to herd cattle. You might go north or south as far as you pleased and there would seem no diminution of their numbers. When they were suddenly frightened and stampeded they made a roar like thunder and the ground seemed to tremble."[37]

But these huge local concentrations of buffalo were deceptive, and an increasing number of astute observers apprehended that the buffalo were slowly but surely being wiped out. In 1841 the western artist George Catlin wrote: "The buffalo's doom is sealed, and with their extinction must assuredly sink into real despair and starvation, the [Indian] inhabitants of these vast plains. . . . It seems hard and cruel, (does it not?) that we civilized people with all the luxuries and comforts of the world about us, should be drawing from the backs of these useful animals the skins for our luxury, leaving their carcasses to be devoured by the wolves . . . and for each of . . . [these] skins the Indian has received but a pint of whiskey!"[38] In 1843 John James Audubon made a prescient observation after watching a bison hunt on the western plains. "This cannot last. Even now there is a perceptible difference in the size of the herds. Before many years," he wrote, "the buffalo, like the Great Auk, will have disappeared; surely this should not be permitted."[39] Josiah Gregg, who had spent many years as a merchant and trader in the American southwest, wrote in 1845 that, were the buffalo "only killed for food, . . . their natural increase would perhaps replenish the loss: yet the continual and wanton slaughter of them by travelers and hunters, and the still greater havoc made among them by the Indians, not only for meat, but often for the skins and tongues alone (for which they find a ready market among their traders), are fast reducing their numbers, and must ultimately effect their total annihilation from the continent."[40] The tocsins of men like Catlin, Audubon, and Gregg failed to halt the slaughter, and despite a growing chorus of pleas for action, the destruction of the buffalo proceeded apace.

*T*HIS SYSTEMATIC PATH TOWARD EXTINCTION TOOK AN abrupt and tragic turn for the worse in the decade that followed the end of the Civil War. In 1865 the Union Pacific Railroad had begun laying track in Omaha, Nebraska, and over the next four years those tracks multiplied until they stretched across the Great Plains to Promontory Point, Utah, where on May 10, 1869, with the driving of the ceremonial golden spike, the Union Pacific and the Central Pacific railroads were joined, creating the first transcontinental railroad. The railroad accelerated the slaughter like no other force. The Union Pacific line cleaved the buffalo population of the Great Plains in two, creating the northern and southern herds. A few years later the Atchison, Topeka & Santa Fe and Kansas Pacific railroads punched their way through the heart of the Southwest, fracturing the southern herd into a number of smaller pieces.[41]

The railroads' most immediate impact on the buffalo came during construction. The thousands of men who laid track needed to eat, and buffalo meat was particularly desirable. The railroad hired hunters to supply the meat, and the most famous hunter of all was William Frederick Cody, who earned his moniker "Buffalo Bill" while working for the Union Pacific in the late 1860s. "I had a wagon with four mules," he recalled, "one driver and two butchers, all brave, well-armed men, [and] myself riding my horse Brigham." Cody would seek out the fattest cows and the youngest heifers in the herd, and then rush in on horseback and shoot them. During his year with the railroad Cody killed an astonishing 4,280 buffalo.[42]

The number of buffalo killed to feed railroad workers pales in comparison to the number that would be killed by the flood of people who would ride the rails west to hunt buffalo for pleasure and profit. Although the railroads created zones as wide as fifty miles around the tracks where the buffalo were sparse, there were enough of them wandering about to sustain a cruel pastime that developed during the early 1870s, whereby buffalo were shot from the comfortable cabins of passing trains and left on the plains to rot.[43] The trains also brought scores of "sportsmen" out west, whose goal was to prove their prowess by killing buffalo and bringing home trophies to mount on their wall. "To shoot buffalo seems a mania," observed a Topeka newspaper in 1872. "Men come from London—cockneys, fops, and nobles—and from all parts of the republic, to enjoy what they call sport. Sport! When no danger is incurred and no skill required. I see no more sport in shooting a buffalo than in shooting an ox nor so much danger as there is hunting Texas cattle."[44]

Along with the tourists and so-called sportsmen, the railroads brought thousands of "professional" or market hunters to the plains, lured by the hope of making quick money. Many of them killed the animals only for their tongues, which had long been a delicacy in eastern restaurants. After shooting the buffalo, all it took was a few slices of a knife to extract the prize, which could be easily prepared in the field by smoking or salting and then packed in barrels for shipping back east, where each one could fetch as much as fifty cents. Most white hunters, however, came for the hides, because of a recent breakthrough in the tanning process that allowed formerly unusable buffalo skins to be transformed into sturdy leather belts that helped turn the wheels of industry. These hunters also took the best skins from the cows and young males, which were turned into robes by tanneries back east. The going rate for a hide might be fifty cents to one dollar, whereas a skin destined to become a robe could sell for three times as much or more. The key to success was volume, and handling the increased traffic in hides and robes was easier now that the railroads were available to haul the skins away quickly and cheaply.[45]

The preferred killing method of the market hunters was the "still hunt." The hunter would walk to within a couple of hundred yards of a herd, staying out of sight and upwind of the animals to avoid being seen or smelled and then, using a powerful long-range rifle, pick off the animals one by one. The sound of the shot would startle the animals but usually only for an instant. Not sensing their adversary, the remaining buffalo might inspect their fallen and bleeding fellow, continue grazing, or perhaps start to slowly amble away, bewildered but largely unaware of the great danger stalking them. At an almost leisurely clip, perhaps one shot every few minutes, the hunter would keep shooting until as many as fifty or one hundred animals lay dead. Then the skinning would begin, with the hides being scraped free of meat, cured, and stretched out on stakes in the ground to dry. The wastefulness was incredible. Many of the "green" hunters were miserable shots and merely wounded animals, which wandered considerable distances before dying, well beyond the reach of the skinner's knife. And the skins themselves were often improperly cut, preserved, staked out, or dried, making them useless to buyers. One knowledgeable observer claimed that each hide or robe that made its way to market represented as many as five dead buffalo, a ratio that was reduced over time as the hunters and skinners became more skilled, but that always left many more buffalo dead than were ultimately utilized.[46]

The U.S. Army also played a role in the fall of the buffalo, although how extensive is still vigorously debated among historians.[47] There is no doubt that many soldiers viewed the killing of the buffalo as one of the best means to resolve the "Indian problem." In 1867 Col. Richard Irving Dodge told a sport hunter to "kill every buffalo you can, every buffalo dead is an Indian gone."[48]

Two years later General Sherman was recorded by the *Army Navy Journal* as having said "that the quickest way to compel the Indians to settle down to civilized life was to send ten regiments of soldiers to the plains, with orders to shoot buffaloes until they became too scarce to support the redskins."[49] And while addressing the Texas legislature in 1875, Gen. Philip Sheridan was reported as saying that bison hunters "have done in the last two years, and will do more in the next year, to settle the vexed Indian question, than the entire regular army has done in the last thirty years. They are destroying the Indians' commissary; and it is a well-known fact that any army losing its base of supplies is placed at a great disadvantage. Send them powder and lead, if you will; but, for the sake of a lasting peace, let them kill, skin, and sell until the buffaloes are exterminated."[50] Although military personnel shot many buffalo for food, sport, and likely for strategic purposes, they had as much if not more of an impact on the herds by providing hunters with protection, shipping and storage facilities, and free ammunition. Not surprisingly they also often looked the other way when hunters illegally trespassed and hunted for buffalo on Indian lands.[51]

The scope of the overall slaughter was staggering, involving not only market hunters, tourists, and the military but also Indians and settlers. Colonel Dodge estimated that between 1872 and 1874 roughly 3.7 million buffalo were killed, and more than 85 percent of that tally was attributable to market hunters. It is hard today to comprehend the carnage. The plains were littered with so many bleached buffalo skeletons that a secondary industry arose, in which people collected the bones and sold them to companies that ground them into fertilizer or animal feed, cooked them to make neat's-foot oil, or burned them to make bone black, a charcoal used in the process of purifying and filtering refined sugar.[52] In Dodge City, where as many as two-thirds of the residents were engaged in the bison hide trade, buffalo bones became a legitimate form of currency. "Could the southern buffalo range have been roofed over at that time," the Smithsonian Institution's chief taxidermist, William Templeton Hornaday, wrote, "it would have made one vast charnel-house. Putrefying carcasses, many of them with the hide still on, lay thickly scattered over thousands of square miles of the level prairie, poisoning the air and water and offending the sight. The remaining herds had become mere scattered bands, harried and driven hither and thither by the hunters, who now swarmed almost as thickly as the buffaloes." Adding considerably to the destruction of the southern herd were a vicious host of environmental factors, including predation, drought, blizzards, and possibly the introduction of Texas fever, a deadly disease that attacked other livestock.[53] By 1875 it all came crashing down. The southern herd "had been utterly annihilated," leaving behind only a few scattered animals.[54] There were, however, still many buffalo in the northern herd, but they too were under attack.

*T*HROUGHOUT THE 1870S THE INDIANS OF THE NORTHERN plains traded up to one hundred thousand robes per year. Then, in the early 1880s, the Northern Pacific Railroad made its way from North Dakota into Montana, bringing thousands of market hunters and skinners who, in a repeat of the dynamic that played out in the South, exacerbated the destruction of the area's buffalo. While the number of buffalo robes traded by the Indians fell by as much as 75 percent, the white hunters picked up the slack. The trajectory of death can be gleaned from the comments of one of the major fur merchants of the era, who said that in 1881, fifty thousand robes and hides were shipped out on the Northern Pacific, a number that rose to two hundred thousand the next year but then fell to forty thousand in 1883, and finally to just three hundred, *or one train carload*, in 1884—at which point the northern herd, too, was virtually annihilated.[55]

Eager to delude themselves during this heady era of manifest destiny, America failed to heed nearly a half century's worth of dire predictions. On March 12, 1882, for example, the *Boston Daily Globe* told its readers that the buffalo population appeared to be in excellent shape. "Thousands are killed every winter for their skins, and thousands more during the summer season by the Indians and by aristocratic sportsmen for the fun of the thing. This has been the case during the past ten or fifteen years, yet the number and extent of the herds on our western plains, judging by the quantity of robes annually shipped east, are as great as ever." Even the white hunters in the North remained blindly optimistic, believing that they would not suffer a replay of the devastation in the South. "In the autumn of 1883," according to Hornaday, "they nearly all outfitted as usual, often at an expense of many hundreds of dollars, and blithely sought 'the range' that had up to that time been so prolific in robes. The end was in nearly every case the same—total failure and bankruptcy. It was indeed hard to believe that not only the millions, but also the thousands, had actually gone, and forever."[56]

Reflecting on the fate of the northern and southern herds, a young

Theodore Roosevelt, who would later become the greatest of our conservation presidents, wrote in 1885: "Never before in all history were so many large wild animals of one species slain in so short a space of time. The extermination of the buffalo has been a veritable tragedy of the animal world. . . . No sight is more common on the plains than that of a bleached buffalo skull." A Montana rancher who had traveled one thousand miles across northern Montana told Roosevelt that "during the whole distance he was never out of sight of a dead buffalo, and never in sight of a live one."[57] The destruction of the buffalo was not merely a tragedy for the "animal world," but also for the Indians, whose very existence—physically, spiritually, economically, even existentially— was linked to this commanding animal now facing extinction. As the buffalo disappeared, so too did the Indians' ability to sustain themselves in the face of mounting pressures from the white man to give up their way of life, their lands, and their independence.[58]

*I*N 1889 A JOURNALIST IN BOSTON NOTICED A SIGN IN A DOWN-town store window that read, "Highest prices paid for buffalo robes." When the journalist entered the store and inquired why the sign had been posted, the proprietor responded, "I suppose you have read long before this that our buffalo are becoming extinct." The proprietor said that he had a standing order from another merchant to purchase all the robes he could find, but he was having scant success. Two of his employees were scouring the streets, knocking on doors, asking people if they had any robes. One of the men found none, while the other found only a few, but the owners were unwilling to sell for any price. "Ten years ago," the proprietor continued, "I could have gone out anywhere and bought up 100 [robes] in less time than it takes to tell it. . . . Hunting for buffalo robes will soon be like hunting for diamonds.' "[59] In fact it already was.

The last documented hunt for buffalo robes had taken place two years before, in late 1887, not far from Tascosa, Texas, when a group of hunters descended on the only remaining remnant of the southern herd, which numbered two hundred head. Fifty-two animals were killed. Ten of them were completely skinned and used to make full-body mounts. All the rest had their heads cut off for mounting, while the skins were made into robes, the best of which sold for twenty dollars apiece.[60]

The same year that the curious journalist walked into that Boston store,

Hornaday tried to determine how many buffalo were left. The results were shocking. According to his survey there were 200 buffalo in Yellowstone National Park, 25 in the panhandle of Texas, 20 in Colorado, 26 in southern Wyoming, ten in Montana, and four in the Dakota Territory. To that were added another 550 in the wilds of Canada and 256 that were in captivity, which brought the total population of buffalo in North America in 1889 to a mere 1,091. It was a simply unfathomable number considering that once tens of millions had roamed the continent.[61]

EPILOGUE

End of an Era

*President Theodore Roosevelt and John
Muir on Glacier Point, Yosemite Valley,
California, in 1903.*

*T*HE AMERICAN FUR TRADE DIDN'T END WITH THE NEAR
extinction of the buffalo; in fact, it hasn't ended at all. From the late
1800s up through the present, Americans have continued to kill animals
for their pelts and sell them for assorted fashion purposes. Today there are
roughly 150,000 mostly part-time fur trappers in the United States, along
with hundreds of fur farms, which contribute to an international fur trade
that in recent years has generated sales of between ten and fifteen billion dollars.[1] This, however, is not the subject of *Fur, Fortune, and Empire*, which concludes at the dawn of the twentieth century with the rise of the conservation
movement.

As it turned out, the buffalo's plight was a symptom of a much larger problem facing America. The nineteenth century, especially the latter half, has
been called the "Age of Extermination," and for good reason.[2] An astounding
number of animals were killed to feed the growing population, to respond
to the demands of fashion, and for sport; while many more perished because

their habitats were destroyed by the relentless expansion of cities, towns, farms, roads, and rail lines. As a result numerous species were dramatically reduced in numbers, some were pushed to the edge of extinction, and a few were wiped off the face of the earth. The buffalo, of course, one of the great American icons, is the poster child for the "Age of Extermination." But there are many other egregious examples, including the passenger pigeon, and a great variety of plume birds, which were killed solely for the sake of their beautiful feathers, used to adorn hats.[3]

During the "Age of Extermination" the buffalo was not, of course, the only animal being killed for its pelt. Ever since the American fur trade commenced, a great variety of furs had been purveyed, and in the late 1800s that continued to be the case. For example, there were years during this period in which more than four hundred thousand skunk were killed for their furs, more than five hundred thousand raccoon, and well over 2 million muskrat— and for each of these animals the tallies sometimes went much higher. The latter part of the century also saw a dramatic increase in the number of beaver killed. After years of not being trapped, their numbers had rebounded, and although the market for beaver hats was small, the pelts were still widely used for trimming coats and making muffs. Fur seals and sea otters, too, were once again fashionable, especially after the United States bought Alaska from Russia in 1867, in the bargain of the century. From 1870 through 1890 the Alaska Commercial Company was given a lease by the United States government to kill up to one hundred thousand male northern fur seals (*Callorhinus ursinus*) annually. For most of those years the company slightly exceeded its quota and sold the skins to furriers who made coats that were very dear. During this time thousands of Alaskan sea otters, prized for their luxurious fur, were also killed.[4]

The "Age of Extermination" led to a fundamental shift in American society. Inspired by the eloquent and stirring words of, among others, Ralph Waldo Emerson, Henry David Thoreau, John Muir, and John Burroughs, who extolled the virtues of living in harmony with the natural world, Americans grew increasingly alarmed at the devastation they were witnessing—not only the great number of animals that were being killed, but also the virgin habitat that was being lost. They were at long last ready to take action, the ravages of the Gilded Age having ironically created an environmental *cri di coeur*. Some were intent on preserving nature by keeping human impacts to a bare minimum or, better yet, by having no impacts at all. Others pursued a philosophy that was more in line with emerging tenets of the embryonic conservation movement, which argued that humans should use natural resources wisely and efficiently so they would be there for the enjoyment and benefit of future generations. Driven by one or perhaps both these impulses, a diverse range of private individuals, hunting and birding organizations, and politicians—most famously Theodore Roosevelt—worked during the late 1800s and early 1900s to implement major changes to the way in which humans and the natural world interacted. The results of their efforts ushered in a whole new age, which witnessed the establishment of America's first national parks, the creation of the National Wildlife Refuge System, the setting aside of the first national forests, and the passage of state and federal laws designed to protect game animals and plume birds.[5]

This nascent movement created a growing tide of conservationism that had a major impact on the operation of the fur trade as well. By the early 1900s the majority of states had enacted laws regulating the killing of fur-bearing animals, most of which included licensing requirements, and instituted closed and open seasons or in some cases, placed bag limits or outright prohibitions on the taking of certain species. These laws in turn were backed by a federal statute, the Lacey Act, that made it illegal to transport across state lines any wildlife killed in violation of state law. The purpose of these laws was not to hinder or stop the fur trade but rather to ensure that the trade continued indefinitely. The thinking went that by offering the animals protection against indiscriminate slaughter, the laws would guarantee that enough fur bearers remained year after year to sustain significant levels of trapping, thereby generating a healthy annual revenue stream for the trappers and the broader economy. In other words the states were interested in preserving the animals primarily because that was the only way to preserve the fur trade itself. Even when states banned the taking of a certain species because its numbers were too low, the expectation was that once the number of animals increased, trapping would resume.[6]

An international effort emerged as well to regulate the fur trade. Until about 1880 the hunt for northern fur seals in Alaska was mainly land based and operated by Americans on the Pribilof Islands, which had the largest concentrations of northern fur seals. By annually killing roughly one hundred thousand seals, the Americans were already threatening the long-term survival of the population. The situation grew direr in subsequent years when the United States, Great Britain (Canada), Russia, and Japan ramped up their pelagic (open ocean) sealing operations beyond the shores of the Pribilofs, killing perhaps as many as 75,000 additional seals per year.[7] This level of slaughter was unsustainable, and once the four countries realized that, they came together in 1911 to sign a treaty that banned pelagic sealing and allowed land-based sealing to continue on a restricted basis. This treaty also included a provision prohibiting the killing of sea otters, whose numbers were so low that they were on the verge of extinction.[8]

The rise of the conservation movement and the passage of these state, federal, and international laws, then, represents a transition point in the history of the American fur trade. It unquestionably marks the end of an era. No longer would market forces alone drive the fur trade. Instead there was now also an expanding list of laws and regulations that placed boundaries on the conduct of the trade. For the first time many fur-bearing animals were afforded a measure of legal protection. It is at this transition point that *Fur, Fortune, and Empire*'s story leaves off, and another begins—one that will have to be written by someone else. Whoever takes up the task of telling the history of the American fur trade in the twentieth and twenty-first centuries will need to consider a whole array of issues—many of them quite prickly—not touched upon here, including the evolution and effectiveness of the laws and regulations; America's transition from a net exporter to a net importer of furs; the dramatic growth of fur farming and the decline of fur trapping; the development and marketing of faux furs and other shifts in fashion; and the rise of the environmental movement. The story of the modern American fur trade will also need to address the controversial, emotionally charged, and sometimes violent political, moral, and ethical debate over the trade itself, in which various sides square off on a wide range of issues, among them animal rights, trappers' rights, individual rights, cruelty to animals, the conditions at fur farms, and whether people should wear furs at all.

*F*OR THE MOST PART THE NEWS ABOUT THE LEADING ANIMAL characters in this book—the beaver, the sea otter, and the buffalo—is encouraging, especially if your base for comparison is where these animal populations stood at the end of the nineteenth century. Beavers, in search of new streams and rivers to dam, have returned to many of the places from which they had vanished long ago. One of the most remarkable reappearances occurred in no less than New York City, when, on February 21, 2007, a keen-eyed observer on the edge of the Bronx River made a startling discovery. There, swimming through the murky water, was a large, brown, furry animal, which looked curiously out of place. It was a beaver, the first one seen in New York City in *two hundred years*. Christened "José"—in honor of José Serrano, the Bronx congressman who had secured nearly $15 million in federal restoration funds to bring the grossly polluted river back to life— this lone, intrepid beaver continued unperturbed to gather wood and build its lodge, while New Yorkers marveled at the city's new resident.[9] Of course not everyone is happy about the nationwide resurgence of beavers, as evidenced by the many newspaper stories that tell of homeowners and town officials who are angry or frustrated about beavers cutting down trees and flooding formerly dry land—in particular, land that used to be someone's backyard.[10]

Also encouraging is that sea otters have rebounded somewhat from their nadir in the early twentieth century, but in many places within their historic North American range, from Alaska down to Baja, there are still either very few or no animals present. And overall the number of sea otters today is but a wisp of a shadow of those that swam majestically in the Pacific before the fur trade commenced. That is why the sea otter populations in most of California and along the coast of Alaska, from the Aleutian Islands to the Kodiak Archipelago, are listed as threatened by the United States Fish and Wildlife Service.[11] As for the hardy buffalo, it too has rebounded. Beginning with private and public efforts in the late 1800s and early 1900s to protect the few individuals that were left, the buffalo was saved from extinction, and today there are more than five hundred thousand spread out over a combination of parks, refuges, ranches, Indian reservations, and zoos, with most of them being raised for meat production, like cattle.[12]

*T*HE RUMBLING ECHOES OF THE FUR TRADE OF YORE REMAIN with us today. Dozens of American cities and towns can trace their origins, if not their actual creation, to the fur trade. These include, among so many others, Springfield, Massachusetts; Augusta, Maine; Saybrook, Connecticut; New York City; Pittsburgh; Detroit; Chicago; St. Paul; Green Bay; Milwaukee; St. Louis; Pierre, South Dakota; Leavenworth, Kansas; Pueblo, Colorado; Fort Benton, Montana; and Astoria. Scores of places are named after fur traders and trappers, among them Williams, Arizona; Ogden and Provo, Utah; Duluth, Minnesota; Culbertson and the Bridger Mountains in

Montana; Bonneville, Washington; Jackson and Laramie, Wyoming; Craig-mont, Idaho; Kit Carson Peak in Colorado; and Walker Lake in Nevada. A mosaic of locales, schools, and sports teams with beaver or buffalo in their name or used as images on their jerseys and flags attests to the ubiquity of these animals at one time, and to their importance in the fur trade. The cultural impact of the mountain man, one of the great icons in American history, remains strong, showing up in our language, our television shows and movies, and at the many reenactments of rendezvous that take place throughout the West. And more broadly, the history of the fur trade is on display at national and state parks, museums, and other historic sights, staffed by trained interpreters who are eager to impart their intimate knowledge of this bygone era.[13] Then there are the hundreds of thousands, if not millions of people who can trace their ancestry back to that diverse parade of early Americans—whites, blacks, Indians, métis, and so many others—who created and sustained the fur trade from the 1600s to the 1800s.

Over time, as the thrills and immediacy of the present crowd out the echoes and lessons of the past, it is all too common for people to lose touch with their heritage. It would be a shame if that were to happen with respect to the fur trade. It is a seminal part of who we are as a nation, and how we came to be.

NOTES

INTRODUCTION

1 James Truslow Adams, *The Founding of New England* (Boston: Atlantic Monthly Press, 1921): 102.

2 In writing this book I had to decide whether to use the term "Indian" or "Native American" when referring broadly to the native inhabitants of North America. I chose "Indian" in large part because many of the authors I admire use that term, and it is the one with which I am most comfortable. Thus I was glad to read in David Hackett Fischer's *Champlain's Dream* that when he asked a gathering of Indian leaders what they preferred to be called, they gave two answers. If one is referring to a specific nation, they said that the name of the nation should be used, for example, Mohawk. But if one is referring to "all of them together," they said that the term "Indian" was "as good as any other," and that "they used it with pride." I will follow that advice. When referring to a specific nation I will use its proper name, but when talking more generically I will use the word "Indian." See David Hackett Fischer, *Champlain's Dream: The European Founding of North America* (New York: Simon & Schuster, 2008), 636n26.

3 Hiram Martin Chittenden, *The American Fur Trade of the Far West*, vol. 1 (1902; reprint, Stanford: Academic Reprints, 1954), xi. The other towering classic on the fur trade—Paul Chrisler Phillip's two-volume set—covers the entire North American fur trade over the course of 1,380 pages. Paul Chrisler Phillips, *The Fur Trade*, 2 vols. (Norman: University of Oklahoma Press, 1961).

CHAPTER 1: *"As Fine a River as Can Be Found"*

1 Donald S. Johnson, *Charting the Sea of Darkness: The Four Voyages of Henry Hudson* (New York: Kodansha International, 1993), 87. See also ibid., 51, 73, 132–42; Russell Shorto, *The Island at the Center of the World: The Epic Story of Dutch Manhattan and the Forgotten Colony That Shaped America* (New York: Vintage Books, 2005), 20–24, 28–31; Emanuel van Meteren, "On Hudson's Voyage," in *Narratives of New Netherland, 1609–1664*, ed. J. Franklin Jameson (New York: Charles Scribner's Sons, 1909), 6; Llewelyn Powys, *Henry Hudson* (New York: Harper & Brothers Publishers, 1928), 70–83; and Douglas Hunter, *Half Moon: Henry Hud-

son and the Voyage That Redrew the Map of the New World (New York: Bloomsbury Press, 2009), 6–11. After Hudson's 1608 voyage was halted by ice, he attempted to find a northwesterly passage to the Orient, writing in his journal, "Void of hope of a Northeast passage. . . . I thereby resolved to use all the means I could to sail to the northwest." Johnson, *Charting the Sea of Darkness*, 73. After sailing in that direction for about ten weeks, his crew, on the verge of mutiny, convinced him to turn around and head back to England. Hudson had also attempted to find a water route to the Orient in 1607, when in the employ of the Muscovy Company he tried to sail to the north, "straight up, over the top of the world." This attempt, too, was halted by ice. Shorto, *The Island at the Center of the World*, 20, 22. There is a huge literature on Henry Hudson and his famed third voyage to find a northern passage to the Far East. The books that I found most useful in recounting Hudson's story as it relates to the origins of America's fur trade include those cited above, as well as E. B. O'Callaghan, *History of New Netherland, Or, New York Under the Dutch*, 2nd ed. vol. 1 (New York: D. Appleton & Company, 1855), 5–42.

2 Van Meteren, "On Hudson's Voyage," 6–7. See also Johnson, *Charting the Sea of Darkness*, 128–29; and Shorto, *The Island at the Center of the World*, 31.

3 Robert Juett, "The Third Voyage of Master Henry Hudson," in Georg Michael Asher, ed., *Henry Hudson The Navigator, The Original Documents in Which His Career is Recorded* (London: Hakluyt Society, 1860), 74; Shorto, *The Island at the Center of the World*, 31; and Hunter, *Half Moon*, 2–3, 93–96.

4 Van Meteren, "On Hudson's Voyage," 7; and Oliver A. Rink, *Holland on the Hudson: An Economic and Social History of Dutch New York* (Ithaca: Cornell University Press, 1986), 28.

5 Robert Juett, "The Third Voyage of Master Henry Hudson," in *Narratives of New Netherland*, 21.

6 Van Meteren, "On Hudson's Voyage," 8; and Rink, *Holland on the Hudson*, 29. According to Martine Gosselink, Hudson was forced to pull into Dartmouth by his eight English crewmen (the other eight being Dutch). Martine Gosselink, *New York, New Amsterdam: The Dutch Origins of New York* (Amsterdam: National Archive, 2009), 41. Other writers claim that the reasons for this move are not clear. See Shorto, *The Island at the Center of the World*, 33; and Edgar Mayhew Bacon, *Henry Hudson, His Times and His Voyages* (New York: G. P. Putnam's Sons, 1907), 173–74.

7 Shorto, *The Island at the Center of the World*, 31–34.

8 Juett, "The Third Voyage of Master Henry Hudson," in *Narratives of New Netherland*, 18–23, 25–26.

9 Van Meteren, "On Hudson's Voyage," 7.

10 As Nathaniel C. Hale observed, "It might be said that man's first true possession was the fur skin of an animal." Nathaniel C. Hale, *Pelts and Palisades: The Story of Fur and the Rivalry for Pelts in Early America* (Richmond, VA: Dietz Press, 1959), 1. For more on the topic of man's nakedness, whose evolutionary reasons scientists are still debating, see James A. Kushlan, "The Evolution of Hairlessness

in Man," *American Naturalist* 116, no. 5 (November 1980): 727–29; and Terrence Kealery, "Glad to be Naked," *New Scientist* (August 7, 1999): 47.

11 Gen. 3:20, *The Oxford Annotated Bible with Apocrypha*, Revised Standard Version, ed. Herbert G. May and Bruce M. Metzger (New York: Oxford University Press, 1965), 5; William E. Austin, *Principles and Practice of Fur Dressing and Fur Drying* (New York: D. Van Nostrand Company, 1922), 128; William Clarence Webster, *A General History of Commerce* (Boston: Ginn & Company, 1903), 7; R. Turner Wilcox, *The Mode in Furs* (New York: Charles Scribner's Sons, 1951), 2; William Smith, William Wayte, and G. E. Marindin, *A Dictionary of Greek and Roman Antiquities*, 3rd ed., vol. 2 (London: John Murray, 1891), 362; Jules Toutain, *The Economic Life of the Ancient World* (New York: Alfred A. Knopf, 1930), 50; Wolfgang Menzel, *The History of Germany From the Earliest Period to the Present Time*, vol. 1 (London: Bell & Daldy, 1869), 127; and James A. Hanson, *When Skins Were Money: A History of the Fur Trade* (Chadron, NE: Museum of the Fur Trade, 2005), 19. Some people claim that the Greek epic of Jason and his journey with the Argonauts to find the Golden Fleece is really a story about "Jason the Fur Trader," and that the Golden Fleece—which was, after all, the skin and golden wool of a sacrificed ram, and therefore an animal pelt—was simply a symbolic representation of the valuable furs that were traded at the time, which could easily make a man rich. Thus Jason's journey is seen in a rather unromantic light, as a highly profitable fur-trading venture. See Captain John C. Sachs, *Furs and the Fur Trade*, 3rd ed. (London: Sir Isaac Pitman & Sons Ltd., 1923), 3–4; and Hale, *Pelts and Palisades*, 2–4.

12 Elspeth M. Veale, *The English Fur Trade* (Oxford: Clarendon Press, 1966), 60, 66; Hanson, *When Skins Were Money*, 21; and Raymond H. Fisher, *The Russian Fur Trade, 1550–1700* (Berkeley: University of California Press, 1943), 1–16, 184–230.

13 Alexander Pulling, *The Order of the Coif* (Boston: Boston Book Company, 1897), 223n3.

14 Patrick Fraser Tyler, *History of Scotland*, vol. 3 (Edinburgh: William Tait, 1829), 271–72.

15 Veale, *The English Fur Trade*, 9.

16 Ibid., 13–14; and E. E. Rich, *Hudson's Bay Company, 1670–1870*, vol. 1 (New York: Macmillan Company, 1961), 1.

17 Veale, *The English Fur Trade*, 17–18, 20, 135, 144; and Wilcox, *The Mode in Furs*, 20.

18 Walter Scott, *Tales of a Grandfather*, vol. 6, *France*, (Edinburgh: Robert Cadell, 1836), 76–77; William Francis Collier, *The Great Events of History* (London: T. Nelson and Sons, 1860), 100; and Veale, *The English Fur Trade*, 4.

19 Helen Zimmern, *The Hansa Towns* (New York: G. P. Putnam's Sons, 1889), 96. The theme of vanity bothered another medieval commentator, but this time the moral of the story valued instead of decried the use of furs. Around 1371 the French knight Geoffrey de la Tour Landry prepared a book for his daughters to

teach them lessons about life and love. One of the stories tells of two sisters, the elder and comelier of whom was about to meet the young and wealthy knight her father had chosen to be her husband. The intended bride, quite proud of her "slender and fair shapen body," chose to wear an "unfurred" gown "which sat right straight upon her." But the "great frost and great wind" were too much for her "simple vesture," and her "color . . . was defaced, and she . . . [became] pale and black of cold." Her younger sister, however, who had the sense to dress in fur-lined garments, looked the picture of health, with cheeks as red as a rose. When the young knight arrived, he took one look at the two sisters, and with the father's permission married the younger, ruddier one. Thinking that he had chosen well, the knight became distressed when, on a subsequent visit to his in-laws, he saw the older sister, now warm and toasty in a fur robe, only to discover that *she* was the fairer sister, but it was too late for him to do anything about it. Quoted in Veale, *The English Fur Trade*, 1; and James Robinson Planche, *A Cyclopædia of Costume or Dictionary of Dress* (London: Chatto and Windus, 1876), 117–18.

20   The number of animals killed in this manner, throughout the medieval era, was certainly in the millions, if not the tens or even hundreds of millions. To get a sense of the scope of the carnage, consider that in 1406, three ships departing from the Baltic port of Riga were carrying in their holds a total of 333,348 pelts, and nearly all of those were from a single species of squirrel. See Veale, *The English Fur Trade*, 134.

21   Frederick Jackson Turner, "The Character and Influence of the Indian Trade in Wisconsin," in *Education, History, and Politics, Johns Hopkins University Studies in Historical and Political Science*, ed. Herbert B. Adams (Baltimore: Johns Hopkins Press, 1891), 551; and Kirsten A. Seaver, *Maps, Myths, and Men, The Story of the Vinland Map* (Stanford: Stanford University Press, 2004).

22   Arthur Middleton Reeves, *The Finding of Wineland the Good: The History of the Icelandic Discovery of America* (London: Henry Frowde Oxford University Press, 1895), 47–48.

23   Susan Tarrow, "Translation of the Cellere Codex," in Lawrence C. Wroth, *The Voyages of Giovanni da Verraçano, 1524–1528* (New Haven: Yale University Press, 1970), 134, 137–38, 140–41; and Neal Salisbury, *Manitou and Providence* (New York: Oxford University Press, 1982), 52–53.

24   Jacques Cartier, "Navigations to Newe France, trans. John Florio," *March of America Facsimile Series*, 10 (1580; reprint, Ann Arbor: University Microfilms, 1966), 15–17. See also James Phinney Baxter, *A Memoir of Jacques Cartier Sieur de Limoilou, His Voyages to the St. Lawrence, a Bibliography and a Facsimile of the Manuscript of 1534 with Annotations, etc.* (New York: Dodd, Mead & Company, 1906), 105.

25   Mark Kurlansky, *Cod: A Biography of the Fish That Changed the World* (New York: Walker and Company, 1997), 28–29, 48–49; and H. P. Biggar, *The Early Trading Companies of New France: A Contribution to the History of Commerce and Discovery in North America* (Toronto: University of Toronto Library, 1901), 24–25. It is pos-

sible that the first Europeans since the Vikings to trade furs with the Indians in the New World were the fishermen who might have been hauling cod and herring from the waters off Newfoundland as early as the late 1400s and, while fishing, could have bartered for furs with the natives. There is, however, only "fragmentary but suggestive evidence" of such activities, which is not surprising, since fishermen, who were loathe to give away trade secrets about prized fishing grounds, rarely left written records of their voyages. Salisbury, *Manitou and Providence*, 51.

26   The Micmac Indians' strenuous efforts to entice Cartier and his men to trade clearly show that the Indians had traded with Europeans before, and the odds are that those Europeans were fishermen.

27   Biggar, *The Early Trading Companies of New France*, 25–26; and Harold A. Innis, *The Fur Trade in Canada* (Toronto: University of Toronto Press, 1956), 9.

28   Francis Parkman, *Pioneers of France in the New World, Huguenots in Florida, Samuel de Champlain* (Boston: Little, Brown & Company, 1907), 234.

29   Biggar, *The Early Trading Companies of New France*, 17, 25, 32–37.

30   Phillips, *The Fur Trade*, vol. 1, 28; and Biggar, *The Early Trading Companies of New France*, 38–67.

31   Juett, *The Third Voyage of Master Henry Hudson*, in Asher, *Henry Hudson the Navigator*, 59–60; and Hunter, *Half Moon*, 93–99.

32   Thomas A. Janiver, *The Dutch Founding of New York* (New York: Harper & Brothers Publishers, 1903), 6–7; John Romeyn Brodhead, *History of the State of New York, First Period, 1609–1664* (New York: Harper & Brothers Publishers, 1853), 43–44; Francis Parkman, *Pioneers of France in the New World, France and England in North America, Part First*, vol. 2 (Boston: Little, Brown & Company, 1897), 276–77; Shorto, *The Island at the Center of the World*, 34; and O'Callaghan, *History of New Netherland*, vol. 1, 32n1, The American fur trade became a complement, not a replacement, of the traditional Dutch fur trade with Russia, and the Dutch continued the latter trade for the balance of the seventeenth century. See Fisher, *The Russian Fur Trade*, 190–91.

CHAPTER 2: *The Precious Beaver*

1   For the beaver's ascent in the world of fashion at this time, see Innis, *The Fur Trade in Canada*, 11; J. F. Crean, "Hats and the Fur Trade," *Canadian Journal of Economics and Political Science*, 28, 3 (August, 1962): 373–86; and Wilcox, *The Mode in Hats and Headdress*, 113.

2   Earl L. Hilfiker, *Beavers, Water, Wildlife and History* (Interlaken, Windswept Press, 1991), 13–16; Björn Kurtén and Elaine Anderson, *Pleistocene Mammals of North America* (New York: Columbia University Press, 1980), 236; and Miles Barton et al., *Prehistoric America: A Journey Through the Ice Age and Beyond* (New Haven: Yale University Press, 2002), 155. The European and the North American beaver have forty-eight and forty chromosomes, respectively, and the Euro-

pean beaver appears to be "more ancient and conservative than its New World cousin," yet there are still some who believe that they are not distinct species. See Dietland Müller-Schwarze and Lixing Sun, *The Beaver: Natural History of a Wetlands Engineer* (Ithaca: Comstock Publishing, 2003), 2–3, 10, 13. The record weight for a beaver is a 110-pounder caught in Wisconsin's Iron River in August 1921. Leonard Lee Rue III, *The World of the Beaver* (Philadelphia: J. B. Lippincott Company, 1964), 15–17.

3   The record appears to be a cottonwood that was thirty-seven inches in diameter, cut down by beavers in British Columbia. Rue, *The World of the Beaver*, 64, 66.

4   Lewis H. Morgan, *The American Beaver* (Philadelphia: J. B. Lippincott & Co., 1868), 18–20, 65–66; Rue, *The World of the Beaver*, 15–16; Müller-Schwarze and Sun, *The Beaver*, 11–12, 23; and Hilfiker, *Beavers, Water, Wildlife and History*, 25–27. Beavers will sometimes eat the bark off standing trees, especially large ones, girdling them in effect, and not cut down the tree. This feeding behavior usually results in the death of the tree.

5   Alice Outwater, *Water: A Natural History* (New York: Basic Books, 1996) 21. See Müller-Schwarze and Sun, *The Beaver*, 48; Hilfiker, *Beavers, Water, Wildlife and History*, 24; and Morgan, *The American Beaver*, 28.

6   Mark Kurlansky, *The Basque History of the World* (New York: Penguin, 1999), 48–49.

7   Thomas Morton, *New English Canaan* (Fairfield, WA: Ye Galleon Press, 2001; facsimile of original 1637 edition), 44, 77. Morton noted that the tail was believed to help with the "advancement of Priapus." Priapus is a minor Greek and Roman God of fertility, whose most distinguishing feature is a huge permanently erect penis. According to one account the beaver's tail, "like all of the beaver is a delicate food, and that is why in Germany beavers are always reserved for the emperor's table on the rare occasions they are caught. The meat excels all other meat of land or water animals . . . and the very finest and best part of all the beaver is the tail, which the Indians will not lightly give up, other than as an exceptional treat or gift for someone." See Adriaen van der Donck, *A Description of New Netherland*, ed. Charles T. Gehring and William A. Starna, trans. Diederick Willem Goedhuys (1655; reprint, Lincoln: University of Nebraska Press, 2008), 123.

8   Müller-Schwarze and Sun, *The Beaver*, 13.

9   Beaver lodges can be aboveground lodges built along the pond's edge, or free-standing, which are dome-shaped mounds of branches, twigs, and mud, rising from the pond's bottom and cresting well above the surface of the water. The lodge is completely enclosed save for a small ventilation hole near the top and plunge holes at the bottom, used by the beavers as an exit or entrance. One of the largest lodges ever documented was in Quebec; it had a base diameter of forty feet and rose eight feet out of the water. See Rue, *The World of the Beaver*, 104; and S. Hodgson, Thomas Bewick, and Ralph Beilby, *A General History of the Quadrupeds*, 3rd ed. (London Newcastle-upon-Tyne: G. G. J. & J. Robinson, & C. Dilly, 1792), 258, 260.

10 Beavers will cut almost any species of deciduous tree to gather building materials; however, they will only rarely cut down a conifer and will never eat conifer bark. Müller-Schwarze and Sun, *The Beaver*, 2.

11 Ibid., 68. Beavers are not buzz saws, and it takes them quite a bit of time to fell a tree, on the order of an hour for trees six or seven inches in diameter, and four hours or more for trees twice that size.

12 Washington Irving, *The Adventures of Captain Bonneville, or Scenes Beyond the Rocky Mountains of the Far West*, vol. 2 (London: Richard Bentley, 1837), 136.

13 For the most extensive discussion of how beavers build dams, see Morgan, *The American Beaver*, 78–131. See also Horace T. Martin, *Castorologia, or the History and Traditions of the Canadian Beaver* (London: Edward Stanford, 1892), 222.

14 Outwater, *Water: A Natural History*, 23; and Enos A. Mills, *In Beaver World* (1913; reprint, Lincoln: University of Nebraska Press, 1990), 4. Certainly one of the largest beaver dams ever discovered was one in Berlin, New Hampshire, which measured four thousand feet, creating a lake behind it that boasted forty beaver lodges. Rue, *The World of the Beaver*, 77.

15 Mills, *In Beaver World*, 36.

16 Outwater, *Water: A Natural History*, 20. See also Müller-Schwarze and Sun, *The Beaver*, 4.

17 Hilfiker, *Beavers, Water, Wildlife and History*, 14–16; and Outwater, *Water*, 21. One estimate even places the number of beavers in prehistoric North America at 1.2 billion. See Hilfiker, *Beavers, Water, Wildlife and History*, 15. It is important to view these estimates with a somewhat skeptical eye. Calculating historic populations is a tricky business, and I can't vouch for the "accuracy" or "rigor" with which the various estimates were made. It seems extremely unlikely that there were ever 200 million beaver roaming North America, given how quickly (relatively speaking) the fur trade greatly diminished their numbers, and I wouldn't be surprised if the actual number was far less than 60 million. In the end we will never truly know how many beaver there were, and therefore how far their populations fell as a result of the fur trade initiated by the coming of the Europeans.

18 Outwater, *Water: A Natural History*, 27; and Everett S. Allen, *A Wind to Shake the World: The Story of the 1938 Hurricane* (Boston: Little, Brown & Company, 1976), 37–39.

19 Mari Sandoz; *The Beaver Men: Spearheads of Empire* (Lincoln: University of Nebraska Press, 1964), 25; J. W. Powell, *Eleventh Annual Report of the Bureau of Ethnology to the Secretary of the Smithsonian Institution*, part 1 (Washington, DC: U.S. Government Printing Office, 1894), 438, 465–66; Jane C. Beck, "The Giant Beaver: A Prehistoric Memory?" *Ethnohistory* 19 (Spring 1972), 109–10; Charles G. Leland, *The Algonquin Legends of New England* (Boston: Houghton, Mifflin & Company, 1884), 342–43; Francis Parkman, *The Jesuits in North America in the Seventeenth Century*, vol. 1 (Boston: Little, Brown & Company, 1906), 63n1;

Katharine Berry Judson, *Myths and Legends of California and the Old Southwest* (Chicago: A. C. McClurg & Co., 1912), 48–49; and Marion Whitney Smith, *Algonquian and Abenaki Indian Myths and Legends* (Lewiston: Central Maine Press, 1962).

20   Pliny, *The Natural History of Pliny*, trans. John Bostock and H. T. Riley, vol. 2 (London: George Bell & Sons, 1890), 297–98.

21   Henry David Thoreau, *The Writings of Henry David Thoreau: Journal*, ed. Bradford Torrey, vol. 13 (Boston: Houghton, Mifflin & Company, 1906), 152.

22   Dante Alighieri, *Readings of the Inferno of Dante*, text and trans. William Warren Vernon, intro. Edward Moore, vol. 2 (London: Methuen & Co., 1906), 8–9n; and Richard Thayer Holbrook, *Dante and the Animal Kingdom* (New York: Columbia University Press, 1902), 197–99.

23   George Cartwright, *Captain Cartwright and his Labrador Journal*, ed. Charles Wendell Townsend (Boston: Dana Estes & Company, 1911), 297; and John D. Godman, *American Natural History*, 3rd ed., vol. 1, (1826; reprint, Philadelphia: Hogan & Thompson, 1836), 284.

24   Sir Thomas Browne, *The Works of Sir Thomas Browne*, ed. Simon Wilkins (London: Henry G. Bohn, 1852), 240–44. Some have claimed that it is from this act of self-castration that the beaver gained its scientific name, *Castor*, a variation of the Latin *castratum*, but the actual origins of the name are debatable: There are those who believe that *Castor* derives from the Greek *gaster*, for belly, or from the Greek god Kastor. See Outwater, *Water*, 21; *Aesop's Fables*, trans. Laura Gibbs (Oxford University Press, 2002), 207–8; and Sandoz, *The Beaver Men*, 22.

25   *Aesop's Fables*, 207–8.

26   Morton, *New English Canaan*, 77. Morton also believed, mistakenly, that when the beaver sits in his lodge, it must have its "tail hanging in the water," or else it "would over heat and rot off." Morton is mum, however, on why the tail doesn't do the same when the beaver is on land cutting down trees.

27   Thoreau, *The Writings of Henry David Thoreau: Journal*, 153. For other myths about beavers, created by Westerners, see Thomas Smith, *The Wonders of Nature and Art*, vol. 9 (London: J. Walker, 1804), 161–65; *The Wonders of Nature and Art*, vol. 2 (Reading, England: C. Corbett, 1750), 173; and Theodore Roosevelt, *Roosevelt's Writings*, ed. Maurice Garland Fulton (New York: Macmillan Company, 1920), 258–59.

28   John James Audubon and John Bachman, *The Viviparous Quadrupeds of North America*, vol. I (New York: J. J. Audubon, 1846), 349.

29   See, for example, W. Bingley, *Animal Biography; or, Anecdotes of the Lives, Manners, and Economy, of the Animal Creation, Arranged According to the System of Linnaeus*, vol. 1, *Quadrupeds* (London: J. Adlard, 1803), 401; Jeremy Belknap, *The History of New Hampshire*, vol. 3 (Boston: Belknap and Young, 1792), 154; and James Burnett Monboddo, *Of the Origin and Progress of Language*, vol. 1 (London: J. Balfour and T. Cadell, 1774), 457–58.

30 Morgan, *The American Beaver*, 17–18.

31 Müller-Schwarze and Sun, *The Beaver*, 11.

32 Sandoz, *The Beaver Men*, 46.

33 Ibid., 46–47; George A. Dorsey, "Games of the Makah Indians of Neah Bay," *American Antiquarian and Oriental Journal* 23 (January–November, 1901): 72; *The Annual Cyclopedia and Register of Important Events of the Year 1899* (New York: D. Appleton & Company, 1900), 19; and Andrew McFarland, "Indian Games," *Bulletin of the Essex Institute* 17 (January–March, 1885): 112–13.

34 George A. Burdock, *Fenaroli's Handbook of Flavor Ingredients*, 5th ed. (Boca Raton; CRC Press, 2005), 276–77. Since castoreum is known to contain salicylic acid—the main ingredient of aspirin—there may be something to these curative claims. Beavers eat willow bark, which contains salicylic acid. Indians also would chew the bark as a treatment for various maladies. Müller-Schwarze and Sun, *The Beaver*, 43; and Marcello Spinella, *The Psychopharmacology of Herbal Medicine: Plant Drugs that Alter Mind, Brain, and Behavior* (Cambridge: MIT Press, 2001), 303–04. Other ailments that were supposedly cured by castoreum include colic, toothaches, tumors of the liver, earaches, deafness, sciatica, lethargy, malignant fever, pleurisy, sleepiness, abscesses, trembling, poison, and vapors. See A. Moquin-Tandon, *Elements of Medical Zoology*, trans. and ed. Robert Thomas Hulm (London: H. Bailliere Publisher, 1861), 121–22; Martin, *Castorologia*, 91–97; George D. Hendricks, "Misconceptions Concerning Western Wild Animals," *Western Folklore* 12, no. 2. (April 1953), 126; and *British Journal of Homeopathy*, ed. J. J. Drysdale, R. E. Dudgeon, and Richard Hughes (London: Henry Turner and Co., 1875), 434. Castoreum ranks in fame alongside other animal-derived fixatives, including ambergris from sperm whales and musk from the African civet cat. Mandy Aftel, *Essence & Alchemy, A Natural History of Perfume* (Layton, UT: Gibbs Smith, 2004), 77; and Nigel Groom, *The New Perfume Handbook*, 2 ed. (London: Blackie Academic & Professional, 1997), 57.

35 Crean, "Hats and the Fur Trade," 374–75. According to one historian of hatmaking, "A perfect beaver hat may be regarded as the highest achievement of the hatter." James Harford Hawkins, *History of the Worshipful Company, of the Art or Mistery of Feltmakers of London* (London: Crowther & Goodman, 1917), 16. No wonder, given the skills involved in making one. Moving from the sorting of pelts by quality, to their preparation, to the shaving of the "beaver wool," to the tangling of the hairs into a thick felt, to the shaping and cutting of the hat, the process of making a beaver hat involved as many as thirty separate steps and could take as long as seven hours. One of the first and most difficult parts of the process was removing the coarse guard hairs to expose the soft undercoat, a task meticulously performed by the hatter who draped the pelt over his knee and plucked the hairs using his thumb and a knife or a pair of tweezers. The opening of the North American beaver trade enabled hatters to often skip this laborious

time-consuming task, because many pelts were imported with guard hairs already rubbed off, as a result of the pelts being worn by the Indians as robes. However the guard hairs were removed, the next step in the felting assembly line was for the fur to be sheared from the pelt, after which it was carded, weighed, bowed, basoned, planked, blocked, trimmed, dyed, stiffened, steamed, ironed, brushed, lined, and finished, resulting in a fashionable beaver hat. Because of beaver's great value, it was not uncommon for beaver hats to be made of more than just beaver, and different parts of the hats, such as the inner lining, were often a combination of beaver fur and less expensive furs, such as rabbit. For a more complete description of how beaver hats were made, please see the White Oak Society Web page on the making of a beaver hat, at http://www.whiteoak.org/learning/furhat .htm, (accessed March 17, 2008); John Thomson, *A Treatise on Hat-Making and Felting* (Philadelphia: Henry Carey Board, 1868), 29–52, 60–61; and Hawkins, *History of the Worshipful Company*, 15–19.

In the early 1700s the feltmaking process experienced a revolution of sorts, with the addition of a new step called Carroting, in which a solution of mercury salts and nitric acid was brushed onto the pelt to roughen the outer casing or scales of the fur, thereby greatly improving its felting qualities. Carroting not only turned the tips of the fur orange or yellowish red, hence the name, but it also placed the hatter's health in great jeopardy. The combination of heat and steam in the feltmaking process created mercury vapors, which the hatters inhaled, and the longer the exposure the greater the chances that the hatters would develop mercury poisoning, characterized by nerve damage, uncontrollable shakes, a shuffling gate, and mental deterioration, a suite of symptoms that likely gave rise to the analogy "mad as a hatter." For more on the impact of mercury on hatters, see John Timbrell, *The Poison Paradox: Chemicals as Friends and Foes* (Oxford: Oxford University Press, 2005), 166.

36 "We find but little of hat-making recorded in history, and anything relating to hats is extremely meager." Thomson, *A Treatise on Hat-Making and Felting*, 26. See also Wilcox, *The Mode in Hats and Headdress*, 41.

37 Geoffrey Chaucer, *The Canterbury Tales of Chaucer*, by Thomas Tyrwhitt, vol. 1 (Edinburgh: James Nichol, 1860), 9.

38 Thomson, *A Treatise on Hat-Making and Felting*, 27; and Eric R. Wolf, *Europe and the People Without History* (Berkeley: University of California Press, 1982), 159.

39 Shorto, *The Island at the Center of the World*, 34.

40 Quotes from Abacuk Pricket, "A Larger Discourse of the Same Voyage, and the Success Thereof," in Johnson, *Charting the Sea of Darkness*, 177–79. See also ibid., 149–52, 195–200; Peter C. Mancall, *Fatal Journey: A Tale of Mutiny and Murder in the Arctic* (New York: Basic Books, 2009), 6–17, 119–30; and Shorto, *The Island at the Center of the World*, 34–35.

41 Mancall, *Fatal Journey*, 144–46, 209–10; and Johnson, *Charting the Sea of Darkness*, 196–200.

CHAPTER 3: *New Amsterdam Rising*

1   Simon Hart, *The Prehistory of the New Netherland Company* (Amsterdam: City of Amsterdam Press, 1959), 21–22; and Gosselink, *New York, New Amsterdam*, 43. According to Hart, "The beginning of Dutch commercial relations with the territory specified as New Netherland and the Hudson River is obscure," 17.

2   There is not much information on Block's voyage in 1612, but what little is available seems to indicate that it was successful. For example, one of Block's supporters, writing to his wife on July 30, 1613, about Block's voyage to the Hudson during the winter of 1612–13, said that it had been "a better voyage even than last year." See Hart, *The Prehistory of the New Netherland Company*, 74; Rink, *Holland on the Hudson*, 32–34. While the official Dutch name for the river at this time was the Mauritius, by 1614 the fur traders in the area were already calling it the Hudson, in honor of that explorer's earlier voyage. See Shorto, *The Island in the Center of the World*, 38. During these early years the Hudson was also called the North River to differentiate it from the South River (the Delaware).

3   Hart, *The Prehistory of the New Netherland Company*, 22–23, 74–75, 80–81; Gosselink, *New York, New Amsterdam*, 43; and Van Cleaf Bachman, *Peltries or Plantations: The Economic Policies of the Dutch West India Company in New Netherland, 1623–1639* (Baltimore: Johns Hopkins Press, 1969), 6–7. Some have claimed that Rodrigues was mulatto or black, but his actual color is not known. Gosselink, *New York, New Amsterdam*, 45.

4   Bachman, *Peltries or Plantations*, 6–7; and Hart, *The Prehistory of the New Netherland Company*, 25–26.

5   Hart, *The Prehistory of the New Netherland Company*, 80–83.

6   Ibid., 28–31.

7   Ibid., 32; and Tom Lewis, *The Hudson: A History* (New Haven: Yale University Press, 2005), 54–55.

8   *Documents Relative to the Colonial History of the State of New-York, Procured in Holland, England and France by John Romeyn Brodhead*, ed. E. B. O'Callaghan, vol. 1 (Albany: Weed, Parsons & Company, 1856), 5–6, 10.

9   John de Laet, ed. and trans., "Extracts from *The New World, or A Description of the West Indies* (1633), in *Collections of the New-York Historical Society*, vol. 1 (New York: New-York Historical Society, 1841), 291, 299. Some accounts claim that Fort Nassau was built on top of an older fortress that French fur traders had built on the island in 1540. See John Fiske, *The Dutch and Quaker Colonies in America*, vol. 1 (Boston: Houghton, Mifflin & Company, 1899), 92.

10 Rink, *Holland on the Hudson*, 49; and Gosselink, *New York, New Amsterdam*, 49.

11 Van der Donck, *A Description of New Netherland*, 139–40.

12 Duffels came by their name because they were originally manufactured in the town of Duffel, in Flanders. Shorto, *The Island at the Center of the World*, 46; Alice Morse Earle, *Costume of Colonial Times* (New York: Charles Scribner's Sons,

1894), 103; Bachman, *Peltries and Plantations*, 21; and Ian K. Steele, *Warpaths: Invasions of North America* (New York: Oxford University Press, 1994), 114–15.

13 William N. Fenton, *The Great Law and the Longhouse: A Political History of the Iroquois Confederacy* (Norman: University of Oklahoma Press, 1998), 224–27; Daniel Gookin, "Historical Collections of the Indians in New England," in *Collections of the Massachusetts Historical Society for the Year 1792*, vol. 1 (1674; reprint, New York: Johnson Reprint Corporation, 1968), 152; and William B. Weeden, "Indian Money as a Factor in New England Civilization," *Johns Hopkins University Studies in Historical Political Science*, (Baltimore: Johns Hopkins University Press, 1884), 9–10.

14 Gookin, "Historical Collections of the Indians in New England," 152. See also Daniel K. Richter, *Facing East from Indian Country: A Native History of Early America* (Cambridge: Harvard University Press, 2001), 45–46; and Harold G. Moulton, *Principles of Money and Banking* (Chicago: University of Chicago Press, 1916), 62–63.

15 Weeden, "Indian Money as a Factor in New England Civilization," 9, 28–29; Ashbel Woodward, *Wampum: A Paper Presented to the Numismatic and Antiquarian Society of Philadelphia*, 2nd ed. (Albany: Munsell, Printer, 1880), 13, 41–42; and Richter, *Facing East from Indian Country*, 45–46.

16 Weeden, *Indian Money as a Factor in New England Civilization*, 9, 28–29; Woodward, *Wampum*, 13, 15, 41–42; Richter, *Facing East from Indian Country*, 45–46; and Brodhead, *History of the State of New York*, 171–72.

17 Weeden, *Indian Money as a Factor in New England Civilization*, 15.

18 One of the difficulties in writing about the American fur trade, especially during the colonial era, is that almost all the historical documents were written by the white people who interacted with the Indians rather than the Indians themselves. Thus it is nearly impossible to say with certainty what the Indians thought about their participation in the trade, and how they perceived the people with whom they were trading. Still, some documents do exist, and historians have used them, and have also carefully analyzed the broader contemporary literature written by whites, to create portraits of the fur trade, and in particular Indian involvement, that are as accurate and balanced as possible.

19 Paul Le Jeune, *Travels and Explorations of the Jesuit Missionaries in New France, 1610–1791*, vol. 6, ed. Reuben Gold Thwaites (Cleveland: Burrows Brothers Company, 1897), 297, 299.

20 As Professor Jennifer Brown, of the University of Winnipeg, points out, "European records made a big thing of how impressed the Indians were with their trade goods; Indian oral tradition tells the reverse—how impressed the Europeans were with the furs that the Indians didn't value particularly highly." Peter C. Newman, *Empire of the Bay: The Company of Adventurers That Seized a Continent* (New York: Penguin Books, 1998), 164.

21 Nicolas Denys, *The Description and Natural History of the Coasts of North America (Acadia)*, trans. and ed. William F. Ganong (Toronto: Champlain Society, 1908), 426.

22 William Cronon, *Changes in the Land: Indians, Colonists, and the Ecology of New England* (New York: Hill & Wang, 1983), 97–99. As Hickerson put it, "Indians, though not conservationists, if only due to limited technology, were not wasteful in precontact times." Harold Hickerson, "Fur Trade Colonialism and the North American Indian," *Journal of Ethnic Studies* 1 (Summer 1973); 24.

23 Some have argued that, in large part, the Indians got involved in the fur trade, and willingly contributed to the destruction of the animals they relied on for their subsistence and held in such high spiritual regard, because they were retaliating against the animals, believing that it was they, not the Europeans, who had brought disease to their tribes. This motivation was in addition to, and more important than, the desire to gain access to European goods. For more about this provocative and controversial interpretation, see Calvin Martin, *Keepers of the Game: Indian-Animal Relationships and the Fur Trade* (Berkeley: University of California Press, 1978); Shepard Krech III, ed., *Indians, Animals, and the Fur Trade: A Critique of Keepers of the Game* (Athens: University of Georgia Press, 1981); and Cronon, *Changes in the Land*, 91.

24 Francis Jennings, *The Ambiguous Iroquois Empire* (New York: W. W. Norton & Company, 1984), 80; and Edmund S. Morgan, *American Heroes: Profiles of Men and Women Who Shaped Early America* (New York: W. W. Norton, 2009), 50–51.

25 Cronon, *Changes in the Land*, 92–98; Jennings, *The Ambiguous Iroquois Empire*, 80.

26 Daniel P. Barr, *Unconquered: The Iroquois League at War in Colonial America* (Westport: Praeger, 2006), 22. According to the historian Richard White, "Indians wanted kettles partly because you can put them on a fire and boil water and they won't break. That's nice. But many of those kettles didn't stay kettles for long. They got cut up and turned into arrowheads that were then used in the hunt. Or they got turned into high-status jewelry. Indians valued kettles because they were such an extraordinarily flexible resource." Richard White, "Indians in the Land," *American Heritage* (August/September 1986), http://www.americanheritage.com/articles/magazine/ah/1986/5/1986_5_18.shtml, (accessed April 2, 2009).

27 Laurel Thatcher Ulrich, *The Age of Homespun: Objects and Stories in the Creation of the American Myth* (New York: Alfred A. Knopf, 2001), 55. See also Cronon, *Changes in the Land*, 102; James Axtell, *Beyond 1492: Encounters in Colonial North America* (Oxford: Oxford University Press, 1992), 138–39; and David Pietrez de Vries, "From the 'Kortee Historiael Ende Journaels Aenteyckeninge, 1633–1634 (1655)," in *Narratives of New Netherland*, 217.

28 Cronon, *Changes in the Land*, 95–96.

29 This Dutchman was later reprimanded and fired by his employers, who were disgusted by his actions. Brodhead, *History of the State of New York*, 146; and Paul Otto, *The Dutch-Munsee Encounter in America: The Struggle for Sovereignty in the Hudson Valley* (Oxford, England: Berghahn Books, 2006), 59. In another, more notorious incident, the Dutchman Hans Hontom kidnapped a Mohawk sachem

and demanded a ransom (likely wampum), which was paid. Nevertheless Hontom proceeded to castrate the sachem, who later died from this wound, and then hung his penis to a stay on his ship. See "Examination of Bastiaen Jansz Krol," in *Van Rensselaer Bowier Manuscripts*, trans. and ed. A. J. F. van Laer (Albany: University of the State of New York, 1908), 302; and Fenton, *The Great Law and the Longhouse*, 270.

30 This perspective of viewing the Indians as customers comes from the author's discussions, in August 2008, with James Hanson, the editor of the *Museum of The Fur Trade Quarterly* and director emeritus of history at the Museum of the Fur Trade.

31 According to the historian Ian K. Steele, "Historians have been irrationally embarrassed by Amerindian economic interests evident in the fur trade of the north and the deerskin trade of the south. Earlier portrayals of naïve Amerindian victims of underpriced furs and overpriced European good have rightly been superseded by more plausible accounts of discerning Amerindian customers able to demand exactly the kind of kettles, blankets, knives, or guns they wanted." Steele, *Warpaths*, 69. See also Axtell, *Beyond 1492*, 132–133; and Hickerson, "Fur Trade Colonialism," 19.

32 Roger Williams, *A Key into the Language of America*, in *Collections of the Massachusett Historical Society for the Year 1794*, vol. 3 (1643; reprint, New York: Johnson Reprint Corporation, 1968), 232.

33 Cronon, "Indians in the Land." As one Indian put it in 1735, "Trade and peace we take to be the same thing." Quoted in Peter Wraxall, *An Abridgement of the Indian Affairs Contained in Four Folio Volumes, Transacted in the Colony of New York, from the Year 1678 to the Year 1751*, ed. Charles Howard McIlwain (Cambridge: Harvard University Press, 1915), 195.

34 It was equally clear that the English were concerned about Dutch encroachments on supposed English territory. Indeed, when Capt. Thomas Dermer encountered Dutch fur traders on the Hudson River in the spring of 1620, he told them they were on His Majesty's land and warned them to leave as soon as possible. The Dutch replied that their country had the rights to the land, and they planned to stay. John Fiske, *The Dutch and Quaker Colonies in America*, vol. 1 (Boston: Houghton, Mifflin & Company, 1903), 100; and Brodhead, *History of the State of New York*, 93.

35 "Petition of the Directors of the New Netherland Company to the Prince of Orange, &c., February 1, 1620," in *The Story of the Pilgrim Fathers, 1606–1623 A.D.; as Told by Themselves, Their Friends, and Their Enemies*, ed. Edward Arber (London: Ward and Downey, 1897), 297–98; and Fiske, *The Dutch and Quaker Colonies in America*, 95.

36 "Resolution of the States General on the Petition of the New Netherland Company, April 11, 1620," in *The Story of the Pilgrim Fathers, 1606–1623 A.D.*," 298. See also Nathaniel Philbrick, *Mayflower: A Story of Courage, Community, and War* (New York: Viking, 2006), 20; and William Bradford, *History of Plymouth Plantation*, ed. Charles Deane (Boston: privately printed, 1856), 42.

37   Bachman, *Peltries or Plantations*, 25–32.

38   Benjamin Schmidt, *Innocence Abroad: The Dutch Imagination and the New World* (Cambridge: Cambridge University Press, 2001), 196–97.

39   Shorto, *The Island at the Center of the World*, 38; and Schmidt, *Innocence Abroad*, 196.

40   Shorto, *The Island at the Center of the World*, 40; and Henry William Elson, *History of the United States of America*, vol. 1 (New York: Macmillan Company, 1908), 184–85.

41   Shorto, *The Island at the Center of the World*, 40–41; Schuyler van Rensselaer, *History of the City of New York in the Seventeenth Century*, vol. 1 (New York: Macmillan Company, 1909), 43–44; and Charles Washington Baird, *History of the Huguenot Emigration to America*, vol. 1 (New York: Dodd, Mead & Company, 1885), 158–69.

42   Shorto, *The Island at the Center of the World*, 43–49.

43   E. B. O'Callaghan, *The Documentary History of the State of New-York*, vol. 4 (Albany: Charles Van Benthuysen, 1851), 132; and Shorto, *The Island at the Center of the World*, 42–43.

44   James Grant Wilson, *The Memorial History of the City of New-York*, vol. 1 (New York: New-York History Company, 1892), 147; and Mary L. Booth, *History of the City of New York, From its Earliest Settlement to the Present Time* (New York: W. R. C. Clark & Meeker, 1859), 52, 140.

45   Letter from Mr. Peter Schagen to the States General (November 5, 1626), in *Documents Relative to the Colonial History of the State of New-York, Procured in Holland, England and France by John Romeyn Brodhead*, vol. 1, 37. Shorto dubbed Schagen's letter "New York City's Birth Certificate." For an interesting and thorough discussion as to why this purchase of Manhattan was not one of history's greatest rip-offs, as many have since stated or implied, see Shorto, *The Island at the Center of the World*, 49–58.

46   Bachman, *Peltries or Plantations*, 94.

47   In 1627, an exceptional year, New France shipped 22,000 pelts. Biggar, *Early Trading Companies*, 129; and Geoffrey J. Matthews, *Historical Atlas of Canada, From the Beginning to 1800* (Toronto: University of Toronto Press, 1993), 84.

48   David A. Price, *Love and Hate in Jamestown: John Smith, Pocahontas, and the Heart of a New Nation* (New York: Alfred A. Knopf, 2003), 14–16, 35–37.

49   John Smith, *The Complete Works of Captain John Smith (1580–1631)*, vol. 1, ed. Philip L. Barbour (Chapel Hill: University of North Carolina Press, 1986), lv–lx.; Bradford Smith, *Captain John Smith, His Life & Legend* (Philadelphia: J. B. Lippincott Company, 1953), 46, 48, 52–53, 58, 61–64, 115–16; E. Keble Chatterton, *Captain John Smith* (New York: Harper & Brothers Publishers, 1927), 16–17, 35–38, 65. 141–48. Some historians have argued that many of Smith's supposed exploits were apocryphal. As Bradford Smith wrote, "No figure in American history has raised such a ruckus among scholars as Captain John Smith." Smith, *Captain John Smith*, 11.

50 John Smith, *The True Travels and Observations of Captaine John Smith in Europe, Asia, Africke, and America, Beginning About the Yeere 1593, and Continued to This Present 1629*, vol. 1 (1629; reprint, Richmond: Franklin Press, 1819), 114.

51 John Smith, *A Map of Virginia, With a Description of the Country, the Commodities, People, Government and Religion (1612)*, vol. 1, *The Complete Works of Captain John Smith, 1580–1631*, 155.

52 William Douglass, *A Summary, Historical and Political of the First Planting, Progressive Improvements, and Present State of the British Settlements in North-America*, vol. 2 (London: R. Baldwin, 1755), 241; "A briefe and true report of the commodities as well merchantable as others, which are to be found and raised in the countrey of Virginia, written by Thomas Harriot: together with Master Ralph Lane his approbation thereof on all points," in *The Principal Navigations Voyages Traffiques & Discoveries of the English Nation Made by Sea or Over-land to the Remote and Farthest Distant Quarters of the Earth at any time within the compasse of these 1600 Yeeres*, vol. 8, compiled by Richard Hakluyt (Glasgow: James MacLehose and Sons, 1914), 355–56; John Brereton, "A Briefe and True Relation of the Discoverie of the North Part of Virginia, 1602, by John Brereton," in *Early English and French Voyages Chiefly from Hakluyt, 1534–1608*, ed. Henry S. Burrage (New York: Charles Scribner's Sons, 1906), 336–37; James Rosier, "A True Relation of the Voyage of Captaine George Waymouth, 1605," in *Early English and French Voyages Chiefly from Hakluyt, 1534–1608*, 371; and Johnson, *Charting the Sea of Darkness*, 140.

53 Smith, *The True Travels and Observations of Captaine John Smith in Europe, Asia, Africke, and America*, 198–99; Hale, *Pelts and Palisades*, 63–64; Phillips, *The Fur Trade*, vol. 1, 162–63; and Frederick J. Thorpe, "Fur Trade," in *Encyclopedia of the North American Colonies*, ed. Jacob Ernest Cooke, vol. 1 (New York: Charles Scribner's Sons, 1993), 644.

CHAPTER 4: *"The Bible and the Beaver"*

1 Samuel Eliot Morison, *The Story of the "Old Colony" of New Plymouth [1620–1692]* (New York: Alfred A. Knopf, 1960), 6.

2 The exact date when beavers became extinct in Great Britain or more narrowly England, is hard to determine. According to a classic book on the history of the beaver, 1526 was the year that the last beaver was seen in England. Martin, *Castorologia*, 29.

3 Bradford, *History of Plymouth Plantation*, 108.

4 Adams, *The Founding of New England*, 102. Adams added, "The original foundations of New York, New England, and Canada all rest on the Indian trade, in which the item of beaver-skins was by far the most important and lucrative." Ibid. See also Francis X. Moloney, *The Fur Trade in New England, 1620–1676* (Cambridge: Harvard University Press, 1931), 17.

5   Adams, *The Founding of New England*, 93; Philbrick, *Mayflower*, 20–21; and Roland G. Usher, *The Pilgrims and their History* (Williamstown, MA: Corner House Publishers, 1984), 59–63.

6   Bradford, *History of Plymouth Plantation*, 45–47, 51.

7   Ibid., 61–63.

8   Ibid., 74.

9   Ibid., 75.

10 Edward Winslow and William Bradford, *Mourt's Relation of Journal of the Plantation at Plymouth*, intro. Henry Martyn Dexter (Boston: John Kimball Wiggin, 1865), 2.

11 Bradford, *History of Plymouth Plantation*, 75–80.

12 Ibid., 87; and Winslow and Bradford, *Mourt's Relation*, 61.

13 Charles Francis Adams, *Three Episodes of Massachusetts History*, vol. 1 (Boston: Houghton, Mifflin & Company, 1896), 1–12; Philbrick, *Mayflower*, 79; Morton *New English Canaan*, 22–24; Alden T. Vaughan, "Introduction, Indian-European Encounters in New England: An Annotated, Contextual Overview," in Alden T. Vaughan, ed., *New England Encounters, Indians and Euroamericans, ca. 1600–1850* (Boston: Northeastern University Press, 1999), 9; and Alden T. Vaughan, *New England Frontier: Puritans and Indians, 1620–1675* (Boston: Little, Brown & Company, 1965), 21–22. This sequence, in which foreigners, in particular Europeans, arrive in a new land, and devastating disease ensues, is not unique to New England or America. As Charles Darwin observed, "Wherever the European has trod, death seems to pursue the aboriginal." Although Darwin did not claim or imply that disease was the only factor that led to this outcome, it was one of the prominent ones mentioned. Charles Darwin, *The Voyage of the Beagle*, ed. Charles W. Eliot (New York: P. F. Collier & Son, 1909), 439.

14 Daniel Gookin, quoted in Jedidiah Morse, *Annals of the American Revolution* (Hartford, CT, 1824), 27.

15 Edward Johnson, *Johnson's Wonder-Working Providence, 1628–1651*, ed. J. Franklin Jameson (1654; reprint, New York: Barnes & Noble, 1952), 41. Johnson, who saw religious significance in almost every event, also argued that the Indians' desire to trade furs for European goods was another sign that God had meant the English to seat themselves in New England. Ibid., 40.

16 Bradford, *History of Plymouth Plantation*, 102. Another contemporary traveler through the area regarded Plymouth as "a new found Golgotha." Morton, *New English Canaan*, 23. For an excellent description of this episode, see Philbrick, *Mayflower*, 48–49, 78–80.

17 Thomas Prince, *A Chronological History of New-England in the form of Annals* (Boston: Cummings, Hilliard, and Company, 1826), 185, 189; Bradford, *History of Plymouth Plantation*, 93; Winslow and Bradford, *Mourt's Relation*, 83; and Philbrick, *Mayflower*, 92.

18 Winslow and Bradford, *Mourt's Relation*, 84; and Usher, *The Pilgrims and Their History*, 88.

19 Winslow and Bradford, *Mourt's Relation*,87; and Philbrick, *Mayflower*, 93–94.

20 Bradford, *History of Plymouth Plantation*, 94–95.

21 Prince, *A Chronological History of New-England in the form of Annals*, 187.

22 Winslow and Bradford, *Mourt's Relation*, 124; and Bradford, *History of Plymouth Plantation*, 104–5.

23 Bradford, *History of Plymouth Plantation*, 105.

24 Smith, *A Description of New England*, in Smith, *The Complete Works of Captain John Smith (1580–1631)*, vol. 1, 340.

25 Winslow and Bradford, *Mourt's Relation*, 130.

26 Bradford, *History of Plymouth Plantation*, 105; and Winslow and Bradford, *Mourt's Relation*, 129.

27 Bradford, *History of Plymouth Plantation*, 107–10.

28 Ibid., 108, 118.

29 Ibid.

30 Salisbury, *Manitou and Providence*, 141.

31 Bradford, *History of Plymouth Plantation*, 127; and Moloney, *The Fur Trade in New England*, 21–22.

32 Bradford, *History of Plymouth Plantation*, 208–11. This new trading stock, combined with that year's corn harvest allowed the Pilgrims to obtain enough furs "to pay their engagements against the time, & to get some clothing for the people." Ibid., 210.

33 Ibid., 204.

34 Ibid., 134; and Francis J. Bremer, *John Winthrop: America's Forgotten Founding Father* (Oxford: Oxford University Press, 2005), 252.

35 Hickerson, "Fur Trade Colonialism and the North American Indians," 39.

36 William Wood, *New England's Prospect* (1634; reprint, Amherst: University of Massachusetts Press, 1977), 48.

37 Reuben Gold Thwaites, ed., *Travels and Explorations of the Jesuit Missionaries in New France, 1610–1791*, vol. 6, *Quebec: 1633–1634* (Cleveland: Burrows Brothers, 1897), 299. See also Carl P. Russell, *Firearms, Traps, & Tools of the Mountain Men* (Albuquerque: University of New Mexico Press, 1977), 97–102.

38 *Travels and Explorations of the Jesuit Missionaries in New France, 1610–1791*, 299–301.

39 Innis, *The Fur Trade in Canada*, 14; Carolyn Gilman, *Where Two Worlds Meet: The Great Lakes Fur Trade* (St. Paul: Minnesota Historical Society, 1982), 40; Sandoz, *The Beaver Men*, 136; James Churchill, *The Complete Book of Tanning Skins and Furs* (Mechanicsburg, PA: Stackpole Books, 1983), 69–70; and Agnes C. Laut, *The Fur Trade of America* (New York: Macmillan Company, 1921), 79–80.

40 There was David Thompson, "a Scottish gentleman," who first settled in the vicinity of present-day Portsmouth, New Hampshire, and then in 1626 relocated to an island in Boston Harbor that now bears his name. See Morton, *New English Canaan*, 22; Bradford, *History of Plymouth Plantation*, 208–9; and Hale, *Pelts and Palisades*, 98. Samuel Maverick established trading operations not far

from Thompson, on Noodle's Island (East Boston), where he built a small fort that boasted "four murderers [small cannons] to protect him from the Indians." Adams, *Three Episodes of Massachusetts History*, vol. 1, 191–92.

41 Bradford, *History of Plymouth Plantation*, 119–20; and George Bancroft, *History of the United States of America, From the Discovery of the Continent*, vol. 1 (New York: D. Appleton & Company, 1888), 211.

42 Bradford, *History of Plymouth Plantation*, 120–24, 128–29; and Morison, *The Story of the "Old Colony" of New Plymouth*, 93.

43 For an excellent description of this battle, see Philbrick, *Mayflower*, 140–55. As Philbrick points out, this victory greatly affected the relations between the Indians and the colonists, and among the Indians themselves. It also affected the fur trade. Standish's onslaught scared off the Indians with whom the colonists most often traded. Therefore, "at least temporarily," the colonists were unable to procure as many furs as they had previously received. Ibid., 155.

44 Morison, *The Story of the "Old Colony" of New Plymouth*, 104–5.

45 Bradford, *History of Plymouth Plantation*, 133–34; and Morison, *The Story of the "Old Colony" of New Plymouth*, 104–5.

46 Moloney, *The Fur Trade in New England*, 32.

47 Bradford, *History of Plymouth Plantation*, 239–40. Later Bradford wrote a very long somewhat stilted poem in which he bemoaned the arming of the Indians. See William Bradford, "A Descriptive and Historical Account of New England in Verse," in *The Collections of the Massachusetts Historical Society for the Year 1794*, vol. 3 (1794; reprint, New York: Johnson Reprint Corporation, 1968), 82–83.

48 Adams, *Three Episodes of Massachusetts History*, vol. 1, 195.

49 Bradford, *History of Plymouth Plantation*, 141; and Phillips, *The Fur Trade*, vol. 1, 71.

50 Adams, *Three Episodes of Massachusetts History*, vol. 1, 169–70; Willison, *The Pilgrim Reader*, 332; and William Heath, "Thomas Morton: From Merry Old England to New England," *Journal of American Studies* 41, no. 1 (2007): 136. Judging by Morton's later activities, it is likely that his early years would make for most interesting reading.

51 Bradford, *History of Plymouth Plantation*, 236–37.

52 Morton, *New English Canaan*, 60.

53 Bradford, *History of Plymouth Plantation*, 237. Even Morton seems to have been in on the play on words, at one point referring to his settlement as "a merry mount." Morton, *New English Canaan*, 132–34.

54 Morton, *New English Canaan*, 55.

55 Although it was assumed by many observers that Morton also traded liquor with the Indians, he maintained that he did not: "Yet in all the commerce that I had with them, I never proffered them any such thing." Even if Morton did trade liquor, it was his trade in guns that truly got the Pilgrims agitated. Morton, *New English Canaan*, 54. Morton claimed that in five years one of his servants made profits of £1,000 through the sale of beavers. Ibid., 78.

56 Ibid., 132, 134–35.

57 Bradford, *History of Plymouth Plantation*, 237.

58 Adams, *Three Episodes of Massachusetts History*, vol. 1, 194–97. It should be noted that the Puritans of Plymouth were not opposed to sex. Indeed, they were quite fond of it, but only within the confines of marriage. It was when people such as Morton had sex outside marriage, and worse, with the Indians, that the Puritans became outraged and condemnatory. For a most illuminating discussion of Puritans and sex, see Morgan, *American Heroes*, 61–74.

59 Vaughan, *New England Frontier: Puritans and Indians*, 89–90.

60 Bradford, *History of Plymouth Plantation*, 238–40.

61 Ibid., 240–41.

62 Morton, *New English Canaan*, 137–43.

63 Bradford, *History of Plymouth Plantation*, 241–42.

64 Morton's trial and departure ended his fur-trading days, but it was hardly the end of him. He returned to New England twice more, and on his last visit was imprisoned as a Royalist agitator, and although not convicted, was banished to Maine, where he died in 1647.

65 Bradford, *History of Plymouth Plantation*, 223.

66 Ibid., 234; and Letter from Isaack de Rasière to William Bradford (1627), in *Collections of the New York Historical Society*, second series, vol. 1, 363–64.

67 Bradford, *History of Plymouth Plantation*, 221, 232–34.

68 Phillips, *The Fur Trade*, vol. 1, 119.

69 Bradford, *History of Plymouth Plantation*, 259–63, 267, 275.

70 Edward Winslow, *Good Newes from New England* (1624; reprint, Bedford: Applewood Books, 1996), 69.

CHAPTER 5: *Competition, Conflict, and Chicanery*

1 Bradford, *History of Plymouth Plantation*, 279, 290–91; Benson J. Lossing, *Lives of Celebrated Americans* (Hartford, CT: Thomas Belknap, 1869), 14. Allerton didn't act alone. The undertakers had also chosen four of the original Merchant Adventurers to become partners in their venture. And although these partners supported most of Allerton's ruinous business decisions, the undertakers cast most of the blame on Allerton. The four partners claimed, with some justification, that Allerton had been chosen by the undertakers as their representative, and therefore they were bound, to some extent, to follow his lead.

2 Bradford, *History of Plymouth Plantation*, 293–94. Although this 1631 attack on the Penobscot post was the first altercation between English *colonists* and the French that affected the colonial fur trade, it was not the first time the English and French had squared off against each other in the New World, with the result being a shift in the control of that trade. In 1628, when England was at war with France,

England's King Charles I issued letters of marque authorizing private individuals to attack French assets. One such letter was granted to London merchant Gervase Kirke and his partners, giving permission to "destroy any French ships . . . and utterly to . . . root out the French settlements in Nova Scotia and Canada." The merchants' motivation for this venture was to gain control of the rich northern fur trade. Over the next two years Kirke and his sons led spectacularly successful raids, resulting in the capture of Quebec and Port Royal, and the merchants' subsequent claim to have taken all of New France. But while the merchants were enjoying the spoils of victory—including more than seven thousand beaver pelts gathered from the surrendering French as well as the local Indians—Charles I decided to give Canada back to the French, entering into a preliminary peace treaty in 1629. Charles's about-face was essentially a quid pro quo designed to improve his financial status. His French wife, Queen Henrietta Maria, whom he married in 1625, had come with a promised dowry of eight hundred thousand crowns, but by 1629 only half of it had been paid. Charles told the French that if they gave him the second half of the dowry, he would restore Canada to their control, and they leaped at the deal. Thus it was, noted Parkman, that "For a sum equal to about two hundred and forty thousand dollars . . . Charles entailed on Great Britain and her colonies a century of bloody wars." From 1629 until 1632, when the final peace treaty restoring France's North American holdings went into effect, there was an "undeclared war" between the English and the French in America. Intermittent skirmishes erupted along the coast, with the English emerging victorious every time. Henry Kirke, *The First English Conquest of Canada* (London: Bemrose & Sons, 1871), 61; Francis Parkman, *Pioneers of France in the New World* (Boston: Little, Brown & Company, 1918), 444–45; Phillips, *The Fur Trade*, vol. 1, 73–78.

3   Henry Sweetser Burrage, *The Beginnings of Colonial Maine, 1602–1658* (Portland: Marks Printing House, 1914), 267; and Henry S. Burrage, "The Plymouth Colonists in Maine," *Collections of the Maine Historical Society*, third series, vol. 1 (Portland: Maine Historical Society, 1904), 138.

4   Bradford, *History of Plymouth Plantation*, 333–34.

5   *Records of the Governor and Company of the Massachusetts Bay in New England*, vol. 1, compiled by Nathaniel B. Shurtleff (Boston: William White, 1853), 53.

6   Bernard Bailyn, *The New England Merchants in the Seventeenth Century* (New York: Harper & Row, 1955), 23

7   Francis Higginson, "Francis Higginson's New-England's Plantation," in Alexander Young, *Chronicles of the First Planters of the Colony of Massachusetts Bay, from 1623 to 1636* (Boston: Charles C. Little and James Brown, 1846), 245–46.

8   Winthrop, quoted in Bailyn, *The New England Merchants in the Seventeenth Century*, 24.

9   Bradford, *History of Plymouth Plantation*, 336–37.

10   Ibid, 316–17.

11 "Affray at Kennebeck, 1634," *New England Historical and Genealogical Register for the Year 1855*, vol. 9 (Boston: Samuel G. Drake, 1855), 80.

12 Bradford, *History of Plymouth Plantation*, 317–18.

13 Augustine Jones, *The Life and Work of Thomas Dudley, the Second Governor of Massachusetts* (Boston: Houghton, Mifflin & Company, 1900), 174; and Samuel Lane Boardman, "A Chapter in the History of Ancient Cushnoc—Now Augusta," in *Collections of the Maine Historical Society*, third series, vol. 2 (Portland: Maine Historical Society, 1906), 322.

14 John Winthrop, *The History of New England from 1630 to 1649, from his Original Manuscripts*, ed. James Savage, vol. 1 (Boston: Little, Brown & Company, 1853), 156; and Bradford, *History of Plymouth Plantation*, 318.

15 Quotes from Bradford, *History of Plymouth Plantation*, 318–22; John S. C. Abbott and Edward H. Elwell, *The History of Maine*, 2nd ed. (Augusta: Brown Thurston Company, 1892), 96; and William D. Williamson, *The History of the State of Maine, From its First Discovery, A.D. 1602 to the Separation, A.D. 1820, Inclusive*, vol. 1 (Hallowell, ME: Glazier, Masters & Smith, 1839), 253–54. See also Burrage, *The Beginnings of Colonial Maine*, 246–47; Jones, *The Life and Work of Thomas Dudley*, 174; and Boardman, "A Chapter in the History of Ancient Cushnoc—Now Augusta," 317–30.

16 It is also spelled Wahquimacut. See, for example, Timothy Dwight, *Travels in New-England and New-York*, vol. 1 (London: William Baynes and Son, 1823), 110. Referring to the Pilgrims' decision to decline the Dutch invitation, Bradford commented, "their hands being full otherwise, they let it pass." Bradford, *History of Plymouth Plantation*, 311.

17 Bradford, *History of Plymouth Plantation*, 311; and G. H. Hollister, *The History of Connecticut, from the First Settlement of the Colony to the Adoption of the Present Constitution*, vol. 1 (New Haven: Durrie and Peck, 1855), 17.

18 Bradford, *History of Plymouth Plantation*, 312n1.

19 Edwin M. Bacon, *The Connecticut River and the Valley of the Connecticut* (New York: G. P. Putnam's Sons, 1907), 19–20.

20 Rink, *Holland on the Hudson*, 119.

21 Shorto, *The Island at the Center of the World*, 81–82; and James Grant Wilson, *The Memorial History of the City of New-York, From its Settlement to the Year 1892*, vol. 1 (New York: New-York Historical Society, 1892), 178.

22 Bayard Tuckerman, *Peter Stuyvesant* (New York: Dodd, Mead & Company, 1893), 24. See also, Shorto, *The Island at the Center of the World*, 82; and Brodhead, *History of the State of New York*, 230.

23 It has also been referred to as the "House of Good Hope" and "Fort Hope." Bacon, *The Connecticut River and the Valley of Connecticut*, 21; and Brodhead, *History of the State of New York*, 234–35.

24 Hollister, *The History of Connecticut*, 18–19. See also Rink, *Holland on the Hudson*, 122–23.

25 Bradford, *History of Plymouth Plantation*, 313–14. See also Rink, *Holland on the

Hudson, 123–24; and Arthur H. Buffinton, "New England and the Western Fur Trade," in *Publications of the Colonial Society of Massachusetts*, vol. 18, *Transactions 1915–1916* (Boston: Colonial Society of Massachusetts, 1917), 167.

26 Adams, *The Founding of New England*, 103; Franklin B. Dexter, "Estimates of Population in the American Colonies," in *Proceedings of the American Antiquarian Society, New Series*, vol. 5 (Worcester: Published by the Society, 1889), 25; and Justin Winsor, *The Memorial History of Boston*, vol. 1 (Boston: James R. Osgood and Company, 1883), 112.

27 Bailyn, *The New England Merchants in the Seventeenth Century*, 28; Henry Hall, *Report on the Ship-Building Industry of the United States* (Washington, DC: U.S. Government Printing Office, 1884), 47; and *A Handbook of New England* (Boston: Porter E. Sargent, 1916), 601.

28 Charles Hosmer Walcott, *Concord in the Colonial Period, Being a History of the Town of Concord, Massachusetts* (Boston: Estes and Lauriat, 1884), 17; Moloney, *The Fur Trade of New England*, 67–69; Bailyn, *The New England Merchants in the Seventeenth Century*, 28–29.

29 A Mr. Savage, quoted in Bradford, *History of Plymouth Plantation*, 312n1.

30 Ibid., 109. *The Blessing of the Bay* was first ship built in Massachusetts.

31 O'Callaghan, *History of New Netherland*, vol. 1, 152.

32 *A Handbook of New England* (Boston: Porter E. Sargent, 1916), 43.

33 John Winthrop, *Winthrop's Journal, "History of New England," 1630–1649*, vol. 1, ed. James Kendall Hosmer (New York: Charles Scribner's Sons, 1908), 108.

34 Bradford, *History of Plymouth Plantation*, 338–39.

35 Ibid., 340–42; and Adams, *The Founding of New England*, 190.

36 Brodhead, *History of the State of New York*, 260.

37 Abiel Holmes, *The Annals of America from the Discovery of Columbus in the Year 1492 to the Year 1826*, vol. 1 (Cambridge: Hilliard and Brown, 1829), 229; Rensselaer, *History of the City of New York*, 129; "The Representation of New Netherland," in *Collections of the New-York Historical Society*, 2nd series, vol. 2, trans. Henry C. Murphy (New York: New-York Historical Society, 1849), 277; and John Gorham Palfrey, *History of New England During the Stuart Dynasty*, vol. 1 (Boston: Little, Brown & Company, 1899), 539.

38 Adams, *The Founding of New England*, 191.

39 Philips, *The Fur Trade*, vol. 1, 131. Other Massachusetts towns that were created "partly as offshoots or rivals of Springfield" included Northampton, Hadley, and Deerfield. See Vaughan, *New England Frontier: Puritans and Indians*, 216.

40 Bradford, *History of Plymouth Plantation*, 346–47; and Bailyn, *The New England Merchants in the Seventeenth Century*, 25.

41 Bailyn, *The New England Merchants in the Seventeenth Century*, 26.

42 Joseph B. Felt, *Annals of Salem from Its First Settlement* (Salem: W. & S. B. Ives, 1827), 70–71; Earle, *Costume of Colonial Times*, 125–26; John Gorham Palfrey, *History of New England During the Stuart Dynasty*, vol. 1 (Boston: Little, Brown & Company, 1859), 552; and Justin Winsor, *The Memorial History of Boston*, 483.

43 Phillips, *The Fur Trade*, vol. 1, 4.

44 *Stuart Royal Proclamations, Royal Proclamations of King Charles I*, vol. 2, ed. James F. Larkin (Oxford: Clarendon Press, 1983), 613–18.

CHAPTER 6: *"Many Hounds Are the Hare's Death"*

1 Buffinton, "New England and the Western Fur Trade," 166.

2 Morton, *New English Canaan*, 99–100.

3 Buffinton, "New England and the Western Fur Trade," 167.

4 "The Assembly of the XIX to the States General [October 23, 1629]," in *Documents Relative to the Colonial History of the State of New-York*, vol. 1, 40.

5 Brodhead, *History of the State of New York*, 184; and Hale, *Pelts and Palisades*, 135.

6 Michael Kammen, *New York, A History* (New York: Oxford University Press, 1975), 38; and Shorto, *The Island at the Center of the World*, 89.

7 Shorto, *The Island at the Center of the World*, 105, 110, 118–28.

8 Figuring out just how many furs New Netherland sent to New Amsterdam during this period is tricky. According to Adriaen van der Donck, who lived near Fort Orange during most of the 1640s, "all told, an average of eighty thousand beavers per year are killed in this part of the country." Jaap Jacobs argues that van der Donck's estimate is "too high." Jacobs's review of the data found that in 1633, 8,800 beavers and 1,383 otters and other peltries were exported from New Netherland, and the following year those numbers increased to 14,891 and 1,413, respectively. Jacobs also points out that "quantitative details for the [fur trade in] the 1640s are scarce," but notes that toward the end of the 1640s the fur trade expanded considerably. For example, a single ship that left Manhattan in 1647, and sank off the coast of Wales, had on board some 16,000 beaver pelts alone. See Adriaen van der Donck, *A Description of New Netherland*, 99; Jaap Jacobs, *New Netherland: A Dutch Colony in Seventeenth-Century America* (Leiden: Brill, 2005), 197–201; and Shorto, *The Island at the Center of the World*, 179.

9 This account of Van den Bogaert's journey is based on his journal and Shorto. All the quotes come from Harmen Meyndertsz van den Bogaert, *A Journey into Mohawk and Oneida Country, 1634–1635*, trans. and ed. Charles T. Gehring and William A. Starna, with a word list and linguistic notes by Gunther Michelson (Syracuse: Syracuse University Press, 1988), 1–22. See also Shorto, *The Island at the Center of the World*, 76–81; and Jacobs, *New Netherland*, 207–8.

10 A hand was a somewhat variable measure that was the length between the thumb and the pinky on an outstretched hand.

11 Amandus Johnson, *The Swedish Settlements on the Delaware, Their History and Relation to the Indians, Dutch and English, 1638–1664*, vol. 1 (New York: D. Apple-

ton & Company, 1911), 182–84; Shorto, *The Island at the Center of the World*, 88, 114–15; and Hale, *Pelts and Palisades*, 147–49.

12 Shorto, *The Island at the Center of the World*, 116. See also Johnson, *The Swedish Settlements*, vol. 1, 186.

13 Johnson, *The Swedish Settlements*, vol. 1, 186–94. Minuit never did get to see New Sweden develop. In August 1638, on his way back to Europe, his ship was lost in a hurricane in the Caribbean. Shorto, *The Island at the Center of the World*, 117.

14 Johnson, *The Swedish Settlements*, vol. 1, 192.

15 Ibid., 208.

16 Ibid., 209–11.

17 Ibid., 211–14, especially 214n31; Hale, *Pelts and Palisades*, 153; O'Callaghan, *History of New Netherland*, vol. 1, 231; and *Documents Relative to the Colonial History of the State of New-York; Procured in Holland, England and France by John Romeyn Brodhead*, vol. 2, ed. E. B. O'Callaghan (Albany: Weed, Parsons and Company, 1858), 144.

18 *Documents Relative to the Colonial History of the State of New-York*, vol. 2, 144.

19 Samuel Hazard, *Annals of Pennsylvania from the Discovery of the Delaware* (Philadelphia: Hazard and Mitchell, 1850), 61.

20 Ibid.

21 It was estimated that the burning of the post resulted in damages to the English of £1,000. See Johnson, *The Swedish Settlements*, vol. 1, 215.

22 Charles H. Levermore, *The Republic of New Haven: A History of Municipal Evolution* (1886; reprint, Port Washington: Kennikat Press, 1966), 93; and Shorto, *The Island at the Center of the World*, 182–83.

23 J. Thomas Scharf and Thompson Westcott, *History of Philadelphia, 1609–1884*, vol. 2 (Philadelphia: L. H. Everts & Co., 1884), 1023.

24 Johnson, *The Swedish Settlements*, vol. 1, 380–88; Hale, *Pelts and Palisades*, 154; Brodhead, *History of the State of New York*, vol. 1, 382; J. Thomas Scharf, *History of Maryland From the Earliest Period to the Present Day*, vol. 1 (Baltimore: John B. Piet, 1879), 240; and John Winthrop, *Winthrop's Journal, "History of New England," 1630–1649*, ed. James Kendall Hosmer, vol. 2 (New York: Charles Scribner's Sons, 1908), 142.

25 Winthrop, *Winthrop's Journal*, vol. 2, 142.

26 Adams, *The Founding of New England*, 229.

27 Johnson, *The Swedish Settlements*, vol. 1, 388–91; Winthrop, *Winthrop's Journal*, vol. 2, 189; Brodhead, *History of the State of New York*, vol. 1, 382–83; and C. William A. Veditz and Bartlett Burleigh James, *The History of North America*, vol. 6, *The Revolution* (Philadelphia: George Barre & Sons, 1904), 169–70.

28 It is usually assumed that this Lake of the Iroquois is Lake Champlain. In 1642 an Irishman named Darby Field, along with two Indian guides, climbed one of the peaks in the White Mountains and claimed to have seen in the distance "a great water which he judged to be about 100 miles broad, but could not see land beyond

it." People assumed he had sighted the Lake of the Iroquois, and this renewed interest in finding a way to get to it by water. Field was apparently the first European to climb to the top of any of the White Mountains. Winthrop, *Winthrop's Journal*, vol. 2, 62–63, and 164; and Johnson, *The Swedish Settlements*, vol. 1, 391–95.

29 Kieft, quoted in Johnson, *The Swedish Settlements*, vol. 1, 396. See also Winthrop, *Winthrop's Journal*, vol. 2, 181.

30 *Winthrop's Journal*, vol. 2, 181, 191. See also Johnson, *The Swedish Settlements*, vol. 1, 396–97.

31 The Pequot War was sparked by the murders of two fur traders, one of whom was John Oldham, the man whose travels and trading along the Old Connecticut Path had spurred the migration of many Massachusetts men to the Connecticut River valley.

32 First quote from Reuben Gold Thwaites, *The Colonies 1492–1750* (New York: Longmans, Green, and Co., 1910), 162. Second quote from Adams, *The Founding of New England*, 206. See also Rensselaer, *History of the City of New York*, vol. 1, 167.

33 Moloney, *The Fur Trade in New England*, 54.

34 Phillips, *The Fur Trade*, vol. 1, 153–54, and Hanson, *When Skins Were Money*, 39.

35 New fur traders were often tutored in the art of grading furs, as was the case when London merchant Francis Kirby instructed John Winthrop, Jr., on the finer points of selecting the best furs. Francis Kirby to John Winthrop, Jr., June 22, 1632, in *Winthrop Papers*, vol. 3, *1631–1637* (Boston: Massachusetts Historical Society, 1943), 82.

36 In addition to Dutch duffels, the Indians had grown fond of a sturdy English woolen cloth called strouds, manufactured for the Indian trade in the Stroud Valley in Gloucestershire, England. See Francis Jennings, *The Invasion of America: Indians, Colonialism, and the Cant of Conquest* (New York: W. W. Norton, 1976), 99.

37 Letter from Peter Stuyvesant to the Directors in Holland (April 21, 1660), in *Documents Relating to the Colonial History of the State of New York*, vol. 14 (1883; reprint, New York: AMS Press, 1969), 470. Wampum was used so widely and liberally in New Netherland and New England that it had become "a universal currency," acceptable for all kinds of transactions, from hiring workers to paying debts and taxes, and in the Dutch colony, Massachusetts and Connecticut wampum was legal tender. Part of the reason that wampum was used so widely was that there was a scarcity of other forms of currency or specie, both coinage and paper money. Wampum's success led to its imitation, as poor-quality and counterfeit beads streamed through colonial economies. There were many ingenious ways to counterfeit wampum. White beads were dyed black to make them more valuable, and beads made of porcelain, stones, or shells other than those traditionally used were passed off as real. There was, however, a limit to the usefulness of counterfeit or poor-quality wampum. While Indians might be willing to trade inferior wampum to the English and the Dutch, they were rarely willing to accept

it for their furs. Weeden, *Indian Money as a Factor in New England Civilization*, 9, 24, 28–29; Woodward, *Wampum*, 13, 41–46; Jerry W. Markham, *A Financial History of the United States*, vol. 1 (Armonk, NY: M. E. Sharpe, 2002), 43–44; Agnes F. Dodd, *History of Money in the British Empire & The United States* (New York: Longmans, Green, and Co., 1911), 228; Walter A. McDougall, *Freedom Just Around the Corner: A New American History, 1585–1828* (New York: Perennial, 2005), 63.

38 Axtell, *Beyond 1492*, 134; and Peter Allen Thomas, "Into the Maelstrom of Change," in *A Place Called Paradise: Culture & Community in Northampton, Massachusetts, 1654–2004* (Amherst: University of Massachusetts Press, 2004), 13. See also Vaughan, *New England Frontier*, 231. For an early discussion (1643) of the Indians' relation to credit and debt, see Williams, *A Key Into the Language of America*, 233.

39 Vaughan, *New England Frontier*, 227–31; Peter C. Mancall, *Deadly Medicine: Indians and Alcohol in Early America* (Ithaca: Cornell University Press, 1995), 26; and Maloney, *The Fur Trade in New England*, 102–8.

40 James D. Knowles, *Memoir of Roger Williams, the Founder of the State of Rhode Island* (Boston: Lincoln, Edmands and Co., 1834), 287. See also Henry C. Dorr, "The Narragansetts," in *Collections of the Rhode Island Historical Society*, vol. 7 (Providence: Kellogg Printing Company, 1885), 179.

41 Denys, *The Description and Natural History of the Coasts of North America*, 440–43. For more on the Indians' loss of traditional ways and the adoption of European goods, see Daniel K. Richter, *The Ordeal of the Long-House: The Peoples of the Iroquois League in the Era of European Colonization* (Chapel Hill: University of North Carolina Press, 1992), 86–87; Richter, *Facing East from Indian Country*, 44; and Gookin, "Historical Collections of the Indians in New England," 152.

42 This argument about the abandonment of native handicrafts and the cycle of dependency on European goods, with the consequent need to hunt more aggressively for furs, is based primarily on Richter, as well as Jennings and Axtell, whom Richter cites as well. Richter, *Facing East from Indian Country*, 50–51; Jennings, *The Invasion of America: Indians*, 85–91; and Axtell, *Beyond 1492*, 128–51.

43 Richter, *Facing East from Indian Country*, 50.

44 For example, John Stuart, a British colonial official, made the following remark in 1761: "A modern Indian cannot subsist without Europeans and would handle a flint ax or any other rude utensil used by his ancestors very awkwardly, what was only conveniency at first is now become necessity." Quoted in Richter, *Facing East from Indian Country*, 174.

45 *Documents Relative to the Colonial History of the State of New-York*, vol. 1, 150; and Jennings, *The Ambiguous Iroquois Empire*, 80–81.

46 Richter, *The Ordeal of the Long-House*, 86. See also Axtel, *Beyond 1492*, 142–43; and Mancall, *Deadly Medicine*, 67, 75.

47 Denys, *The Description and Natural History of the Coasts of North America*, 444. As Mancall points out, "Indian women drank too, and some participated in ritu-

als involving alcohol, but observers took less notice of women." Mancall, *Deadly Medicine*, 67.

48 O'Callaghan, *History of New Netherland*, 264.

49 Gookin, "Historical Collections of the Indians in New England," 151.

50 Mancall, *Deadly Medicine*, xi, 42–43.

51 Unless otherwise noted the background material on the strife between the Dutch and the Swedes comes from the following sources: Johnson, *The Swedish Settlements*, vol. 1, 414–49; Shorto, *The Island at the Center of the World*, 182–83, 278–79; and Hale, *Pelts and Palisades*, 135–63.

52 Shorto, *The Island at the Center of the World*, 183.

53 Stuyvesant, quoted in Johnson, *The Swedish Settlements*, vol. 1, 435.

54 Ibid., 435, 436.

55 Benjamin Nead, "Historical Notes on the Early Government and Legislative Councils and Assemblies of Pennsylvania, Part I," in *Charter to William Penn, and Laws of the Province of Pennsylvania, Passed Between the Years 1682 and 1700, Appendix*, ed. by Staughton George, Benjamin M. Nead, and Thomas McCamant (Harrisburg: Lane S. Hart, 1879), 425–26; and Frederick J. Zwierlein, *Religion in New Netherland* (Rochester: John P. Smith, 1910), 121–22.

56 Brodhead, *History of the State of New* York, 601. In another part of their letter to Stuyvesant, the directors of the company said, "We hardly know whether we are more astonished at the audacious enterprise of the Swedes in taking our for on the South river, or at the cowardly surrender of it by our commander, which is nearly insufferable." Quoted in John S. C. Abbott, *Peter Stuyvesant* (New York: Dodd, Mead and Company, 1898), 177.

57 Brodhead, *History of the State of New York*, 604.

58 Ibid., 605; and Johan Clason Rising, "Relation of the Surrender of New Sweden, by Governor Johan Clason Rising, 1655," in Albert Cook Myers, ed., *Narratives of Early Pennsylvania West New Jersey and Delaware*, 1630–1707 (New York: Charles Scribner's Sons, 1912), 170–76.

59 E. B. O'Callaghan, *History of New Netherland, or New York Under the Dutch*, 2nd ed., vol. 2, (New York: D. Appleton & Company, 1848), 288–89.

60 Stuyvesant pegged New England's numerical superiority at nearly 50 to 1 around 1650, but some historians believe that he was exaggerating. For example, one historian placed the population of New Netherland in 1647 at 1,500, and New England's at 25,000. See Oliver Perry Chitwood, *A History of Colonial America* (New York: Harper & Brothers 1931), 208n20.

61 Bancroft, *History of the United States of America*, vol. 1, 508. See also *The History of New Jersey From its Earliest Settlement to the Present Time*, ed. W. H. Carpenter and T. S. Arthur (Philadelphia: J. B. Lippincott & Co., 1856), 46; Alexander Johnston, *A Study of a Commonwealth-Democracy* (Boston: Houghton, Mifflin & Company, 1903), 147; and Thwaites, *The Colonies*, 163.

62 Shorto, *The Island at the Center of the World*, 236–38; and Hale, *Pelts and Palisades*, 180–82. Fort Good Hope finally was absorbed by the English in 1654, when the

Dutch and the English were at war and Connecticut took over all Dutch property within the colony's limits. Chitwood, *A History of Colonial America*, 153.

63 O'Callaghan, *History of New Netherland*, vol. 2, 153.

64 Levermore, *Republic of New Haven*, 96.

65 Ibid., 97; and Buffinton, "New England and the Western Fur Trade," 171–72.

66 "Minutes of the Court of Fort Orange," August 4, 1659, in *Documents Relating to the Colonial History of the State of New York*, vol. 13, edited by B. Fernow (1881; reprint, New York: AMS Press, 1969), 101; and Buffinton, "New England and the Western Fur Trade," 177–80.

67 Extract from Letter of Director Stuyvesant and Council to the Directors in Holland (September 4, 1659), in *Documents Relating to the Colonial History of the State of New York*, vol. 13, 107–8. At the time the beaver trade in and around Fort Orange and Beverwyck was in decline, but still important to the colony. According to Burke, "The high point of the trade at Beverwyck came in 1656 and 1657 when as many as 40,000 beaver and otter skins were shipped to New Amsterdam each year. Within two years, however, the situation had altered dramatically," with the number of furs being exported dropping significantly. Thomas E. Burke, Jr., *Mohawk Frontier: The Dutch Community of Schenectady, New York, 1661–1710*, 2nd ed. (Albany: State University of New York Press, 2009), 7.

68 "Extract from a Letter of Director Stuyvesant to the Directors in Holland," undated, but late October or early November 1659, in *Documents Relating to the Colonial History of the State of New York*, vol. 13, 126.

69 Ibid., and "Extract from a Letter of the Directors in Holland to Director Stuyvesant," December 22, 1659, in ibid., 129–30.

70 "Extract from a Letter of the Directors in Holland to Director Stuyvesant," March 9, 1660, in ibid., 149–50.

71 Letter from William Torrey, Clerk of the General Court, to Peter Stuyvesant (November 12, 1659), in *Records of the Colony of New Plymouth in New England*, ed. David Pulsifer, vol. 2, *1653–1679* (Boston: William White, 1859), 445–46. See also Buffinton, "New England and the Western Fur Trade," 179.

72 O'Callaghan, *History of New Netherland*, vol. 2, 406.

73 For an excellent and concise history of this transfer of power and the events that led up to it, see Shorto, *The Island at the Center of the World*, 284–300; and O'Callaghan, *History of New Netherland*, vol. 2, 515–38.

CHAPTER 7: *Adieu to the French*

1 According to Fischer, Champlain was denied the title of governor, and instead his official title was "Lieutenant General in New France." But for all intents and purposes he was the governor, and the people of Quebec referred to him as such. Fischer, *Champlain's Dreams*, 445–46.

2   Father Vilmont, "The Journey of Jean Nicolet, 1634," in *Early Narratives of the Northwest, 1634–1699*, ed. Louise Phelps Kellogg (New York: Charles Scribner's Sons, 1917), 11–16. See also Phillips, *The Fur Trade*, vol. 1, 90–91; Reuben Gold Thwaites, *Stories of the Badger State* (New York: American Book Company, 1900), 26–32; Henry Collin Campbell, *Wisconsin in Three Centuries, 1634–1905*, vol. 1 (New York: Century History Company, 1906), 83–93; and Francis Parkman, *Pioneers of France in the New World* (Boston: Little, Brown & Company, 1918), 456–59.

3   Vilmont, "The Journey of Jean Nicolet, 1634," 16. See also Reuben Gold Thwaites, "The Story of Mackinac," in *Papers and Proceedings of the Eighteenth General Meeting of the American Library Association*, (Washington, DC: American Library Association, 1897), 72.

4   The material in this paragraph, including the quote, is from Fischer, *Champlain's Dream*, 512–19.

5   Gilman, *Where Two Worlds Meet*: 30; Bernard DeVoto, *The Course of Empire* (Boston: Houghton, Mifflin & Company, 1952), 239–40; Timothy J. Kent, *Birchbark Canoes of the Fur Trade*, vol. 1 (Ossineke, MI: Silver Fox Enterprises, 1997), vii; and Captain Russell Blakeley, "History of the Discovery of the Mississippi River and the Advent of Commerce in Minnesota," in *Collections of the Minnesota Historical Society*, vol. 8 (St. Paul: Minnesota Historical Society, 1898), 372–75.

6   DeVoto, *The Course of Empire*, 103.

7   Phillips, *The Fur Trade*, vol. 1, 200; and "The American Fur Trade," *Hunt's Merchant's Magazine* (September 1840): 187.

8   J. P. Dunn, *Indiana, A Redemption from Slavery* (Boston: Houghton, Mifflin & Company, 1888), 90–91.

9   Phillips, *The Fur Trade*, vol. 1, 91–92; Fischer, *Champlain's Dream*, 507–8; Clarence A. Vandiveer, *The Fur-Trade and Early Western Exploration* (Cleveland: Arthur H. Clark Company, 1929), 40–42; and Francis Parkman, *The Old Regime in Canada*, vol. 2 (Boston: Little, Brown & Company, 1907), 109–10.

10 Phillips, *The Fur Trade*, vol. 1, 96.

11 Jerome Lalemant, *Travels and Explorations of the Jesuit Missionaries in New France*, vol. 92, ed. Reuben Gold Thwaites (Cleveland: Burrows Brothers, 1898), 307.

12 Francis Parkman, *Count Frontenac and New France Under Louis XIV, France and England in North America, Part Fifth* (Boston: Little, Brown & Company, 1910), 79–80.

13 Richter, *The Ordeal of the Long-House*, 50–74; José António Brandão, *"Your Fyre Shall Burn No More": Iroquois Policy Toward New France and Its Native Allies to 1701* (Lincoln: University of Nebraska Press, 1997); Daniel K. Richter, review of *"Your Fyre Shall Burn No More": Iroquois Policy Toward New France and Its Native Allies to 1701*, by José António Brandão, *William and Mary Quarterly* 55, no. 4 (Oct., 1998): 620–22; Thomas S. Alber, "Iroquois Policy and Iroquois Culture: Two Histories and an Anthropological Ethnohistory," *Ethnohistory*, 47, no. 2 (Spring 2000): 484–91; Barr, *Unconquered*, 37–58; Jerry Keenan, *Encyclopedia*

of American Indian Wars, 1492–1890 (New York: W. W. Norton, 1999), 15; and George T. Hunt, *The Wars of the Iroquois: A Study in Intertribal Trade Relations* (Madison: University of Wisconsin Press, 1940), 32–34.

14 Barr, *Unconquered*, 50–53; Hunt, *The Wars of the Iroquois*, 87–105; Innis, *The Fur Trade in Canada*, 36–37; and DeVoto, *The Course of Empire*, 98.

15 François le Mercier, *Travels and Explorations of the Jesuit Missionaries in New France, 1610–1791*, vol. 40, ed. Reuben Gold Thwaites (Cleveland: Burrows Brothers, 1898), 211–13.

16 Phillips, *The Fur Trade*, vol. 1, 187.

17 Innis, *The Fur Trade in Canada*, 43–44; Hanson, *When Skins Were Money*, 59; and Ted Reese, *Soft Gold: A History of the Fur Trade in the Great Lakes Region and its Impact on Native American Culture* (Bowie, MO: Heritage Books, Inc., 2001), 17.

18 Phillips, *The Fur Trade*, vol. 1, 186; Chitwood, *A History of Colonial America*, 369–70; and W. J. Eccles, *The Canadian Frontier, 1534–1760* (New York: Holt, Rinehart & Winston, 1969), 104–9.

19 E. Bunner, *History of Louisiana, From its First Discovery and Settlement to the Present Time* (New York: Harper & Brothers, Publishers, 1855), 41–43; Vandiveer, *The Fur-Trade*, 57–58; Chittenden, *The American Fur Trade*, vol. 1, 72–73; and Robert Lowrie and William H. McCardle, *A History of Mississippi, From the Discovery of the Great River by Hernando de Soto, Including the Earliest Settlement Made by the French, Under Iberbville, to the Death of Jefferson Davis* (Jackson, MS: R. H. Henry & Co., 1891), 13–14.

20 Henry Tonty, quoted in DeVoto, *The Course of Empire*, 134. See also Francis Parkman, *La Salle and the Discovery of the Great West*, 11th ed. (Boston: Little, Brown & Company, 1879), 275–88; Ray Allen Billington, *Westward Expansion: A History of the American Frontier*, 3rd ed. (New York: Macmillan Company, 1967), 109; and George Bancroft, *History of the United States of America from the Discovery of the Continent*, vol. 2, (New York: D. Appleton & Company, 1884), 159–68; and Eccles, *The Canadian Frontier*, 109.

21 Edwin O. Wood, *Historic Mackinac*, vol. 1 (New York: Macmillan Company, 1918), 64; Louise Phelps Kellogg, *Early Narratives of the Northwest, 1634–1699*, ed. Louise Phelps Kellogg (New York: Charles Scribner's Sons, 1917), 7; Phillips, *The Fur Trade*, vol. 1, 241–43.

22 Phillips, *The Fur Trade*, vol. 1, 203.

23 During this expedition Radisson and Groseilliers became the first white men to explore Lake Superior, and to venture "within the limits of what is now the state of Minnesota." Edward D. Neill, "Groseilliers and Radisson, the First Explorers of Lake Superior and the State of Minnesota," *Magazine of Western History* (February 1888): 412. The brothers-in-law are famed historical figures in Canada, where schoolchildren often refer to them as "Radishes and Gooseberries."

24 Newman, *Empire of the Bay*, 54–57. See also George Bryce, *The Remarkable History of the Hudson's Bay Company* (London: Sampson Low, Marston & Company, 1900), 3–7; Hanson, *When Skins Were Money*, 42; Phillips, *The Fur Trade*, vol. 1,

223–26; DeVoto, *The Course of Empire*, 111, 126–27. The exact dates of the various expeditions of Radisson and Groseilliers are debated by scholars. I have gone with the dates provided by Phillips. See Phillips, *The Fur Trade*, vol. 1, 225–26n.

25 Newman, *Empire of the Bay*, 57–61; Phillips, *The Fur Trade*, vol. 1, 267; Peter Esprit Radisson, *Voyages of Peter Esprit Radisson* (Boston: Prince Society, 1885), 244; and Bryce, *The Remarkable History of the Hudson's Bay Company*, 3.

26 Newman, *Empire of the Bay*, 65–81. See also Hanson, *When Skins Were Money*, 42; and Beckles Willson, *The Great Company, Being a History of the Honourable Company of Merchants-Adventurers Trading into Hudson's Bay* (Toronto: Copp, Clark Company, 1899), 35–39. Many have claimed, either jokingly or sarcastically, that the Hudson's Bay Company initials—stand for "Here Before Christ" or "the Hungry Belly Company." See Newman, *Empire of the Bay*, 4–5.

27 Eccles, *The Canadian Frontier, 1534–1760*, 115.

28 For information on that trade, see Kathryn E. Holland Braund, *Deerskins & Duffels: Creek Indian Trade with Anglo-America, 1685–1815* (Lincoln: University of Nebraska Press, 1993); and Ken Zontek, "Forgotten in the Fur Trade: The Deerskin Trade of the High Plains and Intermountain West, 1540–1882," *Rocky Mountain Fur Trade Journal* 1 (2007): 25–46. One of the by-products of this trade is the rise of the term "buck" to mean dollar, because deerskins cost one dollar each. Hanson, *When Skins Were Money*, 51.

29 Edward Randolph, one of the king's commissioners, commented on this trend in 1688: "New Plymouth Colony have great profit by whale killing. I believe it will be one of our best returns, now beaver and peltry fail us." Quoted in Joseph B. Felt, *Annals of Salem*, 2nd ed., vol. 2 (Salem: W. & S. B. Ives, 1849), 223. Randolph's juxtaposition of the beaver trade and whaling is fascinating—and ironic: Years of hunting beavers had made them scarce in the colonies. With the same ruthless logic, many years of shore whaling would make whales scarcer in coastal waters, thereby pushing the whaling industry offshore. See also Morgan, *The American Beaver*, 227–28; Vaughan, *New England Frontier: Puritans and Indians*, 219, 232–33; and Peter A. Thomas, "Cultural Change on the Southern New England Frontier, 1630–1665," in *Cultures in Contact*, ed. William W. Fitzhugh (Washington, DC: Smithsonian Institution Press, 1985), 155–56.

30 There *were* beavers and other fur-bearing animals in New England, just not enough of them to support anything more than a small, intermittent trade in their pelts. Finally even that could not be sustained in some areas. For example, by the late 1700s and the early to mid-1800s, beavers were virtually extinct in parts of New Hampshire and Vermont. William Ellery Moore, "Contributions to the History of Old Derryfield," in *Manchester Historic Association Collections*, vol. 2, *1900–1901* (Manchester, NH: Manchester Historic Association, 1901), 65; and Zadock Thompson, *History of Vermont, Natural, Civil, and Statistical in Three Parts* (Burlington: Published for the Author by Chauncey Goodrich, 1842), 39.

31 Cronon, *Changes in the Land*, 103. Cronon points out that it wasn't only the loss of furs that forced Indians to use their land as a commodity, but also the devalua-

tion of wampum, another commodity that the Indians had formerly used to obtain European goods. According to the historian Neal Salisbury, the Pawtucket and Massachusett Indians, around the edge of Massachusetts Bay, "had run out of furs to trade," by the early 1630s, and as a result increasingly traded their land. Salisbury, *Manitou and Providence*, 201–2. See also Richter, *Facing East From Indian Country*, 100–101.

32   René Robert Cavelier Sieur de La Salle, *The Journey's of Rene Robert Cavelier Sieur de LaSalle*, ed. Isaac Joslin Cox, vol. 1 (New York: Allerton Book Co., 1922), 198–99; and La Salle, "Memoir of the Sieur de La Salle Reporting to Monseigneur de Siegnelay the Discoveries Made by Him Under Order of his Majesty," in *Collections of the Illinois State Historical Society*, vol. I, ed. H. W. Beckwith (Springfield: H. W. Roker Company, 1903), 121.

33   Phillips, *The Fur Trade*, vol. 1, 326. The patent was never granted.

34   Newman, *Empire of the Bay*, 107–11; Chitwood, *A History of Colonial America*, 376. The Treaty of Ryswyck ended King William's War, and the Treaty of Utrecht concluded Queen Anne's War. Although the wars had little impact on the control of the North American fur trade, the cross-border fighting did disrupt the flow of furs. During King William's War, for example, the Iroquois sided with the English and therefore were a prime target for the French, whose attacks resulted in a marked decrease in the amount of furs that the Indians brought to Albany. Thomas Elliot Norton, *The Fur Trade in Colonial New York, 1686–1776* (Madison: University of Wisconsin Press, 1974), 100.

35   According to Reese, voyageurs "were expected to keep up a speed of 60 strokes per minute, for 12 to 14 hours, stopping to rest only once every hour for ten minutes." Reese, *Soft Gold*, 27. Like the coureurs de bois, the image of the voyageur has been, as the historian Carolyn Podruchny so eloquently shows, glamorized and to some extent caricatured. "Like comic-book heroes, *'voyageurs* have a highly visible reputation, building the Canadian nation with their Herculean strength, while singing, laughing, leaping over waterfalls, and paddling faster than speeding arrows." Carolyn Podruchny, *Making the Voyageur World: Travelers and Traders in the North American Fur Trade* (Lincoln: University of Nebraska, Press, 2006), 2. See also Alexander Ross, *The Fur Hunters of the Far West: A Narrative of Adventures in the Oregon and Rocky Mountains*, vol. 2 (London: Smith, Elder & Co., 1855), 236–37.

36   Hanson, *When Skins Were Money*, 62; Sandoz, *The Beaver Men*, 85–86; and Phillips, *The Fur Trade*, vol. 1, 296–97.

37   Eccles, *The Canadian Frontier*, 145; and Hanson, *When Skins Were Money*, 64.

38   Hanson, *When Skins Were Money*, 49.

39   Phillips, *The Fur Trade*, vol. 1, 338; and "An Act for reducing the several acts for licensing pedlars, and preventing frauds in the duties upon skins and furs, into one set," in *The Statutes at Large; Being a Collection of All the Laws of Virginia, From the First Session of the Legislature, in the Year 1619*, ed. William Waller Hening, vol. 7 (Richmond: Franklin Press, 1820), 284–85.

40 Hanson, *When Skins Were Money*, 51–52; Norton, *The Fur Trade in Colonial New York*, 101–2; Innis, *The Fur Trade in Canada*, 138, 142; and Phillips, *The Fur Trade*, vol. 1, 353, 379, 381, 411.

41 Phillips, *The Fur Trade*, vol. 1, 383–84, 412–16, 424–26.

42 Chitwood, *A History of Colonial America*, 389–90; Hanson, *When Skins Were Money*, 53–57, 64–65; and Phillips, *The Fur Trade*, vol. 1, 378.

43 W. J. Eccles, "The Fur Trade and Eighteenth-Century Imperialism," *William and Mary Quarterly* 40 (July 1983): 362. According to Leach, "There is no doubt that the single most important factor influencing the shifting pattern of Indian alignments was the fur trade." Douglas Edward Leach, *Arms for Empire: A Military History of the British Colonies in North America, 1607–1783* (New York: Macmillan Company, 1973), 177. See also Phillips, *The Fur Trade*, vol. 1, 370–71.

44 Innis, *The Fur Trade in Canada*, 109–11; David J. Weber, *The Spanish Frontier in North America* (New Haven: Yale University Press, 1992), 178; Cadwallader Colden, "A Memorial Concerning the Fur Trade of the Province of New-York, Presented to his Excellency William Burnet, Esq., Captain-General and Governor, December 10,1724," in David Hosack, *Memoir of De Witt Clinton* (New York: J. Seymour, 1829), 236–37; and Richard White, *The Middle Ground: Indians, Empires, and Republics in the Great Lakes Region, 1650–1815* (Cambridge: Cambridge University Prss, 1991), 120–21.

45 Alexander Henry, *Travels and Adventures in Canada and the Indian Territories Between the Years 1760 and 1776* (New York: I. Riley, 1809), 45.

46 Pure alcohol thrown into a fire would cause it to flame; diluted alcohol would not. Thus the Indians, who knew that it was common practice for the traders to dilute their alcohol, would take a draft of the alcohol proffered by a trader, spit it into the fire, and if it flamed he knew it was good stuff—true "firewater"; if it did not he knew he was being cheated. See George E. Ellis, *The Red Man and the White Man in North America from Its Discovery to the Present Time* (Boston: Little, Brown & Company, 1882), 489; Win Blevins, *Dictionary of the American West* (Seattle: Sasquatch Books, 2001), 145.

47 Charles A. Hanna, *The Wilderness Trail*, vol. 2 (New York: G. P. Putnam's Sons, 1911), 307.

48 Mancall, *Deadly Medicine*, 102, 128.

49 Andrew McFarland Davis, "The Indians and the Border Warfare of the Revolution," in *Narrative and Critical History of America*, ed. Justin Winsor (Boston: Houghton, Mifflin & Company, 1888), 668; Wayne Edson Stevens, *The Northwest Fur Trade, 1763–1800* (Urbana: University of Illinois, 1928), 17–18; Writer's Program of the Works Progress Administration in the State of Indiana, *Indian: A Guide to the Hoosier State*, 3rd ed. (New York: Oxford University Press, 1947), 45; and Thorpe, "Fur Trade," in *Encyclopedia of the North American Colonies*, 641. See Hanson for an alternative view: He claims that "it is a myth . . . that the French got on better with the Indians than did other Europeans." Hanson, *When Skins Were Money*, 67. Along the same lines see Saum, *The Fur Trader and the Indian*, 68–88.

50   Leach, *Arms for Empire*, 177.

51   Charles Howard McIlwain, introduction to Wraxall, *An Abridgement of the Indian Affairs*, xl–xli.

52   *Annals of the West: Embracing a Concise Account of Principal Events Which Have Occurred in the Western States and Territories, From the Discovery of the Mississippi Valley to the Year Eighteen Hundred and Fifty-Six*, comp. James R. Albach (Pittsburgh: W. S. Haven, 1858), 148–49.

53   Benjamin Franklin, *The Works of Benjamin Franklin*, comp. and ed. John Bigelow, vol. 3 (New York: G. P. Putnam's Sons, 1904), 140.

54   Homer E. Scolofsky, "Colonial Wars," *in The New Encyclopedia of the American West*, ed. Howard R. Lamar (New Haven: Yale University Press, 1998), 239; Leach, *Arms for Empire*, 177; and Eccles, *The Canadian Frontier*, 158.

55   Vandiveer, *The Fur Trade*, 102–6; Phillips, *The Fur Trade*, vol. 1, 492–95; DeVoto, *Course of Empire*, 200–16.

56   These fur-trading posts and garrisons included Forts Biloxi (MS), Mobile (AL), New Orleans (LA), Miami (near Fort Wayne, IN), Ouiatenon (near Lafayette, IN), de Chartres (Prairie du Rocher, IL), Niagara (Youngstown, NY), Orleans (near Brunswick, MO, although the exact location is not known), St. Louis, Crevecoeur, and Vincennes (IL), and Frontenac (eastern Lake Ontario).

57   The colonies whose charters granted them rights to lands stretching all the way to the Pacific, or "sea-to-sea" claims, included Massachusetts, Connecticut, Virginia, North and South Carolina, and Georgia. See Edward W. Kerson, "Articles of Confederation," in *The New Encyclopedia of the American West*, 57.

58   Parkman, *Montcalm and Wolfe*, vol. 1, 130. See also John W. Monette, *History of the Discovery and Settlement of the Valley of the Mississippi*, vol. 1 (New York: Harper & Brothers, 1846), 165.

59   Cadwallader Colden, "The French and the Fur Trade (1724)," in *American History Told by Contemporaries*, vol. 2, ed. Albert Bushnell Hart (New York: Macmillan Company, 1919), 320–21; and Phillips, *The Fur Trade*, vol. 1, 382.

60   Leach, *Arms for Empire*, 121.

61   Phillips, *The Fur Trade*, vol. 1, 342–46; and Leach, *Arms for Empire*, 166–67.

62   Leach, *Arms for Empire*, 251; *The Cambridge History of British Foreign Policy, 1783–1919*, ed. A. W. Ward and G. P. Gooch (New York: Macmillan Company, 1922), 90–92. According to DeVoto, "All it [the war] settled in either hemisphere was that another war must come." DeVoto, *The Course of Empire*, 220. "The struggle between the French and English in North America which culminated in the seven years' war was really a struggle for the fur trade and for the control of the Indian tribes of the interior." Wayne E. Stevens, "The Organization of the British Fur Trade, 1760–1800," *Mississippi Valley Historical Review* 3, no. 2 (September, 1916): 175.

63   Innis, *The Fur Trade in Canada*, 116.

64   Hanna, *The Wilderness Trail*, 323.

65   Bert Anson, *The Miami Indians* (Norman: University of Oklahoma, 201), 43; and Leach, *Arms for Empire*, 320–21.

66   Francis Parkman, *Montcalm and Wolfe*, vol. 1 (Boston: Little, Brown & Company, 1907), 42–43.

67   Ibid., 46–47, 51.

68   Ibid., 47–48.

69   Joncaire was also referred to as Jean Coeur and Jonquiere. See Emilius O. Randall, *History of Ohio: The Rise and Progress of an American State*, vol. 1 (New York: Century History Company, 1912), 230.

70   Marquis de La Jonquiere, "Conference Between the Marquis de La Jonquiere and the Indians," in *Papers Relating to the French Occupation in Western Pennsylvania, 1631–1674, Pennsylvania Archives, Second Series*, vol. 6, ed. John B. Linn and William H. Egle (Harrisburg: E. K. Meyers, State Printer, 1891), 112.

71   Hanna, *The Wilderness Trail*, 225.

72   Baron de Longueil, quoted in Parkman, *Montcalm and Wolfe*, vol. 1, 88.

73   Ibid., 90; and Leach, *Arms for Empire*, 323–24.

74   Parkman, *Montcalm and Wolfe*, vol. 1, 90, 133–38; Leach, *Arms for Empire*, 324–26; and Fred Anderson, *The War That Made America: A Short History of the French and Indian War* (New York: Viking, 2005), 34–36.

75   A Friend to Publick Liberty, "To the Freeholders and Citizens, Inhabitants of the Province of Pennsylvania," *Pennsylvania Gazette* (September 26, 1754).

76   Richard Frothingham, *The Rise of the Republic of the United States*, 3rd ed. (Boston: Little, Brown & Company, 1881), 131n2.

77   Leach, *Arms for Empire*, 321, 325–26; Parkman, *Montcalm and Wolfe*, vol. 1, 56–57; and Phillips, *The Fur Trade*, vol. 1, 508.

78   Letter from William Trent to Governor Robert Dinwiddie (August 11, 1753), in *The Ohio Company Papers, 1753–1817*, ed. Kenneth P. Bailey (Arcata, CA: Sons of the Revolution Library, 1947), 23–24. Trent was Croghan's brother-in-law. See also Leach, *Arms for Empire*, 326; Justin Winsor, *The Struggle in America Between England and France, 1697–1763* (Boston: Houghton, Mifflin & Company, 1895), 280; William R. Nester, *The Great Frontier War: Britain, France, and the Imperial Struggle for North America, 1607–1755* (Westport, CT: Greenwood Publishing, 2000), 42. See also Phillips, *The Fur Trade*, vol. 1, 514.

79   These words were spoken by the Mohawk chief Tiyanoga, also called Hendrick Peters, at the Albany Conference/Congress in July 1754. "Manuscripts of Sir William Johnson," in O'Callaghan, *The Documentary History of the State of New-York*, vol. 2, 581. See also, Walter Isaacson, *Benjamin Franklin: An American Life* (New York: Simon & Schuster, 2003), 160.

80   Anderson, *The War That Made America*, 39, 45.

81   John Marshall, *The Life of George Washington, Commander in Chief of the American Forces, During the War Which Established the Independence of His Country and First President of the United States*, compiled under the Inspection of the Honourable

Bushrod Washington, from Original Papers, vol. 2 (Philadelphia: C. P. Wayne, 1804), notes section 11. See also George Washington, "Major Washington's Journal of a Tour Over the Allegany Mountains," in Jared Sparks, *The Writings of George Washington, With the Life of the Author*, vol. 2 (Boston: Russell, Odiorne, and Metcalf, 1834), 439–40.

82 Leach, *Arms for Empire*, 331–36; Anderson, *The War That Made America*, 43–47; T. S. Arthur and W. H. Carpenter, *History of Virginia from its Earliest Settlement to the Present Time* (Philadelphia: Claxton, Remsen & Haffelfinger, 1872), 242–45.

83 Two small fishing islands in Canada remained in French hands—Saint-Pierre and Miquelon, both in the Gulf of St. Lawrence. These islands are still French possessions today. The French also retained rights to fish on the Grand Banks southeast of Newfoundland, which had long been the world's most productive codfishing grounds. Colin Gordon Calloway, *The Scratch of a Pen: 1763 and the Transformation of North America* (New York: Oxford University Press, 2006), 8.

84 Hanson, *When Skins Were Money*, 65; and Nancy McPhee, *The Book of Insults Ancient & Modern* (New York: St. Martin's Press, 1978), 101.

85 Sigmund Diamond, "An Experiment in 'Feudalism': French Canada in the Seventeenth Century," *William and Mary Quarterly* (January 1961): 33. See also Leach, *Arms for Empire*, 496–97.

86 A sense of the joy and expectation that the British felt in conquering New France comes through in the writings of Jonathan Mayhew, a pastor at the West Church in Boston. In a speech he delivered on October 25, 1759, a little more than a month after the fall of Quebec, Mayhew expounded upon what he and many other British subjects believed would ensue now that Britain had beaten back the French. "An extensive trade will of course be opened with all the savage nations back of us; particularly the fur trade, of late years almost engrossed by the French, who have had those savages in their interest. They must now hunt for us in our turn, in order to pay us for the necessaries which they must come to us for. Which is also in some measure applicable to the Canadians themselves, that country being reduced, if any of them shall remain therein. They must all be supplied by us, and pay us for it some way or other. So that in short, all the commerce of this part of the world, from the northward of Hudson's Bay to Florida, and back to the Mississippi, or near it, will of course be in the hands of British subjects: A commerce, which will greatly increase the demand for British manufactures, and both well employ and maintain many thousand more people in Great-Britain, than do or can get a livelihood there at present in any honest way. It will also much increase her navigation, and that of her colonies." Jonathan Mayhew, *Two Discourses Delivered October 25th 1759: Being the Day Appointed by Authority to be Observed as a Day of Public Thanksgiving, for the Success of His Majesty's Arms, More Particularly in the Reduction of Quebec, the Capital of Canada* (Boston: Richard Draper, 1759), 44–45.

CHAPTER 8: *Americans Oust the British*

1 Benjamin Franklin, "The Examination of Dr. Benjamin Franklin, [before the English House of Commons, in February, 1766,] relative to the Repeal of the American Stamp Act," in Benjamin Franklin, *Memoirs of the Life and Writings of Benjamin Franklin*, 3rd ed., vol. 2, appendix 4 (London: Henry Colburn, 1818), 379. The other part of Franklin's argument concerned the dispute over the boundary between Canada and Nova Scotia.

2 Billington, *Westward Expansion*, 132.

3 "Purchasing good behavior," in Letter from Jeffrey Amherst to Sir William Johnson (August 9, 1761), in James Sullivan, *The Papers of Sir William Johnson*, vol. 3 (Albany: University of the State of New York, 1921), 515; "Think it necessary," quoted in Billington, *Westward Expansion*, 138. See also Anderson, *The War That Made America*, 233; and Reuben Gold Thwaites et al., *Wisconsin in Three Centuries, 1634–1905*, vol. 2 (New York: Century History Company, 1906), 32.

4 Letter from Amherst to Johnson (August 9, 1761), 515; and Letter from Jeffrey Amherst to Sir William Johnson (February 22, 1761), in Sullivan, *The Papers of Sir William Johnson*, vol. 3, 345. See also Anderson, *The War That Made America*, 233.

5 Letter from George Croghan to General Jeffrey Amherst (April 30, 1763), in *Collections and Researches Made by the Michigan Pioneer and Historical Society*, vol. 19, ed. M. Agnes Burton (Reprint, Lansing: Wynkoop Hallenbeck Crawford Co., 1911), 183–84.

6 Billington, *Westward Expansion*, 138; and N. Matson, *Pioneers of Illinois* (Chicago: Knight & Leonard Printers, 1882), 139.

7 Patrick Carter et al., *American History* (Toronto: Emond Montgomery, 2007), 48; Billington, *Westward Expansion*, 138; and Anderson, *The War That Made America*, 180.

8 Anderson, *The War That Made America*, 236; Billington, *Westward Expansion*, 138; and Leach, *Arms for Empire*, 498–99.

9 Carter et al., *American History*, 48; and DeVoto, *The Course of Empire*, 232–34.

10 Justin Winsor, *Narrative and Critical History of America*, vol. 6 (Boston: Houghton, Mifflin & Company, 1888), 687–88. See also Phillips. *The Fur Trade*, vol. 1, 561–65.

11 Anderson, *The War That Made America*, 240–41.

12 "Report of the Lords Commissioners for Trade and Plantations, on the Petition of the Honourable Thomas Walpole and his Associates, for a Grant of Lands on the River Ohio, in North America," April 15, 1772, In Franklin, *The Writings of Benjamin Franklin*, edited by Albert Henry Smyth, vol. 5, 1767–1772 (New York: Macmillan Company, 1907), 468–69, 472–73, 475; and Thwaites et al., *Wisconsin in Three Centuries, 1634–1905*, vol. 3, 32.

13 Billington, *Westward Expansion*, 154.

14 DeVoto, *Course of Empire*, 238, Stevens, *The Northwest Fur Trade*, 31–33; Billington, *Westward Expansion*, 140–42; Phillips, *The Fur Trade*, vol. 1, 569, 571–72,
580, 618–20; and Henry, *Travels and Adventures in Canada*, 239; Norton, *The Fur
Trade in Colonial New York*, 199; and John Mitchell, *The Present State of Great
Britain and North America with Regard to Agriculture, Population, Trade, and Manufactures, Impartially Considered* (London: T. Becket and P. A. De Hondt, 1767),
174–75.

15 Hanson, *When Skins Were Money*, 69. The Old Northwest "embraces the States
of Ohio, Indiana, Illinois, Michigan, Wisconsin, and the eastern side of Minnesota—a little more than a quarter million square miles of territory." B. A. Hin-
sdale, *The Old Northwest, The Beginnings of Our Colonial System* (Boston: Silver,
Burdett and Company, 1899), v.

16 Clarence Walworth Alvord, *The Mississippi Valley in British Politics*, vol. 1
(Cleveland: Arthur H. Clark Company, 1917), 300–304.

17 *Louisiana, A Guide to the State, compiled by the Writer's Program of the Work Projects Administration in the State of Louisiana* (New York: Hastings House, 1945),
40–41; Henry Rightor, *Standard History of New Orleans, Louisiana* (Chicago:
Lewis Publishing Company, 1900), 20–21; Hanson, *When Skins Were Money*,
107; Chittenden, *The American Fur Trade*, vol. 1, 98–102; William E. Foley and
C. David Rice, *The First Chouteaus: River Barons of Early St. Louis* (Urbana: University of Illinois Press, 1983), 4–5; and Shirley Christian, *Before Lewis and Clark:
The Story of the Chouteaus, the French Dynasty That Ruled America's Frontier* (New
York: Farrar, Straus & Giroux, 2004), 33.

18 Harry Gordon, "Journal of Captain Harry Gordon from Pittsburgh Down the
Ohio and the Mississippi to New Orleans, Mobile, and Pensacola," in *Travels in
the American Colonies*, ed. Newton D. Mereness (New York: Macmillan Company,
1916), 475; and Phillips, *The Fur Trade*, vol. 1, 593, 627.

19 Phillips, *The Fur Trade*, vol. 1, 624–25; DeVoto, *Course of Empire*, 264; Hanson,
When Skins Were Money, 67; Stevens, *The Northwest Fur Trade*, 34–42; and Clar-
ence Walworth Alvord, *The Illinois Country, 1673–1818* (Chicago: A. C. McClurg
& Co., 1922), 306–7.

20 Hamilton Andrews Hill, "The Trade, Commerce and Navigation of Boston,
1780–1880," in *The Memorial History of Boston, Including Suffolk County, Massachusetts*, vol. 4, ed. Justin Winsor (Boston: James R. Osgood and Company,
1881), 199; Phillips, *The Fur Trade*, vol. 1, 636, 638, 648–49; Herbert Eugene Bol-
ton and Thomas Maitland Marshall, *The Colonization of North America, 1492–1783*
(New York: Macmillan Company, 1921), 422; and Stevens, *The Northwest Fur
Trade*, 45–47, 65–67, 77nn22, 24.

21 Benjamin Terry, *A History of England From the Earliest Times to the Death of Queen
Victoria*, 4th ed. (Chicago: Scott, Foresman and Company, 1908), 939.

22 "Definitive Treaty of Peace Between The United States of America, and His Bri-

tannic Majesty," in Joseph Story, *A Familiar Exposition of the Constitution of the United States* (New York: Harper & Brothers, 1847), 324.

23 Ibid., 325–29; John Fiske, "Political Consequences in England of Cornwallis's Surrender at Yorktown," in *Atlantic Monthly* (January 1886): 50; and Phillips, *The Fur Trade*, vol. 1, 649–54.

24 Phillips, *The Fur Trade*, vol. 1, 643.

25 John Adams to Abigail Adams, March 28, 1783, in *Adams Family Correspondence*, vol. 5, ed. Richard Ryerson (Cambridge: Belknap Harvard University Press, 1993), 111.

26 Phillips, *The Fur Trade*, vol. 2, 15.

27 Mr. Powys, quoted in "Debate in the Commons on the Preliminary Articles of Peace," 1783, in *The Parliamentary History of England From the Earliest Period to the Year 1803*, vol. 23 (London: T. C. Hansard, 1814), 457.

28 Lord Shelburne, "Note of the Debates on the Peace in the House of Commons, February 1783, as Confirmatory of the Wisdom of the American Commissioners," in John Jay, *The Peace Negotiations of 1782 and 1783, An Address Delivered Before the New York Historical Society on its Seventy-Fifth Anniversary, Tuesday, November 27, 1883* (New York: New York Historical Society, 1884), 198. See also Phillips, *The Fur Trade*, vol. 1, 649–50.

29 February 17, 1783, "Preliminary Articles of Peace," in *The Parliamentary Register; Or History of the Proceedings and Debates of the House of Lords*, vol. 11 (London: J. Debrett, 1783), 34–35. See also Charles Francis Adams, *The Works of John Adams, Second President of the United States: With the Life of the Author*, vol. 3 (Boston: Charles C. Little and James Brown, 1851), 367–68.

30 McLaughlin, "The Western Posts and the British Debts," 420; and Billington, *Westward Expansion*, 221–22.

31 Phillips, *The Fur Trade*, vol. 2, 22; McLaughlin, "The Western Posts and the British Debts," 414–20, 427, 430–33.

32 Letter from George Washington to the Marquis de Lafayette (May 10, 1786), in *The Writings of George Washington, edited by Worthington Chauncey Ford*, vol. 11, 1785–1790 (New York: G. P. Putnam's Sons, 1891), 28–29.

33 Charles Moore, *History of Michigan*, vol. 1 (Chicago: Lewis Publishing Company, 1915), 214–15; Phillips, *The Fur Trade*, vol. 2, 18–22; and A. C. McLaughlin, "The Western Posts and the British Debts," in *Annual Report of the American Historical Association for the Year 1894* (Washington, DC: U.S. Government Printing Office, 1895), 414–19.

34 Letter from Thomas Jefferson to George Hammond (December 15, 1791), in Thomas Jefferson, *The Writings of Thomas Jefferson*, ed. H. A. Washington, vol. 4 (Washington, DC: Taylor & Maury, 1854), 95.

35 David McCullough, *John Adams* (New York: Simon & Schuster, 2001), 456. See also Eric Jay Dolin, *Leviathan: The History of Whaling in America* (New York: W. W. Norton, 2007), 183.

36   "The Jay Treaty, the Avalon Project at Yale Law School," http://www.yale.edu/lawweb/avalon/diplomacy/britain/jay.htm (accessed September 6, 2008).

37   McLaughlin, "The Western Posts and the British Debts," 433; and Billington, *Westward Expansion*, 222.

38   Samuel Furman Hunt, "General Anthony Wayne and the Battle of Fallen Timbers," in *Orations and Historical Addresses* (Cincinnati: Robert Clarke Company, 1908), 388–41; Hanson, *When Skins Were Money*, 86; and Billington, *Westward Expansion*, 225–26.

39   Hanson, *When Skins Were Money*, 86; and McLaughlin, "The Western Posts and the British Debts," 425, 428.

40   The British were not alone in that thinking. During the debates over the ratification of the treaty, in 1796, at least one American politician predicted that implementation of article 3 would be a disaster for the American fur trade. See William B. Giles, "Speech of William B. Giles on the British Treaty, Delivered in the House of Representatives of the United States, April 18, 1796," in *Eloquence of the United States*, vol. 1, comp. Ebenezer Bancroft Williston (Middletown, CT: E. & H. Clark, 1827), 358–59.

41   George Washington, "Address to Congress, October 25, 1791," in *The Debates and Proceedings in the Congress of the United States, Second Congress* (Washington, DC: Gale and Seaton, 1849), 13.

42   George Washington, "Third Congress—First Session, the President's Speech," in *Addresses of the Successive Presidents of the United States to both Houses of Congress* (Washington, DC: Samuel Harrison Smith, 1805), 62.

43   Hanson, *When Skins Were Money*, 100.

44   Ibid.

45   One of these factories was at Coleraine in Georgia, and the other at Tellico on the Tennessee border. Phillips, *The Fur Trade*, vol. 2, 12; Royal B. Way, "The United States Factory System for Trading with the Indians, 1796–1822," in *Mississippi Valley Historical Review* 6 (September 1919): 224; and Hanson, *When Skins Were Money*, 100–101.

CHAPTER 9: *"A Perfect Golden Round of Profits"*

1   For an excellent and most entertaining education on the voyages of Captain James Cook, see Tony Horwitz, *Blue Latitudes: Boldly Going Where Captain Cook Has Gone Before* (New York: Henry Holt and Company, 2002). One of Horwitz's insights is the similarities between Captain James Cook and Captain James T. Kirk of the Starship *Enterprise*, in *Star Trek*. Both men were cut from the same cloth, and were driven by the same passion—"to boldly go where no man has gone before!" Ibid., 5.

2   James Cook, *The Voyages of Captain James Cook*, vol. I (London: William Smith,

1842), 201–12; Horwitz, *Blue Latitudes*, 14–15, 133–34, 143, 150–52; and J. C. Beaglehole, *The Life of Captain James Cook* (Stanford: Stanford University Press, 1974), 107.

3   James Cook, *The Voyages of Captain James Cook*, vol. 1, 445, 573–74; and Horwitz, *Blue Latitudes*, 210–11, 217–20.

4   James Cook and James King, *The Voyages of Captain James Cook*, vol. 2 (London: William Smith, 1842), 7–8. See also James Cook, "Cook's Second Voyage," in *The English Circumnavigators: The Most Remarkable Voyages Round the World by English Sailors With a Preliminary Sketch of Their Lives and Discoveries*, ed. David Laing Purves (London: William P. Nimmo, 1874), 541; and Alexander Begg, *History of British Columbia from Its Earliest Discovery to the Present Time* (Toronto: William Briggs, 1894), 18.

5   Cook and King, *The Voyages of Captain James Cook*, vol. 2, 233–44; and Horwitz, *Blue Latitudes*, 376.

6   Cook and King, *The Voyages of Captain James Cook*, vol. 2, 232, 258–64; and John Ledyard, *A Journal of Captain Cook's Last Voyage to the Pacific Ocean, and In Quest of a North-West Passage Between Asia and America, Performed in the Years 1776, 1777, 1778, and 1779* (Hartford, CT: Nathaniel Batten, 1783), 70.

7   Cook and King, *The Voyages of Captain James Cook*, vol. 2, 370–87; and Horwitz, *Blue Latitudes*, 378–98.

8   To learn about this debate, see Horwitz, *Blue Latitudes*, 390–92; and 409–11; and J. C. Beaglehole, *The Journals of Captain Cook*, ed. Philip Edwards (London: Penguin, 1999), 610–13.

9   Cook and King, *The Voyages of Captain James Cook*, vol. 2, 382–87; Horwitz, *Blue Latitudes*, 389–410; and Nicholas Thomas, *Cook, The Extraordinary Voyages of Captain James Cook* (New York: Walker and Company, 2003), 391–92. According to Beaglehole, "It is impossible to work out from the reports of eyewitnesses exactly what happened." Beaglehole, *The Journals of Captain Cook*, 610.

10   Cook and King, *The Voyages of Captain James Cook*, vol. 2, 390–407; Horwitz, *Blue Latitudes*, 419–21; and Thomas, *Cook*, 399–401.

11   Cook and King, *The Voyages of Captain James Cook*, vol. 2, 433–527; and Thomas, *Cook*, 401–3.

12   King, quoted in Cook, *The Voyages of Captain James Cook*, vol. 2, 529–32.

13   The general information about sea otters in this section came from the following sources: C. M. Scammon, "The Sea Otters," in *American Naturalist* 4 (April 1870): 65–67; J. A. Estes, "Sea Otter, in *The Smithsonian Book of North American Mammals*, ed. Don E. Wilson (Vancouver: University of British Columbia Press, 1999), 180–82; Richard Ellis, *The Empty Ocean* (Washington, DC: Island Press, 2003), 146–47; James L. Bodkin, "Sea Otter (*Enhydra lutris*)," in *Wild Mammals of North America: Biology, Management, and Conservation*, ed. George A. Feldhamer, Bruce Carlyle Thompson, and Joseph A. Chapman (Baltimore: Johns Hopkins University Press, 2003), 735–43; and Adele Ogden, *The California Sea Otter Trade, 1784–1848* (Berkeley: University of California Press, 1941), 4–11.

14   To get a better sense of the extreme density of sea otter fur, consider that the "average person has about 600,000 hairs on his head." Ellis, *The Empty Ocean*, 146. The number of hairs per square inch on a sea otter pelt depends on who is doing the counting. A variety of sources range from as low as 250,000 to well over one million. See Bodkin, "Sea Otter *(Enhydra lutris)*" 736; and Hans Kruk, *Otters, Ecology, Behaviour and Conservation* (New York: Oxford University Press, 2006).

15   William Sturgis, "The Northwest Fur Trade," *Merchant's Magazine* 14 (June 1846): 534. The sea otter's skin hangs very loosely upon its body, like the skin of a shar-pei, and that is why the pelts end up being larger than the animal, up to six feet long and three feet wide. See Ogden, *The California Sea Otter Trade*, 4–5.

16   C. M. Scammon, "The Sea Otters," in *American Naturalist* 4 (April 1870): 65.

17   James R. Gibson, *Otter Skins, Boston Ships, and China Goods, The Maritime Fur Trade of the Northwest Coast, 1785–1841* (Seattle: University of Washington Press, 1999): 12–13; and Ogden, *The California Sea Otter* Trade, 5–6.

18   Corey Ford, *Where the Sea Breaks its* Back (Boston: Little, Brown & Company, 1966), 65.

19   Ibid., 66; and Harold McCracken, *Hunters of the Stormy Sea* (New York: Double-day & Company, 1957), 12–23.

20   Peter Lauridsen, Julius E. Olson, and Frederick Schwatka, *Vitus Bering, The Discoverer of Bering Strait* (Chicago: S. C. Griggs & Company, 1889), 151.

21   Ibid., 185–86; and Georg Wilhelm Steller, *De Bestiis Marinis or, The Beasts of the Sea*, tran. Walter Miller (1751; reprint, Lincoln: Faculty Publications, UNL Libraries, 2005) 80–81. See also, McCracken, *Hunters of the Stormy Sea*, 24–26.

22   Steller, quoted in Ford, *Where The Sea Breaks Its Back*, 145. See also McCracken, *Hunters of the Stormy Sea*, 25–27. While on this island, Steller became the only naturalist ever to observe what would later be known as Steller's sea cow, described by ecologist and author Carl Safina as "essentially a giant Alaskan manatee," which could reach thirty-five feet in length and twenty-five in girth. Bering Island had the only known colony of this animal, which was exterminated by the Russian sea otter hunters who later visited the area and killed the sea cows for their delectable meat. Carl Safina, *Eye of the Albatross* (New York: Macmillan, 2002), 180; and George Perkins Marsh, *Man and Nature* (New York: Charles Scribner, 1865), 119.

23   Ford, *Where the Sea Breaks Its Back*, 169–78, 187.

24   McCracken, *Hunters of the Stormy Sea*, 16–17, 78–81.

25   Ibid., 38–39, 55–58; Henry Elliot, *Our Arctic Province, Alaska and the Seal Islands* (New York: Charles Scribner's Sons, 1897), 133n; Steller, *de Bestiis Marinis*, 75–76; James R. Gibson, "The Russian Fur Trade," in *Old Trails and New Directions: The Papers of the Third North American Fur Trade Conference* (Toronto: University of Toronto Press, 1980), 218–19; and Agnes C. Laut, *Pioneers of the Pacific Coast: A Chronicle of Sea Rovers and Fur Hunters* (Toronto: Glasgow, Brook & Company, 1915), 36–37.

26 It is estimated that by 1800 the Russians had killed more than one million sea otters for their pelts. Mary E. Wheeler, "Empires in Conflict and Cooperation: The 'Bostonians' and the Russian-American Company," in *Pacific Historical Review* 40 (November 1971): 420.

27 James Zug, *American Traveler, The Life and Adventures of John Ledyard, the Man Who Dreamed of Walking the World* (New York: Basic Books, 2005), 1–34; Bill Gifford, *Ledyard: In Search of the First American Explorer* (Orlando: Harcourt, 2007), 3–55; and David Lavender, *Land of Giants: The Drive to the Pacific Northwest, 1750–1950* (New York: Doubleday & Company, 1958), 16–17.

28 Ledyard's book was "the first copyrighted work of nonfiction to be published in the United States." Gifford, *Ledyard*, 52–54. See also Zug, *American Traveler*, 118–20.

29 Ledyard, *A Journal*, 70.

30 Zug, *American Traveler*, 132. See also Letter from Robert Morris to John Jay (November 27, 1783), in *The Revolutionary Diplomatic Correspondence of the United States*, ed. Francis Wharton, vol. 6 (Washington, DC: U.S. Government Printing Office, 1889), 735.

31 Kenneth Scott Latourette, "The History of Early Relations Between the United States and China, 1784–1844," in *Transactions of the Connecticut Academy of Arts and Sciences* (New Haven: Yale University Press, 1917), 12–13; Jean McClure Mudge, *Chinese Export Porcelain for the American Trade, 1785–1835*, 2nd ed. (Newark: University of Delaware Press, 1981), 35; and Mary Malloy, *"Boston Men" on the Northwest Coast: The American Maritime Fur Trade 1788–1844* (Kingston, ON: Limestone Press, 1998), 23.

32 Zug, *American Traveler*, 132–37, 143–47.

33 Ledyard's comments as recalled by John Paul Jones, in John Paul Jones, *Life and Correspondence of John Paul Jones, Including His Narrative of the Campaign of the Liman* (New York: A. Chandler, 1830), 362; and Zug, *American Traveler*, 157.

34 Gifford, *Ledyard*, 153. See also Samuel Eliot Morrison, *John Paul Jones, A Sailor's Biography* (Boston: Little, Brown & Company, 1959), 342–43; and Zug, *American Traveler*, 158–59.

35 Cook and King, *The Voyages of Captain James Cook*, vol. 2, 273, 532.

36 Robert Greenhow, *Memoir, Historical and Political, on the Northwest Coast of North America and the Adjacent Territories* (New York: Wiley and Putnam, 1840), 87; Malloy, *"Boston Men,"* 25–26; Gibson, *Otter Skins, Boston Ships, and China Goods*, 299; Hubert Howe Bancroft, *History of the Northwest Coast*, vol. 1 (San Francisco: History Company, 1890), 354–55; and Charles Henry Carey, *History of Oregon* (Chicago: The Pioneer Historical Publishing Company, 1922), 255.

37 Barrell, quoted in Thomas Bulfinch, *Oregon and Eldorado, or Romance of the Rivers* (Boston: J. E. Tilton and Company, 1866), 2. See also Agnes Laut, "Gray of Boston Discoverer of the Columbia," in *Leslie's Monthly Magazine* 60 (July 1905): 276; Samuel Eliot Morison, *The Maritime History of Massachusetts, 1783–1860* (Boston: Houghton, Mifflin & Company, 1941), 45–46; Frederic W. Howay, ed.,

Voyages of the Columbia to the Northwest Coast, 1787–1790 and 1790–1793 (1941; reprint, Portland: Oregon Historical Society Press, 1990), vi; Charles Bulfinch, *The Life and Letters of Charles Bulfinch Architect*, ed. Ellen Susan Bulfinch (Boston: Houghton, Mifflin & Company, 1896), 64–65; and E. H. Derby, "Memoir of Elias Hasket Derby, Merchant of Salem, Massachusetts," in *Hunt's Merchants' Magazine*, 36 (February 1857): 168.

38 Quoted in "The Columbia and Washington Medal," from Massachusetts Historical Society Web site, http://www.masshist.org/objects/2004may.cfm#descr (accessed September 20, 2008).

39 Robert Haswell, "A Voyage Round the World" *in Voyages of the Columbia to the Northwest Coast, 1787–1790 and 1790–1793*, ed. Frederic W. Howay, 4.

40 Ibid., 19–20.

41 Ibid., 14–15, 37.

42 Ibid., 34–52, 60–66, 102–7; and Morison, *The Maritime History of Massachusetts*, 47.

43 Malloy, *"Boston Men,"* 28; and Haswell, "A Voyage Round the World," 96.

44 Robert Coarse, *The Seafarers: A History of Maritime America 1620–1820* (New York: Harper & Row, 1964), 214–15; Edward G. Porter, "The Ship Columbia and the Discovery of Oregon," in *New England Magazine* 6 (March–August, 1892): 478–79; Howay, *Voyages of the Columbia to the Northwest Coast*, xi–xii; and Lavender, *The Land of Giants*, 47. At least one observer claims that the cannon shot that killed Kendrick was fired to salute his birthday, not a victory over the natives. See Amaso Delano, *A Narrative of Voyages and Travels in the Northern and Southern Hemispheres, Comprising Three Voyages Around the World* (Boston: E. G. House, 1817), 399–400.

45 It was my intention to show historic dollar amounts in current dollars as well, to give readers a better sense of how to interpret the historic values. But there are many ways to make such calculations, depending on the assumptions one chooses. Because of this great variability I have decided to avoid including such calculations in the book, since I thought it would lead to confusion, not clarity. To explore this issue further, please visit the following Web site: http://www.measuringworth.com/ppowerus/.

46 Morison, *The Maritime History of Massachusetts*, 43–44.

47 Edward G. Porter, "The Ship Columbia and the Discovery of Oregon," in *New England Magazine* (June 1892): 479.

48 Coarse, *The Seafarers*, 215–17 (emphasis in the original); Porter, "The Ship Columbia and the Discovery of Oregon," 479; Sydney and Marjorie Greenbie, *Gold of Ophir: The China Trade in the Making of America* (New York: Wilson-Erickson, Inc., 1937), 59; Samuel Eliot Morison, "Boston Traders in the Hawaiian Islands, 1789–1823," in *Massachusetts Historical Society Proceedings, October 1920–June 1921*, vol. 54 (Boston: Massachusetts Historical Society, 1922), 11; "Ship Columbia," *Boston Gazette* (August 16, 1790); and "Massachusetts, The Columbia," *Massachusetts Spy* (August 19, 1790).

49   "The Oregon Question," in *Speeches and Occasional Addresses by John A. Dix*, vol. 1 (New York: D. Appleton & Company, 1864), 24.

50   Bancroft, *History of the Northwest Coast*, vol. 1, 611; and William Denison Lyman, *The Columbia River, Its History, Its Myths, Its Scenery, Its Commerce* (New York: G. P. Putnam's Sons, 1917), 43–65.

51   Robert Greenhow, *The History of Oregon and California and the Other Territories on the North-West Coast of America*, 2nd ed. (Boston: Charles C. Little and James Brown, 1845), 232.

52   John Boit, "Log of the Columbia," in *Massachusetts Historical Society Proceedings, October 1919–June 1920*, vol. 53 (Boston: Massachusetts Historical Society, 1920), 245–46.

53   Boit, "Log of the Columbia," 247–49; "Remnant of the Official Log of the Columbia," in Howay, *Voyages of the Columbia to the Northwest Coast*, 435–36; and Lavender, *Land of Giants*, 44–45.

54   Boit, "Log of the Columbia," 411; and DeVoto, *Course of Empire*, 329.

55   Greenhow, *The History of Oregon and California*, 248. See also DeVoto, *The Course of Empire*, 329; Lyman, *The Columbia River*, 66–68; and Lavender, *Land of Giants*, 48. Reflecting on the two voyages of the *Columbia*, Morison wrote, "On her first voyage, the *Columbia* had solved the riddle of the China trade. On her second, empire followed in the wake." Morison, *The Maritime History of Massachusetts*, 51.

56   Lavender, *Land of Giants*, 23.

57   Gibson, *Otter Skins, Boston Ships, and China Goods*, 12–35, 299–300; and Malloy, "*Boston Men*," 26–27; Ogden, *The California Sea Otter Trade*, 2.

58   Malloy, "*Boston Men*," 26.

59   Morison, *The Maritime History of Massachusetts*, 53; and Gibson, *Otter Skins, Boston Ships, and China Goods*, 301.

60   James Monroe, "Message from the President of the United States, transmitting the information required by a resolution of the House of Representatives of the 16th of February last, in relation to Claims set up by foreign Governments, to Territory of the United States upon the Pacific Ocean, north of the forty-second degree of latitude, etc., April 17, 1822," in *North American Review*, vol. 6 (Boston: Hilliard & Metcalf Printers, 1822), 372.

61   Gibson, *Otter Skins, Boston Ships, and China Goods*, 57. One 1804 voyage out of Boston, for example, cleared $156,743 after covering all of its expenses. Phillips, *The Fur Trade*, vol. 2, 57. See also "The Fur Trade Between the N. W. Coast of America and China," *Nile's National Register* (March 18, 1843), 40.

62   Frederic Howay, quoted in Gibson, *Otter Skins, Boston Ships, and China Goods*, 58.

63   Sturgis, "The Northwest Fur Trade," 537. John Meares, a British explorer who sailed to the Pacific Northwest in the late 1780s noted "We found to our cost [that those Indians] possessed all the cunning necessary to gains of mercantile

life." John Meares, *Voyages Made in the Years 1788 and 1789, From China to the North West Coast of America* (London: Logographic Press, 1790), 141–42. See also Robin Fisher, "The Northwest from the Beginnings of Trade with Europeans to the 1880s," in *The Cambridge History of the Native Peoples of the Americas*, vol. 1, *North America, Part 2*, ed. Bruce G. Trigger and Wilcomb E. Washburn (Cambridge: Cambridge University Press, 1996), 129.

64   Gibson, *Otter Skins, Boston Ships, and China Goods*, 269; Malloy, *"Boston Men,"* 12; and Fisher, "The Northwest from the Beginnings of Trade with Europeans to the 1880s," 135–48.

65   This account of Jewitt's travails is based mostly on his own account of the events, first published in 1815, and all the quotes come from that source. John R. Jewitt, in collaboration with Richard Alsop, *Narrative of the Adventures and Sufferings of John R. Jewitt* (Middletown, CT: Seth Richards, 1815), 11–16, 24–39, 41, 164, 179–98. This narrative became a best seller that gripped and horrified generations of readers. Other sources include Mary Malloy, *Devil on the Deep Blue Sea: The Notorious Career of Captain Samuel Hill of Boston* (Jersey Shore, PA: Bullbrier Press, 2006), 11–21; John R. Jewitt, *The Adventures and Sufferings of John R. Jewitt, Captive of Maquinna*, annotated and illustrated by Hilary Stewart (Seattle: University of Washington Press, 1987); Lavender, *Land of Giants*, 49–52; and Morison, *The Maritime History of Massachusetts*, 55.

66   Jewitt, *The Adventures and Sufferings of John R. Jewitt, Captive of Maquinna*, 21.

67   Jewitt, *Narrative of the Adventures and Sufferings of John R. Jewitt*, 114.

68   William Sturgis, *"A Most Remarkable Enterprise,"* Lectures on the Northwest Coast trade and Northwest Coast Indian life by Captain William Sturgis, ed. Mary Malloy (Marston Mills, MA: Parnassus Imprints, 1997), 2. See also Gibson, *Otter Skins, Boston Ships, and China Goods*, 158; and John Vaillant, *The Golden Spruce: A True Story of Myth, Madness, and Greed* (New York: W. W. Norton, 2005), 49–50.

69   Sturgis, *"A Most Remarkable Enterprise,"* 77.

70   Gibson, *Otter Skins, Boston Ships, and China Goods*, 158.

71   For an excellent discussion of this history of abuse on both sides, see Gibson, *Otter Skins, Boston Ships, and China Goods*, 153–75.

72   Ibid., 158.

73   Bancroft, *History of the Northwest Coast*, vol. 1, 319; C. L. Andrews, "The Sea Otter in California," in *Overland Monthly* (August 1918): 132; McCracken, *Hunters of the Stormy Sea*, 200, 235–36; Robert Glass Cleland, *A History of California: The American Period* (New York: Macmillan Company, 1922), 23; Hubert Howe Bancroft, *The Works of Hubert Howe Bancroft*, vol. 33, *History of Alaska, 1730–1885* (San Francisco: A. L. Bancroft & Company, 1886), 477–81; William Dane Phelps, "Solid Men of Boston in the Northwest," in *Fur Traders of New England*, 39–40; Ogden, *The California Sea Otter Trade*, 45–47; and Morison, *The Maritime History of Massachusetts*, 60–61.

74 According the Bancroft, the deal was finally "terminated by the Russians when they convinced themselves that their Yankee partners could neither be trusted nor watched, besides arousing the enmity of Spain by their unlawful operations." Bancroft, *History of the Northwest Coast*, vol. 1, 319. See also Wheeler, "Empires in Conflict and Cooperation," 427.

75 According to the marine artist and writer Richard Ellis, by 1823 "only four yearlings could be found" off the California coast. Ellis, *The Empty Ocean*, 144.

76 McCracken, *Hunters of the Stormy Sea*, 268–69; Robin Milner-Gulland, *The Russians* (New York: Blackwell Publishing, 1999), 1; Coman, *Economic Beginnings of the Far West*, 201–2; Albert Hurtado, *John Sutter: A Life on the North American Frontier* (Norman: University of Oklahoma Press, 2006), 50.

77 Briton Cooper Busch, *The War Against the Seals: A History of the North American Seal Fishery* (Kingston, ON: McGill-Queen's University, 1985), 6–36; Edouard A. Stackpole, *The Sea-Hunters: The New England Whalemen During Two Centuries, 1635–1835* (Philadelphia: J. B. Lippincott Company, 1953), 181–93.

78 Busch, *The War Against the Seals*, 7–10; and Delano, *A Narrative of Voyages and Travels*, 306. James Fenimore Cooper, in his classic *The Sea Lions*, has one of his characters talk about how easy it was to kill seals on a newly discovered "sealing-island," because they were not yet fearful of man. "A man might walk in their midst without giving the smallest alarm. In a word, all that a gang of good hands would have to do, would be to kill, and skin, and secure the oil. It would be like picking up dollars on a sea-beach." James Fenimore Cooper, *The Sea Lions; or, The Lost Sealers*, vol. 1 (New York: Stringer & Townsend, 1849), 46. The Russians alone had killed more than 4 million fur seals by 1800. See Wheeler, "Empires in Conflict and Cooperation," 420. According to estimates by Busch, there may have been as many as 5.2 million fur seals killed in the Southern Hemisphere alone. Busch, *The War Against the Seals*, 35–36.

79 Gibson, *Otter Skins, Boston Ships, and China Goods*, 61. See also Kenneth Scott Latourette, *The History of Early Relations Between The United States and China, 1784–1844* (New Haven: Yale University Press, 1917), 54–55; and Phillips, *The Fur Trade*, vol. 2, 57.

80 Benjamin Morrell, *A Narrative of Four Voyages to the South Sea, North and South Pacific Ocean, Chinese Sea, Ethiopic and Southern Atlantic Ocean, Indian and Antarctic Ocean, From the Year 1822 to 1831* (New York: J. & J. Harper, 1832), 363–64. See also "Peru as It Is," *Blackwood's Edinburgh Magazine* 65 (March 1839): 288n, and Callum Roberts, *The Unnatural History of the Sea* (Washington, DC: Island Press, 2007), 103–9.

81 T. Watters, "Letter from Her Britannic Majesty's Consul-General, Canton, to the Behring [sic] Sea Commissioners," December 28, 1891, in *Fur Seal Arbitration, Proceedings of the Tribunal of Arbitration, Convened at Paris*, vol. 6 (Washington, DC: U.S. Government Printing Office, 1895), 251.

CHAPTER 10: *Up the Missouri*

1 DeVoto, *The Course of Empire*, 414. See also Stephen Ambrose, *Undaunted Courage, Meriwether Lewis, Thomas Jefferson, and the Opening of the American West* (New York: Simon & Schuster, 1996), 68.

2 Letter from James Maury to unidentified recipient (January 10, 1756), in *Memoirs of a Huguenot Family*, translated and compiled from the original autobiography of the Reverend James Fontaine by Ann Maury (New York: G. P. Putnam & Sons, 1872), 387, 391; and DeVoto, *The Course of Empire*, 415.

3 Thomas Jefferson to General George Rogers Clarke (December 4, 1783), in *American Historical Review*, vol. 3, *October 1897–July 1898* (New York: Macmillan Company, 1898), 673.

4 George Rogers Clarke, quoted in Donald Jackson, "Thomas Jefferson and the Pacific Northwest," in *Explorations Into the World of Lewis & Clark*, ed. Robert A. Saindon, vol. 1 (Scituate, MA: Digital Scanning Incorporated, 2003), 74.

5 Thomas Jefferson to John Jay (August 14, 1785), in Thomas Jefferson, *The Writings of Thomas Jefferson*, ed. Albert Ellery Bergh, vol. 5 (Washington, DC: Thomas Jefferson Memorial Association, 1907), 63.

6 Letter from Thomas Jefferson to John Jay (October 6, 1785), in *United States State Department, The Diplomatic Correspondence of the United States of America, from the Signing of the Definitive Treaty of Peace, 10th December, 1783, to the Adoption of the Constitution, March 4, 1789*, vol. 1 (Washington, DC: Blair & Rives, 1837), 649; and Ambrose, *Undaunted Courage*, 69.

7 According to the historian Robert J. Miller, the term "manifest destiny" was coined in 1845 by a journalist, John L. O'Sullivan, who wrote an anonymous editorial in the *United States Magazine and Democratic Review*, talking about the annexation of Texas and decrying the efforts of other nations to stand in the way of America's expansion, claiming that they were "checking the fulfillment of our manifest destiny to overspread the continent allotted by Providence for the free development of our yearly multiplying millions." See Robert J. Miller, *Native America, Discovered and Conquered* (Westport, CT: Praeger, 2006), 118; and John L. O'Sullivan, "Annexation," *United States Magazine and Democratic Review* (July and August, 1845), 5. By the time Jefferson became president in 1801, his belief in the concept would only grow stronger. See also Thomas Jefferson to James Monroe (November 24, 1801), in Jefferson, *The Writings of Thomas Jefferson*, vol. 10, 296; and Henry Nash Smith, *Virgin Land, The American West as Symbol and Myth* (Cambridge: Harvard University Press, 1970), 15–16.

8 Letter from Thomas Jefferson to Archibald Stuart (January 25, 1786), in Thomas Jefferson, *The Works of Thomas Jefferson*, vol. 5, ed. Paul Leicester Ford (New York: G. P. Putnam's Sons, 1904), 74–75.

9 Jedidiah Morse, "The American Geography," 1789 1st ed., quoted in Marcus Barker, "A Century of Geography in the United States," *Science* (April 22, 1898):

545. (The 1792 2nd ed. of "The American Geography" contains the same language as the first.) See Jedidiah Morse, *The American Geography; or A View of the Present Situation of the United States of America* (London: John Stockdale, 1792), 469.

10 Thomas Jefferson, "Autobiography," in Jefferson, *The Works of Thomas Jefferson*, vol. 1 103–5.

11 Ibid. See also Zug, *American Traveler*, 161–217; Zug, introduction to *The Last Voyage of Captain Cook, The Collected Writings of John Ledyard*, ed. James Zug (Washington, DC: National Geographic, 2005), xvii; Gifford, *Ledyard*, 156–59; Constance L. Skinner, *Adventures of Oregon: A Chronicle of the Fur Trade* (New Haven: Yale University Press, 1921), 27–29; and George Tucker, *The Life of Thomas Jefferson*, vol. 1 (Philadelphia: Carey, Lea & Blanchard, 1837), 223. Still the roving soul, Ledyard, with the spirited sponsorship of the newly created London-based African Association, was sent to Africa to explore the northern reaches of the continent from the shores of the Red Sea to the Atlantic. However, on January 10, 1789, at thirty-seven, he died in Cairo from an ailment (probably dysentery) that caused him to vomit so violently that he ruptured a blood vessel in his stomach. Ledyard's death was widely covered and mourned in the American and European press. *The American Museum, or Universal Magazine* (November 6, 1789): 405. See also Zug, *American Traveler*, 227–28.

12 Jefferson, "Meriwether Lewis," in Jefferson, *The Writings of Thomas Jefferson*, vol. 18, 144; and Ambrose, Undaunted Courage, 70–71.

13 Thomas Jefferson, "Instructions to André Michaux for Exploring the Western Boundary, (January 1793)," in Thomas Jefferson, *The Writings of Thomas Jefferson*, vol. 6, ed. Paul Leicester Ford (New York: G. P. Putnam's Sons, 1895), 159.

14 Thomas Jefferson, "Memoir of Meriwether Lewis (August 18, 1813)," in Elliot Coues, *History of the Expedition Under the Command of Lewis and Clark*, vol. 1 (New York: Francis P. Harper, 1893), xxn; Ambrose, *Undaunted Courage*, 70–71; and Skinner, *Adventures of Oregon*, 27–29.

15 Ambrose, *Undaunted Courage*, 74; and Derek Hayes, *First Crossing: Alexander Mackenzie, His Expedition Across North America, and the Opening of the Continent* (Seattle: Sasquatch Books, 2001), 254.

16 Alexander Mackenzie, *Voyages from Montreal Through the Continent of North America to the Frozen and Pacific Oceans in 1789 and 1793, With an Account of the Rise and State of the Fur Trade*, vol. 2 (1801; reprint, New York: New Amsterdam Book Company, 1902), 282.

17 Ibid., 358. See also Donald Jackson, *Thomas Jefferson & the Stony Mountains* (Urbana: University of Illinois Press, 1981), 94–96.

18 Thomas Jefferson, "Jefferson's Confidential Message, Recommending a Western Exploring Expedition (January 18, 1803)," in *President's Messages: Inaugural, Annual and Special, from 1789 to 1846*, comp. Edwin Williams, vol. 2, app. (New York: Edward Walker, 1846), xxvi.

19 Ambrose, *Undaunted Courage*, 78.

20 Jefferson, "Jefferson's Confidential Message," xxvii.

21 Smith, *Virgin Land*, 16–17; David J. Wishart, *The Fur Trade of the American West, 1807–1840* (Lincoln: University of Nebraska Press, 1992), 18; and American Philosophical Society Web site, http://www.amphilsoc.org/library/exhibits/treasures/landc.htm (accessed November 3, 2008).

22 Jefferson, "Jefferson's Confidential Message," xxv.

23 Letter from Thomas Jefferson to Governor William H. Harrison (February 27, 1803), in Jefferson, *The Writings of Thomas Jefferson*, vol. 9, 370.

24 Jefferson, "Jefferson's Confidential Message," xxvi.

25 Ibid., xxvii; and Ambrose, *Undaunted Courage*, 77. It is no surprise that the Europeans were not fooled by Jefferson's claim that the expedition's purpose was primarily "literary": America's interest in colonizing western lands and taking advantage of western resources was an open secret. See Frederick Jackson Turner, *The Frontier in American History* (New York: Henry Holt and Company, 1921), 183–84.

26 Thomas Jefferson, "Memoir of Meriwether Lewis," xix–xx; and Jefferson, *The Writings of Thomas Jefferson*, vol. 17, 145–46. The number of people in the corps fluctuated throughout the journey, but the so-called permanent party numbered thirty-three. See, Irving W. Anderson, "The Corps," on the Public Broadcasting Service Web site, "Lewis & Clark, The Journey of the Corps of Discovery, A Film by Ken Burns," http://www.pbs.org/lewisandclark/inside/idx_corp.html, accessed October 30, 2008. According to Hanson, "Of the fifty-nine people who left Missouri with the expedition or joined it enroute, thirty were involved with the fur trade, either before, during, or after the trip." Hanson, *When Skins Were Money*, 108.

27 Jefferson, "Memoir of Meriwether Lewis", xxvi–xxxi.

28 Ibid., xxxiv; and Ambrose, *Undaunted Courage*, 101.

29 Jefferson, "Memoir of Meriwether Lewis," xxxiv.

30 William Clark, "Journal entry for November 7, 1805," in Reuben Gold Thwaites, *Original Journals of the Lewis and Clark Expedition, 1804–1806*, vol. 3 (New York: Dodd, Mead & Company, 1905), 207n, and 210n2.

31 They named this peninsula, on the south side of the river about twelve miles from the ocean, Point William (today it is known as Tongue Point). William Clark, "Journal entry for December 3, 1805," in Thwaites, *Original Journals of the Lewis and Clark Expedition*, 264; and Olin D. Wheeler, *The Trail of Lewis and Clark, 1804–1904*, vol. 2 (New York: G. P. Putnam's Sons, 1904), 189.

32 Jefferson, "Memoir of Meriwether Lewis," xxxi. As it turns out, however, there might have been an American vessel in the area—the *Lydia*. After rescuing John Jewitt and John Thompson from captivity in Nootka Sound, Captain Sam Hill sailed the *Lydia* north to Queen Charlotte Islands, and then south, arriving at the mouth of the Columbia River sometime in late 1805. "We proceeded about ten miles up the river, to a small Indian village," Jewitt recalled, "where we heard from the inhabitants, that Captains Clark and Lewis, from the United States of America,

had been there about a fortnight before, on their journey over land, and had left several medals with them, which they showed us." Jewitt, *Narrative of the Adventures and Sufferings*, 161–62. Those medals were Jefferson Peace Medals, at least 89 of which Lewis and Clark had brought with them to present to Indian chiefs as a token of friendship from the "Great Father" in Washington. Although it is unclear from Jewitt's narrative exactly when this encounter occurred, it is possible that it was about the time that the Corps was building Fort Clatsop. Why the Indians didn't tell Hill that Lewis and Clark were still in the vicinity—perhaps as close as ten miles away—is a mystery. Similarly, we will never know how Lewis and Clark's expedition might have been altered had the two explorers crossed paths with Hill. In any event, the meeting never took place, and the *Lydia* soon departed.

    The story of the near meeting of the *Lydia* and Lewis and Clark is the subject of controversy among historians, in large part because of uncertainly about the timing of the *Lydia*'s return to the Columbia, and the puzzling silence of the Indians as to the proximity of Lewis and Clark. Historian David Lavender, who in his 1956 book *Land of Giants* claimed that the *Lydia* had been on the Columbia while the Corps was in the area, recanted in his later book, *The Way to the Western Sea*, claiming that based on a fuller reading of the relevant documents, "there was no ship there during the Americans' [read Lewis and Clark's] stay." Nevertheless, it is certainly plausible that the *Lydia* and the Corps were in the vicinity of the Columbia at the same time. See, Lavender, *Land of Giants*, 73; David Lavender, *The Way to the Western Sea: Lewis and Clark Across the Continent* (New York: Doubleday, 1988), 400; Malloy, *Devil on the Deep Blue Sea*, 46–48, 70–72; Stephen Ambrose Tubbs and Clay Straus Jenkinson, *The Lewis and Clark Companion* (New York: Macmillan, 2003), 201; Gold Thwaites, *Original Journals of the Lewis and Clark Expedition*, 327–28n1; and Wheeler, *The Trail of Lewis and Clark*, 191–93.

33   Meriwether Lewis, "Journal entry for March 23, 1806," in Thwaites, *Original Journals of the Lewis and Clark Expedition*, vol. 4, 197; and Meriwether Lewis, William Clark, et al., (winter 1804–5,n.d.) in *The Journals of the Lewis and Clark Expedition*, http://lewisandclarkjournals.unl.edu/hilight.php?id=416. On June 8, 1805, Lewis wrote that he had "little doubt" that the Marias River (in northern Montana) "will become one of the most interesting branches of the Missouri in a commercial point of view . . . as it abounds with animals of the fur kind, and most probably furnishes a safe and direct communication to that productive country of valuable furs exclusively enjoyed at present by the subjects of His Britannic Majesty." He added that the river was "destined to become . . . an object of contention between the two great powers of America and Great Britain with respect to the adjustment of the northwesterly boundary of the former." Meriwether Lewis, William Clark, et al., June 8, 1805, entry in *The Journals of the Lewis and Clark Expedition*, http://lewisandclarkjournals.unl.edu/hilight.php?id=598.

34   Letter from Meriwether Lewis to Thomas Jefferson (September 23, 1806), in *The Original Journals of the Lewis and Clark Expedition, edited by Reuben Gold Thwaites*

as Published in 1904, vol. 7, part 2, appendix 61 (Scituate, MA: Digital Scanning Inc, 2001), 334.

35 Ambrose, *Undaunted Courage*, 407.

36 Letter from Meriwether Lewis to Thomas Jefferson (September 23, 1806), in *The Original Journals of the Lewis and Clark Expedition*, 335–36.

37 "Arrival of Captains Lewis and Clark at St. Louis," in *Western World* (October 11, 1806), quoted in James P. Ronda, "St. Louis Welcomes and Toasts the Lewis and Clark Expedition: A Newly Discovered 1806 Newspaper Account," in *Explorations Into the World of Lewis & Clark*, ed. Robert A. Saindon, vol. 3 (Scituate, MA: Digital Scanning, Inc., 2003), 1280–81. See also Betty Houchin Winfield, "The Press Response to the Corps of Discovery: The Making of Heroes in an Egalitarian Age," *Journalism & Mass Communication Quarterly* 80.4 [2003]: 866–83.

38 Arlen J. Large, "Expedition Aftermath: The Jawbone Journals," in *Explorations Into the World of Lewis & Clark*, vol. 3, 1172. See also Ambrose, *Undaunted Courage*, 412–13.

39 This point has been made by a number of historians. See James P. Ronda, "Imagining the West Through the Eyes of Lewis and Clark," in *Explorations Into the World of Lewis & Clark*, 464; and James E. Hanson, "Expansion of the Fur Trade Following Lewis and Clark," in ibid., vol. 2, 1167–68.

40 Chittenden, *The American Fur Trade*, vol. 1, 125–26; Kathryn M. French, "Manuel Lisa," in *South Dakota Historical Collections*, vol. 4 (Pierre: South Dakota Historical Society, 1908), 121; and Hanson, *When Skins Were Money*, 111.

41 Thomas James, *Three Years Among the Indians and Mexicans* (1846; reprint, St. Louis: Missouri Historical Society, 1916), 47.

42 Lewis, quoted in *The Lewis and Clark Companion*, ed. Stephanie Ambrose Tubbs with Clay Straus Jenkinson (New York: Macmillan, 2003), 8. See also Bil Gilbert, *The Trailblazers* (New York: Time-Life Books, 1973), 55.

43 Chittenden, *The American Fur Trade*, vol. 1, 113, 130. See also William Finley Wagner, introduction to *Adventures of Zenas Leonard Fur Trader and Trapper, 1831–1836*, ed. W. F. Wagner (Cleveland: Burrows Brothers Company, 1904), 21.

44 Richard H. Thornton, *An American Glossary*, vol. 1 (Philadelphia: J. B. Lippincott Company, 1912), 62; Stanley Vestal, *The Missouri* (Lincoln: University of Nebraska Press, 1996), 5; Chittenden, *The American Fur Trade*, vol. 1, 32–34; Paul O'Neil, *The Rivermen* (New York: Time-Life Books, 1975), 64–67; and Hiram Martin Chittenden, *History of Early Steamboat Navigation on the Missouri: Life and Adventures of Joseph La Barge*, vol. 1 (New York: Francis P. Harper, 1903), 102.

45 James Marquette, "Relation of the Voyages, Discoveries, and Death, of Father James Marquette, and the Subsequent Voyages of Father Claudius Allouez, by Father Claudius Dablon," in John Gilmary Shea, *Discovery and Exploration of the Mississippi Valley, With Original Narratives of Marquette, Allouez, Membre, Hennepin, and Anastase Douay*, (1678; reprint, New York: J. S. Redfield, 1853, 39.

46 O'Neil, *The Rivermen*, 64–65; and Chittenden, *History of Early Steamboat Navigation on the Missouri*, 103–6.

47 Harris, *John Colter*, 55–58; Gilbert, *The Trailblazers*, 55; O'Neil, *The Rivermen*, 62–63; Barbara Kubik, "John Colter—One of Lewis and Clark's Men," in *Explorations Into the World of Lewis & Clark*, vol. 1, 296–97.

48 Quoted in Coman, *Economic Beginnings of the Far West*, 300; and Hanson, *When Skins Were Money*, 153.

49 David Lavender, *Westward Vision: The Story of The Oregon Trail* (Lincoln: University of Nebraska Press, 1985), 124; Bill Harris, *The Lives of Mountain Men* (Guilford, CT: Lyons Press, 2005), 32; Bernard DeVoto, *Across the Wide Missouri* (Boston: Houghton, Mifflin & Company, 1947), 157; John James Audubon, *Audubon and His Journals*, ed. Maria R. Audubon, vol. 2 (New York: Charles Scribner's Sons, 1897), 163; William A. Baillie-Grohman, *Camps in the Rockies* (New York: Charles Scribner's Sons, 1910), 250; and personal communication with James Hanson, August 2008.

50 Hanson, *When Skins Were Money*, 153; Chittenden, *A History of the American Fur Trade of the Far West*, vol. 1, 113–19; Harris, *John Colter*, 70; Kate Hammond Fogarty, *The Story of Montana* (New York: A. S. Barnes Company, 1916), 28–29; and Eugene Morrow Violette, *A History of Missouri* (Boston: D. C. Heath & Co., 1918), 173–74.

51 Harris, *John Colter*, 73–74, 82–83.

52 Chittenden, *The American Fur Trade*, vol. 2 (1902; reprint, Stanford: Academic Reprints, 1954), 717.

53 See, for example, Merrill J. Mattes, "Behind the Legend of Colter's Hell: The Early Exploration of Yellowstone National Park," in *Mississippi Valley Historical Review* 36, no. 2 (September 1949): 251–82; Harris, *John Colter*, 73–114; and Kubik, "John Colter—One of Lewis and Clark's Men," 297–300. The main source for assessing where Colter went is the map William Clark drew up based on conversations with Colter upon the latter's return to St. Louis in 1810 or 1811. The map, published as part of the history of the expedition in 1814, has a dotted line labeled "Colter's Route in 1807." See Harris, *John Colter* (reproduced images between pages 80 and 81).

54 Harris, *John Colter*, 73–114. The first person to use the term "Colter's Hell" in print was Washington Irving. Irving, *Adventures of Captain Bonneville*, vol. 2, 80–81.

55 A number of writers have made basically this same claim. See, for example, Chittenden, *The American Fur Trade*, vol. 2, 717; and Gilbert, *The Trailblazers*, 55.

56 Manuel Lisa, quoted in W.E.S., "Journal of James H. Bradley", in *Contributions to the Historical Society of Montana*, vol. 2 (Helena: State Publishing Company, 1896), 228.

57 It was incorporated as the St. Louis Missouri Fur Company, but people universally referred to it as the Missouri Fur Company. See Chittenden, *The American Fur Trade*, vol. 1, 137.

58 "Missouri Fur Company," *Missouri Gazette* (March 8, 1809), in *Publications of the Nebraska State Historical Society*, vol. 20, ed. Albert Watkins (1809; reprint,

Lincoln: Nebraska State Historical Society, 1922), 1–2. See also Chittenden, *The American Fur Trade*, vol. 1, 137–38.

59 Henry Marie Brackenridge, "Journal of a Voyage Up the River Missouri, Performed in Eighteen Hundred and Eleven," in *Early Western Travels, 1748–1846*, ed. Reuben Gold Thwaites, vol. 6, (1816; reprint, Cleveland: Arthur H. Clark Company, 1904), 28–29; and Chittenden, *American Fur Trade*, vol. 1, 141–42.

60 Meriwether Lewis, William Clark, et al., July 26, 1806, entry in *The Journals of the Lewis and Clark Expedition*, http://libtextcenter.unl.edu/examples/servlet/transform/tamino/Library/lewisandclarkjournals?&_xmlsrc=http://libtextcenter.unl.edu/lewisandclark/files/xml/1806-07-26.xml&_xslsrc=http://libtextcenter.unl.edu/lewisandclark/LCstyles.xsl; Meriwether Lewis, William Clark, et al., July 27, 1806, entry in *The Journals of the Lewis and Clark Expedition*, http://libtextcenter.unl.edu/examples/servlet/transform/tamino/Library/lewisandclarkjournals?&_xmlsrc=http://libtextcenter.unl.edu/lewisandclark/files/xml/1806-07-27.xml&_xslsrc=http://libtextcenter.unl.edu/lewisandclark/LCstyles.xsl; and David Lavender, *The Way to the Western Sea*, 342–51.

61 According to Ronda, it was the Americans' supplying guns to the Blackfeet's enemies and threatening their control over the region, and not the deaths of the two braves, that sparked the hatred of the Blackfeet toward Americans. "In the face of a massive assault on their plains empire, Blackfeet warriors and diplomats hardly had time to think about avenging the deaths under the three cottonwoods. But they did remember Lewis's words. The explorer was the prophet of violence to come." However, comments by the Canadian explorer, cartographer, fur trader David Thompson, strongly suggest that the deaths played at least a partial if not determining role in the Blackfeet's attitude. Ronda, "Imagining the West," 465–66; David Thompson, *David Thompson's Narrative of His Explorations in Western America, 1784–1812*, ed. J. B. Tyrrell (Toronto: Champlain Society, 1916), 375; Lavender, *The Way to the Western Sea*, 351–52; Washington Irving, *Astoria; or, Enterprise Beyond the Rocky Mountains* (Paris: Baudry's European Library, 1836), 90; Ken Burns, Lewis & Clark Web site, Public Broadcasting System, http://www.pbs.org/lewisandclark/native/bla.html (accessed November 9, 2008).

62 James, *Three Years Among the Indians*, 52–53; and Chittenden, *The American Fur Trade*, vol. 2, 715.

63 There are two early-nineteenth-century versions of this encounter, which differ in many particulars, but basically tell the same story—Colter and Potts being stopped by the Blackfeet, Potts being killed, Colter running for his life, hiding in the river, and then hiking many days to Fort Manuel. It is likely that the broad outlines of the story are true, even if many of the more fantastic flourishes are embellishments, added either by Colter or those to whom he told the story. I have chosen the version by John Bradbury, who published the first account of the story and who heard it from Colter when the latter arrived back in St. Louis in May 1810. The other version comes from Thomas James, a man

who traveled with Colter in 1808, and heard the story from him. The Colter historian Burton Harris believes James's rendition is "more realistic and logical than" Bradbury's. I invite readers to decide for themselves. John Bradbury, *Travels in the Interior of America, in the Years 1809, 1810, and 1811* (Liverpool: Smith and Galway, 1817), 17–21; and James, *Three Years Among the Indians*, 58–63.

The history surrounding Lewis's interaction with the Blackfeet and Colter's subsequent exploits with that tribe are incredibly confusing because the information is at times sparse, the accounts are often contradictory, and the interpretations of what happened, why it happened, when it happened, and what it meant in terms of the evolving relationship between the Blackfeet and the Americans don't always agree. For a sampling of various differences of opinion on this issue, see "Letter of Major Thomas Biddle to Col. Henry Atkinson "29 October 1819," in *American State Papers, Indian Affairs*, vol. 2, p. 201, quoted in James, *Three Years Among the Indians*, 52n; Robert A. Saindon, editor's note, in Arlen J. Large, "Riled-up Blackfeet: Did Meriwether Lewis Do it?" in Saindon, *Explorations Into the World of Lewis & Clark*, vol. 2, 614–23; and DeVoto, *Across the Wide Missouri*, 396.

64 James, *Three Years Among the Indians*, 80; George Laycock, *The Mountain Men* (Guilford, CT: Lyons Press, 1988), 62–63; and Chittenden, *The American Fur Trade*, vol. 1, 142–43.

65 Chittenden, *The American Fur Trade*, vol. 1, 144–45, 251.

CHAPTER 11: *Astoria*

1 Until just after the end of the American Revolution, Pearl Street was actually called Queen Street.

2 Axel Madsen, *John Jacob Astor: America's First Multimillionaire* (New York: John Wiley & Sons, Inc., 2001), 8–13; John Upton Terrell, *Furs by Astor* (New York: William Morrow & Company, 1963) 23–32; Kenneth Wiggins Porter, *John Jacob Astor, Business Man*, vol. 1 (New York: Russell & Russell, 1966), 3–7; and John Denis Haeger, *John Jacob Astor: Business and Finance in the Early Republic* (Detroit: Wayne State University Press, 1991), 42–44.

3 According to one history of Baltimore, "The winter of 1783–4 proved exceedingly severe; the bay was closed by ice almost to the mouth of it, and the harbor, which closed the 2d of January, was not clear to admit vessels until the 25th of March— nor then, but with much labor in cutting passages." J. Thomas Scharf, *The Chronicles of Baltimore: Being a Complete History of "Baltimore Town" and Baltimore City from the Earliest Period to the Present Time* (Baltimore: Turnbull Brothers, 1874), 235. See also Madsen, *John Jacob Astor*, 12–15; Terrell, *Furs by Astor*, 28–35; and Virginia Cowles, *The Astors* (New York: Alfred A. Knopf, 1979), 11–14.

4   James Parton, "John Jacob Astor," in *Harper's New Monthly Magazine* (February 1865): 317; Booth, *History of the City of New York*, 575–76.

5   There is considerable disagreement about what did and did not happen to Astor during not only his early years in Walldorf but also his early years in New York. For example, John Denis Haeger claims that "The popular stories that Astor was beating furs in the backrooms of New York merchants or that he was selling trinkets along the harbor docks are obviously total fabrications." I am not as convinced as Haeger that this is the case, but without proof one way or the other, I have presented Astor's early years in a way that makes sense to me or is at least plausible, and is supported by many authors who have preceded me. See Haeger, *John Jacob Astor*, 47; Porter, *John Jacob Astor*, vol. 1, 3–12, 18–27; Terrell, *Furs by Astor*, 21–49; Madsen, *John Jacob Astor*, 7–20; and Newman, *Empire of the Bay*, 348–49.

6   Charles Burr Todd, *The Story of the City of the New York* (New York: G. P. Putnam's Sons, 1890), 392; and Madsen, *John Jacob Astor*, 20–21.

7   "John Jacob Astor," *Merchants' Magazine and Commercial Review* vol. 11, *From July to December, 1844* (New York: Published at 142 Fulton-Street, 1844), 155.

8   It is not clear exactly how much money Astor had at this time. Most sources quote $250,000, but Astor was also secretive about his finances, telling a friend later in life that he had become a millionaire well before people thought he had. Cowles, *The Astors*, 28. In his old age Astor was fond of saying, "The first hundred thousand dollars—that was hard to get; but afterward it was easy to make more." John Jacob Astor, quoted in Parton, "John Jacob Astor," 314.

9   Madsen, *John Jacob Astor*, 18–34, 52; Terrell, *Furs by Astor*, 47–60, 122; Parton "John Jacob Astor," 315. and Porter, *John Jacob Astor*, 129–56.

10 Parton, "John Jacob Astor," 314. See also Alexander Starbuck, *History of the American Whale Fishery* (1878; reprint, Secaucus: Castle Books, 1989), 77; Burton J. Hendrick, "The Astor Fortune," *McClure's Magazine* (April 1905): 571; "William B. Astor," in *The Great and Eccentric Characters of the World, Their Lives and Their Deeds, Representing All Ages and All Countries* (New York: Hurst & Co. Publishers, 1877), 791–92; Madsen, *John Jacob Astor*, 53; Terrell, *Furs by Astor*, 116–17; and Hershel Parker, *Herman Melville: A Biography*, vol. 1, *1819–1851* (Baltimore: Johns Hopkins University Press, 2005), 373.

11 Matthew Hale Smith, *Sunshine and Shadow in New York* (Hartford: J. B. Burr and Company, 1869), 117.

12 Freeman Hunt, *Lives of American Merchants*, vol. 2 (New York: Derby & Jackson, 1858), 397.

13 Terrell, *Furs by Astor*, 138–45. See also James P. Ronda, *Astoria & Empire* (Lincoln: University of Nebraska Press, 1990), 40–41. Irving—Astor's first and most adoring biographer—claims that Astor's interest in the Astoria enterprise was motivated by much more than just money. "He considered his projected establishment at the mouth of the Columbia as the emporium to an immense commerce; as a colony that would form the germ of a wide civilization; that would, in fact, carry the American population across the Rocky Mountains and spread it along

the shores of the Pacific, as it already animated the shores of the Atlantic." While Astor certainly mentioned imperial aspirations to Irving years later, there is little evidence that they were on his mind at the time he launched the enterprise; In contrast, profits clearly were. Of course, empire and the prospects for settlement might have been motivating factors from the beginning. As Ronda notes, "Many crucial episodes in the history of Astoria remain shrouded in mystery, which is partly the result of Astor's passion for secrecy." Even Porter, one of Astor's most thorough biographers, muses that Astor might have had colonization and civilization building as one of his main goals. See Irving, *Astoria*, 18; Ronda, *Astoria & Empire*, 44–46; and Porter, *John Jacob Astor*, 243.

14   Thompson, *David Thompson's Narrative of His Explorations in Western America*, 204–6; and Andrew C. Isenberg, *The Destruction of the Bison* (New York: Cambridge University Press, 2000), 53.

15   Terrell, *Furs by Astor*, 137–46; Haeger, *John Jacob Astor*, 102–5; Zebulon Montgomery Pike, *Exploratory Travels Through the Western Territories of North America* (1811; reprint, Denver: W.H. Lawrence & Co., 1889), 142; Irving, *Astoria*, 164–65.

16   Thomas Jefferson to John Jacob Astor (April 13, 1808), in Jefferson, *The Writings of Thomas Jefferson*, vol. 11, 28.

17   Irving, *Astoria*, 20, 37–41; Ronda, *Astoria & Empire*, 50–59; Chittenden, *The American Fur Trade*, vol. 1, 167–69; and Terrell, *Furs by Astor*, 157–59.

18   Haeger, *John Jacob Astor*, 121; and Ronda, *Astoria & Empire*, 94–101.

19   Gabriel Franchère, "Narrative of a Voyage to the Northwest Coast of America in the Years, 1811, 1812, and 1813, or the First Settlement on the Pacific," in *Early Western Travels 1748–1846*, vol. 6, ed. Reuben Gold Thwaites (1854; reprint, Arthur H. Clark Company, 1904), 207.

20   Irving, *Astoria*, 26–27.

21   Ibid., 29–30.

22   Richard L. Neuberger, "Bloody Trek to Empire," *American Heritage* (August 1958): 59. See also Franchère, "Narrative of a Voyage to the Northwest Coast of America," 207; and Irving, *Astoria*, 48–49.

23   Franchère, "Narrative of a Voyage to the Northwest Coast of America," 202–4; Irving, *Astoria*, 31–33.

24   Irving, *Astoria*, 33–34.

25   Ibid., 43.

26   Ibid., 45.

27   Alexander Ross, *Adventures of the First Settlers on the Oregon or Columbia River: Being a Narrative of the Expedition Fitted Out by John Jacob Astor to Establish the "Pacific Fur Company"* (London: Smith, Elder and Co., 1849), 55; and Neuberger, "Bloody Trek to Empire," 60.

28   Ross, *Adventures of the First Settlers on the Oregon or Columbia River*, 55.

29   Franchère, *Narrative of a Voyage to the Northwest Coast of America*, 234–37.

30   Ross, *Adventures of the First Settlers on the Oregon or Columbia River*, 81, 159. See

also Irving, *Astoria*, 54, 64; Franchère, "Narrative of a Voyage to the Northwest Coast of America," 250; and Ronda, *Astoria & Empire*, 196–220.

31 My account of the *Tonquin* disaster is based on the following sources, which don't all agree on the specifics, thereby requiring some creative cobbling, based on what I perceive to be the most plausible story line. Franchère, "Narrative of a Voyage to the Northwest Coast of America," 289–92; Ross, *Adventures of the First Settlers on the Oregon or Columbia River*, 158–66; Irving, *Astoria*, 64–70; Ronda, *Astoria & Empire*, 235–37; Chittenden, *The American Fur Trade*, vol. 1, 176–81; and "September," in *The Annual Register, or a View of the History, Politics, and Literature, for the Year 1813* (London: Baldwin, Craddock, and Joy, 1823), 83–84.

32 Franchère, "Narrative of a Voyage to the Northwest Coast of America," 290.

33 Irving, *Astoria*, 69.

34 Franchère, "Narrative of a Voyage to the Northwest Coast of America," 292; "September," *The Annual Register*, 84; and Chittenden, *The American Fur Trade*, vol. 2, 909–11.

35 McDougall, quoted in Irving, *Astoria*, 71. See also Franchère, "Narrative of a Voyage to the Northwest Coast of America," 255–56.

36 Franchère, "Narrative of a Voyage to the Northwest Coast of America," 255, 259; Ronda, *Astoria & Empire*, 97, 205–6; Silas B. Smith, "Beginnings in Oregon," in *Proceedings of the Oregon Historical Society* (December 16, 1899) (Salem, OR: W. H. Leeds, 1900), 94; and Irving, *Astoria*, 74–75.

37 Irving, *Astoria*, 81–83; Ronda, *Astoria & Empire*, 130–34.

38 Lavender, *The Way to the Western Sea*, 111; and Irving, *Astoria*, 86–87.

39 Irving, *Astoria*, 86–87; Chittenden, *The American Fur Trade*, vol. 1, 184; and Ronda, *Astoria & Empire*, 138–39.

40 Bradbury, *Travels in the Interior of America*, 11–13, 23; Irving, *Astoria*, 88–89; and Ronda, *Astoria & Empire*, 122–23, 133, 137–40.

41 Bradbury, *Travels in the Interior of America*, 17–20.

42 Brackenridge, "Journal of a Voyage Up the River Missouri," 31.

43 Irving, *Astoria*, 104.

44 Brackenridge, "Journal of a Voyage Up the River Missouri," 45; Chittenden, *The American Fur Trade*, vol. 1, 185; and O'Neil, *The Rivermen*, 65.

45 W.E.S., "Journal of James H. Bradley," vol. 2, 228.

46 Brackenridge, "Journal of a Voyage up the River Missouri," 32–33.

47 Ibid., 43, 66, 72, 83–84; and Bradbury, *Travels in the Interior of America*, 76.

48 Bradbury, *Travels in the Interior of America*, 77.

49 Ibid., 77–78; Ronda, *Irving & Astoria*, 128–30, 149–51; Irving, *Astoria*, 138–40.

50 Bradbury, *Travels in the Interior of America*, 102–3; Brackenridge, "Journal of a Voyage Up the River Missouri," 99, 106–7; Irving, *Astoria*, 119–22; and Chittenden, *The American Fur Trade*, vol. 1, 185.

51 Chittenden, *The American Fur Trade*, vol. 1, 189–98; Ronda, *Astoria & Empire*, 165–79.

52 Neuberger, "Bloody Trek to Empire," 81.

53 Robert Stuart, quoted in Ronda, *Astoria & Empire*, 183. See also Irving, *Astoria*, 174–80. This dangerous stretch of the Snake River was later dubbed "the Devil's Scuttle Hole."

54 Neuberger, "Bloody Trek to Empire," 82. See also Irving, *Astoria*, 179–210; and Franchère, "Narrative of a Voyage to the Northwest Coast of America," 269.

55 Irving, *Astoria*, 211.

56 Chittenden, *The American Fur Trade*, vol. 1, 203–5; Ronda, *Astoria & Empire*, 221, 231, 238–42.

57 Astor, quoted in Irving, *Astoria*, 70. See also Ronda, *Astoria & Empire*, 250.

58 As the historian Julius Pratt claimed of the War of 1812, "to the British and Canadians, at least, it was a war for control of the vast fur trade of the Northwest." Julius Pratt, "Fur Trade Strategy and the American Left Flank in the War of 1812," *American Historical Review* 40 (January 1935): 246. See also Thwaites, "The Story of Mackinac," 77. While many fur traders were in favor of fighting for their rights, many other Americans believed that the fur trade was not a cause worth fighting for. See, for example, J. Randolph, "Speech of the Hon. J. Randolph, Representative for the State of Virginia," in the *General Congress of America, for the Non-Importation of British Merchandize, Pending the Present Disputes Between Great Britain and America* (London: J. Butterworth, 1806), 11–12.

59 Washington McCartney, *The Origins and Progress of the United States* (Philadelphia: E. H. Butler & Co., 1847), 322–23; Benson J. Lossing, "The Indians Instigated to Make War," *American Historical Record* (October 1872): 448; and Willis Mason West, *History of the American People* (Boston: Allyn and Bacon, 1918), 398.

60 John Jacob Astor to James Monroe (February 1813), in *Message from the President of the United States, Communicating the Letter of Mr. Prevost, and other Documents, Relating to an Establishment Made at the Mouth of Columbia River, January 27, 1823* (Washington, DC: U.S. Government Printing Office, 1823), 14–15.

61 "Expedition to the Pacific, from the *Missouri Gazette*," *The Portfolio* (October 1813): 396.

62 William H. Goetzmann, *New Lands, New Men, America and the Second Great Age of Discovery* (New York: Viking, 1986), 131–32. See also Frederick V. Holman, "Some Important Results from the Expeditions of John Jacob Astor to, and from the Oregon Country," in *Quarterly of the Oregon Historical Society*, vol. 12, ed. Frederic George Young (Portland: Ivy Press, 1911), 215–16.

63 Irving, *Astoria*, 296–97.

64 Ronda, *Astoria & Empire*, 72–73, 240–42, 250–84; Irving, *Astoria*, 305; and David A. White, "Robert Stuart and Wilson P. Hunt," in *News of the Plains and Rockies, 1803–1865*, vol. 1, comp. David A. White (Spokane: Arthur H. Clark Company, 1996), 134.

65 Irving, *Astoria*, 285–87.

66 Ronda, *Astoria & Empire*, 282–83.

67 Irving, *Astoria*, 307–11.

68　Ibid., 313. The actual value of the items purchased by McTavish, as well as their purported full value, is debatable. See John Jacob Astor to John Quincy Adams, (January 4, 1823), in *Message from the President of the United States, Communicating the Letter of Mr. Prevost, and other Documents, Relating to an Establishment Made at the Mouth of Columbia River, January 27, 1823* (Washington, DC.: U.S. Government Printing Office, 1823), 17–18; and Irving, *Astoria*, 313.

69　Cox, *Adventures on the Columbia River*, 132n.

70　Ronda, *Astoria & Empire*, 297–301.

71　This telling of Marie Dorion's ordeal is based on Franchère's journal and Irving's *Astoria*, with Franchère's account being relied on more heavily where the two accounts diverge since he was there and heard the story from Marie firsthand. Franchère, "Narrative of a Voyage to the Northwest Coast of America," 342–44; and Irving, *Astoria*, 294, 319–21.

72　Astor and the newspaper, both quoted in Ronda, *Astoria & Empire*, 301. See also Porter, *John Jacob Astor*, vol. 1, 235.

73　Irving, *Astoria*, 314. Franchère agreed with Astor's and Irving's assessment. Franchère, "Narrative of a Voyage to the Northwest Coast of America," 303.

74　Astor, quoted in Porter, *John Jacob Astor*, vol. 1, 239.

75　Treaty of Ghent, 1814, quoted from Yale University Law School's Avalon Project Web site, http://avalon.law.yale.edu/19th_century/ghent.asp (accessed December 22, 2008).

76　Porter, *John Jacob Astor*, vol. 1, 240.

77　Greenhow, *The History of Oregon and California*, 307. See also Charles Henry Carey, *History of Oregon* (Chicago: Pioneer Historical Publishing Company, 1922), 247.

78　Irving, *Astoria*, 322; Porter, *John Jacob Astor*, vol. 1, 239–42; and T. C. Elliot, "The Surrender at Astoria in 1818," *Quarterly of the Oregon Historical Society* (December 1918): 271–82. The historian James P. Ronda uses a letter Astor wrote Albert Gallatin in 1818 to highlight another reason why Astor decided to drop his Astorian aspirations at this time: "If I was a young man, I would again resume that trade—as it is I am too old and I am withdrawing from all business as fast as I can." Ronda, *Astoria & Empire*, 315. (But, as will be seen, Astor still had plenty of energy left.)

79　Greenhow, *The History of Oregon*, 315; "The Oregon Treaty," *American Review: A Whig Journal of Politics, Literature, Art, and Science* (August 1846): 109; Porter, *John Jacob Astor*, vol. 1, 242; Ronda, *Astoria & Empire*, 314–15; and Irving, *Astoria*, 321–22. For more on this intricate "ballet," see Ronda, *Astoria & Empire*, 305–15; and Haeger, *John Jacob Astor*, 182.

80　Irving, *Astoria*, vi.

81　U.S. Congress, "An Act supplementary to the act passed the thirtieth of March, one thousand eight hundred and two, to regulate trade and intercourse with the Indian tribes, and to preserve peace on the frontiers," in *The Debates and Pro-*

ceedings in the Congress of the United States, Fourteenth Congress—First Session (Washington, DC: Gales and Seaton, 1854), 1901–3; Kenneth Wiggins Porter, *John Jacob Astor, Business Man*, vol. 2 (New York: Russell & Russell, 1966), 686–718; Phillips, *The Fur Trade*, vol. 2, 348–59, 389, 391; Way, "United States Factory System," 226; Hanson, *When Skins Were Money*, 117; Terrell, *Furs by Astor*, 216–32, 249, 254–259; Johnson, *The Michigan Fur Trade*, 122–26; Chittenden, *The American Fur Trade*, vol. 1, 310–11; and Isaac Holmes, *Account of the United States of America, Derived from Actual Observation During a Residence of Four Years in That Republic* (London: Caxton Press, 1823), 203–4.

CHAPTER 12: *Mountain Men*

1 The date of Ashley's birth is debatable; of 1778, 1782, and 1785, the earlier ones seem more likely. Similarly the exact date of his departure from Virginia, and arrival on the Mississippi is also unknown, with dates ranging from 1799 to 1808. Dale L. Morgan, ed., *The West of William H. Ashley* (Denver: Old West Publishing Company, 1964), xv–xxi; Don Berry, *A Majority of Scoundrels: An Informal History of the Rocky Mountain Fur Company* (New York: Harper & Brothers, 1961), 4; Harvey L. Carter, "William H. Ashley," in *The Mountain Men and Fur Traders of the Far West*, ed. LeRoy R. Hafen (Lincoln: University of Nebraska Press, 1972), 79–80; and *Dictionary of Missouri Biography*, ed. Lawrence O. Christensen et al. (Columbia: University of Missouri Press, 1999), 396.

2 Morgan, *The West of William H. Ashley*, 1.

3 Berry, *A Majority of Scoundrels*, 7.

4 James Clyman, quoted in Morgan, *The West of William H. Ashley*, 23.

5 Berry, *A Majority of Scoundrels*, 8–9.

6 *The St. Louis Enquirer*, quoted in Chittenden, *The American Fur Trade*, vol. 1, 263; and Dale L. Morgan, *Jedediah Smith and the Opening of the West* (Lincoln: University of Nebraska Press, 1964), 29.

7 "Expedition to the Rocky Mountains," *Niles' Weekly Register* (June 8, 1822): 227; and "Expedition to the Rocky Mountains, *Philosophical Magazine and Journal* (July 1822): 73–74.

8 Carter, "William H. Ashley," 81–83; Robert M. Utley, *A Life Wild and Perilous, Mountain Men and the Paths to the Pacific* (New York: Henry Holt & Company, 1997), 55–64; Berry, *A Majority of Scoundrels*, 76–77; Fred R. Gowans, *Rocky Mountain Rendezvous: A History of the Fur Trade Rendezvous, 1825–1840* (Layton, MD: Gibbs M. Smith, Inc., 1985), 12–13; and Chittenden, *The American Fur Trade*, vol. 1, 262–73.

9 Berry, *A Majority of Scoundrels*, 100–105.

10 Gowans, *Rocky Mountain Rendezvous*, 15. The exact location of many of the ren-

dezvous is debatable. See Gowans, *Rocky Mountain Rendezvous*, 18; and Carter, "William H. Ashley," 85.

11 William Ashley, *The Ashley-Smith Explorations and Discovery of a Central Route to the Pacific, 1822–1829*, ed. Harrison Clifford Dale (Cleveland: Arthur H. Clark Company, 1918), 156–57.

12 The exact number and value of furs that Ashley brought back to St. Louis varies slightly depending on which newspaper account one wants to believe, but the numbers I use are within the range of those available. Gowans, *Rocky Mountain Rendezvous*, 20–21, 31; Carter, "William H. Ashley," 86; Morgan, *The West of William H. Ashley*, xxiii; and Hanson, *When Skins Were Money*, 157.

13 Fred R. Gowans, *The Great Fur Trade Road: Discovery and Exploration, 1739–1843* (Salt Lake City: California Trails Association, 1995), 106.

14 According to the historian Robert M. Utley, "Colter, Drouillard, and Lisa's other men were the earliest of the mountain trappers"; and of Colter and Drouillard in particular he says they were "two great mountain men, prototypes of those to come." As for Robinson, Hoback, and Reznor, "their exploits rank them as precursors of the mountain man generation." Utley, *After Lewis and Clark*, 12, 22, 38; and Frances F. Victor, *Eleven Years in the Rocky Mountains and Life on the Frontier* (Hartford, CT: Columbian Book Company, 1879), 48.

15 Richard J. Fehrman, "The Mountain Men—A Statistical View," in *The Mountain Men and the Fur Trade of the Far West*, vol. 10, ed. LeRoy R. Hafen (Spokane: Arthur H. Clark Company, 2004), 10–11. Some of the most noteworthy companies to operate in the Rockies included Ashley and Henry's outfit; the Smith, Jackson and Sublette Company; the Rocky Mountain Fur Company; the American Fur Company, and the Pratte, Chouteau and Company.

16 Frances F. Victor, *Eleven Years in the Rocky Mountains and Life on the Frontier*, 49–50.

17 According to Despain, "Scholarly estimates [of the number of mountain men] are around 3,000 or so. But that number reflects a dilemma of definition about who the mountain men were. In reality, . . . the number might easily be halved." S. Matthew Despain, "The Image," in *The Mountain Men*, ed Fred R. Gowans and Brenda D. Francis, *Museum of the Fur Trade Quarterly* (Summer 2006): 14.

18 The most famous black mountain man was James Beckwourth, the son of an Irish father and a mulatto slave mother. With relatively light skin and European features, Beckwourth might have passed for white, but he went through life as a free black man. The story of his life, filled with derring-do, close escapes, and heroism, recounts Beckwourth's close association with Ashley, Smith, and other famed mountain men, as well as stints in the gold fields of California, as a chief of the Crow, as an interpreter and guide, and as an Indian fighter. For many years historians dismissed Beckwourth as a "gaudy liar," but more recent scholarship has redeemed his reputation somewhat, and it appears that the basic outlines of many of his stories are true, if a bit embellished. See James P. Beckwourth, *The*

Life and Adventures of James P. Beckwourth, Mountaineer, Scout, Pioneer, and Chief of the Crow Nation of Indians, written from his own dictation by T.D. Bonner (New York: Harper & Brothers, 1858); Elinor Wilson, *Jim Beckwourth: Black Mountain Man and War Chief of the Crows* (Norman: University of Oklahoma Press, 1972); and Gordon B. Dodds, "James Pierson Beckwourth," in *The New Encyclopedia of the American West*, 89–90.

19 William R. Swagerty, "Marriage and Settlement Patterns of Rocky Mountain Trappers and Traders," *Western Historical Quarterly* 11 (April 1980): 159–80; and Fehrman, "The Mountain Men—A Statistical View," vol. 10, 9–15.

20 Alfred Jacob Miller, "The Trapper's Bride," in *The West of Alfred Jacob Miller* (1837) (Norman: University of Oklahoma Press, 1951), 12.

21 Thomas Jefferson Farnham, *Travels in the Great Western Prairies, the Anahuac and Rocky Mountains, and the Oregon Country*, in *Travels in the Far Northwest, 1839–1846*, edited by Reuben Gold Thwaites, vol. 1 (1843; reprint, Cleveland: Arthur H. Clark Company, 1906), 255; Topham, "The 'Fair of the Wilderness,'" in *The Fur Trade & Rendezvous of the Green River Valley* (Pinedale, WY: Museum of the Mountain Man, 2005), 47; and Farnham, *Travels in the Great Western Prairies*, 254–55.

22 In addition to what is already cited, much of the information in the last three paragraphs comes from the following sources. Harris, *The Lives of Mountain Men*, 8–10; Jay H. Buckley, "Indian Participation in the Rocky Mountain Fur Trade," in *The Fur Trade & Rendezvous of the Green River Valley*, 87–88; Hansen, *When Skins Were Money*, 154; Despain, "The Image," 10–15; and Fehrman, "The Mountain Men—A Statistical View," 9–15.

23 According to Don D. Walker, "considering the relatively small number of [mountain] men involved and the work and survival demands made upon those men, the length of the list of journals is impressive." Don D. Walker, "The Mountain Man Journal: Its Significance in a Literary History of the Fur Trade," *Western Historical Quarterly* 5 (July 1974): 307.

24 Russell, *Journal of a Trapper*, 55, 109.

25 William T. Hamilton, *My Sixty Years on the Plains, Trapping, Trading, and Indian Fighting* (New York: Forest and Stream Publishing, Co., 1905), 68. See also Stephen V. Banks, "Attire, Arms & Accoutrements," in *The Fur Trade & Rendezvous of the Green River Valley*, 61; Swagerty, "Marriage and Settlement Patterns," 163; and Levette J. Davidson, "Shakespeare in the Rockies," *Shakespeare Quarterly* 4 (January 1953): 39–49.

26 "Expectant capitalist" is a term that William Goetzmann applied to mountain men, but as he makes abundantly clear, the term was created by another historian, Richard Hofstadter, who had used it in describing the "Jacksonian man." See William H. Goetzmann, *Exploration and Empire, The Explorer and the Scientist in the Winning of the American West* (New York: History Book Club, Francis Parkman Prize Edition, 2006), 107. See also Utley, *A Life Wild and Perilous*, xiv; and

Swagerty, "Marriage and Settlement Patterns of Rocky Mountain Trappers and Traders," 163.

27 Zenas Leonard, *Adventures of Zenas Leonard, Fur Trader and Trapper, 1831–1836*, edited by W. F. Wagner (Cleveland: Burrows Brothers, 1904), 142.

28 Many writers have commented on the strong attachment that many mountain men developed to the mountains, and how they would rather stay in the wild than reenter "civilization." See Peter Skene Ogden, *Peter Skene Ogden's Snake Country Journal, 1826–27*, ed. K.G. Davies (London: Hudson's Bay Record Society, 1961), 94. See also "The Peter Skene Ogden Journals," with editorial notes by T.C. Elliot, in *Quarterly of the Oregon Historical Society*, vol. 11 (Portland: Ivy Press, 1911), 216; and Bradbury, *Travels in the Interior of America*, 190–91.

29 Rufus B. Sage, *Rocky Mountain Life: or Startling Scenes and Perilous Adventures in the Far West, During an Expedition of Three Years* (1846; reprint, Boston: Wentworth & Company, 1857), 37–39.

30 Ibid., Banks, "Attire, Arms & Accoutrements," 56–59; Osborne Russell, *Journal of a Trapper or Nine Years in the Rocky Mountains, 1834–1843* (Boise: Syms-York Company, 1921), 85; Russell, *Firearms, Traps, and Tools of the Mountain Men*, 34–96; Laycock, *The Mountain Men*, 102–6; and personal communication with James A. Hanson, August 2008.

31 Utley, *A Life Wild and Perilous*, 86.

32 Victor, *Eleven Years in the Rocky Mountains*, 83–84.

33 Irving offers an excellent description of how caches were constructed. See Irving, *Astoria*, 181–82.

34 Warren Angus Ferris, *Life in the Rocky Mountains: A Diary of Wanderings on the Sources of the Rivers Missouri, Columbia, and Colorado, 1830–1835*, ed. LeRoy R. Hafen (1843–44; reprint, Denver: Old West Publishing Company, 1983), 123–24.

35 Harris, *The Lives of Mountain Men*, 38.

36 Captain Benjamin Louis Eulalie de Bonneville, quoted in Irving, *Adventures of Captain Bonneville*, vol. 1, 235–37. See also Berry, *A Majority of Scoundrels*, 291.

37 Frederick A. Wislizenus, *A Journey to the Rocky Mountains in the Year 1839* (St. Louis: Missouri Historical Society, 1912), 88; Robert Glass Cleland, *This Reckless Breed of Men: The Trappers and Fur Traders of the Southwest* (Albuquerque: University of New Mexico Press, 1950), 24–26; Chittenden, *The American Fur Trade*, 39–40; and Gowans, *Rocky Mountain Rendezvous*.

38 Bonner, *The Life and Adventures of James P. Beckwourth*, 107. In 1832 Meek recorded his impressions of one of, if not the largest, rendezvous ever held, at Pierre's Hole, near present-day Driggs, Idaho. "All the parties were now safely in. The lonely mountain valley was populous with the different camps.... Altogether there could not have been less than one thousand souls, and two or three thousand horses and mules gathered in this place." Victor, *Eleven Years in the Rocky Mountains*, 110. See also Russell, *Journal of a Trapper*, 62.

39 George F. Ruxton, *Adventures in Mexico and the Rocky Mountains* (New York: Harper & Brothers, 1848), 236–37.

40 Leonard, *Adventures of Zenas Leonard*, 248. According to Chittenden, "It was a sort of mountain pride, a convention of the business, to squander wages as fast as earned." Chittenden, *The American Fur Trade*, vol. 1, 59.

41 Wislizenus, *A Journey to the Rocky Mountains*, 86–88; and Russell, *Journal of a Trapper*, 63.

42 Utley, *A Life Wild and Perilous*, xiv; and Cleland, *This Reckless Breed of Men*, 54–55.

43 Goetzmann, *Exploration and Empire*, 112.

44 Morgan, *Jedediah Smith*, 23–26. As Morgan notes, because of Smith's "reticence" to write about himself, "not much will ever be known of" his youth.

45 Ibid., 24–27.

46 Jedediah Smith, quoted in "Captain Jedediah Strong Smith: A Eulogy of That Most Romantic and Pious of Mountain Men, First American by Land Into California," *Illinois Magazine* (June 1832): reproduced in Edwin L. Sabin, *Kit Carson Days (1809–1868)* (Chicago: A. C. McClurg & Co., 1914), 512.

47 There is circumstantial evidence, however, that another mountain man, Etienne Provost, had seen the Great Salt Lake a bit earlier than Bridger. Utley, *A Life Wild and Perilous*, 72–73; and Goetzmann, *Exploration and Empire*, 118–20.

48 The following story about Smith's first expedition to California is based on Utley, *A Life Wild and Perilous*, 89–94; Goetzmann, *Exploration and Empire*, 130–35; and Morgan, *Jedediah Smith*, 193-215.

49 Utley, *A Life Wild and Perilous*, 90. See also Goetzmann, *Exploration and Empire*, 130.

50 Letter from Cunningham, quoted in Robert G. Cleland, "The First Expedition of Jedediah S. Smith to California," in *Publications, Historical Society of Southern California, 1912–1913*, vol. 9 (Los Angeles: Historical Society of Southern California, 1914), 203.

51 The Spaniards named the Sierra Nevada. *Sierra* means "saw-toothed mountain range," while *Nevada* means "snowy".

52 John Muir, *My First Summer in the Sierra* (Boston: Houghton, Mifflin & Company, 1911), 354.

53 Francis P. Farquhar, *History of the Sierra Nevada* (Berkeley: University of California Press, 1965), 26.

54 Utley, *A Life Wild and Perilous*, 92.

55 Morgan, *Jedediah Smith*, 215.

56 This next section on Smith's second trip to California and then on to Oregon is based on information from Morgan, *Jedediah Smith*, 236–79; and Utley, *A Life Wild and Perilous*, 94–97.

57 Morgan, *Jedediah Smith*, 241.

58 Carter, "Jedediah Smith," 91.

59 Jedediah S. Smith to his brother (December 24, 1829), in Morgan, *Jedediah Smith*,

354; and David A. White, "Jedediah S. Smith, 1827," in *News of the Plains and Rockies, 1803–1865*, vol. 1 comp. David A. White (Spokane: Arthur H. Clark Company, 1996), 273.

60　The following section on Walker is based on the following sources. Leonard, *Adventures of Zenas Leonard*, 146–243; Utley, *A Life Wild and Perilous*, 117–29; Chittenden, *The American Fur Trade*, vol. 1, 396–421; Cleland, *This Reckless Breed of Men*, 276–310; Ardis M. Walker, "Joseph R. Walker," in *Mountain Men and Fur Traders of the Far West*, 291–310; and Goetzmann, *Exploration and Empire*, 151–56.

61　Leonard, *Adventures of Zenas Leonard*, 147.

62　Ibid., 159, 162, 165.

63　This account of the course they took is based on Goetzmann and Utley. See Goetzmann, *Exploration and Empire*, 153; and Utley, *A Life Wild and Perilous*, 125–26.

64　Leonard, *Adventures of Zenas Leonard*, 85–87, 174, 180.

65　Ibid., 186–92. For a fascinating discussion of the trade in cowhides along the West Coast in the early 1800s, see Richard Henry Dana, Jr., *Two Years Before the Mast* (1840; reprint, New York: D. Appleton & Company, 1912).

66　Leonard, *Adventures of Zenas Leonard, 204–26*.

67　Ibid., 214–17.

68　Ibid., 226–27.

69　Goetzmann, *Exploration and Empire*, 154.

70　Ferris, *Life in the Rocky Mountains*, 278–79.

71　Russell, *Journal of a Trapper or Nine Years in the Rocky Mountains*, 118–19.

72　Leonard, *Adventures of Zenas Leonard*, 85–87, 180.

73　Wislizenus, *A Journey to the Rocky Mountains*, 51–52.

74　George Frederick Ruxton, *Life in the Far West* (Edinburgh: William Blackwood and Sons, 1851), 123; and "Life in the 'Far West,'" part 3, *Blackwood's Edinburgh Magazine* (August *1848): 139–40.

75　Edwin L. Sabin, *Kit Carson Days, 1809–1868*, vol. 1 (1935; reprint, Lincoln: University of Nebraska, 1995), 154; and Wislizenus, *A Journey to the Rocky Mountains*, 51.

76　James, *Three Years Among the Indians and Mexicans*, 116; Ruxton, *Adventures in Mexico and the Rocky Mountains*, 255; and Ruxton, "Life in the 'Far West,'" part 4, 302.

77　Hamilton, *My Sixty Years on the Plains*, 33.

78　Sage, *Rocky Mountain Life*, 69. See also Farnham, *Travels in the Great Western Prairies*, 202–4.

79　Leonard, *Adventures of Zenas Leonard*, 75–76; DeVoto, *Across the Wide Missouri*, 163–65; Blevins, *Dictionary of the American West*, 203–4; and Richard C. Poulsen, *The Mountain Man Vernacular: Its Historical Roots, Its Linguistic Nature, and its Literary Uses* (New York: Peter Lang, 1985), 172.

80　William T. Hamilton, *My Sixty Years on the Plains, Trapping, Trading, and Indian Fighting* (New York: Forest and Stream Publishing, 1905), 32.

81 Rufus. B. Sage, *Rocky Mountain Life*, 71; and Victor, *Eleven Years in the Rocky Mountains*, 120.

82 Leonard, *Fur Trader and Trapper*, 77–78; and Ferris, *Life in the Rocky Mountains*, 100. When wood wasn't readily available, mountain men often built fires by using dried buffalo excrement, or buffalo chips. According to some mountain men, meat cooked over buffalo-chip fires tasted better. Ferris wrote, "Certainly some of the veterans of the party affirm that our cooking exhibits a decided improvement, which they attribute to this cause, and to no other. That our steaks are particularly savory I can bear witness." Ibid., 101.

83 Irving, *The Adventures of Captain Bonneville*, vol. 3, 152–53; and G. Gage Skinner, "Sweet Encounters: Mountain Men and the Honey Bee on the Fur Trade Frontier," *Rocky Mountain Fur Trade Journal*, 2 (2008): 55–56. That the mountain men had any honey at all is a fascinating. Honeybees are not native to North America, and were introduced by Europeans on the East Coast sometime during the early seventeenth century, and then they started expanding their range westward. See ibid., 52–53; and Bradbury, *Travels in the Interior of America*, 33–34.

84 G. Turner, *Traits of Indian Character*, vol. 2 (Philadelphia: Key & Biddle, 1836), 116; Harris, *The Lives of Mountain Men*, 13–14; and Poulsen, *The Mountain Man Vernacular*, 172.

85 Chittenden, *The American Fur Trade*, vol. 1, 63. See also Ferris, *Life in the Rocky Mountains*, 364. For a scholarly look at the speech of the mountain men, and a perspective that questions the extent to which mountain men actually had a unique language, see Poulsen, *The Mountain Man Vernacular*.

86 Levette Jay Davidson, "Old Trapper Talk," *American Speech* 13 (April 1938), 85.

87 Poulsen, *The Mountain Man Vernacular*, 159–88; Harris, *The Lives of Mountain Men*, 138–41; Davidson, "Old Trapper Talk," 86–91; and Blevins, *Dictionary of the American West*, 337, 407. For an extended sample of the mountain-man vernacular, see Ruxton, *Life in the Far West*, 16–17, 127.

88 *Ursus arctos horribilis* is Latin for "horrible northern bear." Robert H. Busch, *The Grizzly Almanac* (New York: Lyons Press, 2000), 9. One of the first white men to see these awe-inspiring, intelligent, and incredibly powerful animals was Henry Kelsey, an employee of the Hudson's Bay Company, who killed one on an exploring expedition in 1691 in northern Manitoba. This encounter impressed him sufficiently enough to write about what he called the "outgrown silver-haired bear" in his journal, noting that "he is man's food & he makes food of man." See Henry Kelsey, "Henry Kelsey his Book Being the Gift of James Hubbard in the year of our Lord 1693," from the CanText eLibrary, at the following Web site, http://www .northernblue.ca/canchan/cantext/european/1693kels.html (accessed December 30, 2008).

89 Miller, "The Grizzly Bear," in *The West of Alfred Jacob Miller*, 32. And by all accounts there were a huge number of grizzly bears in the West, many more than there are today, so that encountering one in the wild was not an unusual occur-

rence. See F. H. Day, "Sketches of the Early Settlers of California, George C. Yount," *The Hesperian* (March 1859): 1.

90 Although some believe that the story of Hugh Glass and the bear is apocryphal, or at least largely made up, many more believe—as I do—that the basic story is true. The story presented here is based on the earliest known written account of the Glass affair, which appeared in *The Port Folio* in 1825, and Chittenden's account. See, "Letters from the West, No. XIV, The Missouri Trapper," *The Port Folio*, vol. 19, (January to June 1825), ed. J. E. Hall (Philadelphia: Harrison Hall, 1825), 214–19; and Chittenden, *The American Fur Trade*, vol. 2, 698–706. The literature on mountain men contains numerous stories of grizzly attacks. See, for example, James O. Pattie, "The Personal Narrative of James O. Pattie of Kentucky," in *Early Western Travels 1748–1846*, ed. Reuben Gold Thwaites, vol. 18 (Cleveland: Arthur H. Clark Company, 1905). Although grizzlies clearly posed the greatest potential threat to the humans in the mountains, they were not the only animal that put mountain men on guard. So too did mountain lions, also called panthers or cougars, and wolves.

91 David A. White, "James Hall [re Hugh Glass], 1825," in *News of the Plains and Rockies, 1803–1865*, vol. 1, comp. David A. White (Spokane: Arthur H. Clark Company, 1996), 190–91; Laycock, *The Mountain Men*, 132–34; and Edgley W. Todd, "James Hall and the Hugh Glass Legend," *American Quarterly* 7 (Winter 1955), 362–70. An entire book on Hugh Glass, which concludes that all the dramatic stories about him were true, is John Myers Myers, *The Saga of Hugh Glass: Pirate, Pawnee, and Mountain Man* (Lincoln: University of Nebraska Press, 1976).

92 It is generally believed that the two men were John S. Fitzgerald and a very young and inexperienced Jim Bridger. See Utley, *A Life Wild and Perilous*, 57.

93 Quoted in *The Yale Book of Quotations*, ed. Fred R. Shapiro (New Haven: Yale University Press, 2006), 781. Most people believe that Twain said, "Reports of my death have been greatly exaggerated"; that is not what he actually said, although it does sound more melodious and dramatic.

94 Buckley, "Indian Participation in the Rocky Mountain Fur Trade," 82–95; Charles Wilkinson, *Blood Struggle: The Rise of Modern Indian Nations* (New York: W. W. Norton, 2005), 32; report from R. Graham, U.S. Indian Agent, to Thomas H. Benton (February 10, 1824), in *Messages from the President on the State of the Fur Trade, 1824–1832* (Fairfield, WA: Ye Galleon Press, 1985), 35; and personal communication with James Hanson, August 2008.

95 My account of the battle at Pierre's Hole is based primarily on Victor (Meek), Chittenden, and Irving. See Victor, *Eleven Years in the Rocky Mountains and Life on the Frontier*, 112–17; Chittenden, *The American Fur Trade*, vol. 2, 657–64; and Irving, *Adventures of Captain Bonneville*, vol. 1, 118–32. According to DeVoto, "There are more eyewitness accounts of 'the battle of Pierre's Hole' than of any other episode in the mountain fur trade. They differ in both fundamentals and

details so much that any modern account must be to some extent arbitrary and even conjectural." De Voto, *Across the Wide Missouri*, 398.

96 Many contemporary accounts of this battle claim that the Indians were Blackfeet, not Atsina, but that is only because mountain men didn't distinguish between the two tribes, and called them all Blackfeet. So even though the Indians who fought the mountain men in Pierre's Hole were Atsina, they were labeled Blackfeet by many of the participants and subsequent writers. As Stanley Vestal points out, "Since their own language was difficult and little known, [the Atsina] generally talked to strangers in the tongue of the Blackfeet, with whom they fought and hunted. Therefore the Mountain Men lumped both tribes under the one name, Blackfeet." Stanley Vestal, *Jim Bridger, Mountain Man* (Lincoln: University of Nebraska Press, 1970), 73. See also DeVoto, *Across the Wide Missouri*, 81–82; Gowans, *The Rocky Mountain Rendezvous*, 71–77, 199–211; Chittenden, *The American Fur Trade*, vol. 2, 850–55; and Henry G. Waltman, "Blackfoot Indians," in *The New Encyclopedia of the American West*, 107. Also, personal communication with Fred R. Gowans, June 2009.

97 Another observer at the scene claims that it was Godin who shot the Atsina chief, not the Flathead, and that the Flathead grabbed the scarlet robe. Either way, the Atsina chief's death precipitated the ensuing battle. See John B. Wyeth, "Oregon; Or a Short History of a Long Journey from the Atlantic Ocean to the Region of the Pacific, By Land," in *Early Western Travels, 1748–1846*," vol. 21, ed. Reuben Gold Thwaites (Cleveland: Arthur H. Clark Company, 1905), 70.

98 George Nidever, as quoted in Gowans, *Rocky Mountain Rendezvous*, 207.

99 Chittenden, *The American Fur Trade*, vol. 1, 306; Harris, *The Lives of Mountain Men*, 10; and Letter from William Gordon to Lewis Cass (October 3, 1831), in *Messages from the President on the State of the Fur Trade, 1824–1832* (Fairfield, WA: Ye Galleon Press, 1985), 68.

100 Irving, *Adventures of Captain Bonneville*, vol. 1, 25–27, 36–38. About a decade later James Hall, building on Irving's theme, claimed that "There is no page in the history of our country more surprising, or richer in the romance of real life, than that which depicts the adventures and the perils of the traders and trappers in the wilderness beyond our Western frontier." James Hall, *The West: Its Commerce and Navigation* (Cincinnati: H. W. Derby & Co., 1848), 15. See also "The American Fur Trade," *Hunt's Merchant's Magazine*, 202.

101 Ruxton, *Adventures in Mexico and the Rocky Mountains*, 233–34. Another example of this stereotype comes from Timothy Flint, who in his 1830 novel, *The Shoshone Valley*, claims that all mountain men are "more or less, imbued with an instinctive fondness for the reckless savage life, alternately indolent and laborious, full and fasting, occupied in hunting, fighting, feasting, intriguing, and amours, interdicted by no laws, or difficult morals, or any restraints, but the invisible ones of Indian habit and opinion." Timothy Flint, "Extract from the work, 'The Shoshone Valley: A Romance,'" in Timothy Flint, *Western Monthly Review*, vol. 3,

July 1829 to June 1830 (Cincinnati: E. H. Flint, 1830), 571–72; and Smith, *Virgin Land*, 82.

102 See, for example, Goetzmann, *Exploration and Empire*, 106–7; and Wishart, *The Fur Trade of the American West*, 206–7; Smith, *Virgin Land*, 81–89; Harvey Lewis Carter and Marcia Carpenter Spencer, "Stereotypes of the Mountain Man," *Western Historical Quarterly* 6 (January 1975): 17–32; William H. Goetzmann and Harvey L. Carter, "Mountain Man Stereotypes," *Western Historical Quarterly*, 6 (July 1975): 295–302; and Bernard DeVoto, *The Year of Decision, 1846* (New York: Houghton, Mifflin & Company, 1989), 58–60.

CHAPTER 13: *Taos Trappers and Astor's Empire*

1 David Dary, *The Santa Fe Trail: Its History, Legends, and Lore* (New York: Alfred A. Knopf, 2000), 23–67; Chittenden, *The American Fur Trade*, vol. 2, 489–500; David J. Weber, *The Taos Trappers: The Fur Trade in the Far Southwest, 1540–1846* (Norman: University of Oklahoma Press, 1970), 12–52.

2 Letter from Julius De Mun to William Clark (November 25, 1817), quoted in U.S. Congress, *The Debates and Proceedings in the Congress of the United States*, Fifteenth Congress—First Session (Washington, DC: Gales and Seaton, 1854), 1965–66. See also Utley, *A Life Wild and Perilous*, 70; Chittenden, *The American Fur Trade*, vol. 2, 499; and Dary, *The Santa Fe Trail*, 60–61.

3 Dary, *The Santa Fe Trail*, 72.

4 F. F. Stephens, "Missouri and the Santa Fe Trade," in Missouri Historical Review, vol. 9, October 1916–July 1917 (Columbia: State Historical Society of Missouri, 1917), 292. See also Chittenden [who quotes the date of the ad incorrectly as June 10, 1822], The American Fur Trade, vol. 2, 501–2; and Dary, The Santa Fe Trail, 68–73; and William Becknell, "Journal of Two Expeditions from Boone's Lick to Santa Fe, by Capt. Thomas Becknell," in Missouri Historical Review, vol. 4, October, 1909–July 1910 (Columbia: State Historical Society of Missouri, 1910), 71–81.

5 Becknell, "Journal of Two Expeditions from Boone's Lick to Santa Fe," 77. See also David J. Weber, *The Mexican Frontier, 1821–1846* (Albuquerque: University of New Mexico Press, 1982), 125.

6 Becknell, "Journal of Two Expeditions from Boone's Lick to Santa Fe," 81. See also Dary, *The Santa Fe Trail*, 73; and Weber, *The Mexican Frontier*, 128.

7 According to Chittenden, "To William Becknell, of Missouri, belongs the honor of being the founder of the Santa Fe trade and the father of the Santa Fe Trail. It was he who took the first successful trading expedition to Santa Fe. He first passed along the general route later followed and he was the first to take wagons over the route." Chittenden, *The American Fur Trade*, vol. 2, 501. See also Dary, *The Santa*

Fe Trail, 78; and Grace Raymond Hebard, *The Pathbreakers from River to Ocean* (Chicago: Lakeside Press, 1913), 79–80.

8 Hebard, *The Pathbreakers from River to Ocean*, 80. See also Dary, *The Santa Fe Trail*, 77; and Josiah Gregg, *Commerce of the Prairies, Or, The Journal of a Santa Fe Trader, During Eight Expeditions Across the Great Western Prairies, and a Residence of Nearly Nine Years in Northern Mexico*, vol. 1 (New York: J & H. Langley, 1845), 22–24.

9 The *Missouri Intelligencer*, quoted in Chittenden, *The American Fur Trade*, vol. 2, 515.

10 Cleland, *This Reckless Breed of Men*, 136–37.

11 As Goetzmann observed, prior to Mexico's independence the Spaniards "chose to leave the beaver in the streams and instead embarked on a plan to sweep the country of American adventurers." Goetzmann, *Exploration and Empire*, 55.

12 Weber, *The Taos Trappers*, 15–31. See also Hanson, *When Skins Were Money*, 164; and David J. Weber, "Spanish Fur Trade from New Mexico, 1540–1821," *The Americas*, 24 (October 1967): 124.

13 Cleland, *This Reckless Breed of Men*, 131–32.

14 Utley, *A Life Wild and Perilous*, 71.

15 Stephens, "Missouri and the Santa Fe Trade," 304. See also Gregg, *Commerce of the Prairies*, vol. 1, 307.

16 Letter from William Gordon to Lewis Cass (October 3, 1831), in *Messages from the President on the State of the Fur Trade, 1824–1832* (Fairfield, WA: Ye Galleon Press, 1985), 67.

17 "Contrary to common opinion, many of the desert or semi-desert rivers of the Southwest were major trapping fields." Cleland, *This Reckless Breed of Men*, 10.

18 Phillips, *The Fur Trade*, vol. 2, 469–509; Despain, "The Image," 12.

19 Carson, quoted in Kit Carson, *Kit Carson's Autobiography*, ed. Milo Milton Quaife (Lincoln: University of Nebraska Press, 1966), 5. See also Hampton Sides, *Blood and Thunder: An Epic of the American West* (New York: Doubleday, 2006), 8–15.

20 Utley, *A Life Wild and Perilous*, 109–10; Carson, *Kit Carson's Autobiography*, 6–9; Sides, *Blood and Thunder*, 13–14; Carter, "Kit Carson," 168; and Utley, *After Lewis and Clark*, 210.

21 Carson, *Kit Carson's Autobiography*, 21–22.

22 Many contemporaries of Carson's, including some who witnessed the fight, wrote about the event, and they don't all agree on the particulars, which is not surprising since this tale, one of the most famous of all mountain-man stories, was retold many times, and elaborated upon by later writers. I have relied primarily on Carson's autobiography, as well as Hampton Sides's excellent description of the fight. All the quotes are from Carson, unless otherwise noted. See Carson, *Kit Carson's Autobiography*, 42–44; and Sides, *Blood and Thunder*, 29–31. See also, Samuel Parker, *Journal of an Exploring Tour Beyond the Rocky Mountains, Under the Direction of A. B. C. F. M. Performed in the Years 1835, '36, and '37* (Ithaca: Published by the Author, 1838), 79–80.

23 "Bully" quote from Parker, *Journal of an Exploring Tour Beyond the Rocky Mountains*, 79. Other quote from Carson, *Kit Carson's Autobiography*, 43.

24 William T. Sherman, *Memoirs of General William T. Sherman*, vol. 1 (New York: D. Appleton & Company, 1886), 75. See also Ruxton, *Life in the Far West*, 254–55.

25 Carson, *Kit Carson's Autobiography*, 44; and Sides, *Blood and Thunder*, 31.

26 John E. Sunder, *Bill Sublette: Mountain Man* (Norman: University of Oklahoma Press, 1959), 83–87; and Gowans, *Rocky Mountain Rendezvous*, 56–57.

27 Sunder, *Bill Sublette*, 88.

28 Josiah Gregg, *Commerce of the Prairies*. In November, just after the three men arrived back in St. Louis, Governor Miller of Missouri said that the Santa Fe trade was " 'an essential and important branch of the commerce' of the state." Sunder, *Bill Sublette*, 93.

29 There is some disagreement over the exact size of the party. I have used Morgan's numbers. See Morgan, *Jedediah Smith*, 326–28; and Sunder, *Bill Sublette*, 95–96. See also Chittenden, *The American Fur Trade*, vol. 2, 552.

30 Sunder, *Bill Sublette*, 97.

31 The retelling of the story is based primarily on "Captain Jedediah Strong Smith: A Eulogy of That Most Romantic and Pious of Mountain Men," 515–17. See also Morgan, *Jedediah Smith*, 329–30; and Sunder, *Bill Sublette*, 97.

32 Sunder, *Bill Sublette*, 99–107.

33 There were factories at places such as Chicago, Green Bay, Prairie du Chien, Detroit, Chickasaw Bluffs on the Mississippi, and Sandusky on Lake Erie. Katherine Coman, "Government Factories: An Attempt to Control Competition in the Fur Trade," *American Economic Review* 1 (April 1911): 369 n2. The grand total for the number of factories the government established was twenty-two, but the most operating at one time was twelve. See Hanson, *When Skins Were Money*, 101; and Berry, *A Majority of Scoundrels*, 376.

34 Chittenden, *The American Fur Trade*, vol. 1, 12.

35 Ibid., 12–16; Berry, *A Majority of Scoundrels*, 375–78; Hanson, *When Skins Were Money*, 99–103; Terrell, *Furs by Astor*, 302–4; and Royal B. Way, "The United States Factory System for Trading with the Indians, 1796–1822," *Mississippi Valley Historical Review* 6 (September 1919):228–29.

36 Way, "The United States Factory System for Trading with the Indians," 229. See also James H. Lockwood, "Early Times and Events in Wisconsin," in *Second Annual Report and Collections of the State Historical Society of Wisconsin*, vol. 2 (Madison: Calkins & Proudfit, 1856), 130–31.

37 Jacob Van Der Zee, "Fur Trade Operations in the Eastern Iowa Country from 1800 to 1833," *Iowa Journal of History and Politics* (October 1914): 529. See also Way, "The United States Factory System for Trading with the Indians," 234; Hanson, *When Skins Were Money*, 102; and Terrell, *Furs by Astor*, 310.

38 Biddle, quoted in Coman, "Government Factories," 378. See also John C. Calhoun, "Indian Trade, Report from the War Department" (December 5,

1818), in *The Debates and Proceedings in the Congress of the United States, Fifteenth Congress—Second Session* (Washington, DC: Gales and Seaton, 1855), 2457.

39 Terrell, *Furs by Astor*, 304, 308–9. See also Thomas Hart Benton, "Indian Factory System" (March 1822), *The Debates and Proceedings in the Congress of the United States, Seventeenth Congress, First Session, Comprising the Period from December 3, 1821, to May 8, 1822* (Washington, DC: Gales and Seaton, 1855), 319, 331; and Way, "The United States Factory System," 232 n26.

40 Way, "The United States Factory System," 234.

41 Terrell, *Furs by Astor*, 373.

42 Ibid., 357–59; and Chittenden, *The American Fur Trade*, vol. 2, 375.

43 Berry, *A Majority of Scoundrels*, 234.

44 Terrell, *Furs by Astor*, 347–48, 369–84; and Chittenden, *The American Fur Trade*, vol. 1, 322–26;

45 Phillips, *The Fur Trade*, vol. 2, 414–17.

46 Barton H. Barbour, *Fort Union and the Upper Missouri Fur Trade* (Norman: University of Oklahoma Press, 2001), 121–22; Chittenden, *The American Fur Trade*, vol. 1, 343, 386; and A. C. Laut, *The Story of the Trapper*, 44.

47 Terrell, *Furs by Astor*, 394–97; Chittenden, *The American Fur Trade*, vol. 1, 327–29; and David Lavender, *The First in the Wilderness* (Lincoln: University of Nebraska Press, 1998), 386.

48 As they approached the Indians, some of the men exclaimed, "now for the butcher shop!" Charles Larpenteur, *Forty Years a Fur Trader on the Upper Missouri: The Personal Narrative of Charles Larpenteur, 1833–1872*, vol. 1, ed. Elliot Coues (New York: Francis P. Harper, 1898), 113.

49 Chittenden, *The American Fur Trade*, vol. 1, 333–34.

50 Charles Larpenteur, *Forty Years a Fur Trader*, 109–15; Terrell, *Furs by Astor*, 410–21; Chittenden, *The American Fur Trade*, vol. 1, 331–35; Berry, *A Majority of Scoundrels*, 296–98; and Lavender, *The Fist in the Wilderness*, 393.

51 Chittenden, *The American Fur Trade of the Far West*, vol. 1, 106. See also E. W. Gould, *Fifty Years on the Mississippi; or, Gould's History of River Navigation* (Saint Louis: Nixon-Jones Printing, 1889), 113.

52 Lavender, *The Fist in the Wilderness*, 394; and Chittenden, *The American Fur Trade*, vol. 1, 338–39.

53 Chittenden, *The American Fur Trade*, vol. 1, 340.

54 Ibid., 341.

55 Letter from Thomas Forsyth to Lewis Cass (October 24, 1831), in Chittenden, *The American Fur Trade*, vol. 2, 927–28; Terrell, *Furs by Astor*, 365–66; Hanson, *When Skins Were Money*, 114–18; and Phillips, *The Fur Trade*, vol. 2, 362.

56 Gilman, *Where Two Worlds Meet*, 78; Susan Sleeper-Smith, *Indian Women and French Men: Rethinking Cultural Encounter in the Western Great Lakes* (Amherst: University of Massachusetts Press, 2001), 5; John C. Jackson, *Children of the Fur Trade: The Forgotten Métis of the Pacific Northwest* (Corvallis: Oregon State Uni-

versity Press, 2007); Gerhardt J. Ens, "Métis," in *Encyclopedia of the Great Plains*, ed. David J. Wishart (Lincoln: University of Nebraska Press, 2007), 124–26; and Fischer, *Champlain's Dream*, 510–11.

57 Chittenden, *The Fur Trade of the Far West*, vol. 1, 11–31; and Henry R. School-craft, *Oneota or Characteristics of the Red Race in America* (New York: Wiley & Putnam, 1845), 420–21. The best example of a fur trader setting up his own still is provided by McKenzie, who decided that becoming a distiller was his only option after a series of his liquor shipments up the Missouri were seized and confiscated by the government inspectors at Fort Leavenworth. See Clement A. Lounsberry, *Early History of North Dakota* (Washington, DC: Liberty Press, 1919), 179.

58 Chittenden, *The American Fur Trade*, vol. 1, 23.

59 Letter from William Clark and Lewis Cass to Thomas H. Benton (December 27, 1828), in *Public Documents Printed by Order of the Senate of the United States at the Second Session of the Twenty-First Congress* (December 6, 1830), vol. 1, doc. 39 (Washington, DC: Duff Green, 1831), 28. See also Haeger, *John Jacob Astor*, 233–34.

60 Personal communication with Carolyn Gilman, Special Projects Historian, Missouri History Museum, February 24, 2009. For another comment on the commercial savvy of the Indians, see Daniel Walker Howe, *What Hath God Wrought: The Transformation of America, 1815–1848* (Oxford: Oxford University Press, 2007), 48.

61 Terrell, *Furs by Astor*, 397–98.

62 Letter from Thomas Forsyth to Lewis Cass (October 24, 1831), in Chittenden, *A History of the American Fur Trade of the Far West*, vol. 2, 929.

63 Terrell, *Furs by Astor*, 403–4.

64 Letter from Lewis Cass to Andrew Jackson (February 8, 1832), "Message from the President of the United States, in Compliance With a Resolution of the Senate Concerning the Fur Trade, and Inland Trade to Mexico, February 9, 1832," in *Messages from the President on the State of the Fur Trade, 1824–1832* (Fairfield, WA: Ye Galleon Press, 1985), 39.

65 According to the best estimate available, Astor personally cleared a bit more than one hundred thousand dollars in profits per year. And those profits were generated from the annual sales of furs valued at half a million dollars or more. Phillips, *The Fur Trade*, vol. 2, 354–59; Porter, *John Jacob Astor*, vol. 2, 820–23; and W. F. Reuss, *Calculations and Statements Relative to the Trade Between Great Britain and the United States of America* (London: Effingham Wilson, Royal Exchange, 1833), 271. Such an impressive income is not hard to believe when the value of furs collected at the Northern Department's headquarters on Mackinac Island in some years approached three hundred thousand dollars. See, Phillips, *The Fur Trade*, vol. 2, 360. Astor wrote in 1829 that the "American fur company have for years past, and do now employ a capital of a million or more dollars." See Letter from John Jacob Astor to Thomas Hart Benton (January 29, 1829), in *Messages from the President on the State of the Fur Trade, 1824–1832* (Fairfield, WA:

Ye Galleon Press, 1985), 103. Some authors claim personal profits for Astor that are way too high. According to Terrell, in the late 1820s, when his empire was at its zenith, Astor was earning almost one million dollars annually from all aspects of his involvement in the fur trade. According to Madsen, "Astor received interest on the capital he invested in both departments [the Western and Northern]. At one time the interest reached $1 million. He also paid himself a salary, the size of which he kept secret." See Terrell, *Furs by Astor*, 387; and Madsen, *John Jacob Astor*, 207.

66 Chittenden, *The American Fur Trade*, vol. 1, 344–45, 380.

67 *Report of the Secretary of the Interior Being Part of the Message and Documents Communicated to the Two Houses of Congress at the Beginning of the Second Session of the Forty-First Congress, House of Representatives* (Washington, DC: U.S. Government Printing Office, 1869), 555.

68 James L. Clayton, "The Growth and Economic Significance of the American Fur Trade, 1790–1890," in *Aspects of the Fur Trade, Selected Papers of the 1965 North American Fur Trade Conference* (St. Paul: Minnesota Historical Society, 1965), 70–71; and Sunder, "The Decline of the Fur Trade on the Upper Missouri," 132.

CHAPTER 14: *Fall of the Beaver*

1 Chittenden, *The American Fur Trade*, vol. 2, 342.

2 Ibid., 343. One of the gilded Astor Medals sold at a Stack's (New York) auction in 2006 for $29,900, and at an earlier auction by the same firm, a silver Astor Medal sold for $54,625. Personal communication with Vicken Yegparian, Stack's Rare Coins, April 30, 2009.

3 Madsen, *John Jacob Astor*, 218.

4 Porter, *John Jacob Astor*, vol. 2, 777.

5 Chittenden, *The American Fur Trade*, vol. 1, 343, 363.

6 Utley, *A Life Wild and Perilous*, 145.

7 Chittenden, *The American Fur Trade*, vol. 1, 364. Although silk hats appeared to be something of a novelty to Astor, they first appeared in Europe in the late eighteenth century, and since that time had been a threat to the beaver hat's market dominance. See Hanson, "The Myth of the Silk Hat and the End of the Rendezvous System," *Museum of the Fur Trade Quarterly* (Spring 2000): 2–3.

8 "*Nutria* is the fur of a small animal called the *coypu*, the *quoiya*, or the *Myopotamus Bonariensis*, found in various parts of South America. The long or coarse hairs are generally of a reddish color; and the inner or soft hairs brownish ash color. It was not until about thirty years ago that hatters, influenced by the high price of beaver fur (which within a century has risen from 20s. to 80s. per pound), began to use nutria fur; but since that time the employment of them has become so extensive, that one million nutria skins have sometimes been imported in one

year." George Dodd, *Days at the Factories: or, The Manufacturing Industry of Great Britain Described* (London: Charles Knight & Co., 1843), 140.

9   Terrell, *Furs by Astor*, 462; and Madsen, *John Jacob Astor*, 229.

10 William Astor, quoted in Weber, *The Taos Trappers*, 207–8. See also Utley, *A Life Wild and Perilous*, 174.

11 Porter, *John Jacob Astor*, vol. 2, 1,114.

12 "For nearly forty years, [Astor] has been characterized as, perhaps, the greatest merchant of this, if not of any age—the Napoleon of commerce." See "John Jacob Astor," *The Merchants' Magazine and Commercial Review* (July to December, 1844), 154.

13 Philip Hone, *The Diary of Philip Hone, 1828–1851*, ed. Bayard Tuckerman, vol. 2 (New York: Dodd, Mead & Company, 1889), 347–48. According to a table compiled by *Forbes*, which shows the 75 richest people in history, based on the value of their fortunes in current dollars, John Jacob Astor ranks number 18, and his fortune in 2008 dollars would be 115 billion, putting some contemporary billionaires, such as Bill Gates and Warren Buffett to shame (20 and 40, respectively). Also on the list are Astor's heirs, William Backhouse Astor, Jr. (grandson, number 27), Vincent Astor (great-great-grandson, and number 32) and John Jacob Astor IV (great-grandson, at number 62). See Wikipedia Web site, http://en.wikipedia.org/wiki/Wealthy_historical_figures_2008 (accessed on April 11, 2009).

14 Hanson, "The Myth of the Silk Hat," 2–11. The literature provides numerous examples of authors pointing to the rise in silk, nutria, as well as other substitutes, as the main reason for the fall in the American beaver trade. See, for example, J. S. Newberry, "Report Upon the Zoology of the Route," in *Reports of Explorations and Surveys to Ascertain the Most Practicable and Economical Route for a Railroad From the Mississippi River to the Pacific Ocean*, vol. 6, *U.S. Congress, House of Representatives, 33rd Congress, Second Session* (Washington, DC: A.O.P. Nicholson, 1857), 58; Ruxton, *Adventures in Mexico and the Rocky Mountains*, 231; Morgan, *The American Beaver*, 227–28; and Hafen, *Mountain Men and the Fur Trade of the Far West*, vol. 1, 174–75.

15 Hanson, "The Myth of the Silk Hat," 3–4.

16 This argument about the relative impact of silk, nutria, and the Panic of 1837 on the beaver trade is based on the work of James A. Hanson. According to Hanson, the role of the introduction of the silk hat on the decline of the beaver trade in America has been much overblown: "This concept [that the silk hat ended the beaver trade] built upon faulty assumptions of cause and effect, is a myth and cannot be supported when the chronology of events is examined." Hanson, "The Myth of the Silk Hat," 2. Hanson also disputes the impact of the Panic of 1837 on beaver prices. See also ibid., 5; and Utley, *A Life Wild and Perilous*, 174–75.

17 "On the Fur Trade, and Fur-Bearing Animals," *American Journal of Science* 25 (1834), 329, http://ajs.library.cmu.edu/books/pages.cgi?layout=vol0/part0/copy0&call=AJS_1834_025_1834&file=00000336 (accessed February 24, 2009).

18 Godman, *American Natural History*, 277–78; and John D. Godman, "Natural History: The Beaver," in *Franklin Journal, and American Mechanic's Magazine*, ed. Thomas P. Jones, vol. 3 (Philadelphia: Judah Dobson, 1827), 161. While disease is not mentioned in these quotes, it likely also contributed to the demise of the beaver in some places, although far less than hunting. According to the American trapper and interpreter John Tanner, who was trapping near what is now Pembina, North Dakota, disease had devastated the local beaver population. John Tanner, *Narrative of the Captivity and Adventures of John Tanner, During Thirty Years Residence Among the Indians*, ed. Edwin James (New York: G. & C. & H. Carvill, 1830), 104. See also Arthur J. Ray, *Indians in the Fur Trade* (Toronto: University of Toronto Press, 1974), 119.

19 Utley, *A Life Wild and Perilous*, 115. See also Weber, *The Taos Trappers*, 225.

20 Letter from William Gordon to Lewis Cass (October 3, 1831), in *Messages from the President on the State of the Fur Trade, 1824–1832* (Fairfield, WA: Ye Galleon Press, 1985), 68.

21 Letter from Lewis Cass to Andrew Jackson (February 8, 1832), "Message from the President of the United States, in Compliance with a Resolution of the Senate Concerning the Fur Trade, and Inland Trade to Mexico, February 9, 1832," in ibid., 41.

22 Hafen, *The Mountain Men and the Fur Trade of the Far West*, vol. 1, 160. That same year Newell's friend and fellow mountain man Joseph Meek declared: "Though the amount of furs taken on the spring hunt was considerable, it was by no means equal to former years. The fact was becoming apparent that the beaver was being rapidly exterminated." Victor, *Eleven Years in the Rocky Mountains and Life on the Frontier*, 237.

23 Wislizenus, *A Journey to the Rocky Mountains*, 86–88.

24 The discussion of the diplomatic wrangling between the United States and Great Britain over the Oregon Territory is based on the following sources, the first of which was particularly helpful. Miller, *Native America, Discovered and Conquered*, 121–45; Bashford, *The Oregon Missions*, 82–83; Greenhow, *Memoir, Historical and Political*, 2–3, 381, 389; and Frederick Merk, "An Episode of Fur Trade and Empire," *Mississippi Valley Historical Review* 21 (June 1934): 49–51.

25 Utley, *A Life Wild and Perilous*, 74; Merk, "An Episode of Fur Trade and Empire," 51; and John Phillip Reid, *Contested Empire: Peter Skene Ogden and the Snake River Expeditions* (Norman: University of Oklahoma Press, 2002), 6, 42–43.

26 Simpson, quoted in Lavender, *Westward Vision*, 205; and Lorne Hammond, "Marketing Wildlife: The Hudson's Bay Company and the Pacific Northwest, 1821–1849," in David Freeland Duke, *Canadian Environmental History: Essential Readings* (Toronto: Canadian Scholar's Press, 2006), 206.

27 Merk, "An Episode of Fur Trade and Empire," 51.

28 Goetzmann, *Exploration and Empire*, 92; and Wishart, *The Fur Trade of the American West*, 32.

29 For a fuller description of this rotating policy, see Wishart, *The Fur Trade of the*

American West, 32. In 1827 Ashley considered the value of having Americans employ conservation practices similar to those being used by the Canadians. There is no evidence, however, that any American trappers ever did so. One advantage the Canadians had was that they all fell under a single company— the Hudson's Bay Company—which could dictate and enforce broad policies. American trappers, in contrast, worked for many companies or no company at all. Letter from William H. Ashley to Thomas H. Benton (November 1827), in J. Henry Brown, *Brown's Political History of Oregon*, vol. 1 (Portland: Wiley B. Allen, 1892), 45–46.

30   Between 1840 and 1890, for example, the number of beaver pelts exported by the Hudson's Bay Company to England never fell below 26,000, and most years it was much higher. Indeed, between 1859 and 1885 the number of beaver pelts exported never fell below 100,000. Henry Poland, *Fur-Bearing Animals in Nature and Commerce* (London: Gurney & Jackson, 1892), xxiv, xxvi.

31   Simpson called the Snake River country to the south and east of the Columbia "a rich preserve of beaver . . . which for political reasons we should endeavor to destroy as soon as possible." Simpson, quoted in Wishart, *The Fur Trade of the American West*, 32.

32   The expeditions actually began in 1818, under the oversight of the Northwest Company, but those sent out with the explicit purpose of creating a "fur desert" below the Columbia didn't begin until later, after the merging of the North West Company into the Hudson's Bay Company, and the arrival of Simpson.

33   Goetzmann argues: "As an explorer, Ogden deserves to be ranked with the giants of the West." Goetzmann, *Exploration, and Empire*, 99.

34   Ibid., 92–99; Ted J. Warner, "Peter Skene Ogden," in Hafen, *Mountain Men and Fur Traders of the Far West*, 120–23; and Merk, "An Episode of Fur Trade and Empire," 53.

35   On his trip to California with Ewing Young, Kit Carson said they ran across Ogden's party, some sixty men strong, on the San Joaquin River in California. Carson, *Kit Carson's Autobiography*, 14. Ogden had one thousand beaver pelts with him, and he and his men trapped for a while with the Americans, along the San Joaquin and Sacramento rivers. Utley, *A Life Wild and Perilous*, 111.

36   Reid, *Contested Empire*, 103; and Utley, *A Life Wild and Perilous*, 76.

37   Utley, *A Life Wild and Perilous*, 75.

38   As Reid notes, the poor treatment of the trappers was "a grievance that the fiercely independent mountain men could readily understand and, if given a chance, actively resent." See Reid, *Contested Empire*, 106–7.

39   Ibid., 105–7; and Utley, *A Life Wild and Perilous*, 76; Phillips, *The Fur Trade*, vol. 2, 453–54; and J. Cecil Alter, *Jim Bridger* (1925; reprint, Norman: University of Oklahoma Press, 1962), 67–68.

40   Warner, "Peter Skene Ogden," 125.

41   Ibid., 126.

42   Michael S. Durham, *Desert Between the Mountains, Mormons, Miners, Padres,*

Mountain Men, and the Opening of the Great Basin, 1772–1869 (Norman: University of Oklahoma Press, 1997), 51; and Goetzmann, *Exploration and Empire*, 96.

43 Warner, "Peter Skene Ogden," 126; and Lavender, *Land of Giants*, 129–30.

44 "The permission which was given to the British after the late war, to trade on our own country," Gordon complained, "has been most liberally used, and the [British] country trappers kill, over and over again, young ones of six months old, the dams never being spared. At present, the [American] trappers are only gleaning where the British have been reaping." Letter from William Gordon to Lewis Cass (October 3, 1831); in *Messages from the President*, 68. See also Greenhow, *Memoir, Historical and Political*, 197.

45 Letter from William H. Ashley to Thomas H. Benton (November 1827), ed. J. Henry Brown, *Brown's Political History of Oregon*, vol. 1 (Portland: Wiley B. Allen, 1892), 45–46.

46 Letter from Jedediah S. Smith, David E. Jackson, and W. L. Sublette to John H. Eaton (October 29, 1830), in Morgan, *Jedediah Smith*, 347. Simpson, too, noticed the diminution of beaver in the Snake Country, commenting in 1832 that the area "was overrun with Americans and so nearly trapped." Phillips, *The Fur Trade*, vol. 2, 458.

47 Hiram Marin Chittenden and Alfred Talbot Richardson, *Life, Letters and Travels of Father Pierre-Jean de Smet, S.J.*, vol. 1 (New York: Francis P. Harper, 1905), 108.

48 Father Pierre Jean de Smet, "Letters and Sketches, with a Narrative of a Year's Residence among the Indian Tribes of the Rocky Mountains," in *Travels in the Far West, 1836–1841*, ed. Reuben Gold Thwaites, vol. 2 (1843; reprint, Cleveland: Arthur H. Clark Company, 1906), 138.

49 Hanson offers evidence that there were other rendezvous after this time, but also notes that most historians agree that the 1840 rendezvous was the last. Hanson, "The Myth of the Silk Hat," 8.

50 Newell, quoted in Hafen, *The Mountain Men and the Fur Trade of the Far West*, vol. 1, 164. This same year Kit Carson decided to leave the fur trade. "Beaver was getting very scarce," Carson said, "and finding that it was necessary to try our hand at something else, [five other mountain men] . . . and myself concluded to start for Bent's Fort on the Arkansas [where he hired on as a hunter to supply meat to the fort, at a salary of one dollar per day]." Carson, *Kit Carson's Autobiography*, 63–64. As the historian James A. Hanson observed, "The simple reason for the collapse of the rendezvous system is that there was not enough beaver to make it worthwhile." Hanson, "The Myth of the Silk Hat," 8. See also Utley, *A Life Wild and Perilous*, 175.

51 Victor, *Eleven Years in the Rocky Mountains*, 175–76.

52 Much of the following discussion is based on Goetzmann's seminal book *Exploration and Empire*, 105–80. According to Robert Utley, "As beaver trappers and fur traders, the mountain men wrote one chapter in the history of the West. As explor-

ers and discoverers, they wrote another. As national expansionists, they wrote still another. This single generation of frontiersmen played a momentous role in the history of the West and in the history of the nation." See Utley, *A Life Wild and Perilous*, xiv. For another view, which is rather dismissive of mountain men and their role in the settlement of the West, see Stewart L. Udall, *The Forgotten Founders: Rethinking the History of the Old West* (WA: City Island Press, 2002), 79–90.

53   James Hall, *The West: Its Commerce and Navigation* (Cincinnati: H. W. Derby & Co., 1848), 15. The same year Ruxton observed: "Not a hole or corner in the vast wilderness of the 'Far West' but has been ransacked by these hardy men. . . . The mountains and streams still retain the names assigned to them by the rude hunters; and these alone are the hardy pioneers who have paved the way for the settlement of the western country." Ruxton, *Adventures in Mexico and the Rocky Mountains*, 234. See also "The American Fur Trade," *Hunt's Merchant's Magazine*, 186.

54   Chittenden, *The American Fur Trade*, vol. 1, xxv. According to Theodore Roosevelt, "These old-time hunters [and trappers] have been the forerunners of the white advance throughout all our Western land." Theodore Roosevelt, *Ranch Life and The Hunting Trail* (1888; reprint, New York: Century Co., 1911), 81–82. See also Charles M. Harvey, "Fur Traders as Empire-Builders," in *Atlantic Monthly* 103 (April 1909): 523.

55   "General Ashley's Expedition," *Niles' Register* (December 9, 1826), reprinted from *Missouri Herald and St. Louis Advertiser*, 229. Also quoted in part in Goetzmann, *Exploration and Empire*, 129.

56   Goetzmann, *Exploration and Empire*, 129.

57   Ibid., 139, 147–58; letter from Jedediah S. Smith, David E. Jackson, and W. L. Sublette to John H. Eaton (October 29, 1830), in Morgan, *Jedediah Smith*, 346.

58   Irving, *The Adventures of Captain Bonneville*, vol. 3, 274.

59   Goetzmann, *Exploration and Empire*, 155.

60   Leonard, *Adventures of Zenas Leonard*, 192–93; and Goetzmann, *Exploration and Empire*, 155.

61   Utley, *A Life Wild and Perilous*, 263, 207–22; Ferol Egan, *Fremont: Explorer for a Restless Nation* (New York: Doubleday & Company, 1977); Arthur Chapman, "Jim Bridger, Master Trapper and Trail Maker," *Outing Magazine* (January 1906): 341; and Grenville M. Dodge, *Biographical Sketch of James Bridger* (New York: Unz & Company, 1905), 25.

62   Newman, *Empire of the Bay*, 511.

63   Ibid., 510–11; Robert H. Ferrell, "Oregon Controversy," in *The New Encyclopedia of the American West*, 833–34; Skinner, *Adventures of Oregon*, 262–64; Stewart Richardson, *Rivers of America: The Columbia* (New York: Rinehart and Co., 1956), 84; Smith, *Virgin Land*, 18; and John C. Calhoun, *The Works of John C. Calhoun*, vol. 4 (New York: D. Appleton & Company, 1888), 245–46.

CHAPTER 15: *The Last Robe*

1   Phillip Manning, *Islands of Hope: Lessons from North America's Great Wildlife Sanctuaries* (Winston-Salem: John F. Blair, 1999), 123; Scott C. Zeman, *Chronology of the American West* (Santa Barbara: ABC-CLIO Inc., 2002), 10; Isenberg, *The Destruction of the Bison*, 22. Plenty of ink has been used to debate the merits of calling these animals buffalo or bison. "Bison" is the scientifically accurate name, but "buffalo" is the one most people use. See, for example, David Dary, *The Buffalo Book: The Full Saga of the American Animal* (Chicago: Sage Books, 1974), 6, 10–11; Isenberg, *The Destruction of the Bison*, 22, 22n31; Ernest Thompson Seton, "The American Bison or Buffalo," *Scribner's Magazine* (October 1906): 385–86; Jack W. Brink, *Imaging Head-Smashed-In, Aboriginal Buffalo Hunting on the Northern Plains* (Edmonton: Athabasca Press, 2008), 32–33; and Dale F. Lott, *American Bison: A Natural History* (Berkeley: University of California Press, 2002), xiv–xv.

2   Allen, *History of the American Bison*, Bison Americanus, 445–46; and George Catlin, *Illustrations of the Manners, Customs, and Condition of the North American Indians*, vol. 1 (1841; reprint, London: Henry G. Bohn, 1866), 24.

3   A few sources claim that buffalo once roamed to the shores of the Atlantic, north into New England and coastal Canada. Trying to figure out exactly where the buffalo lived before the arrival of the Europeans is a mind-numbing exercise. Consider the following sources—Allen, *History of the American Bison*, Bison Americanus, 473–520; William Temple Hornaday, *The Extermination of the American Bison* (1889; reprint, Washington, DC: Smithsonian Institution Press, 2002), 376–86; and Ted Franklin Belue, *The Long Hunt: Death of the Buffalo East of the Mississippi* (Mechanicsburg: Stackpole Books, 1996), 8–10. Although many people are surprised to learn that buffalo lived east of the Mississippi, the following story shows just how abundant they once were: In 1750 the former governor of New France, the Marquis de La Gallisonière, wrote a *Memoir on the French Colonies in North America*, in which he urged the king to strengthen France's position in the Illinois country—which encompassed much of the present-day states of Illinois, Indiana, and Ohio—to keep the British out and maintain Canada's strategically important connection to the Mississippi River. In touting the area's value for colonization, Galissonière spoke glowingly about the wide-open and fertile prairies, and the "innumerable multitude of buffaloes," which he thought might prove useful in cultivating the land. If a buffalo were "caught and attached to the plow," Galissonière contended, it "would move [the plow] . . . at a speed superior to that of the domestic ox!" Quoted in Edward G. Mason, *Chapters from Illinois History* (Chicago: Herbert S. Stone and Company, 1901), 227. Galissonière also predicted that the buffalo were so numerous they would "probably not run out for many centuries hence, both because the country is not sufficiently peopled to make their consumption perceptible, and because . . . it will never happen that

the animals will be killed solely for the sake of their skins." On this, of course, he was dead wrong. Quoted in Allen, *History of the American Bison*, Bison Americanus, 571. See also Edward G. Mason, "Old Fort Chartres," *Atlantic Monthly* (May 1882): 623.

4   The complex question of the number of buffalo that were in North America before the arrival of the Europeans has been debated for years. The number 75 million comes from an estimate made by the naturalist Ernest Thompson Seton in 1929, which subsequent scholars have attacked as being too high on a number of grounds. But whereas Seton tried to estimate the number for the entire continent, some of the later estimates have focused solely on the Great Plains, where the greatest concentration of buffalo are thought to have roamed. The historian Dan Flores estimates that "during prehorse times" the Great Plains might have supported "perhaps 28–30 million" buffalo. For more on this debate see Dan Flores, "Bison Ecology and Bison Diplomacy: The Southern Plains from 1800 to 1850," *Journal of American History* 78 (September 1991): 470–71; Isenberg, *The Destruction of the Bison*, 24–30; Dary, *The Buffalo Book*, 27–29; and Shepard Krech III, *The Ecological Indians: Myth and History* (New York: W. W. Norton & Company, 1999), 125–26.

5   Solis, quoted in Ernest Thompson Seton, "The American Bison or Buffalo," *Scribner's Magazine* (October 1906): 385. See also Hornaday, *The Extermination of the American Bison*, 373; and Valerius Geist, *Buffalo Nation: History and Legend of the North American Bison* (Stillwater, MN: Voyageur Press, 1996), 59.

6   Álvar Núñez Cabeza de Vaca," The Account and Commentaries of Governor Álvar Núñez Cabeza de Vaca, of what occurred on the two journeys that he made to the Indies," Southwestern Writers Collection of Texas State University, http://alkek.library.txstate.edu/swwc/cdv/book/54.html (accessed March 13, 2009). For a fascinating account of how Cabeza de Vaca found himself in Texas and what he did there, see Steven Rinella, *American Buffalo: In Search of a Lost Icon* (New York: Spiegel & Grau, 2008), 17–19.

7   Samuel Argall, "A Letter of Sir Samuel Argoll touching his Voyage to Virginia, and Actions there: Written to Master Nicholas Hawes. June 1613," in *Hakluytus Postumous or Purchas His Pilgrimes*, ed. Samuel Purchas, vol. 19 (1613; reprint New York: Macmillan Company, 1906), 92; and Dary, *The Buffalo Book*, 9. It is not clear how the word "kine" came to be used to designate buffalo, but perhaps it goes back to the Spanish. See, for example, Tom McHugh, *The Time of the Buffalo* (Lincoln: University of Nebraska Press, 1979), 43.

8   Hansen, *When Skins Were Money*, 163–65. See also Weber, *The Spanish Frontier in North America*, 177; and *Robes of Splendor: Native American Painted Buffalo Hides*, with contributions by George P. Horse Capture et al. (New York: New Press, 1993).

9   Thomas Ashe, *Travels in America, Performed in 1806* (London: Edmund M. Blunt, 1808), 48–49.

10 Geist, *Buffalo Nation*, 80. The chief's name has also been spelled as "Sabonee," "Shabbona," and so on.

11   Thomas Mails, *The Mystic Warriors of the Plains* (Garden City, NY: Doubleday & Company, 1972), 188.

12   Ibid., 190–92; and Tom McHugh, *The Time of the Buffalo*, 103–9.

13   Henry R. Schoolcraft, *Narrative Journal of Travels From Detroit Northwest Through the Great Chain of American Lakes to the Sources of the Mississippi River in the Year 1820* (Albany: E. & E. Hosford, 1821), 278–80. See also Wayne Gard, *The Great Buffalo Hunt* (Lincoln: University of Nebraska Press, 1959), 43.

14   Hornaday, *The Extermination of the American Bison*, 444.

15   Chittenden, *The American Fur Trade*, vol. 1, 7.

16   Hornaday, *The Extermination of the American Bison*, 443–44.

17   Ibid., 414–15, 444; Theodore R. Davis, "The Buffalo Range," *Harper's New Monthly Magazine* (January 1869): 159; Alexander Henry, *The Manuscript Journals of Alexander Henry, Fur Trader of the Northwest Company, and of David Thompson, Official Geographer and Explorer of the Same Company, 1799–1814*, ed. Elliot Coues, vol. 1 (New York: Francis P. Harper, 1897), 242, 253; Kurz, *On the Upper Missouri*, 28, and E. Douglas Branch, *The Hunting of the Buffalo* (1929; reprint, Lincoln: University of Nebraska Press, 1962), 51. On May 3, 1933, an almost-pure-white buffalo calf was born on the National Bison Range, in Montana, named "Big Medicine" in honor of the great sacred powers attributed to white bison by the Native Americans. Because Big Medicine had some pigmentation—tan hooves, brown topknot, and blue eyes—he was not a true albino. Nevertheless his birth was an extremely rare event, perhaps a one in five million occurrence. See Hornaday, *The Extermination of the American Bison*, 414; and Eric Jay Dolin, *Smithsonian Book of National Wildlife Refuges* (Washington, DC: Smithsonian Institution Press, 2003); 21.

18   George Bird Grinnell, "In Buffalo Days," in *American Big-Game Hunting*, ed. Theodore Roosevelt and George Bird Grinnell (New York: Forest and Stream Publishing, 1893), 183–86.

19   Richard Irving Dodge, *The Plains of the Great West and Their Inhabitants* (New York: G. P. Putnam's Sons, 1877), 127. See also Francis Parkman, *Prairie and Rocky Mountain Life; or, The California and Oregon Trail* (New York: George P. Putnam, 1852), 256–58; and Francis Haines, *The Buffalo, The Story of the American Bison and Their Hunters from Prehistoric Times to the Present* (New York: Thomas Y. Crowell, 1970), 1–2.

20   Rudolph Friedrich Kurz, *On the Upper Missouri: the Journal of Rudolph Friedrich Kurz*, ed. Carla Kelly (Norman: University of Oklahoma Press, 2005), 195–96; Isenberg, *The Destruction of the Bison*, 99–101; and George P. Belden, *The White Chief; or, Twelve Years Among the Wild Indians of the Plains* (Cincinnati: E. W. Starr & Co., 1875), 126.

21   Hornaday, *The Extermination of the American Bison*, 443; T. Lindsay Baker, "Beaver to Buffalo Robes: Transition in the Fur Trade," in *Museum of the Fur Trade Quarterly* (Summer 1987): 6–8 Chittenden, *The American Fur Trade*, vol. 1, 34–35; Maria R. Audubon, *Audubon and His Journals*, vol. 1 (New York:

Charles Scribner's Sons, 1897), 500; and Wishart, *The Fur Trade of the American West*, 85.

22   Wishart, *The Fur Trade of the American West*, 67. See also letter from John Dougherty to William Clark (October 29, 1831), doc. 190, U. S. House of Representatives, 22nd Congress, 1st Session, in *Executive Documents, Printed by Order of the House of Representatives at the First Session of the Twenty-Second Congress, Begun and Held at the City of Washington, December 7, 1831* (Washington, DC: Duff Green, 1832), 1–2.

23   Chittenden, *The American Fur Trade*, vol. 2, 620–27; Isenberg, *Destruction of the Bison*, 115–18; Barbour, *Fort Union and the Upper Missouri Fur Trade*, 135–38; Wishart, *The Fur Trade of the American West*, 67–69; DeVoto, *Across the Wide Missouri*, 280–95.

24   W. P. Clark, *The Indian Sign Language* (Philadelphia: L. R. Hamersly & Co., 1885), 351–52.

25   Captain Marryat, *A Diary in America With Remarks and Illustrations, part Second*, vol. 3 (London: Longman, Orme, Brown, Green, & Longmans, 1839), 228.

26   Larpenteur, *Forty Years a Fur Trader*, 134–35.

27   Mark L. Gardner, " 'Where the Buffalo Was Plenty': Bent, St. Vrain & Co. and the Robe Trade of the Southern Plains," in *Museum of the Fur Trade Quarterly* (Fall/Winter 2007): 22–25; and Gard, *The Great Buffalo Hunt*, 53–57.

28   Gardner, " 'Where the Buffalo Was Plenty,' " 22–23.

29   John E. Sunder, *The Fur Trade on the Upper Missouri, 1840–1865* (Norman: University of Oklahoma Press, 1965), 17; Baird, "Native Ruminating Animals of North America, and Their Susceptibility of Domestication," 41; "Fur Trade of St. Louis—Great West," in *Hunt's Merchant's Magazine and Commercial Review*, vol. 42, *January to June 1860* (New York: George W. & Jno. A. Wood, 1860), 617; "Arrival of Red River Traders at St. Paul," in *The Great Lakes, Or Inland Seas of America; Embracing a Full Description of Lakes Superior, Huron, Michigan, Erie, and Ontario; Rivers St. Mary, St. Clair, Detroit, Niagara, and St. Lawrence; Commerce of the Lakes, Etc., Etc.*, comp. John Disturnell (New York: American News Co., 1868), 191; Thomas P. Kettell, "Furs and Fur Trade," in *One Hundred Years' Progress of the United States* (Hartford CT: L. Stebbins, 1870), 345; and John C. Frémont, *Narrative of the Exploring Expedition to the Rocky Mountains, in the Year 1842, and to Oregon and North California in the Years 1843–44* (London: Wiley and Putnam, 1846), 135.

30   Baker, "Beaver to Buffalo Robes," 6–7; *Missouri Democrat*, "Fur Trade of St. Louis—Great West," 617; and Rinella, *American Buffalo*, 167. An example of the value of a finished robe can be gleaned from the following interesting tidbit: "A few days ago an elegant buffalo robe was taken from the possession of a loaferish looking chap by a policeman in Broadway and placed in charge of the property clerk at the Tombs Police Court, on suspicion of being stolen. Meanwhile, the party from whom the robe was taken was committed to the Tombs to await the result of advertising for an owner of the property. Scarcely had 48 hours elapsed

when one of the 'shyster' lawyers that infest the City Prison and Police Courts, procured a discharge from the sitting magistrate and the accused was set at liberty. . . . However the article advertised according to law, and yesterday it was identified by a livery stable keeper, who valued it at $50, and said it was stolen from one of his coaches." "New York City," *New York Daily Times* (February 22, 1855).

31 Sunder, *The Fur Trade on the Upper Missouri*, 16–17; and Branch, *The Hunting of the Buffalo*, 101–2.

32 Isenberg, *The Destruction of the Bison*, 93–94.

33 From 1820 through the mid-1860s, the métis who lived along the Red River in Manitoba conducted annual buffalo hunts. Entire villages would empty out as all the inhabitants traveled to the hunting grounds in western Manitoba, Saskatchewan, Montana, the Dakotas, and even northern Minnesota in search of sizable herds. One of the largest hunts took place in the summer of 1840, when 1,630 people, including men, women, and children, headed out. Alexander Ross, *The Red River Settlement: Its Rise, Progress, and Present State* (London: Smith, Elder and Co., 1856), 243–56; Rinella, *American Buffalo*, 166–67; and Hornaday, *The Extermination of the Buffalo*, 435.

34 Writing in 1845, Josiah Gregg said, "It is believed that the annual 'export' of buffalo [robes] . . . from the Prairies and bordering 'buffalo range,' is about a hundred thousand: and the number killed wantonly, or exclusively for meat, is no doubt still greater, as the skins are fit to dress scarcely half the year." Josiah Gregg, *Commerce of the Prairies, Or, the Journal of a Santa Fe Trader, During Eight Expeditions Across the Great Western Prairies, and a Residence of Nearly Nine Years in Northern Mexico*, vol. 2 (New York: J & H. Langley, 1845), 213.

35 Isenberg, *The Destruction of the Bison* 30, 93.

36 Thomas J. Farnham, *Travels in the Great Western Prairies, The Anahuac and Rocky Mountains*, vol. 1 (London: Richard Bentley, 184), 81. See also George Catlin, *Letters and Notes on the Manners, Customs, and Condition of the North American Indians*, vol. 2, 3rd ed. (New York: Wiley and Putnam, 1844), 13–14.

37 Robert M. Wright, "Personal Reminiscences of Frontier Life in Southwest Kansas," in *Transactions of the Kansas State Historical Society, 1901–1902*, vol. 3 (Topeka: W. Y. Morgan, 1902), 50.

38 George Catlin, *Letters and Notes on the Manners, Customs, and Condition of the North American Indians*, vol. 1 (London: Published by the Author, 1841), 263. Catlin continued by offering a potential solution to the plight of the buffalo, suggesting that the capital then tied up in the fur trade could "much more advantageously . . . be employed, both for the weal of the country and for the owners, if it were invested in machines for the manufacture of *woolen robes*." Ibid.

39 Audubon, *Audubon and His Journals*, vol. 2, 131.

40 Gregg, *Commerce of the Prairies*, vol. 2, 213. See also *A Pictorial Geography of the World*, vol. 2 (Boston, Charles D. Strong, 1856), 41; Allen, *History of the American*

Bison, 561; and "Report of the Secretary of War," Senate Doc. 77, 40th Congress, 1st Sess. (July 19, 1867), 11.

41 Hornaday, *The Extermination of the American Bison*, 492; and Rinella, *American Buffalo*, 167.

42 William F. Cody, *True Tales of the Plains* (New York: Empire Book Company, 1908), 66–68.

43 An observer described this pernicious form of "entertainment" as follows. "When the iron-horse comes rushing into their solitudes, and snorting out his fierce alarms the [buffalo] herds, though perhaps a mile away from his path, will lift their heads and gaze intently for a few moments toward the object thus approaching them with a roar which causes the earth to tremble, and enveloped in a white cloud that streams further and higher than the dust of the old stage-coach ever did; and then, having determined its course, instead of fleeing back to the distant valleys, away they go, charging across the ridge over which the iron rails lie, apparently determined to cross in front of the locomotive at all hazards. The rate per mile of passenger trains is slow upon the plains, and hence it often happens that the cars and buffalo will be side by side for a mile or two, the brutes abandoning the effort to cross only when their foe has merged entirely ahead. During these races the car-windows are opened, and numerous breech-loaders fling hundreds of bullets among the densely crowded and flying masses. Many of the poor animals fall, and more go off to die in the ravines." W. E. Webb, *Buffalo Land, An Authentic Account of the Discoveries, Adventures, and Mishaps of a Scientific and Sporting Party in the Wild West* (Cincinnati: E. Hannaford & Company, 1873), 313–14. See also Peter D. Ridenour, *Autobiography of Peter D. Ridenour* (New York: Hudson Press, 1908), 215.

44 Quoted in Dary, *The Buffalo Book*, 124.

45 Hornaday, *The Extermination of the American Bison*, 435, 440, 496–98; Isenberg, *The Destruction of the Buffalo*, 130–31; William Cronon, *Nature's Metropolis: Chicago and the Great West* (New York: W. W. Norton, 1991), 216; and Joel Asaph Allen, *History of the American Bison*, Bison Americanus (Washington, DC: U.S. Government Printing Office, 1877), 570.

46 Hornaday, *The Extermination of the American Bison*, 494; and Allen, *History of the American Bison*, Bison Americanus, 579–80.

47 See, for example, David D. Smits, "The Frontier Army and the Destruction of the Buffalo: 1865–1833," *Western Historical Quarterly* 25 (Autumn 1994): 313–38; and Isenberg, *The Destruction of the Bison*, 129.

48 William Butler, *Sir William Butler, An Autobiography* (New York: Charles Scribner's Sons, 1911), 97; and Smits, "The Frontier Army and the Destruction of the Buffalo," 328.

49 Smits, "The Frontier Army and the Destruction of the Buffalo," 317.

50 John R., Cook, *The Border and the Buffalo* (Topeka: Crane & Company, 1907), 113; and Smits, "The Frontier Army and the Destruction of the Buffalo," 330.

51 Isenberg, *The Destruction of the Bison*, 129; and Smits, "The Frontier Army and the Destruction of the Buffalo," 319–21, 332–33.

52 Hornaday, *The Extermination of the American Bison*, 501; Hansen, *When Skins Were Money*, 187; and Eugene D. Flaherty, *Wild Animals and Settlers on the Great Plains* (Norman: University of Oklahoma Press, 1995), 62. Over a three-year period, from 1872 to 1874, the Atchison, Topeka & Santa Fe Railroad alone transported 10,793,350 pounds of bison bones. Hornaday, *The Extermination of the American Bison*, 498.

53 Isenberg, *The Destruction of the Bison*, 139–40; and Flores, "Bison Ecology," 481–83.

54 Hornaday, *The Extermination of the American Bison*, 496, 501.

55 Ibid., 503, 505–9, and 513; and Isenberg, *The Destruction of the Bison*, 140.

56 "Where the Buffalo Robes Come From," *Boston Daily Globe* (March 12, 1882); and Hornaday, *The Extermination of the American Bison*, 512.

57 Theodore Roosevelt, *Hunting Trips of a Ranchman*, vol. 2 (New York: G. P. Putnam's Sons, 1885), 74–76. At this early stage of his life, although Roosevelt viewed the demise of the buffalo as a tragedy of the animal world, and a personal loss, he did not think it a tragedy for humankind. Later in this same book, he wrote that because huge populations of buffalo were incompatible with human settlement, and further because eliminating the buffalo "was the only way of solving the Indian question. . . . From the standpoint of humanity at large, the extermination of the buffalo has been a blessing." Ibid., 82–83.

58 Isenberg, *The Destruction of the Bison*, 162.

59 "The Extinct Buffalo," *Boston Daily Globe* (September 22, 1889). See also "The Extermination of the Bison," *New York Times*, reprinted from the *London Daily Telegraph* (July 28, 1885).

60 Hornaday, *The Extermination of the American Bison*, 502. See also A. L. Belden, *The Fur Trade of America, and Some of the Men Who Made and Maintain It* (New York: Peltries Publishing Company, 1917), 450–51.

61 Hornaday, *The Extermination of the American Bison*, 525; and William T. Hornaday, *Our Vanishing Wildlife, Its Extermination and Preservation* (New York: New York Zoological Society, 1913), 180.

EPILOGUE: *End of an Era*

1 Clive Roots, *Domestication* (Westport, CT: Greenwood Press, 2007), 127–29; Helen Coster, "Adventures in the Skin Trade," *Fortune* (November 26, 2007), 142; Lauren Letter, "Slowing Economy Pelts the Global Fur Business," *Wall Street Journal* (February 12, 2009); Jerry Harkavy, "Beaver Trapper Carries on Centuries-Old Tradition," *Boston Globe* (March 6, 2009); Harold Faber, "Becoming Rare Species: The American Trapper," *New York Times* (February 9, 1992); Sam Smith, "Fur Trappers are Taking on the Scourge of the Marshlands," *New*

York Times (May 28, 2002); Kate Galbraith, "Back in Style: The Fur Trade," *New York Times* (December 24, 2006); Katie Weisman, "Fur's Quiet Comeback," *New York Times* (November 23, 2007); fact sheets on International Fur Trade Federation Web site, http://www.iftf.com/iftf_3_1_1.php?id=173 and http://www.iftf.com/iftf_3_2_2.php (accessed April 6, 2009); and Fur Commission USA Web site, http://www.furcommission.com/who/index.html (accessed April 6, 2009).

2   Frank Graham, Jr., *Man's Dominion, The Story of Conservation in America* (New York: M. Evans and Company, 1971), 14.

3   For information on the fate of the passenger pigeon, which became extinct in 1914, as well as the diminution of game animals and plume birds during the "Age of Extermination," see A. W. Schorger, *The Passenger Pigeon, Its Natural History and Extinction* (Norman: University of Oklahoma Press, 1955); and Dolin, *The Smithsonian Book of National Wildlife Refuges*, 13–15; Peter Matthiessen, *Wildlife in America* (New York: Viking, 1987); Eric Jay Dolin and Bob Dumaine, *The Duck Stamp Story: Art, Conservation, History* (Iola, WI: Krause Publications, 2000), 15; and Frank Graham, Jr., *The Audubon Ark, A History of the National Audubon Society* (Austin: University of Texas, 1990).

4   Poland, *Fur-Bearing Animals in Nature and Commerce*, xxxii–xxxiii, 252; Busch, *The War Against the Seals*, 110–11; and Roberts, *The Unnatural History of the Sea*, 110–11. Even at this early period, not everyone looked favorably upon the use of furs for bodily adornment. A religious magazine in 1858 began an article on the fur trade with the following caveat. "We doubt not that our readers will mostly agree with us, that money spent in the purchase of costly furs is poorly applied, especially when the object is to minister to pride and the love of ostentatious display. The fur business, however, in its various branches, affords a subsistence to not a few of the human family, and therefore, the information contained in the following extract is not devoid of interest." "The Fur Trade," *The Friend, A Religious and Literary Journal* (December 25, 1858).

5   For more on the rise of the conservation movement, see Stephen Fox, *John Muir and His Legacy: The American Conservation Movement* (Boston: Little, Brown and Company, 1981); Frank Graham, Jr., *Man's Dominion, The Story of Conservation in America* (New York: M. Evans and Company, 1971); Dolin, *The Smithsonian Book of National Wildlife Refuges*, 23–82; and James B. Trefethen, *An American Crusade for Wildlife* (New York: Winchester Press, 1975).

6   Agnes C. Laut, *The Fur Trade of America* (New York: Macmillan Company, 1921), 151–86; Hanson, *When Skins Were Money*, 189–90; Henry Fairfield Osborn and Harold Elmer Anthony, "Can We Save the Mammals?" *Natural History* (September–October 1922); 389–405; Cameron Jenks, *The Bureau of Biological Survey* (1929; reprint, New York: Arno Press, Inc., 1974), 10. The earliest state law protecting fur-bearing animals I was able to find comes from 1791, when Massachusetts passed "An Act for the Preservation and Encouragement of the Fur Trade Within This Commonwealth," which made it illegal to kill any beavers, otters,

wolverines, muskrats, sable, fox, fisher, mink, or martin during the months of June, July, August, and September, and set a fine of "not less than *twenty shillings* nor more than *three pounds*" per violation. "An Act for the Preservation and Encouragement of the Fur Trade Within This Commonwealth," June 10, 1791, in *Acts and Laws of the Commonwealth of Massachusetts* (Boston: Adams & Nourse, 1895), 262. According to the 1909 report of the National Conservation Commission, "Our wild game and fur-bearing animals have been largely exterminated. To prevent their complete extinction the States and the United States have taken in hand their protection, and their numbers are now increasing." National Conservation Commission, *Report of the National Conservation Commission*, vol. 1, U.S. Senate, 60th Congress, 2nd sess., doc. 676 (Washington, DC: U.S. Government Printing Office, 1909), 18. The report also states, "Our game animals and birds supply food, skins, furs, and feathers to the annual value of several million dollars, and the amount is increasing." Ibid., 82. In an appendix to the report, C. Hart Merriam, chief of the Biological Survey, provided some excellent background on the depletion of fur-bearing animals in the United States and efforts to put a halt to it: "North America was formerly the richest fur-producing region in the world, but now the stock of furbearing animals is greatly depleted, and the supply falls far short of the demand. . . . The present value of the annual catch of furs in the United States is between \$15,000,000 and \$20,000,000. The growing scarcity of the more valuable furbearers has produced in the lower grades a great increase in both demand and price. What is needed . . . is wise husbanding of the wild stock, which everywhere is diminishing under the growing demand for furs and the rapid encroachment on their original domain by our ever-expanding civilization. . . . The remedy seems to lie in the prevention of overgrazing and in the enactment of laws limiting the open season for trapping. Many of the States have already realized the necessity for such legislation and have acted accordingly. It remains only for other States and the National Government to follow their example in order to provide for the preservation and utilization of an important natural resource which, at no cost for maintenance, may be made to yield a substantial annual revenue." C. Hart Merriam, "Relations of Birds and Mammals to the National Resources," in National Conservation Commission, *Report of the National Conservation Commission*, vol. 3, United States Senate, 60th Congress, 2nd sess., doc. 676 (Washington, DC: U.S. Government Printing Office, 1909), 318–31.

7   This includes both those animals that were hauled aboard the boats after being shot and those that sank. Busch, *The War Against the Seals*, 145–47.

8   Ibid., 197. This was the first international environmental treaty. See Roberts, *The Unnatural History of the Sea*, 111–12.

9   Remarking on the sighting of José, Steven Sanderson, the President of the Wildlife Conservation Society, declared the beaver's appearance to be "a symbolic moment for our great city. . . . The fact that an animal which represents the wild frontier of North America can live and thrive in a river that runs through the

Bronx Zoo is proof that we can coexist with nature anywhere on the planet. Anything is possible." Quoted in Live Science, "Beaver Returns to New York City Centuries After Eradication" (February 23, 2007), at the Web site http://www .livescience.com/animals/070223bronx_beaver.html (accessed April 9, 2009). See also Bob Kappstter, "Bronx River Beaver 'Alive and Well,'" *Daily News* (May 7, 2008); and Peter Miller, "Before New York," *National Geographic* (September 2009): 126.

10   See, for example, Cornelia Dean, "Return of the Once-Rare Beaver? Not in My Yard," *New York Times*, June 9, 2009.

11   See the following U.S. Fish and Wildlife Service Web sites on sea otters for more background: Northern sea otter *(Enhydra lutris kenyoni)*, http://ecos.fws .gov/speciesProfile/SpeciesReport.do?spcode=A0HK; and Southern sea otter *(Enhydra lutris nereis)*, http://ecos.fws.gov/speciesProfile/SpeciesReport.do?sp code=A0A7. See also Roberts, *The Unnatural History of the Sea*, 172–73. The sea otter population along the Aleutian Islands experienced a precipitous drop between 1990 and 2000, and scientists are still trying to figure out why. For a fascinating discussion of this situation, and one of the theories—that killer whale predation is partly to blame—see ibid., 171–83.

12   Eric W. Sanderson et al., "The Ecological Future of the North American Bison: Conceiving Long-Term, Large-Scale Conservation of Wildlife," *Conservation Biology* 22 (April 2008): 254; and C. H. Freese et al., "Second Chance for the Plains Bison," *Biological Conservation* 136 (April 2007): 175–84.

13   The two best museums in the country that deal exclusively with the fur trade are the Museum of the Fur Trade in Chadron, Nebraska (www.furtrade.org), and the Museum of the Mountain Man in Pinedale, Wyoming (www.museumofthemount ainman.com). Both are excellent and well worth visiting.

SELECT BIBLIOGRAPHY

This bibliography, which is intended as a starting point for those who want to learn more about the history of the fur trade in America, contains a small fraction of the sources cited in this book. For additional information about specific topics covered in the text, please refer to the endnotes.

Adams, James Truslow. *The Founding of New England*. Boston: Atlantic Monthly Press, 1921.

Bailyn, Bernard. *The New England Merchants in the Seventeenth Century*. New York: Harper & Row, 1955.

Barbour, Barton H. *Fort Union and the Upper Missouri Fur Trade*. Norman: University of Oklahoma Press, 2001.

Berry, Don. *A Majority of Scoundrels: An Informal History of the Rocky Mountain Fur Company*. New York: Harper & Brothers, 1961.

Branch, E. Douglas. *The Hunting of the Buffalo*. 1929. Reprint, Lincoln: University of Nebraska Press, 1962.

Buffinton, Arthur H. "New England and the Western Fur Trade." In *Publications of the Colonial Society of Massachusetts*. Vol. 18, *Transactions 1915–1916*. Boston: Colonial Society of Massachusetts, 1917.

Busch, Briton Cooper. *The War Against the Seals, A History of the North American Seal Fishery*. Kingston, ON: McGill-Queen's University, 1985.

———, and Barry M. Gough, eds. *Fur Traders from New England: The Boston Men in the North Pacific, 1787–1800*. Spokane: Arthur H. Clark Company, 1997.

Chittenden, Hiram Martin. *The American Fur Trade of the Far West*. 2 vols. 1902. Reprint, Stanford: Academic Reprints, 1954.

Cleland, Robert Glass. *This Reckless Breed of Men: The Trappers and Fur Traders of the Southwest*. Albuquerque: University of New Mexico Press, 1950.

Crean, J. F. "Hats and the Fur Trade," *Canadian Journal of Economics and Political Science* 28, no. 3 (Aug. 1962): 373–86.

Dary, David. *The Buffalo Book: The Full of Saga of the American Animal*. Chicago: Sage Books, 1974.

———. *The Santa Fe Trail: Its History, Legends, and Lore*. New York: Alfred A. Knopf, 2000.

DeVoto, Bernard. *Across the Wide Missouri*. Boston: Houghton, Mifflin & Company, 1947.

Gibson, James R. *Otter Skins, Boston Ships, and China Goods: The Maritime Fur Trade of the Northwest Coast. 1785–1841*. Seattle: University of Washington Press, 1999.

Goetzmann, William H. *Exploration and Empire, The Explorer and the Scientist in the Winning of the American West*. Francis Parkman Prize ed. New York: History Book Club, 2006.

Gowans, Fred R. *Rocky Mountain Rendezvous, A History of the Fur Trade Rendezvous, 1825–1840*. Layton, UT: Gibbs M. Smith, Inc., 1985.

Hale, Nathaniel C. *Pelts and Palisades: The Story of Fur and the Rivalry for Pelts in Early America*. Richmond, VA: Dietz Press, 1959.

Hanson, James A. *When Skins Were Money: A History of the Fur Trade*. Chadron, NE: Museum of the Fur Trade, 2005.

Harris, Bill. *The Lives of Mountain Men*. Guilford, CT: Lyons Press, 2005.

Hornaday, William Temple. *The Extermination of the American Bison*. 1889. Reprint, Washington, DC: Smithsonian Institution Press, 2002.

Horwitz, Tony. *Blue Latitudes: Boldly Going Where Captain Cook Has Gone Before*. New York: Henry Holt and Company, 2002.

Innis, Harold. *The Fur Trade in Canada*. Toronto: University of Toronto Press, 1970.

Irving, Washington. *Astoria; or, Enterprise Beyond the Rocky Mountains*. Paris: Baudry's European Library, 1836.

———. *The Adventures of Captain Bonneville, Or Scenes Beyond the Rocky Mountains of the Far West*. 2 vols. London: Richard Bentley, 1837.

Isenberg, Andrew C. *The Destruction of the Bison*. New York: Cambridge University Press, 2000.

Johnson, Amandus. *The Swedish Settlements on the Delaware: Their History and Relation to the Indians, Dutch and English, 1638–1664*. 2 vols. New York: D. Appleton & Company, 1911.

Krech, Shepard, III. *The Ecological Indians: Myth and History*. New York: W. W. Norton & Company, 1999.

Lavender, David. *Land of Giants: The Drive to the Pacific Northwest, 1750–1950*. New York: Doubleday & Company, 1958.

———. *The First in the Wilderness*. Lincoln: University of Nebraska Press, 1998.

Laycock, George. *The Mountain Men*. Guilford, CT: Lyons Press, 1988.

Madsen, Axel. *John Jacob Astor: America's First Multimillionaire*. New York: John Wiley & Sons, Inc., 2001.

Malloy, Mary. *"Boston Men" on the Northwest Coast: The American Maritime Fur Trade 1788–1844*. Kingston, ON: Limestone Press, 1998.

Mancall, Peter C. *Deadly Medicine, Indians and Alcohol in Early America*. Ithaca: Cornell University Press, 1995.

McCracken, Harold. *Hunters of the Stormy Sea*. New York: Doubleday & Company, 1957.

Mills, Enos A. *In Beaver World* 1913. Reprint, Lincoln: University of Nebraska Press, 1990.

Moloney, Francis X. *The Fur Trade in New England, 1620–1676*. Cambridge: Harvard University Press, 1931.

Morgan, Dale L. *Jedediah Smith and the Opening of the West*. Lincoln: University of Nebraska Press, 1964.

Morgan, Lewis H. *The American Beaver*. Philadelphia: J. B. Lippincott & Co., 1868.

Morison, Samuel Eliot. *The Maritime History of Massachusetts, 1783-1860*. Boston: Houghton, Mifflin & Company, 1941.

Müller-Schwarze, Dietland, and Lixing Sun. *The Beaver: Natural History of a Wetlands Engineer*. Ithaca: Comstock Publishing, 2003.

Newman, Peter C. *Empire of the Bay: The Company of Adventurers That Seized a Continent*. New York: Penguin Books, 1998.

Norton, Thomas Elliot. *The Fur Trade in Colonial New York, 1686–1776*. Madison: University of Wisconsin Press, 1974.

Outwater, Alice. *Water, A Natural History*. New York: Basic Books. 1996.

Phillips, Paul Chrisler. *The Fur Trade*. 2 vols. Norman: University of Oklahoma Press, 1961.

Richter, Daniel K. *Facing East from Indian Country: A Native History of Early America*. Cambridge: Harvard University Press, 2001.

Rink, Oliver A. *Holland on the Hudson: An Economic and Social History of Dutch New York*. Ithaca: Cornell University Press, 1986.

Ronda, James P. *Astoria & Empire*. Lincoln: University of Nebraska Press, 1990.

Shorto, Russell. *The Island at the Center of the World*. New York: Vintage Books, 2005.

Sunder, John E. *The Fur Trade on the Upper Missouri, 1840–1865*. Norman: University of Oklahoma Press, 1965.

Terrell, John Upton. *Furs by Astor*. New York: William Morrow & Company, 1963.

Utley, Robert M. *A Life Wild and Perilous: Mountain Men and the Paths to the Pacific*. New York: Henry Holt and Company, 1997.

Vanidiveer, Clarence A. *The Fur-Trade and Early Western Exploration*. Cleveland: Arthur H. Clark Company, 1929.

Veale, Elspeth M. *The English Fur Trade in the Later Middle Ages*. Oxford: Clarendon Press, 1966.

Weber, David J. *The Taos Trappers: The Fur Trade in the Far Southwest, 1540–1846*. Norman: University of Oklahoma Press, 1970.

Wishart, David J. *The Fur Trade of the American West, 1807–1840*. Lincoln: University of Nebraska Press, 1992.

ACKNOWLEDGMENTS

*F*OR ME THIS BOOK WAS A THOROUGHLY ENJOYABLE EXPLO-
ration of a fascinating part of the American experience, and along the
way I had many helpful guides. First, of course, are the people who have written about the fur trade, whose work enabled me to piece together the story.
This includes individuals who lived the history and left first-person accounts,
as well as those who recorded and interpreted history after the fact. The literature on the American fur trade is particularly rich, and I encourage those
who have enjoyed *Fur, Fortune, and Empire* to use the endnotes and the select
bibliography as a jumping-off point for further adventures into the past.

I owe special thanks to the reviewers of the manuscript, whose excellent
feedback greatly improved the book. First in line is Bruce Belason, a retired
aerospace engineer with a keen interest in history, whose passion is the American fur trade. I met Bruce just after I had begun working on the book, and
he not only placed his extensive library at my disposal but also served as my
first audience, reading and commenting on each chapter as it was finished.
He and his wife, Ann, were also very welcoming when I visited their home.
Next in line is James A. Hanson, the director emeritus of the Museum of the
Fur Trade, in Chadron, Nebraska. Jim has an encyclopedic knowledge of the
North American fur trade, and he is a storyteller par excellence. The two days
I spent with him, and with his wife, Ann, during my trip out west were great
fun and very informative. Fred R. Gowans, professor emeritus of Western
American History at Brigham Young University, and Robert M. Utley, the
former chief historian of the National Park Service, both offered very helpful insights. Mary Malloy, a professor of maritime history at the Sea Semes-
ter in Woods Hole, Massachusetts, thoughtfully critiqued the chapter on the
sea otter trade in the Pacific Northwest, while buffalo aficionado Bob Doerk,
reviewed the chapter on the buffalo robe trade. Finally Peter Drummey, the
Stephen T. Riley Librarian at the Massachusetts Historical Society, read the

entire manuscript and shared with me his great enthusiasm for the project. Any errors in the book, of course, are mine alone.

Other people who were helpful include Gail DeBuse Potter, the director of the Museum of the Fur Trade; Laurie Hartwig, the director of the Sublette County Historical Society and the Museum of the Mountain Man; the staff at the Abbot Public Library, in my hometown of Marblehead; the staff at the Massachusetts Historical Society; the staff at the Swampscott Public Library; Henry Armstrong; Jennifer Belt; Mary Lynne Bird; Marge Bollack; Ruth Bowler; Jennifer A. Bryan; Sean Campbell; Caitlin Deane; Eric Esau; Laura A. Foster; Gina Garden; Katie Gardner; Clint Gilchrist; Ronald E. Grimm; Elaine Grublin; Lori Holmberg; Jeannie Gales; Alan Gehret; Carrie Anne Hamel; Margaret Kieckhefer; Daniel Kosharek; Peter Lewis; Lorraine C. Miller; Ken Robison; Roger Ryley; Joshua Shaw; Nancy Sherbert; Doug Smith; Kelly-Ann Turkington; Thomas Warren; Brenda J. Wetzel; Vicken Yegparian; and Chuck Young. For the names of the institutions that provided artwork, for which I am very grateful, please see the credit section that follows.

Russell Galen, my agent, as always, astounds me with his sagacity and his uncanny ability to solve problems or, better yet, keep them from arising in the first place. He continues to teach me about the intricacies of publishing, and, in general, smoothes the way so I can focus on research and writing. W. W. Norton provided me with one of the most important things a writer can have—the backing and encouragement of a great publishing house. My indefatigable and highly skilled editor, Bob Weil, put an incredible amount of time and thought into this book, and his numerous suggestions improved virtually every page. This is my second book with Bob, and I hope there are many more. It is great to have him on my side. Lucas Wittmann, Bob's assistant for almost the entire time I was working on the book, was extremely helpful, and a pleasure to work with. Whenever I had a question, he had an answer, or got me one soon. The same can be said for his replacement, Phil Marino. Bill Rusin, director of trade sales and marketing, does a fantastic job of getting a book into the hands of readers, and his enthusiastic support of me and my work is most appreciated. I am also very thankful for receiving the same type of support from publishing director Jeannie Luciano. Louise Brockett, vice president and director of publicity, and Rachel Salzman, associate director of publicity, are extremely creative and effective in their work, giving me confidence that my book will be noticed.

Managing editor Nancy Palmquist oversaw the editing and indexing process, and picked Sue Llewellyn to copyedit the book, an excellent choice indeed. With humor—including a reasonable dose of constructive ribbing—and a deft pen, Sue sharpened my prose in many ways. Don Rifkin, project editor, made sure that the text was as flawless as possible. Ingsu Liu, vice president and art director, and her team created a beautiful cover. And production manager Andy Marasia did a fantastic job pulling everything together to create the book you are holding in your hands. I also thank David Cain, of Able Illustrator, for producing the magnificent map that appears on the endpapers and in the text.

*T*HE MOST IMPORTANT CONSTANT THROUGHOUT THE WRITING process for this book was my family. My dad, Stanley Dolin, I have to admit, was a poor critic—since he unreservedly praises everything I write—but I still loved hearing his comments on the manuscript, and am very happy that my writing fills him with pride. My mom, Ruth, was equally encouraging and interested in the project. My children, Lily and Harry, never complained about all the time I spent in the basement, but loved making fun of my "writing cave," and the fact that *all* I did *all* day was sit in a chair, stare at the computer screen, and, every now and then, type a few words and mutter incoherently. Harry always made me laugh when he asked, "So, dad, you done with that fur book yet?" Jennifer, my wife, was my biggest booster, and greatest source of strength. Although she abhors clichés, I have to say, with utmost sincerity, that I couldn't have written this book without her.

ILLUSTRATION
CREDITS

6. Courtesy Winston E. Banko and U.S. Fish and Wildlife Service
7. Courtesy Library and Archives of Canada, C-016758
8. Courtesy New York Public Library / Art Resource, NY
9. Courtesy Library and Archives Canada, 194
10. Courtesy Museum of the Mountain Man, Pinedale, Wyoming
11. Courtesy Library of Congress
12. Courtesy Ledyard National Bank
13. Courtesy Palace of the Governors Photo Archives (NMHM/DCA), neg. # 070636
14. George Henry Mason, *Costumes of China* (London: W. Miller, 1804)
15. Courtesy U.S. Fish and Wildlife Service
16. Courtesy Library and Archives Canada, C-017338
17. Courtesy Museum of the Fur Trade, Chadron, Nebraska
18. Courtesy Kansas Historical Society
19. Courtesy Colorado Historical Society (scan 10026611)
20. Courtesy Library of Congress
21. Courtesy Museum of the Fur Trade, Chadron, Nebraska
22. Courtesy Library of Congress
23. Courtesy Library of Congress
24. Courtesy Overholser Historical Research Center, Fort Benton, Montana
25. Courtesy Fred R. Gowans
26. Courtesy American Geographical Society and Norman B. Leventhal Map Center at the Boston Public Library
27. Courtesy Library of Congress
29. Courtesy Library of Congress
30. Courtesy Kansas Historical Society
31. Courtesy Library and Archives Canada, C-001229
32. Courtesy Library of Congress
33. Courtesy Library and Archives Canada, PA-051498

COLOR INSERT

34. Courtesy Collections & Archives Department, Nimitz Library, U.S. Naval Academy
35. Courtesy National Gallery, London / Art Resource, NY
36. Courtesy State Museum of PA, PA Historical and Museum Commission
37. Courtesy Library of Congress
38. Courtesy Buffalo Bill Historical Center, Cody, Wyoming; gift of Mrs. Karl Frank, 14.86
39. Courtesy Museum of the Fur Trade, Chadron, Nebraska

40. Courtesy © The Trustees of the British Museum / Art Resource, NY
41. Courtesy Library and Archives Canada, R9266
42. Courtesy National Maritime Museum, London
43. Courtesy Library of Congress, Geography and Map Division
44. Courtesy Library and Archives Canada, C-002773
45. Courtesy Library of Congress
46. Courtesy John James Audubon Museum, Henderson, KY
47. Courtesy Library and Archives Canada, C-013415
48. Courtesy Rare Books and Special Collections Division of Library of Congress
49. Courtesy Library of Congress
50. Courtesy Independence National Historical Park
51. Courtesy Independence National Historical Park
52. Courtesy Library and Archives Canada, C-114375
53. Courtesy Library and Archives Canada, C-046498
54. Courtesy Missouri History Museum, St. Louis
55. Courtesy Dakota Discovery Museum, Mitchell, South Dakota
56. Courtesy Stack's Rare Coins, New York City
57. Courtesy Gift of CliffsNotes, Museum of Nebraska Art, Kearney, Nebraska
58. Courtesy Library and Archives Canada, C-00439
59. Courtesy Library and Archives Canada, C-000426
60. Courtesy © Metropolitan Museum of Art / Art Resource, NY
61. Photo courtesy © Walters Art Museum, Baltimore
62. Photo courtesy © Walters Art Museum, Baltimore
63. Courtesy New York Public Library / Art Resource, NY
64. Courtesy Library of Congress
65. Courtesy Buffalo Bill Historical Center, Cody, Wyoming; Gertrude Vanderbilt Whitney Trust Fund Purchase, 2.60

INDEX

Note: Page numbers in *italics* refer to illustrations.

ABOUT THE AUTHOR

ERIC JAY DOLIN, who grew up near the coasts of New York and Connecticut, graduated from Brown University, where he majored in biology and environmental studies. After getting a master's degree in environmental management from the Yale School of Forestry and Environmental Studies, he received his Ph.D. in environmental policy and planning from the Massachusetts Institute of Technology.

Dolin has worked as a program manager at the U.S. Environmental Protection Agency, an environmental consultant stateside and in London, an intern at the National Wildlife Federation and on Capitol Hill, a fisheries policy analyst at the National Marine Fisheries Service, and an American Association for the Advancement of Science Mass Media Science and Engineering Fellow at *BusinessWeek*.

Much of Dolin's writing reflects his interest in wildlife, the environment, and American history. His books include the *Smithsonian Book of National Wildlife Refuges*, *Snakehead: A Fish Out of Water*, and *Political Waters*, a history of the degradation and cleanup of Boston Harbor. His most recent book, *Leviathan: The History of Whaling In America* (W. W. Norton), was chosen as one of the best nonfiction books of 2007 by the *Los Angeles Times* and the *Boston Globe*. *Leviathan* has also won a number of awards, including the 2007 John Lyman Award for U. S. Maritime History, the eighth annual Massachussetts Book Award (nonfiction honors), and the twenty-third annual L. Byrne Waterman Award, given by the New Bedford Whaling Museum, for outstanding contributions to whaling research and history.

Dolin and his family reside in Marblehead, Massachusetts.

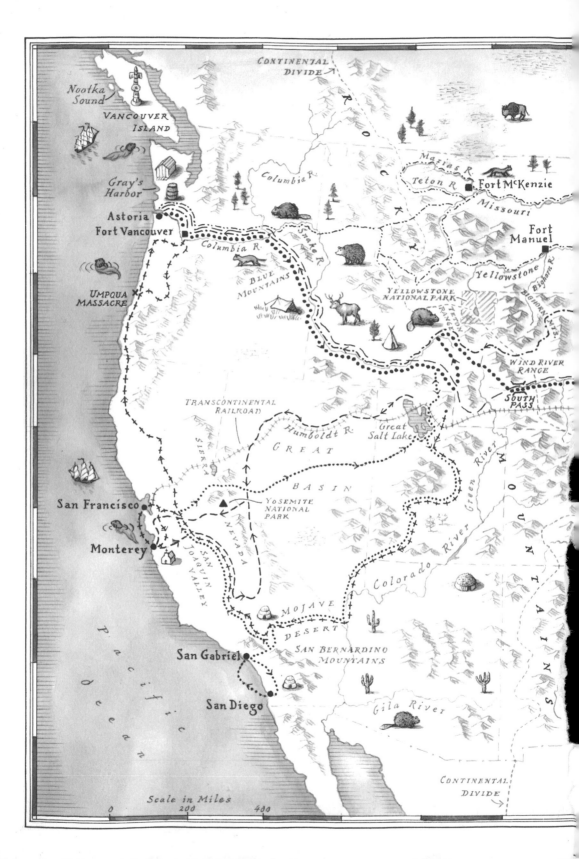